PRISON SCHOOL

Akira Hiramoto

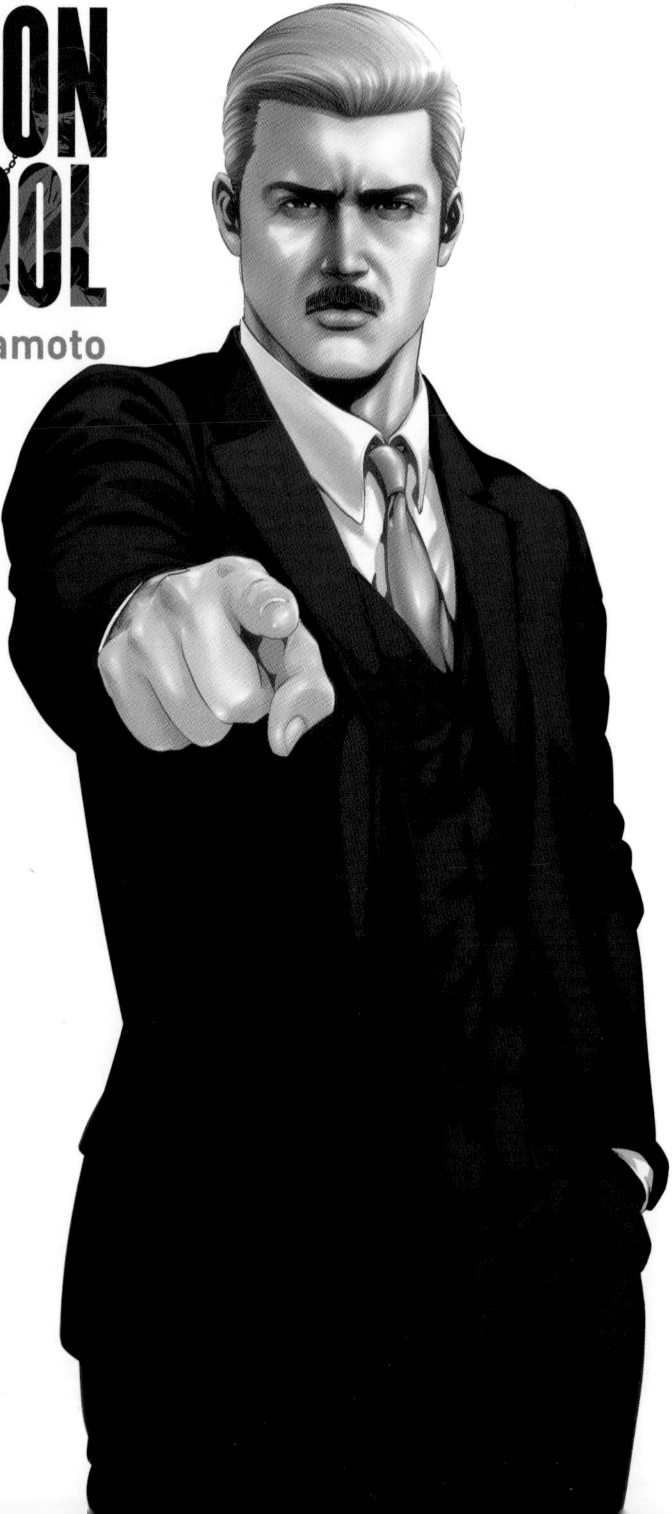

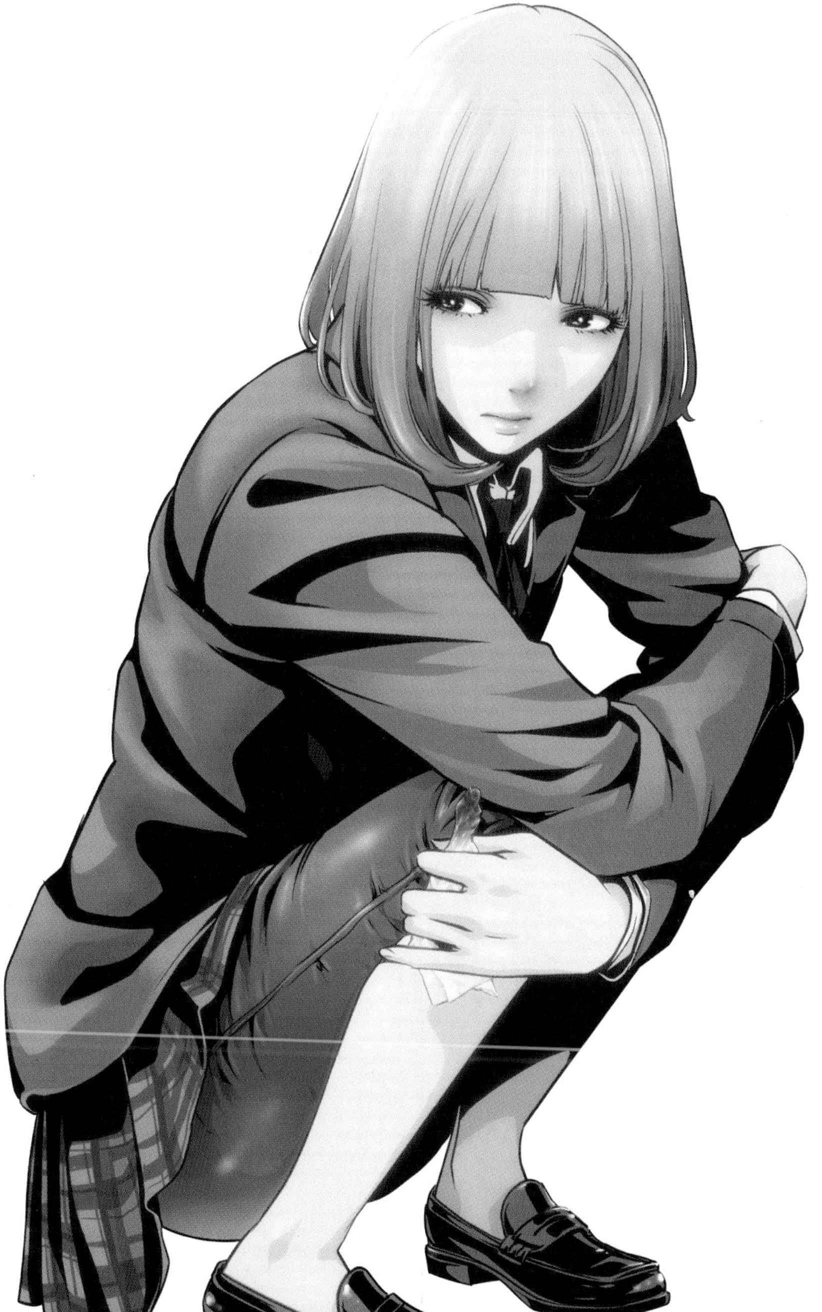

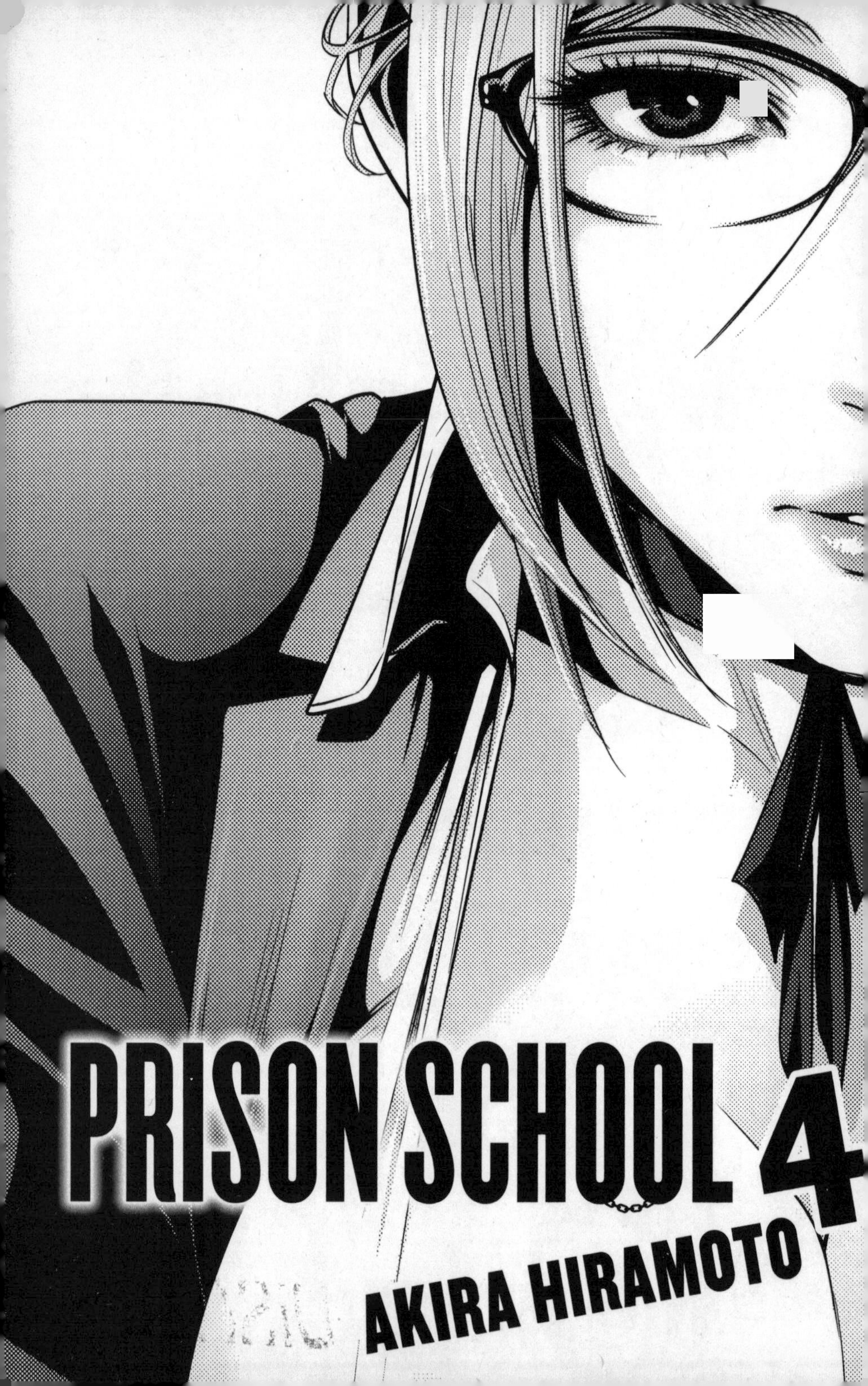
PRISON SCHOOL 4
AKIRA HIRAMOTO

THE PRISONERS

GACKT

TAKEHITO MOROKUZU

Something of a commander among the boys, nothing can overcome this man's convictions when it comes to his beloved *Romance of the Three Kingdoms*, not even forced haircuts or public defecation.

KIYOSHI

KIYOSHI FUJINO

In the very enviable position of being one of five boys in a former all-girls school. Forced to enter the school's prison with the other boys for the crime of peeping into the girls' bath. On the verge of expulsion after falling into the grip of the Expel the Boys Operation (E.B.O.) run by the Shadow Student Council, but issues a challenge in order to change his fortune!!

SHINGO

SHINGO WAKAMOTO

Gets permission to go on a date outside the school, but it was a trap. Becomes the third prisoner to attempt an escape as a result of the E.B.O.

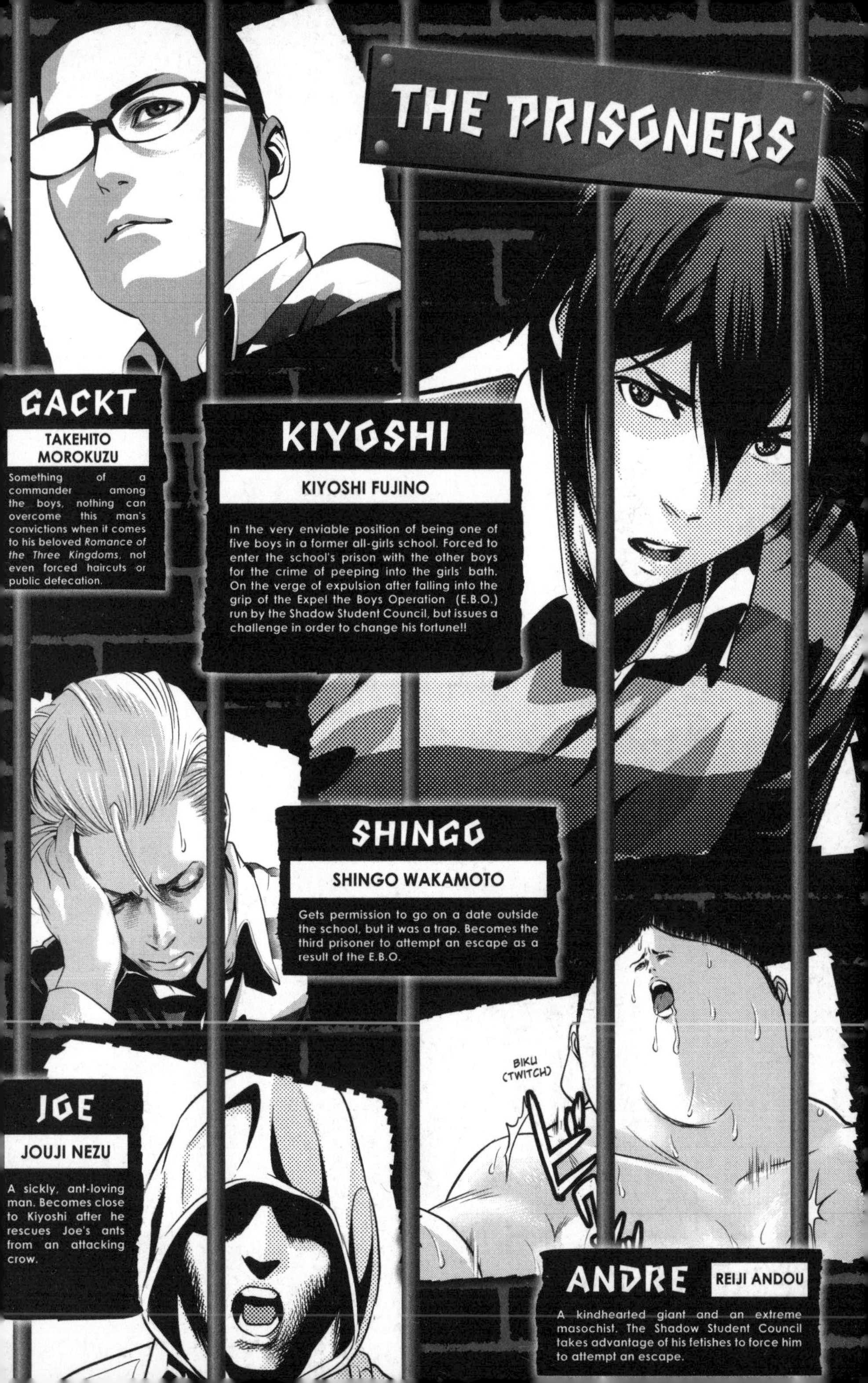
BIKU (TWITCH)

JOE

JOUJI NEZU

A sickly, ant-loving man. Becomes close to Kiyoshi after he rescues Joe's ants from an attacking crow.

ANDRE

REIJI ANDOU

A kindhearted giant and an extreme masochist. The Shadow Student Council takes advantage of his fetishes to force him to attempt an escape.

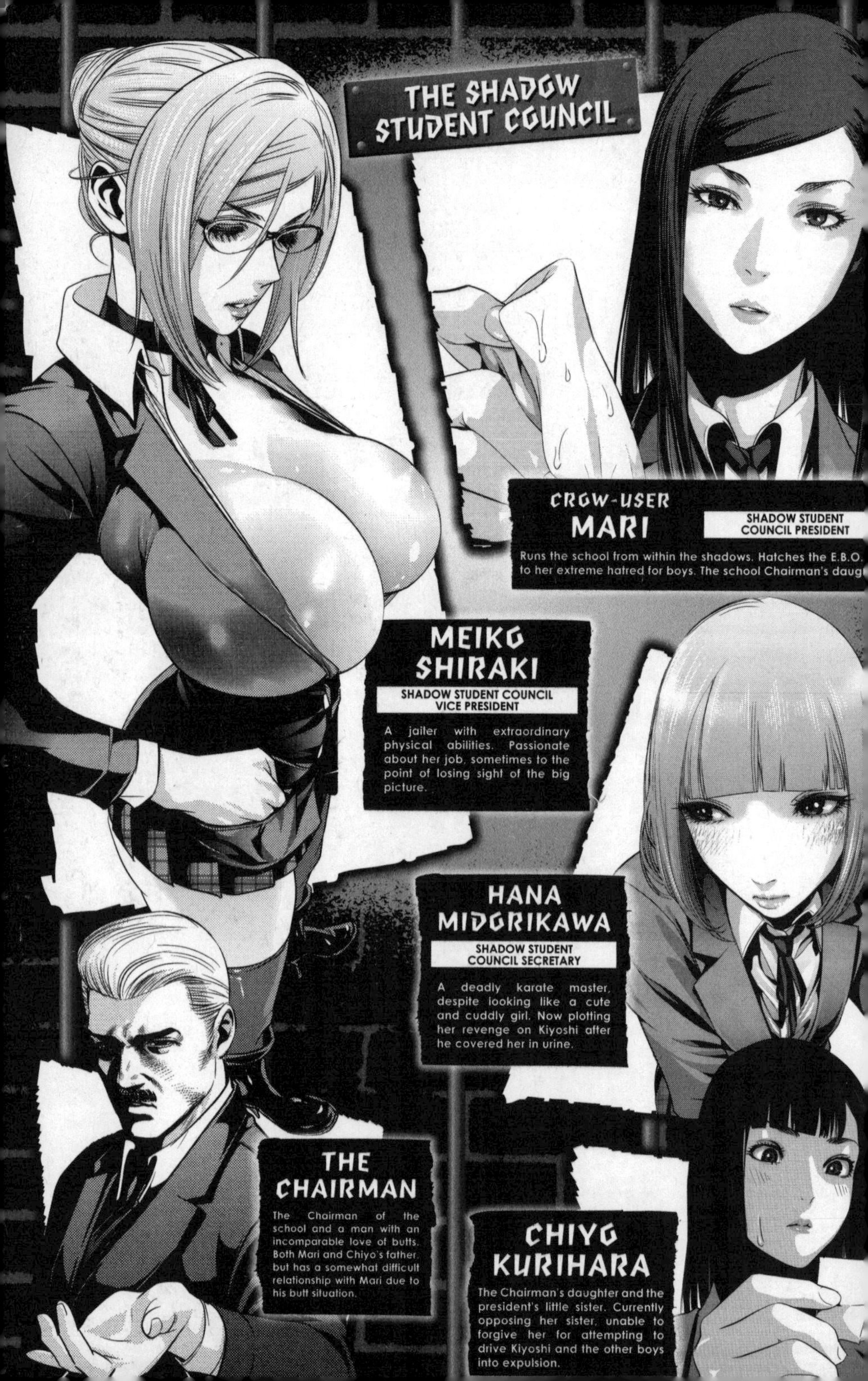
THE SHADOW STUDENT COUNCIL
CROW-USER
MARI
SHADOW STUDENT COUNCIL PRESIDENT
Runs the school from within the shadows. Hatches the E.B.O. to her extreme hatred for boys. The school Chairman's daug
MEIKO SHIRAKI
SHADOW STUDENT COUNCIL VICE PRESIDENT
A jailer with extraordinary physical abilities. Passionate about her job, sometimes to the point of losing sight of the big picture.
HANA MIDORIKAWA
SHADOW STUDENT COUNCIL SECRETARY
A deadly karate master, despite looking like a cute and cuddly girl. Now plotting her revenge on Kiyoshi after he covered her in urine.
THE CHAIRMAN
The Chairman of the school and a man with an incomparable love of butts. Both Mari and Chiyo's father, but has a somewhat difficult relationship with Mari due to his butt situation.
CHIYO KURIHARA
The Chairman's daughter and the president's little sister. Currently opposing her sister, unable to forgive her for attempting to drive Kiyoshi and the other boys into expulsion.

CONTENTS

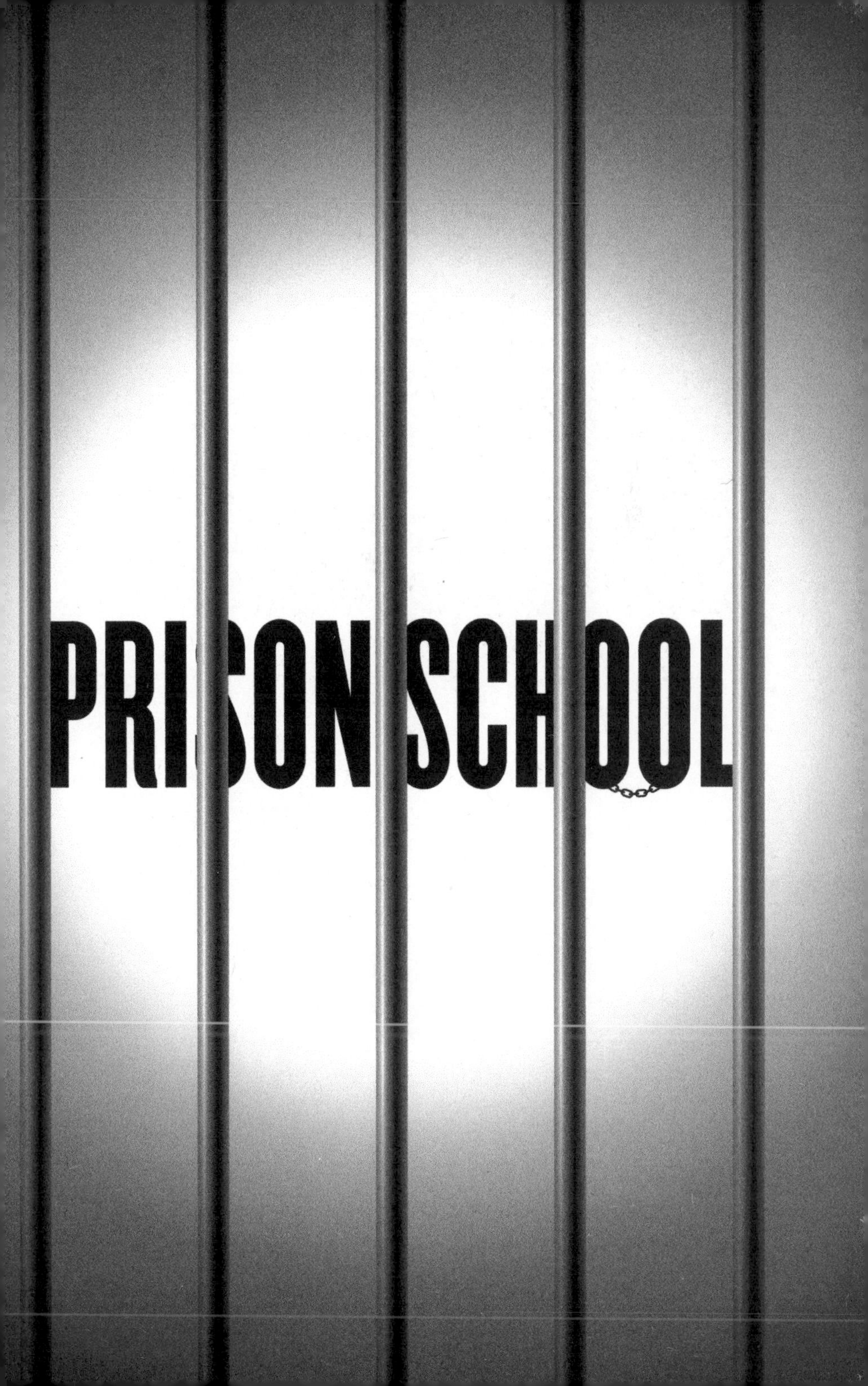
PRISON SCHOOL

CHAPTER 59: VERTIGO

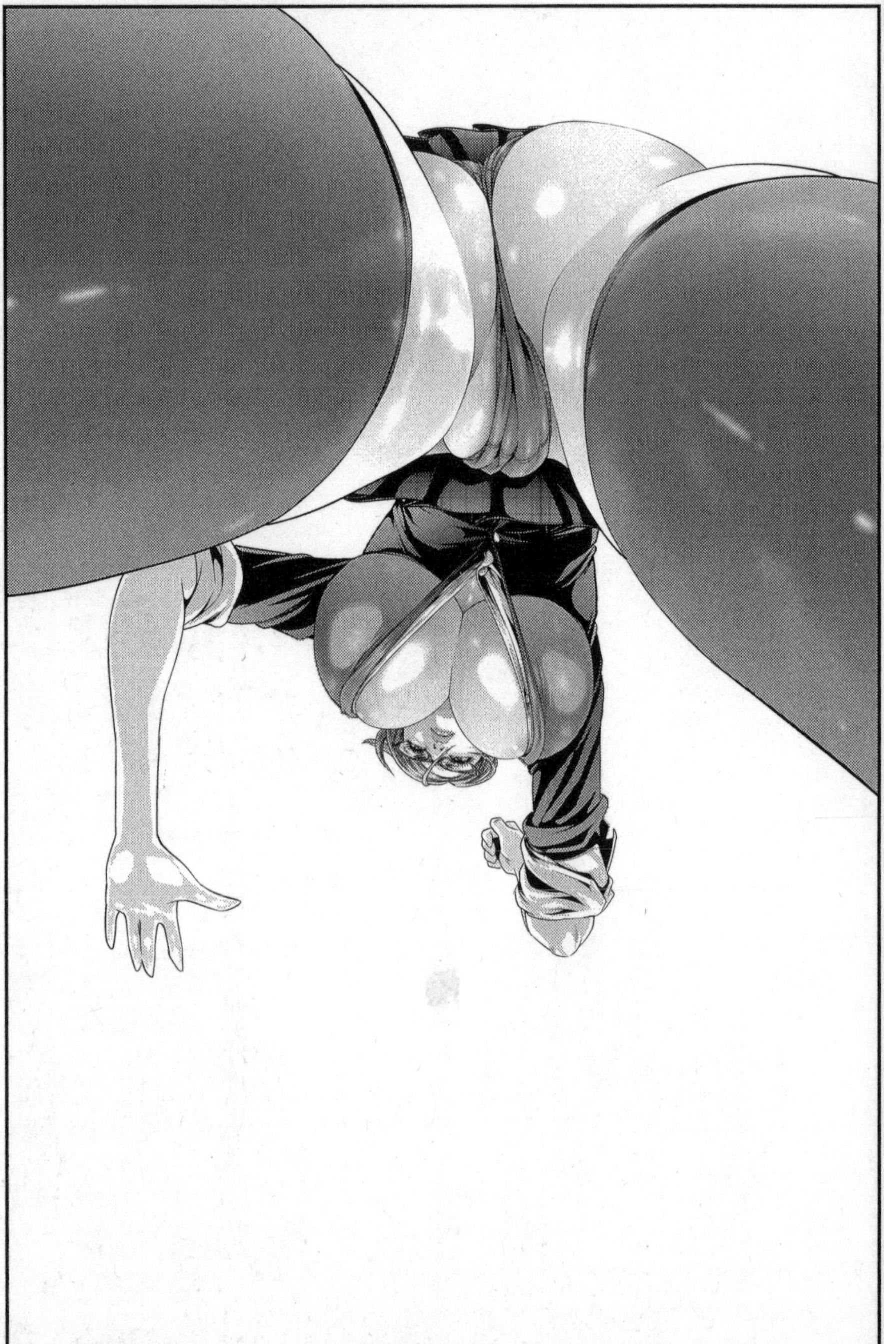

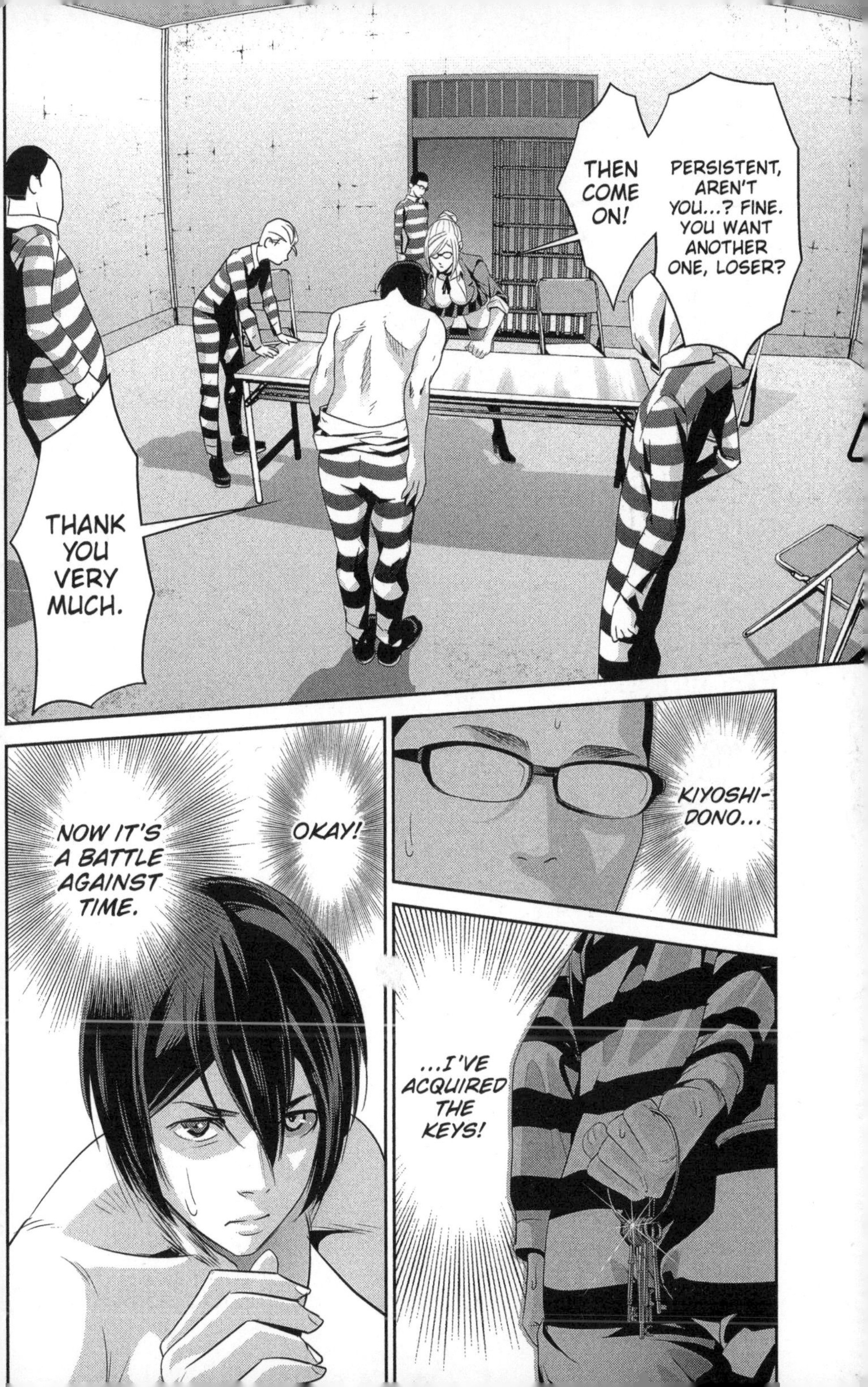
PERSISTENT, AREN'T YOU...? FINE. YOU WANT ANOTHER ONE, LOSER?
THEN COME ON!
THANK YOU VERY MUCH.
KIYOSHI-DONO...
...I'VE ACQUIRED THE KEYS!
OKAY!
NOW IT'S A BATTLE AGAINST TIME.

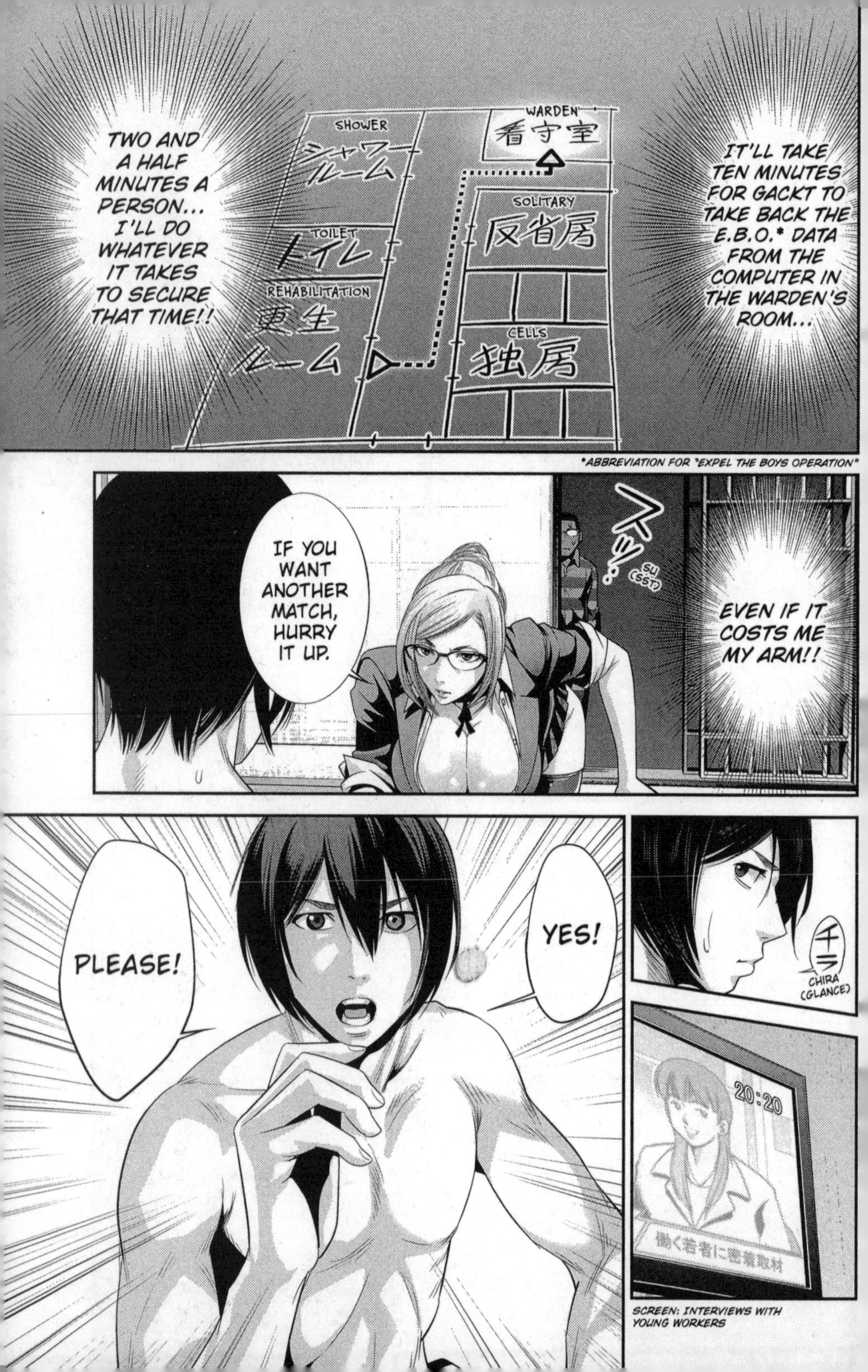
IT'LL TAKE TEN MINUTES FOR GACKT TO TAKE BACK THE E.B.O.* DATA FROM THE COMPUTER IN THE WARDEN'S ROOM...
WARDEN
看守室
SOLITARY
反省房
CELLS
独房
SHOWER
シャワールーム
TOILET
トイレ
REHABILITATION
更生ルーム
TWO AND A HALF MINUTES A PERSON... I'LL DO WHATEVER IT TAKES TO SECURE THAT TIME!!
*ABBREVIATION FOR "EXPEL THE BOYS OPERATION"
EVEN IF IT COSTS ME MY ARM!!
SU (SST)
IF YOU WANT ANOTHER MATCH, HURRY IT UP.
CHIRA (GLANCE)
20:20
働く若者に密着取材
SCREEN: INTERVIEWS WITH YOUNG WORKERS
YES!
PLEASE!

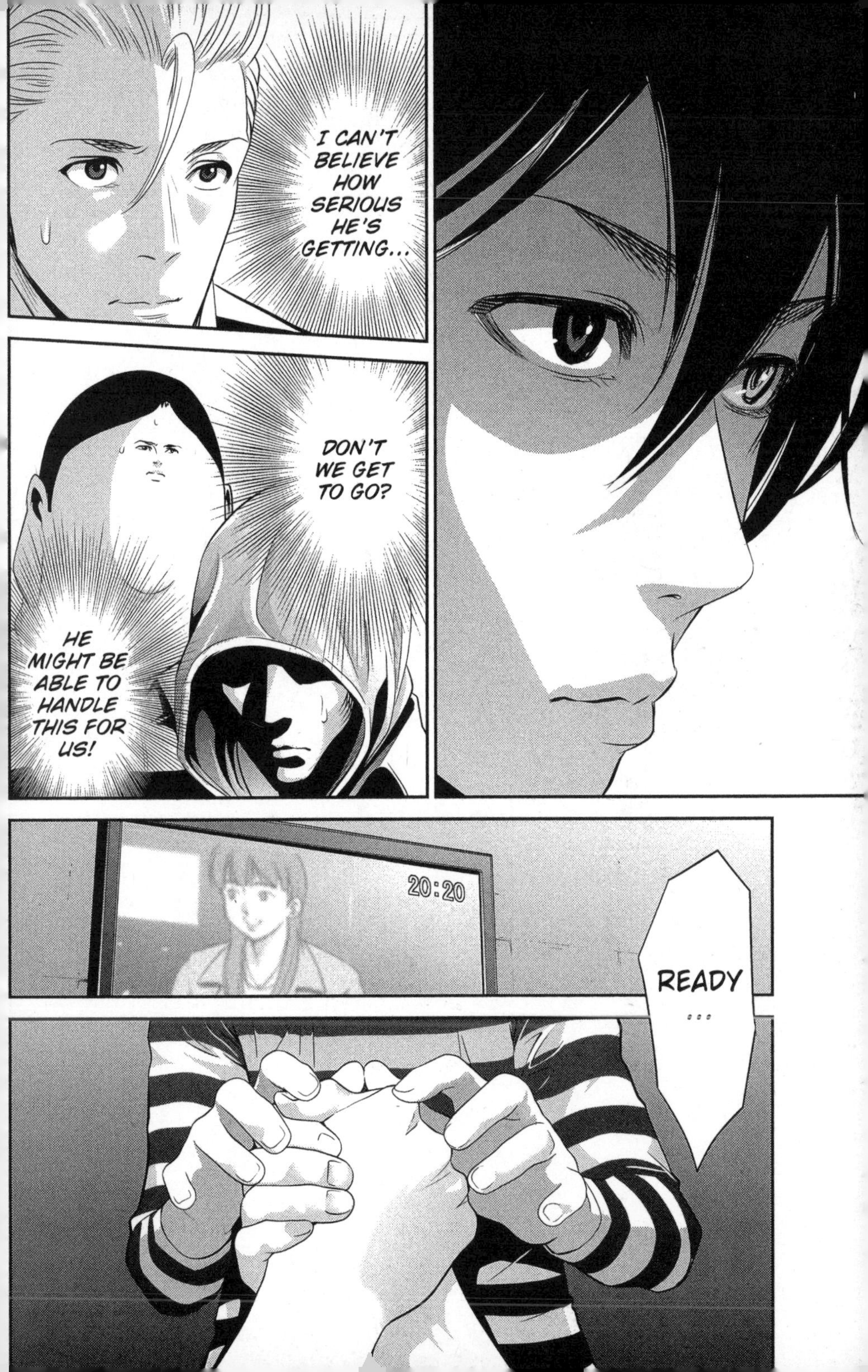
I CAN'T BELIEVE HOW SERIOUS HE'S GETTING...
DON'T WE GET TO GO?
HE MIGHT BE ABLE TO HANDLE THIS FOR US!
20:20
READY ...

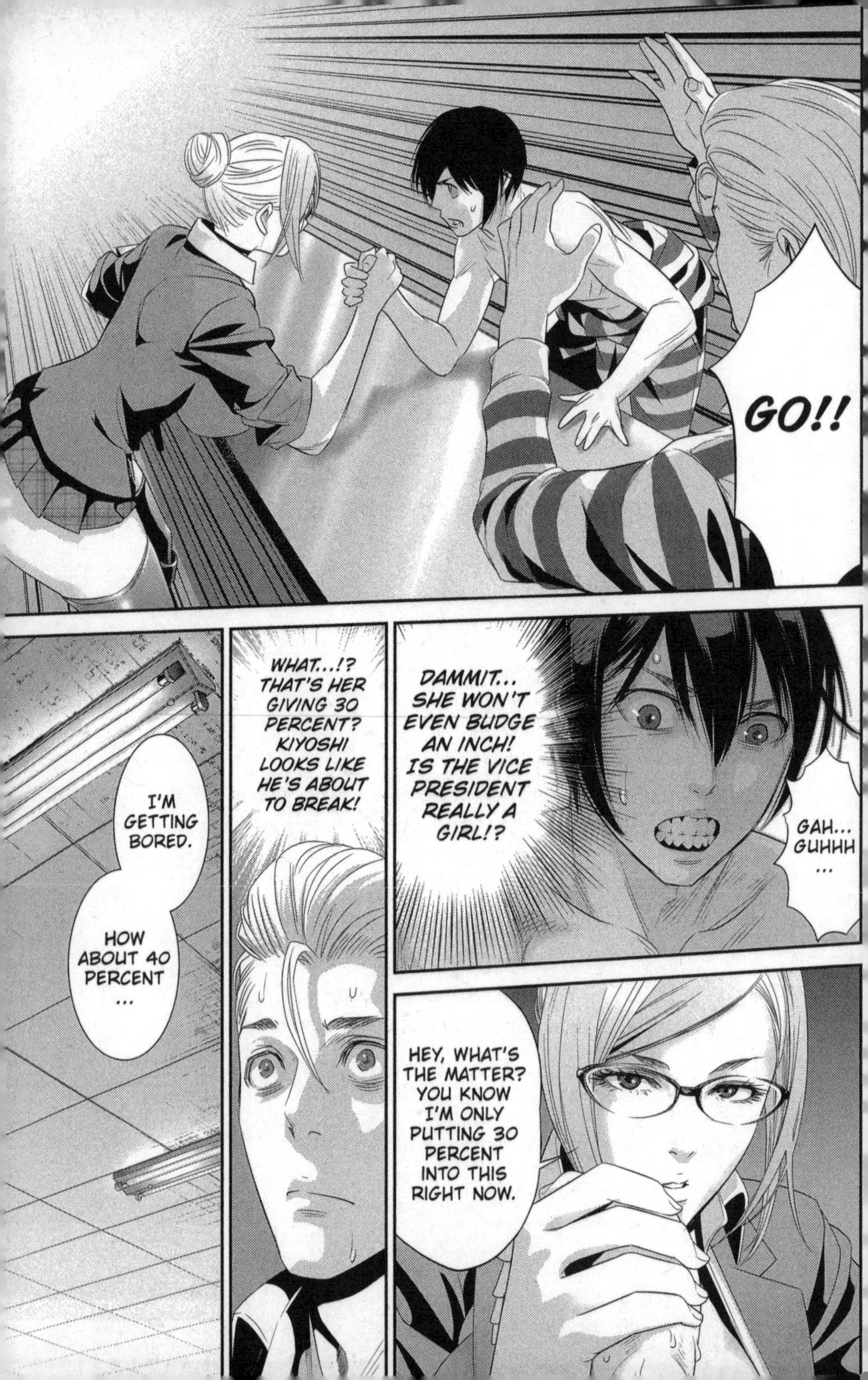
GO!!
GAH... GUHHH ...
DAMMIT... SHE WON'T EVEN BUDGE AN INCH! IS THE VICE PRESIDENT REALLY A GIRL!?
HEY, WHAT'S THE MATTER? YOU KNOW I'M ONLY PUTTING 30 PERCENT INTO THIS RIGHT NOW.
WHAT...!? THAT'S HER GIVING 30 PERCENT? KIYOSHI LOOKS LIKE HE'S ABOUT TO BREAK!
I'M GETTING BORED.
HOW ABOUT 40 PERCENT ...

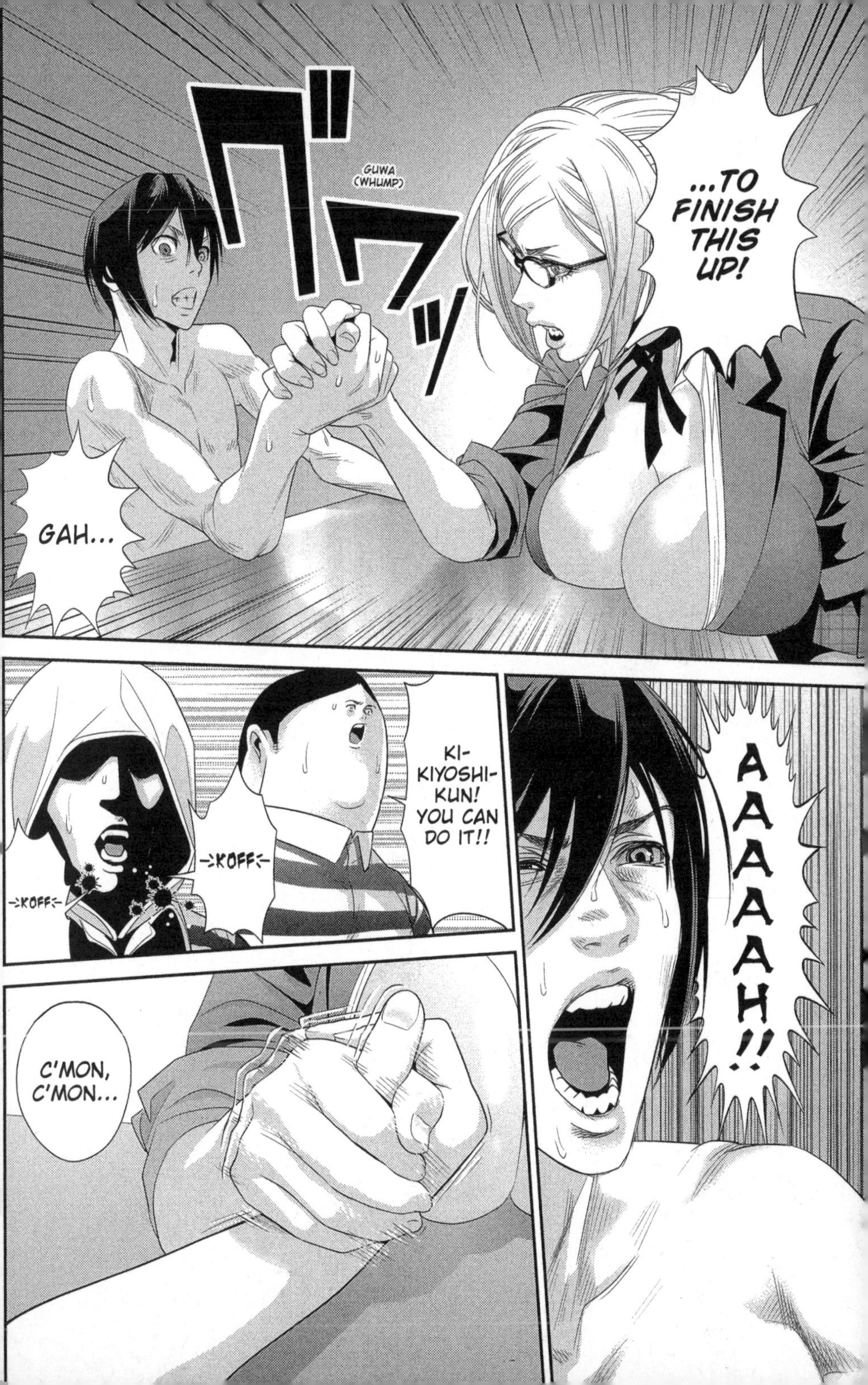
...TO FINISH THIS UP!
GUWA (WHUMP)
GAH...
AAAAAH!!
KI-KIYOSHI-KUN! YOU CAN DO IT!!
KOFF
KOFF
C'MON, C'MON...

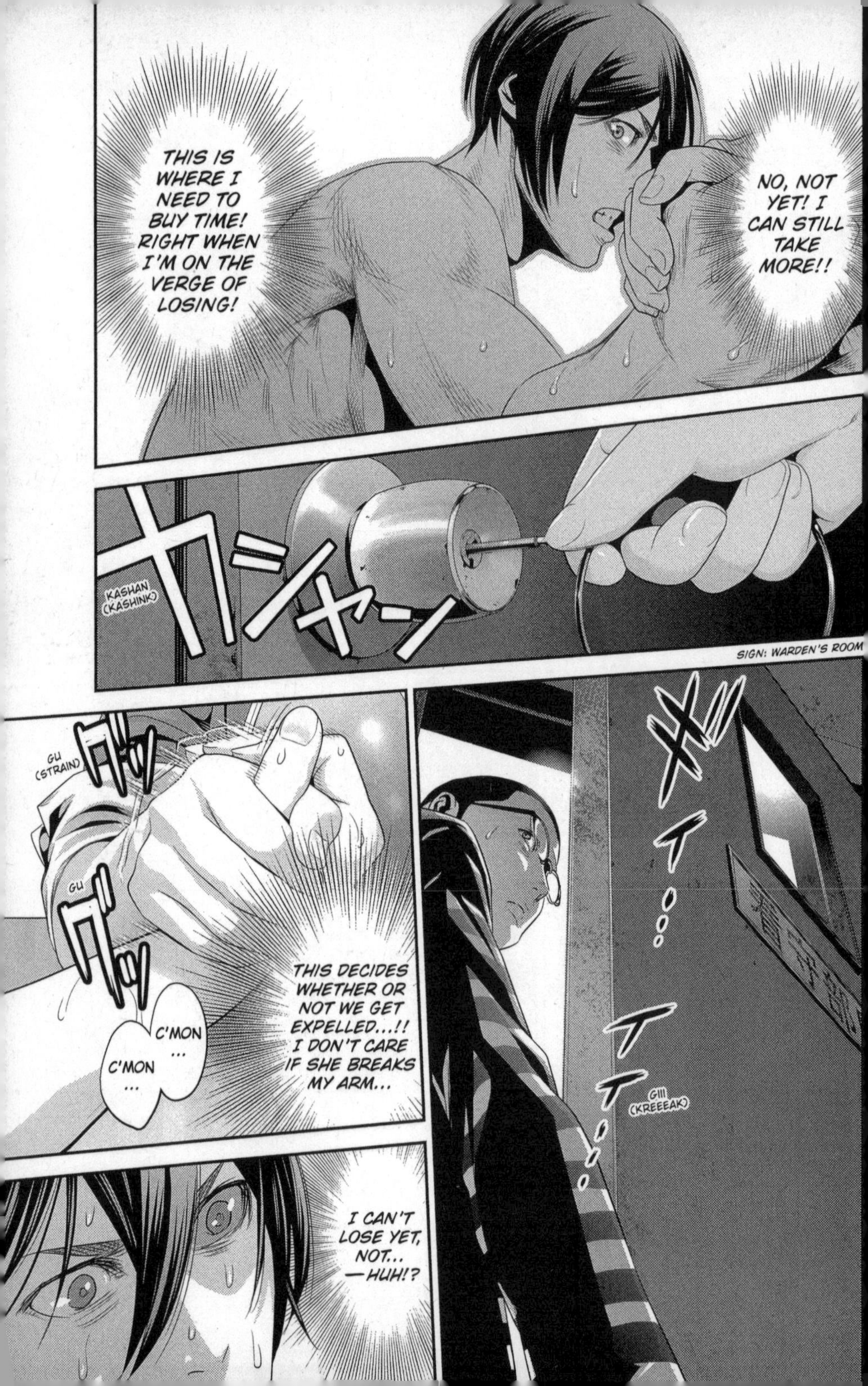
NO, NOT YET! I CAN STILL TAKE MORE!!
THIS IS WHERE I NEED TO BUY TIME! RIGHT WHEN I'M ON THE VERGE OF LOSING!
SIGN: WARDEN'S ROOM
KASHAN (KASHINK)
GIII (KREEEAK)
GU (STRAIN)
GU
THIS DECIDES WHETHER OR NOT WE GET EXPELLED...!! I DON'T CARE IF SHE BREAKS MY ARM...
C'MON ...
C'MON ...
I CAN'T LOSE YET, NOT... —HUH!?

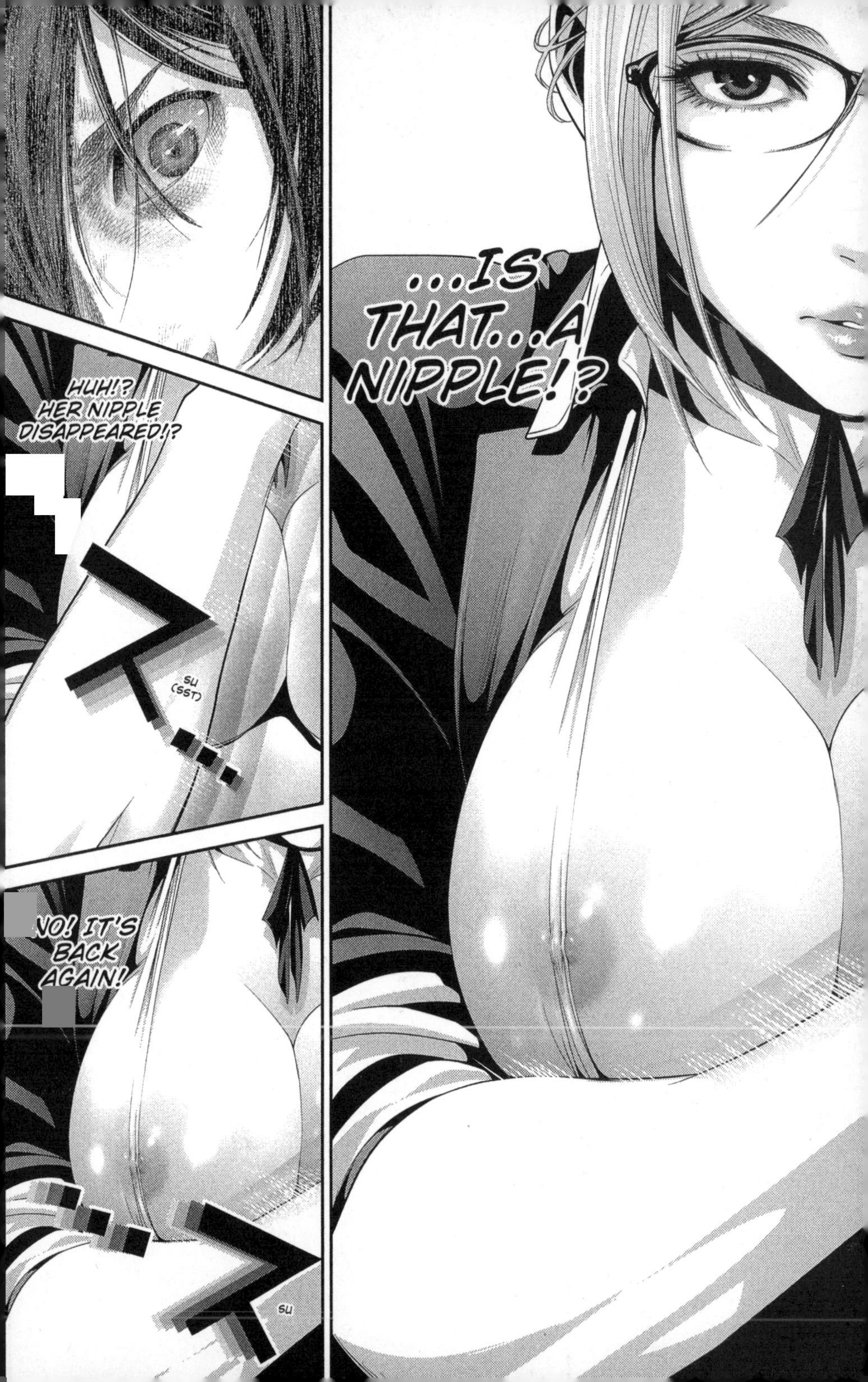
...IS THAT...A NIPPLE!?
HUH!? HER NIPPLE DISAPPEARED!?
SU (SST)
NO! IT'S BACK AGAIN!
SU

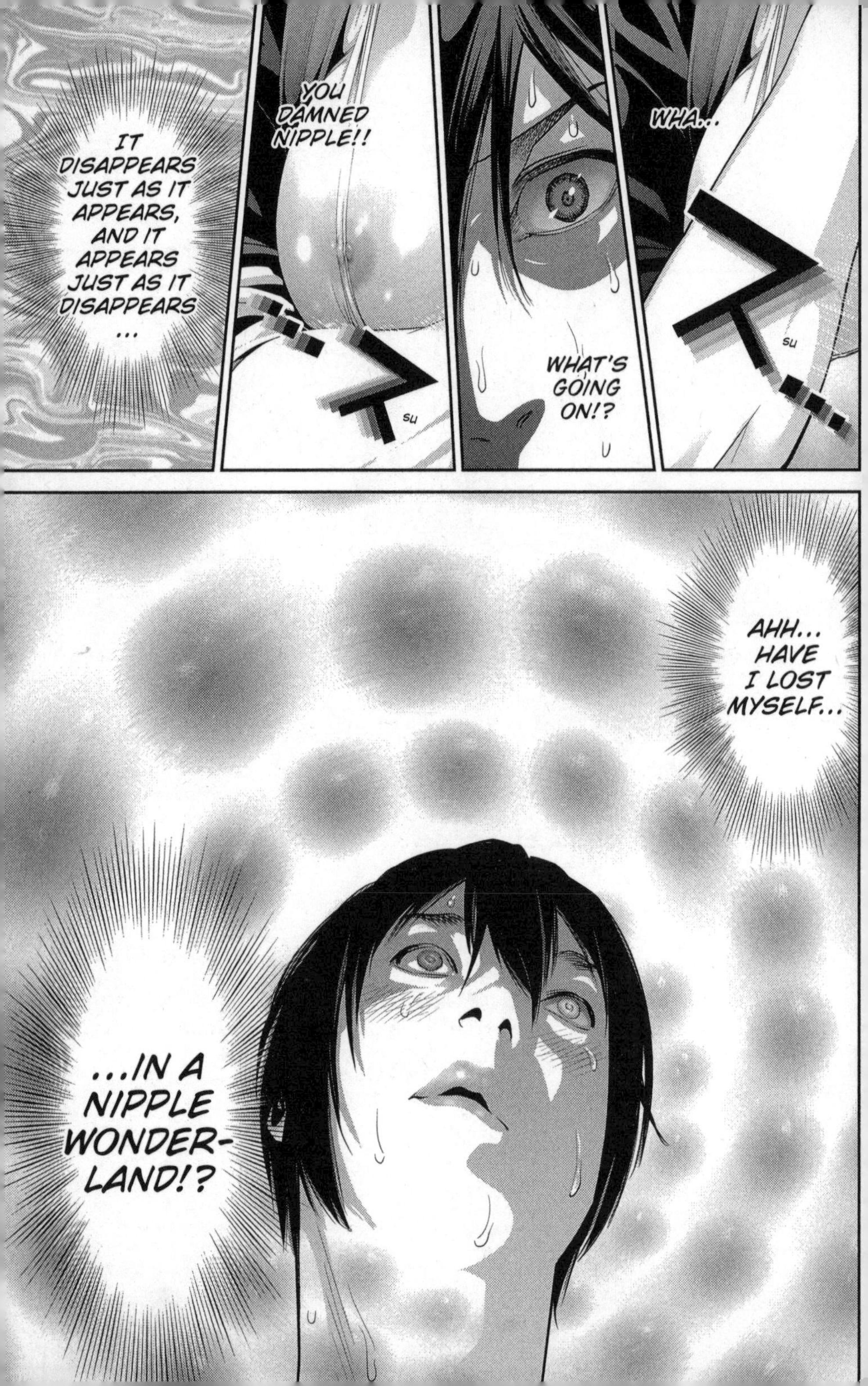
WHA...
SU
WHAT'S GOING ON!?
YOU DAMNED NIPPLE!!
SU
IT DISAPPEARS JUST AS IT APPEARS, AND IT APPEARS JUST AS IT DISAPPEARS...
AHH... HAVE I LOST MYSELF...
...IN A NIPPLE WONDER-LAND!?

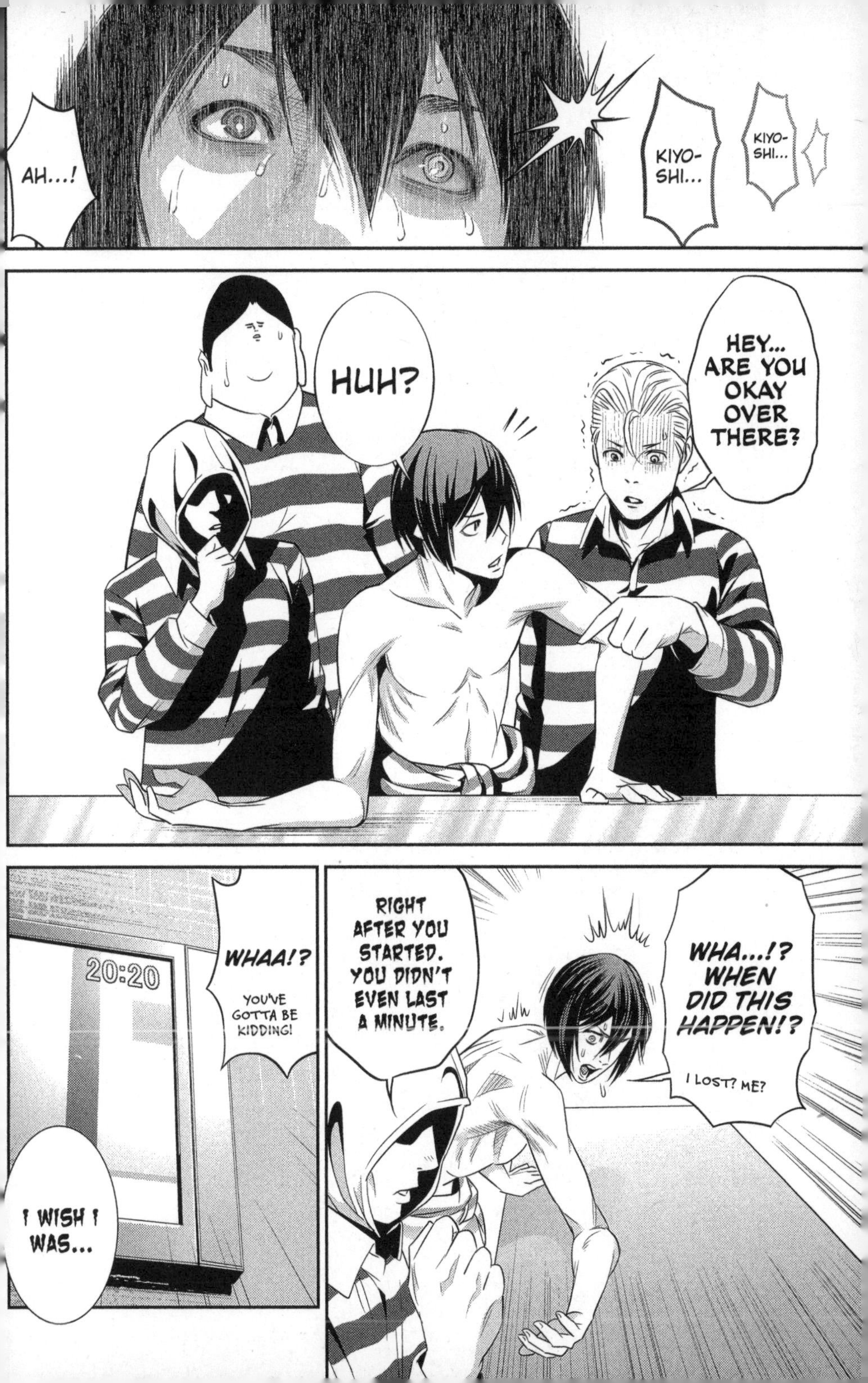
KIYO-SHI...
KIYO-SHI...
AH...!
HEY... ARE YOU OKAY OVER THERE?
HUH?
WHA...!? WHEN DID THIS HAPPEN!?
I LOST? ME?
RIGHT AFTER YOU STARTED. YOU DIDN'T EVEN LAST A MINUTE.
20:20
WHAA!?
YOU'VE GOTTA BE KIDDING!
I WISH I WAS...

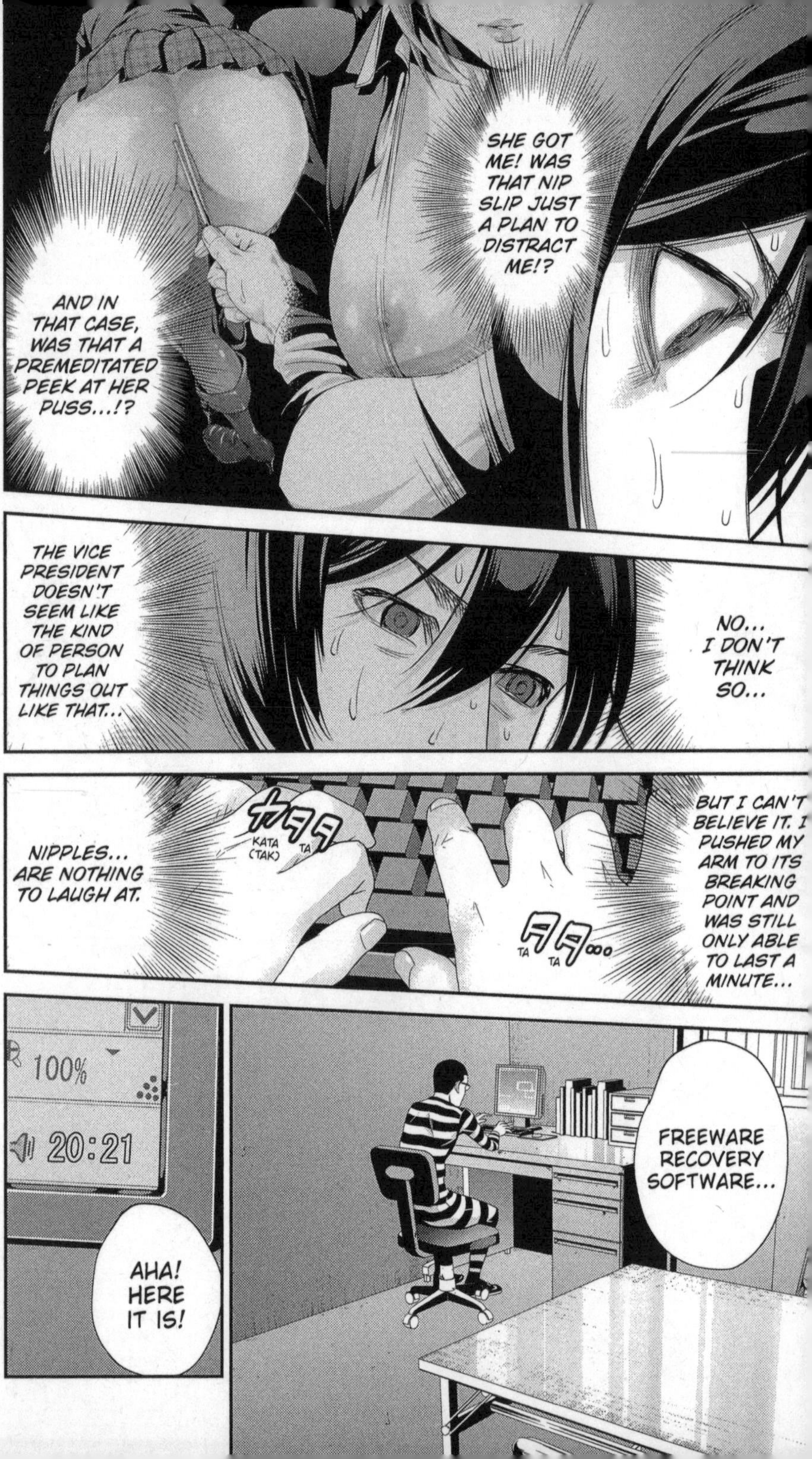
SHE GOT ME! WAS THAT NIP SLIP JUST A PLAN TO DISTRACT ME!?
AND IN THAT CASE, WAS THAT A PREMEDITATED PEEK AT HER PUSS...!?
NO... I DON'T THINK SO...
THE VICE PRESIDENT DOESN'T SEEM LIKE THE KIND OF PERSON TO PLAN THINGS OUT LIKE THAT...
BUT I CAN'T BELIEVE IT. I PUSHED MY ARM TO ITS BREAKING POINT AND WAS STILL ONLY ABLE TO LAST A MINUTE...
TA TA
KATA (TAK) TA
NIPPLES... ARE NOTHING TO LAUGH AT.
FREEWARE RECOVERY SOFTWARE...
100%
20:21
AHA! HERE IT IS!

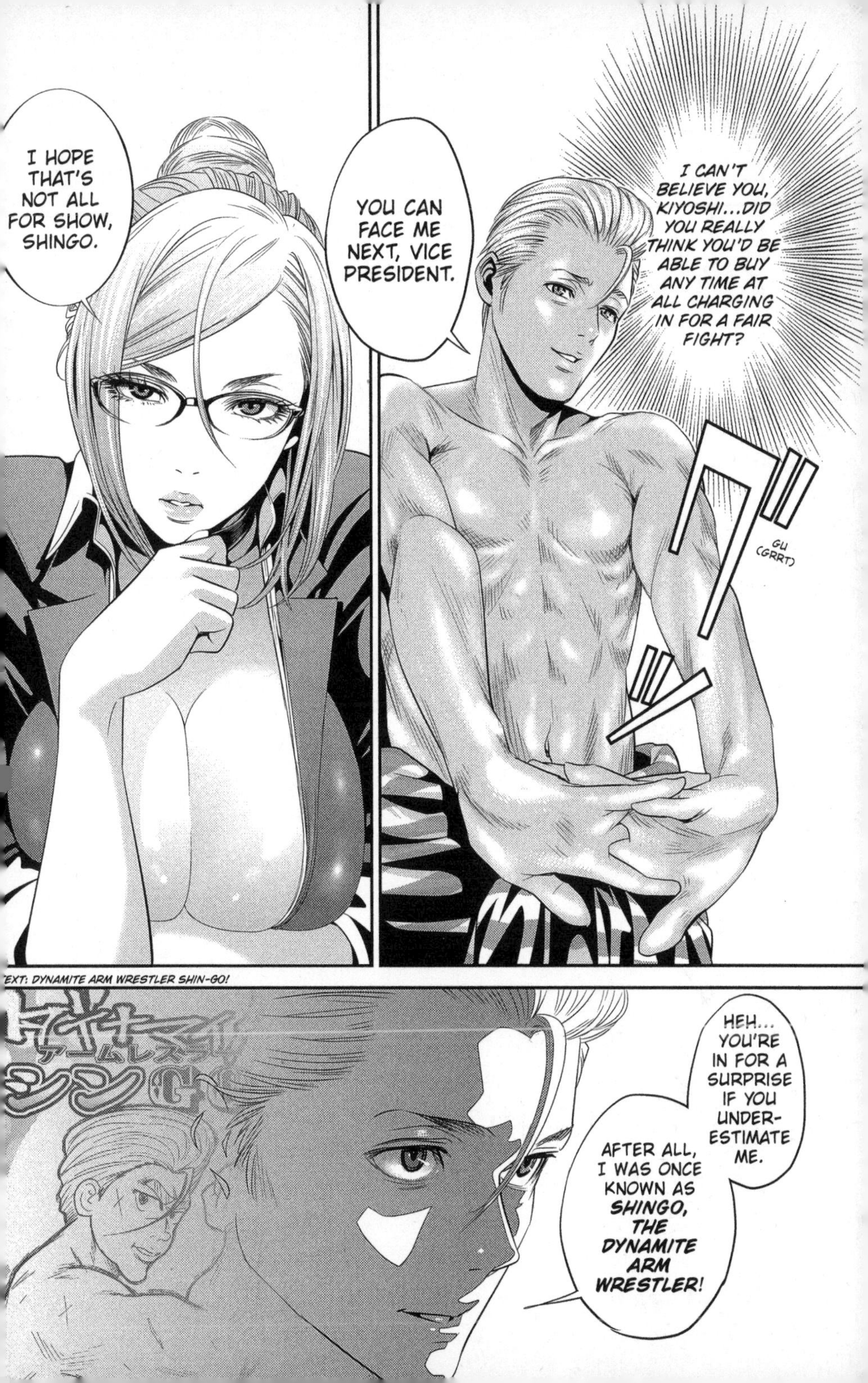
I CAN'T BELIEVE YOU, KIYOSHI...DID YOU REALLY THINK YOU'D BE ABLE TO BUY ANY TIME AT ALL CHARGING IN FOR A FAIR FIGHT?
YOU CAN FACE ME NEXT, VICE PRESIDENT.
GU (GRRT)
I HOPE THAT'S NOT ALL FOR SHOW, SHINGO.
EXT: DYNAMITE ARM WRESTLER SHIN-GO!
HEH... YOU'RE IN FOR A SURPRISE IF YOU UNDER-ESTIMATE ME.
AFTER ALL, I WAS ONCE KNOWN AS ***SHINGO, THE DYNAMITE ARM WRESTLER!***

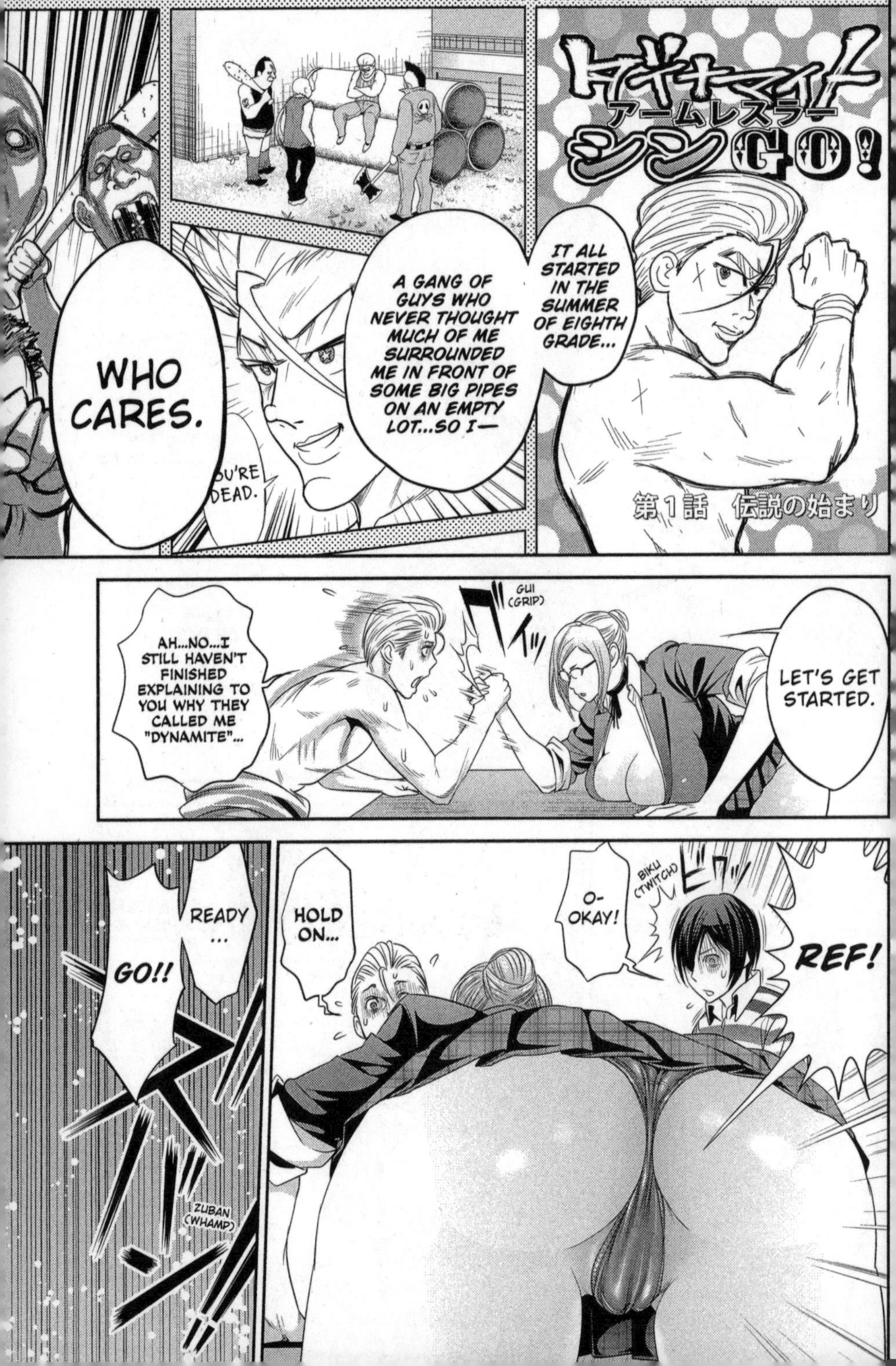
ダイナマイト
アームレスラー
シンGO!
IT ALL STARTED IN THE SUMMER OF EIGHTH GRADE...
第1話 伝説の始まり
A GANG OF GUYS WHO NEVER THOUGHT MUCH OF ME SURROUNDED ME IN FRONT OF SOME BIG PIPES ON AN EMPTY LOT...SO I—
OU'RE DEAD.
WHO CARES.
LET'S GET STARTED.
GUI (GRIP)
AH...NO...I STILL HAVEN'T FINISHED EXPLAINING TO YOU WHY THEY CALLED ME "DYNAMITE"...
REF!
BIKU (TWITCH)
O-OKAY!
HOLD ON...
READY...
GO!!
ZUBAN (WHAMP)

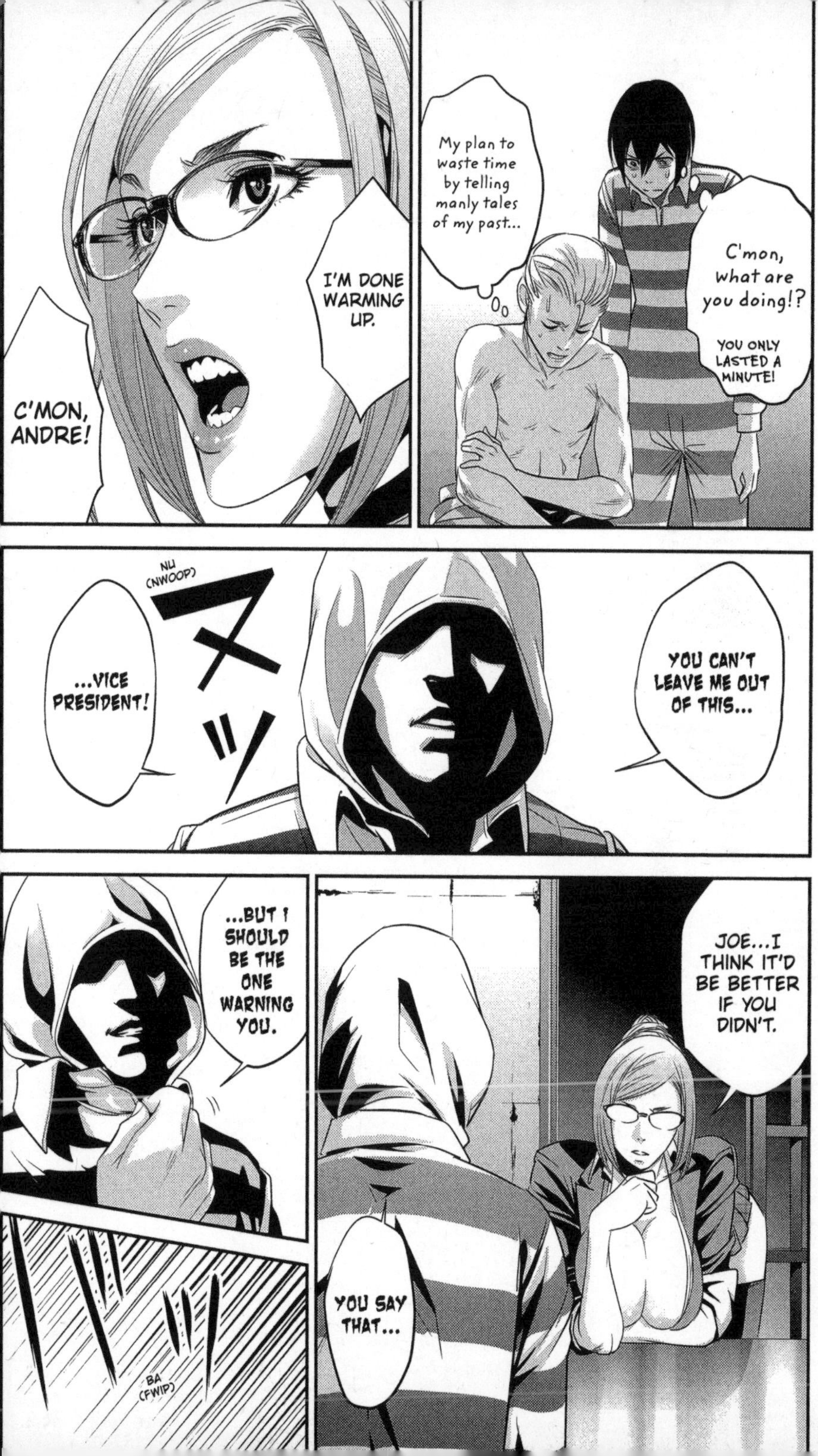
C'mon, what are you doing!?
YOU ONLY LASTED A MINUTE!
My plan to waste time by telling manly tales of my past...
I'M DONE WARMING UP.
C'MON, ANDRE!
YOU CAN'T LEAVE ME OUT OF THIS...
NU (NWOOP)
...VICE PRESIDENT!
JOE...I THINK IT'D BE BETTER IF YOU DIDN'T.
YOU SAY THAT...
...BUT I SHOULD BE THE ONE WARNING YOU.
BA (FWIP)

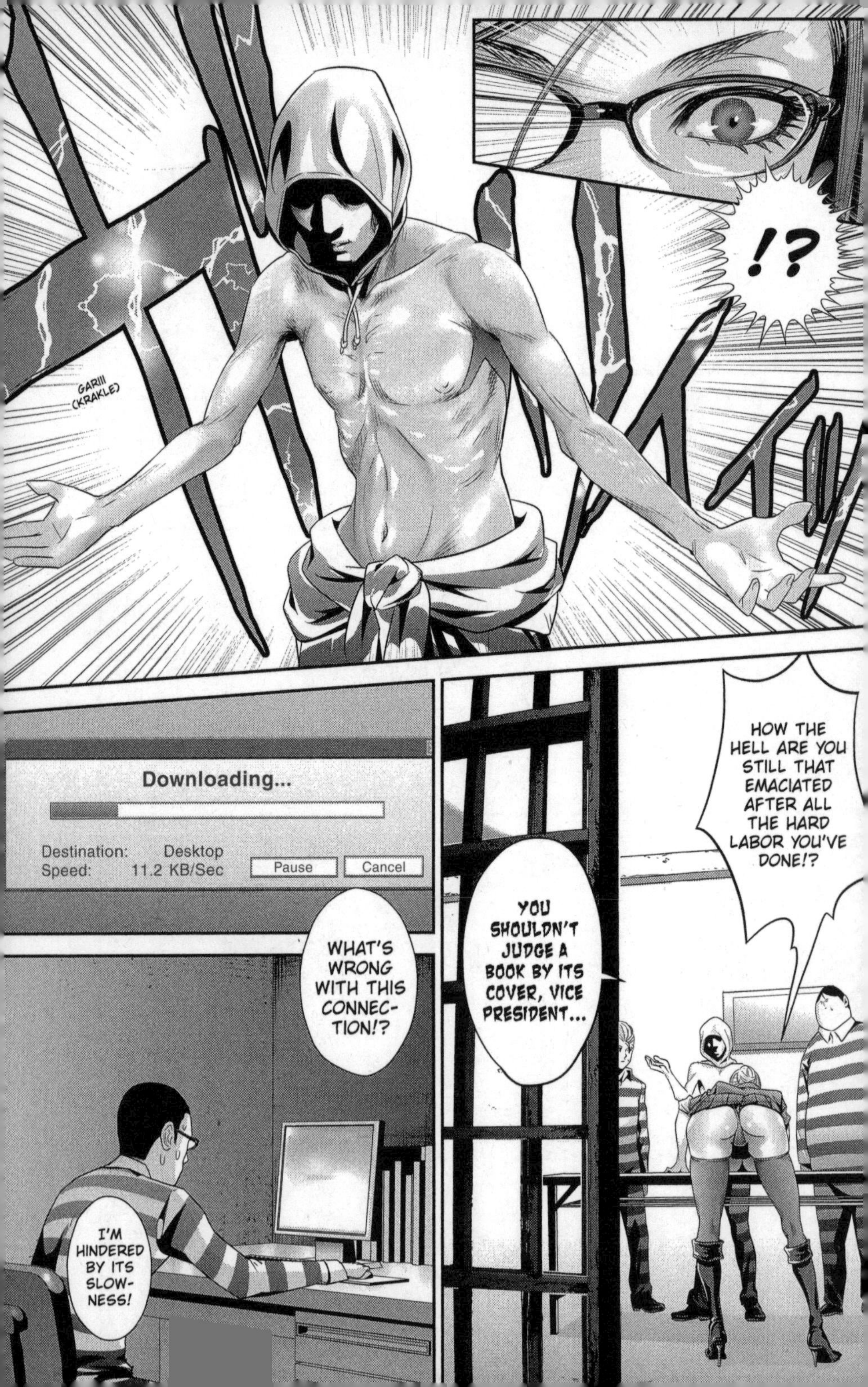
!?
GARIII (KRAKLE)
HOW THE HELL ARE YOU STILL THAT EMACIATED AFTER ALL THE HARD LABOR YOU'VE DONE!?
YOU SHOULDN'T JUDGE A BOOK BY ITS COVER, VICE PRESIDENT...
Downloading...
Destination: Desktop
Speed: 11.2 KB/Sec
Pause
Cancel
WHAT'S WRONG WITH THIS CONNEC-TION!?
I'M HINDERED BY ITS SLOW-NESS!

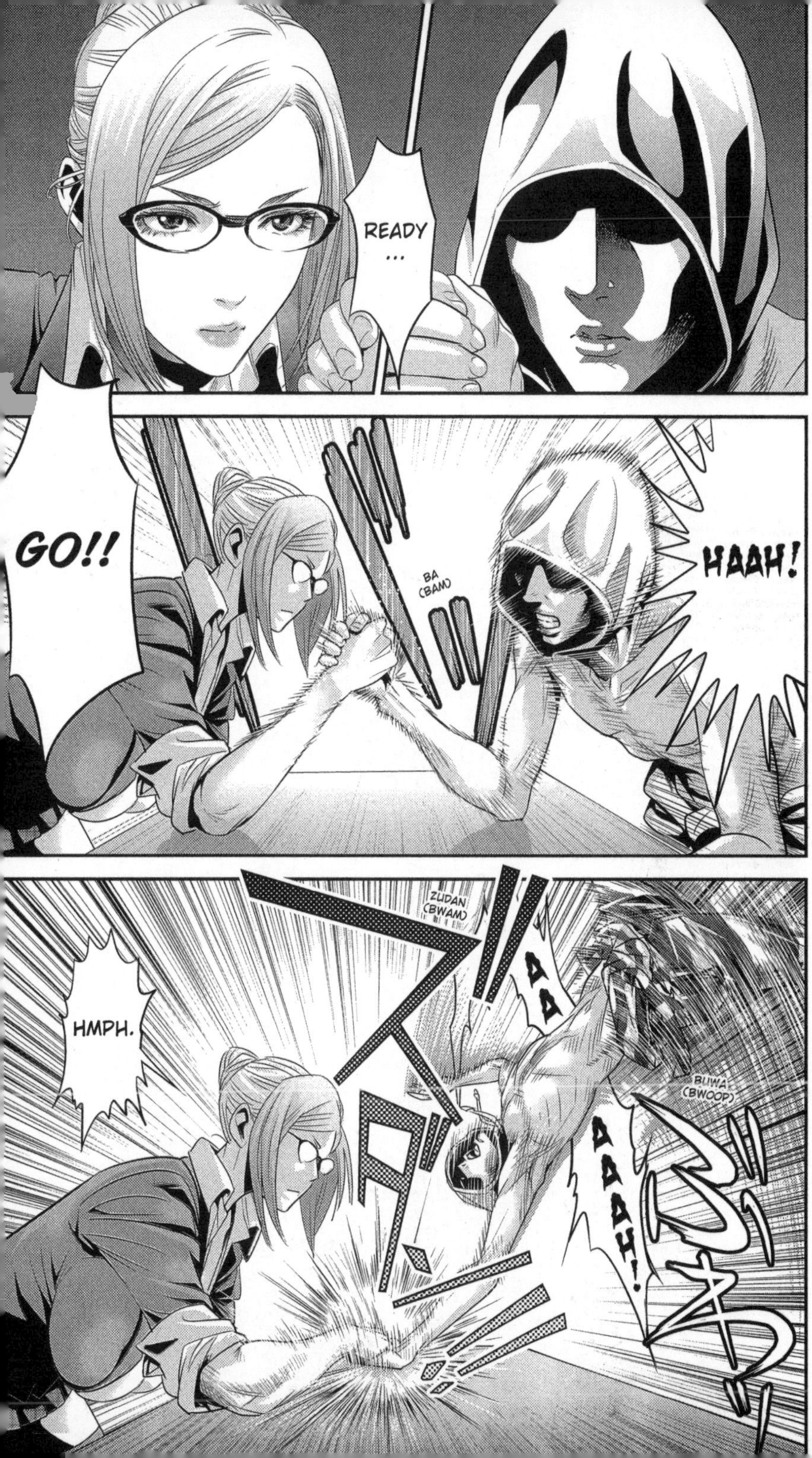

READY ...
GO!!
HAAH!
BA (BAM)
ZUDAN (BWAM)
AAAAAH!
BUWA (BWOOP)
HMPH.

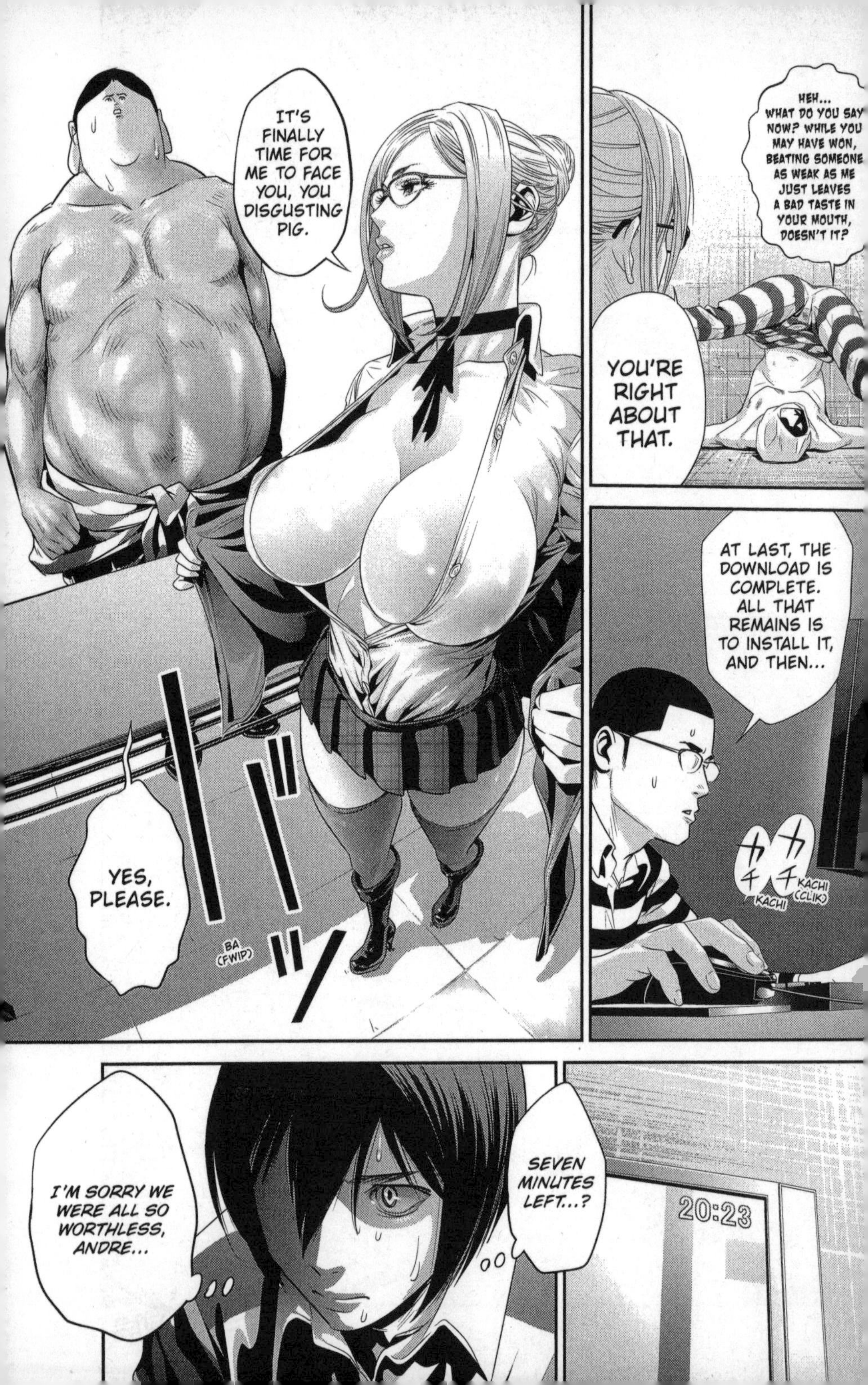
HEH... WHAT DO YOU SAY NOW? WHILE YOU MAY HAVE WON, BEATING SOMEONE AS WEAK AS ME JUST LEAVES A BAD TASTE IN YOUR MOUTH, DOESN'T IT?
YOU'RE RIGHT ABOUT THAT.
AT LAST, THE DOWNLOAD IS COMPLETE. ALL THAT REMAINS IS TO INSTALL IT, AND THEN...
カチ カチ
KACHI (CLIK)
KACHI
IT'S FINALLY TIME FOR ME TO FACE YOU, YOU DISGUSTING PIG.
YES, PLEASE.
BA (FWIP)
20:23
SEVEN MINUTES LEFT...?
I'M SORRY WE WERE ALL SO WORTHLESS, ANDRE...

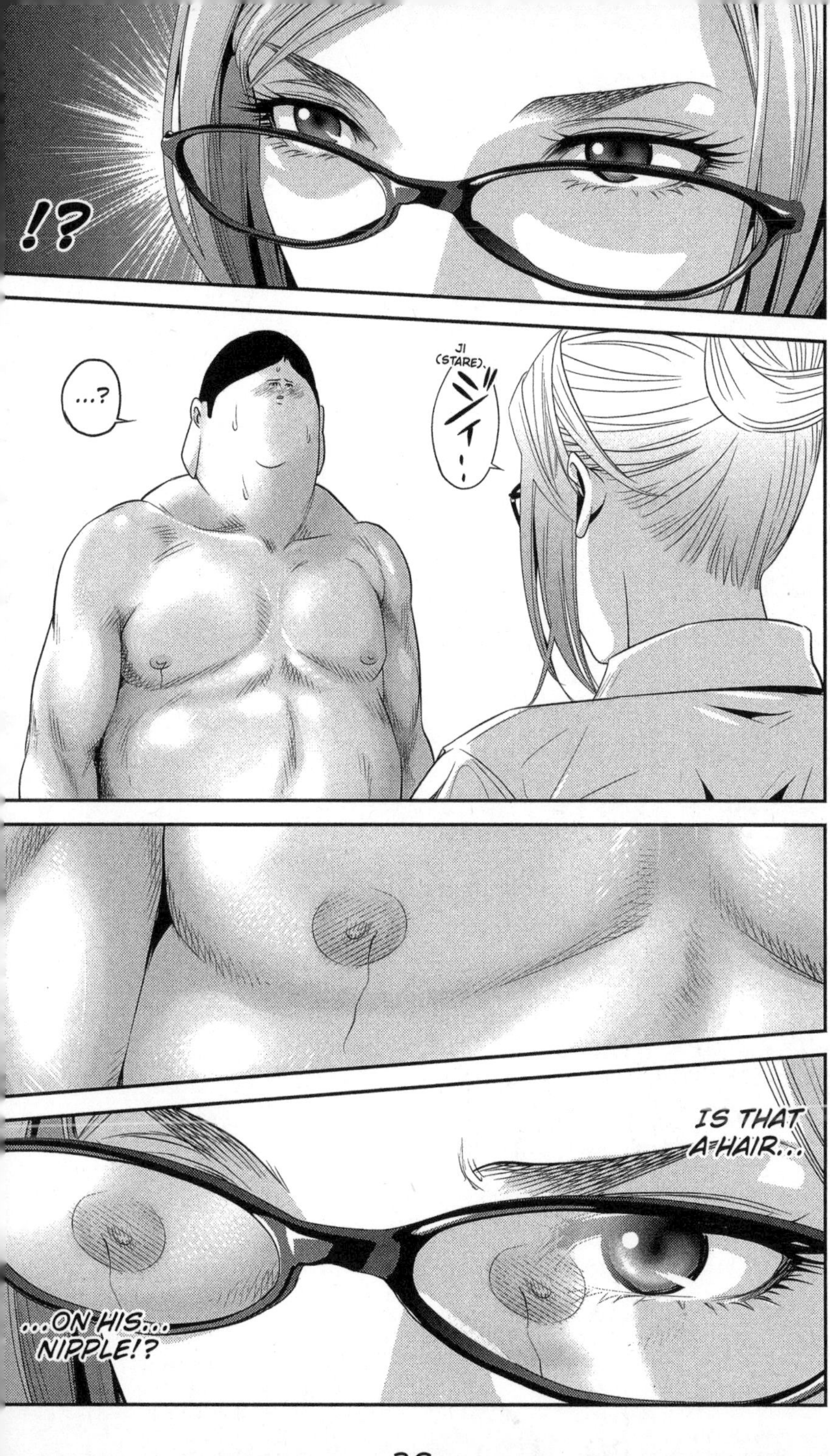
!?
JI (STARE)
...?
IS THAT A HAIR...
...ON HIS... NIPPLE!?

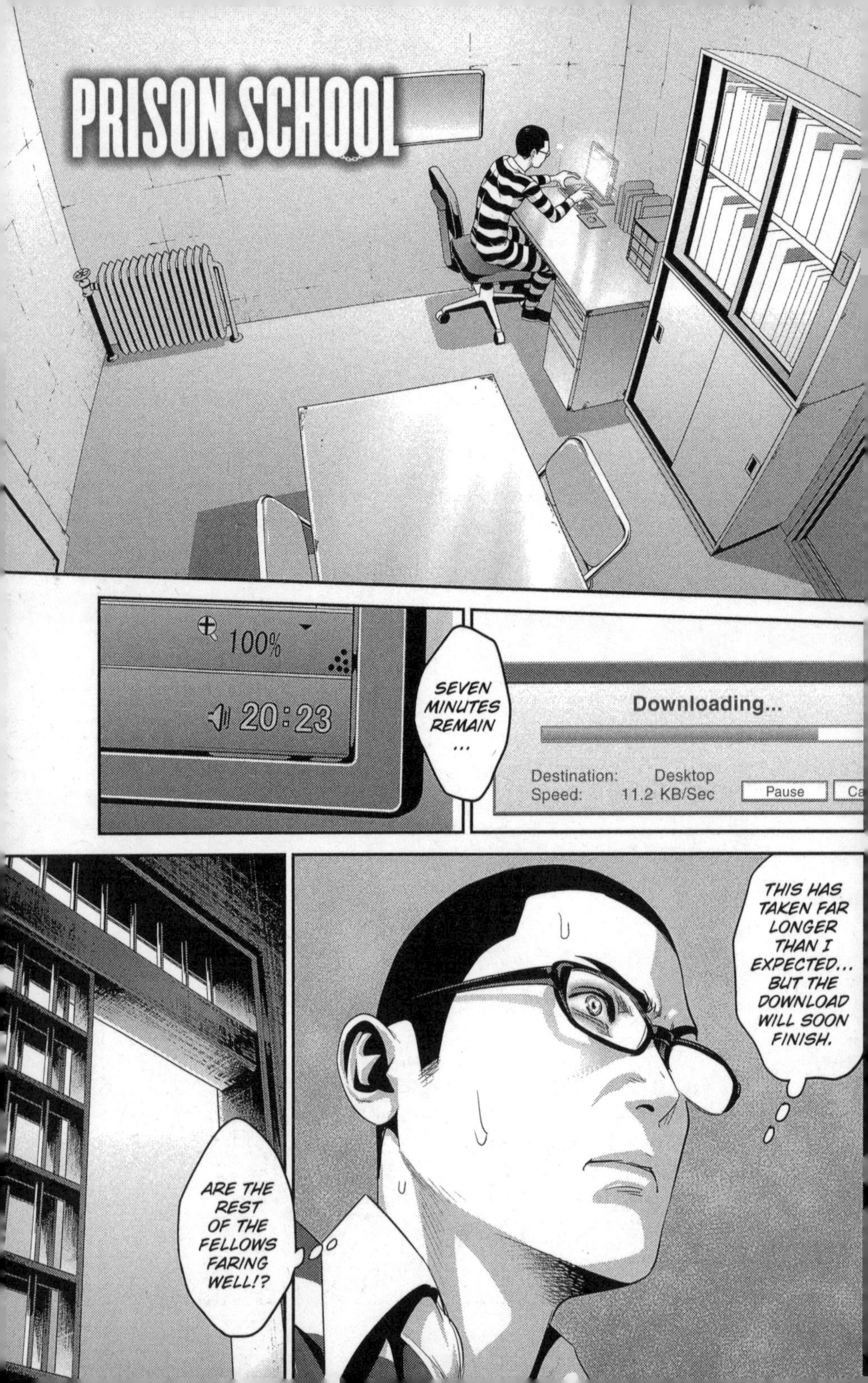
PRISON SCHOOL
Downloading...
Destination: Desktop
Speed: 11.2 KB/Sec
Pause
SEVEN MINUTES REMAIN ...
100%
20:23
THIS HAS TAKEN FAR LONGER THAN I EXPECTED... BUT THE DOWNLOAD WILL SOON FINISH.
ARE THE REST OF THE FELLOWS FARING WELL!?

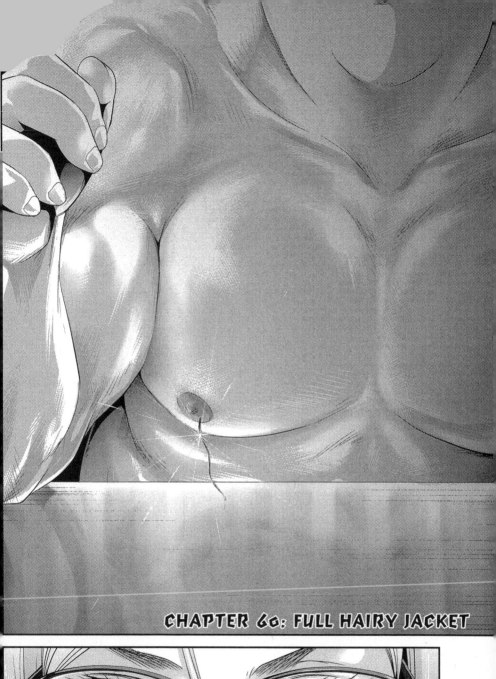

CHAPTER 60: FULL HAIRY JACKET

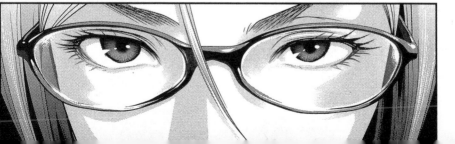

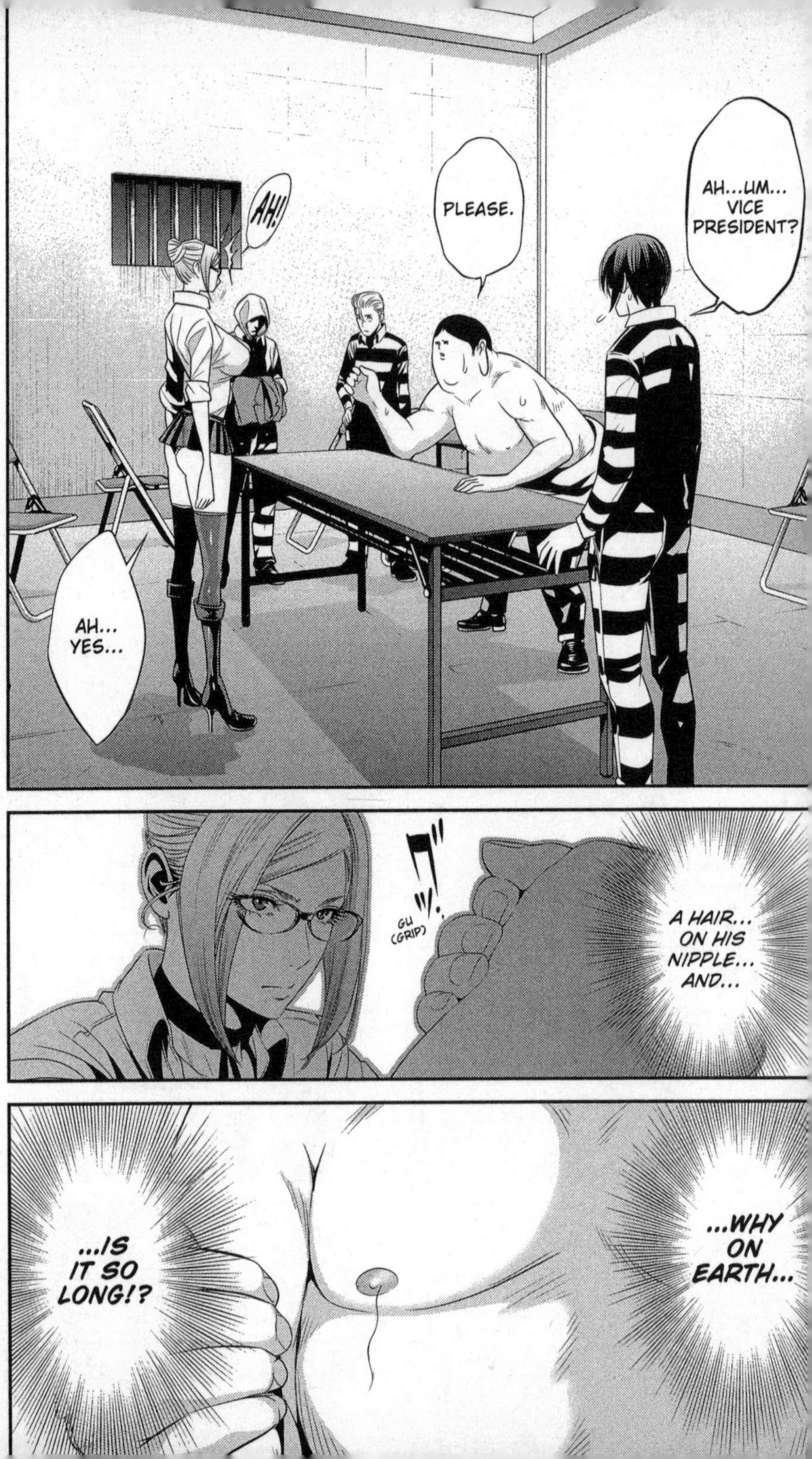
AH...UM... VICE PRESIDENT?
PLEASE.
AH!
AH... YES...
A HAIR... ON HIS NIPPLE... AND...
GU (GRIP)
...WHY ON EARTH...
...IS IT SO LONG!?

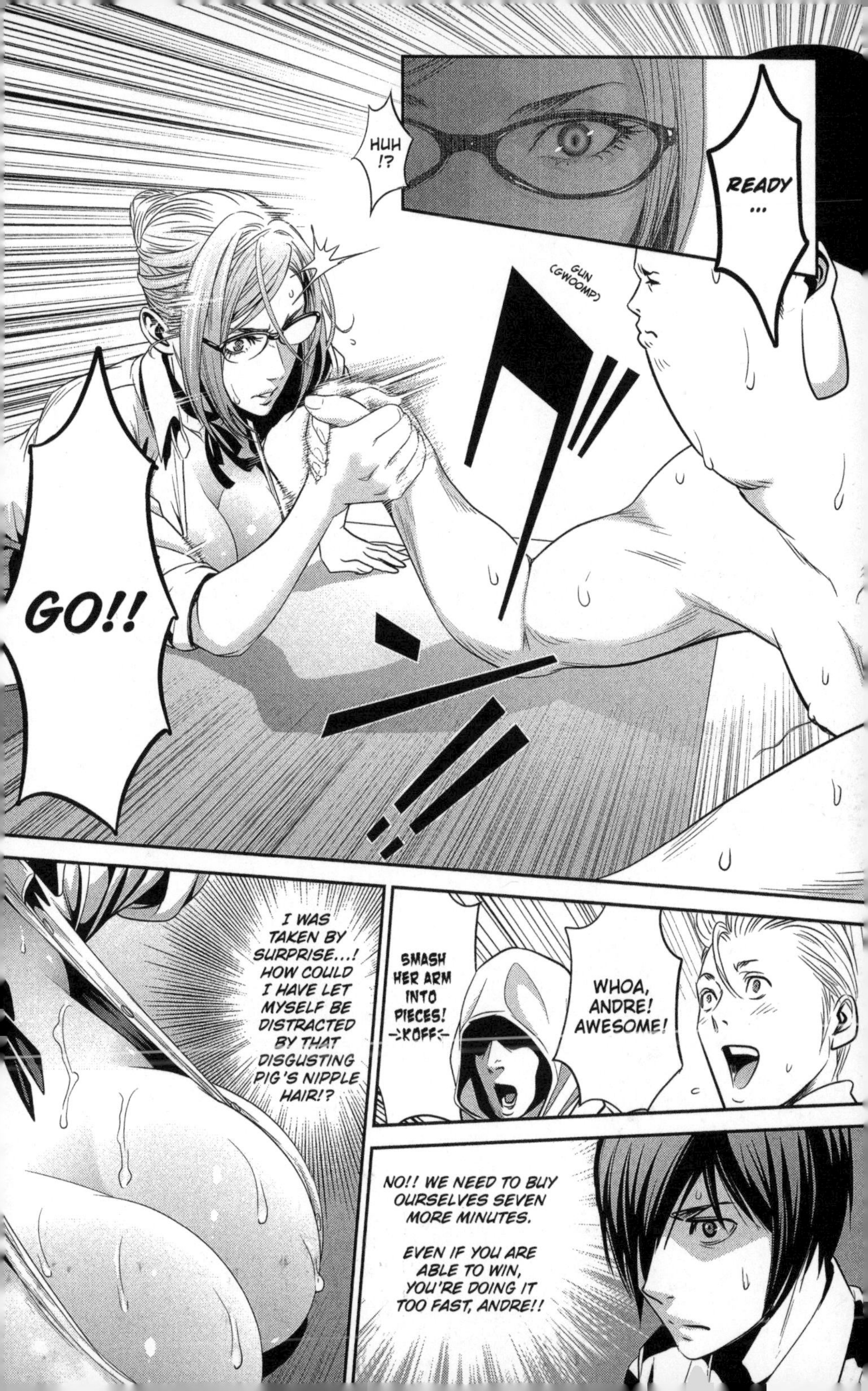
READY ...
HUH !?
GUN (GWOOMP)
GO!!
WHOA, ANDRE! AWESOME!
SMASH HER ARM INTO PIECES! -KOFF-
NO!! WE NEED TO BUY OURSELVES SEVEN MORE MINUTES.
EVEN IF YOU ARE ABLE TO WIN, YOU'RE DOING IT TOO FAST, ANDRE!!
I WAS TAKEN BY SURPRISE...! HOW COULD I HAVE LET MYSELF BE DISTRACTED BY THAT DISGUSTING PIG'S NIPPLE HAIR!?

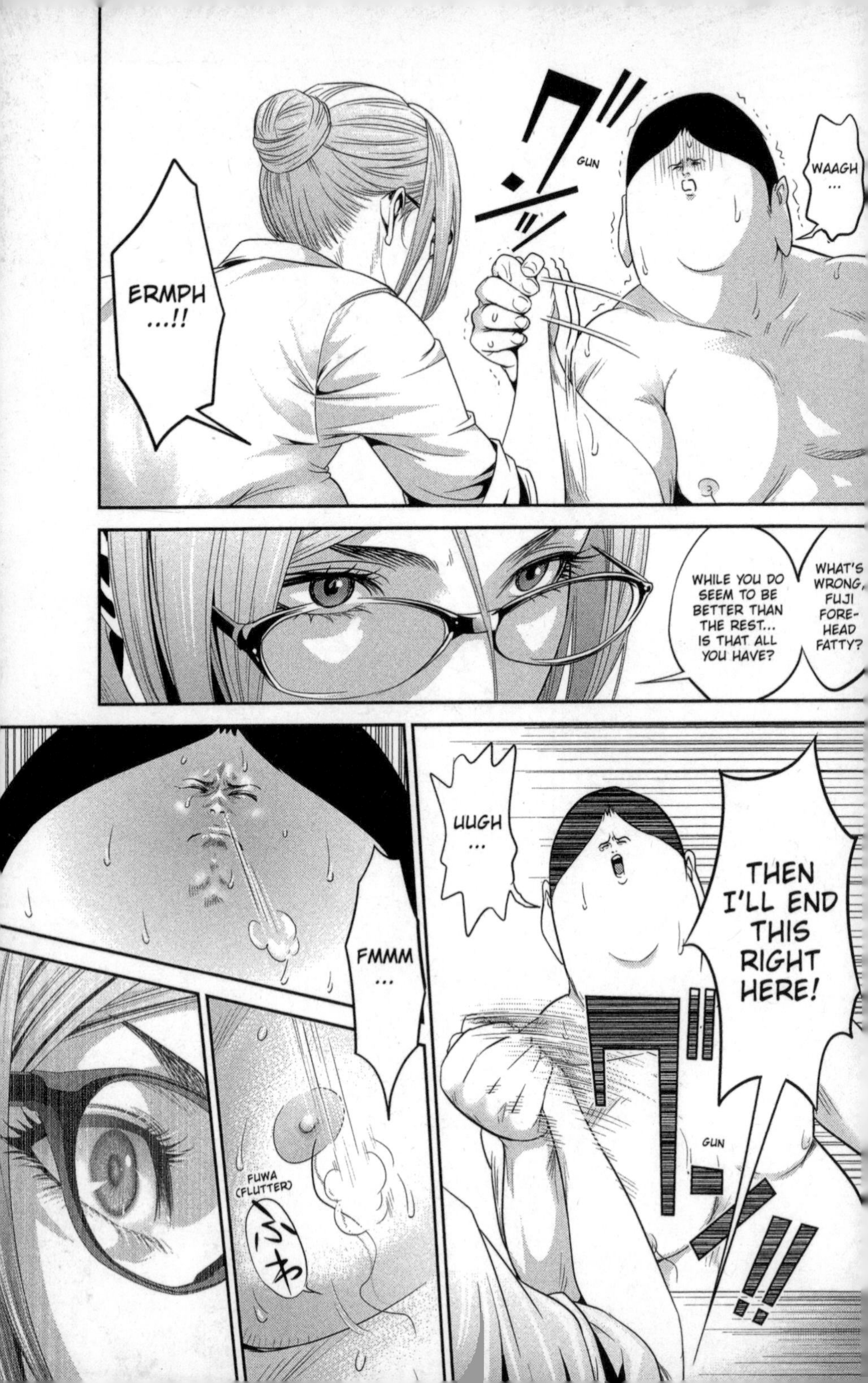
WAAGH ...
GUN
ERMPH ...!!
WHAT'S WRONG, FUJI FORE-HEAD FATTY?
WHILE YOU DO SEEM TO BE BETTER THAN THE REST... IS THAT ALL YOU HAVE?
THEN I'LL END THIS RIGHT HERE!
GUN
UUGH ...
FMMM ...
FUWA (FLUTTER)
ふわ

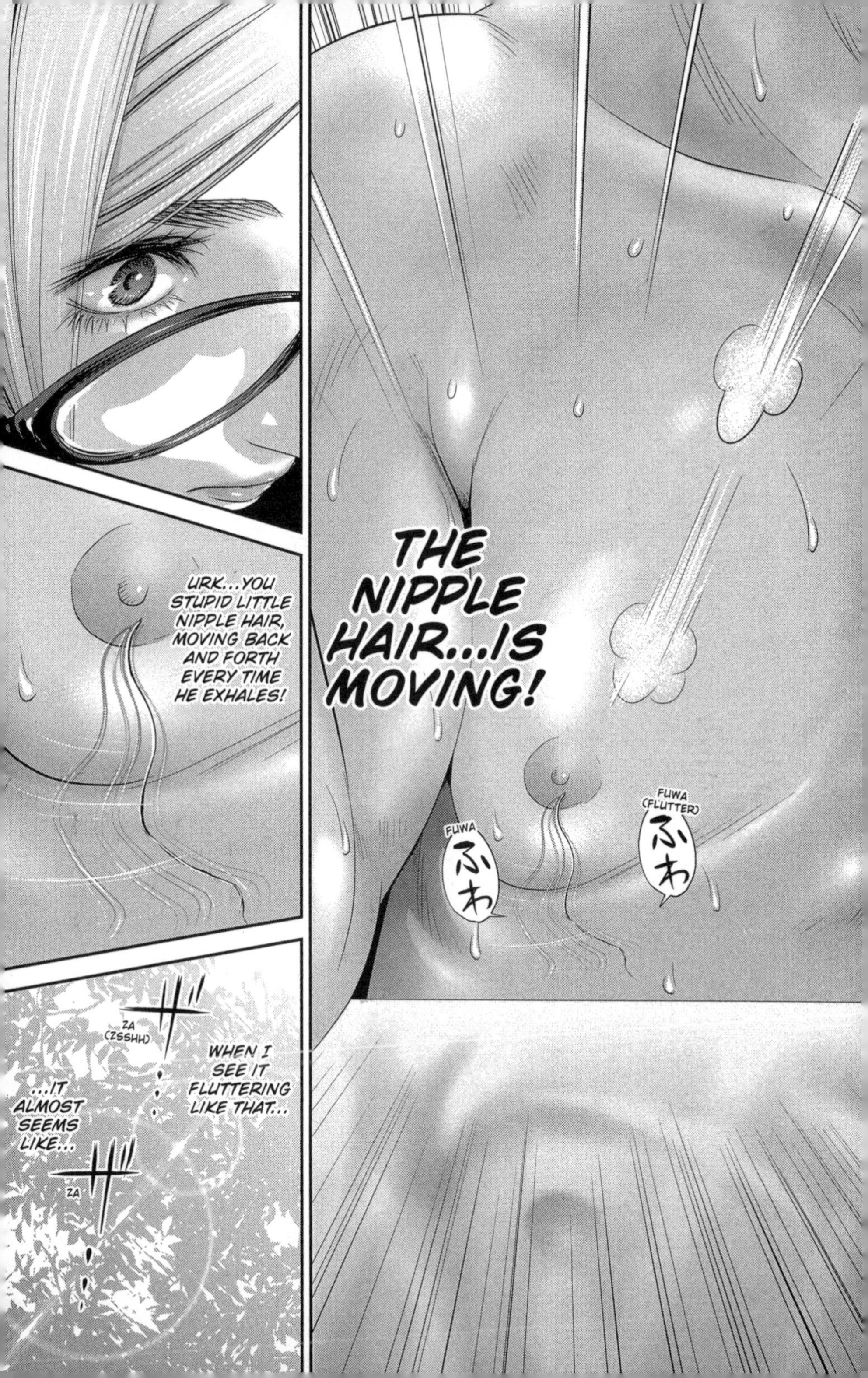
THE NIPPLE HAIR...IS MOVING!
FUWA (FLUTTER)
ふわ
FUWA
ふわ
URK...YOU STUPID LITTLE NIPPLE HAIR, MOVING BACK AND FORTH EVERY TIME HE EXHALES!
ZA (ZSSHH)
WHEN I SEE IT FLUTTERING LIKE THAT...
...IT ALMOST SEEMS LIKE...
ZA

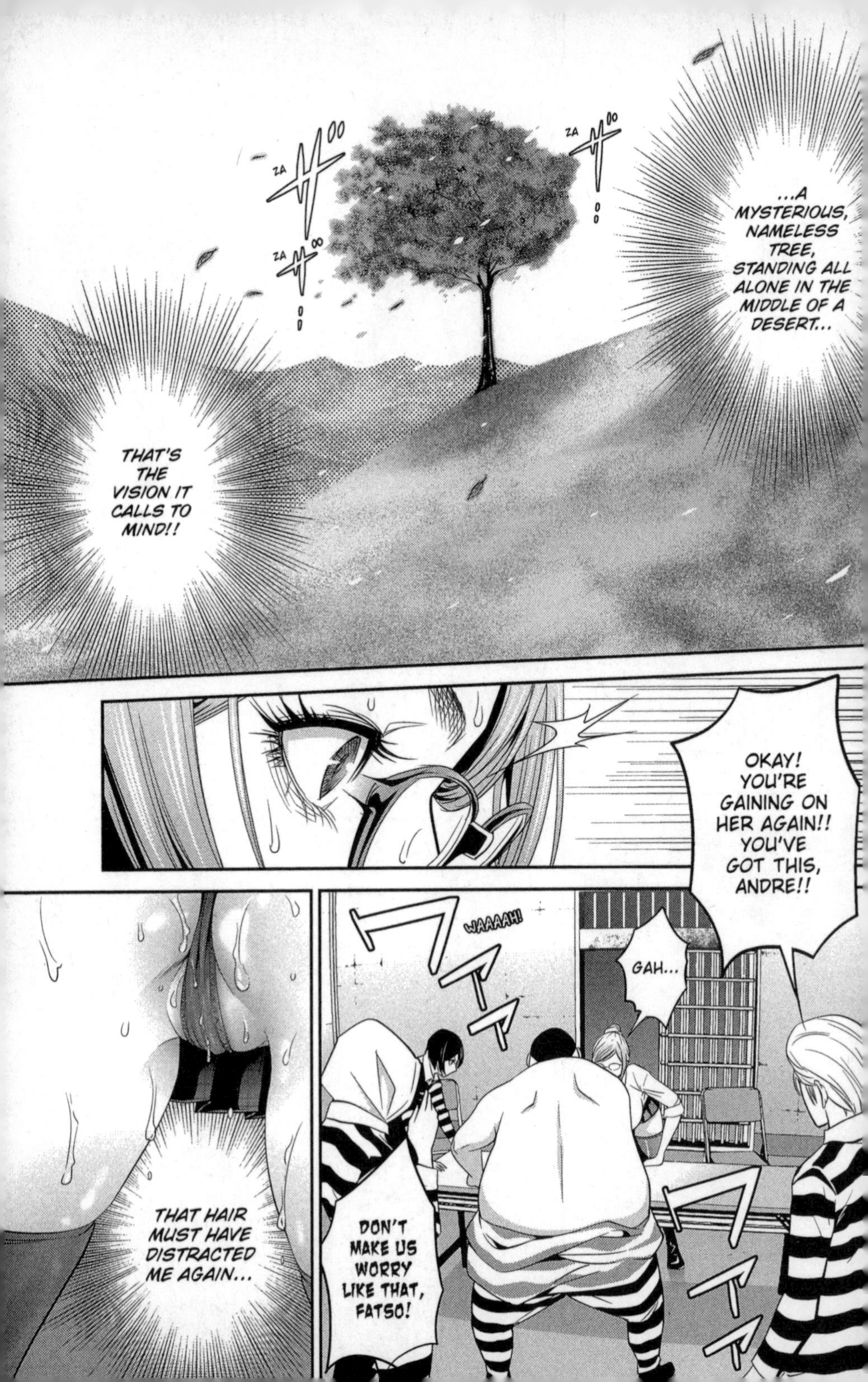
ZA
ZA
ZA
...A MYSTERIOUS, NAMELESS TREE, STANDING ALL ALONE IN THE MIDDLE OF A DESERT...
THAT'S THE VISION IT CALLS TO MIND!!
OKAY! YOU'RE GAINING ON HER AGAIN!! YOU'VE GOT THIS, ANDRE!!
GAH...
WAAAAH!
DON'T MAKE US WORRY LIKE THAT, FATSO!
THAT HAIR MUST HAVE DISTRACTED ME AGAIN...

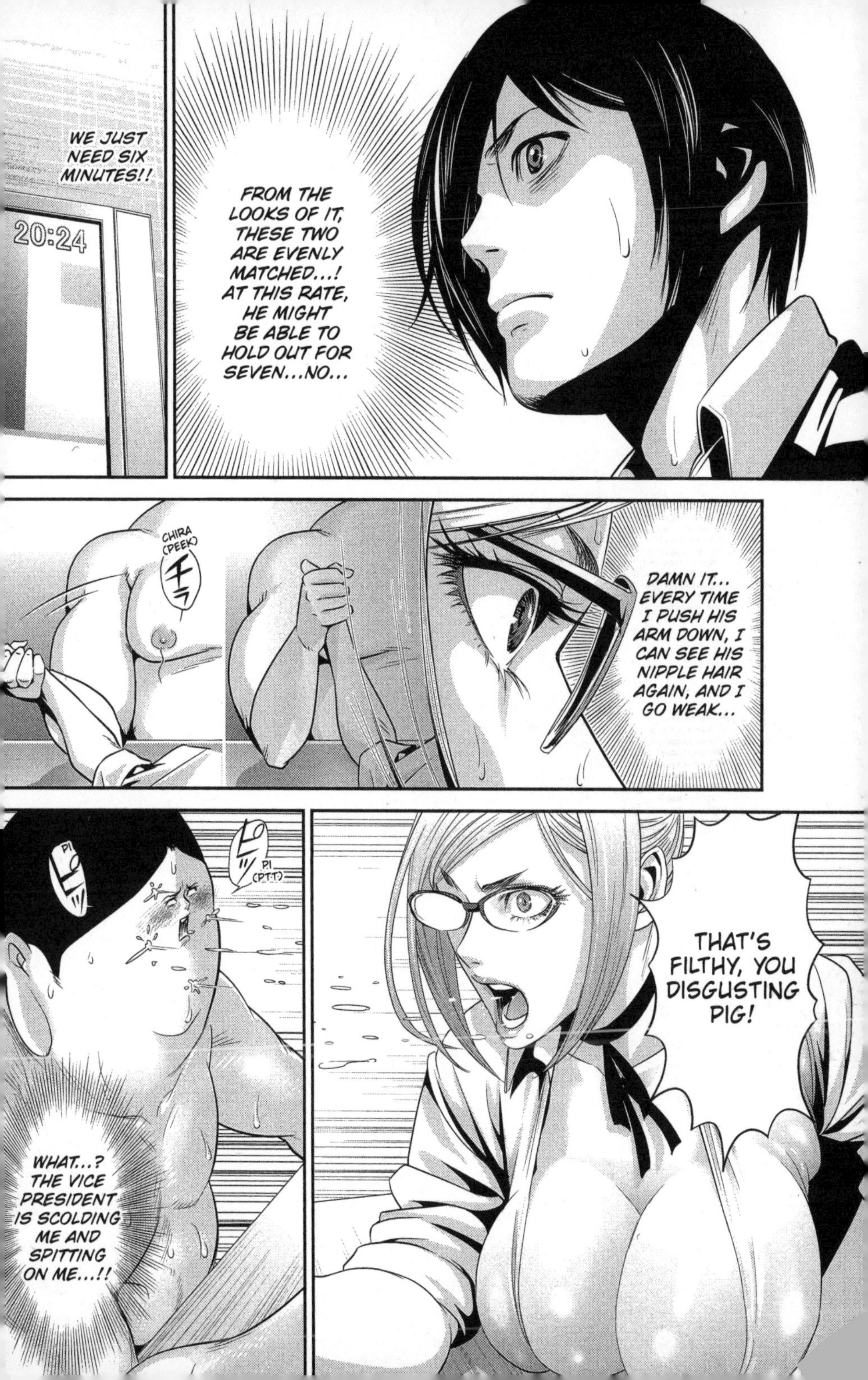
FROM THE LOOKS OF IT, THESE TWO ARE EVENLY MATCHED...! AT THIS RATE, HE MIGHT BE ABLE TO HOLD OUT FOR SEVEN...NO...
WE JUST NEED SIX MINUTES!!
20:24
DAMN IT... EVERY TIME I PUSH HIS ARM DOWN, I CAN SEE HIS NIPPLE HAIR AGAIN, AND I GO WEAK...
CHIRA (PEEK)
チラ
THAT'S FILTHY, YOU DISGUSTING PIG!
PI (PT-T)
PI
WHAT...? THE VICE PRESIDENT IS SCOLDING ME AND SPITTING ON ME...!!

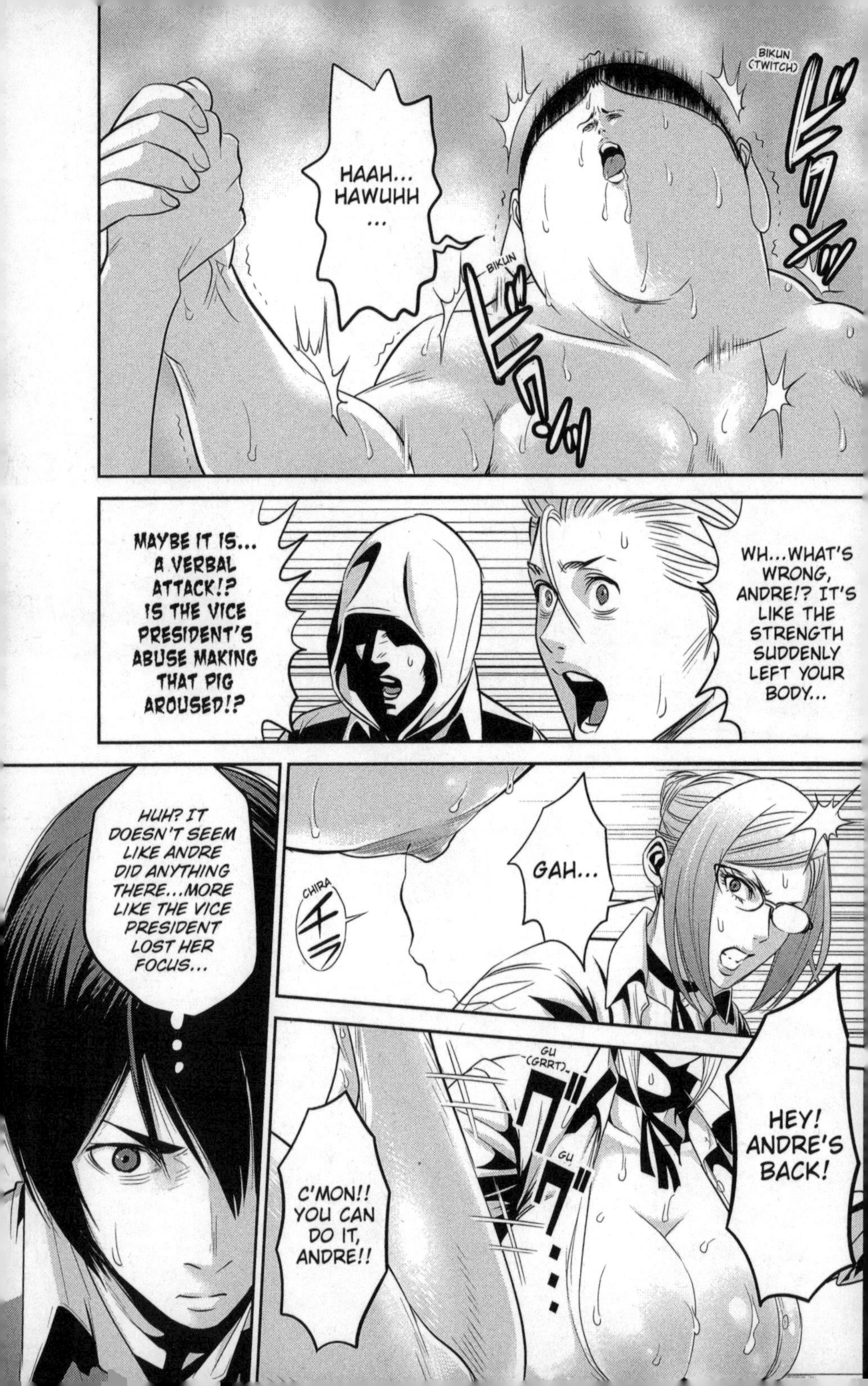
BIKUN (TWITCH)
HAAH... HAWUHH ...
BIKUN
WH...WHAT'S WRONG, ANDRE!? IT'S LIKE THE STRENGTH SUDDENLY LEFT YOUR BODY...
MAYBE IT IS... A VERBAL ATTACK!? IS THE VICE PRESIDENT'S ABUSE MAKING THAT PIG AROUSED!?
GAH...
CHIRA
HEY! ANDRE'S BACK!
GU (GRRT)
GU
C'MON!! YOU CAN DO IT, ANDRE!!
HUH? IT DOESN'T SEEM LIKE ANDRE DID ANYTHING THERE...MORE LIKE THE VICE PRESIDENT LOST HER FOCUS...

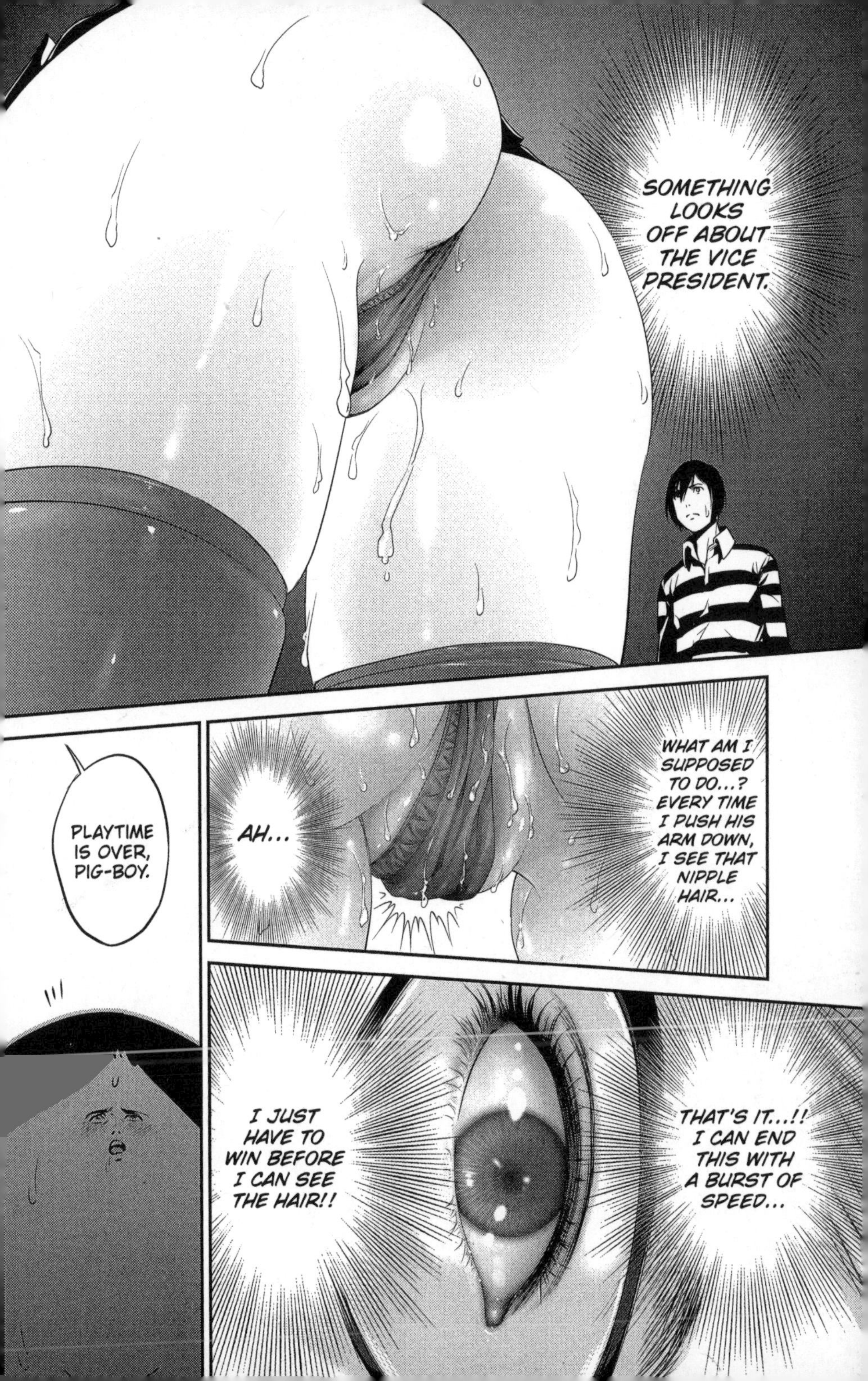
SOMETHING LOOKS OFF ABOUT THE VICE PRESIDENT.
WHAT AM I SUPPOSED TO DO...? EVERY TIME I PUSH HIS ARM DOWN, I SEE THAT NIPPLE HAIR...
AH...
PLAYTIME IS OVER, PIG-BOY.
THAT'S IT...!! I CAN END THIS WITH A BURST OF SPEED...
I JUST HAVE TO WIN BEFORE I CAN SEE THE HAIR!!

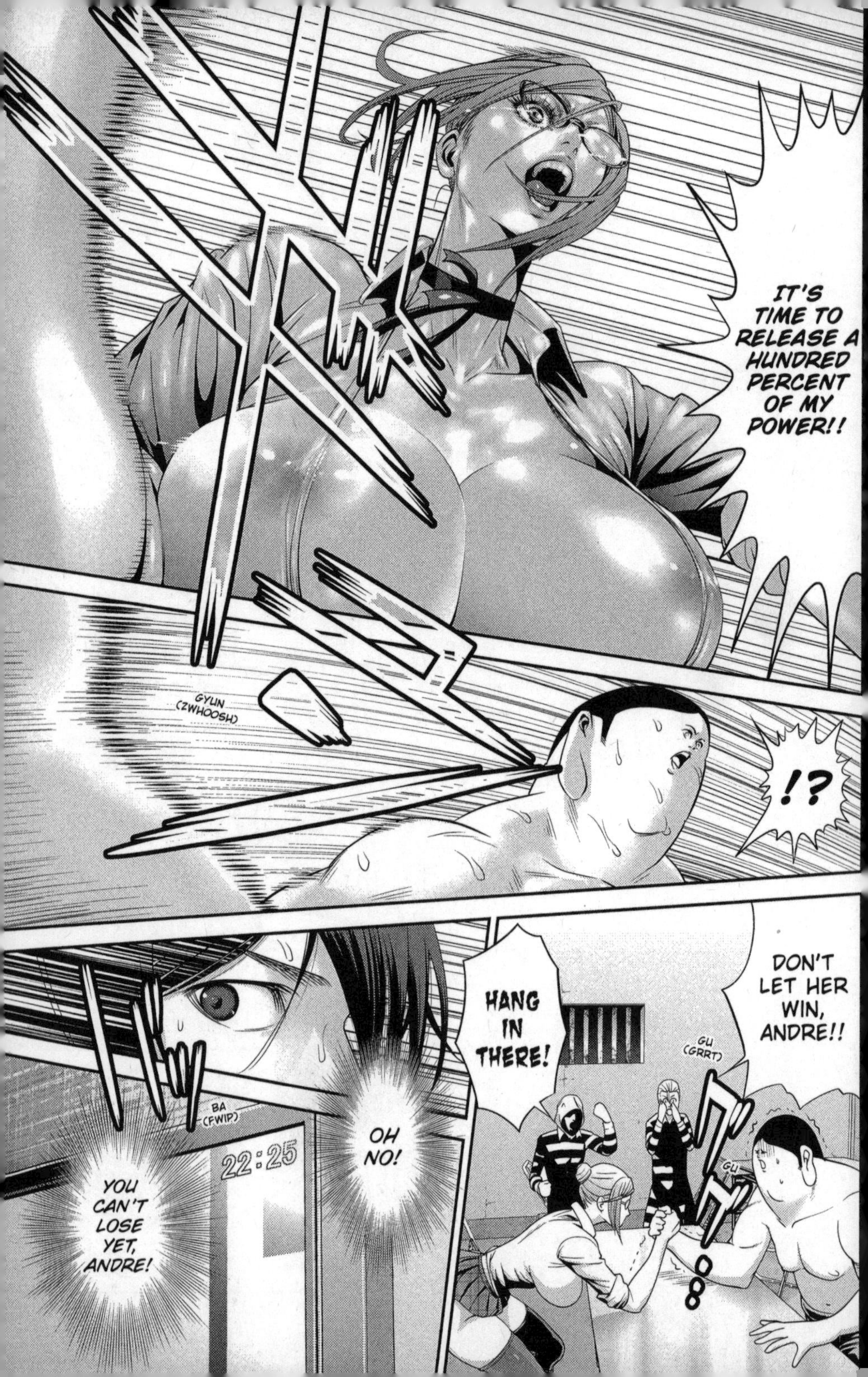
IT'S TIME TO RELEASE A HUNDRED PERCENT OF MY POWER!!
!?
GYUN (ZWHOOSH)
DON'T LET HER WIN, ANDRE!!
HANG IN THERE!
GU (GRRT)
GU
BA (FWIP)
OH NO!
22:25
YOU CAN'T LOSE YET, ANDRE!

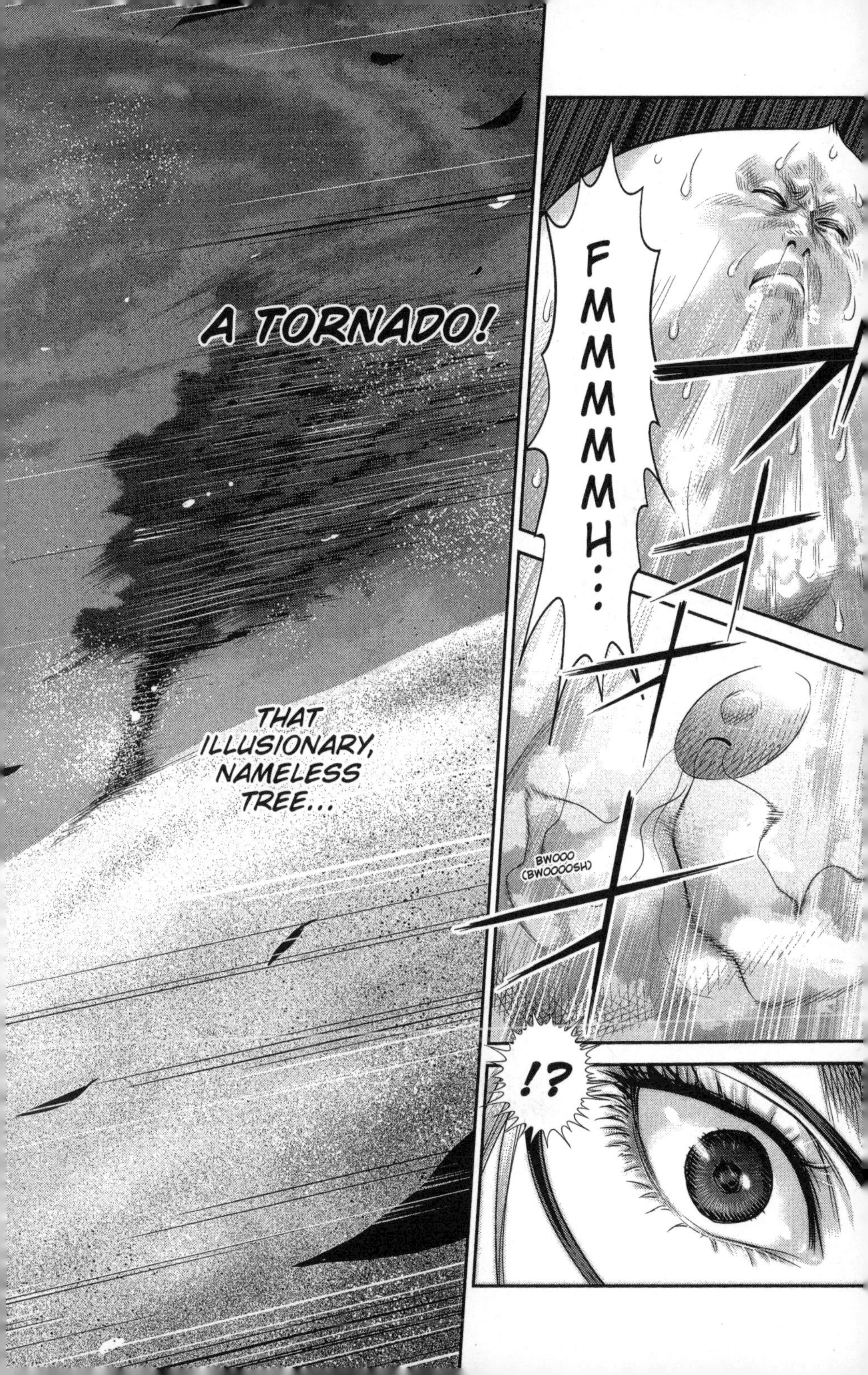
FMMMMMMH...
BWOOO (BWOOOOSH)
!?
A TORNADO!
THAT ILLUSIONARY, NAMELESS TREE...

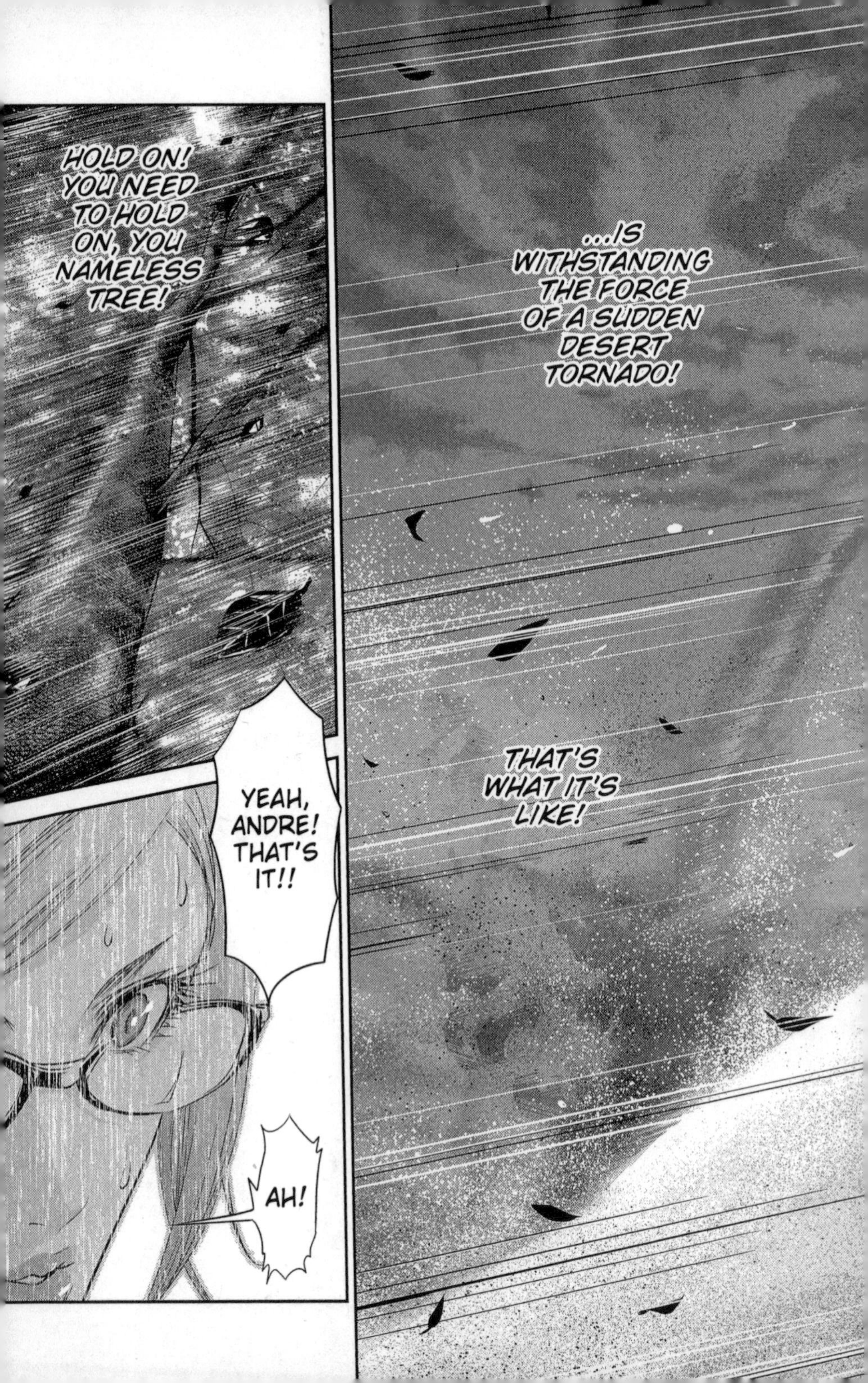
...IS WITHSTANDING THE FORCE OF A SUDDEN DESERT TORNADO!
THAT'S WHAT IT'S LIKE!
HOLD ON! YOU NEED TO HOLD ON, YOU NAMELESS TREE!
YEAH, ANDRE! THAT'S IT!!
AH!

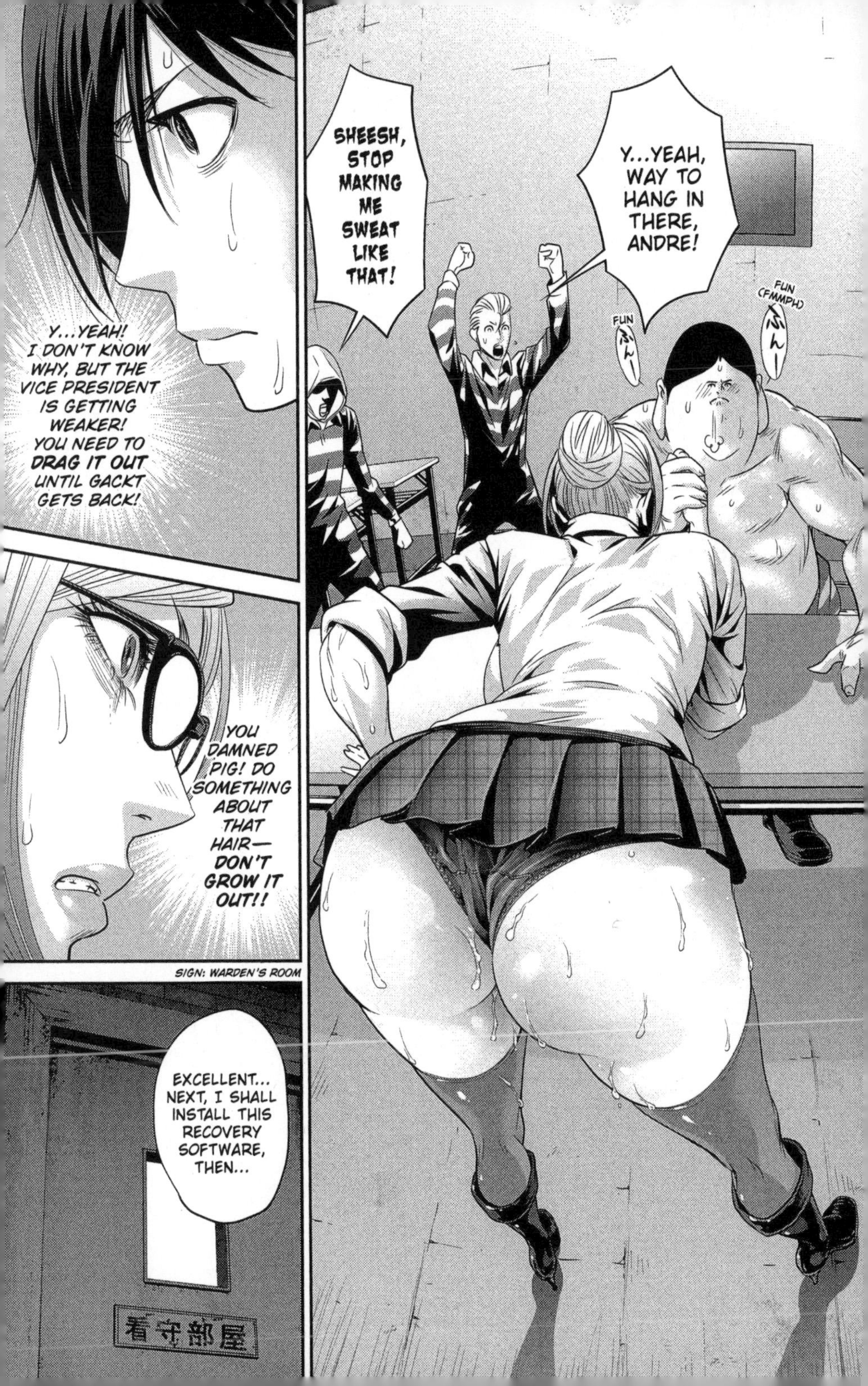
Y...YEAH, WAY TO HANG IN THERE, ANDRE!
FUN (FMMPH) ふん—
FUN ふん—
SHEESH, STOP MAKING ME SWEAT LIKE THAT!
Y...YEAH! I DON'T KNOW WHY, BUT THE VICE PRESIDENT IS GETTING WEAKER! YOU NEED TO DRAG IT OUT UNTIL GACKT GETS BACK!
YOU DAMNED PIG! DO SOMETHING ABOUT THAT HAIR—DON'T GROW IT OUT!!
SIGN: WARDEN'S ROOM
EXCELLENT... NEXT, I SHALL INSTALL THIS RECOVERY SOFTWARE, THEN...
看守部屋

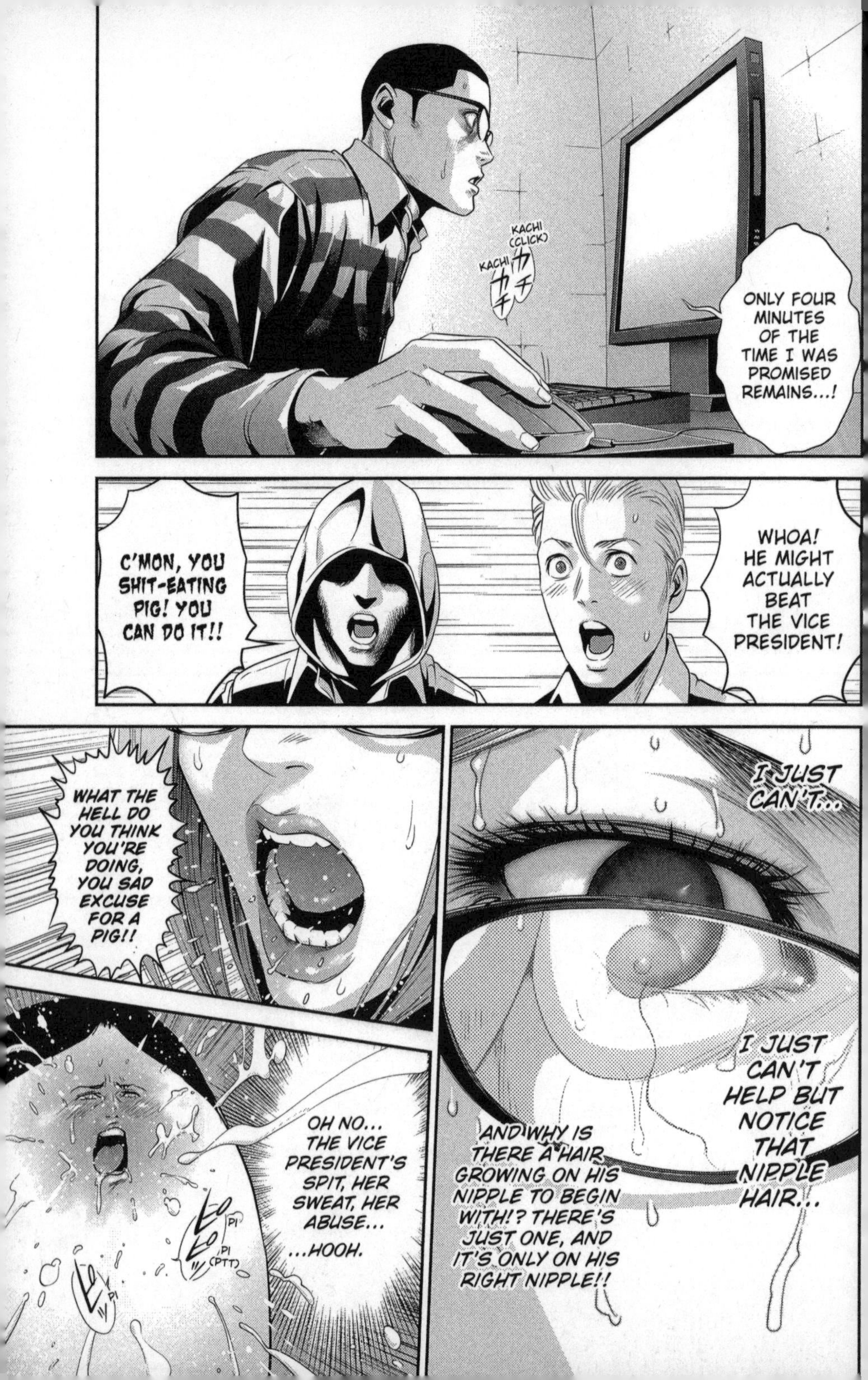
ONLY FOUR MINUTES OF THE TIME I WAS PROMISED REMAINS...!
KACHI (CLICK)
KACHI
WHOA! HE MIGHT ACTUALLY BEAT THE VICE PRESIDENT!
C'MON, YOU SHIT-EATING PIG! YOU CAN DO IT!!
I JUST CAN'T...
I JUST CAN'T HELP BUT NOTICE THAT NIPPLE HAIR...
AND WHY IS THERE A HAIR GROWING ON HIS NIPPLE TO BEGIN WITH!? THERE'S JUST ONE, AND IT'S ONLY ON HIS RIGHT NIPPLE!!
WHAT THE HELL DO YOU THINK YOU'RE DOING, YOU SAD EXCUSE FOR A PIG!!
OH NO... THE VICE PRESIDENT'S SPIT, HER SWEAT, HER ABUSE... ...HOOH.
PI
PI (PTT)
PI

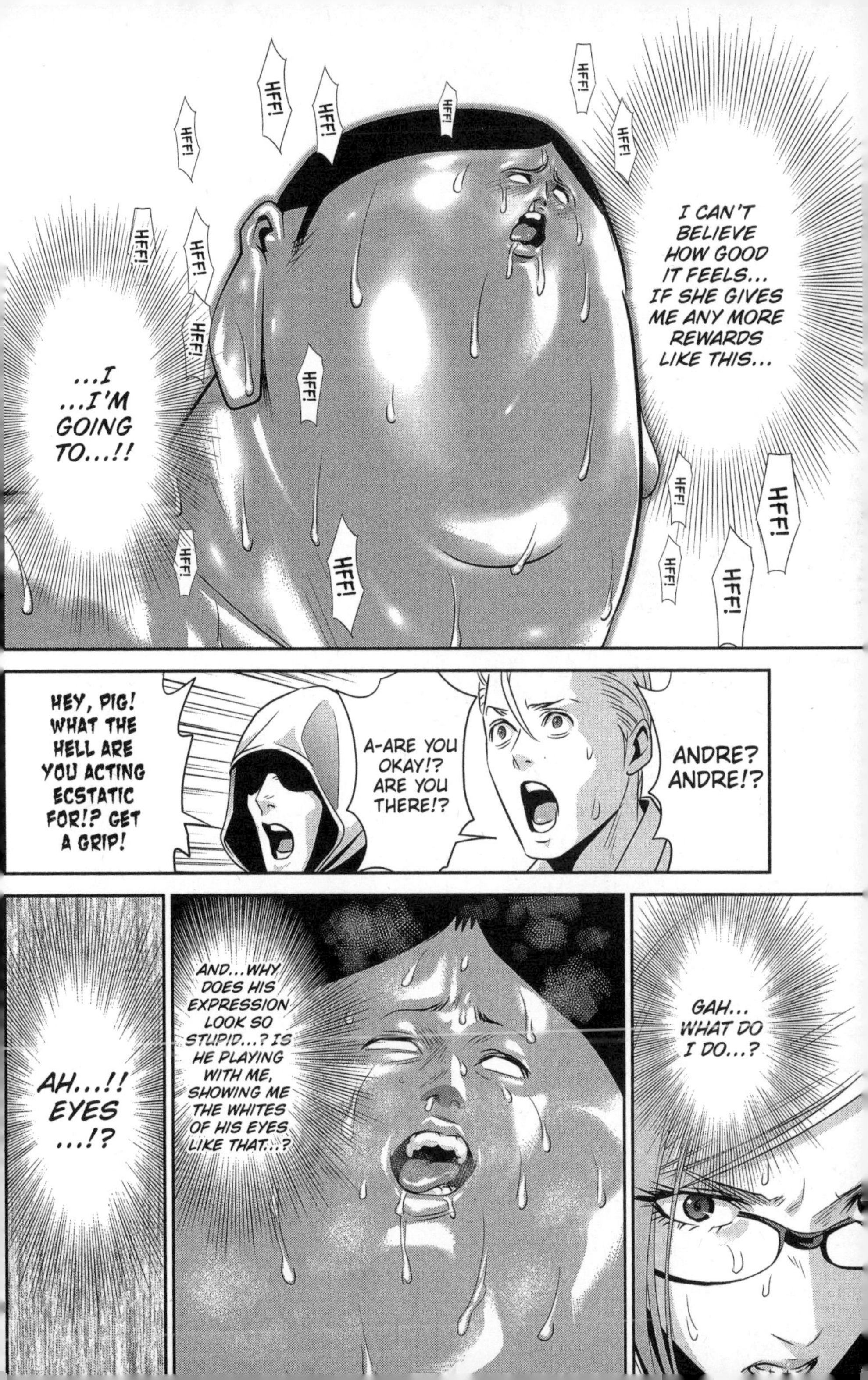
HFF!
HFF!
HFF!
HFF!
I CAN'T BELIEVE HOW GOOD IT FEELS... IF SHE GIVES ME ANY MORE REWARDS LIKE THIS...
HFF!
HFF!
HFF!
HFF!
HFF!
HFF!
HFF!
HFF!
HFF!
HFF!
HFF!
HFF!
...I ...I'M GOING TO...!!
ANDRE? ANDRE!?
A-ARE YOU OKAY!? ARE YOU THERE!?
HEY, PIG! WHAT THE HELL ARE YOU ACTING ECSTATIC FOR!? GET A GRIP!
GAH... WHAT DO I DO...?
AND...WHY DOES HIS EXPRESSION LOOK SO STUPID...? IS HE PLAYING WITH ME, SHOWING ME THE WHITES OF HIS EYES LIKE THAT...?
AH...!! EYES ...!?

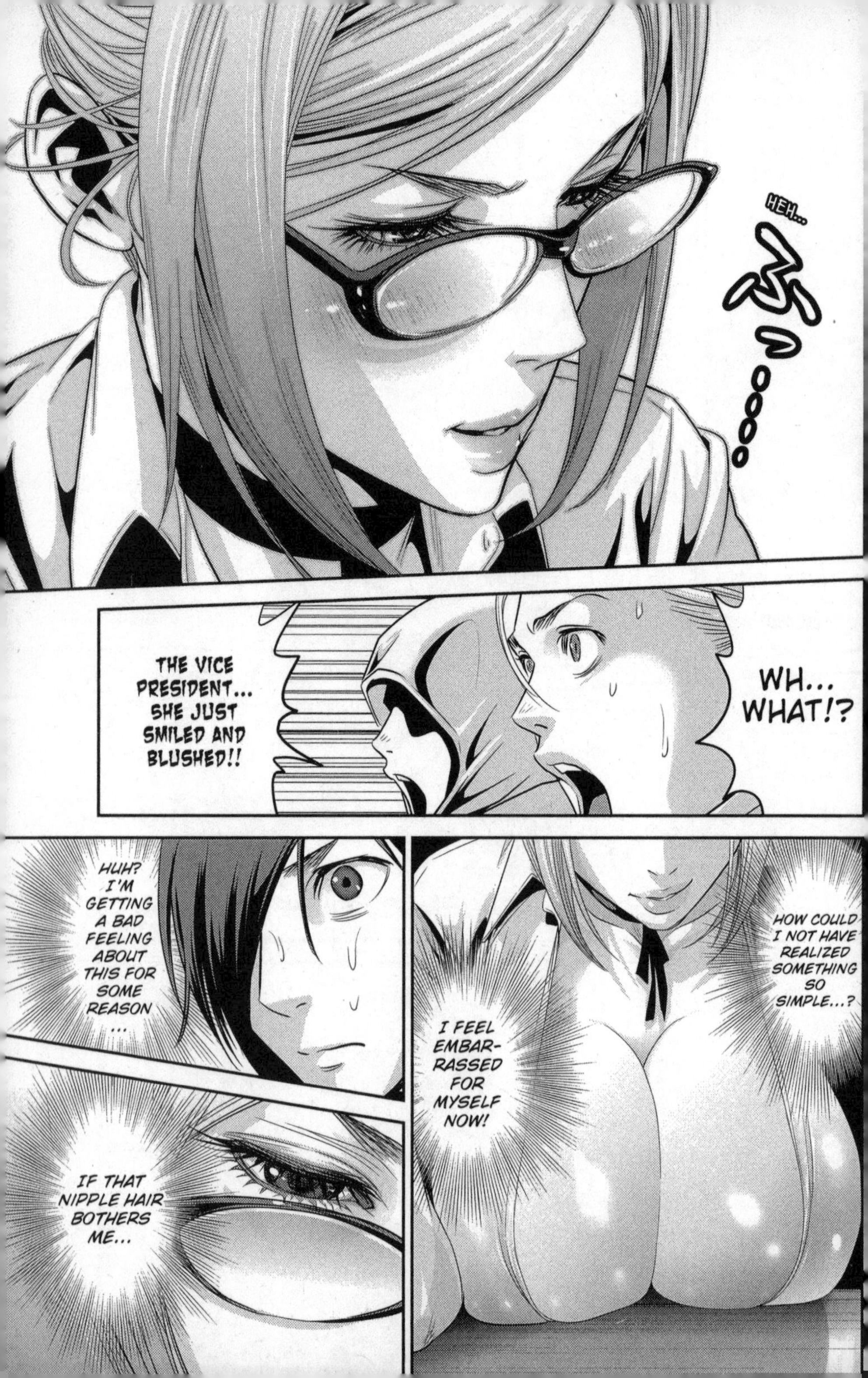
HEH...
WH... WHAT!?
THE VICE PRESIDENT... SHE JUST SMILED AND BLUSHED!!
HOW COULD I NOT HAVE REALIZED SOMETHING SO SIMPLE...?
I FEEL EMBARRASSED FOR MYSELF NOW!
HUH? I'M GETTING A BAD FEELING ABOUT THIS FOR SOME REASON...
IF THAT NIPPLE HAIR BOTHERS ME...

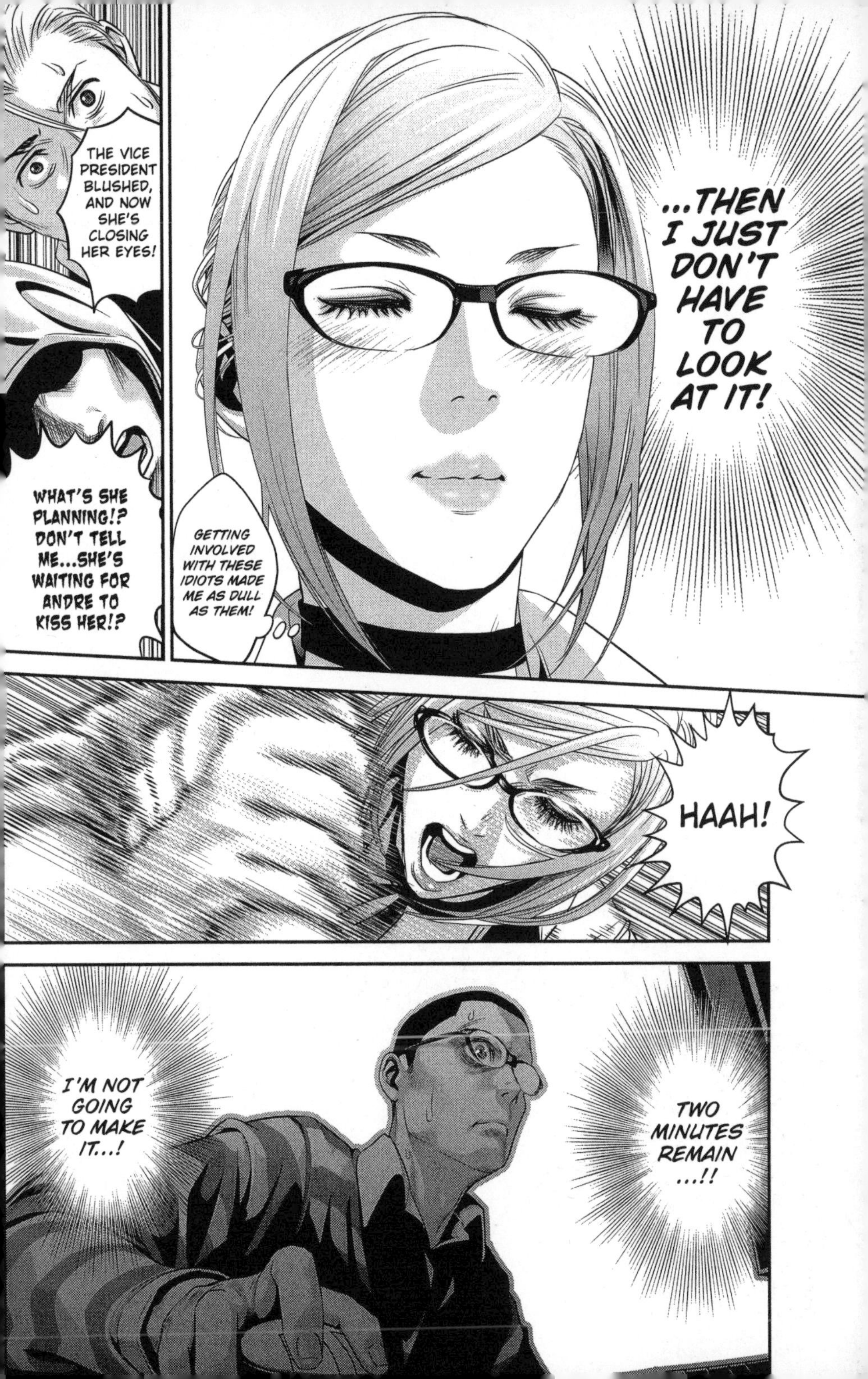
...THEN I JUST DON'T HAVE TO LOOK AT IT!
GETTING INVOLVED WITH THESE IDIOTS MADE ME AS DULL AS THEM!
THE VICE PRESIDENT BLUSHED, AND NOW SHE'S CLOSING HER EYES!
WHAT'S SHE PLANNING!? DON'T TELL ME...SHE'S WAITING FOR ANDRE TO KISS HER!?
HAAH!
TWO MINUTES REMAIN ...!!
I'M NOT GOING TO MAKE IT...!

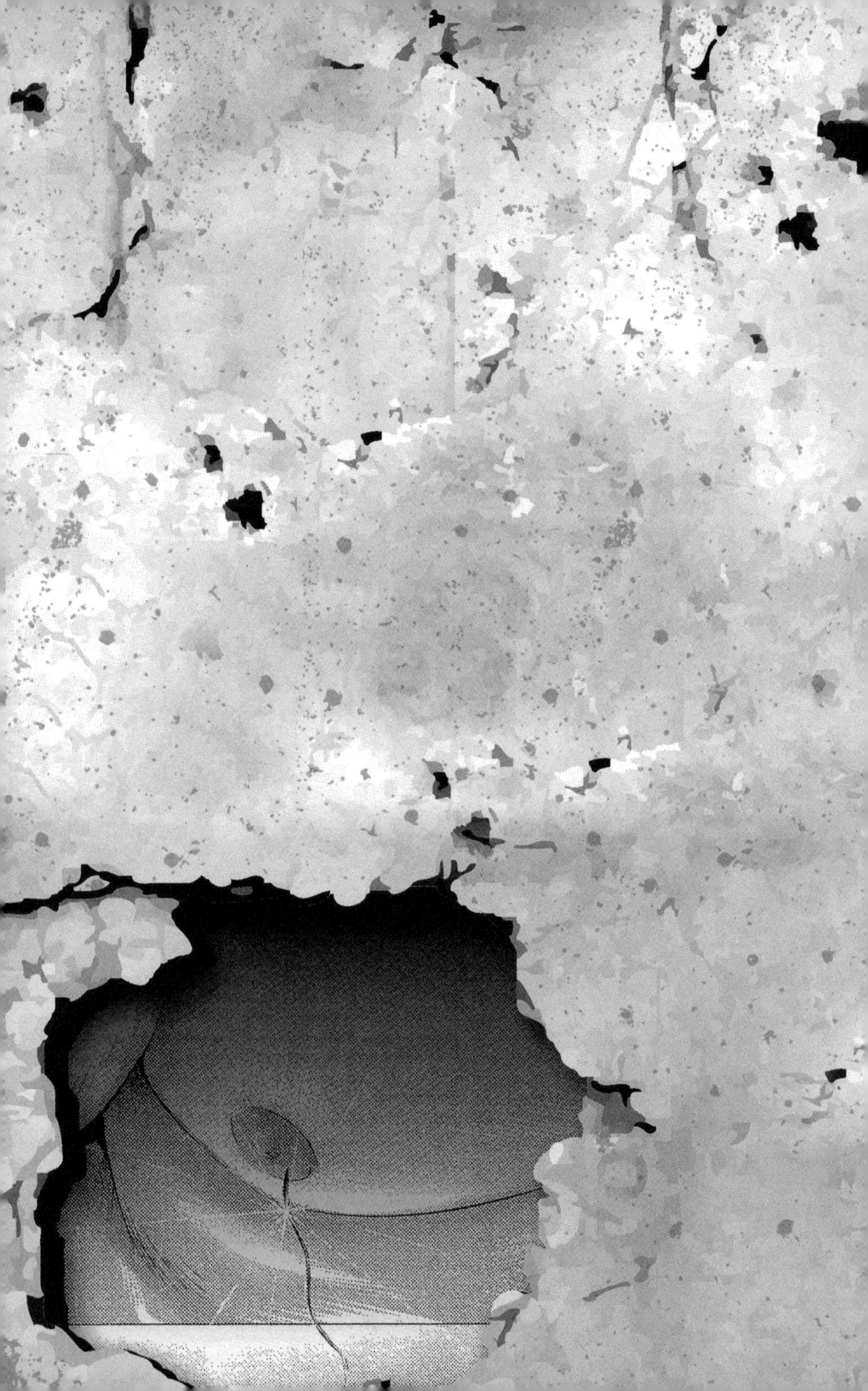

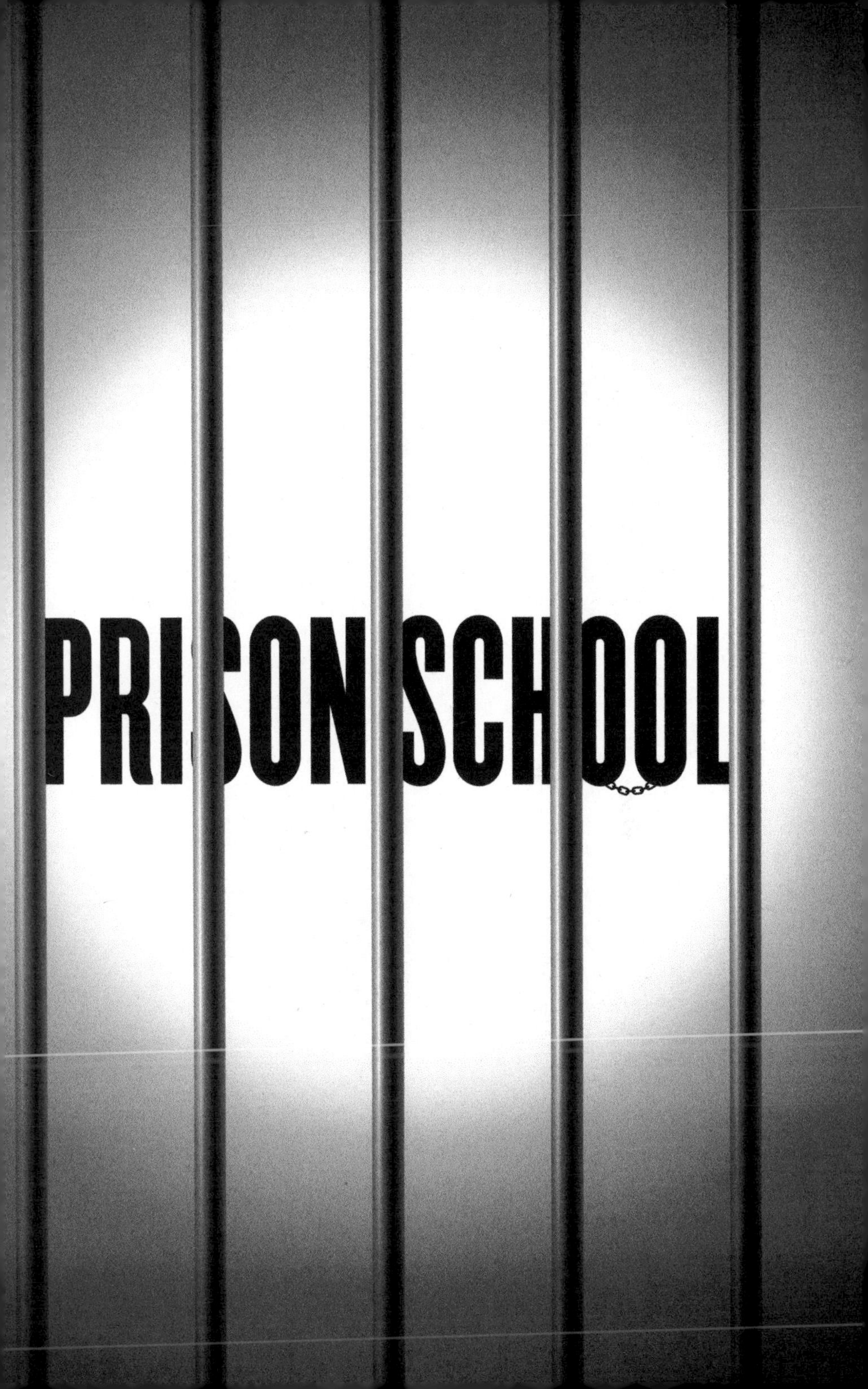
PRISON SCHOOL

CHAPTER 61: LIQUID SKY

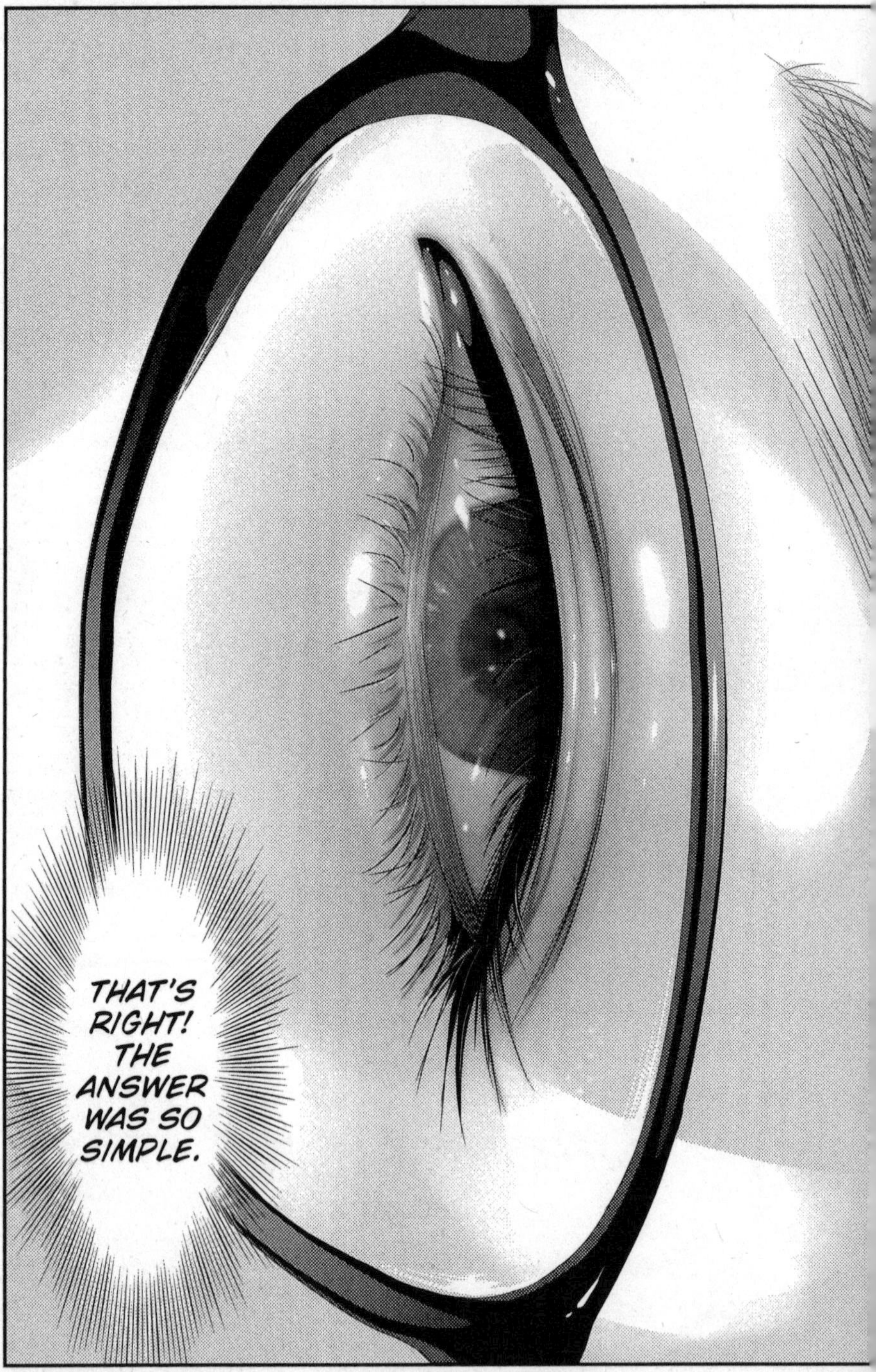
THAT'S RIGHT! THE ANSWER WAS SO SIMPLE.

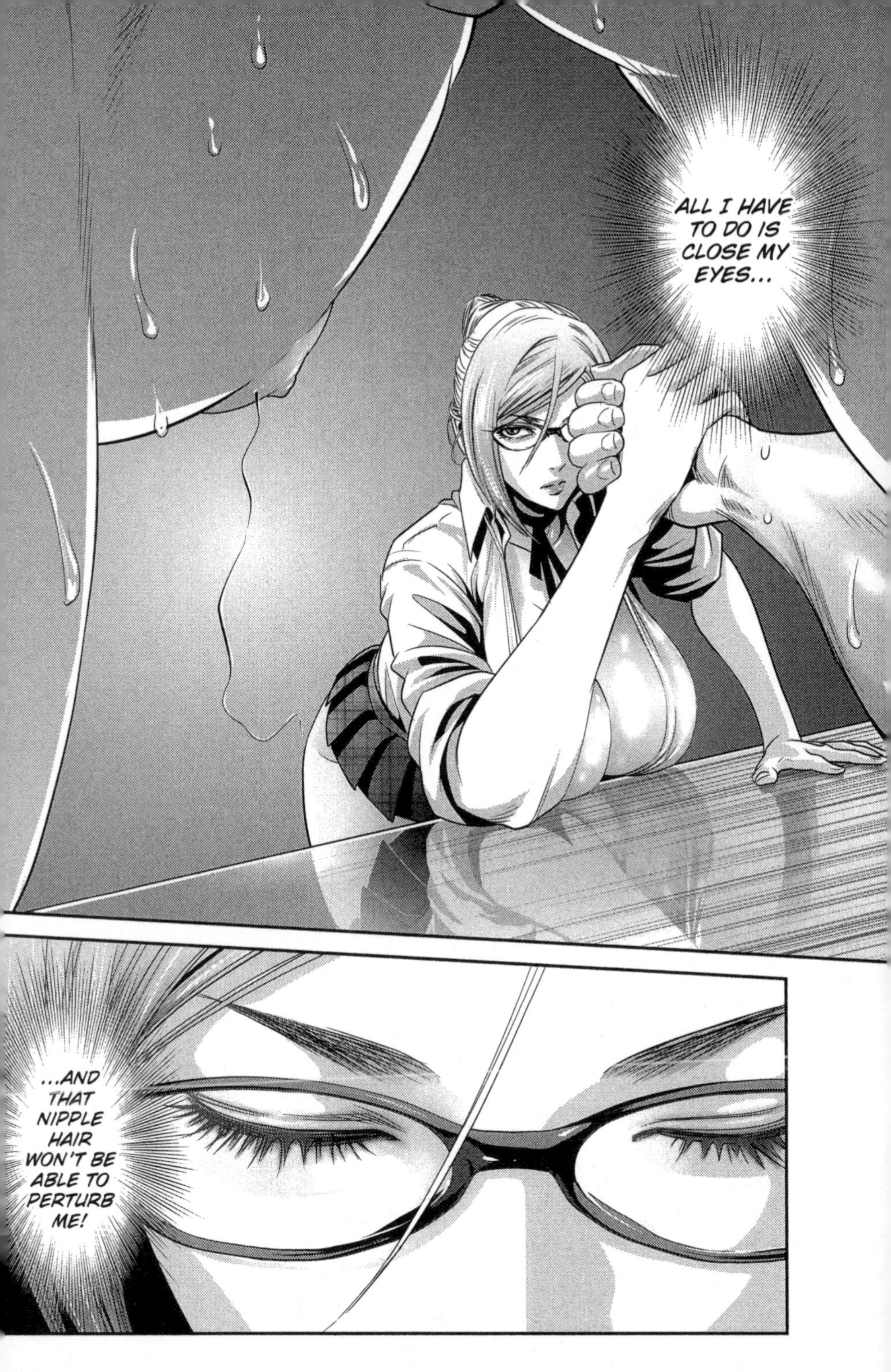
ALL I HAVE TO DO IS CLOSE MY EYES...
...AND THAT NIPPLE HAIR WON'T BE ABLE TO PERTURB ME!

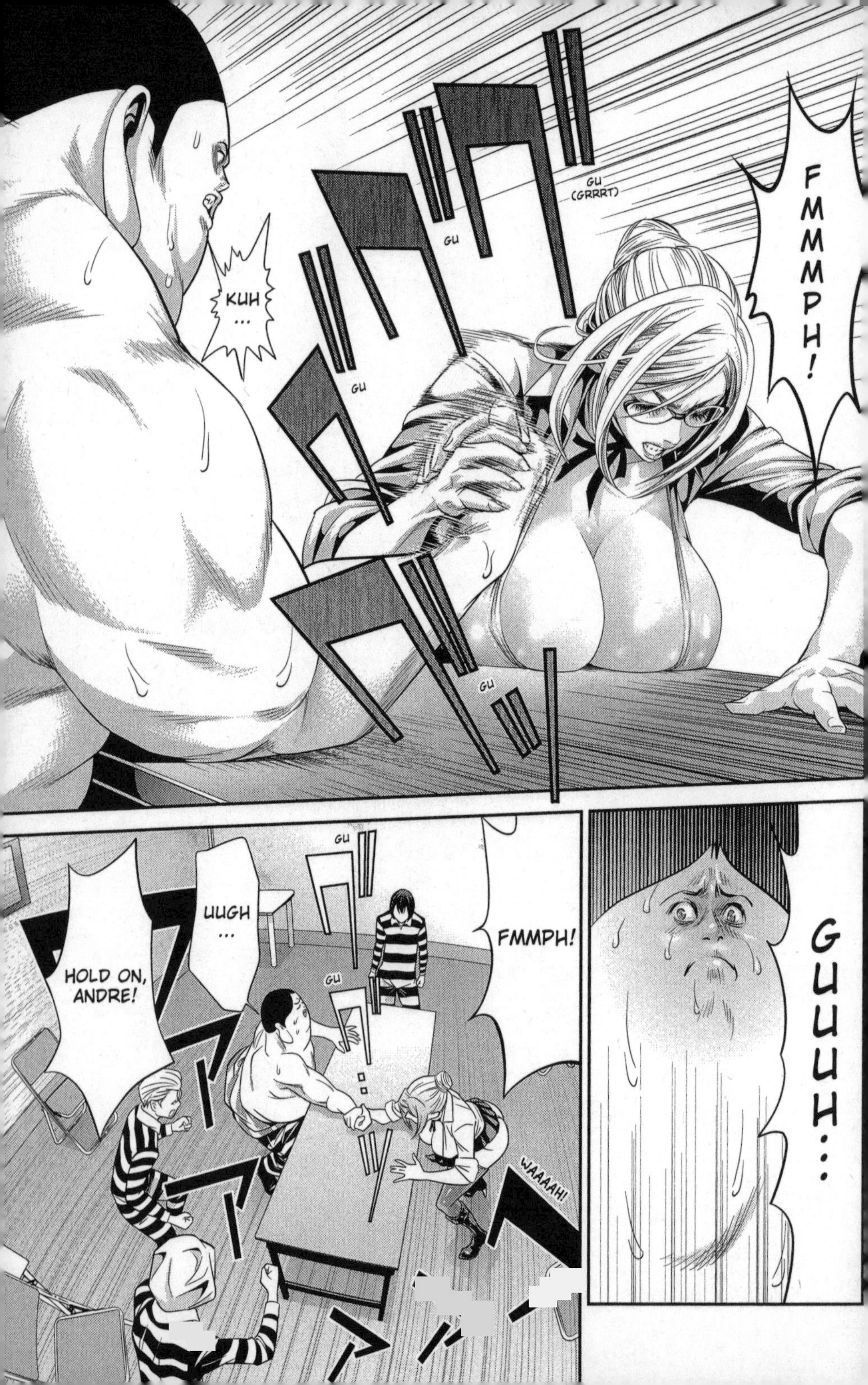
FMMMPH!
GU (GRRRT)
GU
KUH ...
GU
GU
GUUUH...
FMMPH!
GU
UUGH ...
HOLD ON, ANDRE!
GU
WAAAAH!

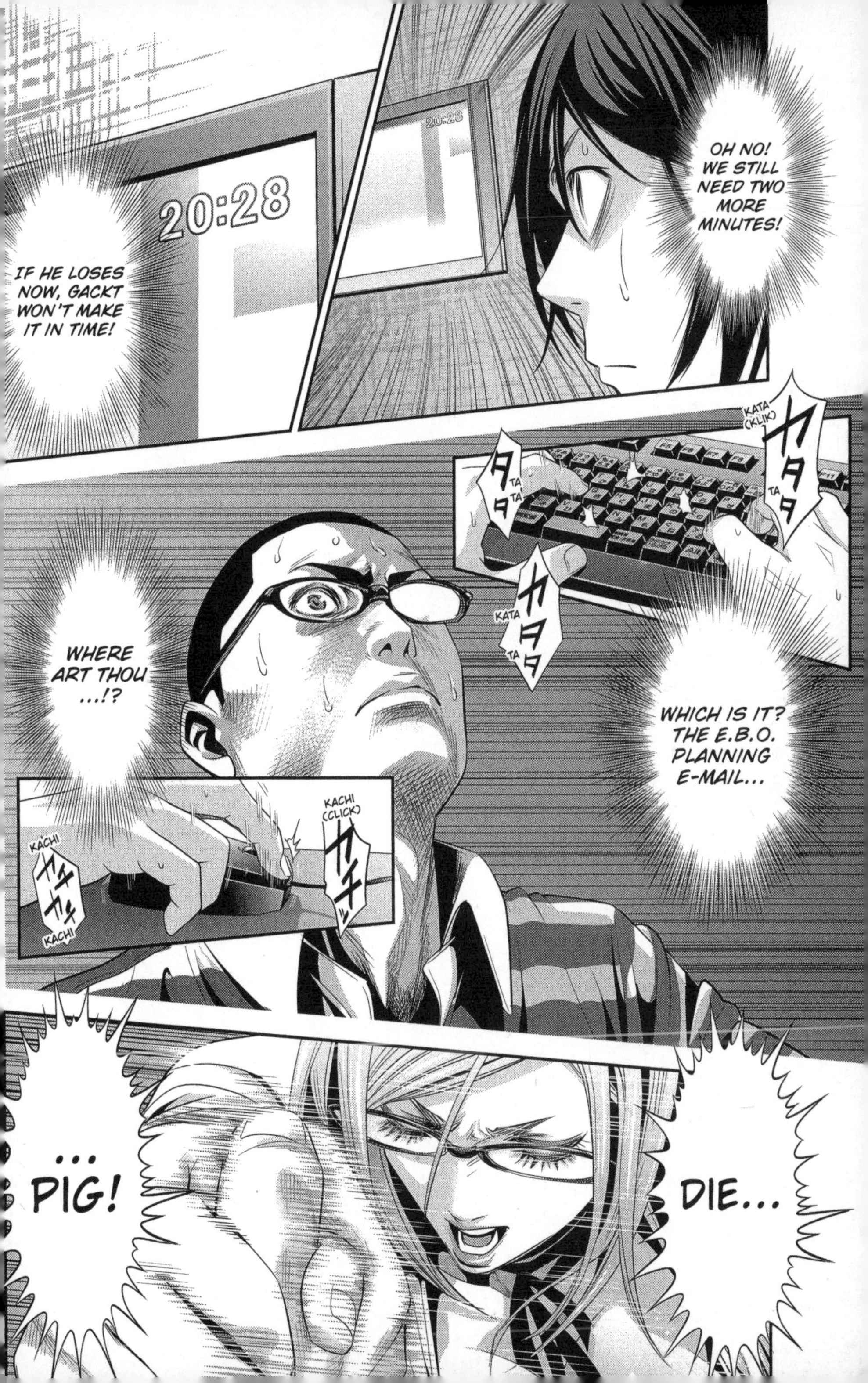
20:28
OH NO! WE STILL NEED TWO MORE MINUTES!
20:28
IF HE LOSES NOW, GACKT WON'T MAKE IT IN TIME!
KATA (KLIK)
TA
TA
TA
KATA
TA
WHICH IS IT? THE E.B.O. PLANNING E-MAIL...
WHERE ART THOU ...!?
KACHI (CLICK)
KACHI
KACHI
DIE...
...PIG!

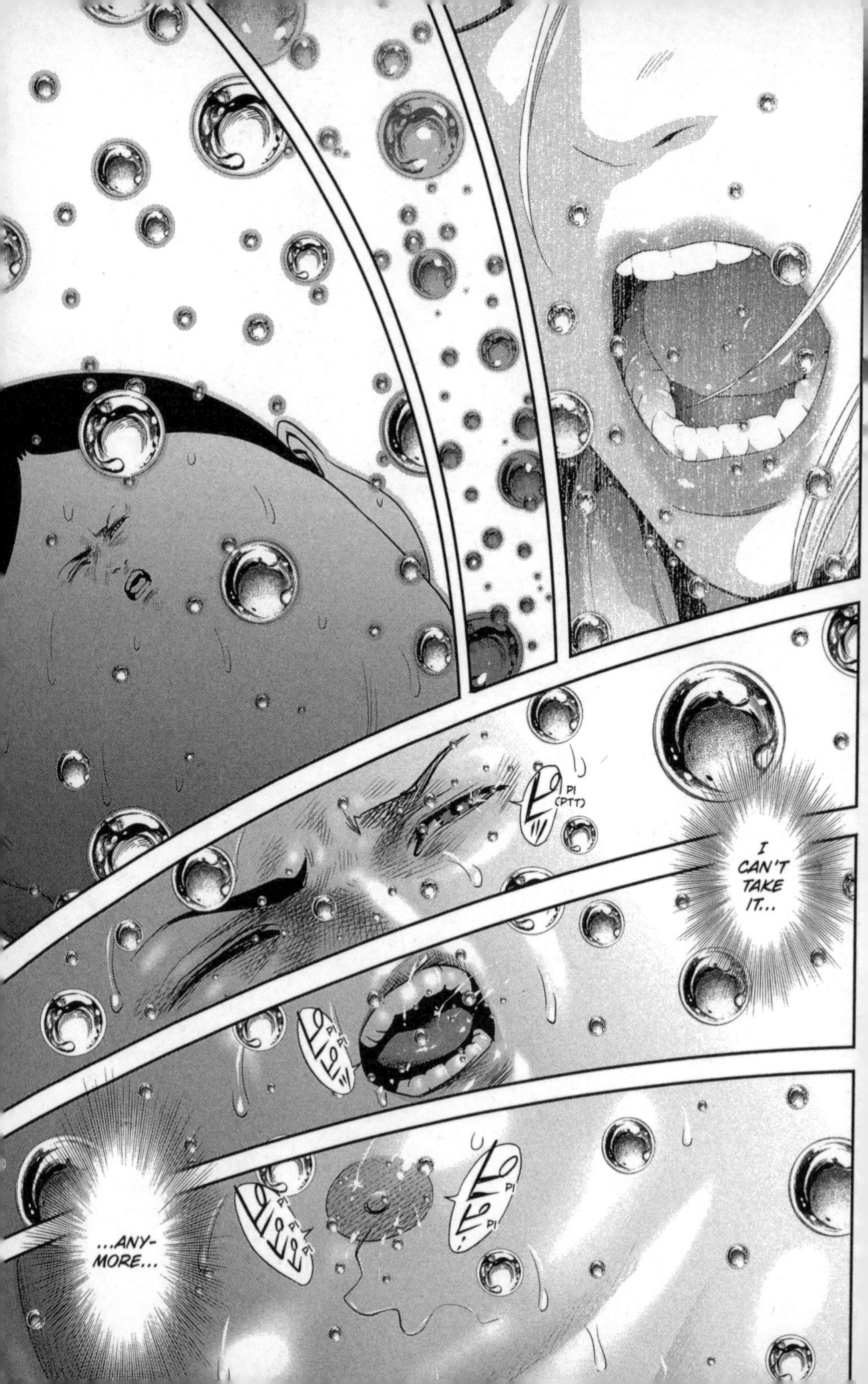

PI (PTT)
I CAN'T TAKE IT...
PI PI
PI PI
PI PI PI
...ANY-MORE...

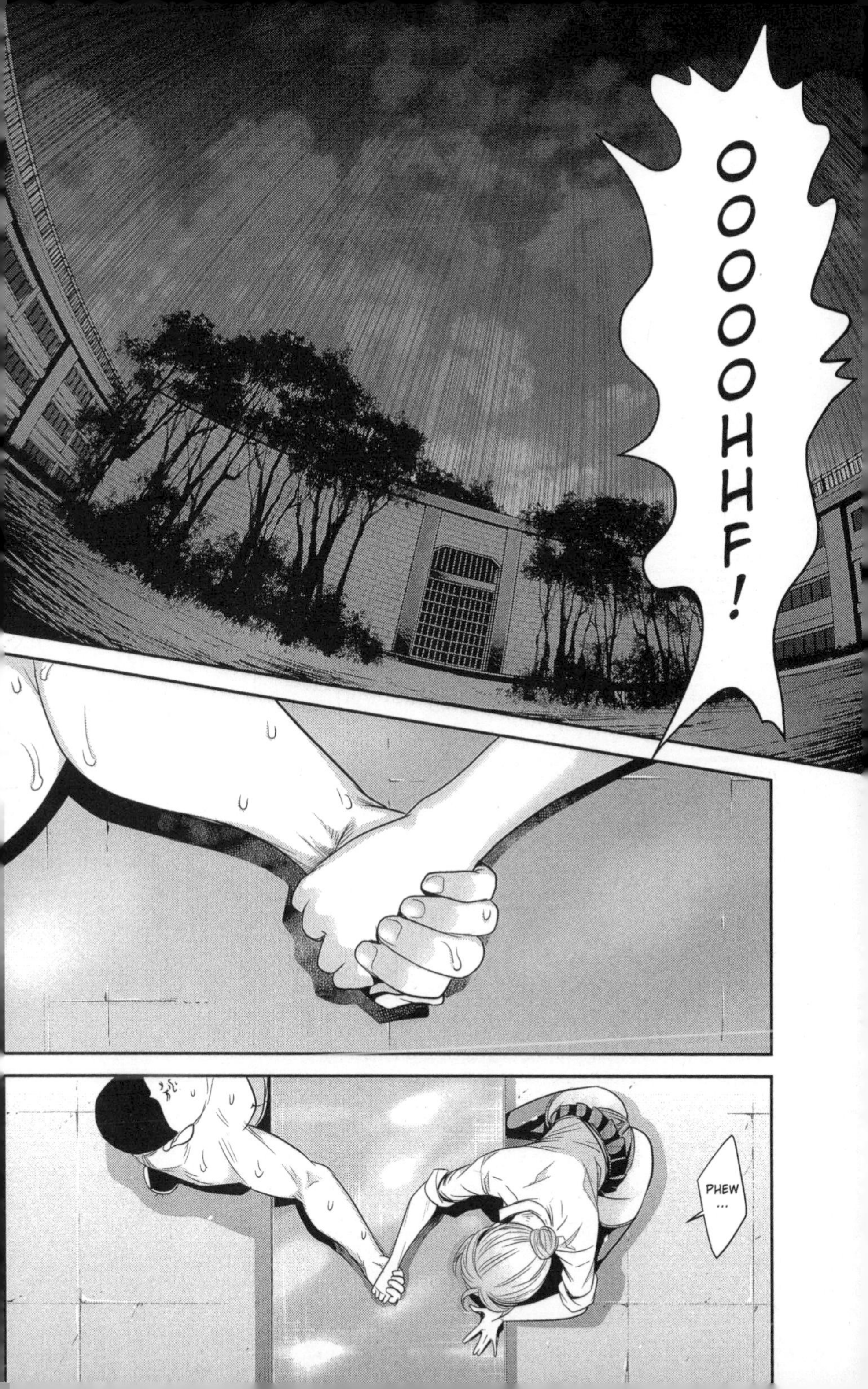
OOOOOOHHF!
PHEW ...

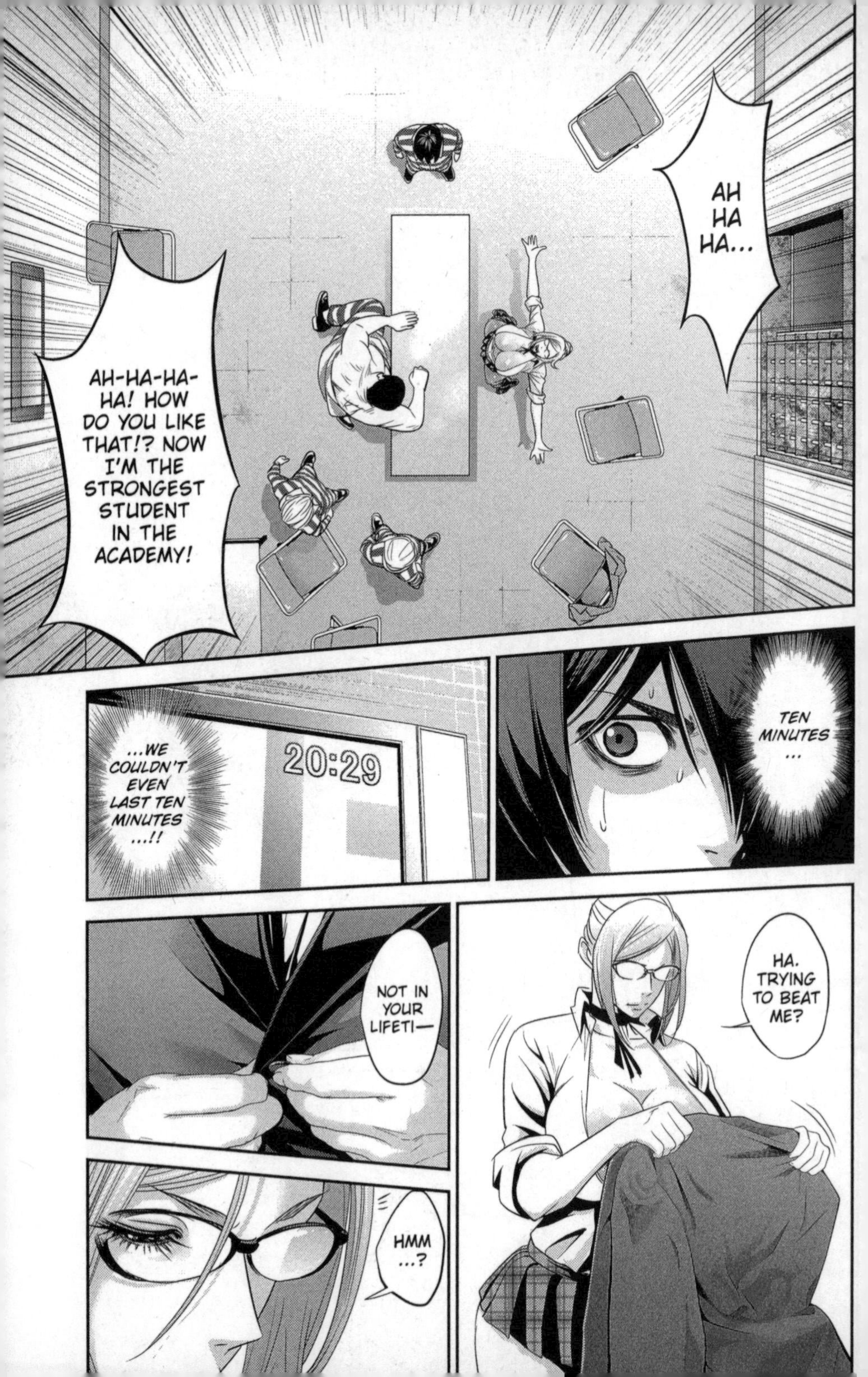
AH HA HA...
AH-HA-HA-HA! HOW DO YOU LIKE THAT!? NOW I'M THE STRONGEST STUDENT IN THE ACADEMY!
TEN MINUTES ...
20:29
...WE COULDN'T EVEN LAST TEN MINUTES ...!!
HA. TRYING TO BEAT ME?
NOT IN YOUR LIFETI—
HMM ...?

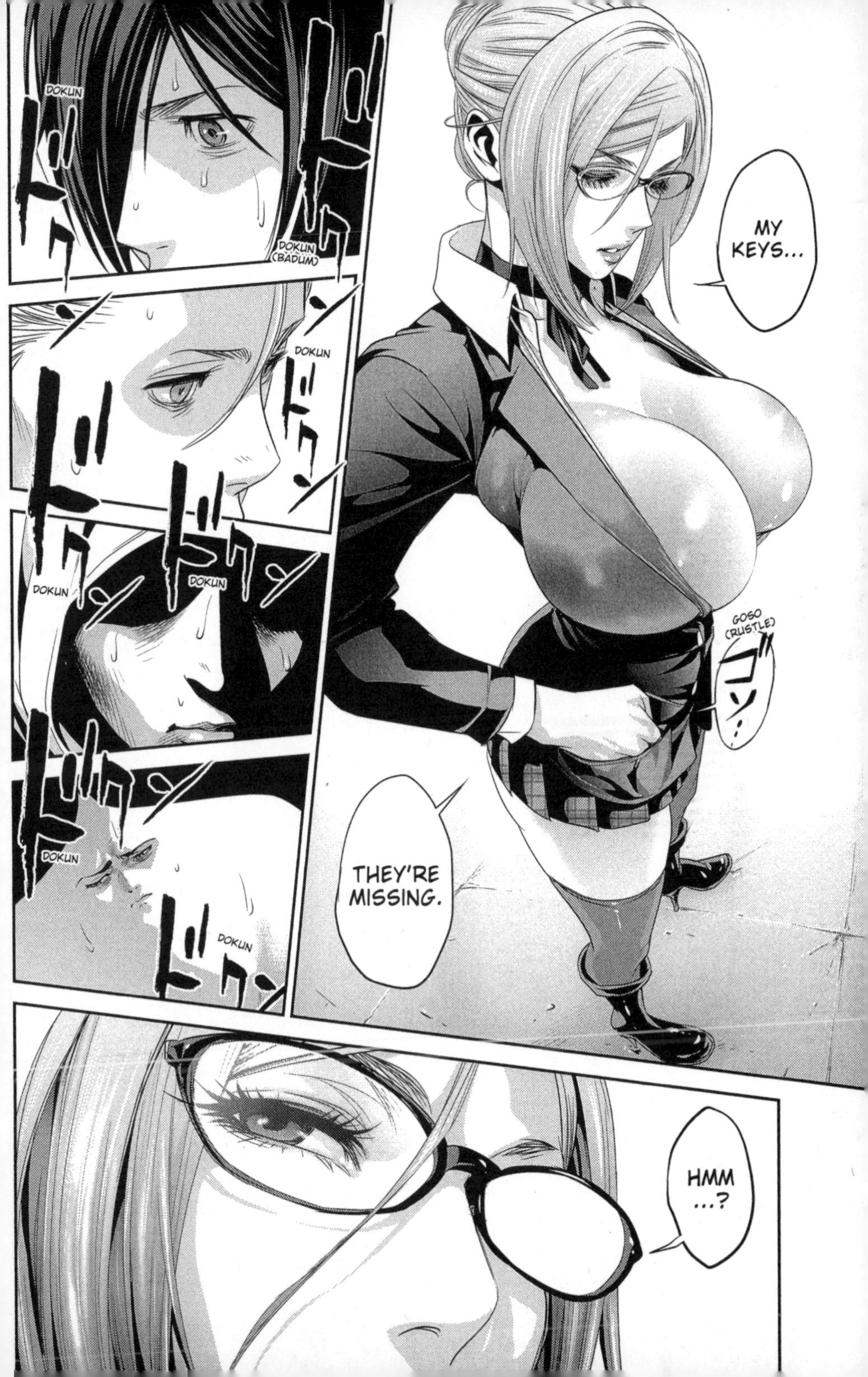
MY KEYS...
GOSO (RUSTLE)
THEY'RE MISSING.
DOKUN (BADUM)
DOKUN
DOKUN
DOKUN
DOKUN
DOKUN
DOKUN
HMM ...?

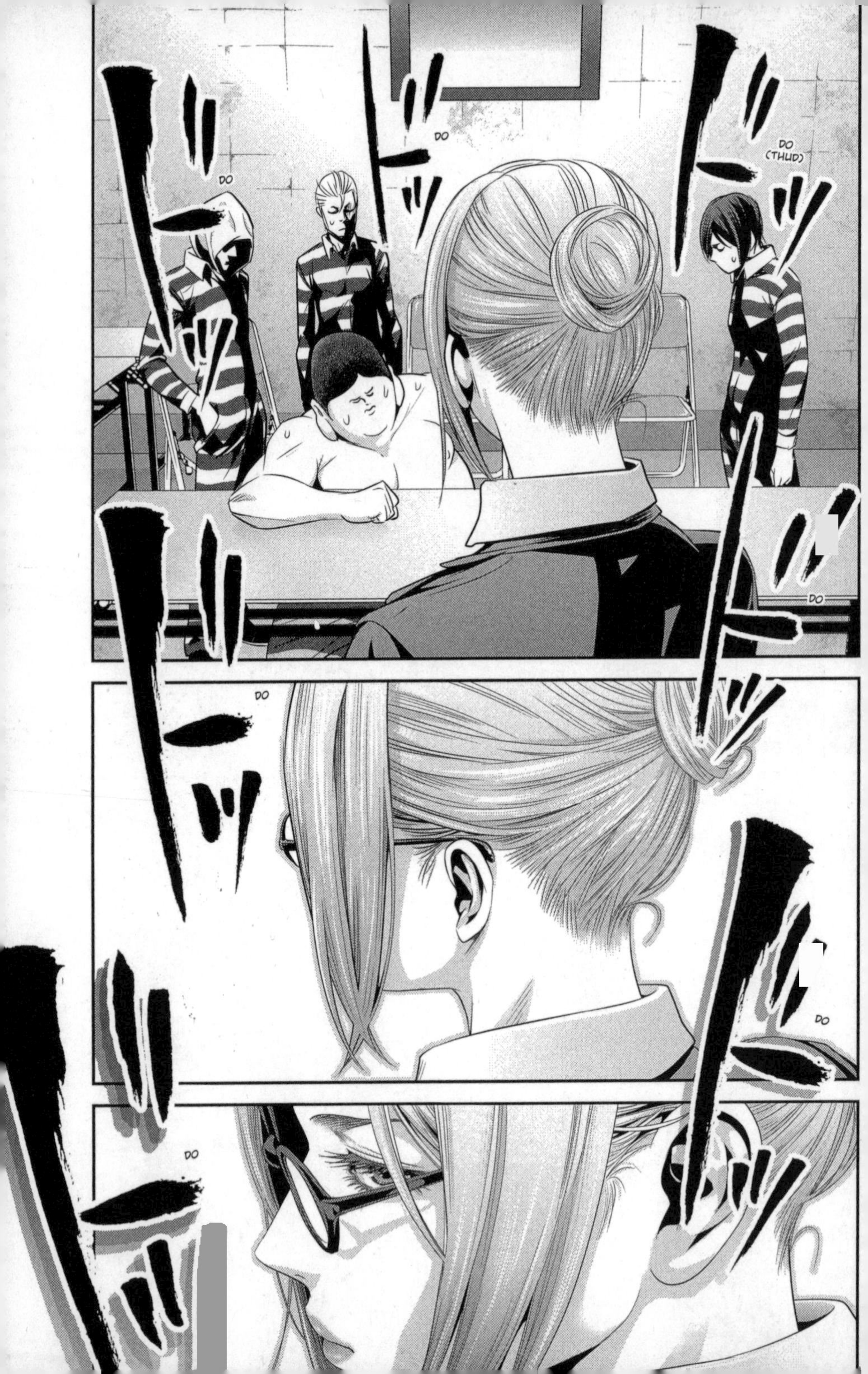
DO
(THUD)
DO
DO
DO
DO
DO
DO

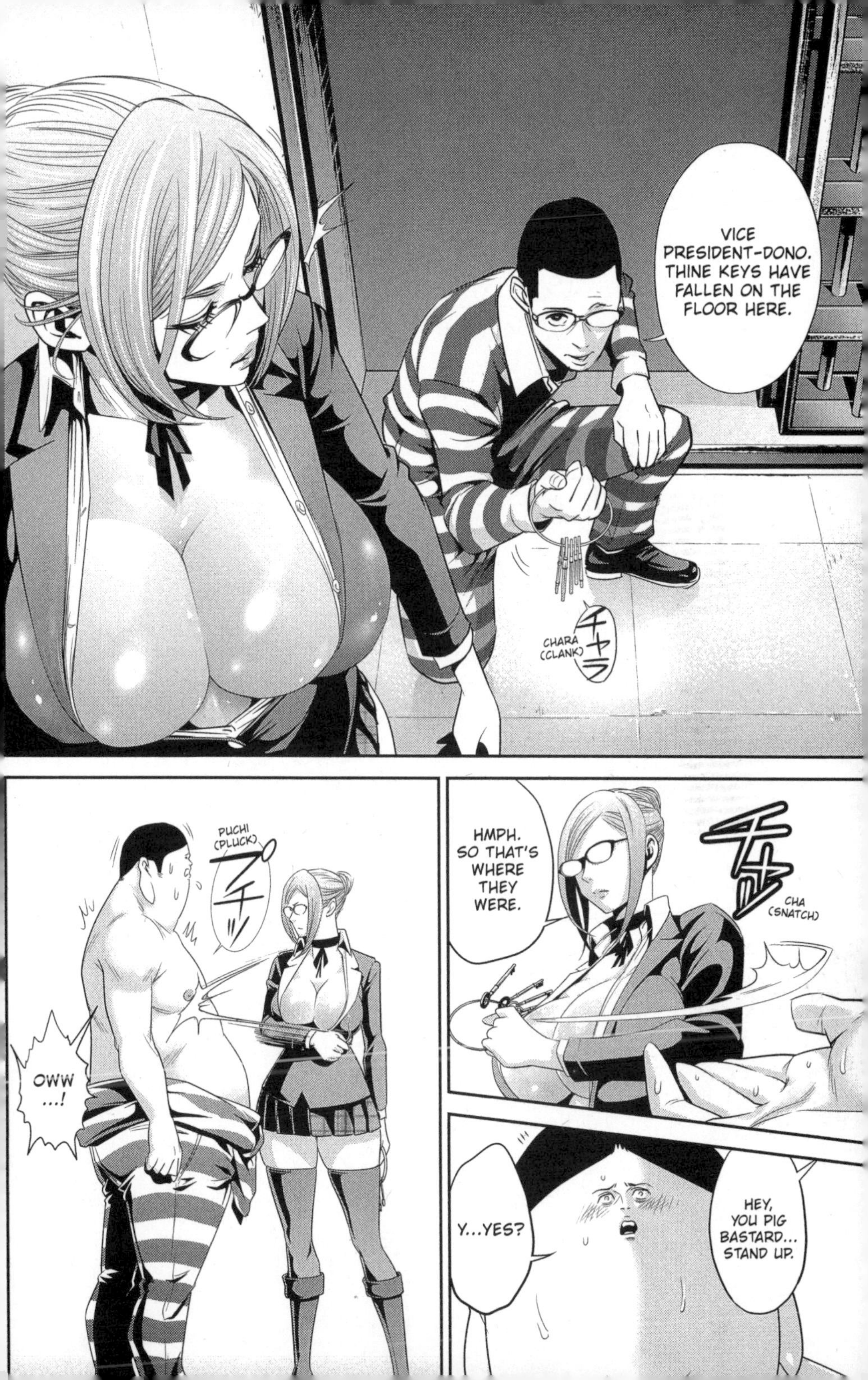
VICE PRESIDENT-DONO. THINE KEYS HAVE FALLEN ON THE FLOOR HERE.
チャラ
CHARA (CLANK)
HMPH. SO THAT'S WHERE THEY WERE.
CHA (SNATCH)
HEY, YOU PIG BASTARD... STAND UP.
Y...YES?
PUCHI (PLUCK)
プチッ
OWW ...!

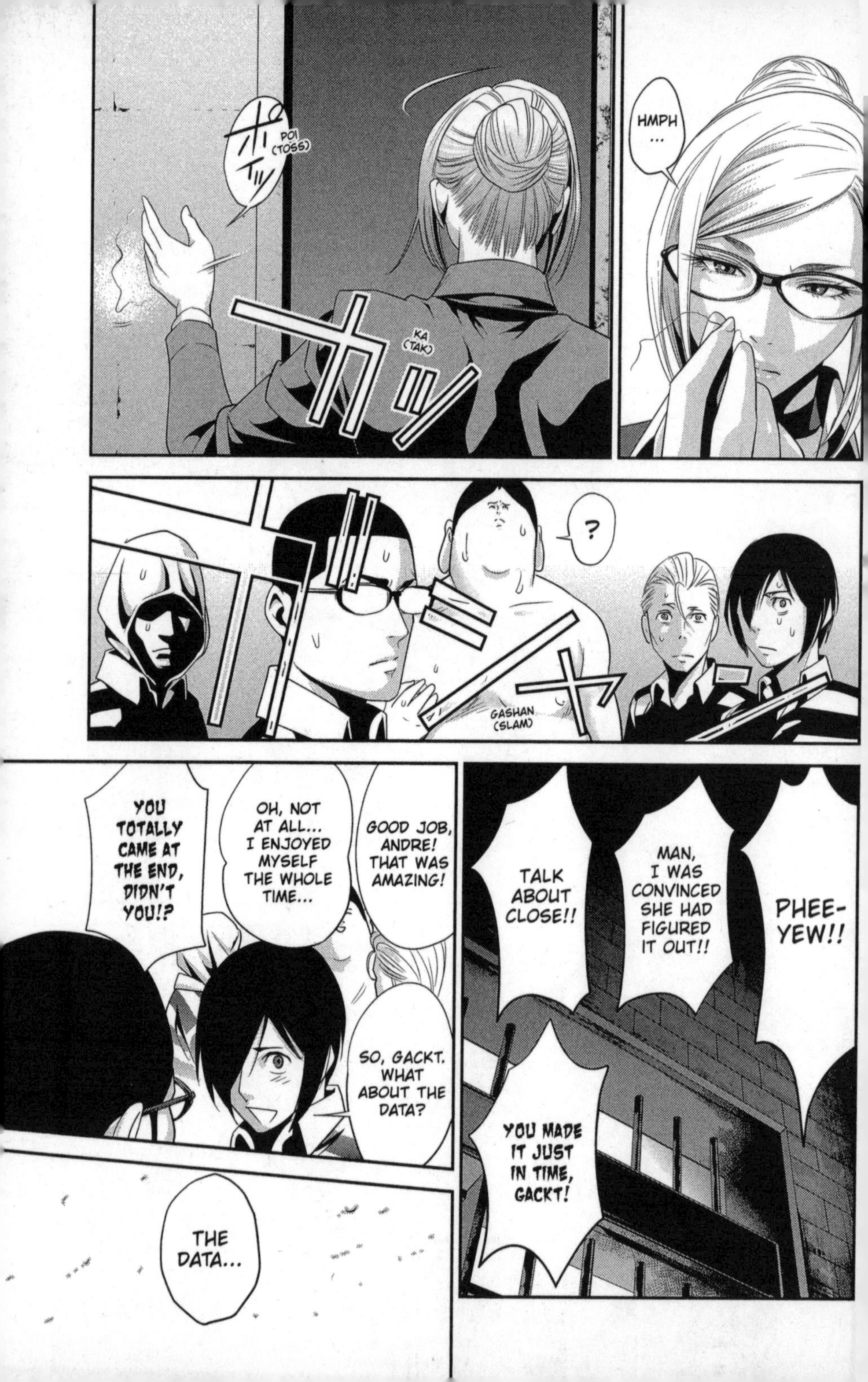

HMPH...
ポイッ
POI (TOSS)
カッ
KA (TAK)
?
GASHAN (SLAM)
PHEE-YEW!!
MAN, I WAS CONVINCED SHE HAD FIGURED IT OUT!!
TALK ABOUT CLOSE!!
YOU MADE IT JUST IN TIME, GACKT!
GOOD JOB, ANDRE! THAT WAS AMAZING!
OH, NOT AT ALL... I ENJOYED MYSELF THE WHOLE TIME...
YOU TOTALLY CAME AT THE END, DIDN'T YOU!?
SO, GACKT. WHAT ABOUT THE DATA?
THE DATA...

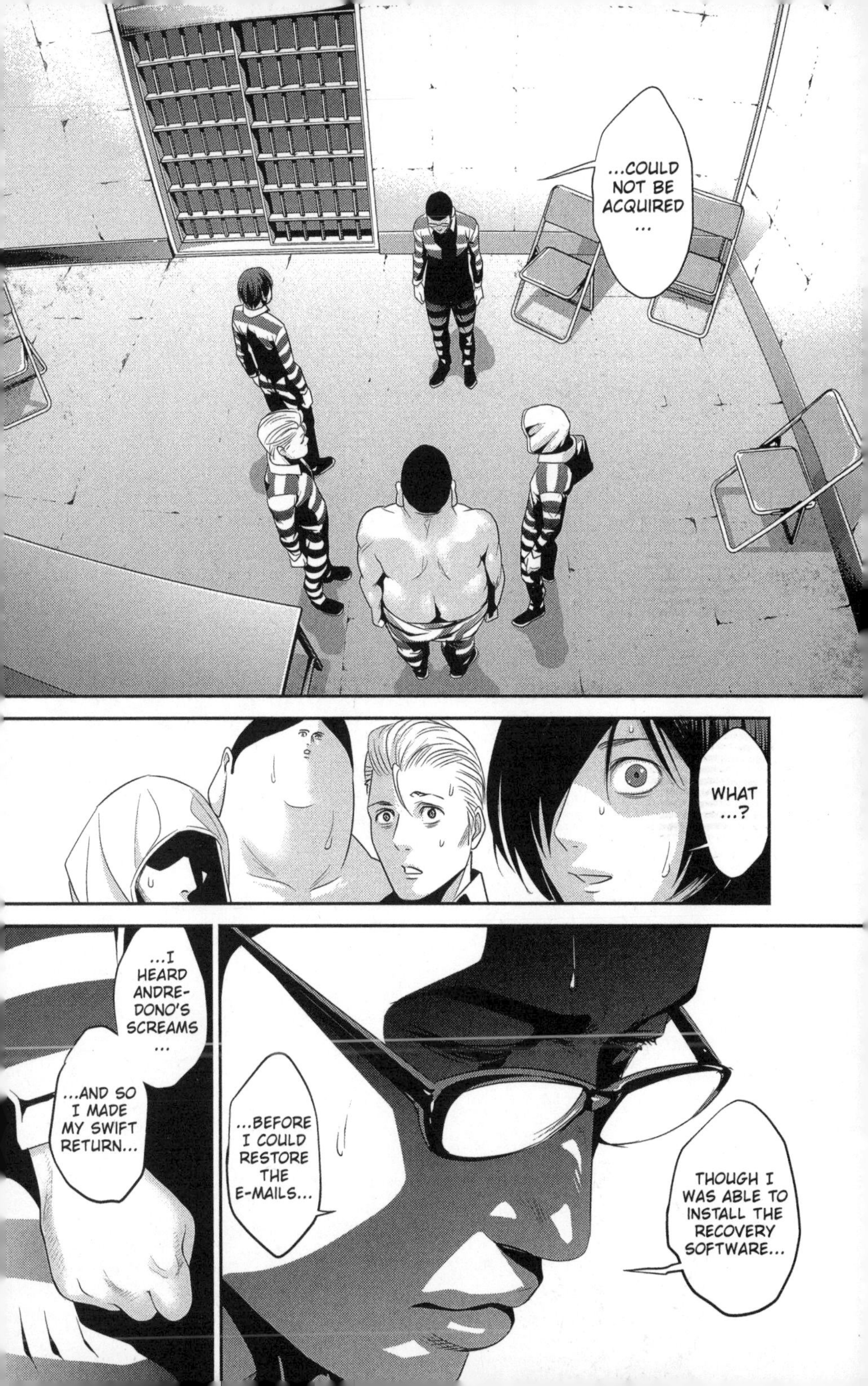
...COULD NOT BE ACQUIRED ...
WHAT ...?
THOUGH I WAS ABLE TO INSTALL THE RECOVERY SOFTWARE...
...BEFORE I COULD RESTORE THE E-MAILS...
...I HEARD ANDRE-DONO'S SCREAMS ...
...AND SO I MADE MY SWIFT RETURN...

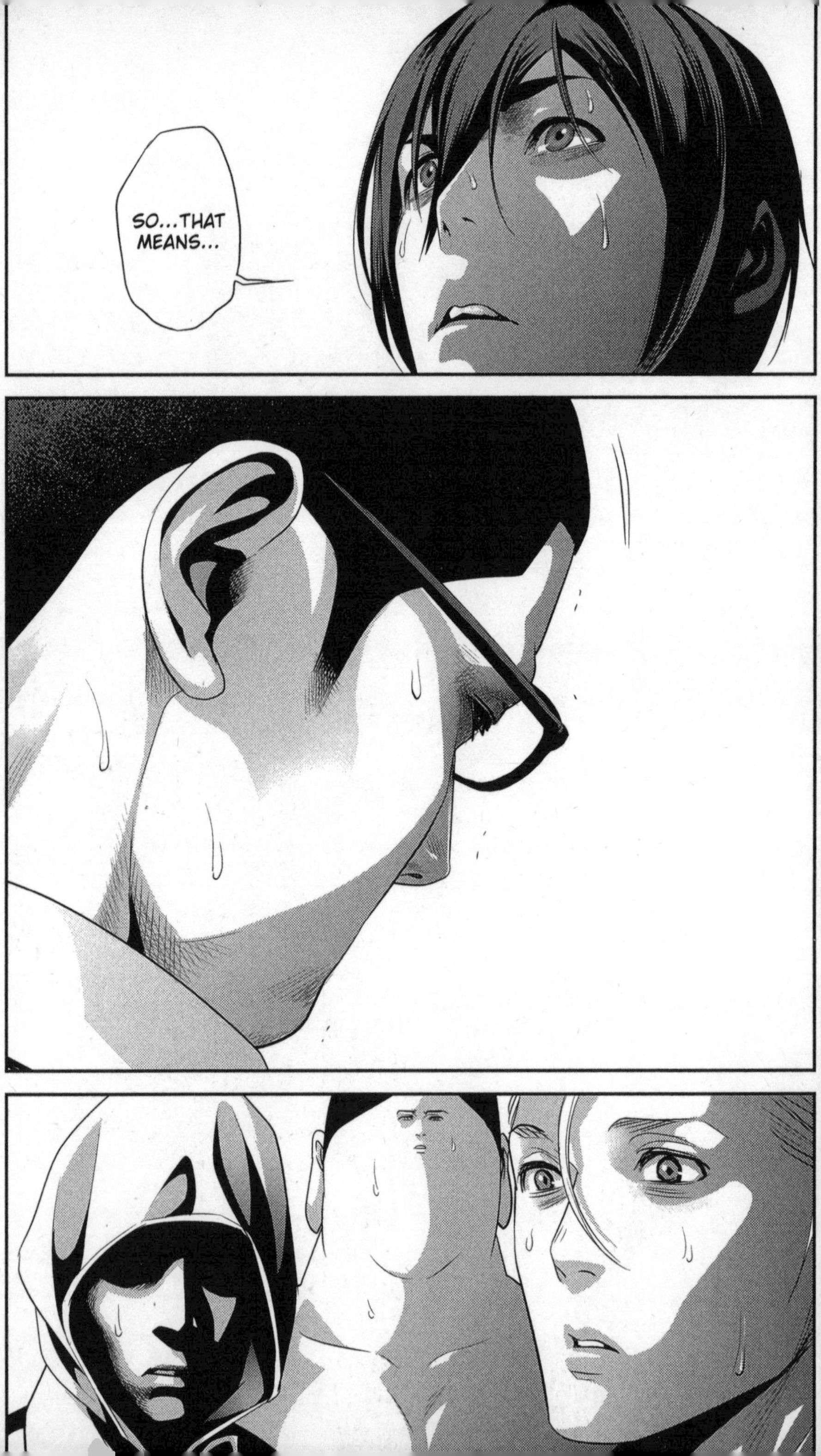
SO...THAT MEANS...

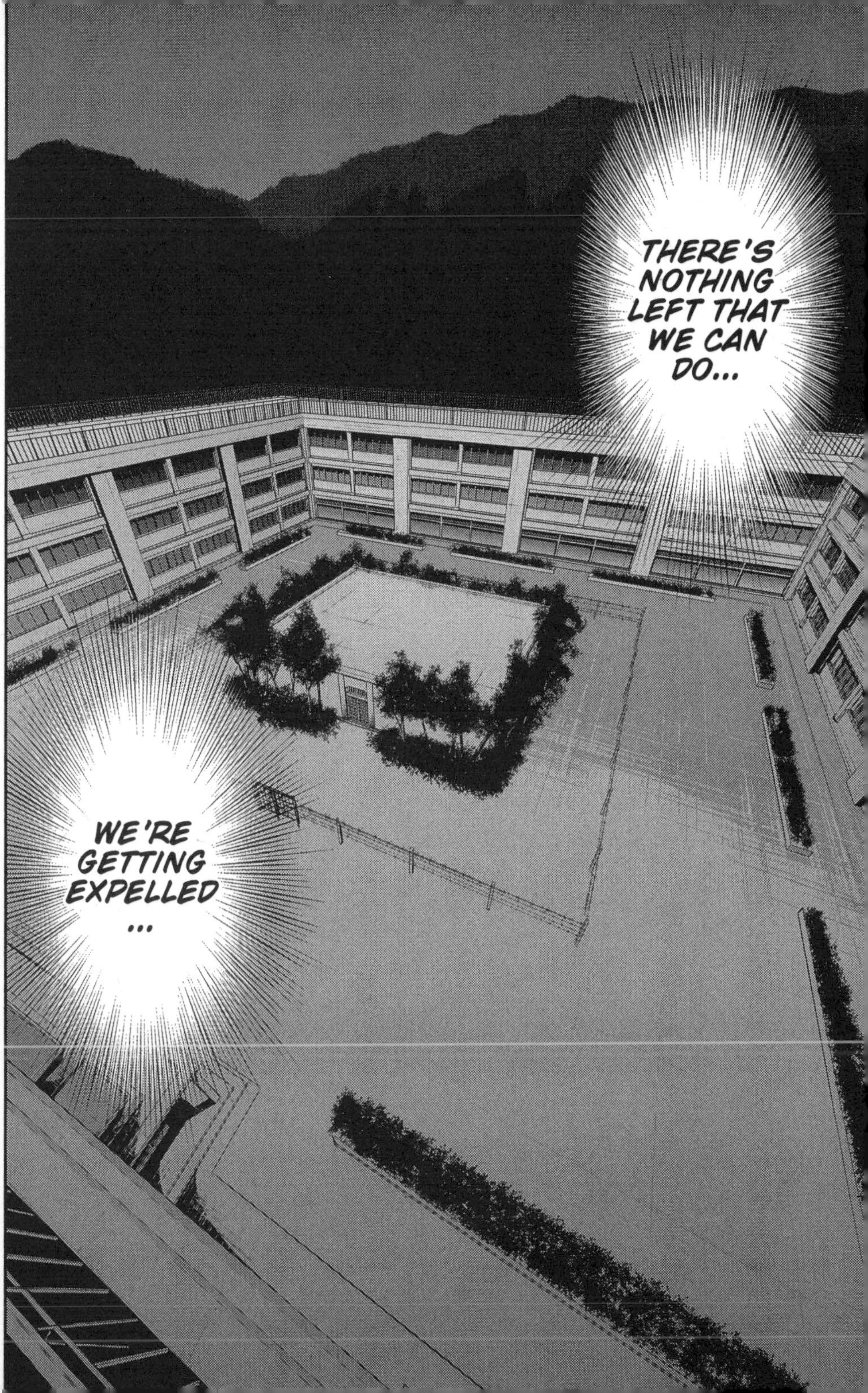
THERE'S NOTHING LEFT THAT WE CAN DO...
WE'RE GETTING EXPELLED ...

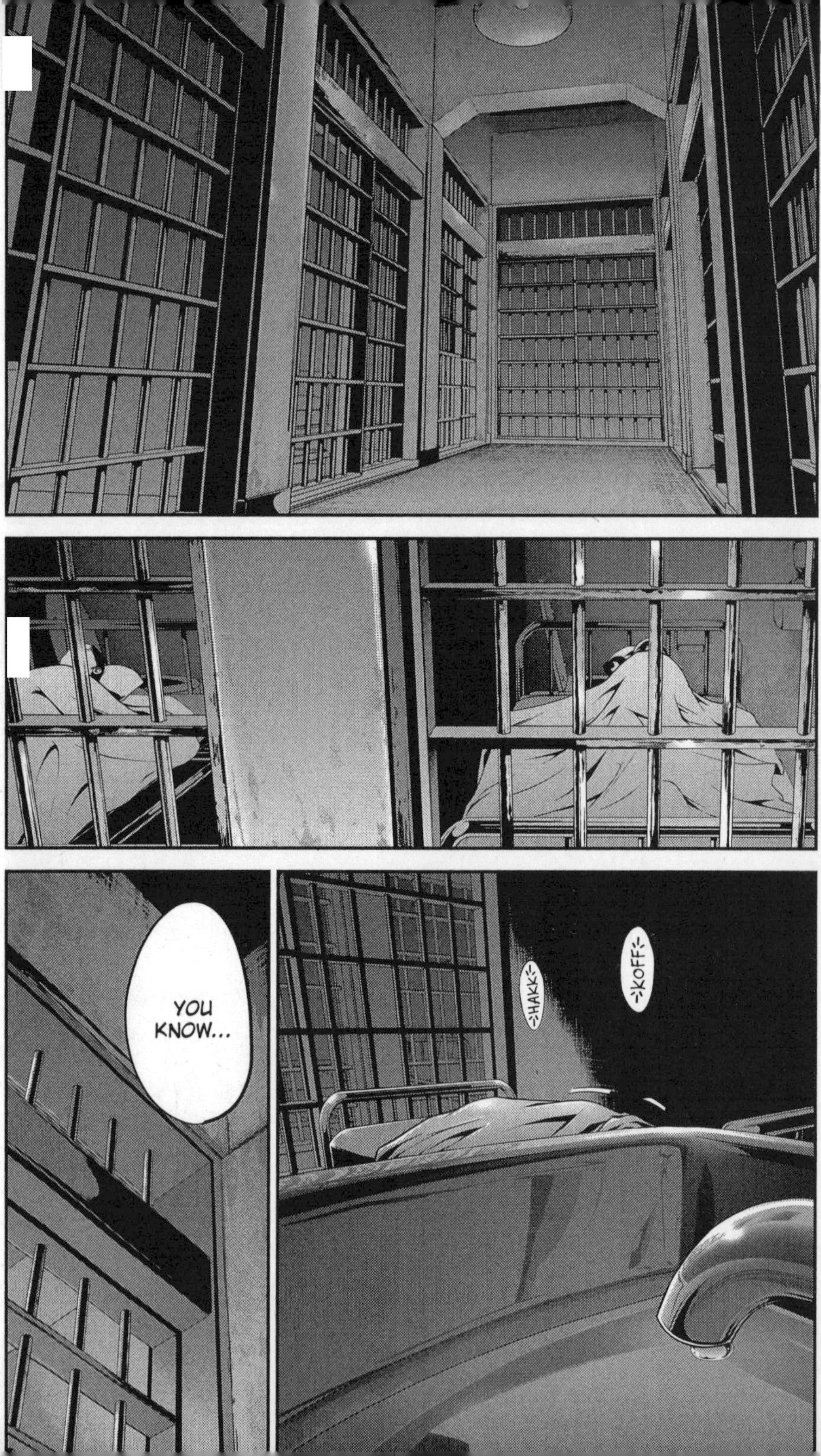
-KOFF-
-HAKK-
YOU KNOW...

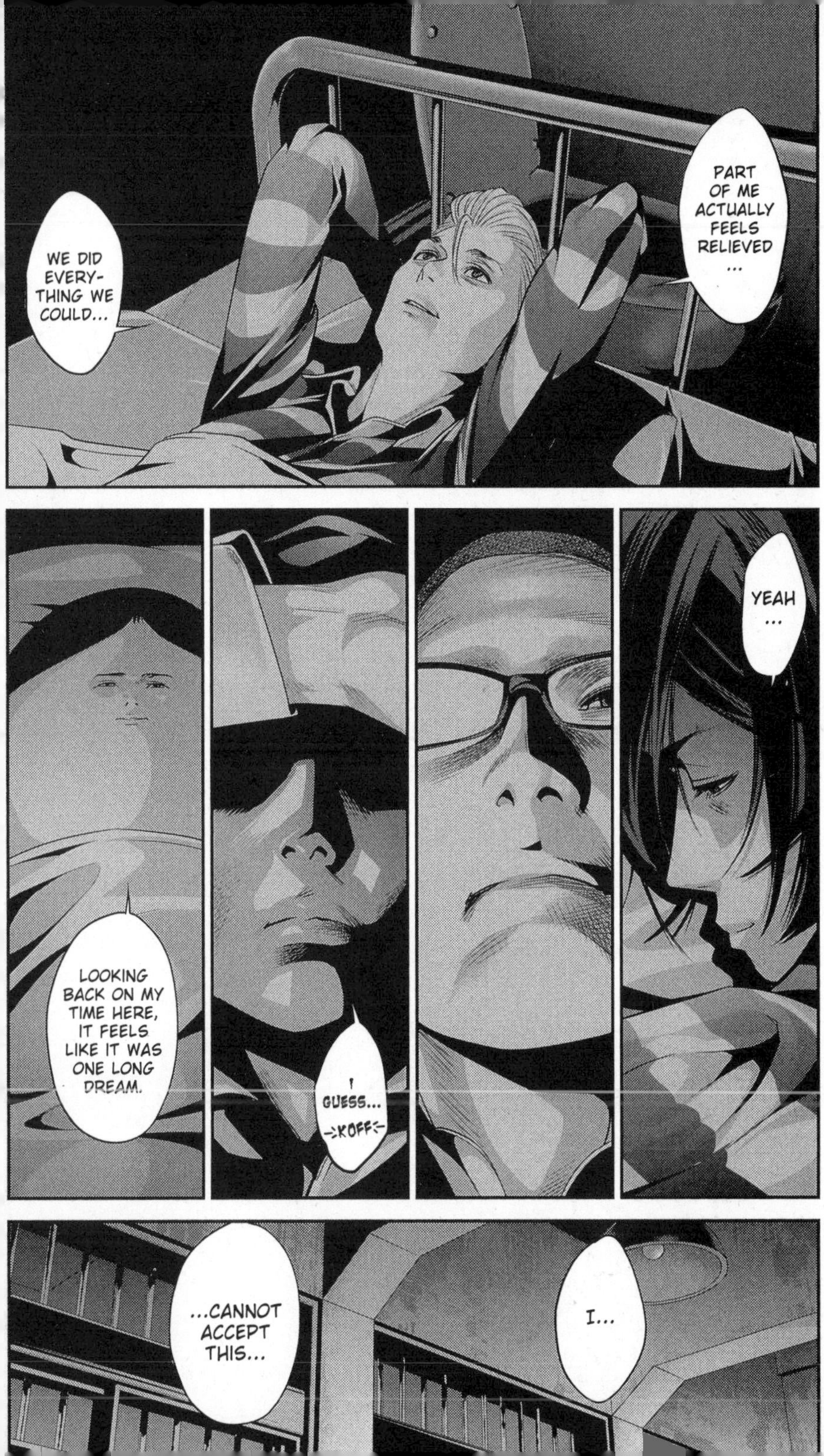
PART OF ME ACTUALLY FEELS RELIEVED ...
WE DID EVERY-THING WE COULD...
YEAH ...
I GUESS... -KOFF-
LOOKING BACK ON MY TIME HERE, IT FEELS LIKE IT WAS ONE LONG DREAM.
I...
...CANNOT ACCEPT THIS...

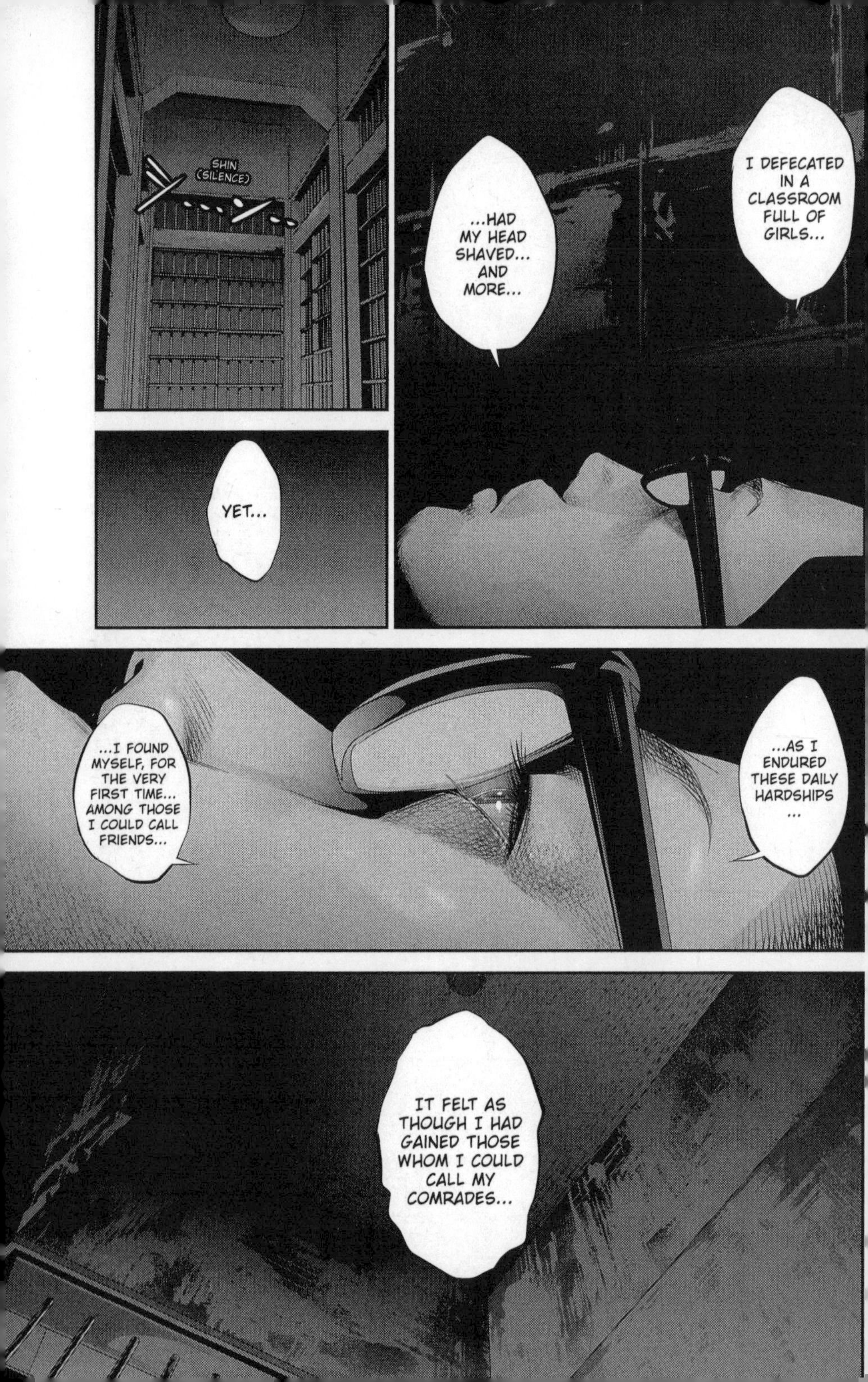

I DEFECATED IN A CLASSROOM FULL OF GIRLS...
...HAD MY HEAD SHAVED... AND MORE...
SHIN (SILENCE)
YET...
...AS I ENDURED THESE DAILY HARDSHIPS ...
...I FOUND MYSELF, FOR THE VERY FIRST TIME... AMONG THOSE I COULD CALL FRIENDS...
IT FELT AS THOUGH I HAD GAINED THOSE WHOM I COULD CALL MY COMRADES...

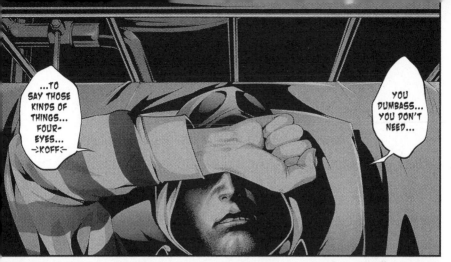

YOU DUMBASS... YOU DON'T NEED...
...TO SAY THOSE KINDS OF THINGS... FOUR-EYES... -KOFF-
OUR HIGH SCHOOL LIVES...
...HAVE COME TO AN END...

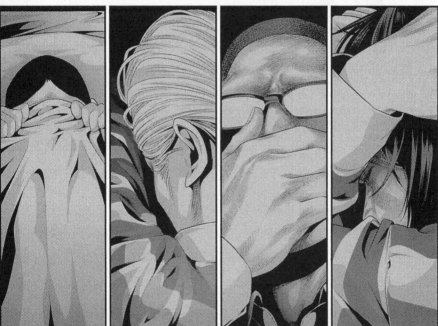

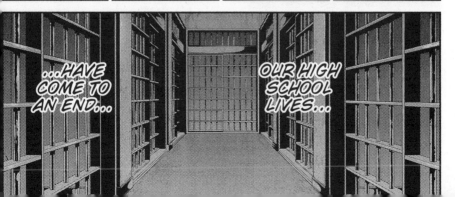

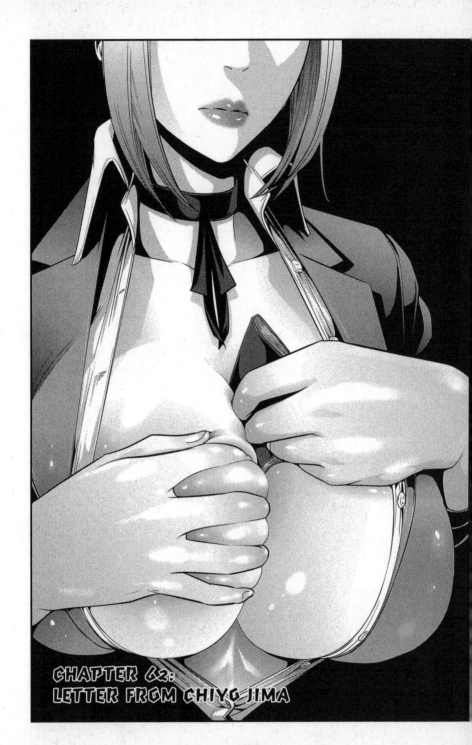

CHAPTER 62:
LETTER FROM CHIYO JIMA

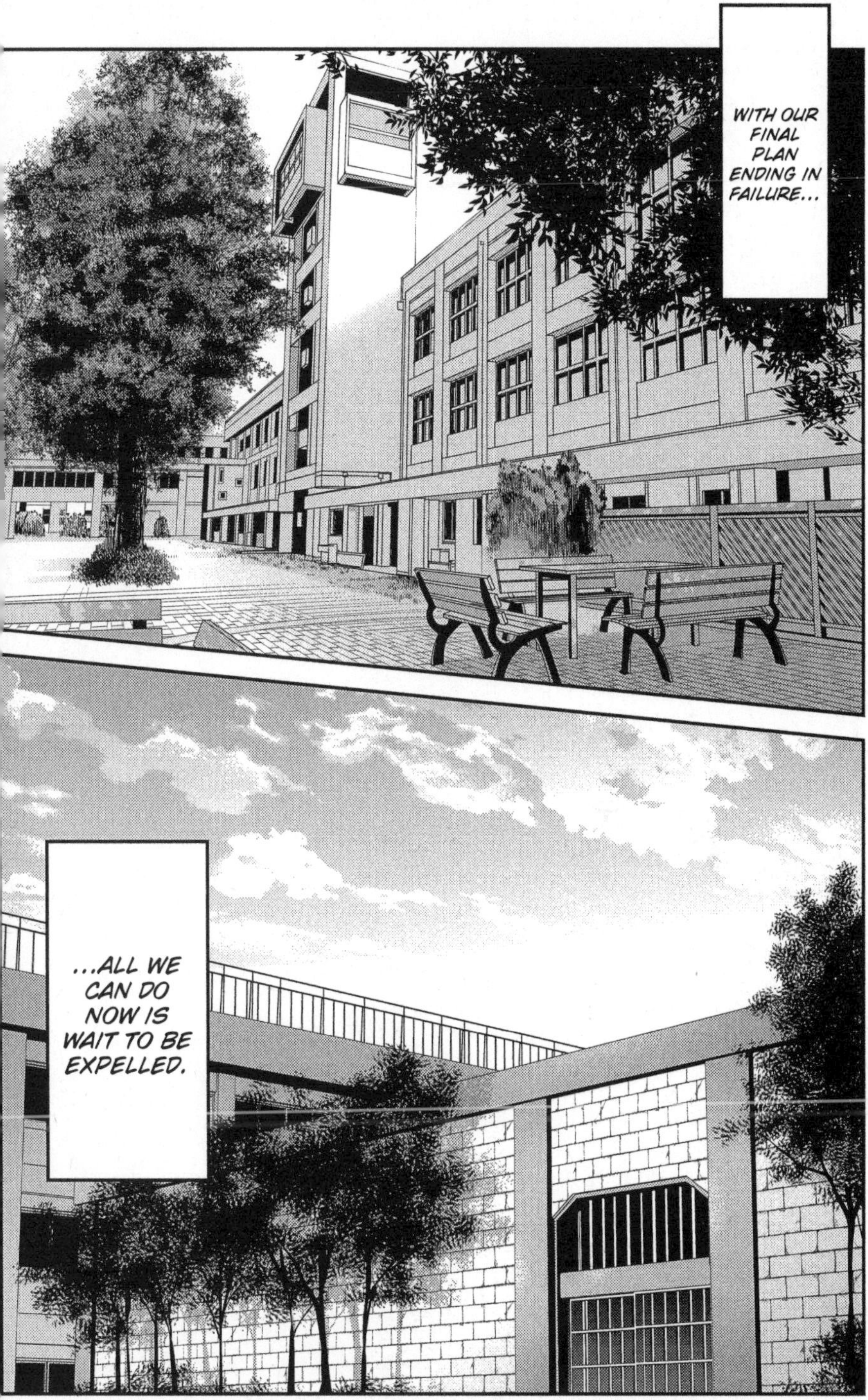
WITH OUR FINAL PLAN ENDING IN FAILURE...
...ALL WE CAN DO NOW IS WAIT TO BE EXPELLED.

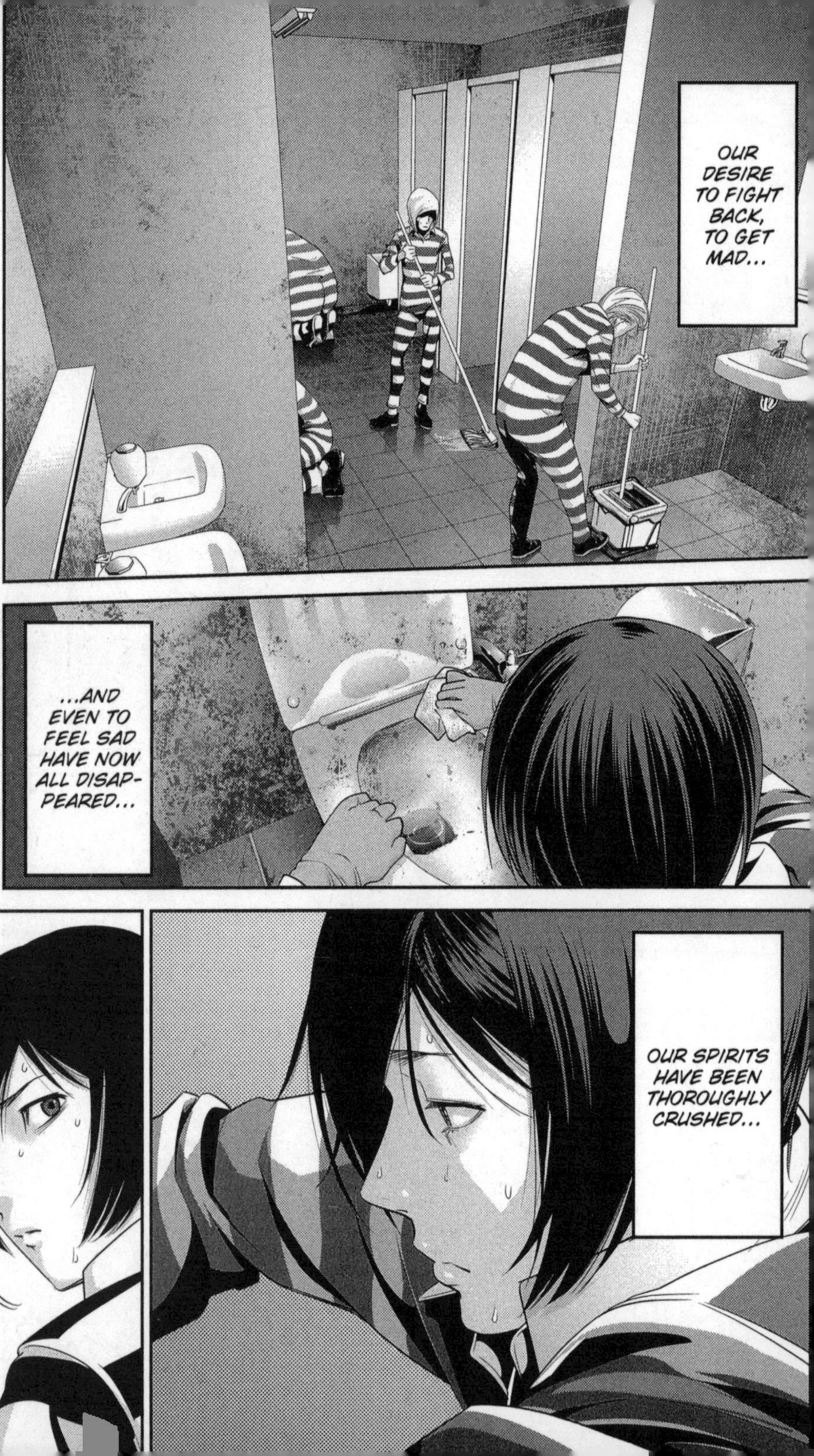
OUR DESIRE TO FIGHT BACK, TO GET MAD...
...AND EVEN TO FEEL SAD HAVE NOW ALL DISAP-PEARED...
OUR SPIRITS HAVE BEEN THOROUGHLY CRUSHED...

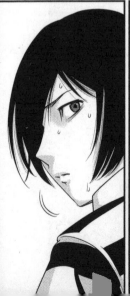

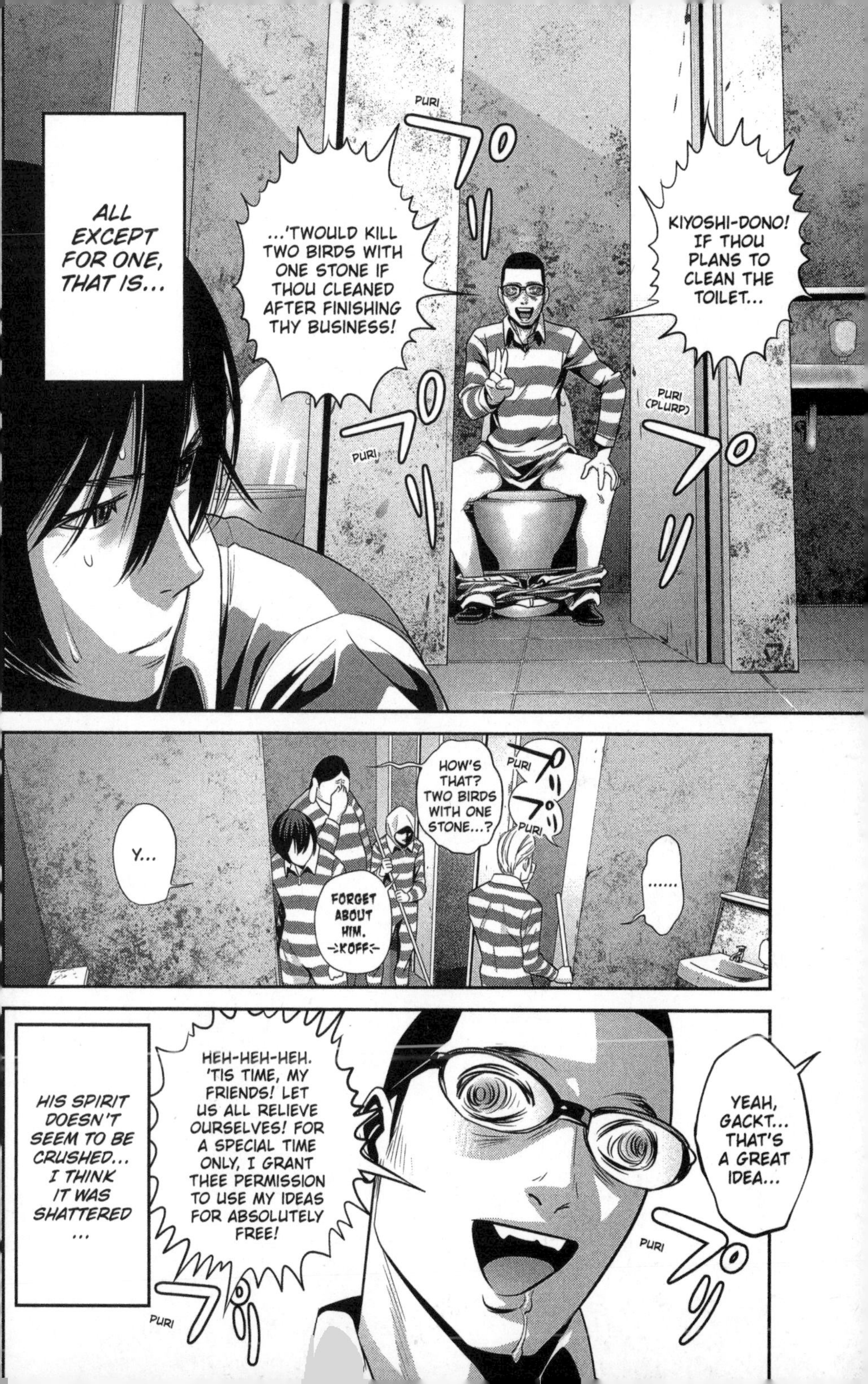

KIYOSHI-DONO! IF THOU PLANS TO CLEAN THE TOILET...
PURI
...'TWOULD KILL TWO BIRDS WITH ONE STONE IF THOU CLEANED AFTER FINISHING THY BUSINESS!
PURI (PLURP)
PURI
ALL EXCEPT FOR ONE, THAT IS...
......
PURI
PURI
HOW'S THAT? TWO BIRDS WITH ONE STONE...?
FORGET ABOUT HIM. -KOFF-
Y...
YEAH, GACKT... THAT'S A GREAT IDEA...
PURI
HEH-HEH-HEH. 'TIS TIME, MY FRIENDS! LET US ALL RELIEVE OURSELVES! FOR A SPECIAL TIME ONLY, I GRANT THEE PERMISSION TO USE MY IDEAS FOR ABSOLUTELY FREE!
PURI
HIS SPIRIT DOESN'T SEEM TO BE CRUSHED... I THINK IT WAS SHATTERED ...

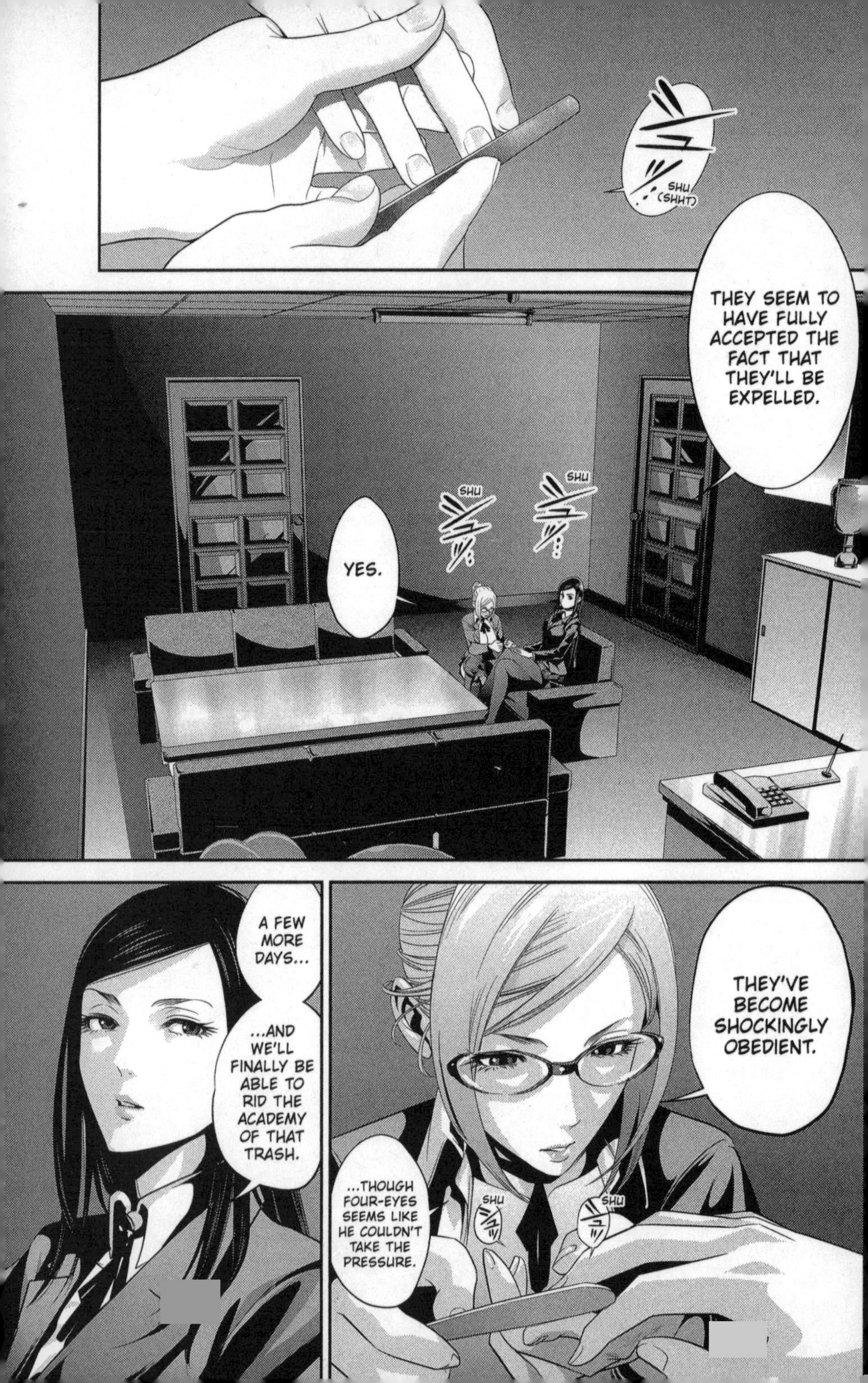
SHU (SHHT)
THEY SEEM TO HAVE FULLY ACCEPTED THE FACT THAT THEY'LL BE EXPELLED.
SHU
SHU
YES.
THEY'VE BECOME SHOCKINGLY OBEDIENT.
SHU
SHU
...THOUGH FOUR-EYES SEEMS LIKE HE COULDN'T TAKE THE PRESSURE.
A FEW MORE DAYS...
...AND WE'LL FINALLY BE ABLE TO RID THE ACADEMY OF THAT TRASH.

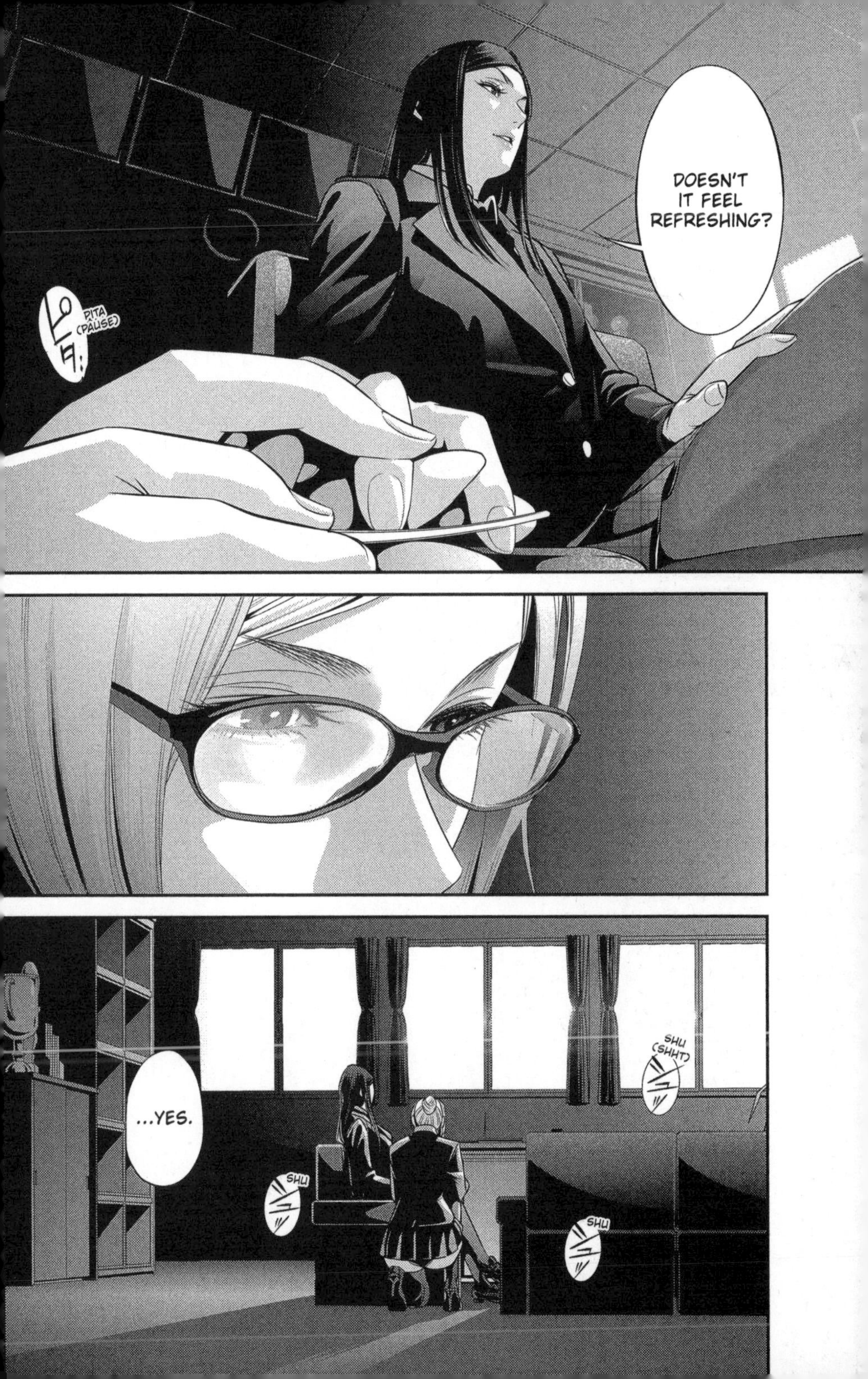
DOESN'T IT FEEL REFRESHING?
PITA (PAUSE)
SHU (SHHT)
...YES.
SHU
SHU

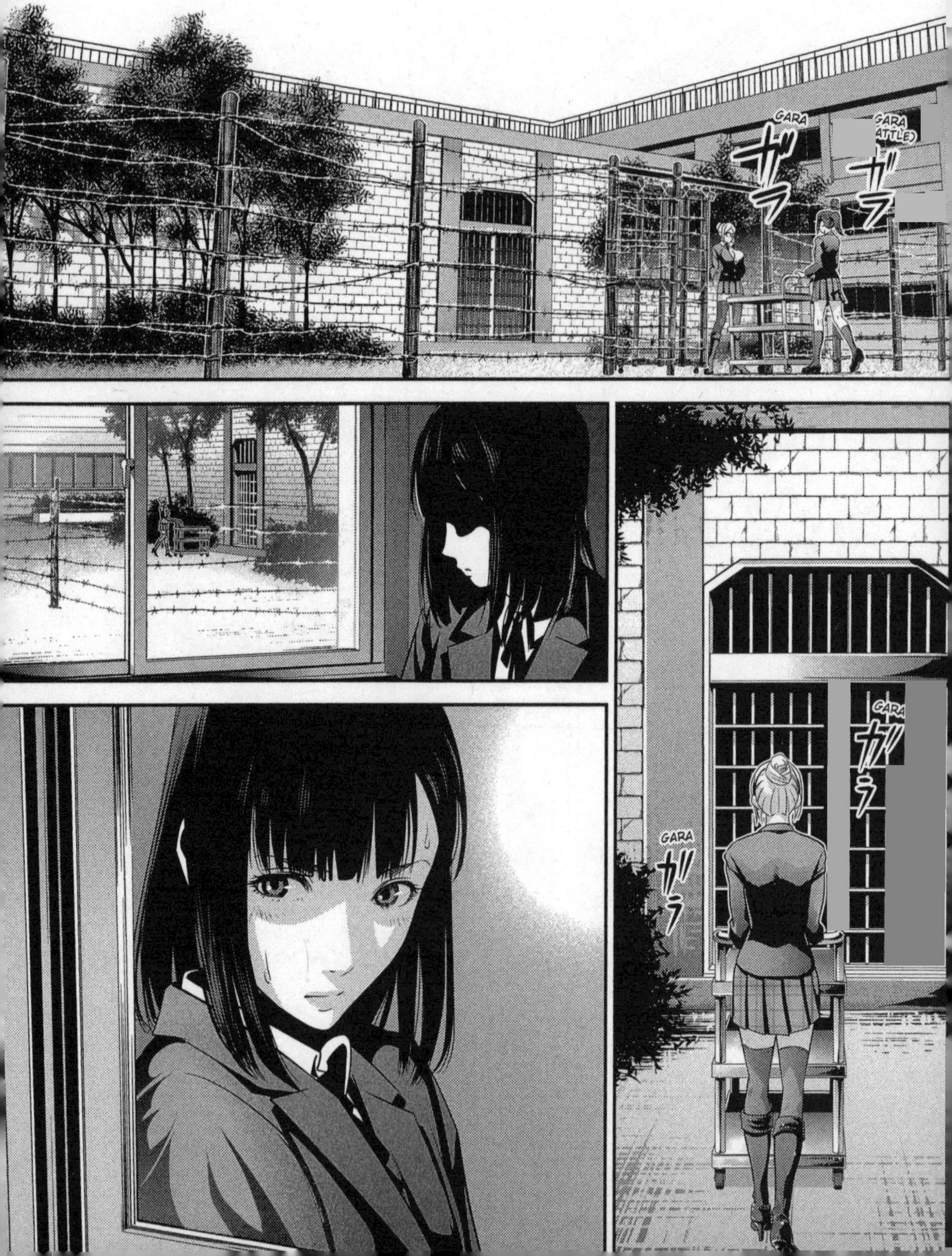
GARA
ATTLE)
ガラ
GARA
ガラ
GARA
ガラ
GARA
ガラ

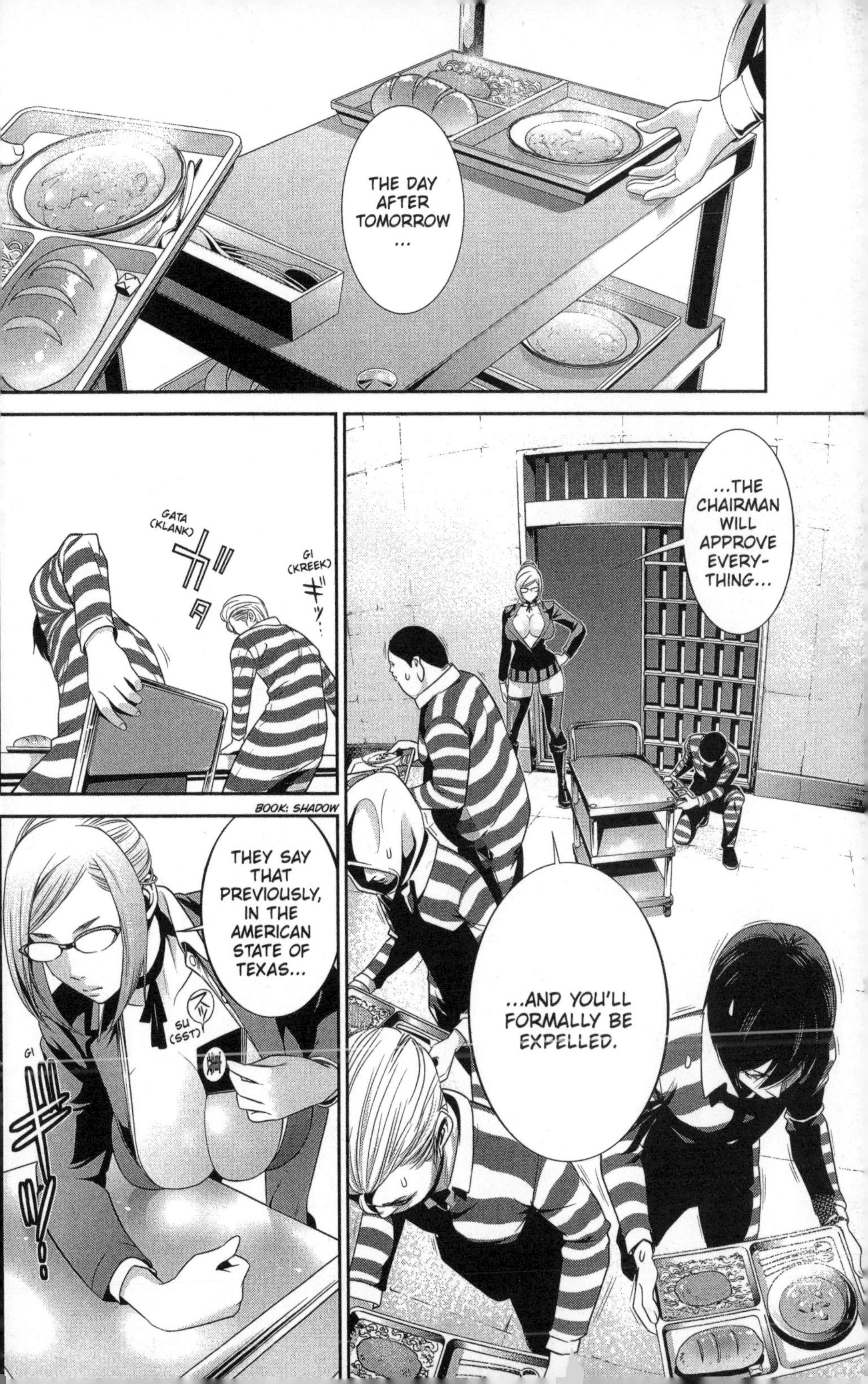
THE DAY AFTER TOMORROW ...
...THE CHAIRMAN WILL APPROVE EVERY-THING...
...AND YOU'LL FORMALLY BE EXPELLED.
GATA (KLANK)
GI (KREEK)
BOOK: SHADOW
THEY SAY THAT PREVIOUSLY, IN THE AMERICAN STATE OF TEXAS...
SU (SST)
GI

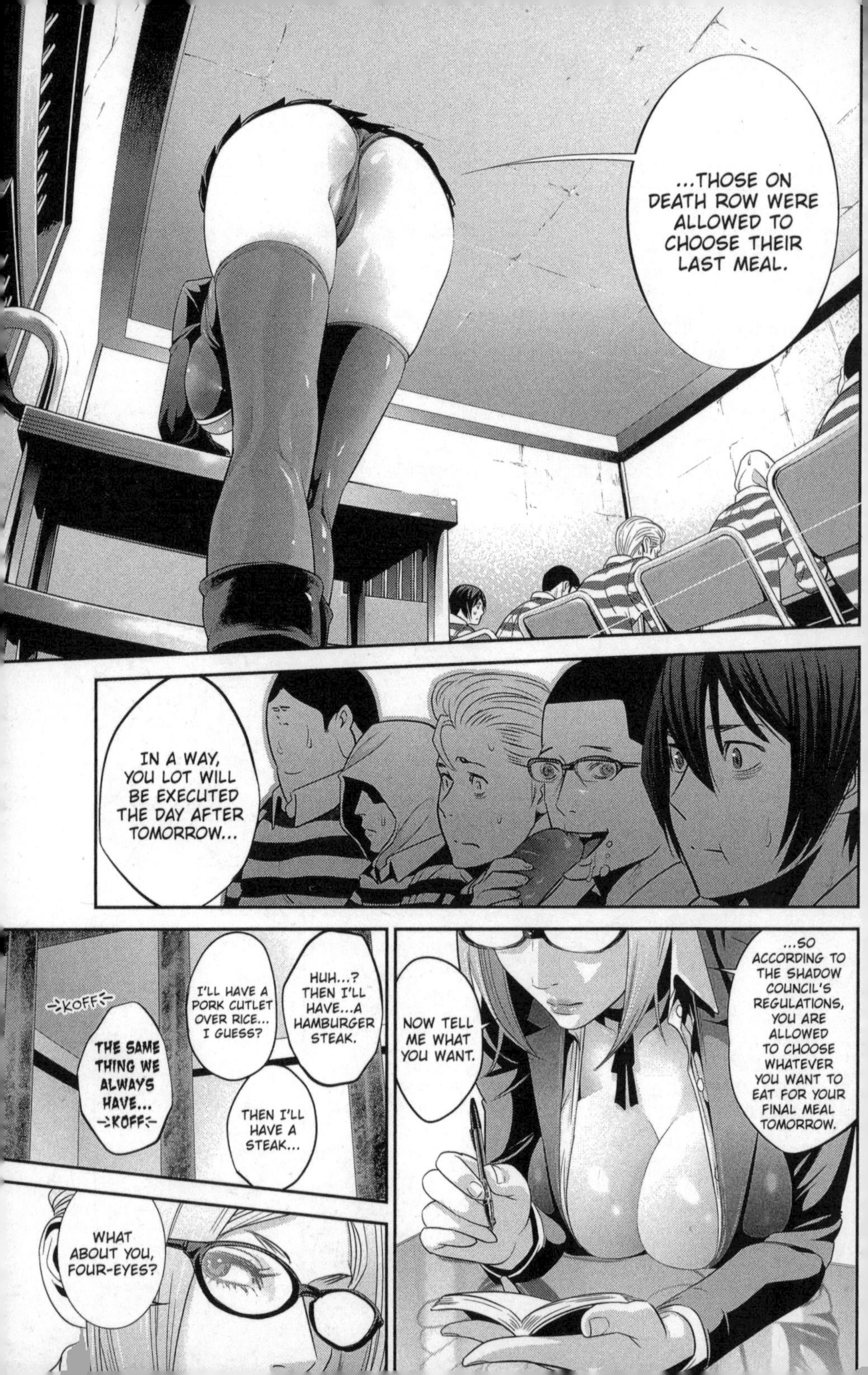
...THOSE ON DEATH ROW WERE ALLOWED TO CHOOSE THEIR LAST MEAL.
IN A WAY, YOU LOT WILL BE EXECUTED THE DAY AFTER TOMORROW...
...SO ACCORDING TO THE SHADOW COUNCIL'S REGULATIONS, YOU ARE ALLOWED TO CHOOSE WHATEVER YOU WANT TO EAT FOR YOUR FINAL MEAL TOMORROW.
NOW TELL ME WHAT YOU WANT.
HUH...? THEN I'LL HAVE...A HAMBURGER STEAK.
I'LL HAVE A PORK CUTLET OVER RICE... I GUESS?
THEN I'LL HAVE A STEAK...
KOFF
THE SAME THING WE ALWAYS HAVE... KOFF
WHAT ABOUT YOU, FOUR-EYES?

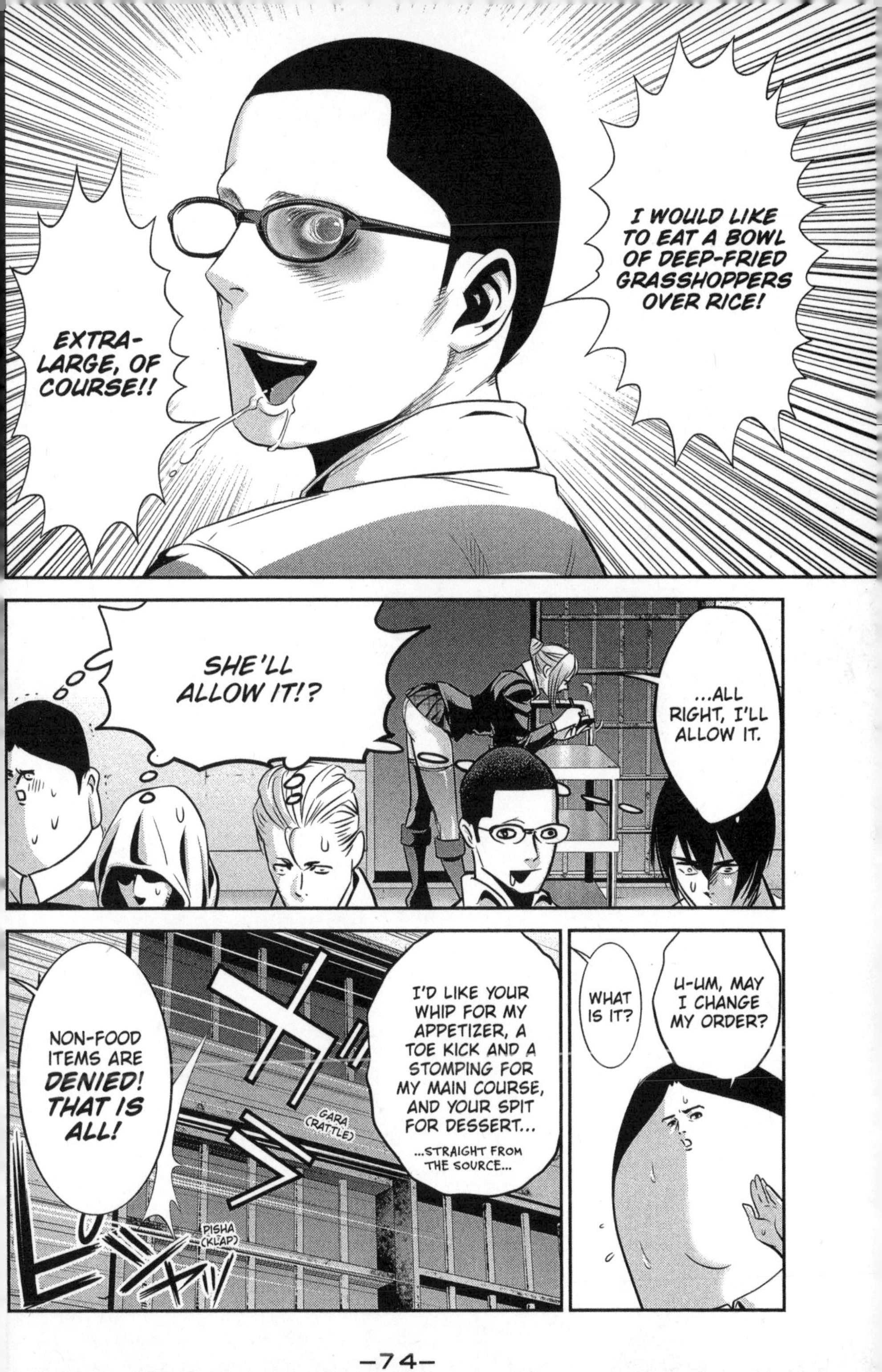
I WOULD LIKE TO EAT A BOWL OF DEEP-FRIED GRASSHOPPERS OVER RICE!
EXTRA-LARGE, OF COURSE!!
...ALL RIGHT, I'LL ALLOW IT.
SHE'LL ALLOW IT!?
...
U-UM, MAY I CHANGE MY ORDER?
WHAT IS IT?
I'D LIKE YOUR WHIP FOR MY APPETIZER, A TOE KICK AND A STOMPING FOR MY MAIN COURSE, AND YOUR SPIT FOR DESSERT...
...STRAIGHT FROM THE SOURCE...
GARA (RATTLE)
NON-FOOD ITEMS ARE DENIED! THAT IS ALL!
PISHA (KLAP)

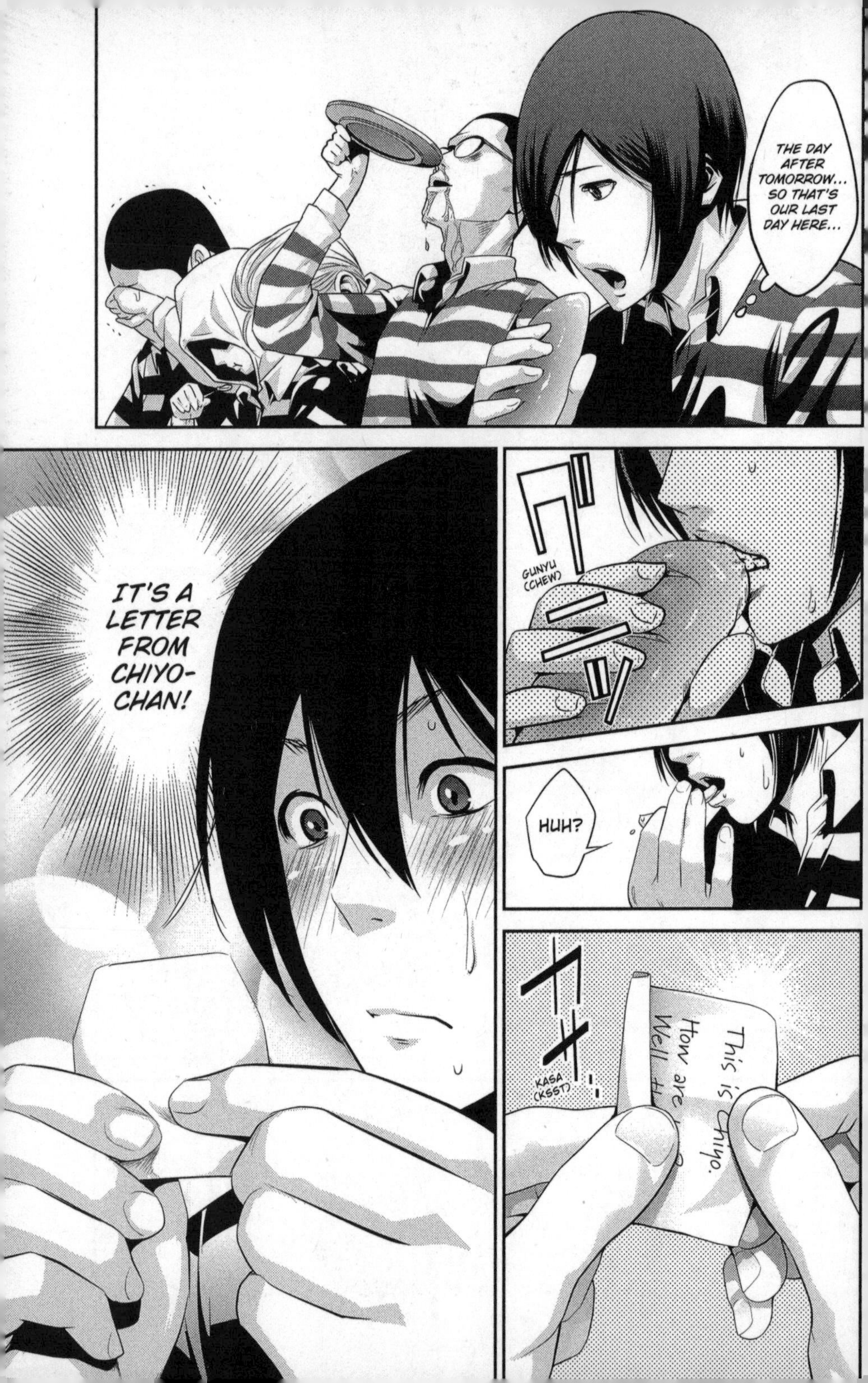
THE DAY AFTER TOMORROW... SO THAT'S OUR LAST DAY HERE...
GUNYU (CHEW)
HUH?
KASA (KSST)
This is Chiyo.
How are
Well
IT'S A LETTER FROM CHIYO-CHAN!

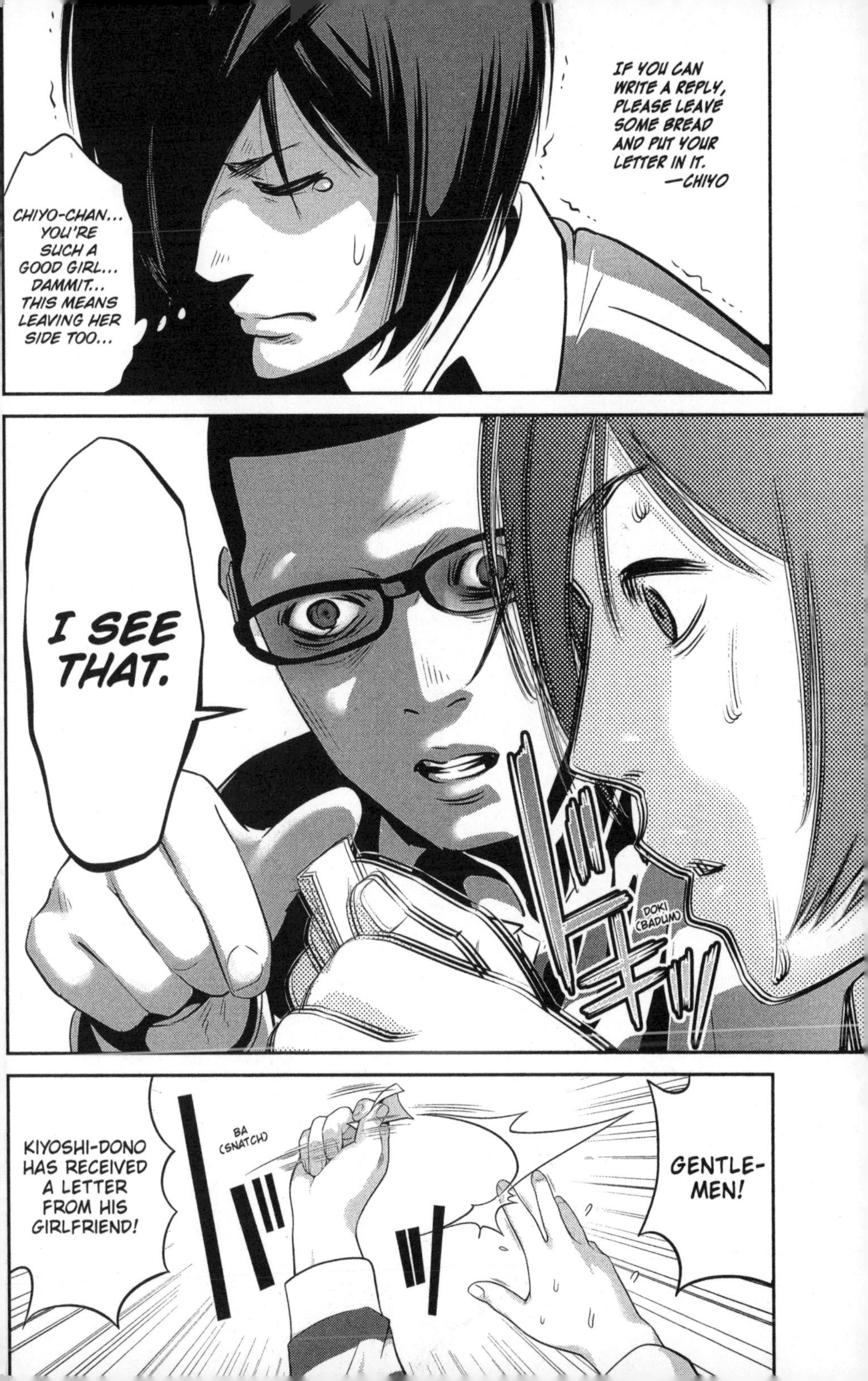
IF YOU CAN WRITE A REPLY, PLEASE LEAVE SOME BREAD AND PUT YOUR LETTER IN IT. —CHIYO
CHIYO-CHAN... YOU'RE SUCH A GOOD GIRL... DAMMIT... THIS MEANS LEAVING HER SIDE TOO...
I SEE THAT.
DOKI (BADUM)
GENTLE-MEN!
BA (SNATCH)
KIYOSHI-DONO HAS RECEIVED A LETTER FROM HIS GIRLFRIEND!

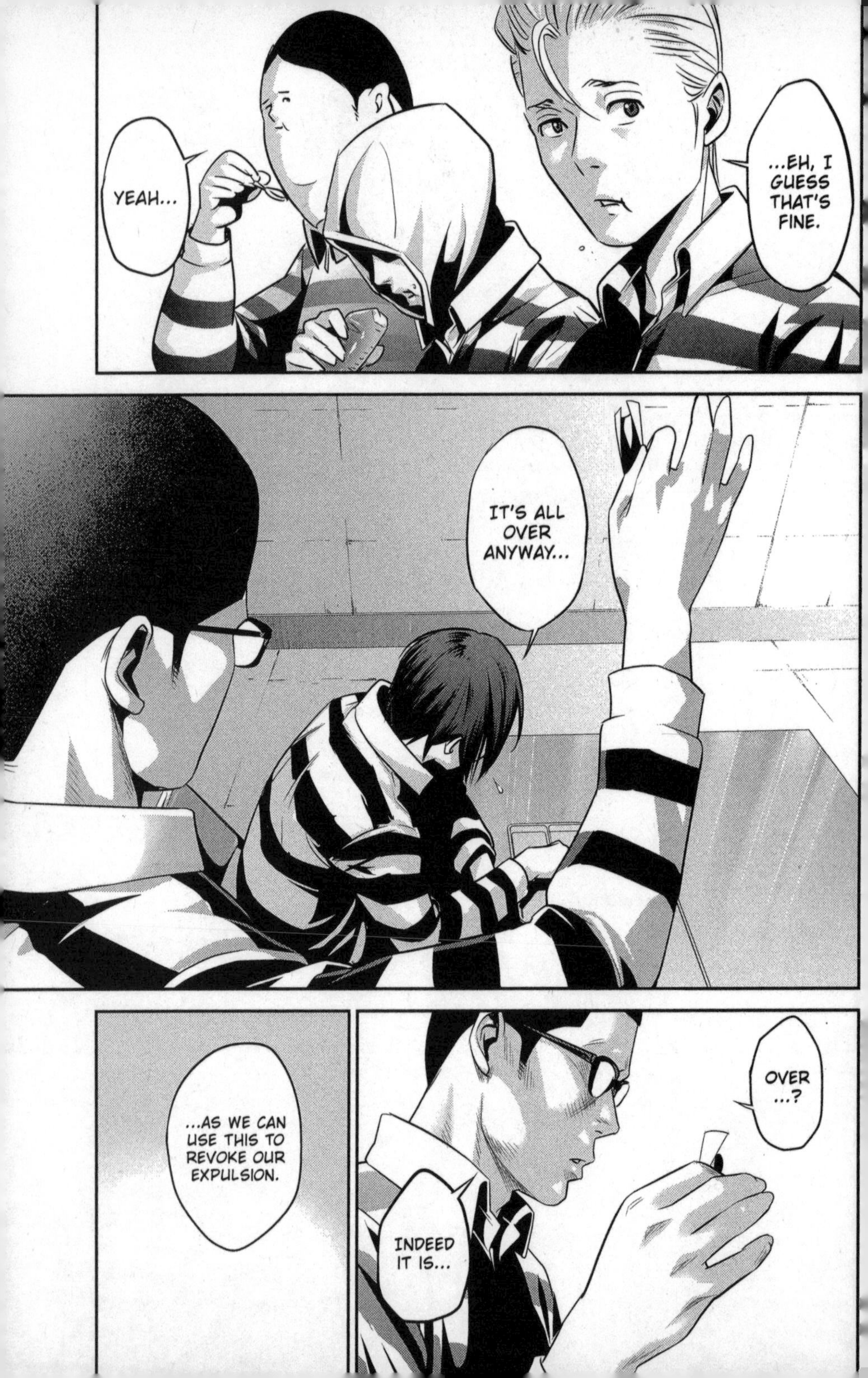
...EH, I GUESS THAT'S FINE.
YEAH...
IT'S ALL OVER ANYWAY...
OVER ...?
INDEED IT IS...
...AS WE CAN USE THIS TO REVOKE OUR EXPULSION.

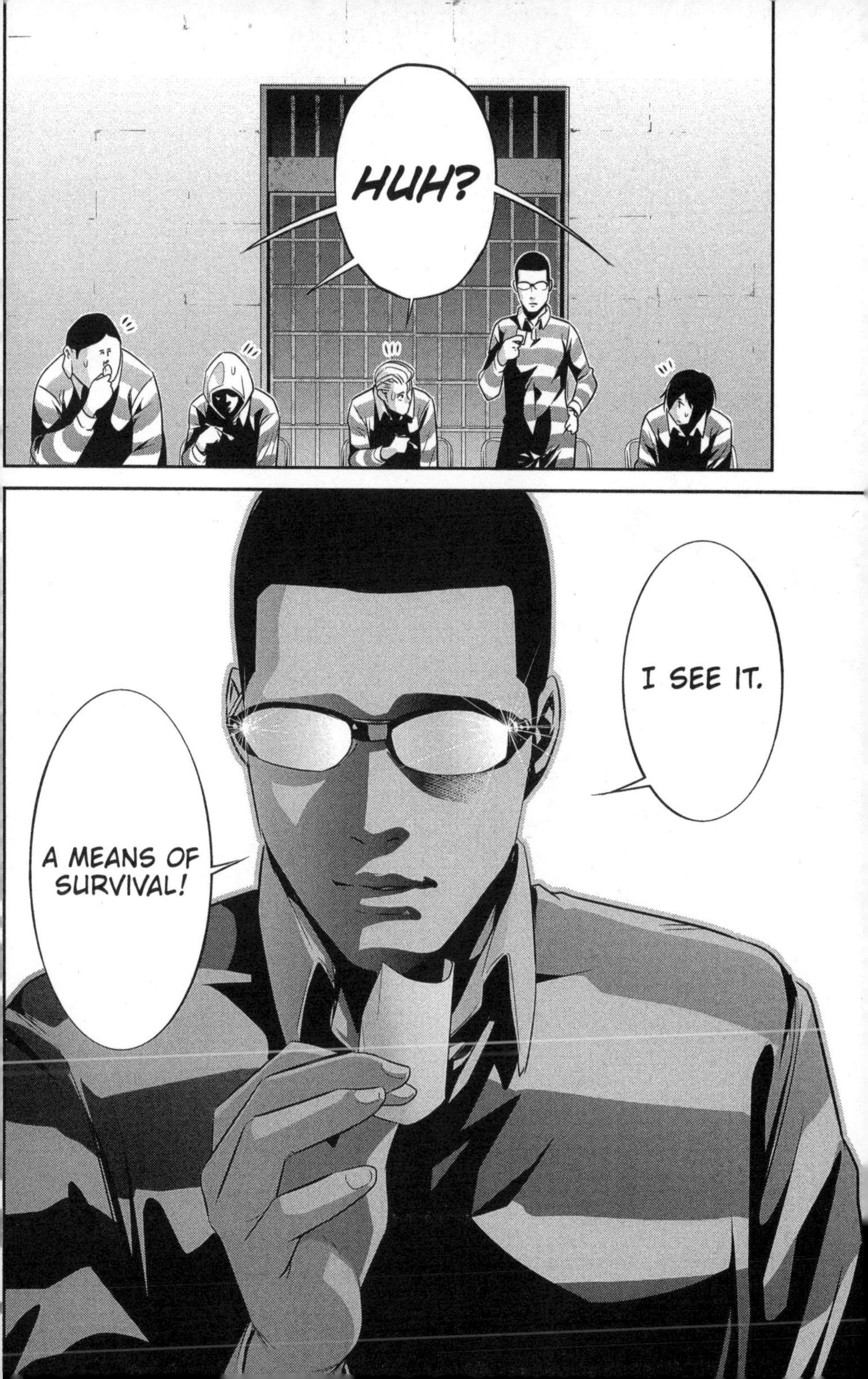
HUH?
I SEE IT.
A MEANS OF SURVIVAL!

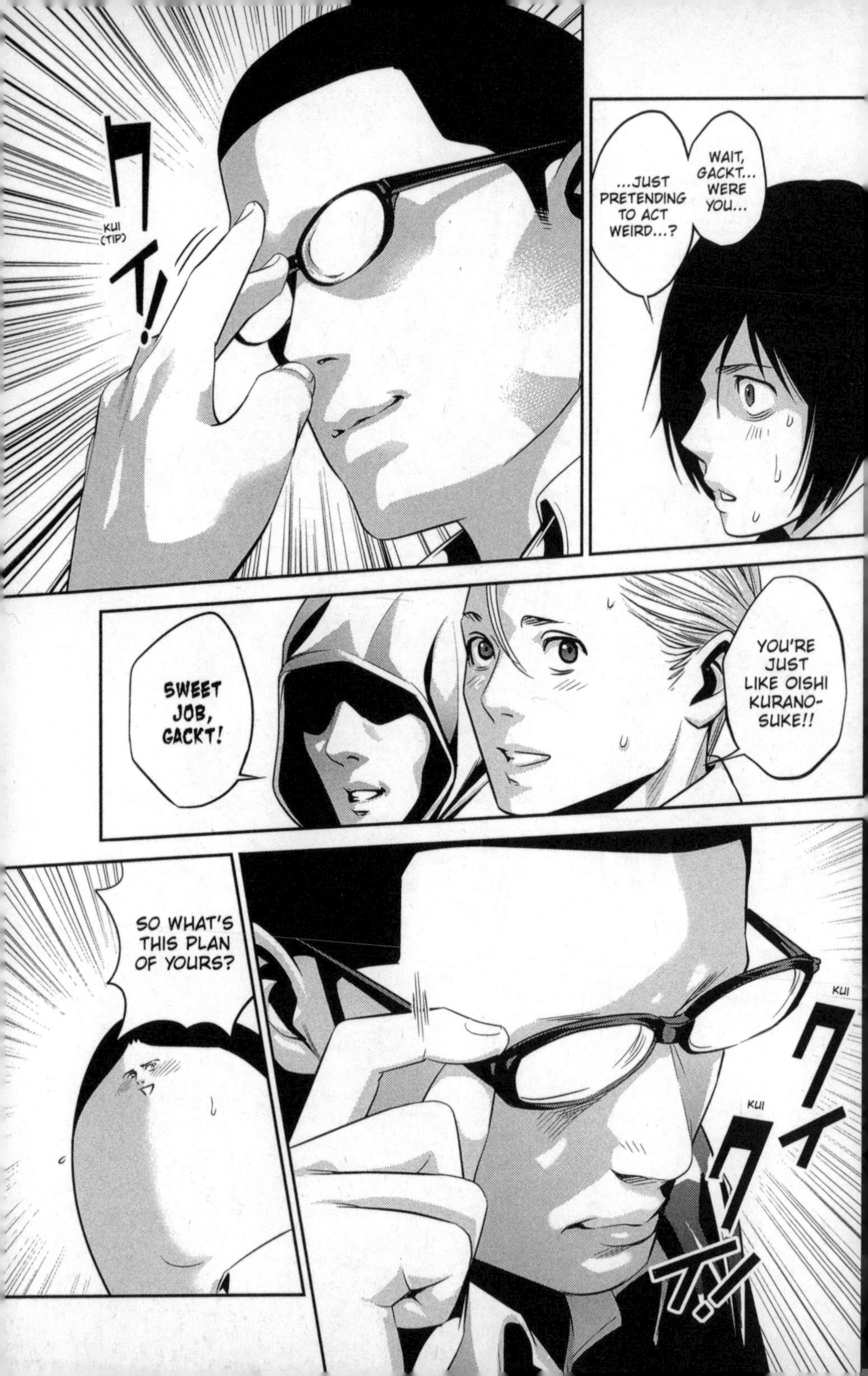
WAIT, GACKT... WERE YOU...
...JUST PRETENDING TO ACT WEIRD...?
KUI (TIP)
YOU'RE JUST LIKE OISHI KURANO-SUKE!!
SWEET JOB, GACKT!
KUI
KUI
SO WHAT'S THIS PLAN OF YOURS?

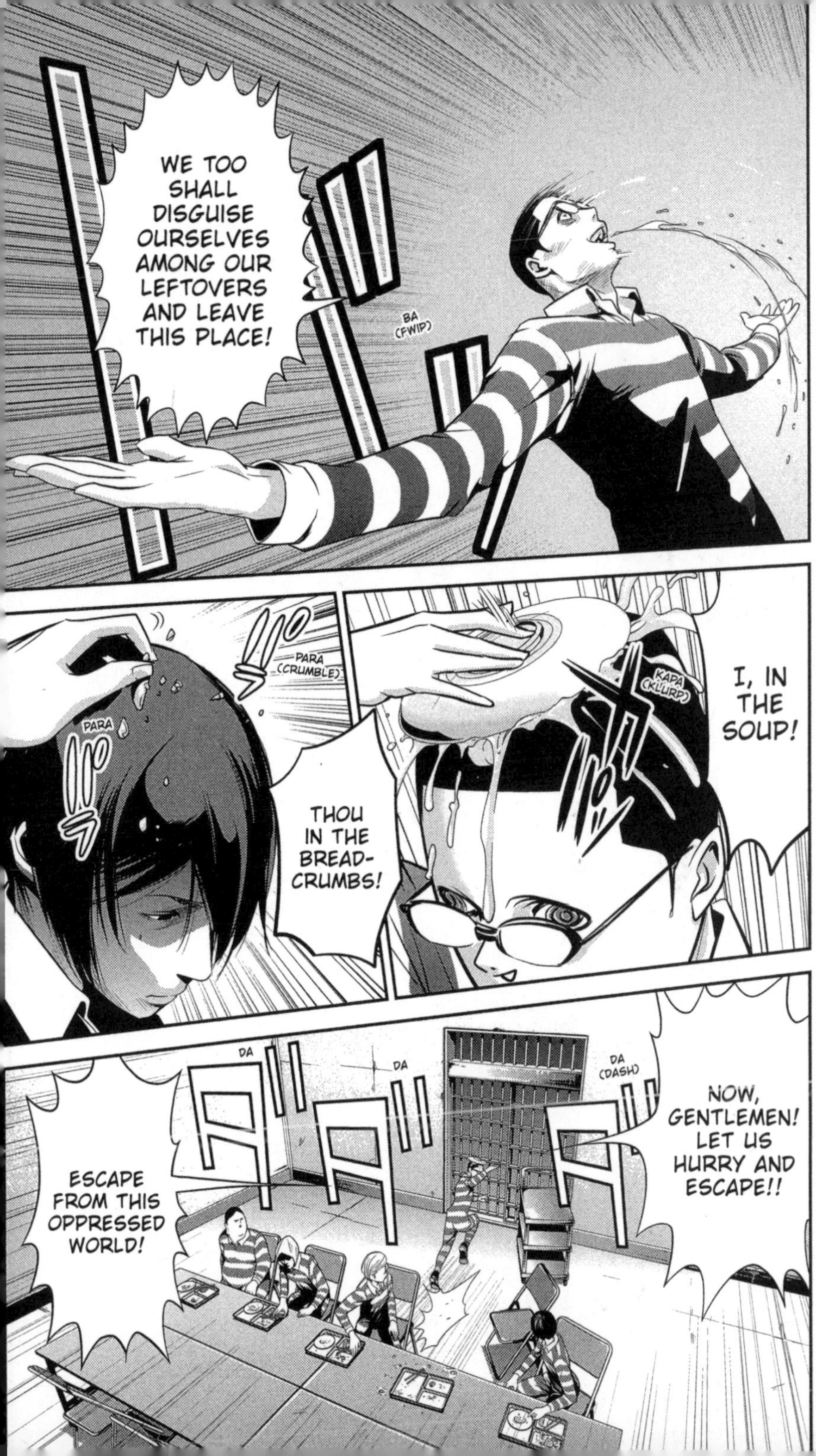
BA (FWIP)
WE TOO SHALL DISGUISE OURSELVES AMONG OUR LEFTOVERS AND LEAVE THIS PLACE!
KAPA (KLURP)
I, IN THE SOUP!
PARA (CRUMBLE)
PARA
THOU IN THE BREAD-CRUMBS!
DA (DASH)
NOW, GENTLEMEN! LET US HURRY AND ESCAPE!!
DA
DA
ESCAPE FROM THIS OPPRESSED WORLD!

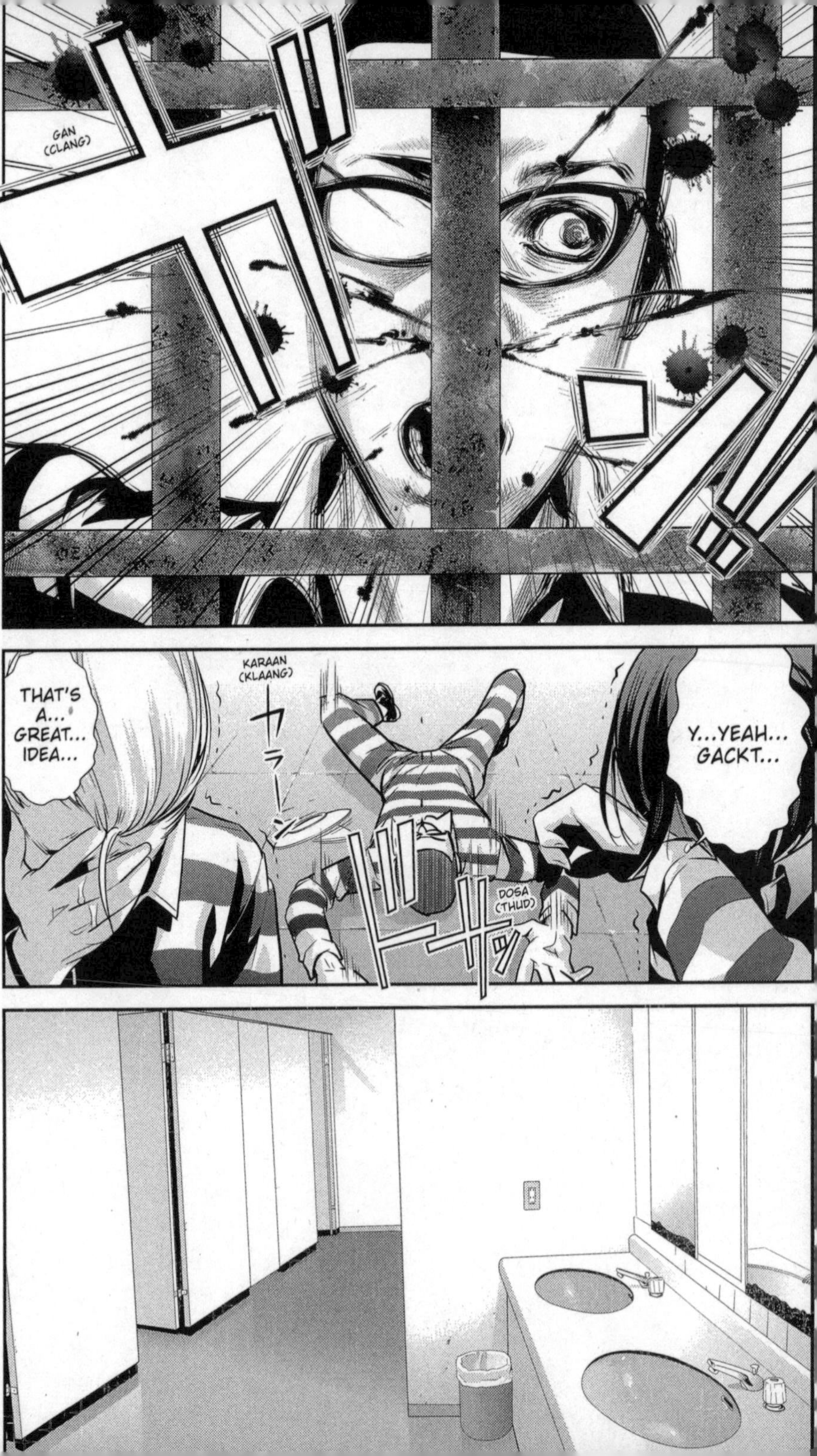
GAN (CLANG)
Y...YEAH... GACKT...
KARAAN (KLAANG)
THAT'S A... GREAT... IDEA...
DOSA (THUD)

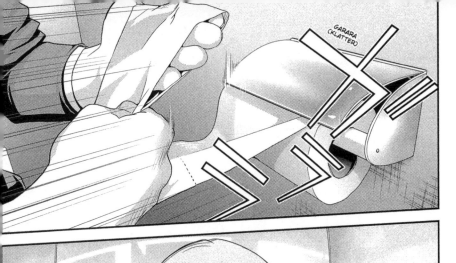

GARARA
(KLATTER)

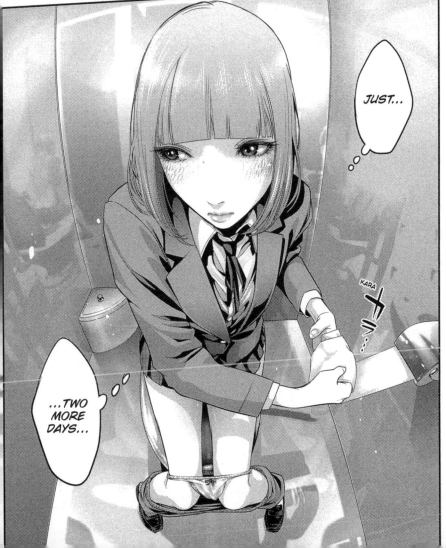

JUST...

KARA

...TWO
MORE
DAYS...

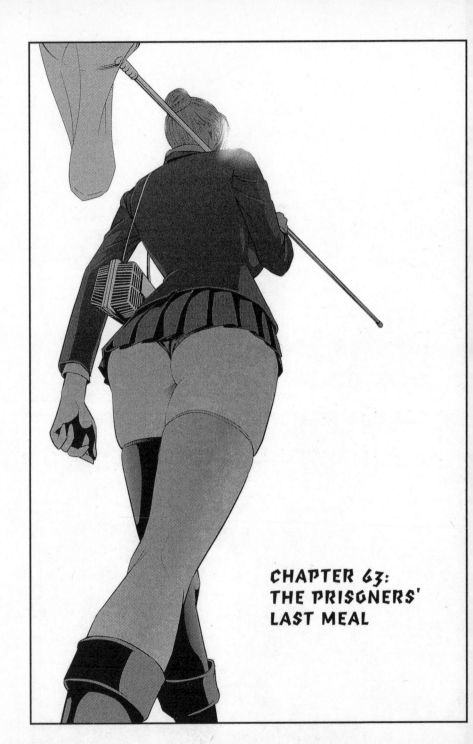

CHAPTER 63:
THE PRISONERS'
LAST MEAL

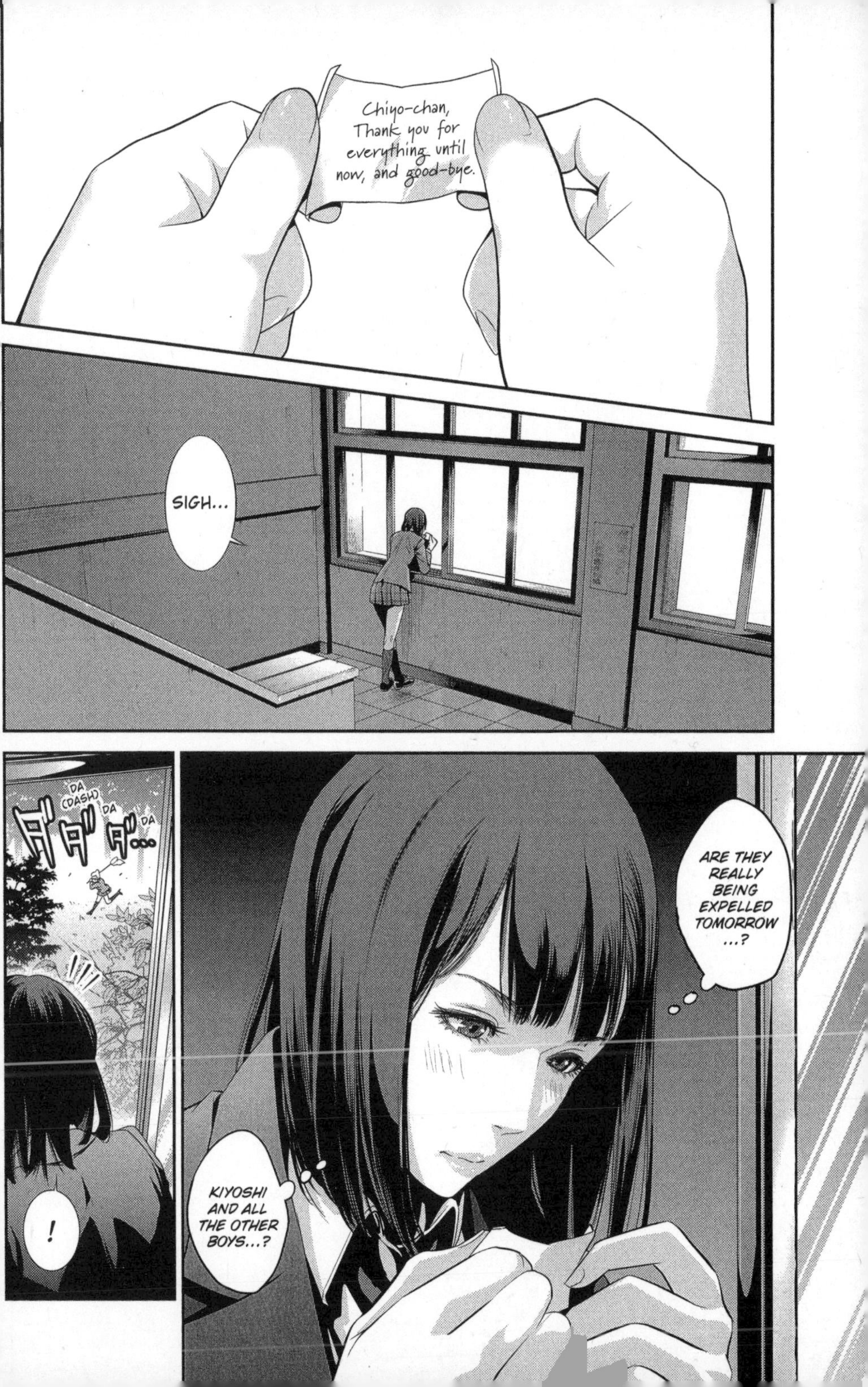
Chiyo-chan, Thank you for everything until now, and good-bye.
SIGH...
ARE THEY REALLY BEING EXPELLED TOMORROW ...?
KIYOSHI AND ALL THE OTHER BOYS...?
ダダダ...
DA (DASH) DA DA
!!
!

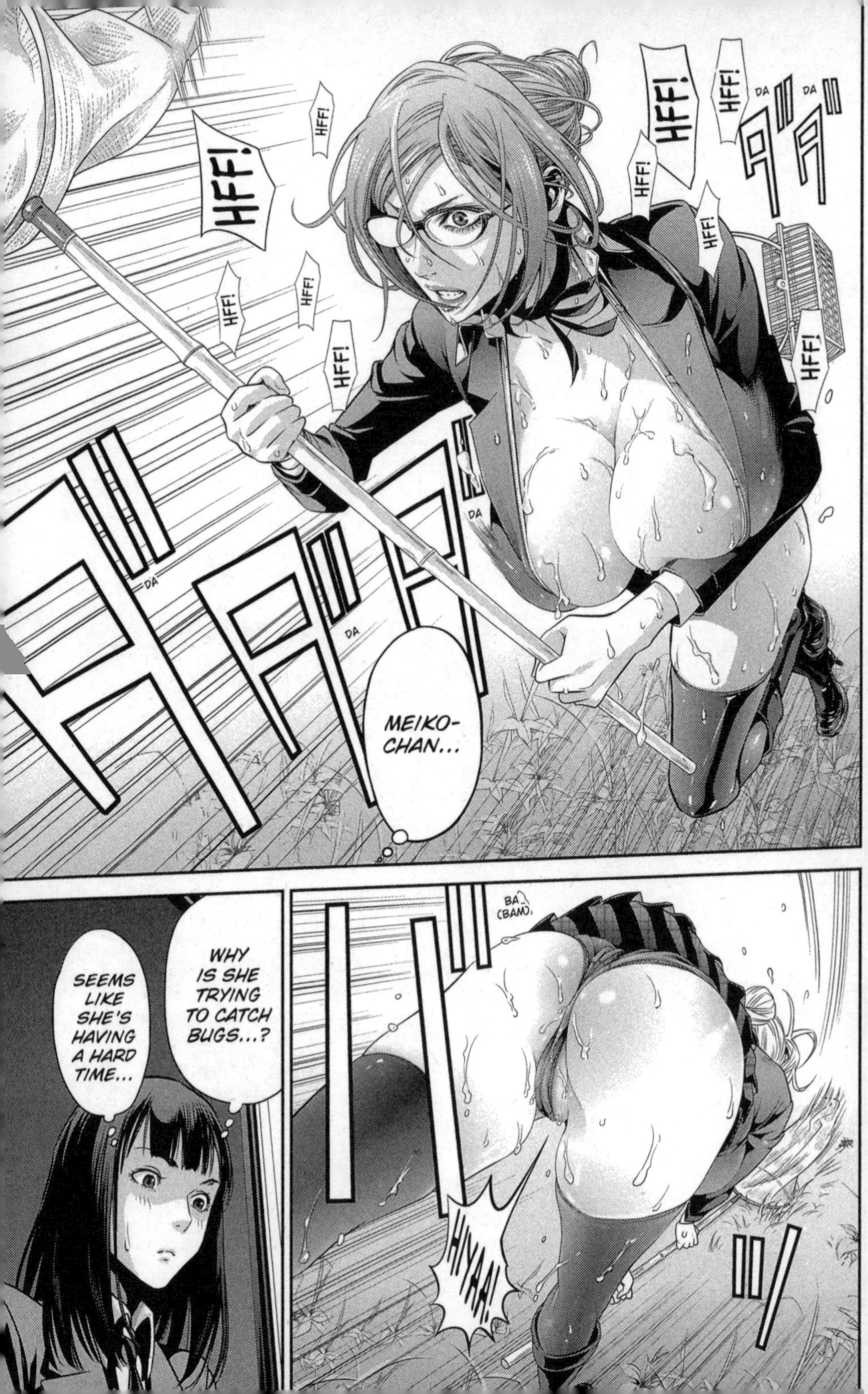
DA
DA
HFF!
HFF!
HFF!
HFF!
HFF!
HFF!
HFF!
HFF!
HFF!
HFF!
DA
DA
DA
MEIKO-CHAN...
BA (BAM)
HIYAA!
WHY IS SHE TRYING TO CATCH BUGS...?
SEEMS LIKE SHE'S HAVING A HARD TIME...

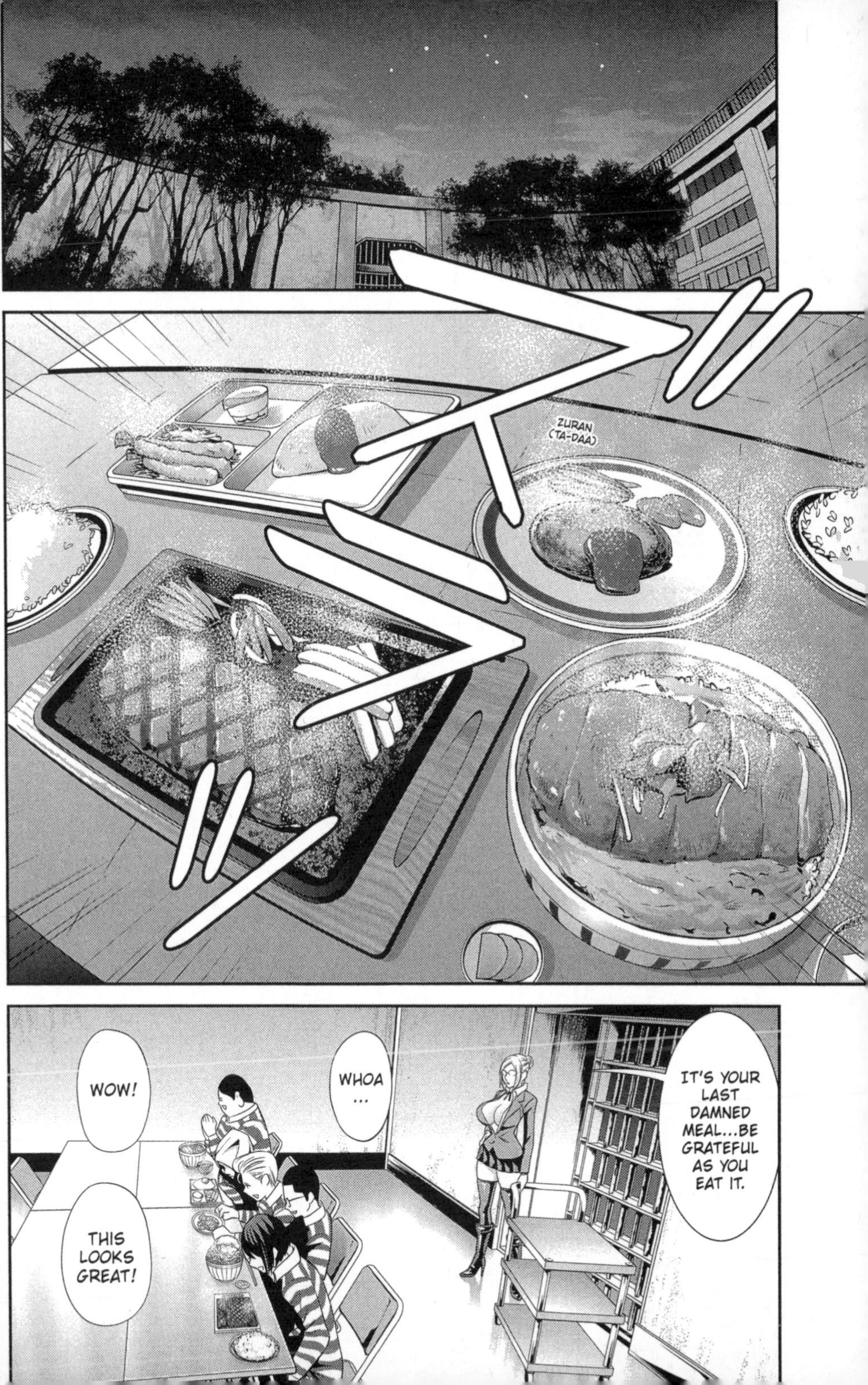
ZURAN (TA-DAA)
IT'S YOUR LAST DAMNED MEAL...BE GRATEFUL AS YOU EAT IT.
WHOA ...
WOW!
THIS LOOKS GREAT!

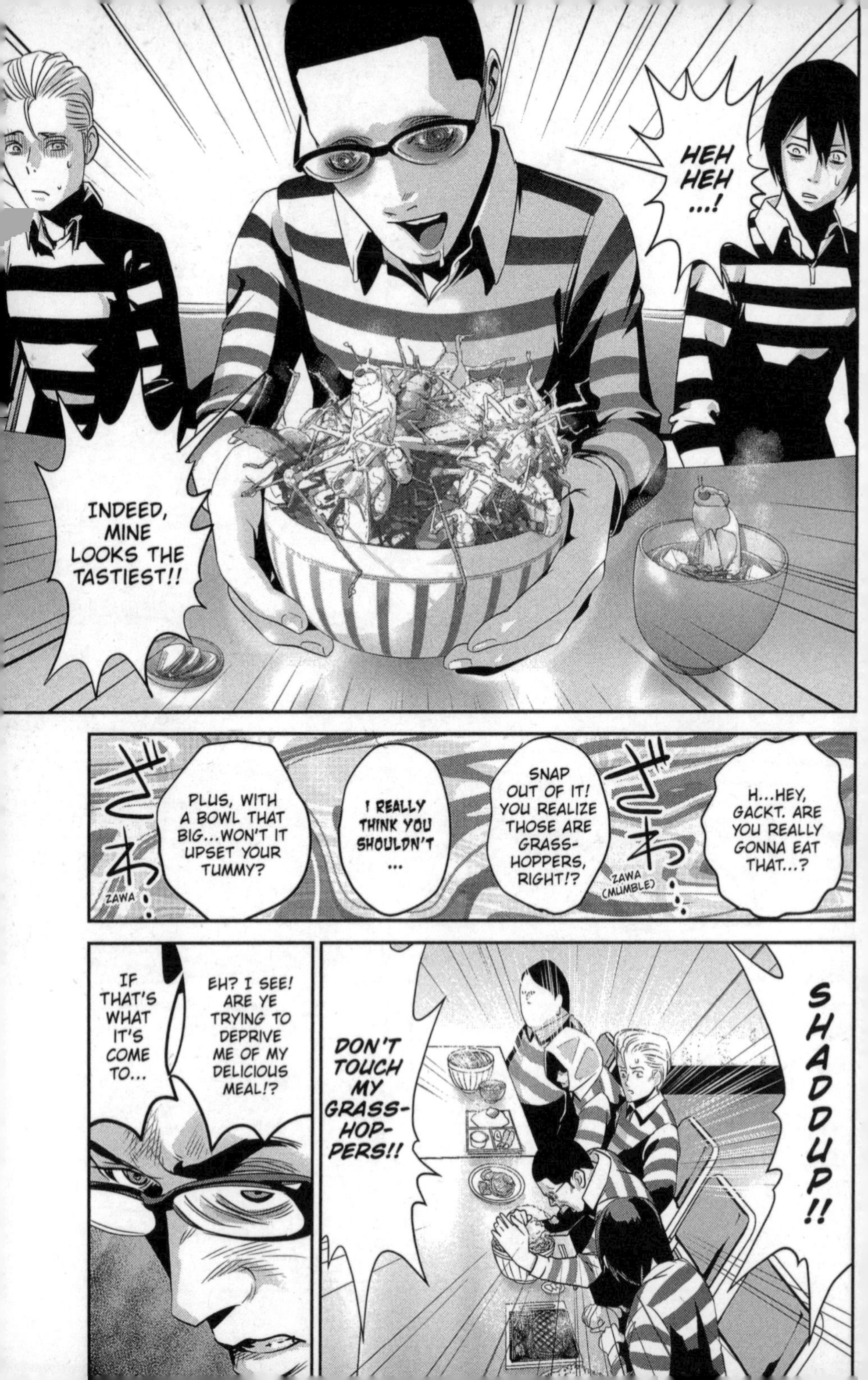
HEH HEH ...!
INDEED, MINE LOOKS THE TASTIEST!!
H...HEY, GACKT. ARE YOU REALLY GONNA EAT THAT...?
ざわ
ZAWA (MUMBLE)
SNAP OUT OF IT! YOU REALIZE THOSE ARE GRASS-HOPPERS, RIGHT!?
I REALLY THINK YOU SHOULDN'T ...
PLUS, WITH A BOWL THAT BIG...WON'T IT UPSET YOUR TUMMY?
ざわ
ZAWA
SHADDUP!!
DON'T TOUCH MY GRASS-HOP-PERS!!
EH? I SEE! ARE YE TRYING TO DEPRIVE ME OF MY DELICIOUS MEAL!?
IF THAT'S WHAT IT'S COME TO...

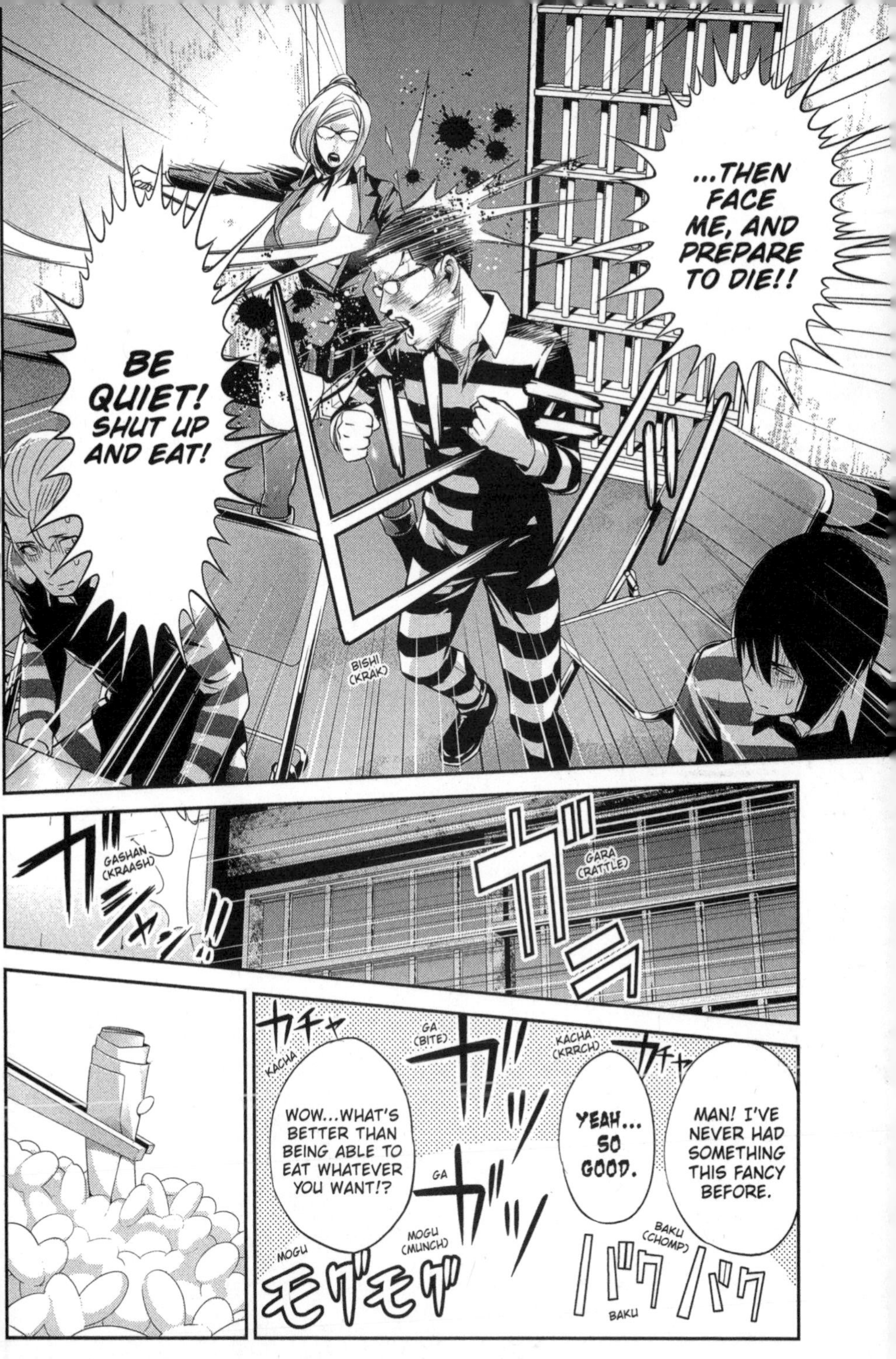
...THEN FACE ME, AND PREPARE TO DIE!!
BE QUIET! SHUT UP AND EAT!
BISHI (KRAK)
GARA (RATTLE)
GASHAN (KRAASH)
MAN! I'VE NEVER HAD SOMETHING THIS FANCY BEFORE.
KACHA (KRRCH)
YEAH... SO GOOD.
BAKU (CHOMP)
BAKU
GA (BITE)
KACHA
WOW...WHAT'S BETTER THAN BEING ABLE TO EAT WHATEVER YOU WANT!?
GA
MOGU (MUNCH)
MOGU

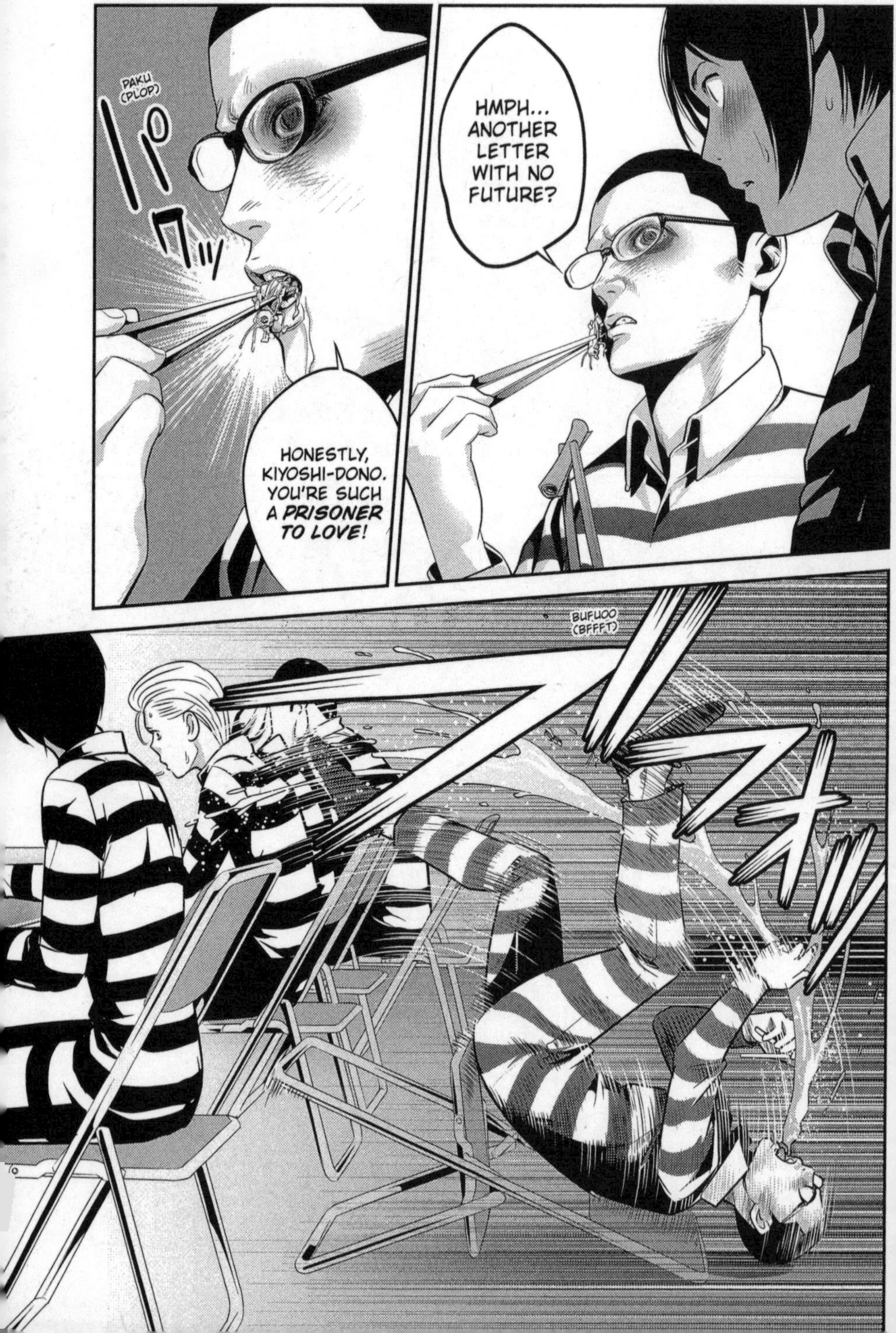
HMPH... ANOTHER LETTER WITH NO FUTURE?
PAKU (PLOP)
HONESTLY, KIYOSHI-DONO. YOU'RE SUCH A *PRISONER TO LOVE*!
BUFUOO (BFFFT)

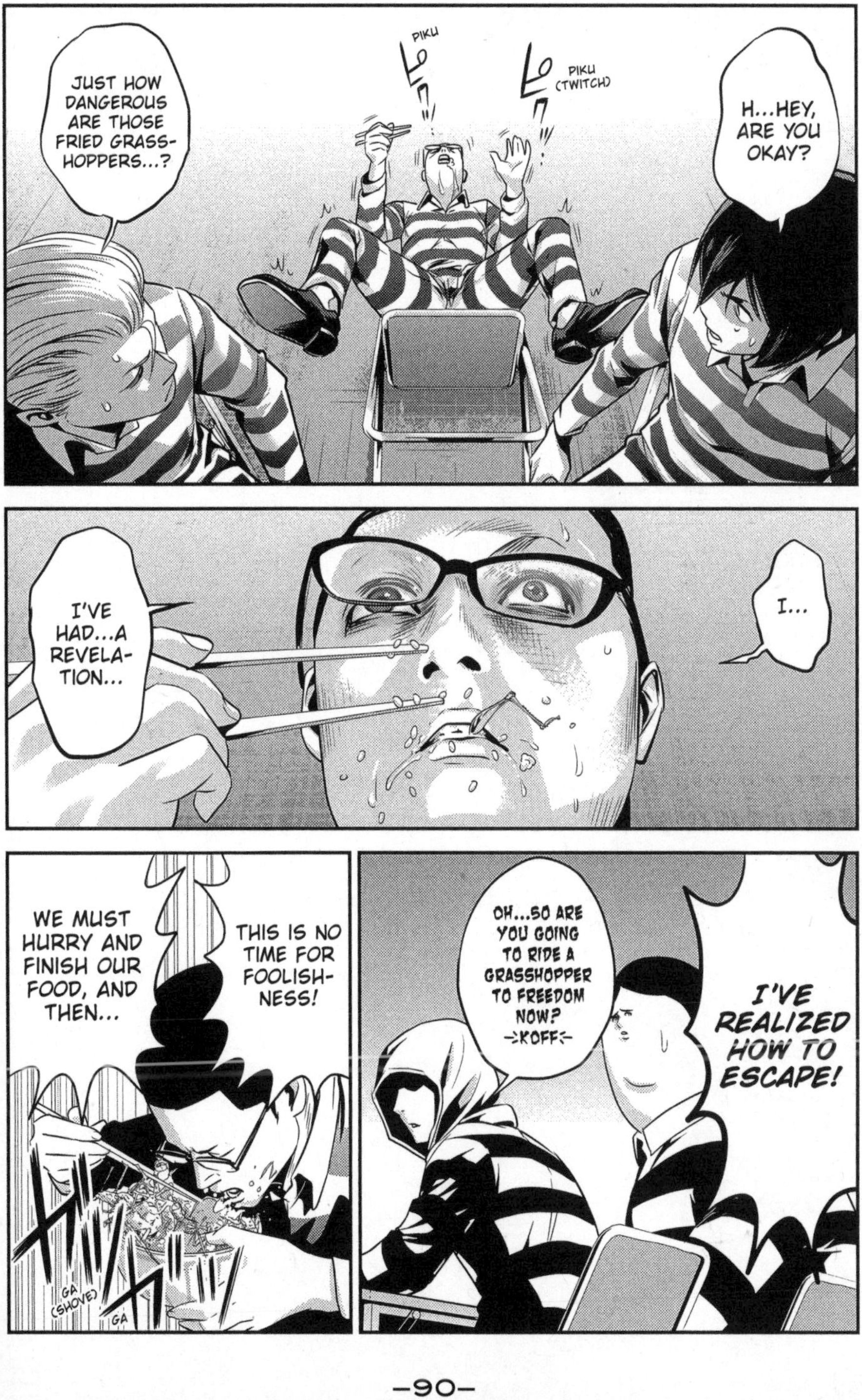
H...HEY, ARE YOU OKAY?
PIKU (TWITCH)
PIKU
JUST HOW DANGEROUS ARE THOSE FRIED GRASS-HOPPERS...?
I...
I'VE HAD...A REVELATION...
I'VE REALIZED HOW TO ESCAPE!
OH...SO ARE YOU GOING TO RIDE A GRASSHOPPER TO FREEDOM NOW? -KOFF-
THIS IS NO TIME FOR FOOLISH-NESS!
WE MUST HURRY AND FINISH OUR FOOD, AND THEN...
GA (SHOVE)
GA

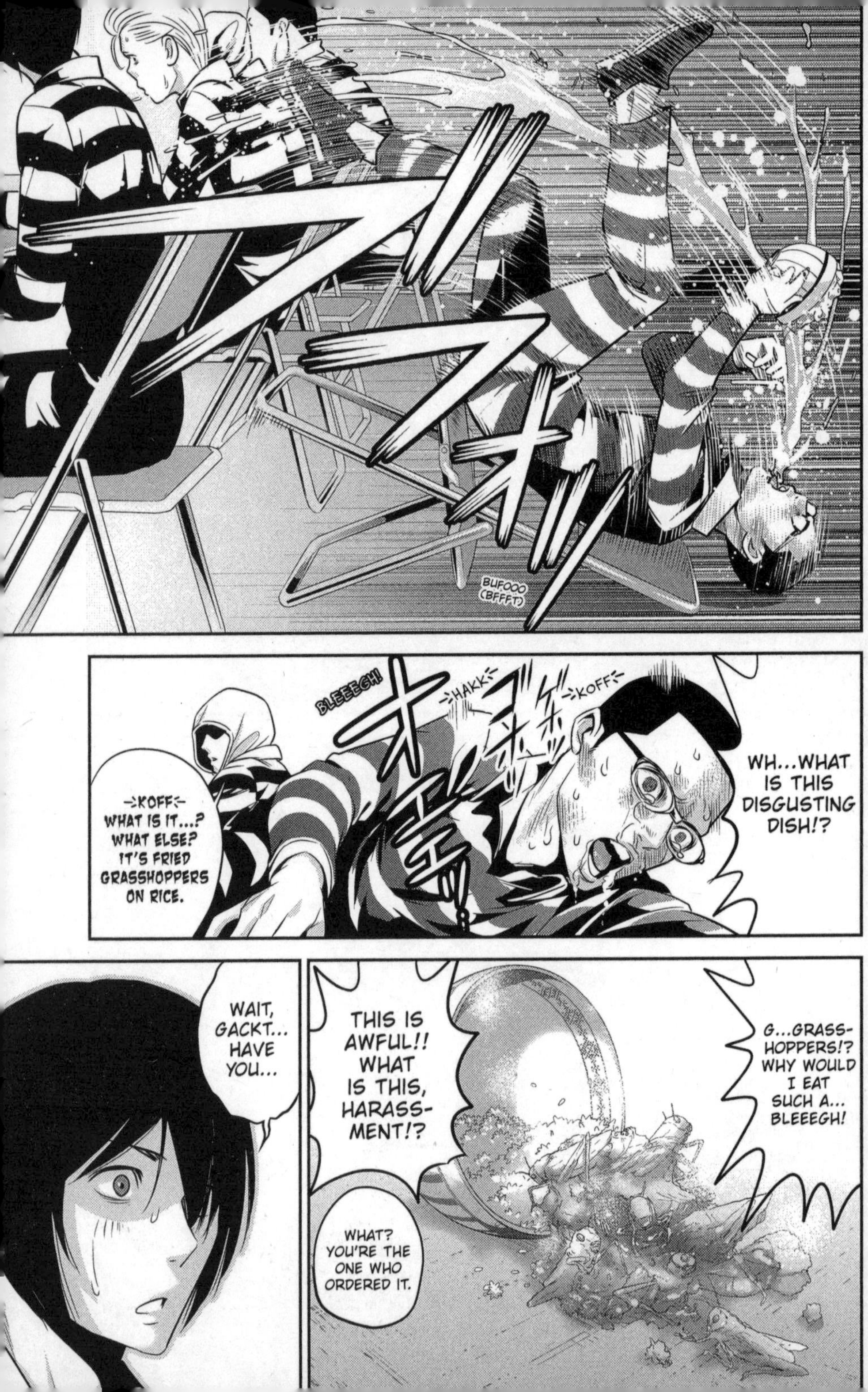
BUFOOO (BFFFT)
WH...WHAT IS THIS DISGUSTING DISH!?
-KOFF
-HAKK
BLEEEGH!
-KOFF- WHAT IS IT...? WHAT ELSE? IT'S FRIED GRASSHOPPERS ON RICE.
G...GRASSHOPPERS!? WHY WOULD I EAT SUCH A... BLEEEGH!
THIS IS AWFUL!! WHAT IS THIS, HARASSMENT!?
WHAT? YOU'RE THE ONE WHO ORDERED IT.
WAIT, GACKT... HAVE YOU...

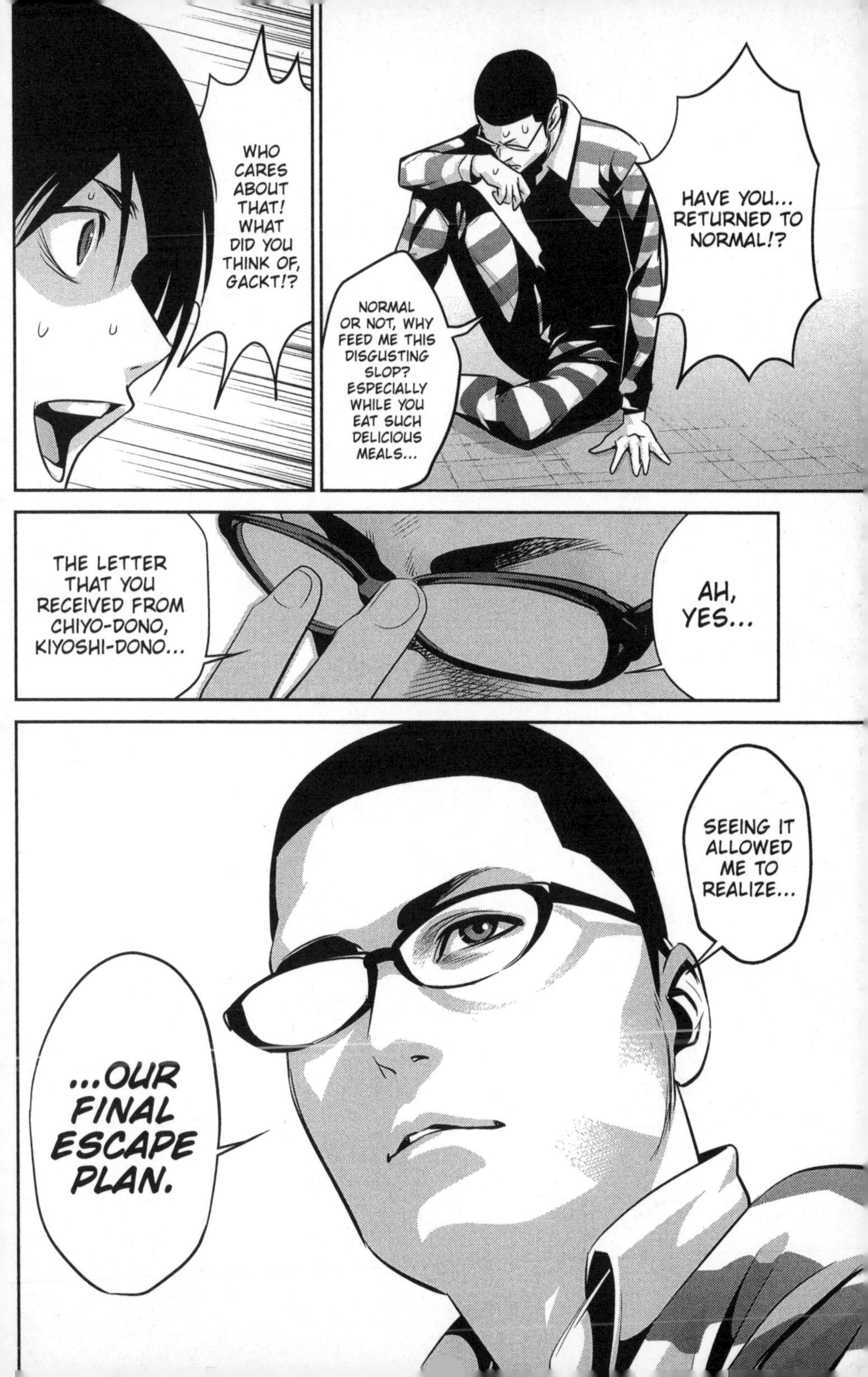
HAVE YOU... RETURNED TO NORMAL!?
NORMAL OR NOT, WHY FEED ME THIS DISGUSTING SLOP? ESPECIALLY WHILE YOU EAT SUCH DELICIOUS MEALS...
WHO CARES ABOUT THAT! WHAT DID YOU THINK OF, GACKT!?
AH, YES...
THE LETTER THAT YOU RECEIVED FROM CHIYO-DONO, KIYOSHI-DONO...
SEEING IT ALLOWED ME TO REALIZE...
...OUR FINAL ESCAPE PLAN.

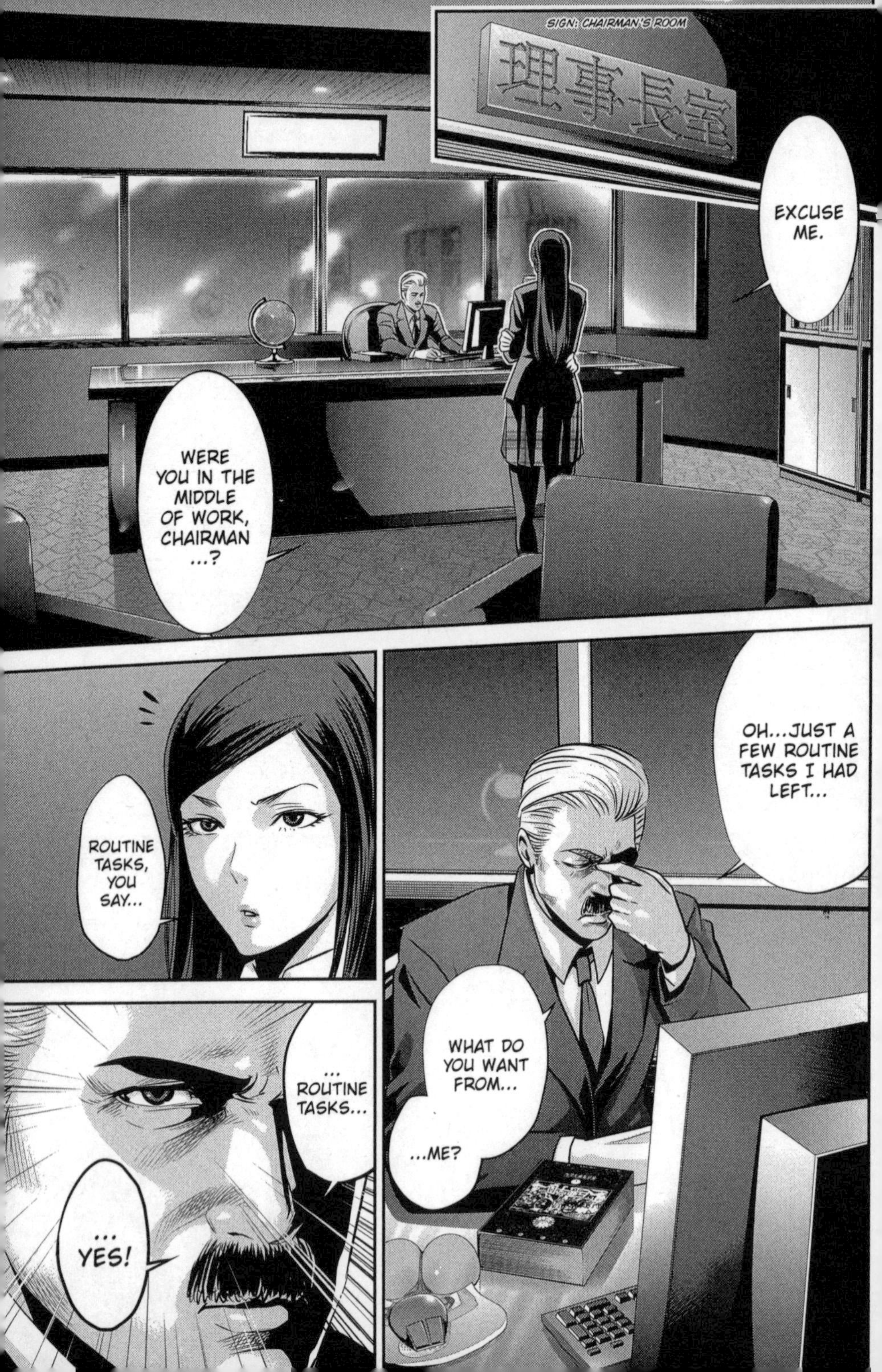
SIGN: CHAIRMAN'S ROOM
理事長室
EXCUSE ME.
WERE YOU IN THE MIDDLE OF WORK, CHAIRMAN ...?
OH...JUST A FEW ROUTINE TASKS I HAD LEFT...
WHAT DO YOU WANT FROM...
...ME?
ROUTINE TASKS, YOU SAY...
... ROUTINE TASKS...
... YES!

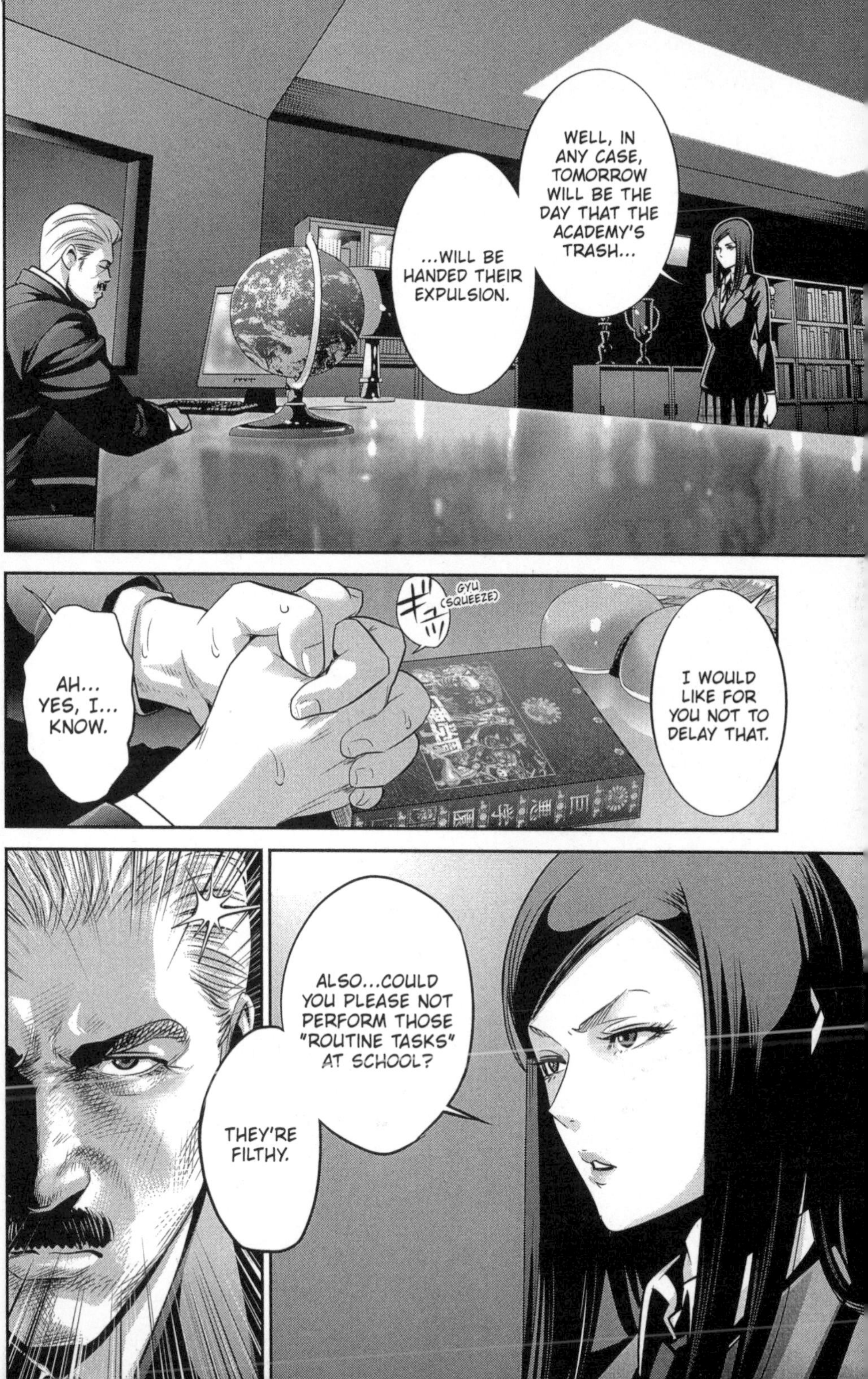
WELL, IN ANY CASE, TOMORROW WILL BE THE DAY THAT THE ACADEMY'S TRASH...
...WILL BE HANDED THEIR EXPULSION.
I WOULD LIKE FOR YOU NOT TO DELAY THAT.
GYU (SQUEEZE)
AH... YES, I... KNOW.
ALSO...COULD YOU PLEASE NOT PERFORM THOSE "ROUTINE TASKS" AT SCHOOL?
THEY'RE FILTHY.

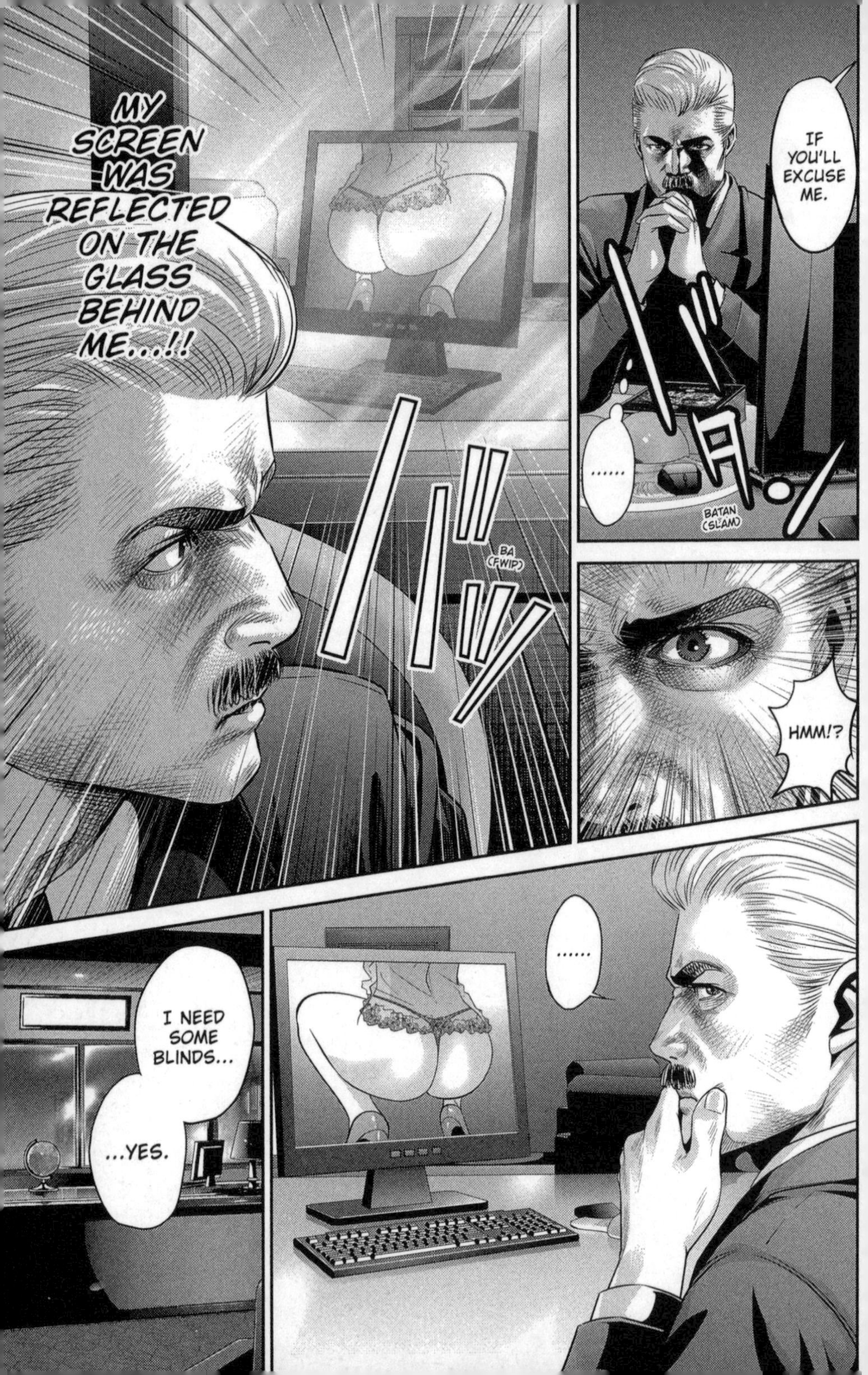
IF YOU'LL EXCUSE ME.
......
BATAN (SLAM)
HMM!?
MY SCREEN WAS REFLECTED ON THE GLASS BEHIND ME...!!
BA (FWIP)
......
I NEED SOME BLINDS...
...YES.

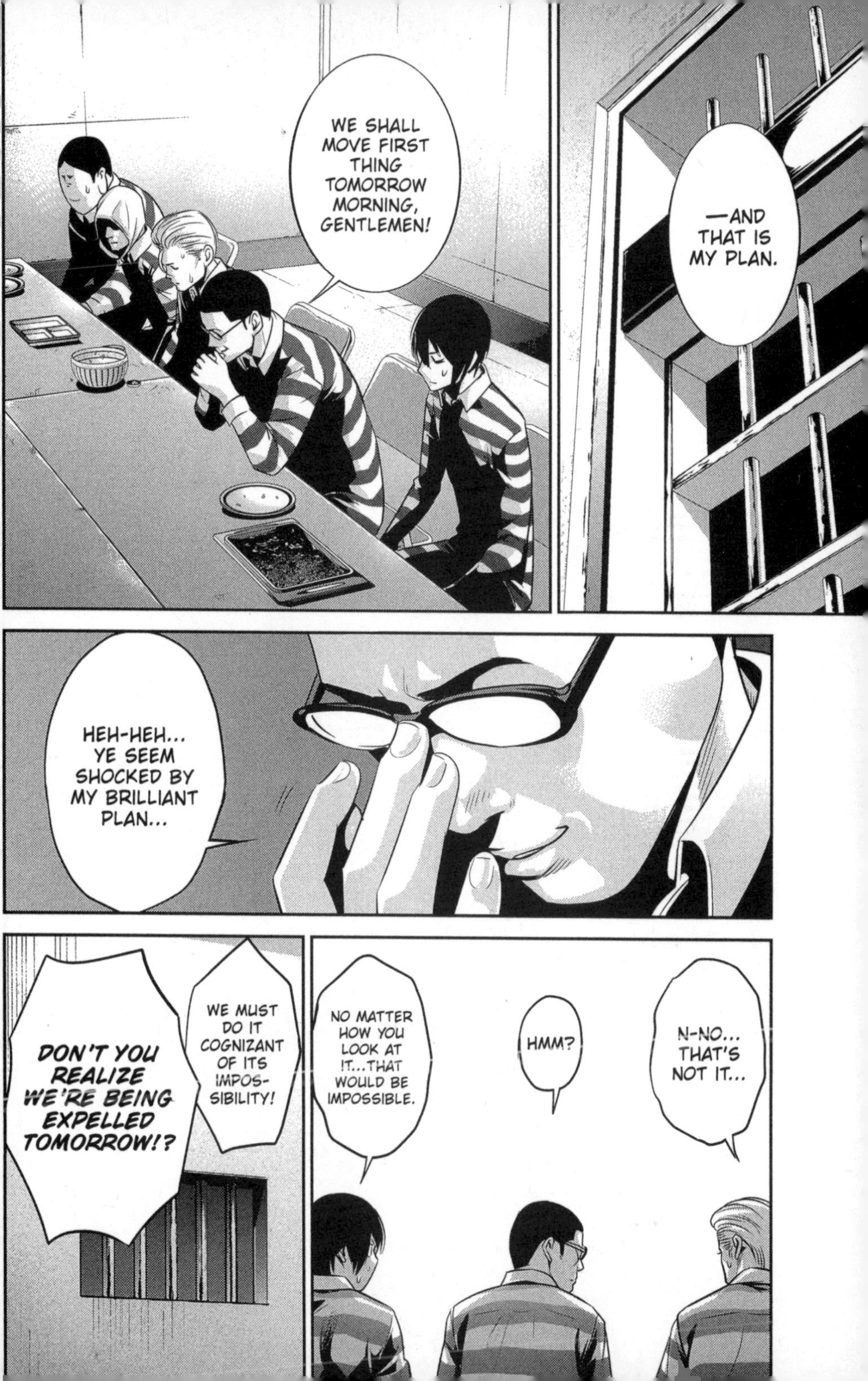
—AND THAT IS MY PLAN.
WE SHALL MOVE FIRST THING TOMORROW MORNING, GENTLEMEN!
HEH-HEH... YE SEEM SHOCKED BY MY BRILLIANT PLAN...
N-NO... THAT'S NOT IT...
HMM?
NO MATTER HOW YOU LOOK AT IT...THAT WOULD BE IMPOSSIBLE.
WE MUST DO IT COGNIZANT OF ITS IMPOS-SIBILITY!
DON'T YOU REALIZE WE'RE BEING EXPELLED TOMORROW!?

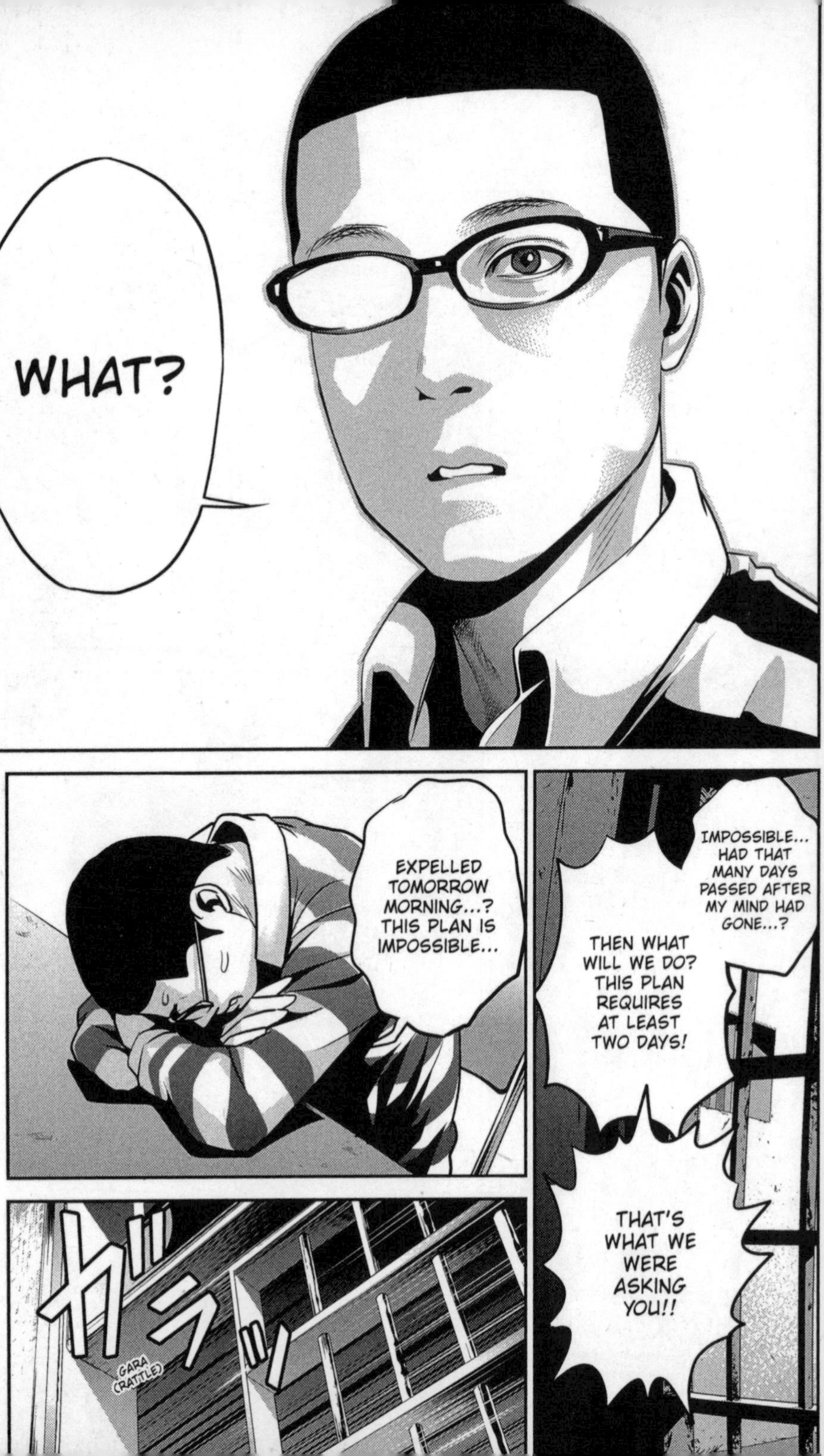
WHAT?
IMPOSSIBLE... HAD THAT MANY DAYS PASSED AFTER MY MIND HAD GONE...?
THEN WHAT WILL WE DO? THIS PLAN REQUIRES AT LEAST TWO DAYS!
THAT'S WHAT WE WERE ASKING YOU!!
EXPELLED TOMORROW MORNING...? THIS PLAN IS IMPOSSIBLE...
GARA (RATTLE)

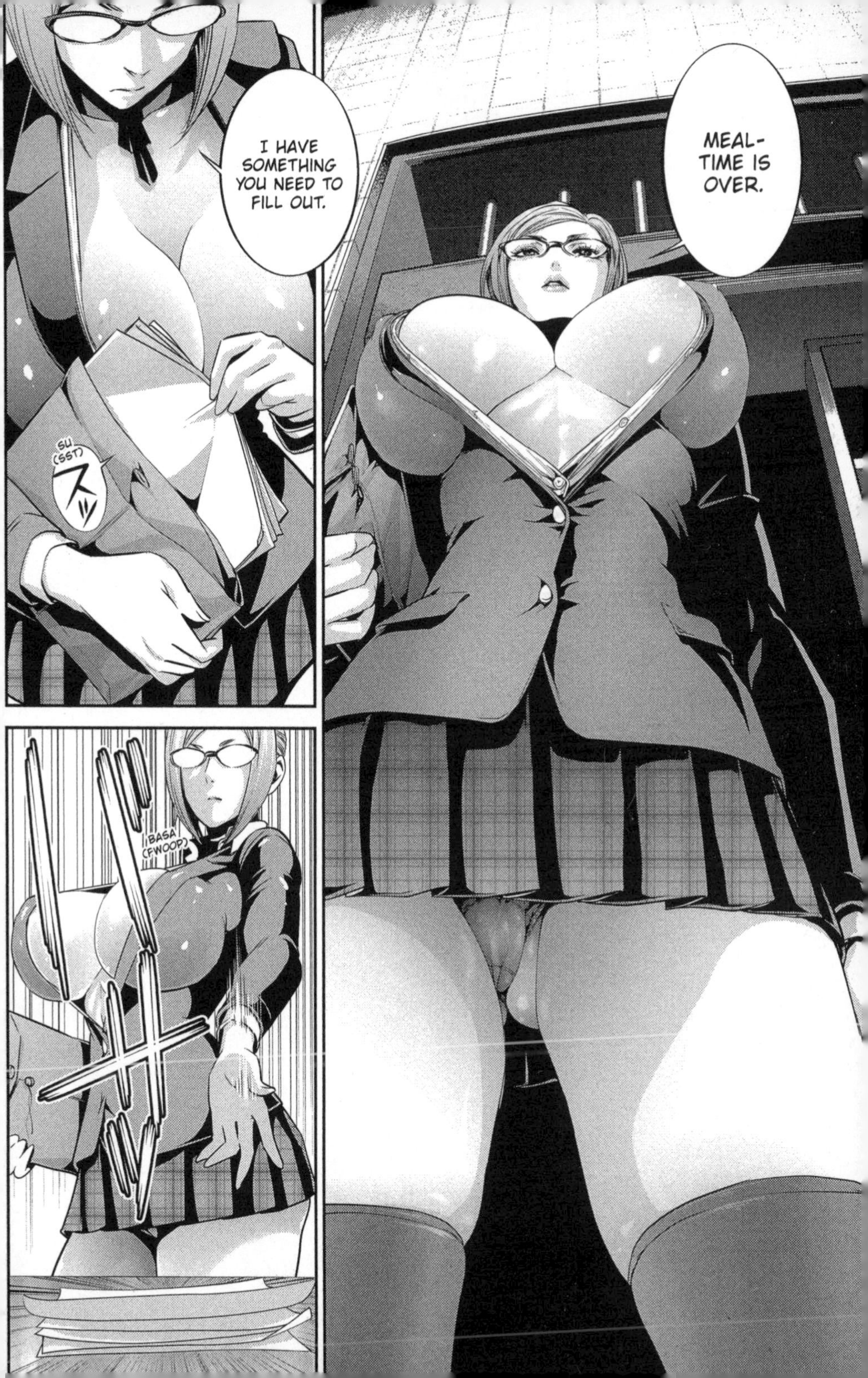
MEAL-
TIME IS
OVER.
I HAVE
SOMETHING
YOU NEED TO
FILL OUT.
SU
(SST)
スッ
BASA
(FWOOP)

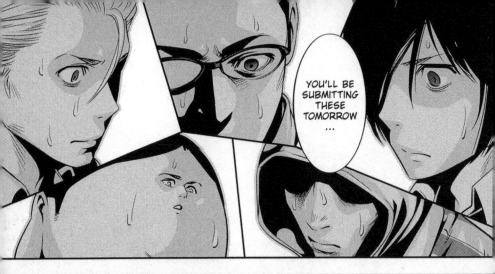

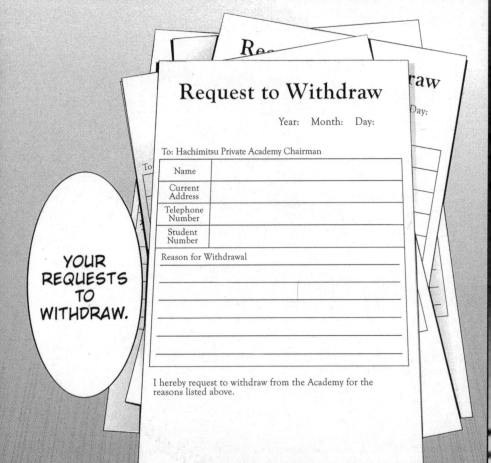

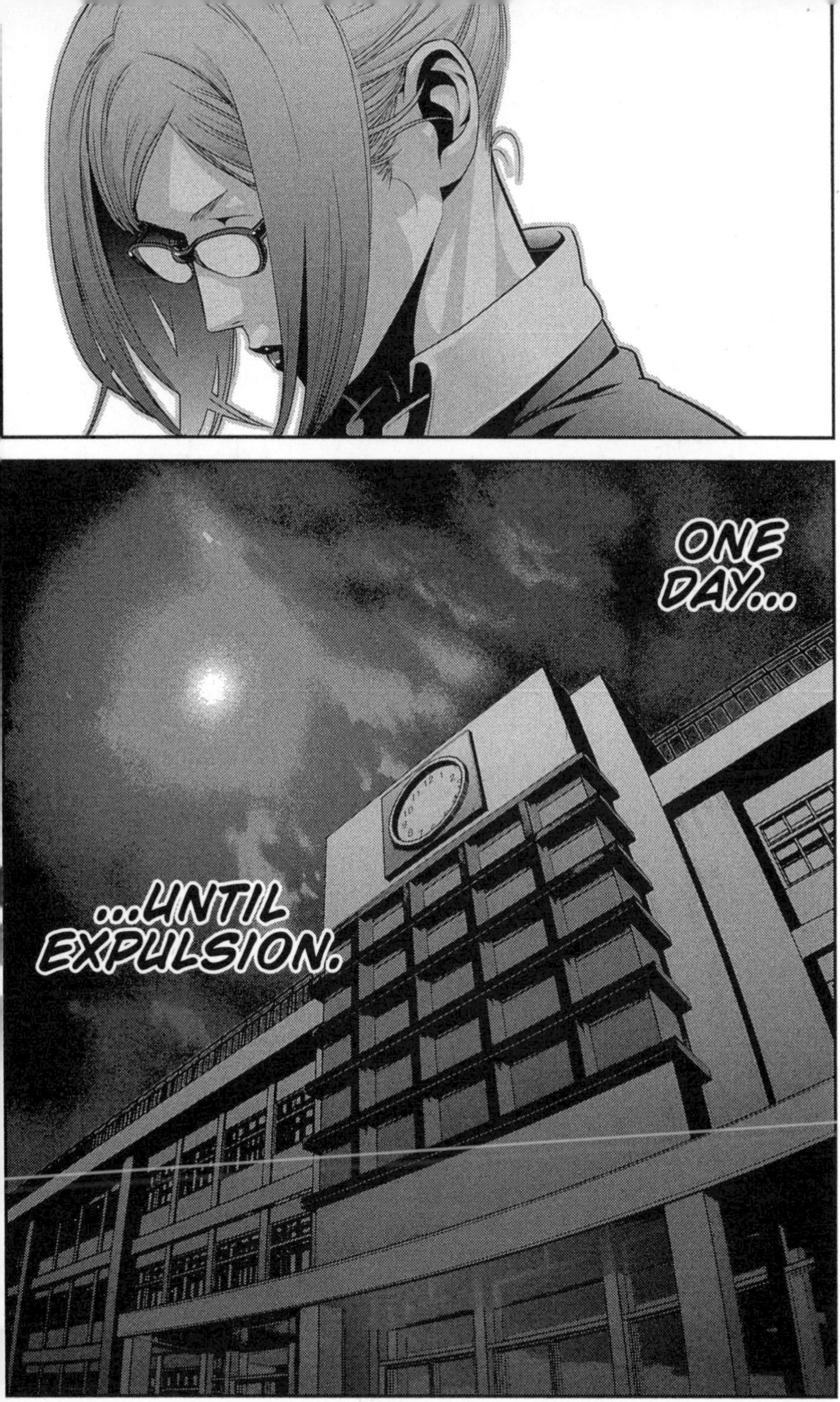
ONE DAY...
...UNTIL EXPULSION.

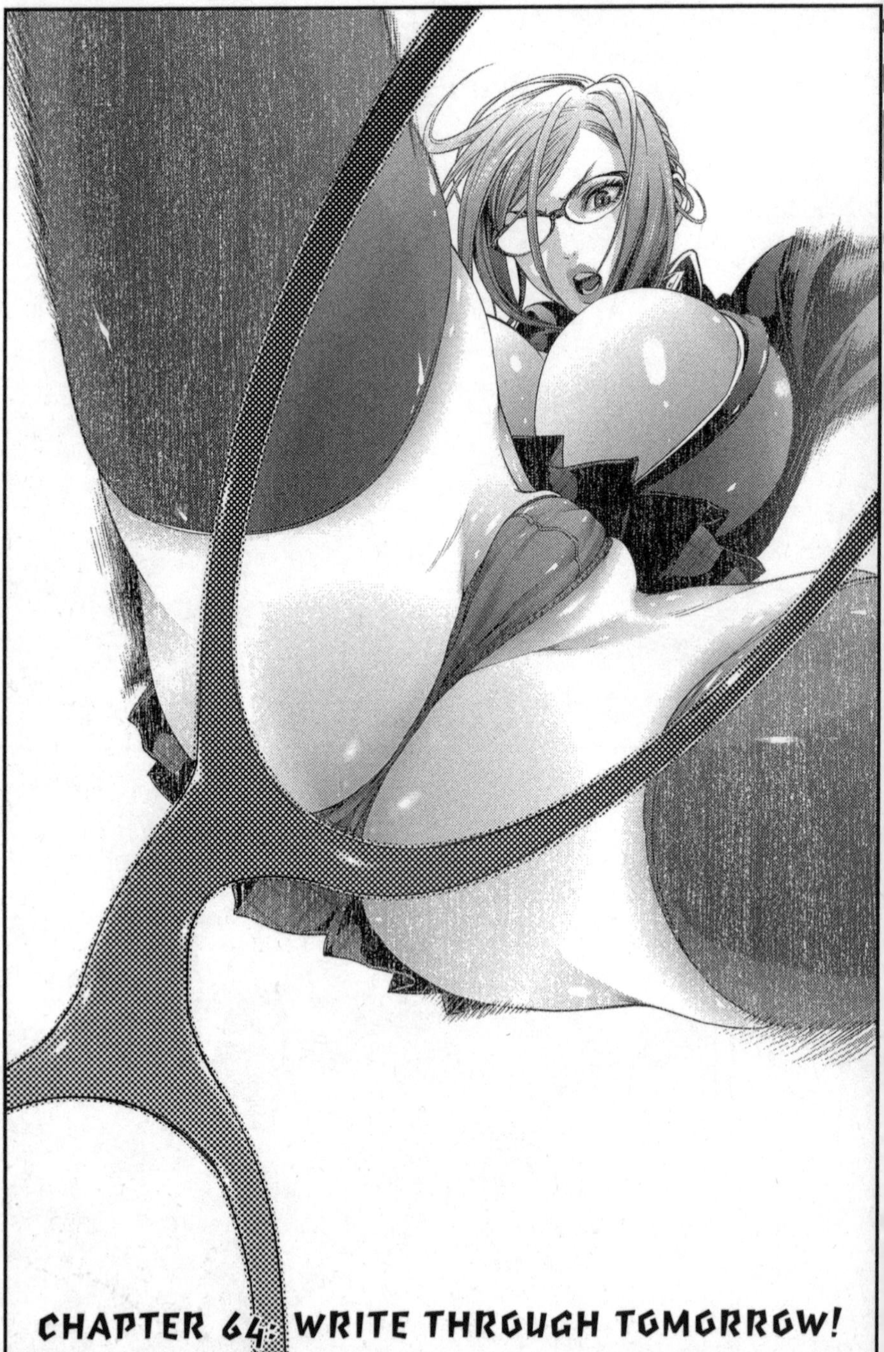
CHAPTER 64: WRITE THROUGH TOMORROW!

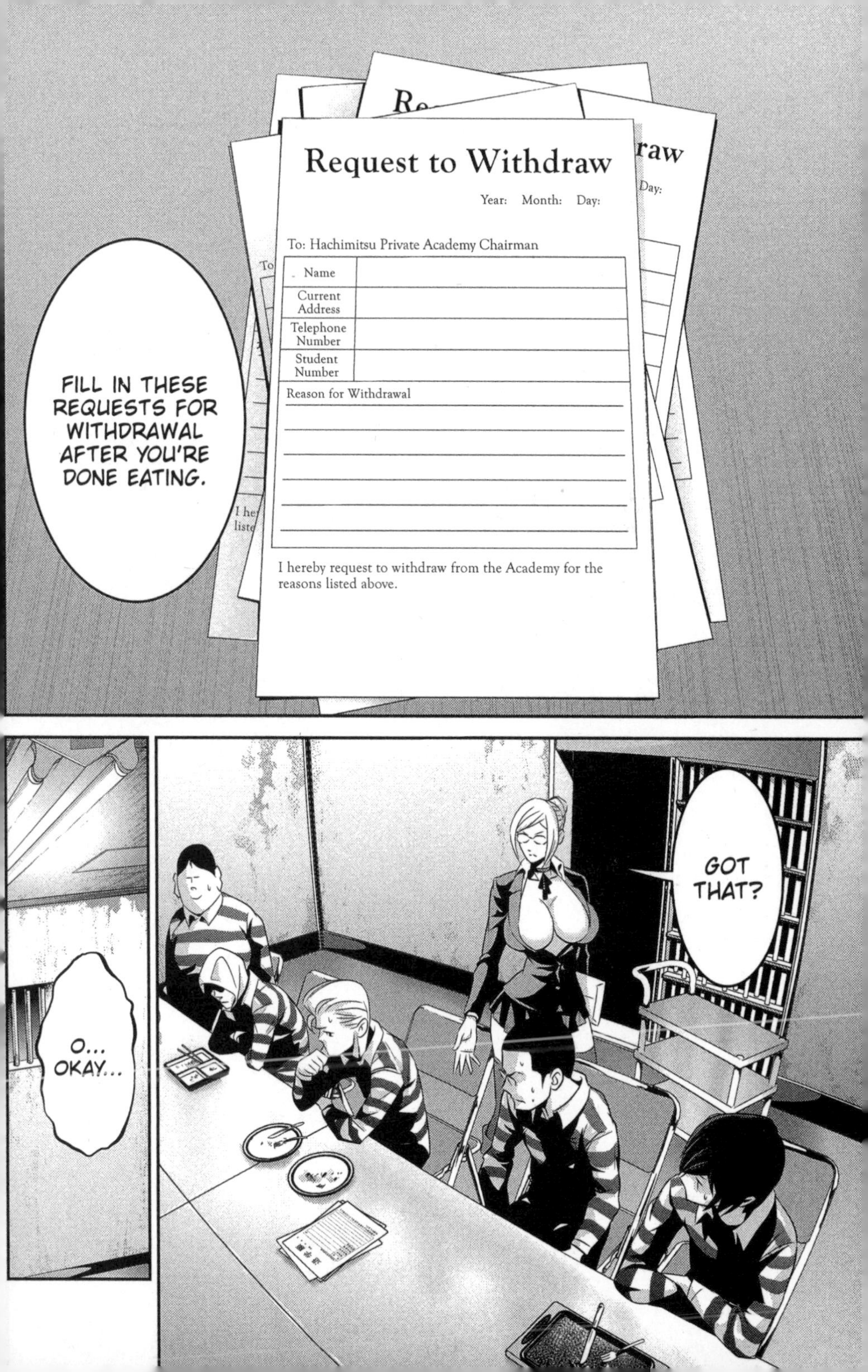
Request to Withdraw
Year: Month: Day:
To: Hachimitsu Private Academy Chairman
Name
Current Address
Telephone Number
Student Number
Reason for Withdrawal
I hereby request to withdraw from the Academy for the reasons listed above.
FILL IN THESE REQUESTS FOR WITHDRAWAL AFTER YOU'RE DONE EATING.
GOT THAT?
O... OKAY...

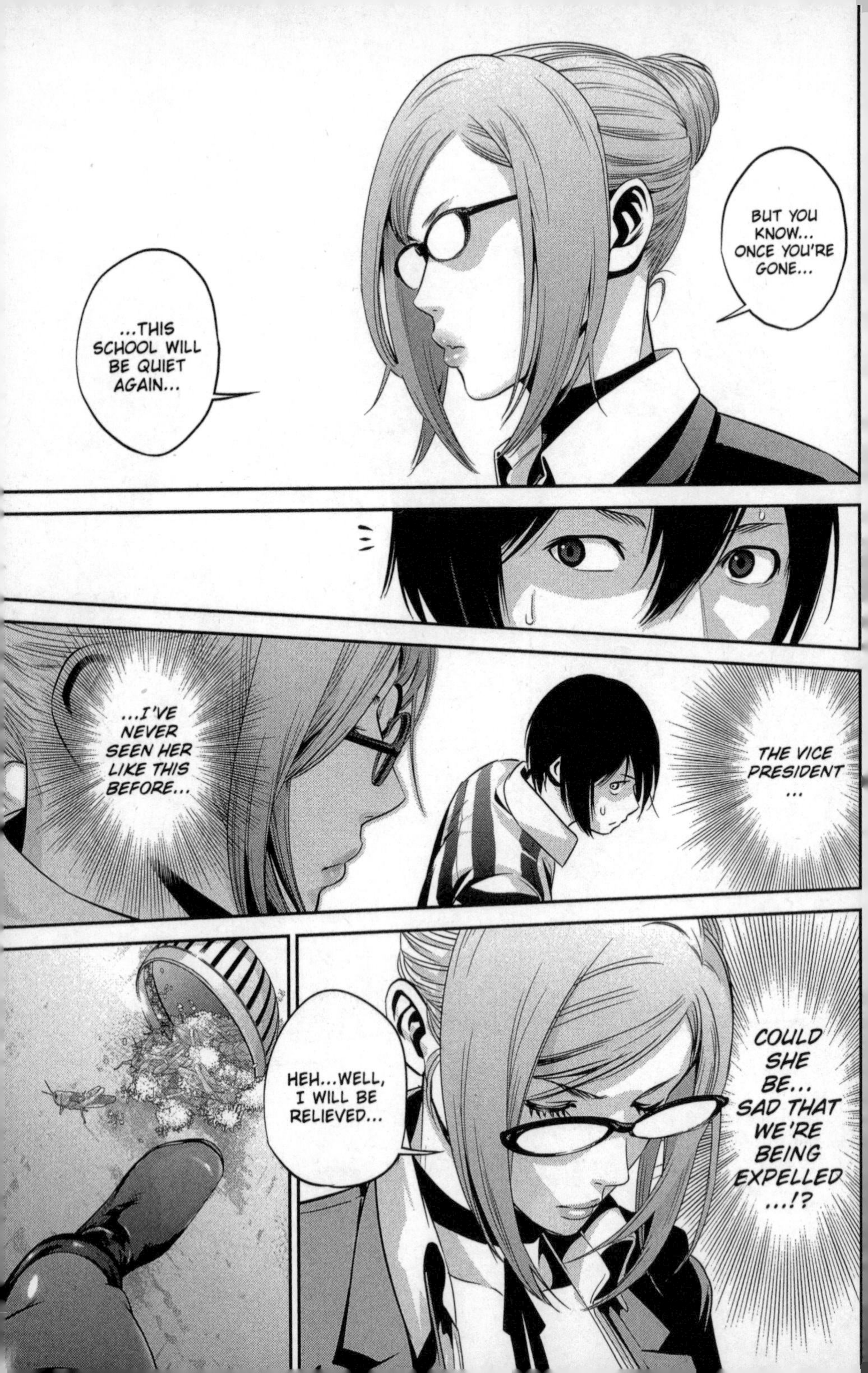
BUT YOU KNOW... ONCE YOU'RE GONE...
...THIS SCHOOL WILL BE QUIET AGAIN...
THE VICE PRESIDENT ...
...I'VE NEVER SEEN HER LIKE THIS BEFORE...
COULD SHE BE... SAD THAT WE'RE BEING EXPELLED ...!?
HEH...WELL, I WILL BE RELIEVED...

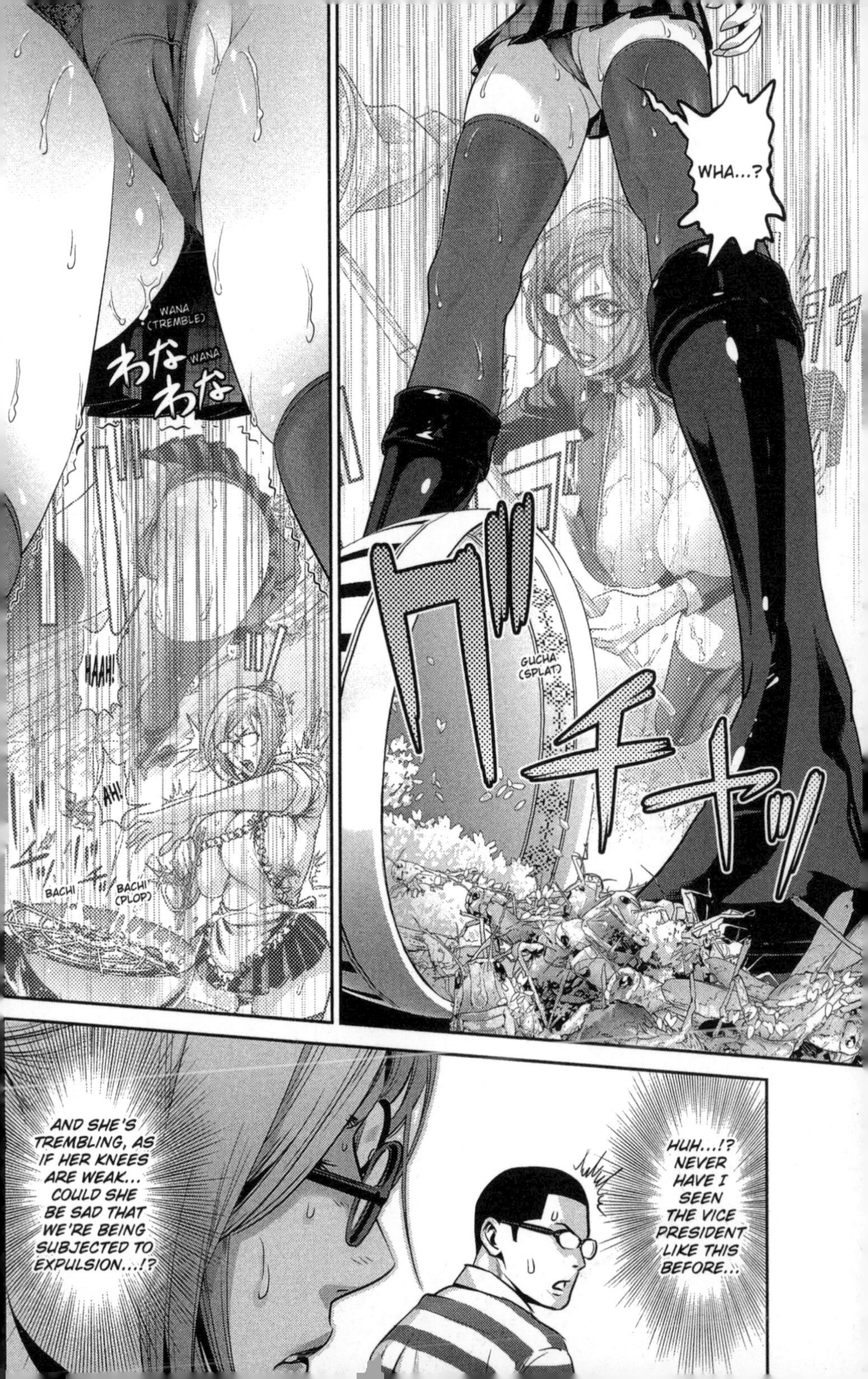

WHA...?
GUCHA (SPLAT)
グチャッ
WANA (TREMBLE)
わなわな
WANA
HAAH!
AH!
BACHI
BACHI (PLOP)
HUH...!? NEVER HAVE I SEEN THE VICE PRESIDENT LIKE THIS BEFORE...
AND SHE'S TREMBLING, AS IF HER KNEES ARE WEAK... COULD SHE BE SAD THAT WE'RE BEING SUBJECTED TO EXPULSION...!?

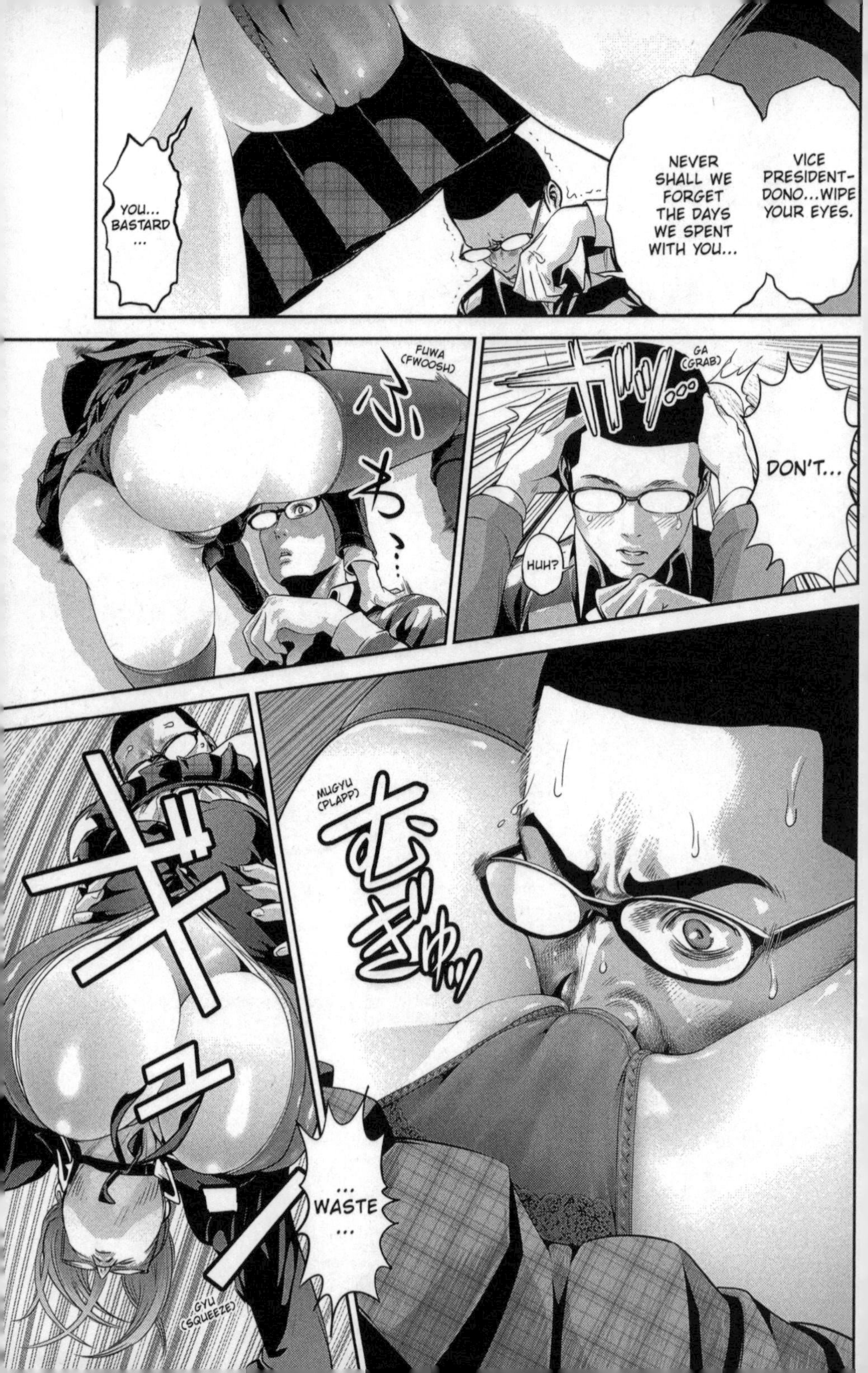
VICE PRESIDENT-DONO...WIPE YOUR EYES.
NEVER SHALL WE FORGET THE DAYS WE SPENT WITH YOU...
YOU... BASTARD ...
GA (GRAB)
DON'T...
HUH?
FUWA (FWOOSH)
MUGYU (PLAPP)
... WASTE ...
GYU (SQUEEZE)

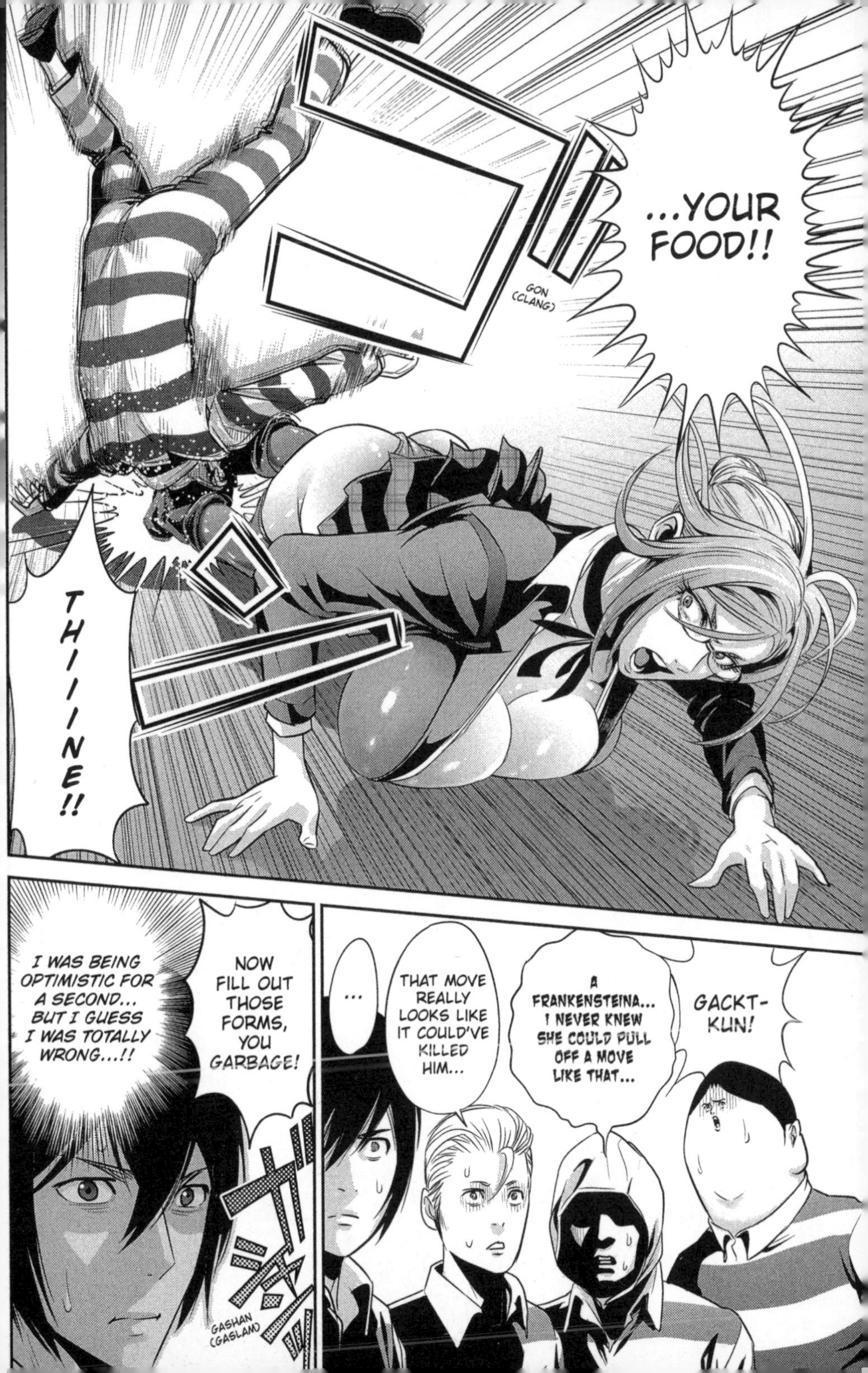
...YOUR FOOD!!
GON (CLANG)
THIIIINE!!
GACKT-KUN!
A FRANKENSTEINA... I NEVER KNEW SHE COULD PULL OFF A MOVE LIKE THAT...
THAT MOVE REALLY LOOKS LIKE IT COULD'VE KILLED HIM...
...
NOW FILL OUT THOSE FORMS, YOU GARBAGE!
I WAS BEING OPTIMISTIC FOR A SECOND... BUT I GUESS I WAS TOTALLY WRONG...!!
GASHAN (GASLAM)

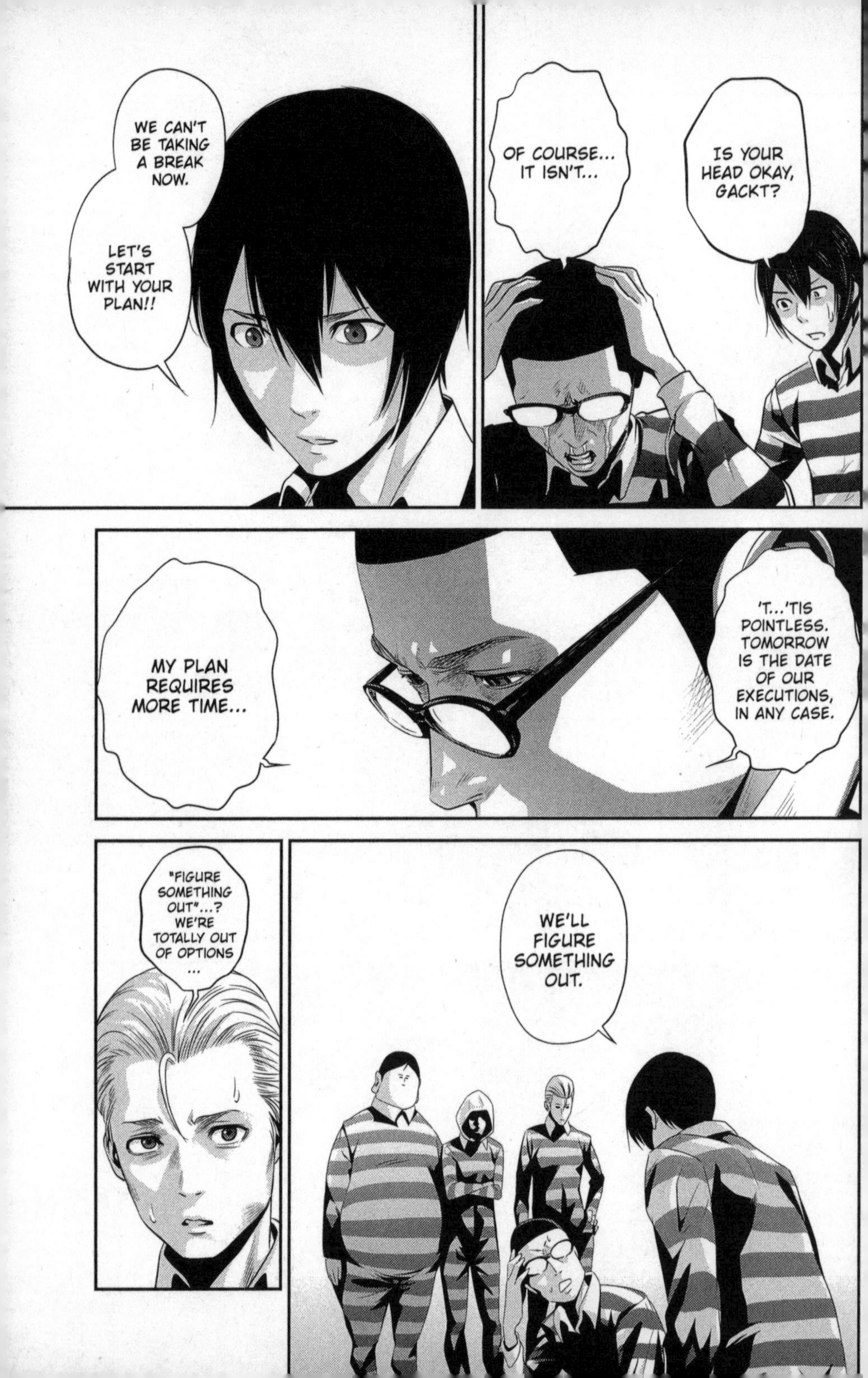
IS YOUR HEAD OKAY, GACKT?
OF COURSE... IT ISN'T...
WE CAN'T BE TAKING A BREAK NOW.
LET'S START WITH YOUR PLAN!!
'T...'TIS POINTLESS. TOMORROW IS THE DATE OF OUR EXECUTIONS, IN ANY CASE.
MY PLAN REQUIRES MORE TIME...
WE'LL FIGURE SOMETHING OUT.
"FIGURE SOMETHING OUT"...? WE'RE TOTALLY OUT OF OPTIONS ...

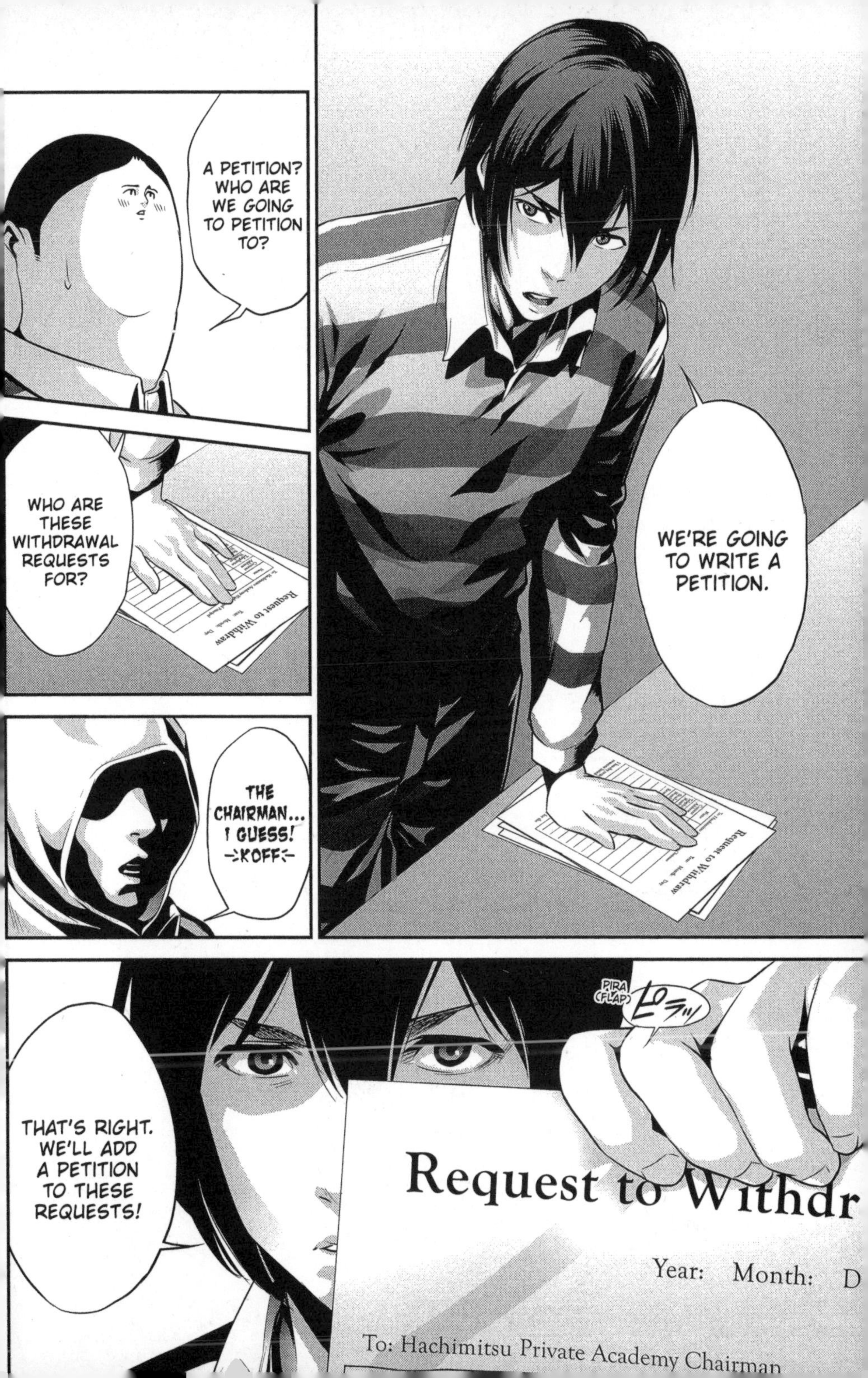
WE'RE GOING TO WRITE A PETITION.
Request to Withdraw
A PETITION? WHO ARE WE GOING TO PETITION TO?
WHO ARE THESE WITHDRAWAL REQUESTS FOR?
Request to Withdraw
THE CHAIRMAN... I GUESS! -KOFF-
PIRA (FLAP)
THAT'S RIGHT. WE'LL ADD A PETITION TO THESE REQUESTS!
Request to Withdr
Year: Month: D
To: Hachimitsu Private Academy Chairman

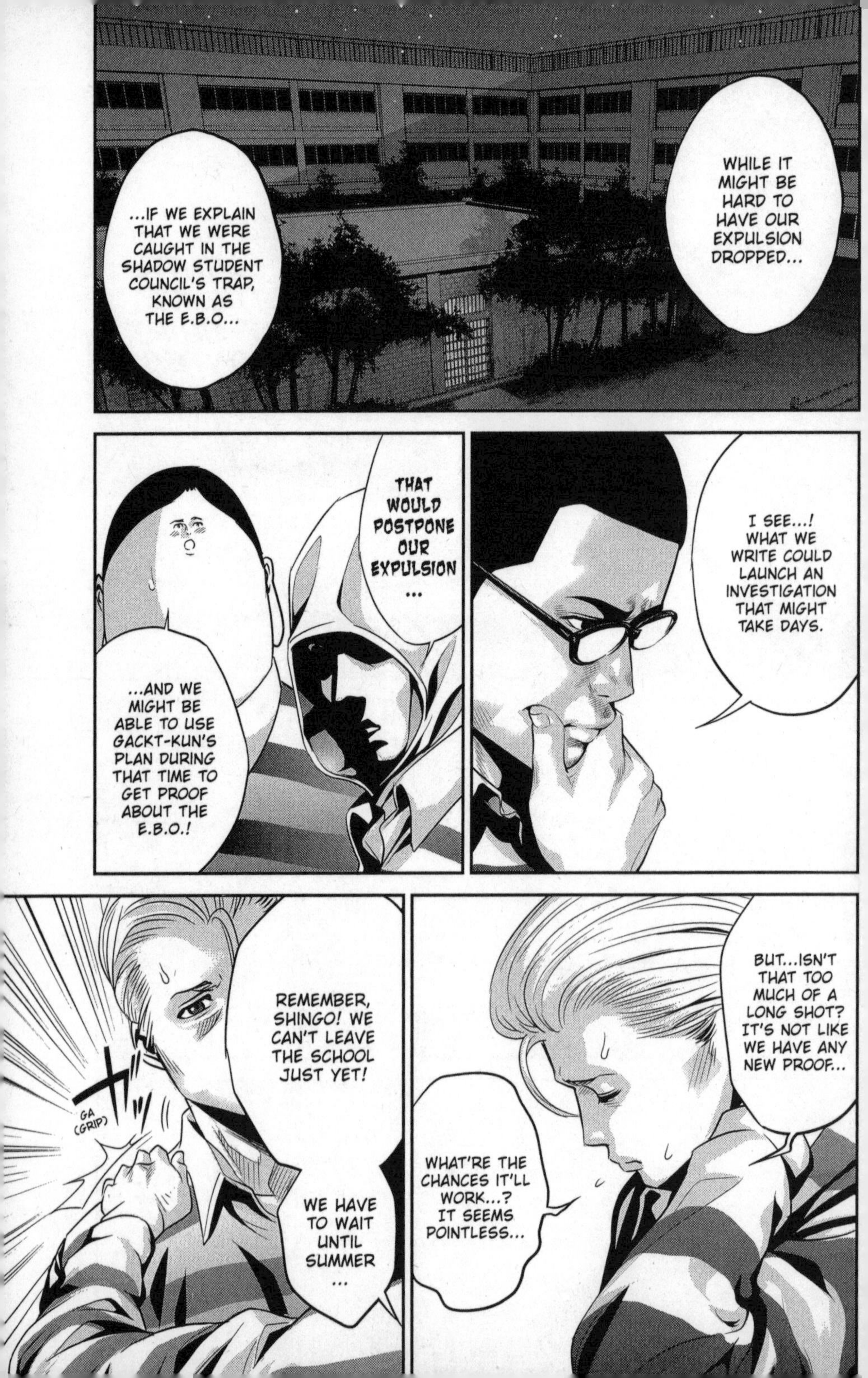
WHILE IT MIGHT BE HARD TO HAVE OUR EXPULSION DROPPED...
...IF WE EXPLAIN THAT WE WERE CAUGHT IN THE SHADOW STUDENT COUNCIL'S TRAP, KNOWN AS THE E.B.O...
I SEE...! WHAT WE WRITE COULD LAUNCH AN INVESTIGATION THAT MIGHT TAKE DAYS.
THAT WOULD POSTPONE OUR EXPULSION ...
...AND WE MIGHT BE ABLE TO USE GACKT-KUN'S PLAN DURING THAT TIME TO GET PROOF ABOUT THE E.B.O.!
BUT...ISN'T THAT TOO MUCH OF A LONG SHOT? IT'S NOT LIKE WE HAVE ANY NEW PROOF...
WHAT'RE THE CHANCES IT'LL WORK...? IT SEEMS POINTLESS...
REMEMBER, SHINGO! WE CAN'T LEAVE THE SCHOOL JUST YET!
GA (GRIP)
WE HAVE TO WAIT UNTIL SUMMER ...

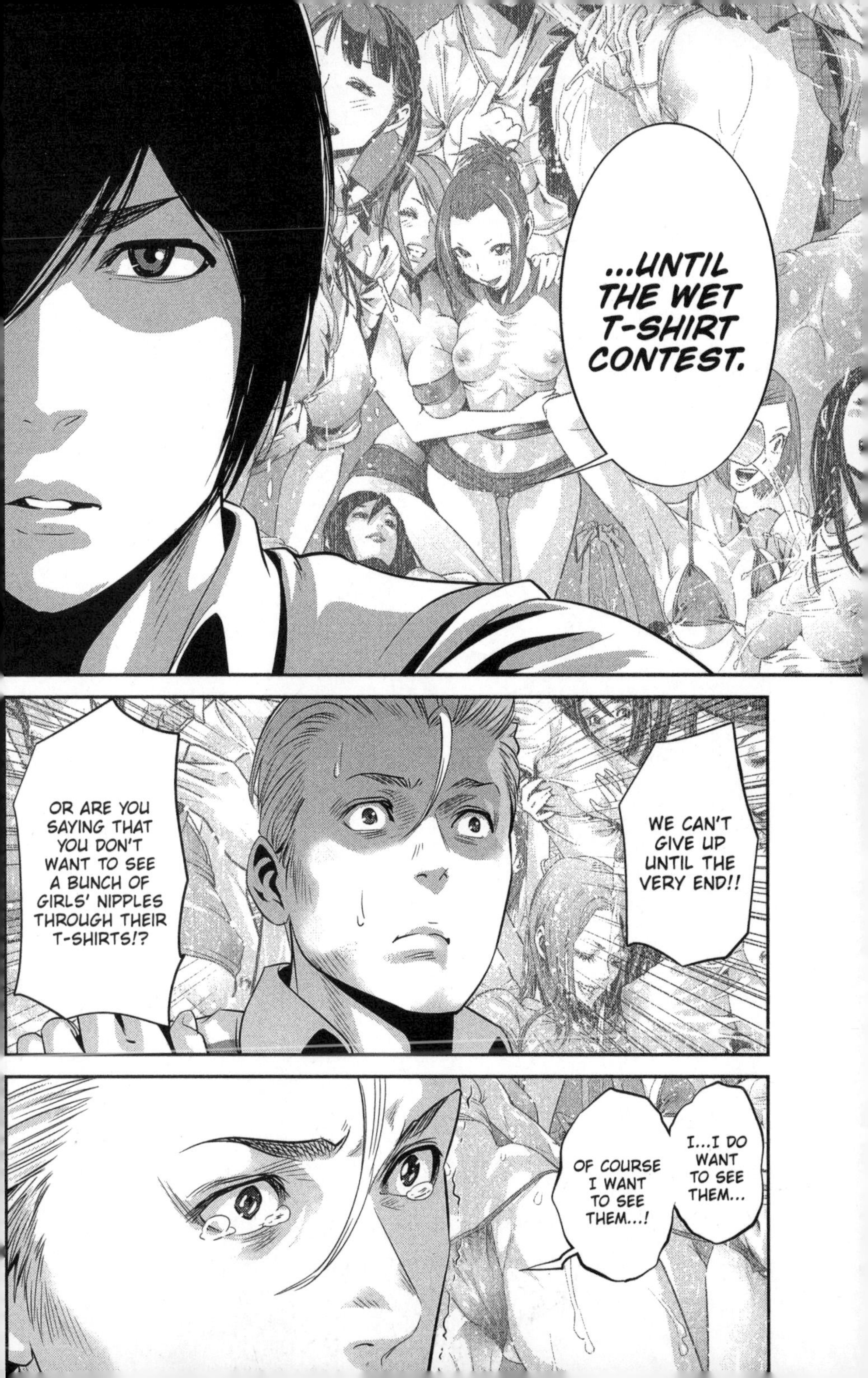
...UNTIL THE WET T-SHIRT CONTEST.
WE CAN'T GIVE UP UNTIL THE VERY END!!
OR ARE YOU SAYING THAT YOU DON'T WANT TO SEE A BUNCH OF GIRLS' NIPPLES THROUGH THEIR T-SHIRTS!?
I...I DO WANT TO SEE THEM...
OF COURSE I WANT TO SEE THEM...!

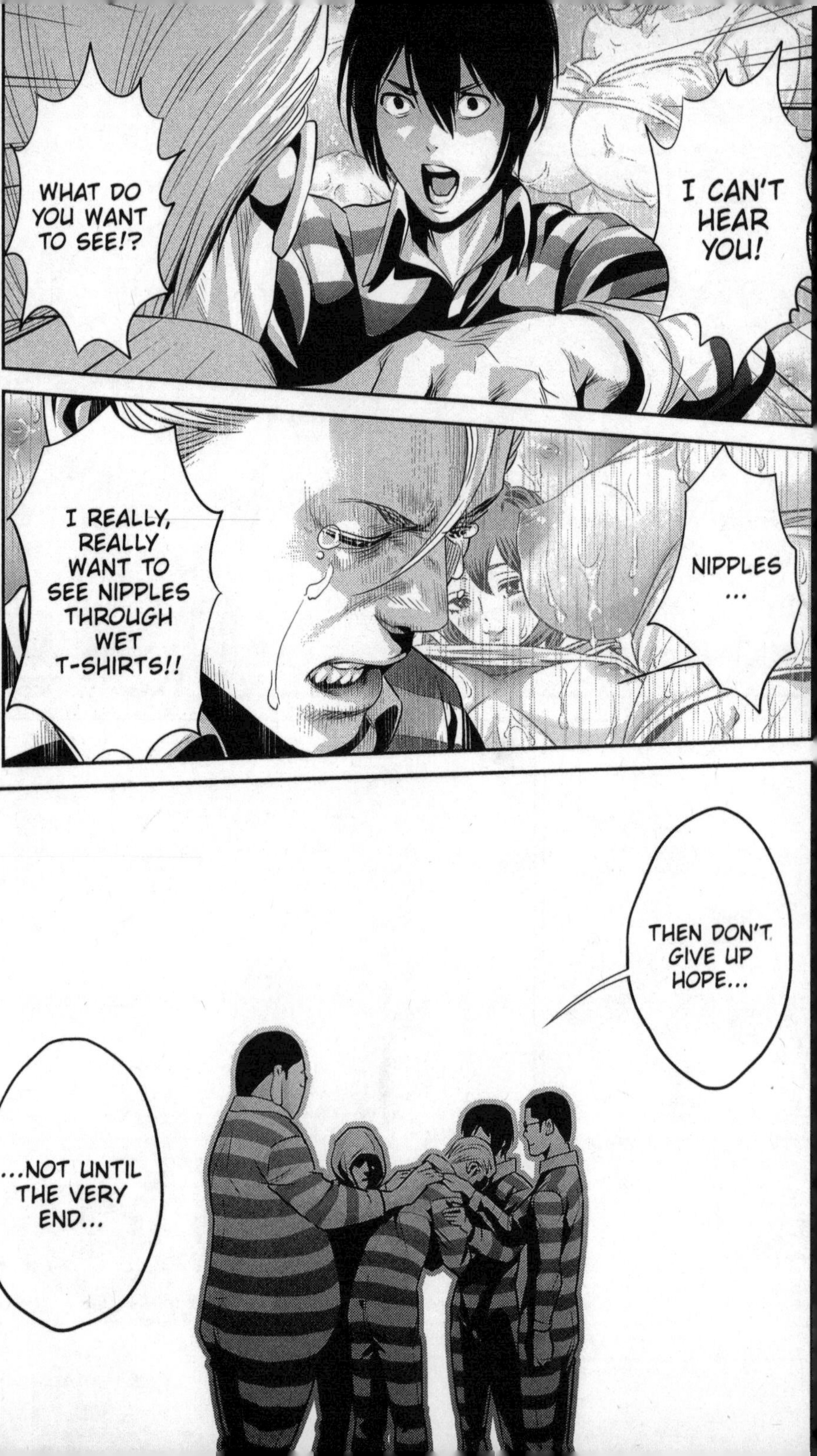
I CAN'T HEAR YOU!
WHAT DO YOU WANT TO SEE!?
NIPPLES ...
I REALLY, REALLY WANT TO SEE NIPPLES THROUGH WET T-SHIRTS!!
THEN DON'T GIVE UP HOPE...
...NOT UNTIL THE VERY END...

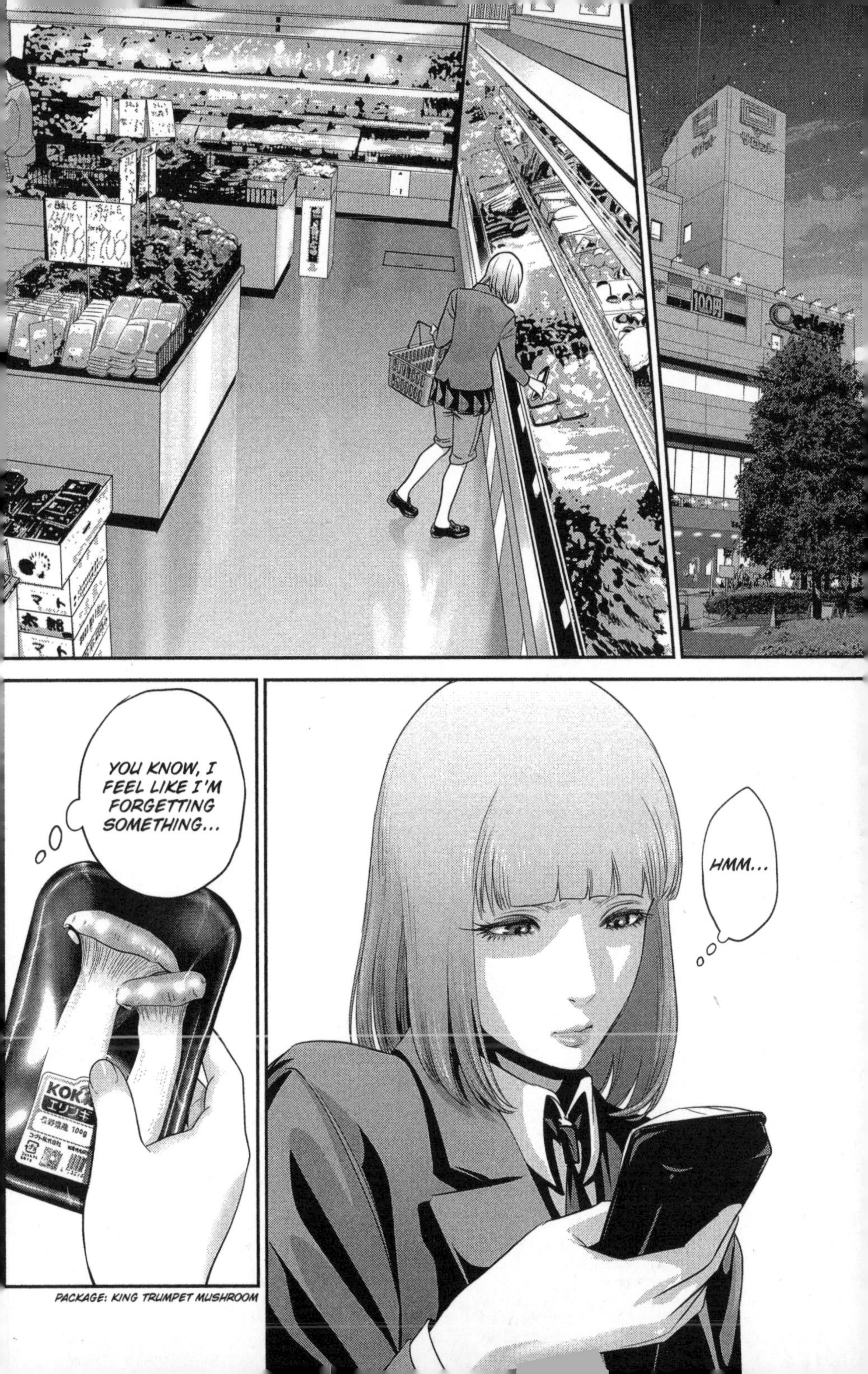
HMM...
YOU KNOW, I FEEL LIKE I'M FORGETTING SOMETHING...
PACKAGE: KING TRUMPET MUSHROOM

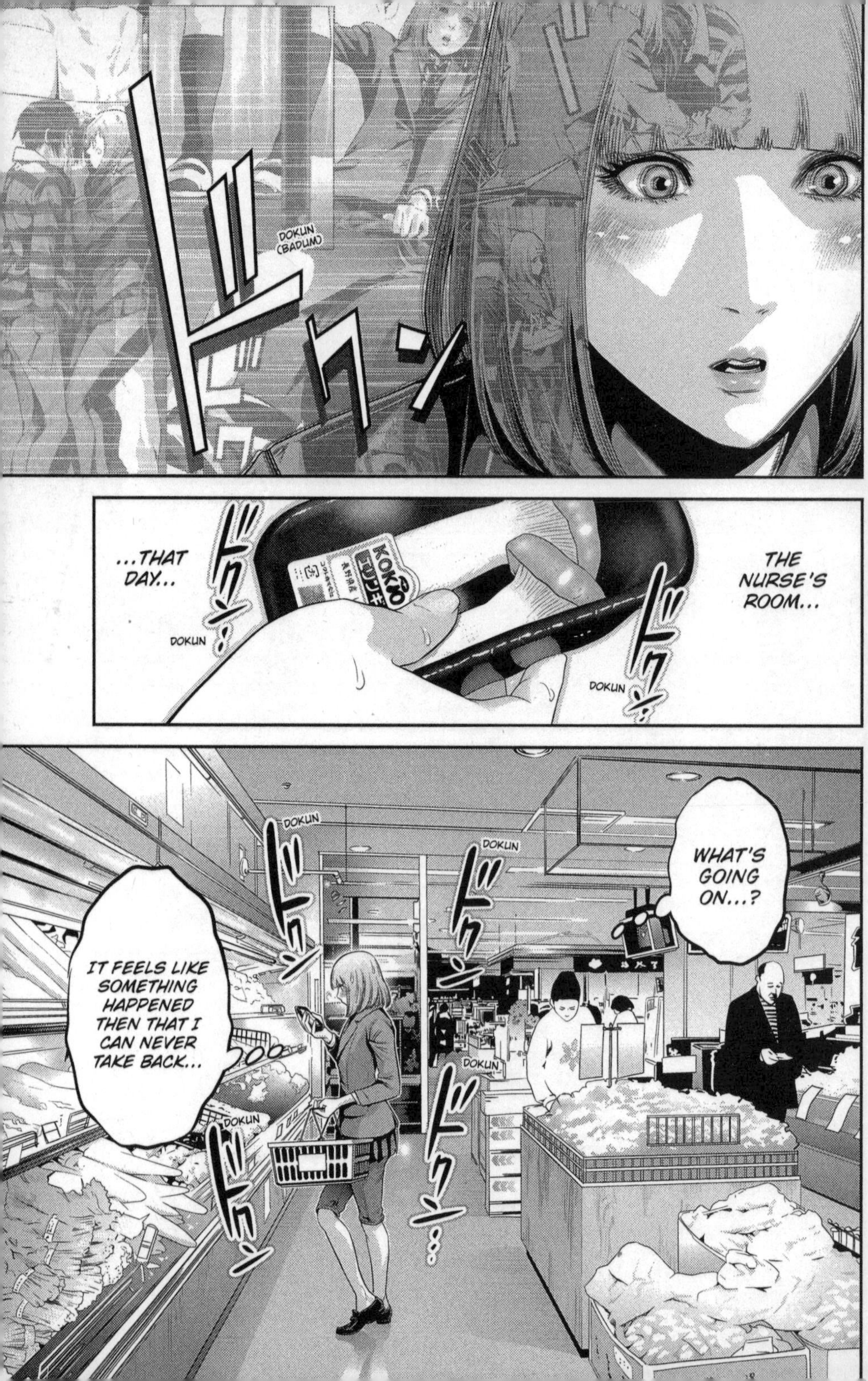
DOKUN (BADUM)
THE NURSE'S ROOM...
DOKUN
KOKO
DOKUN
...THAT DAY...
WHAT'S GOING ON...?
DOKUN
DOKUN
DOKUN
IT FEELS LIKE SOMETHING HAPPENED THEN THAT I CAN NEVER TAKE BACK...
DOKUN

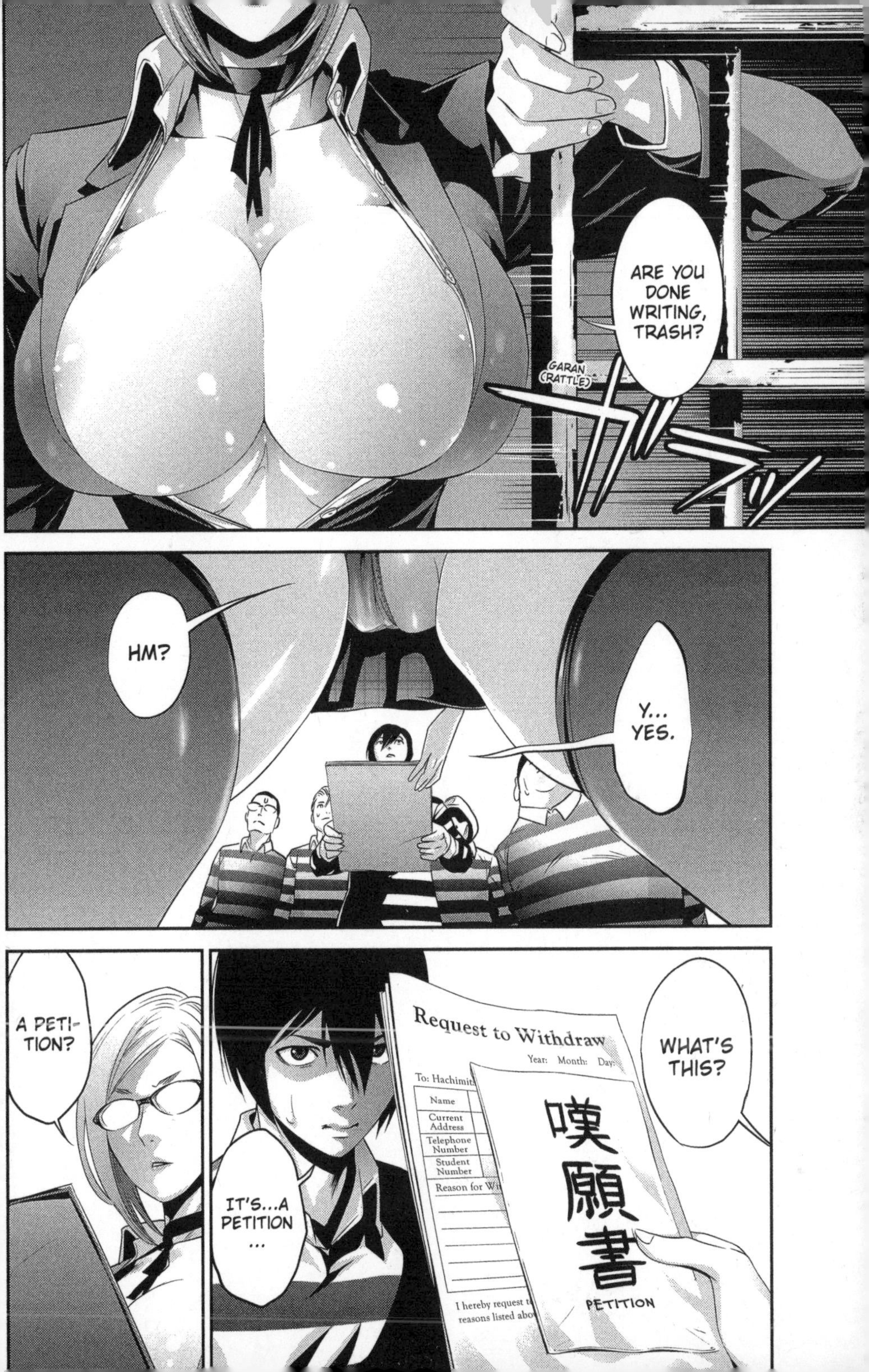
ARE YOU DONE WRITING, TRASH?
GARAN (RATTLE)
Y... YES.
HM?
WHAT'S THIS?
IT'S...A PETITION ...
Request to Withdraw
Year: Month: Day:
Name
Current Address
Telephone Number
Student Number
嘆願書
PETITION
A PETI- TION?

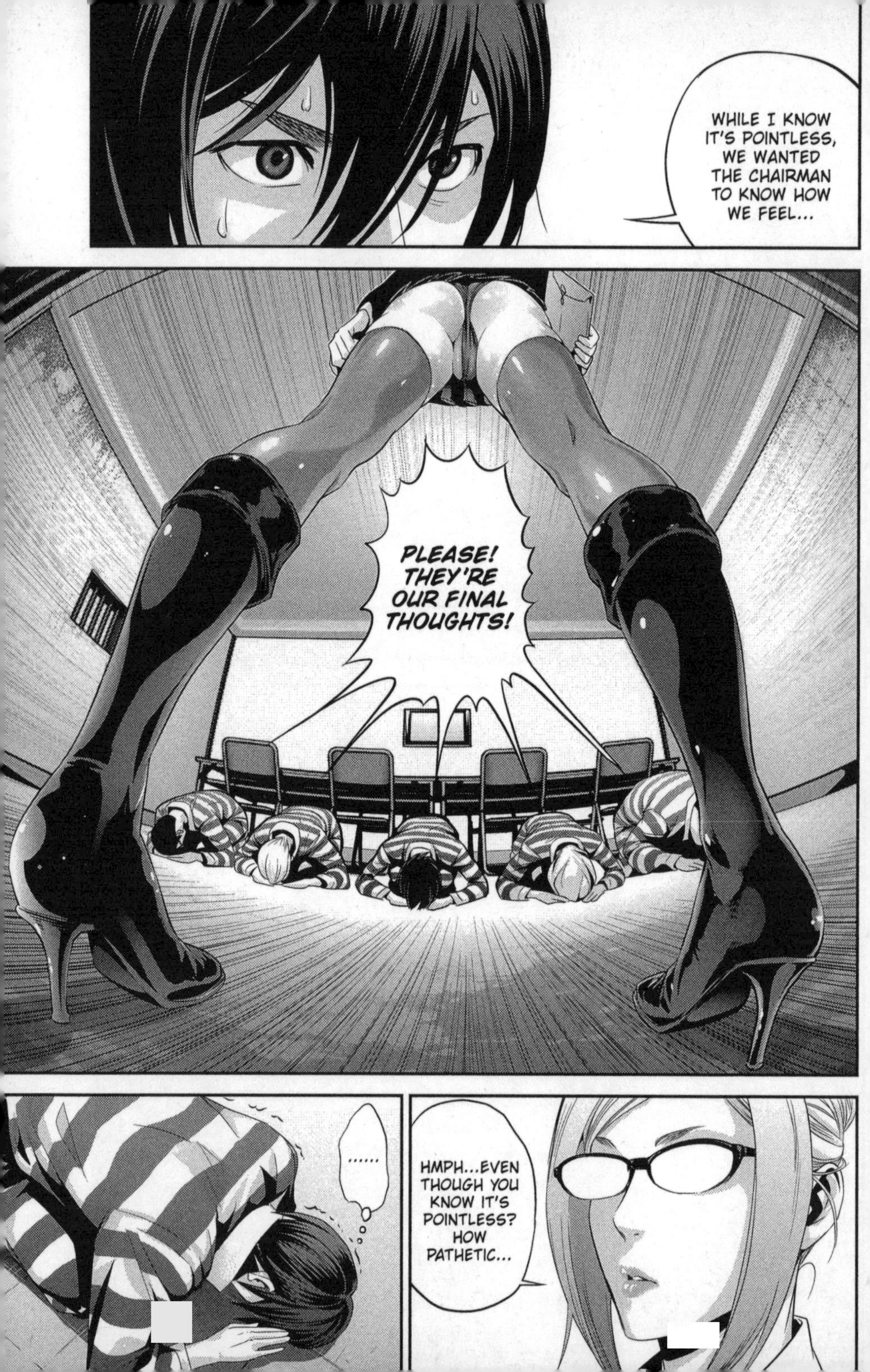
WHILE I KNOW IT'S POINTLESS, WE WANTED THE CHAIRMAN TO KNOW HOW WE FEEL...
PLEASE! THEY'RE OUR FINAL THOUGHTS!
HMPH...EVEN THOUGH YOU KNOW IT'S POINTLESS? HOW PATHETIC...
......

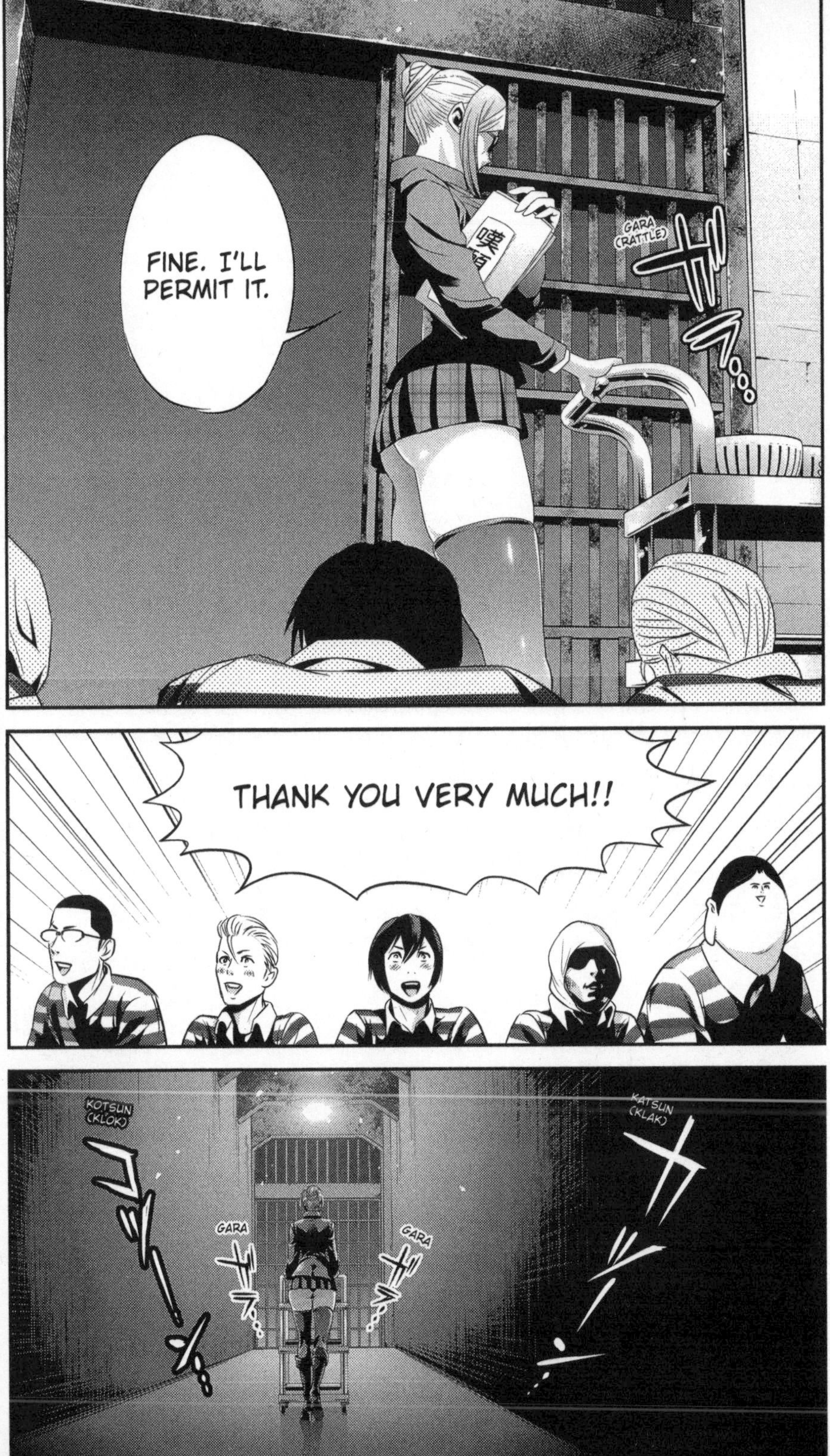
GARA (RATTLE)
FINE. I'LL PERMIT IT.
THANK YOU VERY MUCH!!
KATSUN (KLAK)
GARA
GARA
KOTSUN (KLOK)

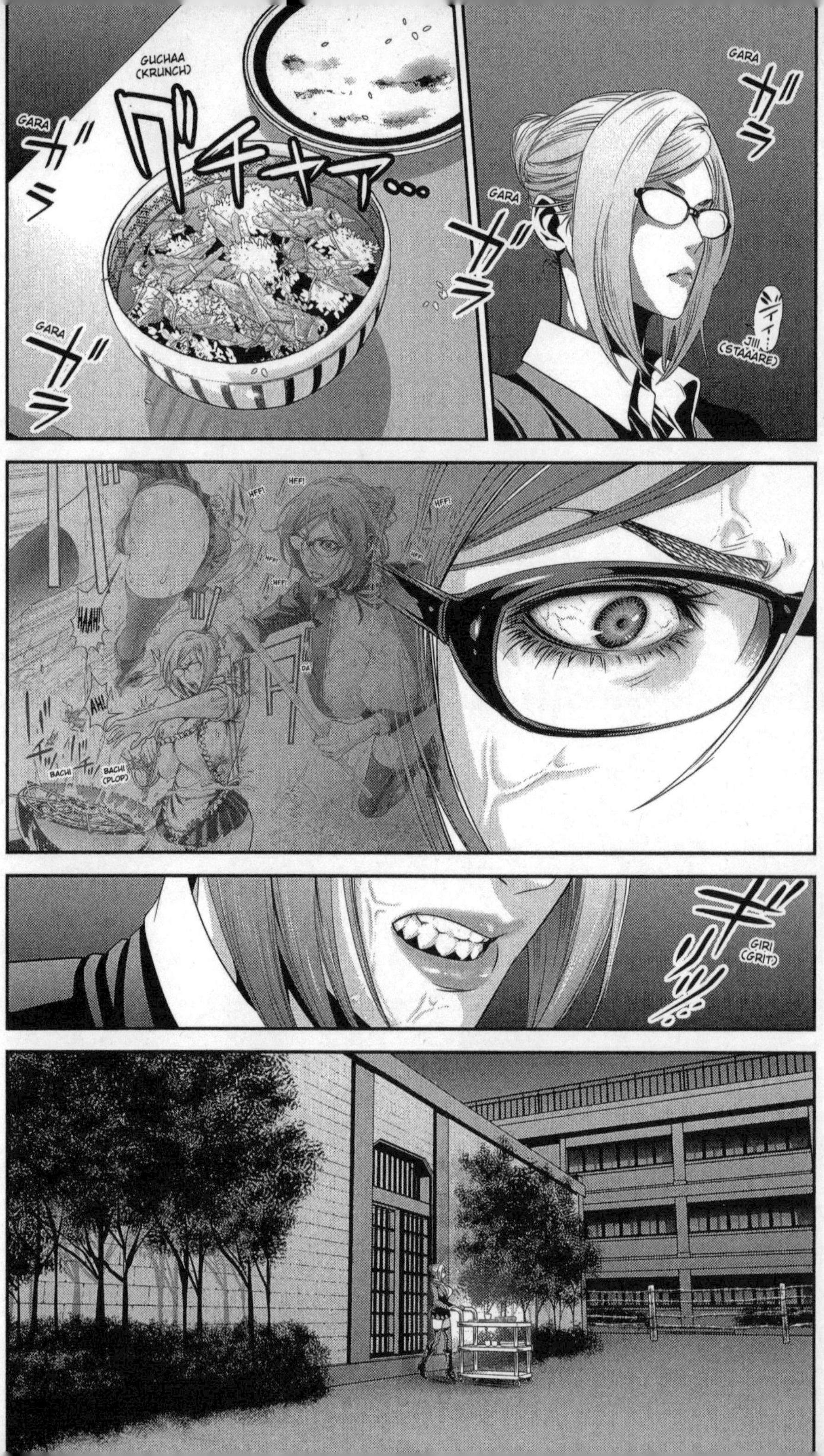
GARA
ガラ
GARA
ガラ
JIII… (STAAARE)
GUCHAA (KRUNCH)
グチャア…
GARA
ガラ
GARA
ガラ
HFF!
HFF!
HFF!
HAAH!
AH!
BACHI
BACHI (PLOP)
GIRI (GRIT)
ギリ

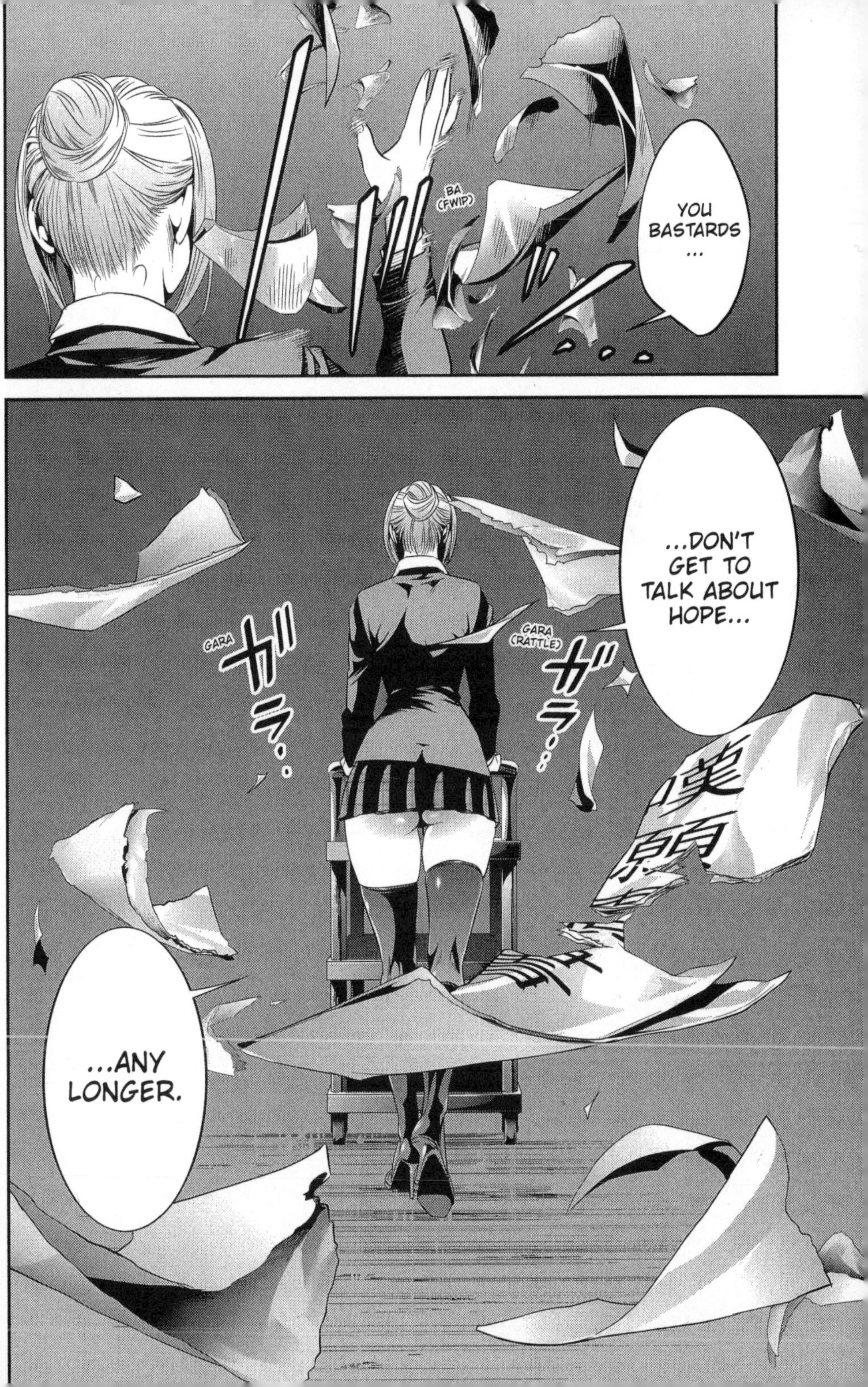
YOU BASTARDS ...
BA (FWIP)
...DON'T GET TO TALK ABOUT HOPE...
GARA (RATTLE)
GARA
...ANY LONGER.

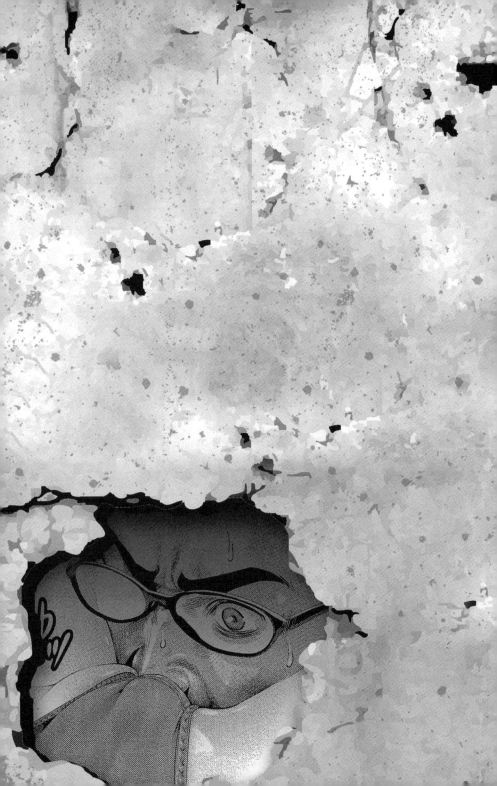

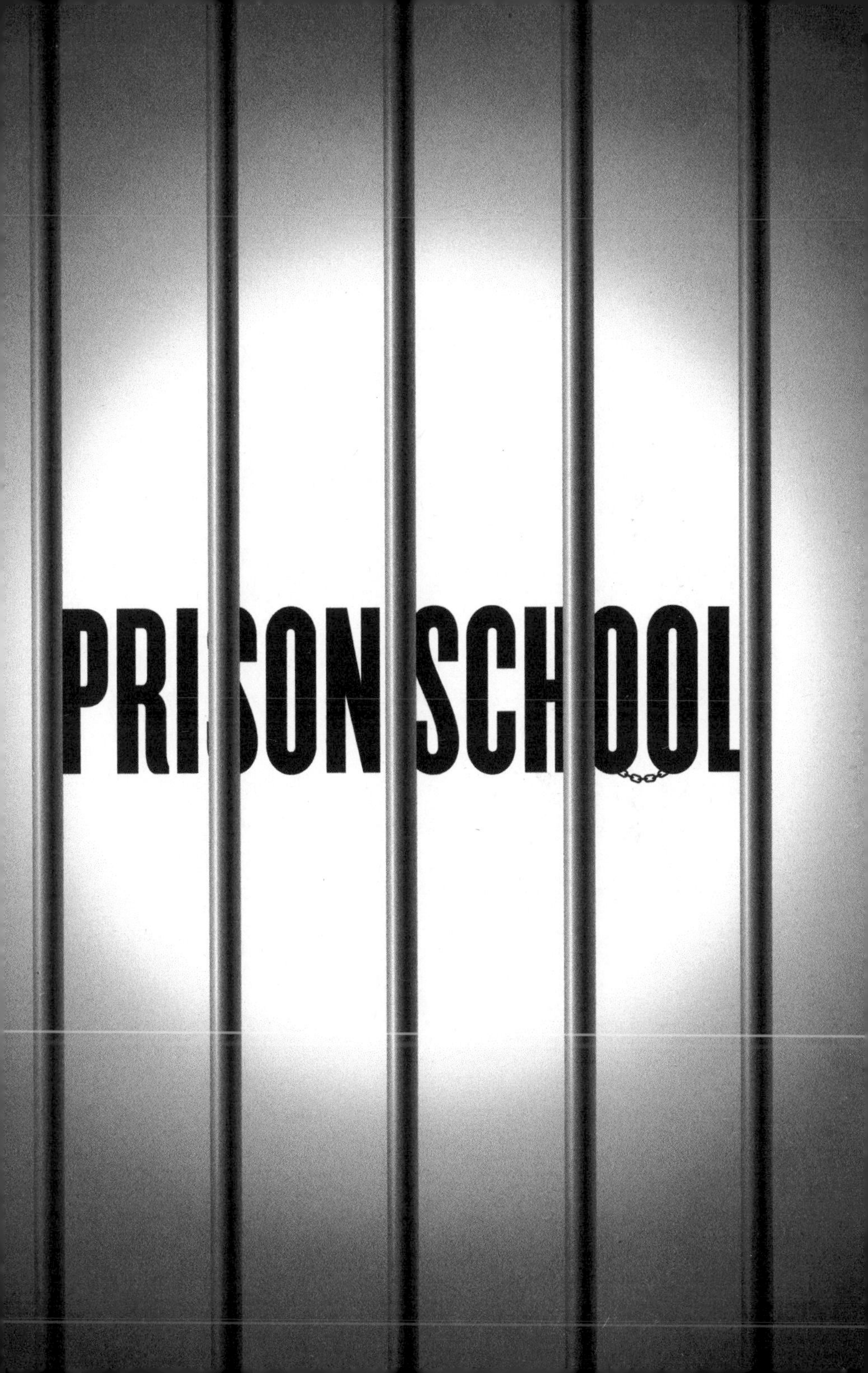
PRISON SCHOOL

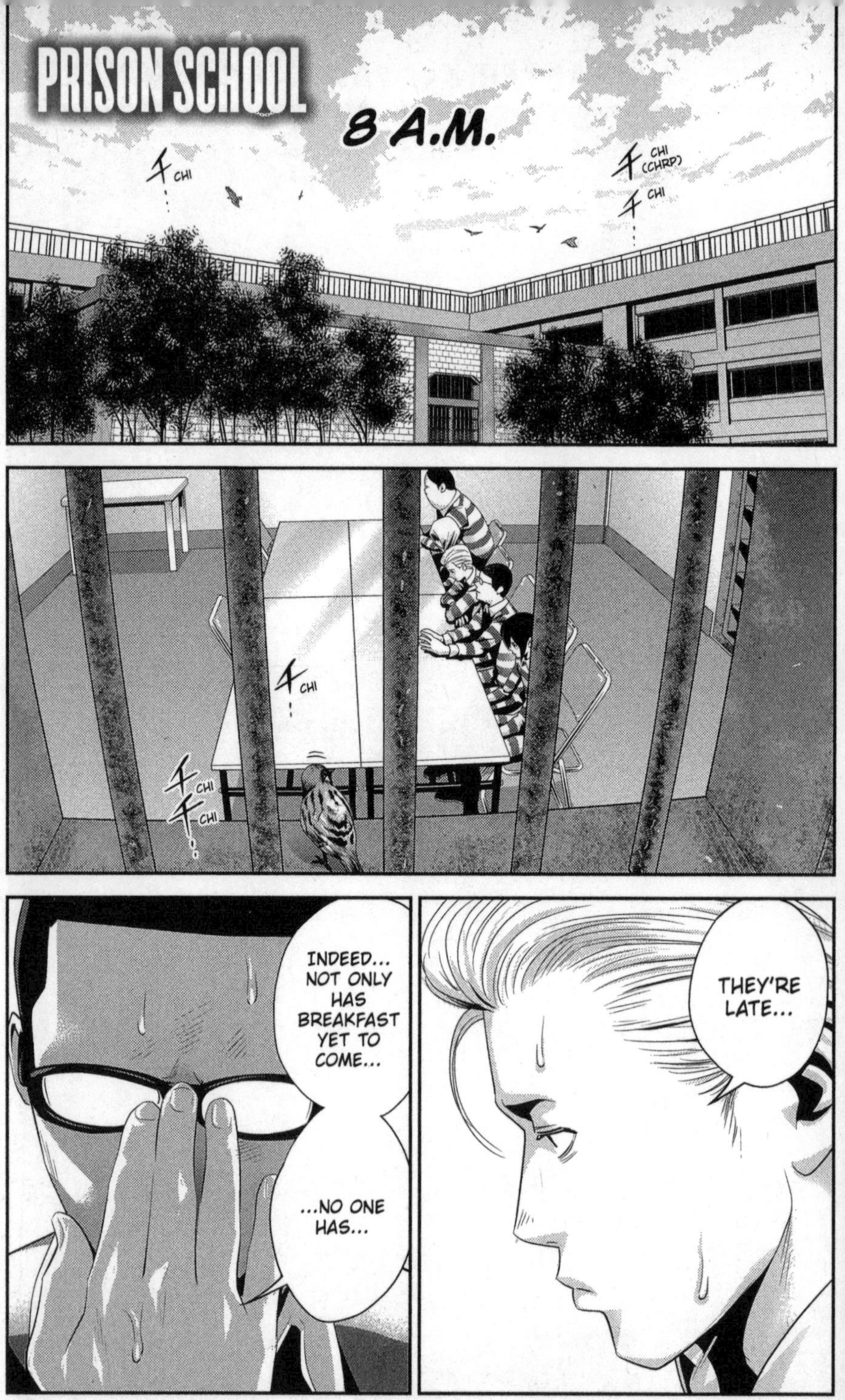
PRISON SCHOOL
8 A.M.
CHI (CHRP)
CHI
CHI
CHI
CHI
CHI
THEY'RE LATE...
INDEED... NOT ONLY HAS BREAKFAST YET TO COME...
...NO ONE HAS...

CHAPTER 65: SACCO AND VANZETTI

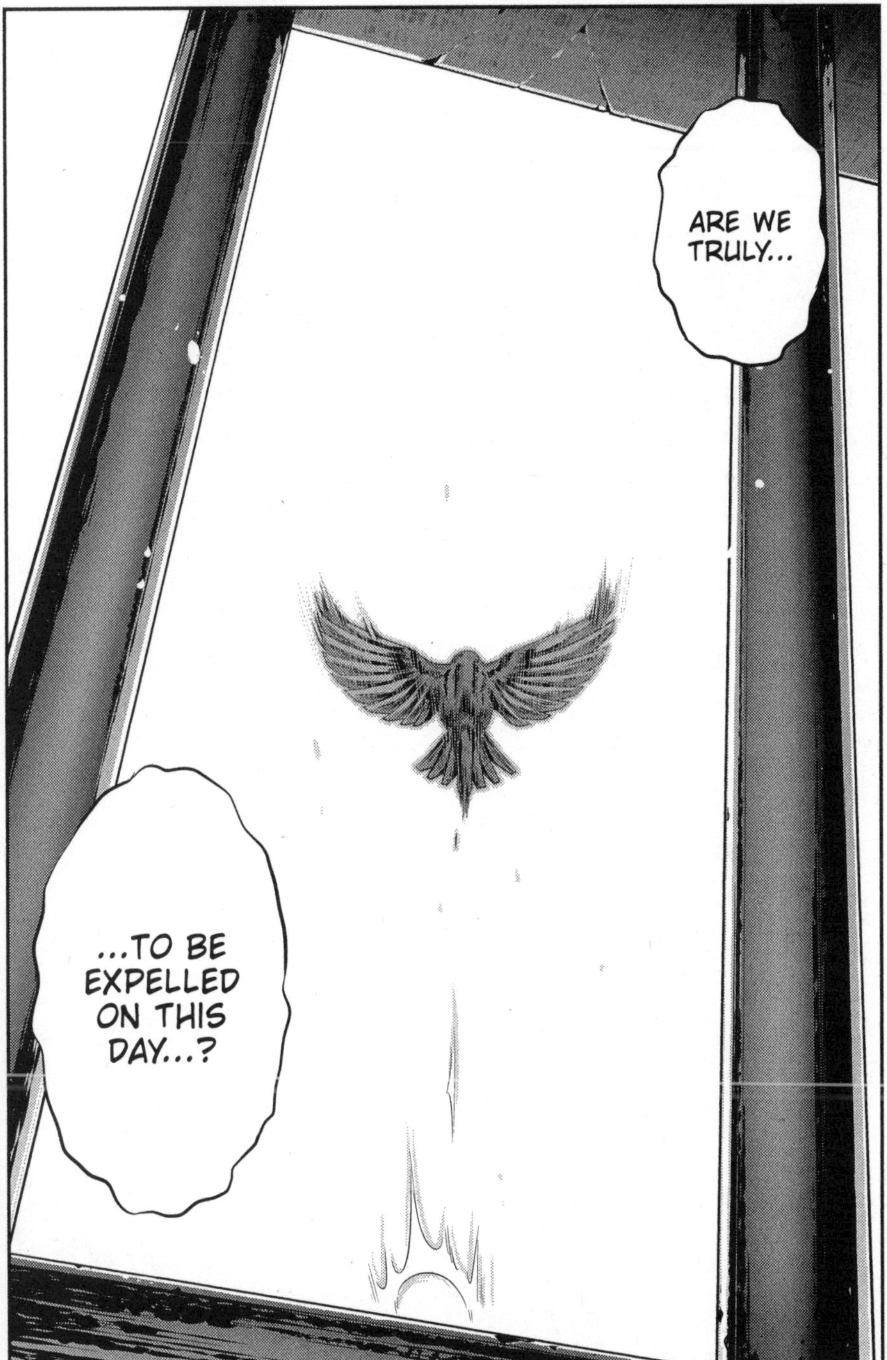
ARE WE TRULY...
...TO BE EXPELLED ON THIS DAY...?

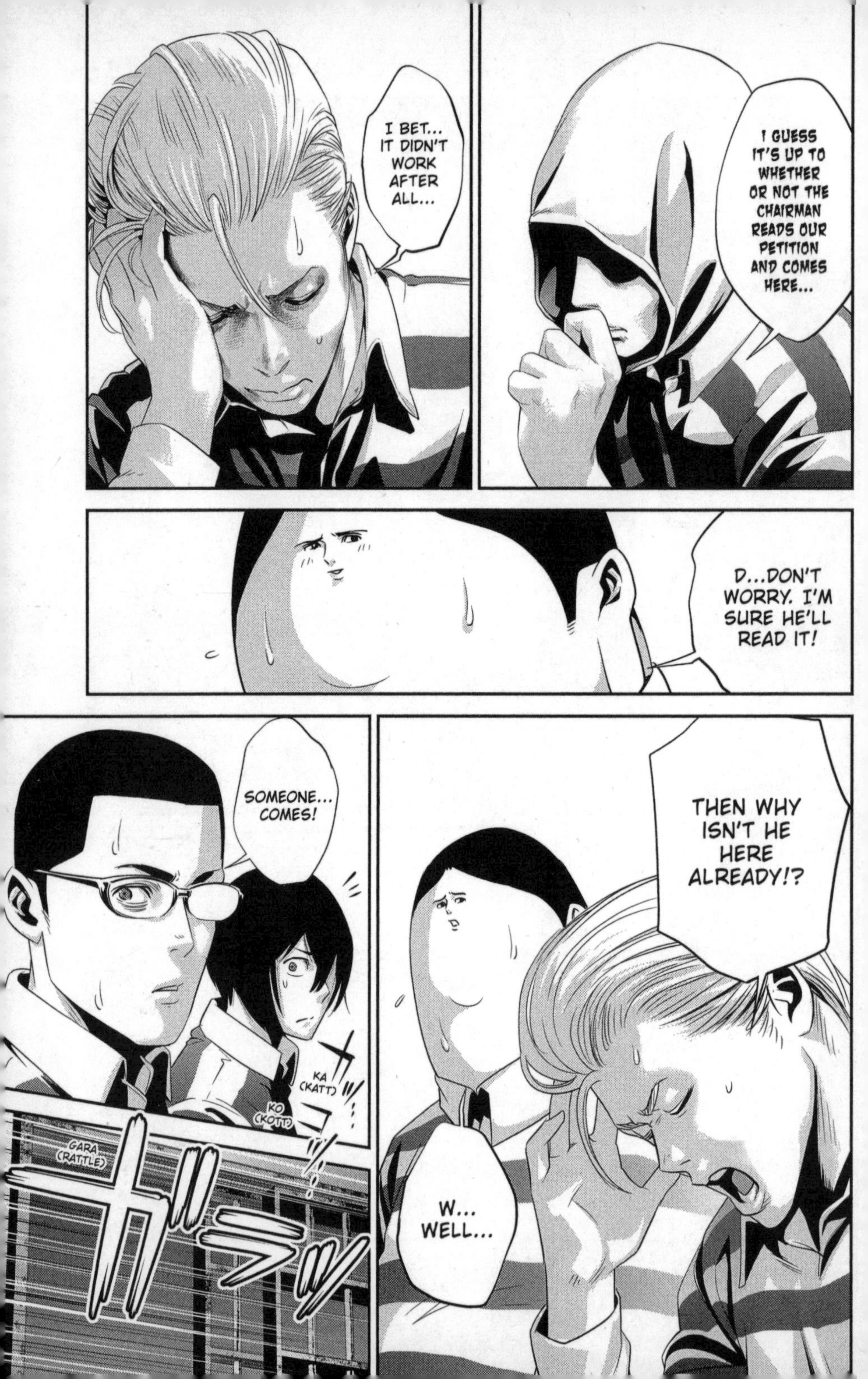
I GUESS IT'S UP TO WHETHER OR NOT THE CHAIRMAN READS OUR PETITION AND COMES HERE...
I BET... IT DIDN'T WORK AFTER ALL...
D...DON'T WORRY. I'M SURE HE'LL READ IT!
THEN WHY ISN'T HE HERE ALREADY!?
W... WELL...
SOMEONE... COMES!
KA (KATT)
KO (KOTT)
GARA (RATTLE)

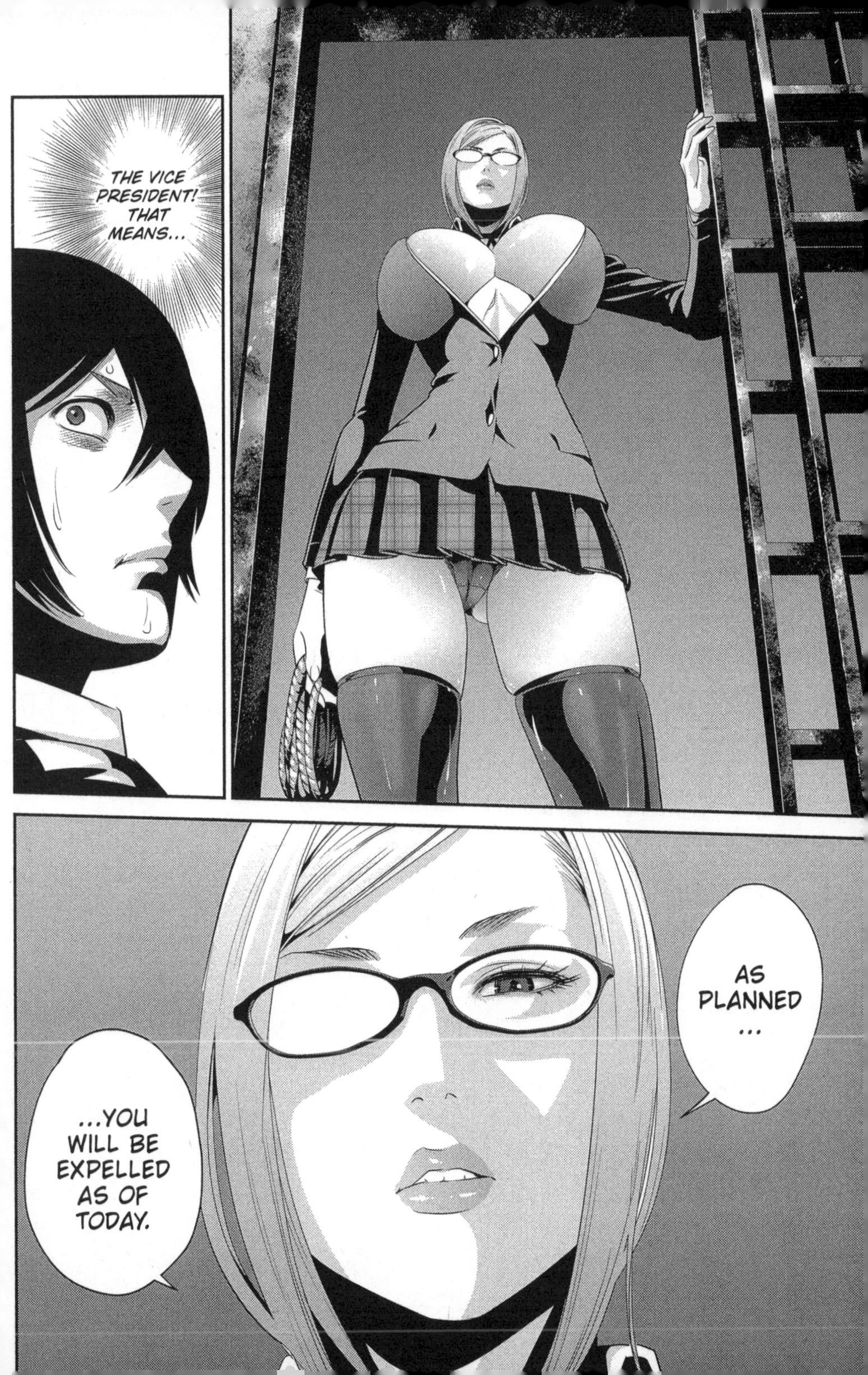
THE VICE PRESIDENT! THAT MEANS...
AS PLANNED...
...YOU WILL BE EXPELLED AS OF TODAY.

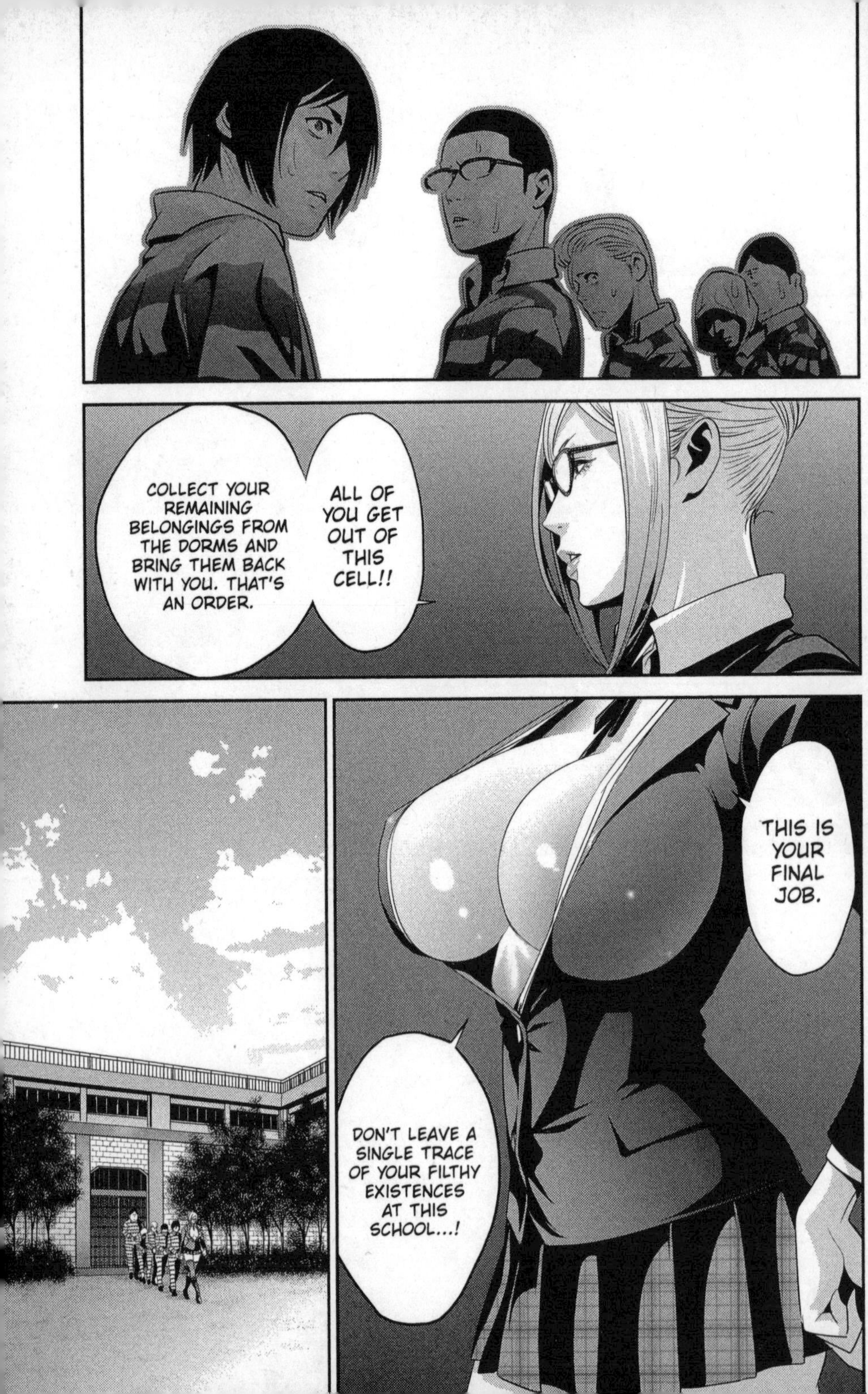
ALL OF YOU GET OUT OF THIS CELL!!
COLLECT YOUR REMAINING BELONGINGS FROM THE DORMS AND BRING THEM BACK WITH YOU. THAT'S AN ORDER.
THIS IS YOUR FINAL JOB.
DON'T LEAVE A SINGLE TRACE OF YOUR FILTHY EXISTENCES AT THIS SCHOOL...!

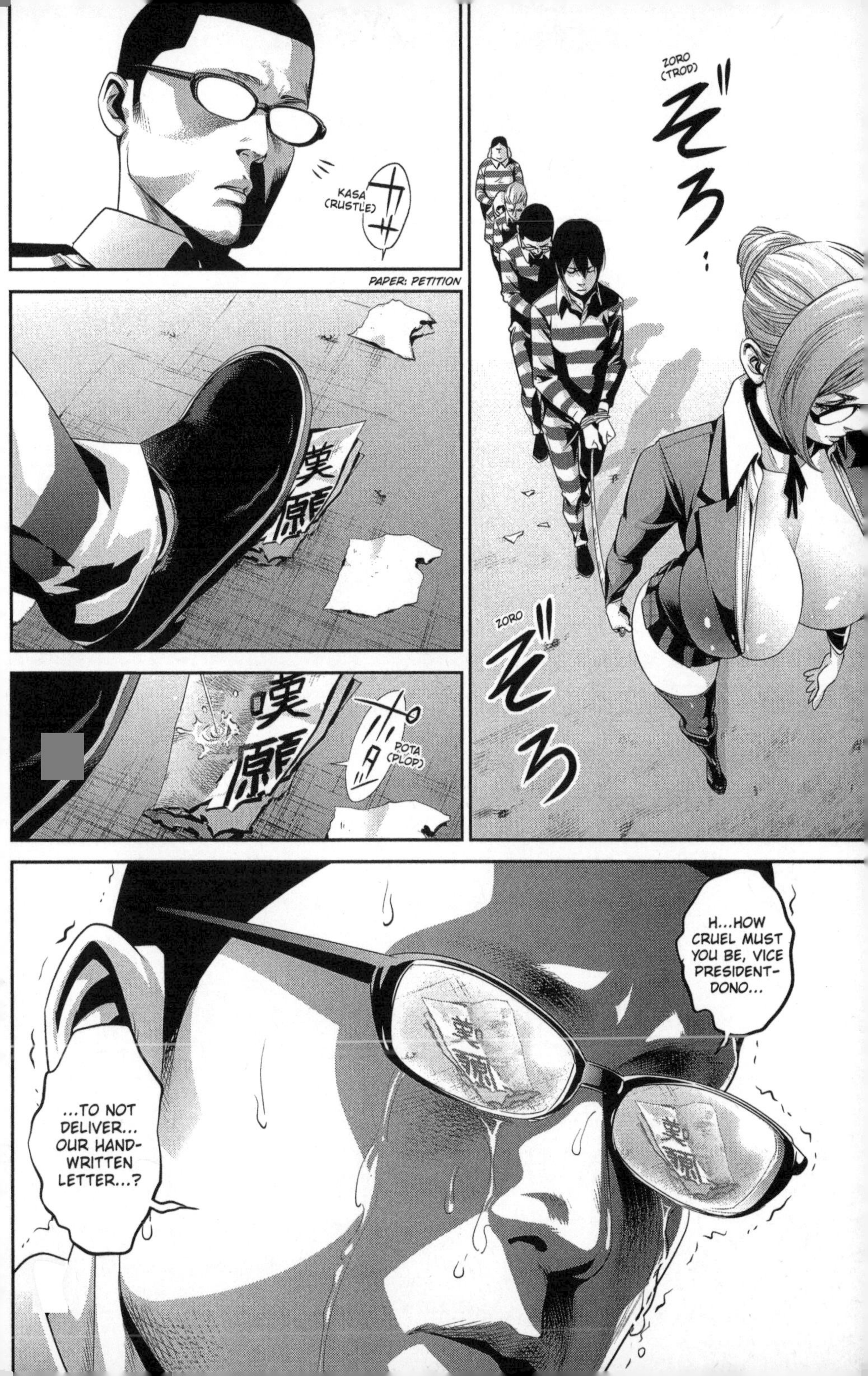
ZORO (TROD)
ぞろ
ZORO
ぞろ
KASA (RUSTLE)
カサ
PAPER: PETITION
POTA (PLOP)
ポタ
H...HOW CRUEL MUST YOU BE, VICE PRESIDENT-DONO...
...TO NOT DELIVER... OUR HAND-WRITTEN LETTER...?

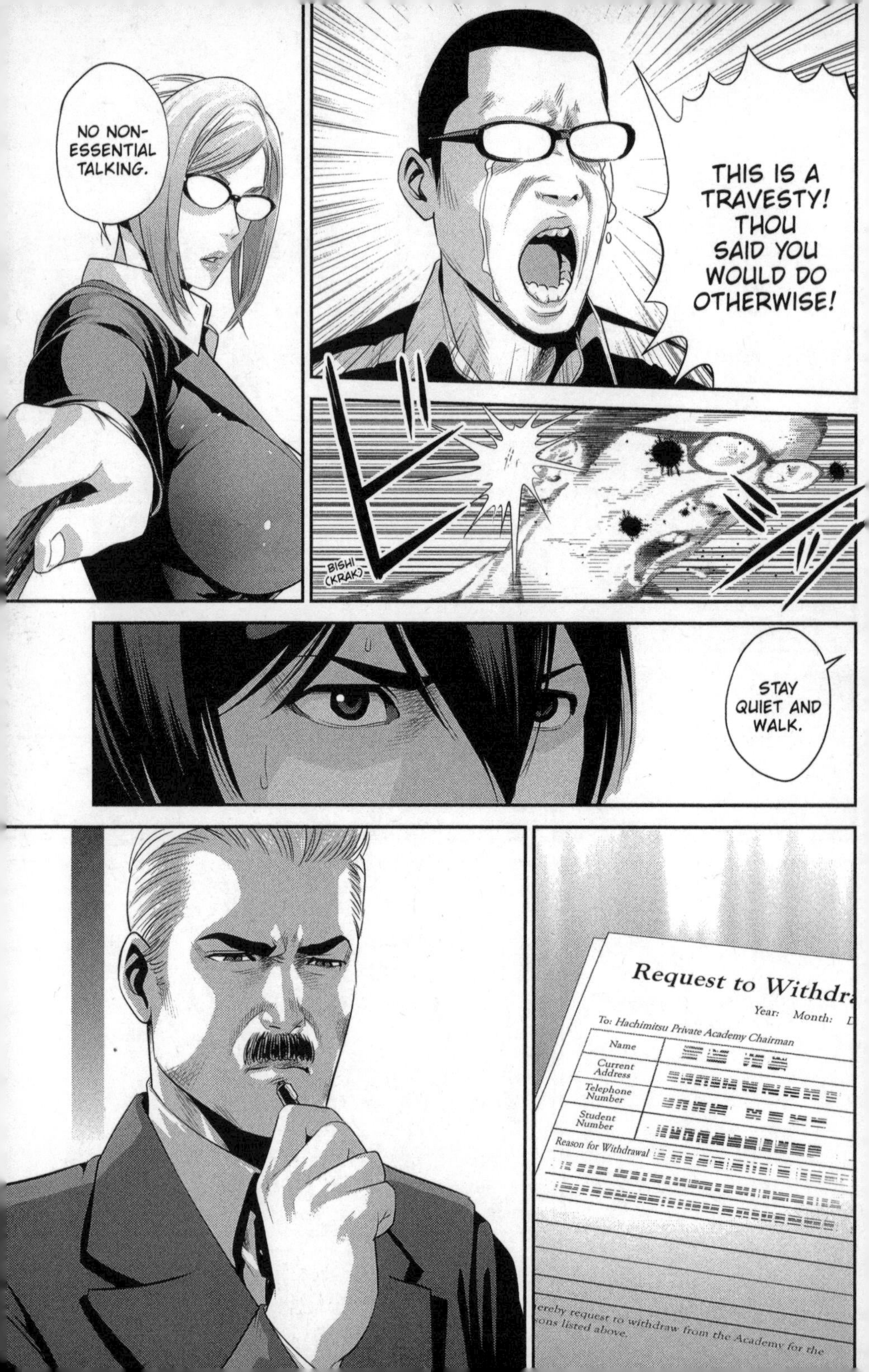
THIS IS A TRAVESTY! THOU SAID YOU WOULD DO OTHERWISE!
BISHI (KRAK)
NO NON-ESSENTIAL TALKING.
STAY QUIET AND WALK.
Request to Withdra
Year: Month: D
To: Hachimitsu Private Academy Chairman
Name
Current Address
Telephone Number
Student Number
Reason for Withdrawal
ereby request to withdraw from the Academy for the
sons listed above.

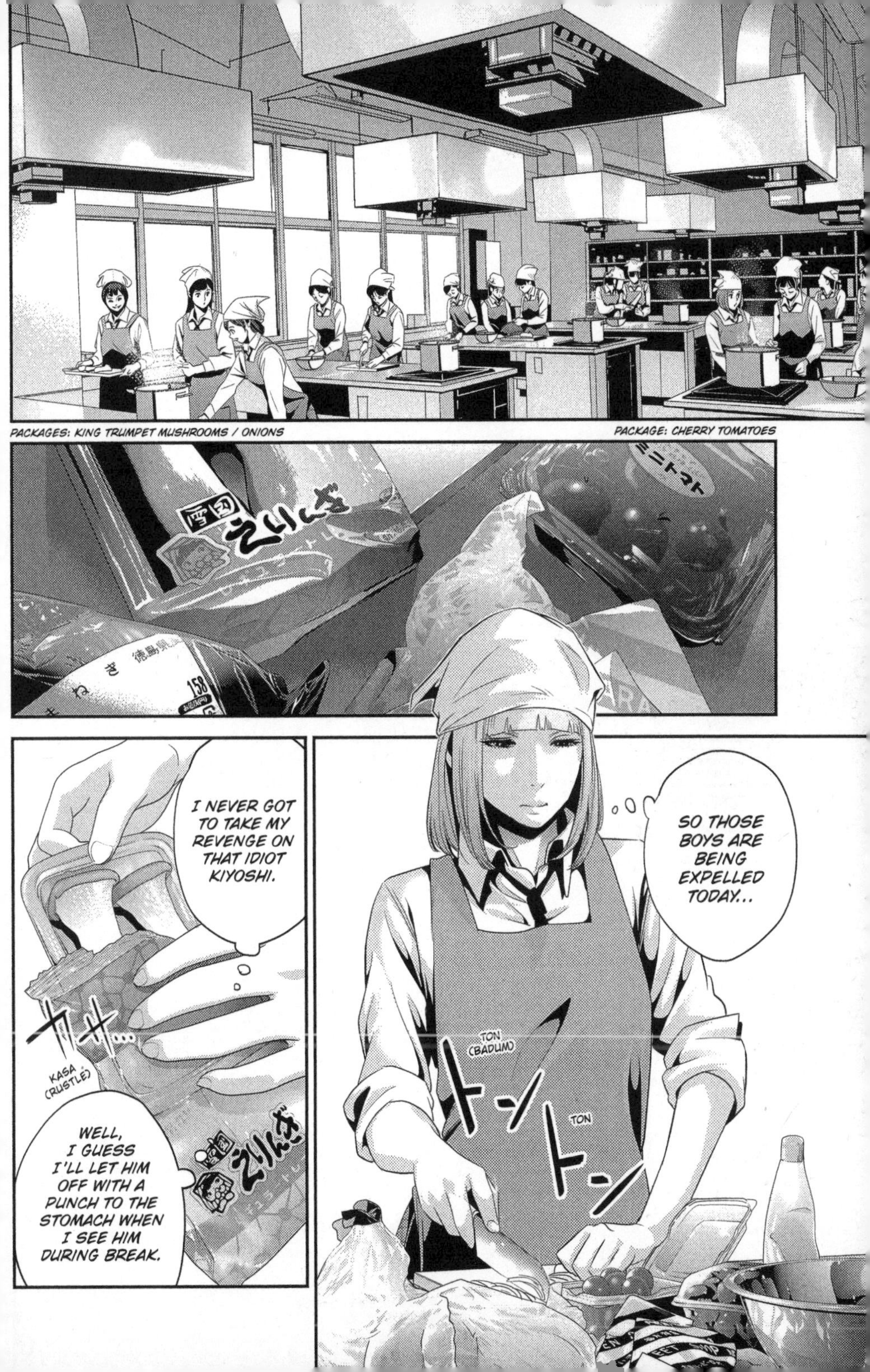
PACKAGE: CHERRY TOMATOES
PACKAGES: KING TRUMPET MUSHROOMS / ONIONS
ミニトマト
雪国
えりんぎ
SO THOSE BOYS ARE BEING EXPELLED TODAY...
TON (BADUM)
TON
I NEVER GOT TO TAKE MY REVENGE ON THAT IDIOT KIYOSHI.
KASA (RUSTLE)
WELL, I GUESS I'LL LET HIM OFF WITH A PUNCH TO THE STOMACH WHEN I SEE HIM DURING BREAK.

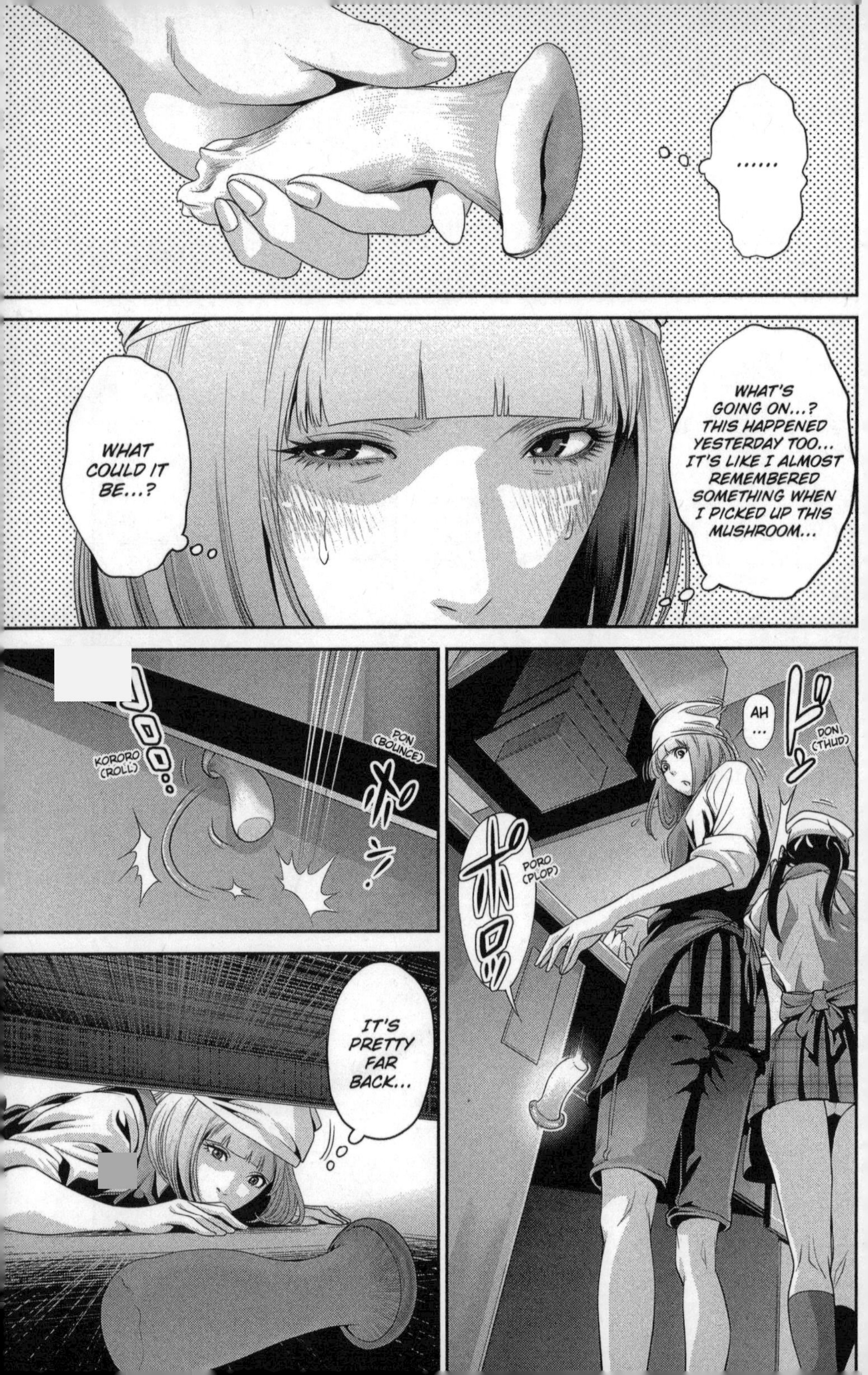
......
WHAT'S GOING ON...? THIS HAPPENED YESTERDAY TOO... IT'S LIKE I ALMOST REMEMBERED SOMETHING WHEN I PICKED UP THIS MUSHROOM...
WHAT COULD IT BE...?
DON (THUD)
AH ...
PORO (PLOP)
PON (BOUNCE)
KORORO (ROLL)
IT'S PRETTY FAR BACK...

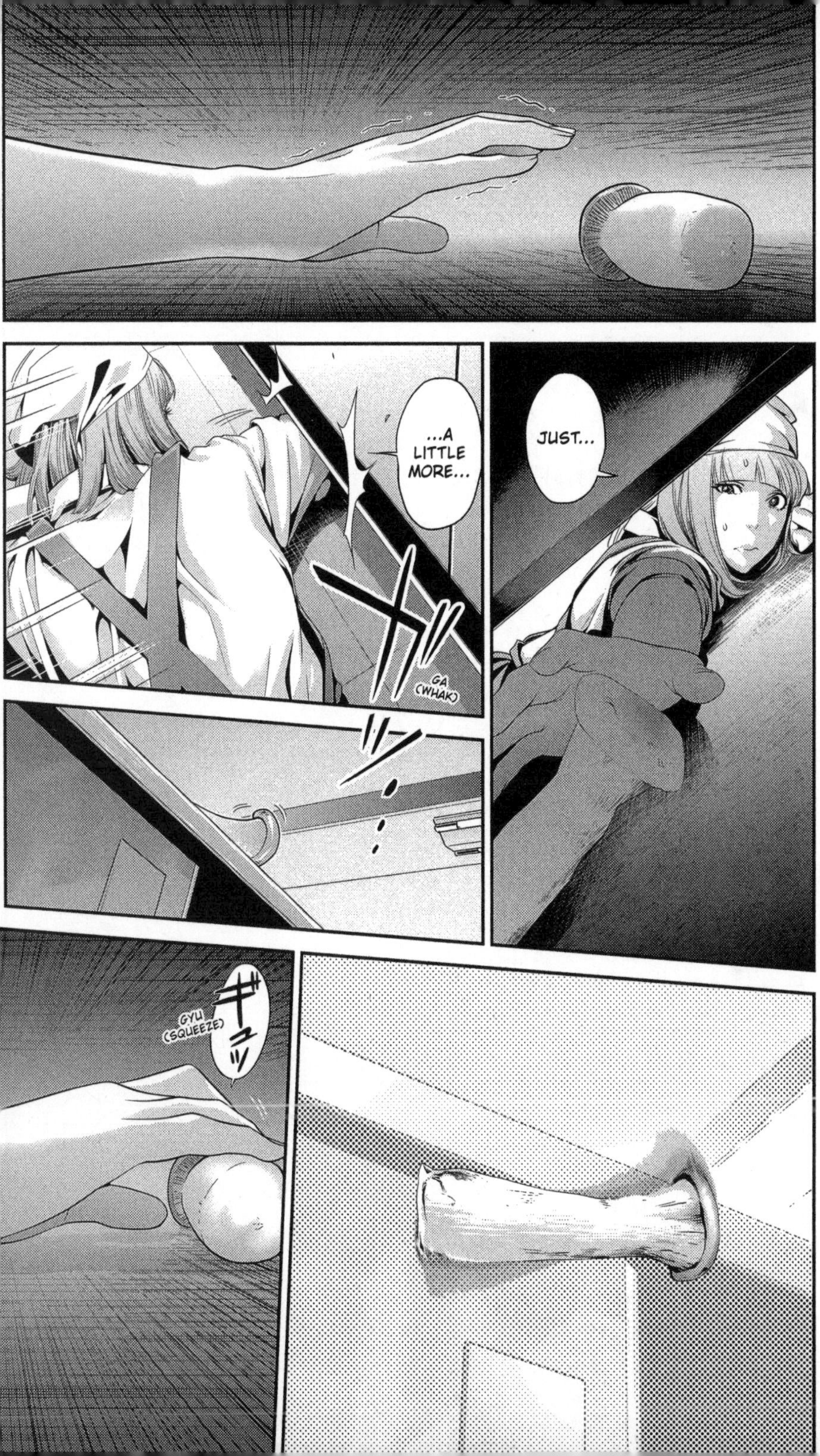
JUST...
...A LITTLE MORE...
GA (WHAK)
ギュッ
GYU (SQUEEZE)

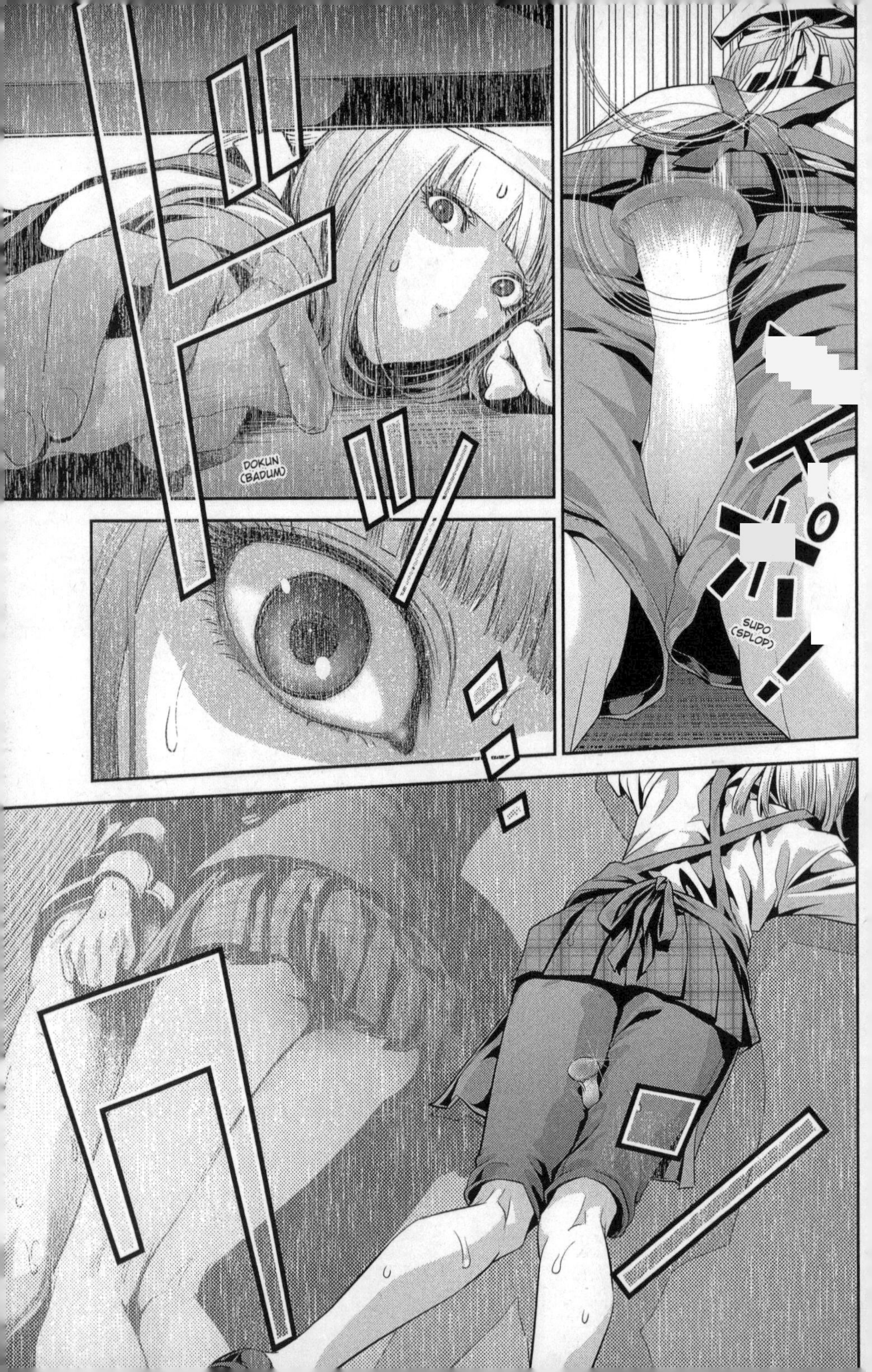
SUPO (SPLOP)
DOKUN (BADUM)

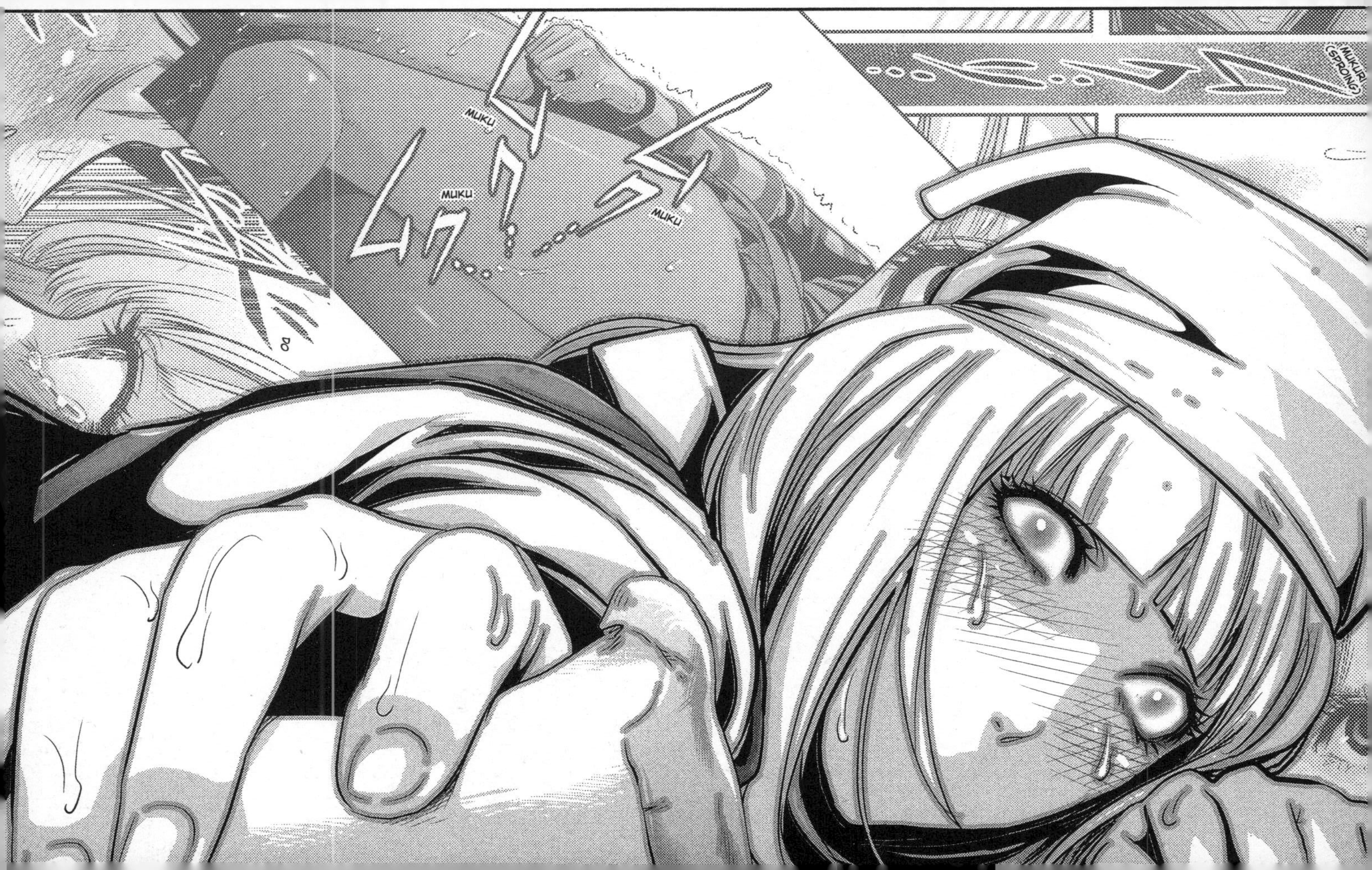
MUKURI (SPROING)
MUKU
MUKU
MUKU
DO

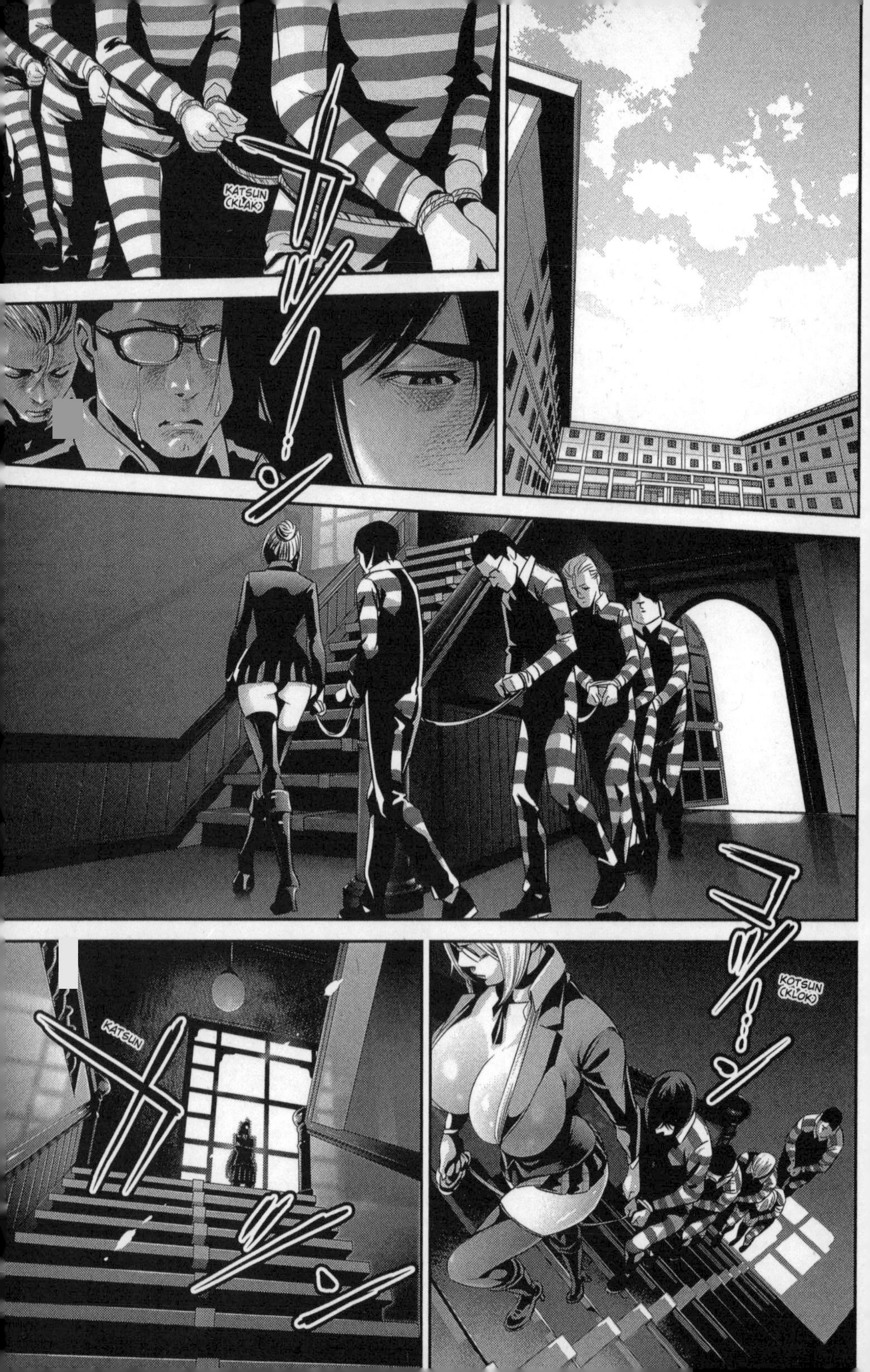
KATSUN (KLAK)
KOTSUN (KLOK)
KATSUN

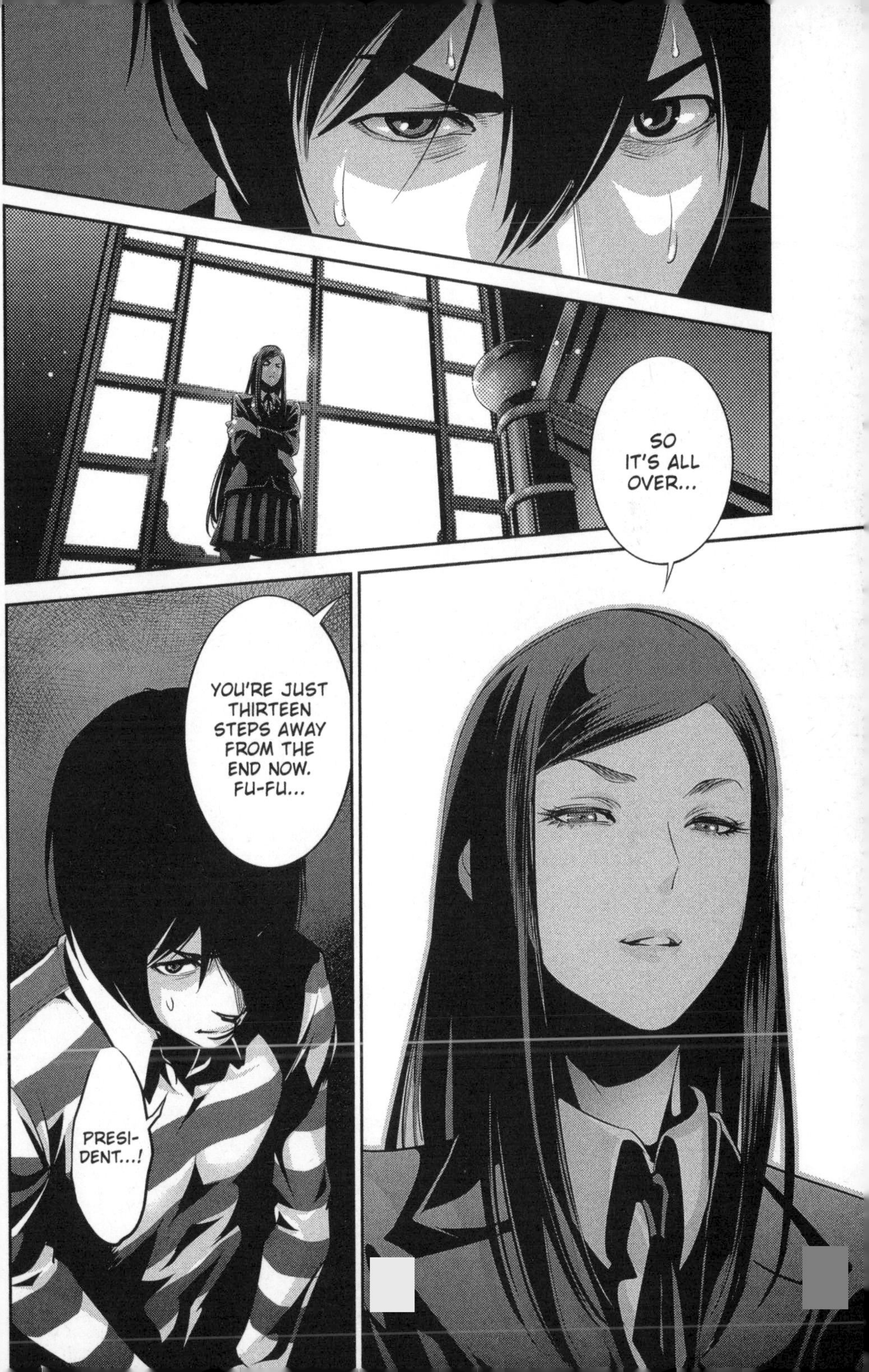
SO IT'S ALL OVER...
YOU'RE JUST THIRTEEN STEPS AWAY FROM THE END NOW. FU-FU...
PRESI-DENT...!

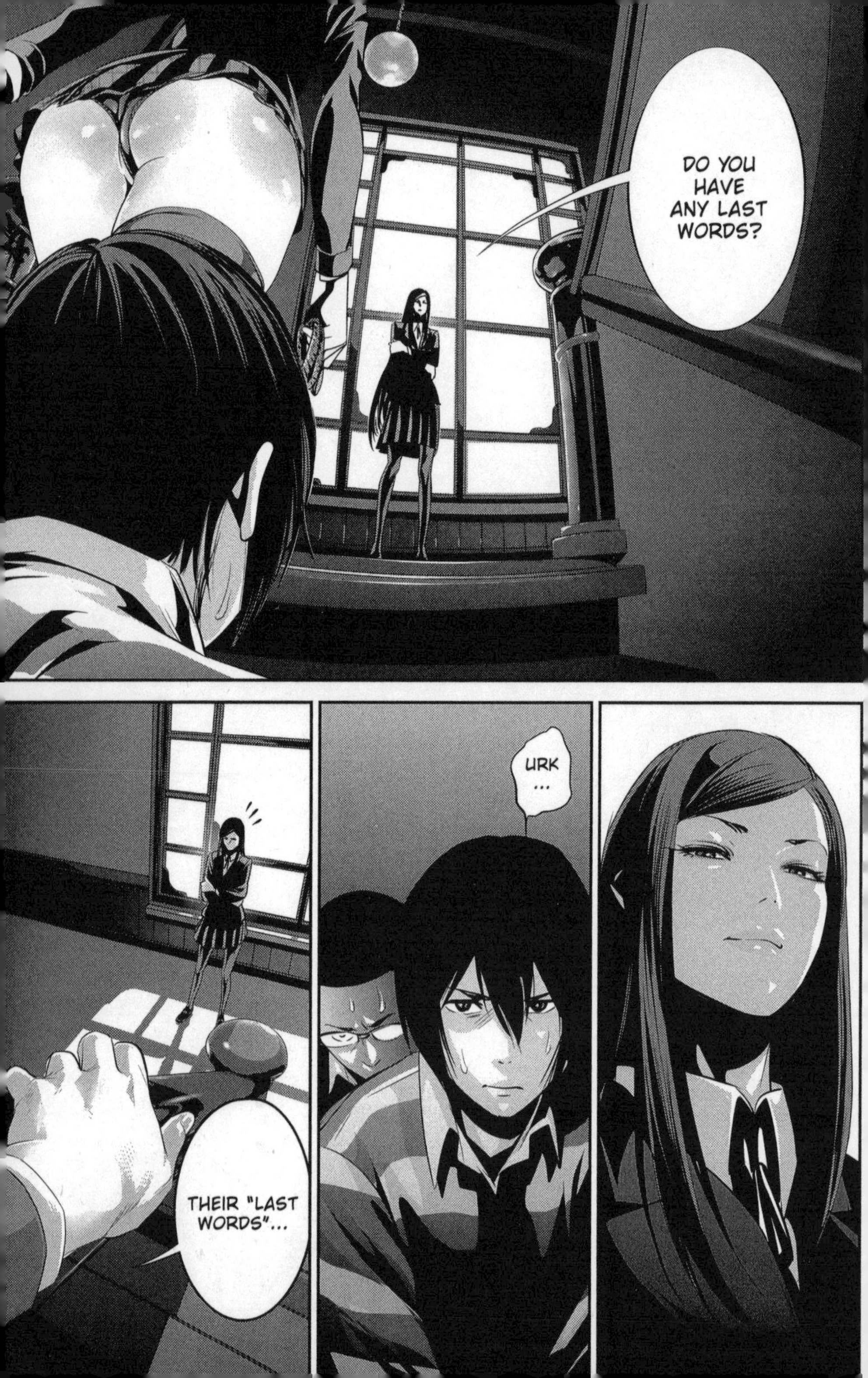
DO YOU HAVE ANY LAST WORDS?
URK ...
THEIR "LAST WORDS"...

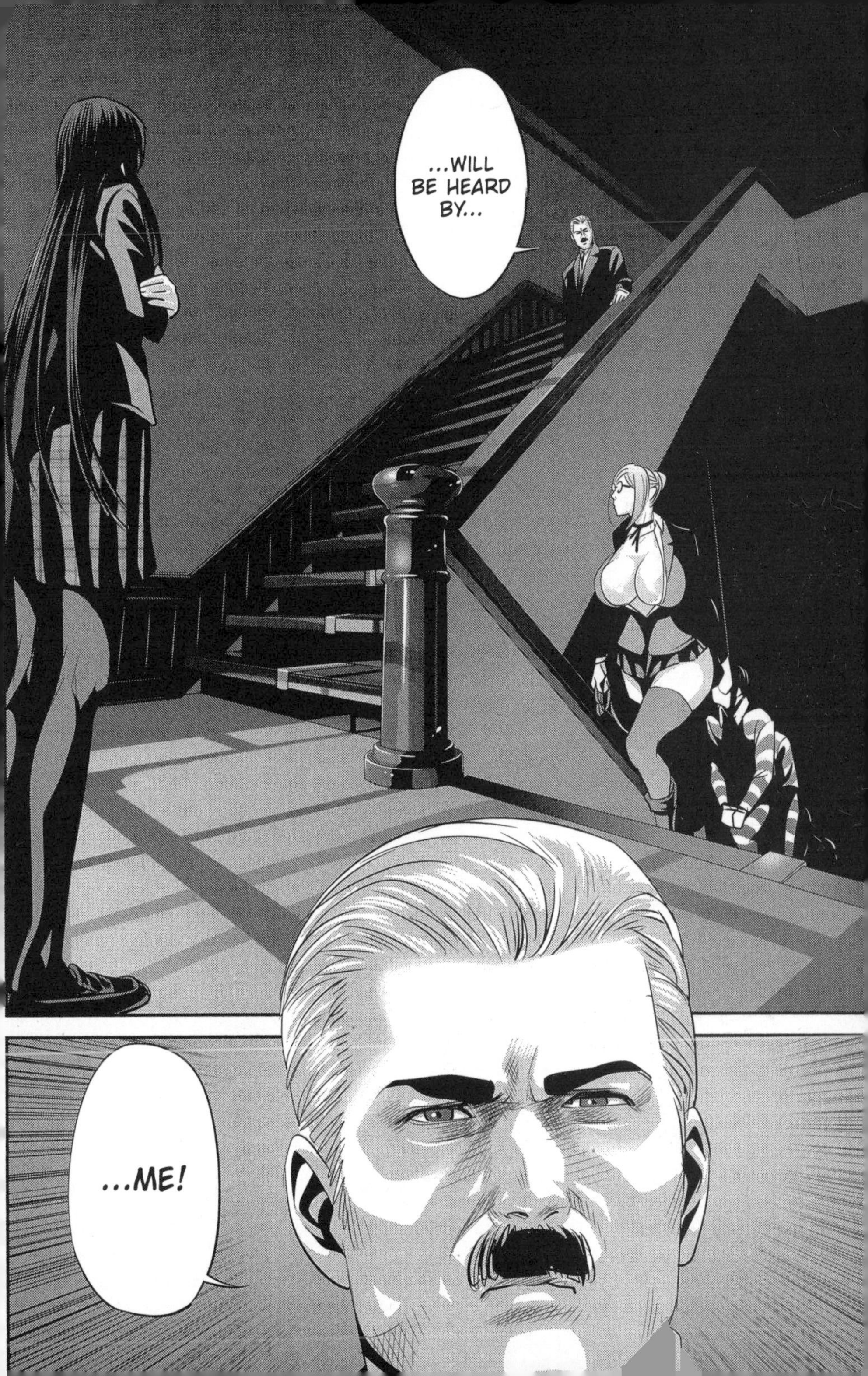
...WILL BE HEARD BY...
...ME!

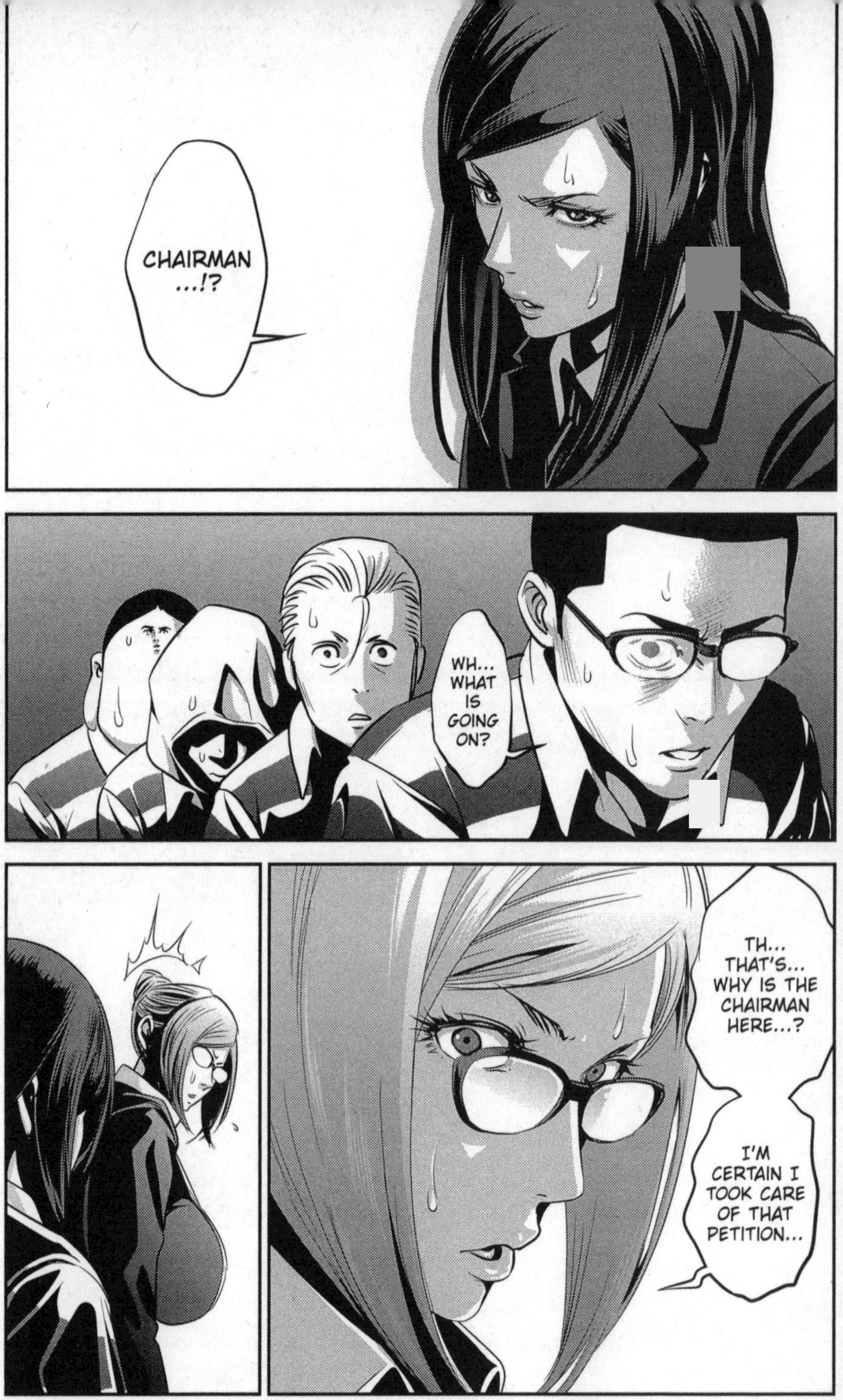
CHAIRMAN ...!?
WH... WHAT IS GOING ON?
TH... THAT'S... WHY IS THE CHAIRMAN HERE...?
I'M CERTAIN I TOOK CARE OF THAT PETITION...

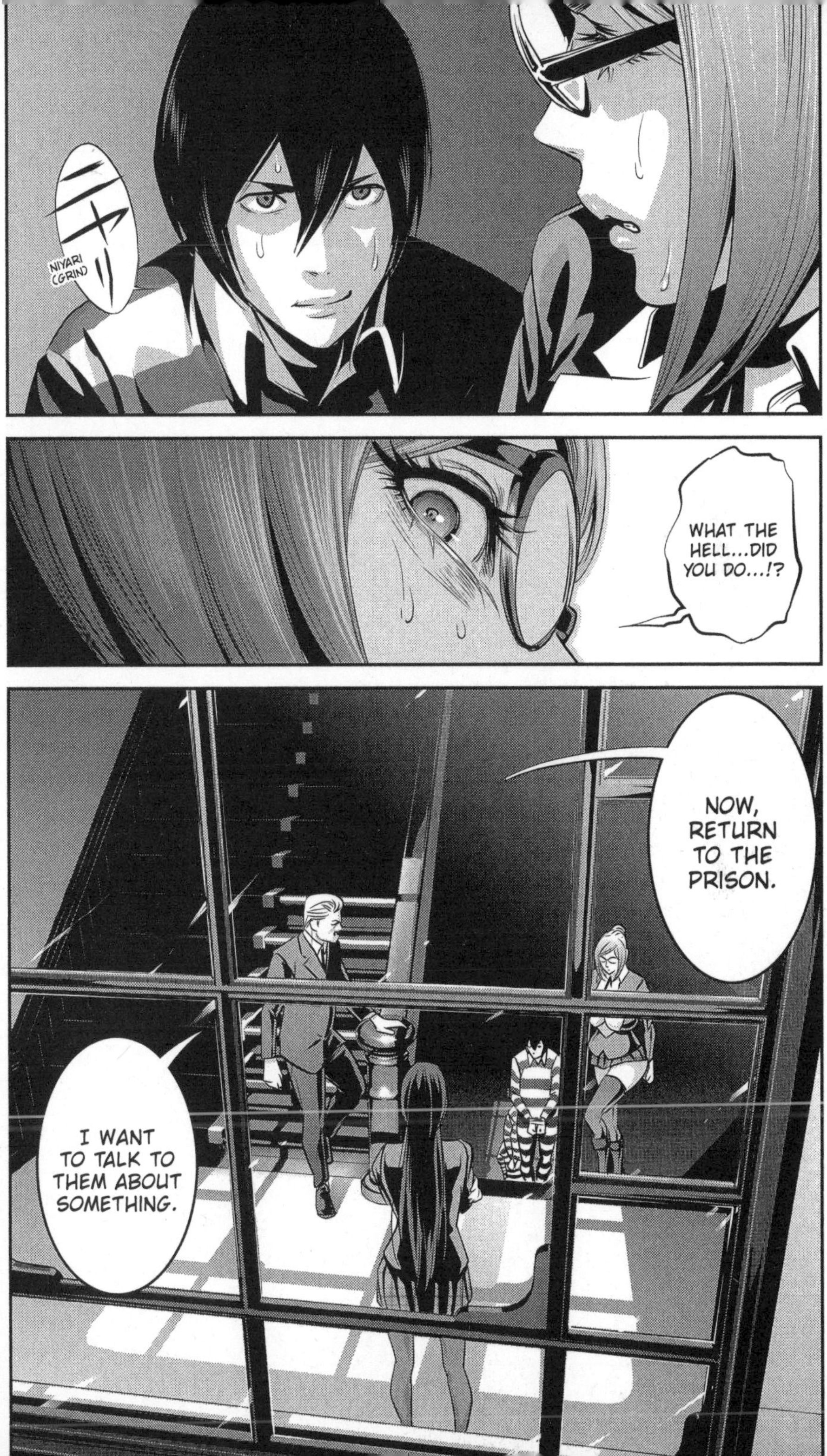
ニヤリ
NIYARI (GRIN)
WHAT THE HELL...DID YOU DO...!?
NOW, RETURN TO THE PRISON.
I WANT TO TALK TO THEM ABOUT SOMETHING.

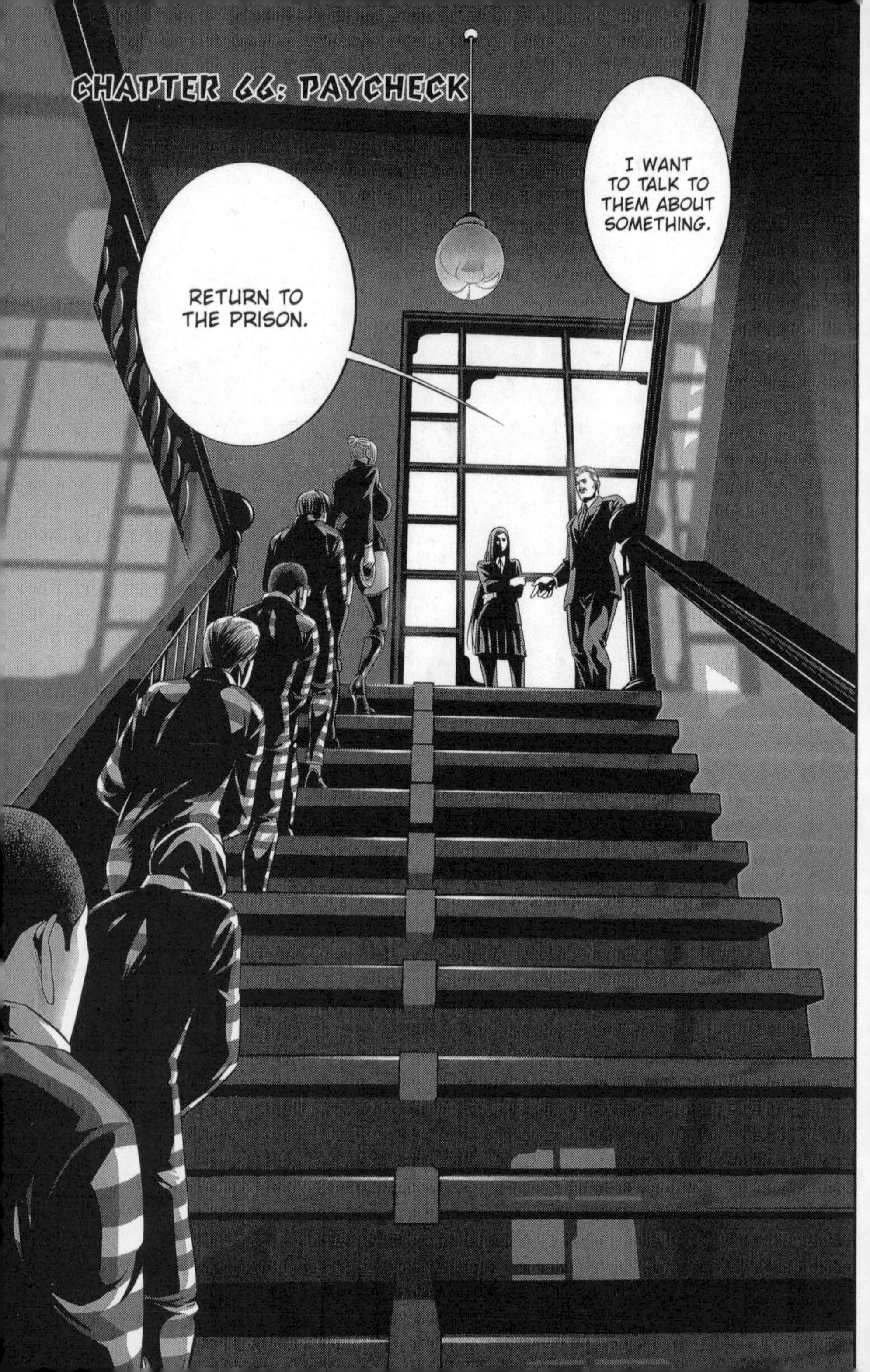
CHAPTER 66: PAYCHECK
I WANT TO TALK TO THEM ABOUT SOMETHING.
RETURN TO THE PRISON.

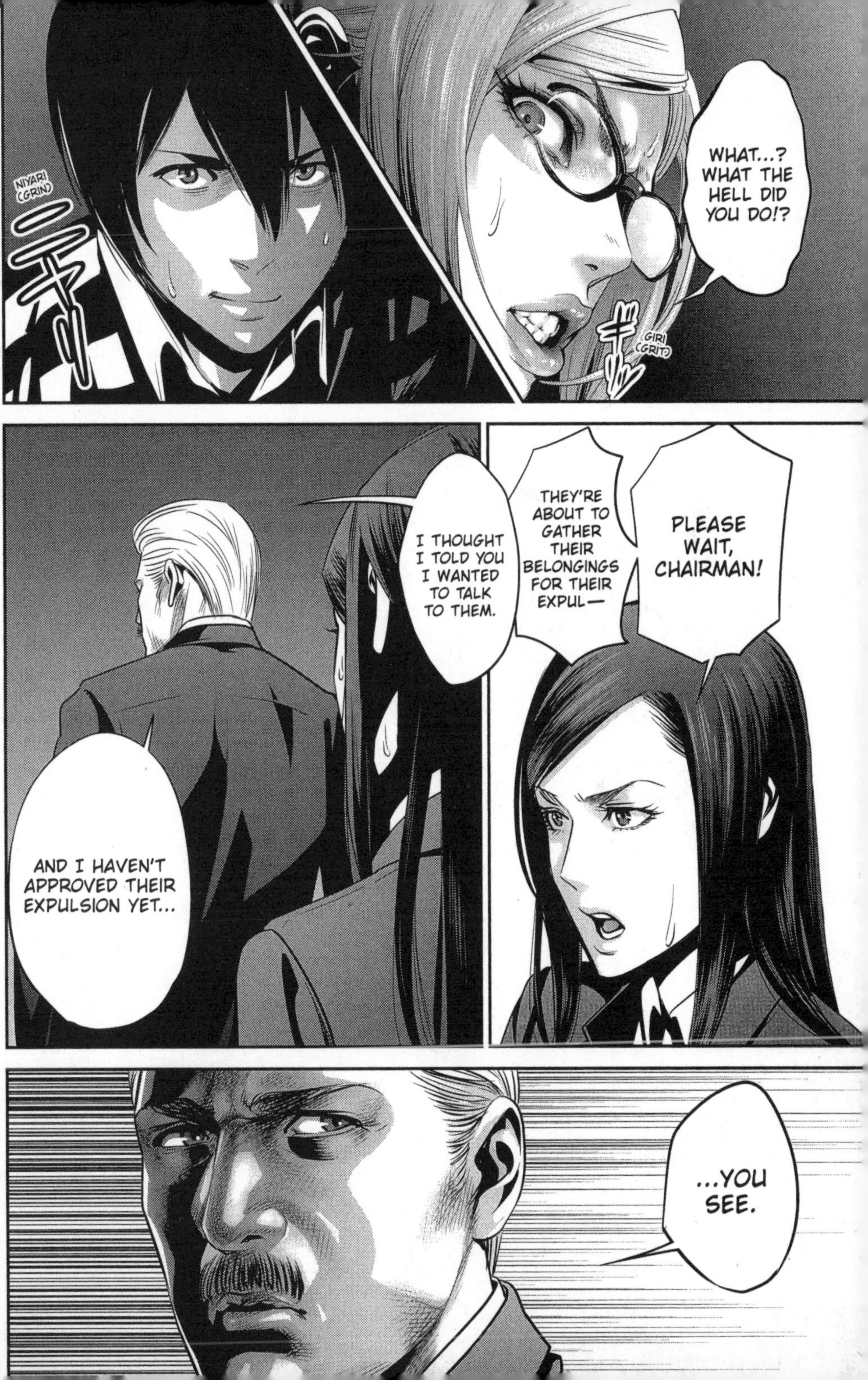
WHAT...? WHAT THE HELL DID YOU DO!?
GIRI (GRIT)
NIYARI (GRIN)
PLEASE WAIT, CHAIRMAN!
THEY'RE ABOUT TO GATHER THEIR BELONGINGS FOR THEIR EXPUL—
I THOUGHT I TOLD YOU I WANTED TO TALK TO THEM.
AND I HAVEN'T APPROVED THEIR EXPULSION YET...
...YOU SEE.

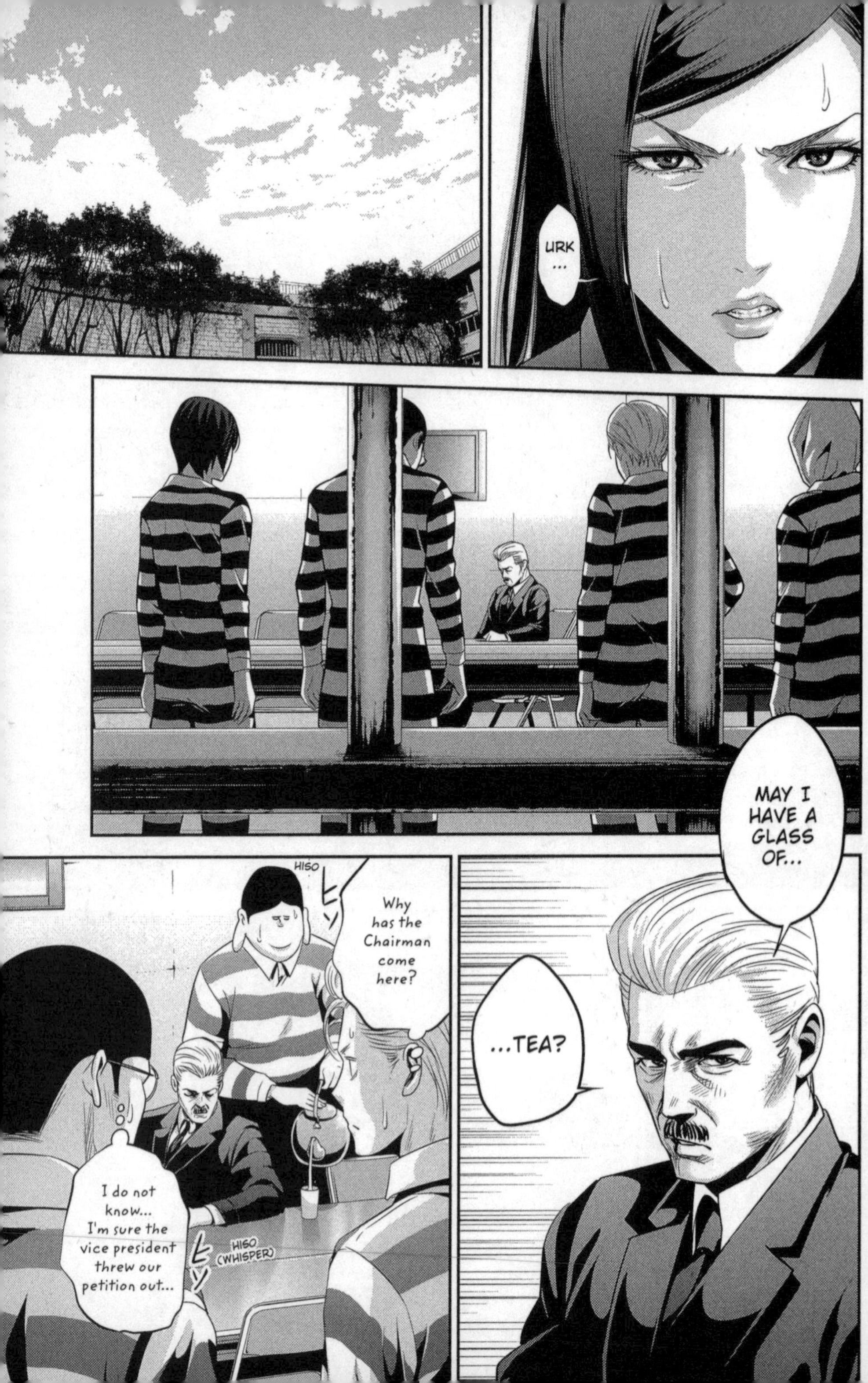
URK ...
MAY I HAVE A GLASS OF...
...TEA?
HISO
Why has the Chairman come here?
I do not know... I'm sure the vice president threw our petition out...
HISO (WHISPER)

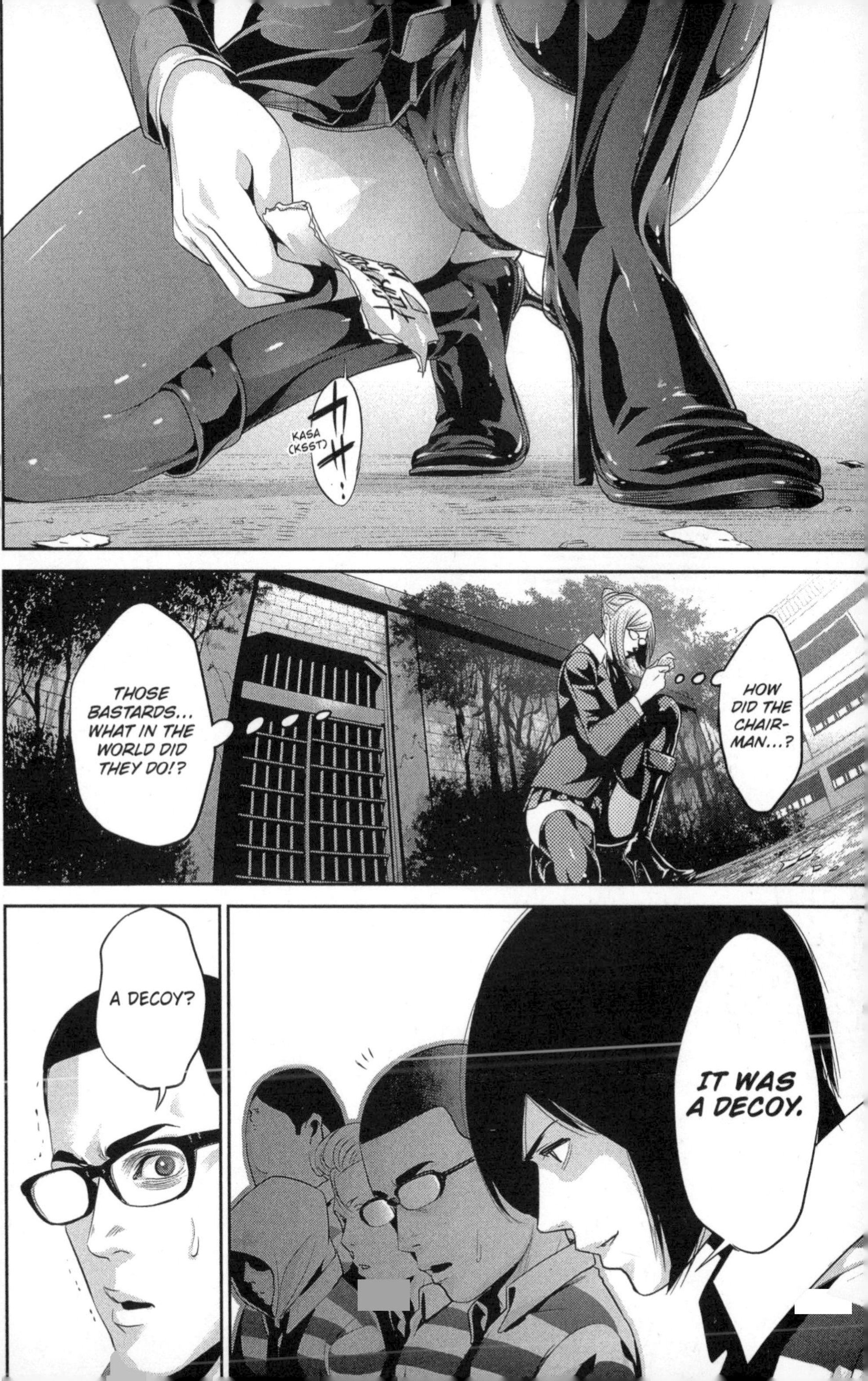
KASA (KSST)
HOW DID THE CHAIRMAN...?
THOSE BASTARDS... WHAT IN THE WORLD DID THEY DO!?
IT WAS A DECOY.
A DECOY?

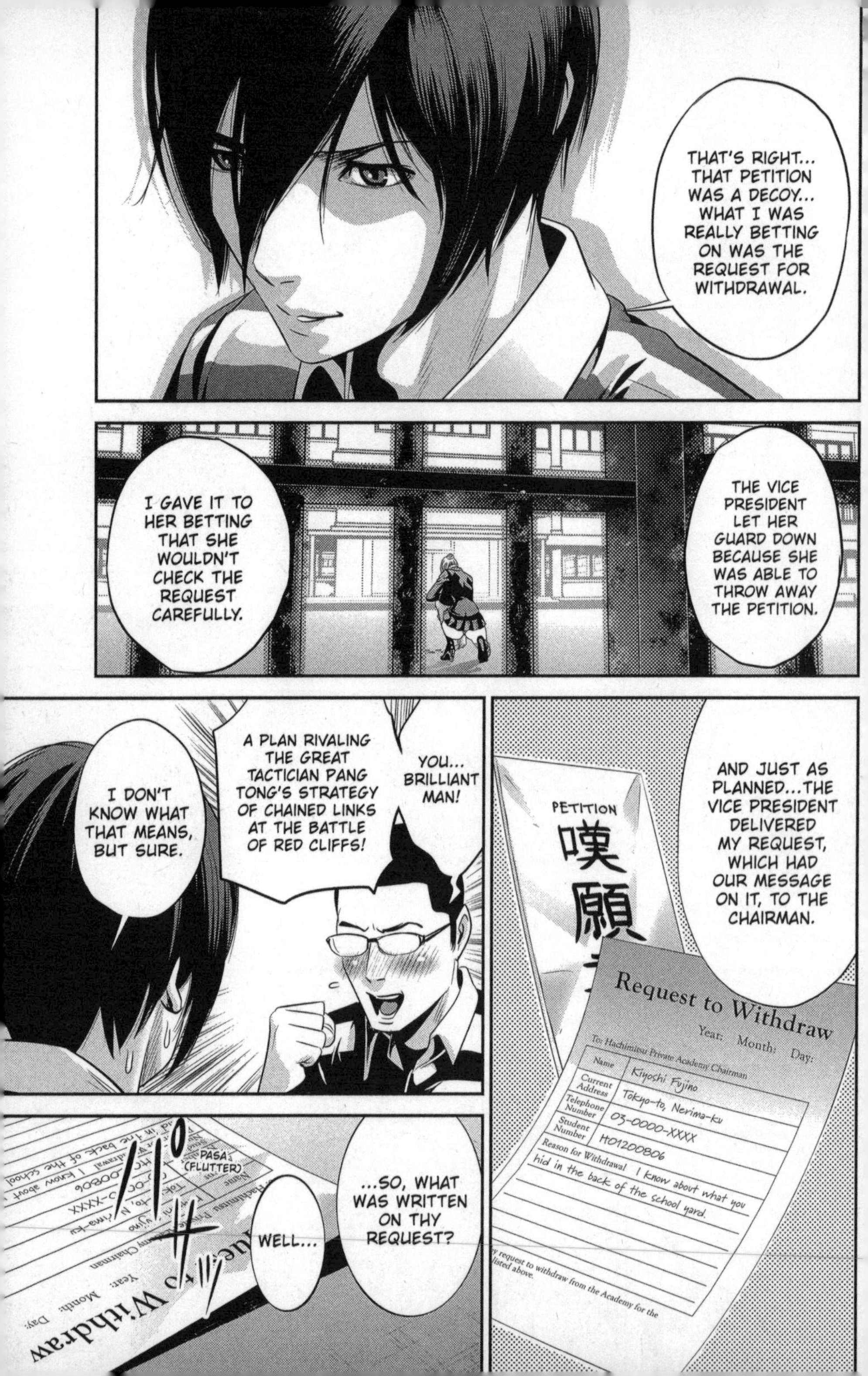
THAT'S RIGHT... THAT PETITION WAS A DECOY... WHAT I WAS REALLY BETTING ON WAS THE REQUEST FOR WITHDRAWAL.
THE VICE PRESIDENT LET HER GUARD DOWN BECAUSE SHE WAS ABLE TO THROW AWAY THE PETITION.
I GAVE IT TO HER BETTING THAT SHE WOULDN'T CHECK THE REQUEST CAREFULLY.
AND JUST AS PLANNED...THE VICE PRESIDENT DELIVERED MY REQUEST, WHICH HAD OUR MESSAGE ON IT, TO THE CHAIRMAN.
PETITION
嘆願
Request to Withdraw
Year: Month: Day:
To: Hachimitsu Private Academy Chairman
Name Kiyoshi Fujino
Current Address Tokyo-to, Nerima-ku
Telephone Number 03-0000-XXXX
Student Number H01200806
Reason for Withdrawal I know about what you hid in the back of the school yard.
YOU... BRILLIANT MAN!
A PLAN RIVALING THE GREAT TACTICIAN PANG TONG'S STRATEGY OF CHAINED LINKS AT THE BATTLE OF RED CLIFFS!
I DON'T KNOW WHAT THAT MEANS, BUT SURE.
...SO, WHAT WAS WRITTEN ON THY REQUEST?
WELL...
PASA (FLUTTER)

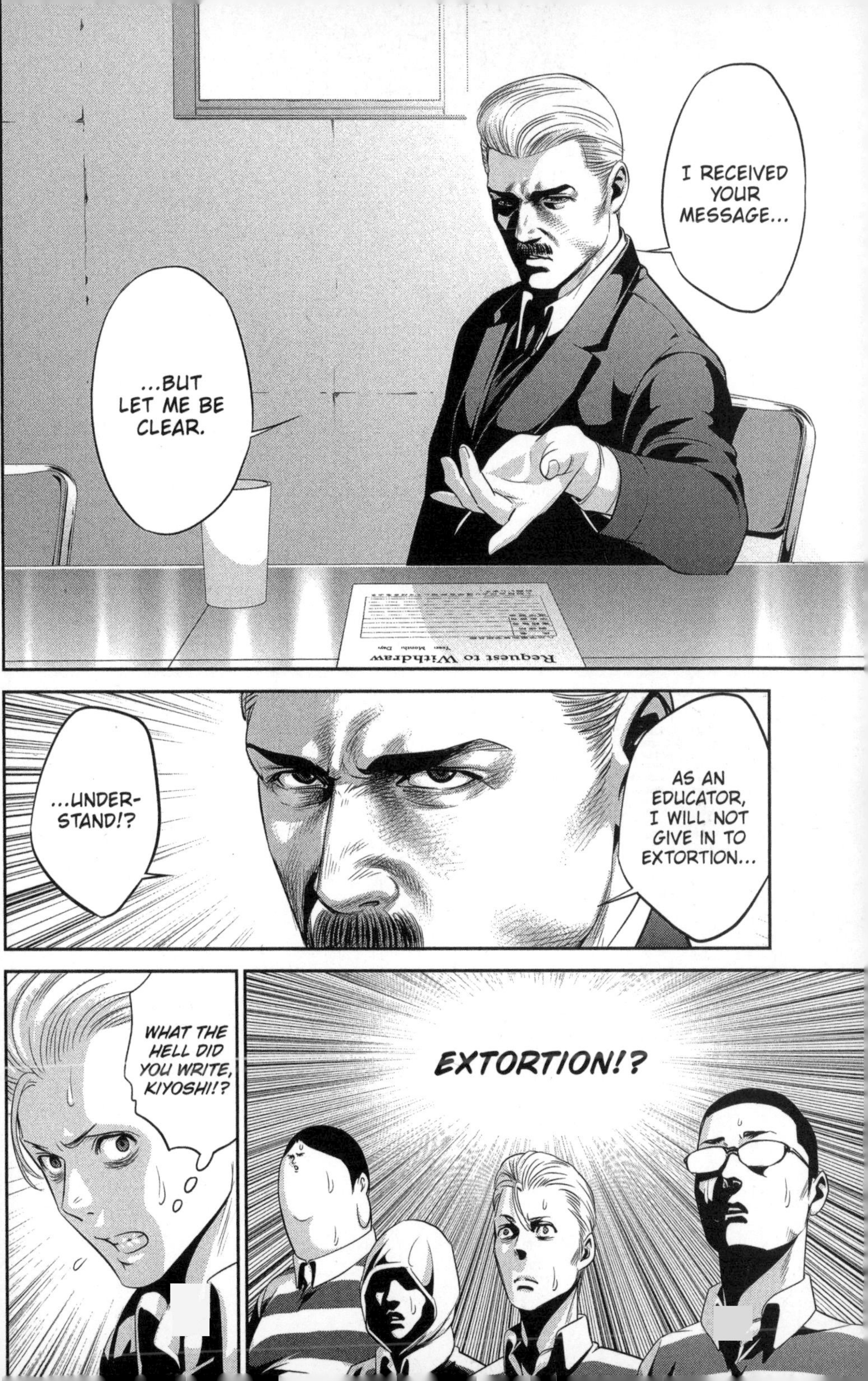
I RECEIVED YOUR MESSAGE...
...BUT LET ME BE CLEAR.
Request to Withdraw
AS AN EDUCATOR, I WILL NOT GIVE IN TO EXTORTION...
...UNDER-STAND!?
EXTORTION!?
WHAT THE HELL DID YOU WRITE, KIYOSHI!?

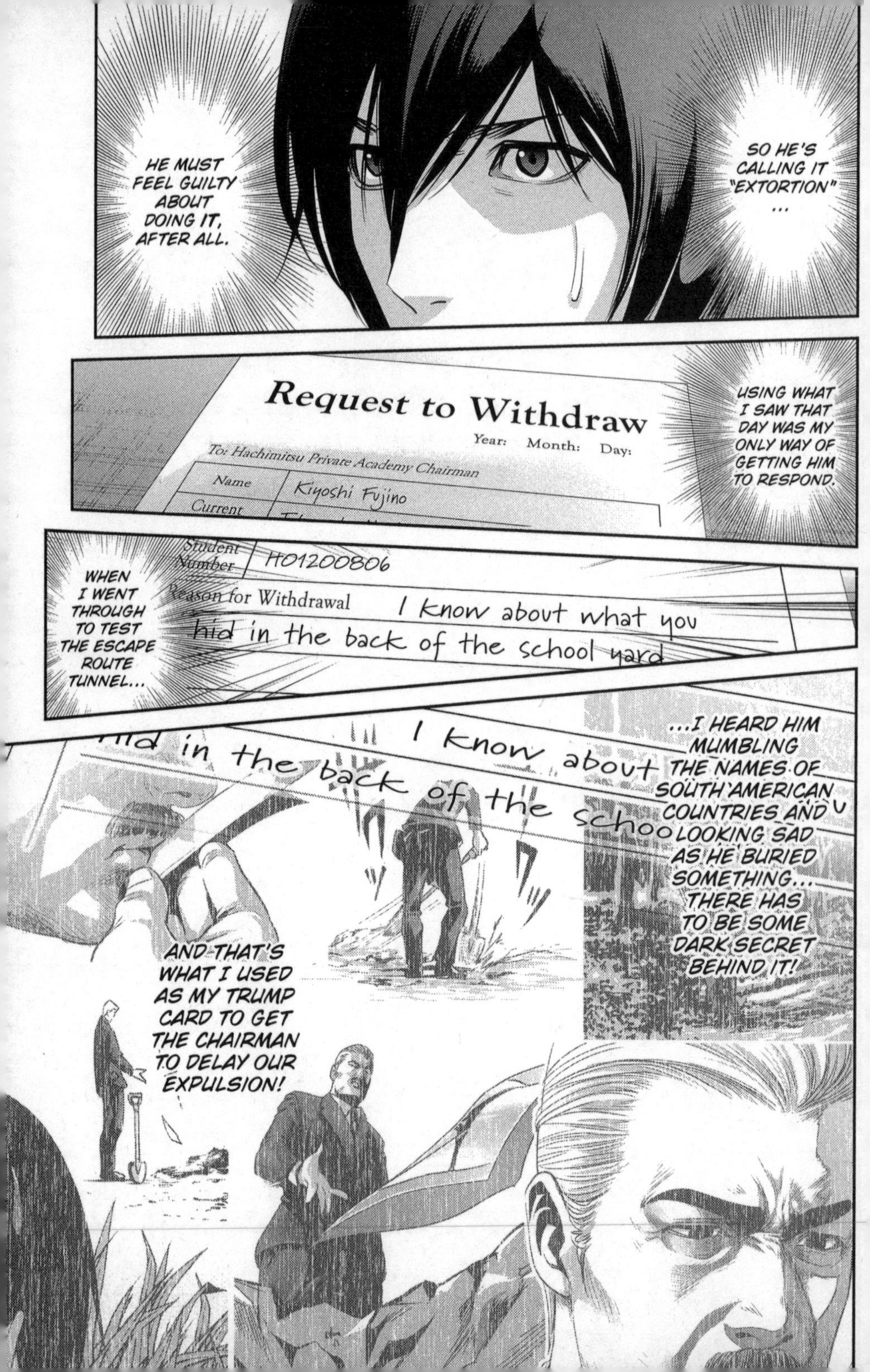

SO HE'S CALLING IT "EXTORTION"...
HE MUST FEEL GUILTY ABOUT DOING IT, AFTER ALL.
USING WHAT I SAW THAT DAY WAS MY ONLY WAY OF GETTING HIM TO RESPOND.
Request to Withdraw
Year: Month: Day:
To: Hachimitsu Private Academy Chairman
Name
Kiyoshi Fujino
Current
Student Number
H01200806
Reason for Withdrawal
I know about what you hid in the back of the school yard
WHEN I WENT THROUGH TO TEST THE ESCAPE ROUTE TUNNEL...
...I HEARD HIM MUMBLING THE NAMES OF SOUTH AMERICAN COUNTRIES AND LOOKING SAD AS HE BURIED SOMETHING... THERE HAS TO BE SOME DARK SECRET BEHIND IT!
I know about
hid in the back of the schoo
AND THAT'S WHAT I USED AS MY TRUMP CARD TO GET THE CHAIRMAN TO DELAY OUR EXPULSION!

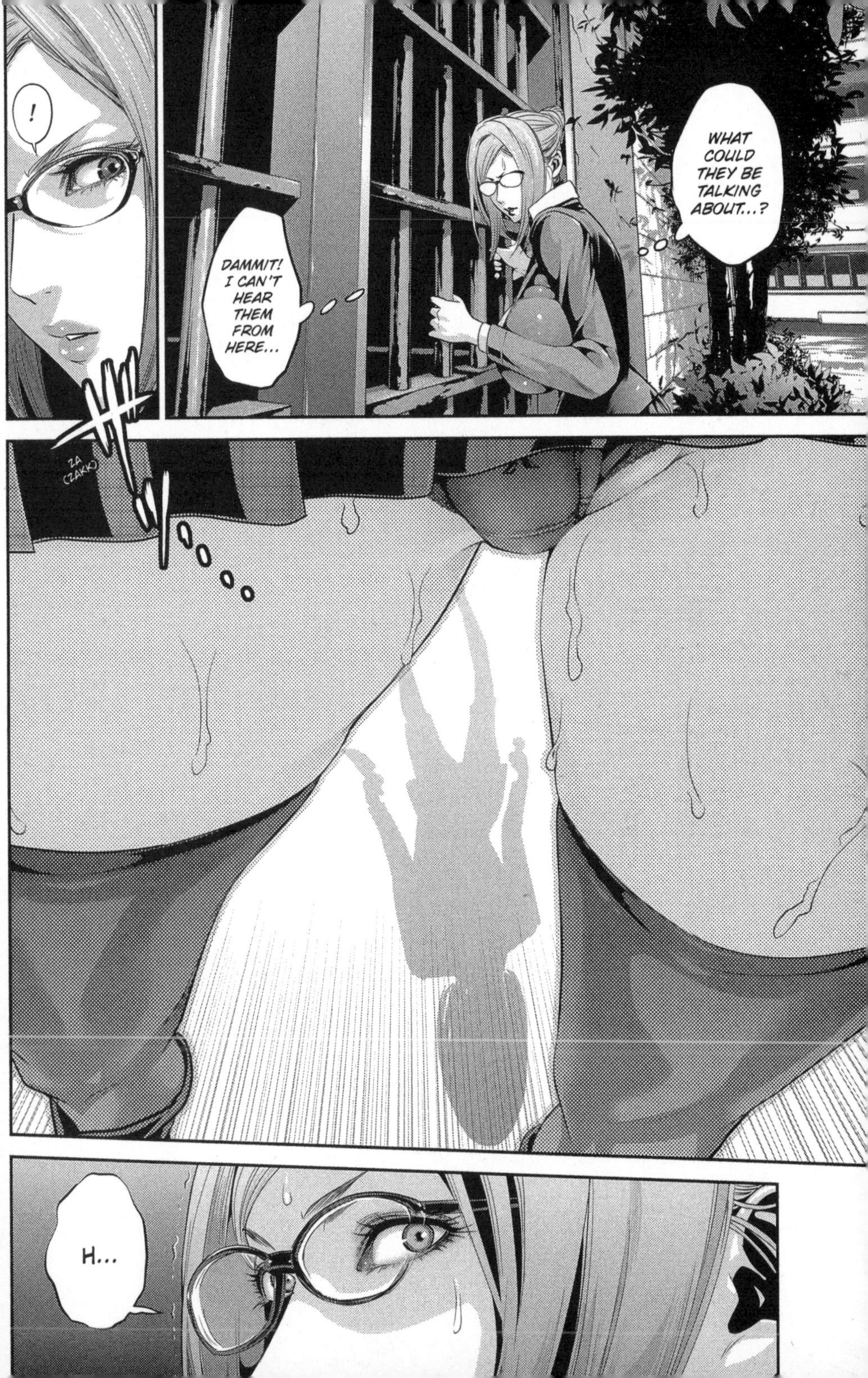
WHAT COULD THEY BE TALKING ABOUT...?
DAMMIT! I CAN'T HEAR THEM FROM HERE...
!
ZA (ZAKK)
H...

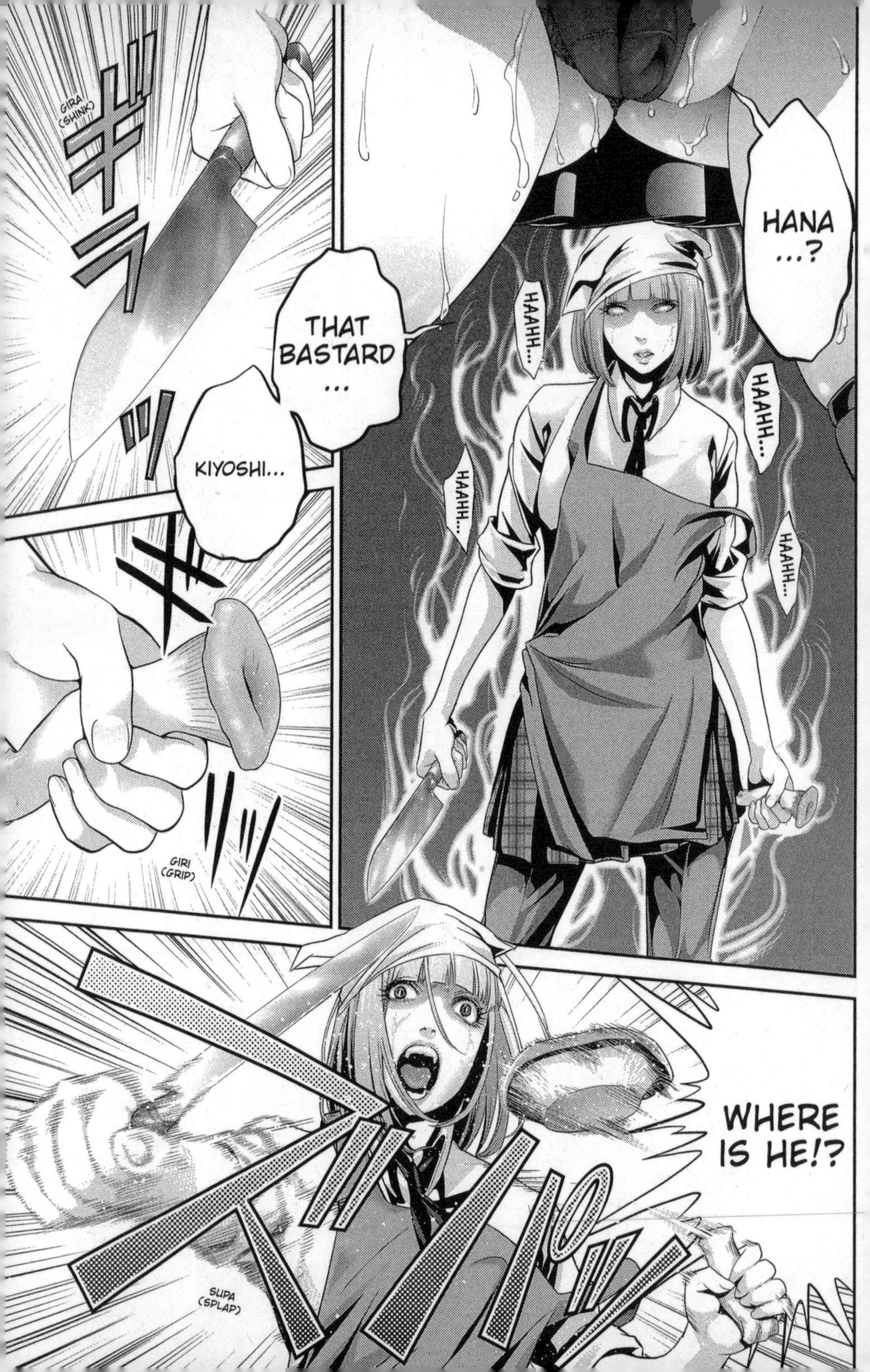
HANA ...?
THAT BASTARD ...
HAAHH...
HAAHH...
HAAHH...
HAAHH...
GIRA (SHINK)
KIYOSHI...
GIRI (GRIP)
WHERE IS HE!?
SUPA (SPLAP)

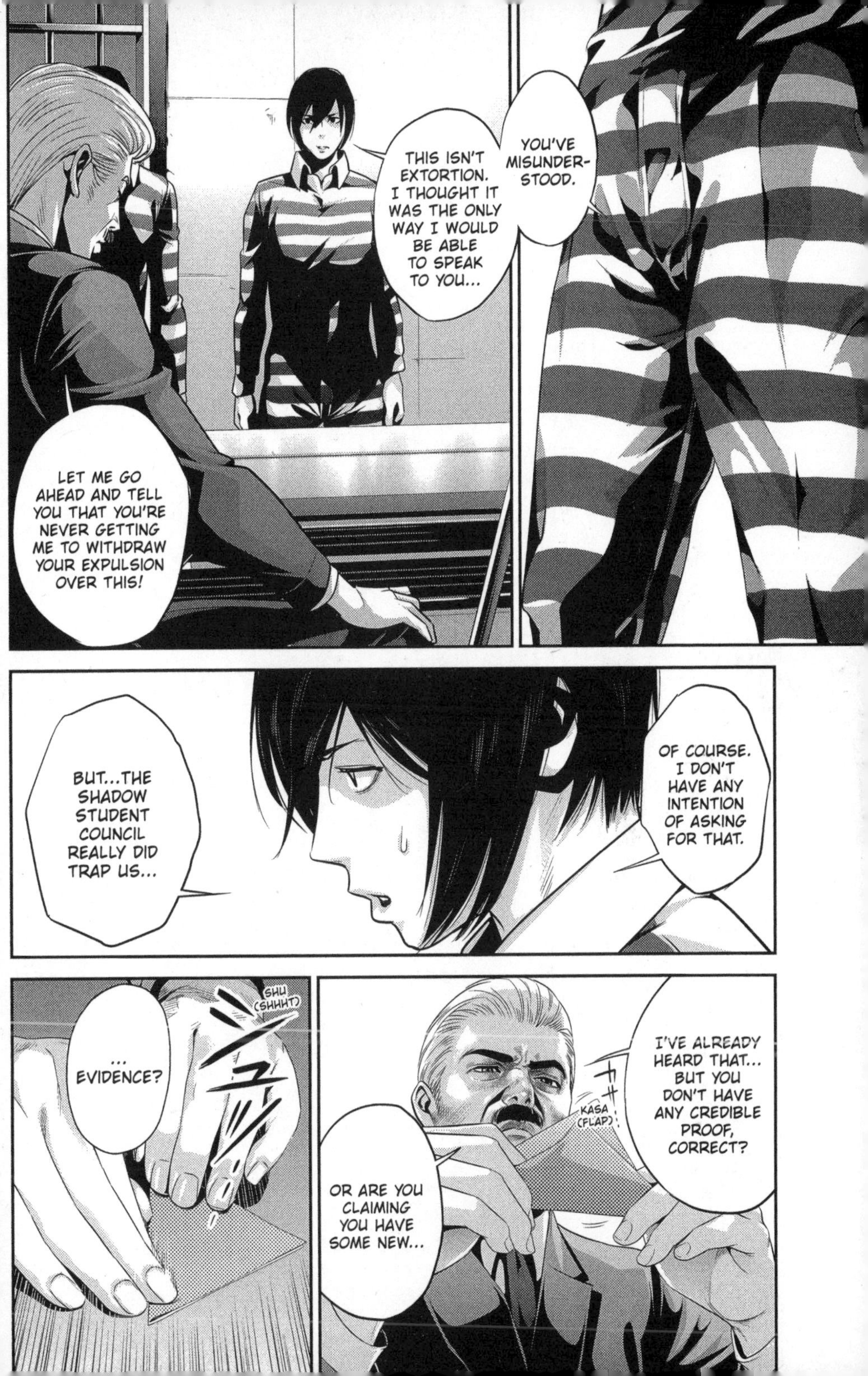
YOU'VE MISUNDER-STOOD.
THIS ISN'T EXTORTION. I THOUGHT IT WAS THE ONLY WAY I WOULD BE ABLE TO SPEAK TO YOU...
LET ME GO AHEAD AND TELL YOU THAT YOU'RE NEVER GETTING ME TO WITHDRAW YOUR EXPULSION OVER THIS!
OF COURSE. I DON'T HAVE ANY INTENTION OF ASKING FOR THAT.
BUT...THE SHADOW STUDENT COUNCIL REALLY DID TRAP US...
I'VE ALREADY HEARD THAT... BUT YOU DON'T HAVE ANY CREDIBLE PROOF, CORRECT?
KASA (FLAP)
OR ARE YOU CLAIMING YOU HAVE SOME NEW...
SHU (SHHHT)
...EVIDENCE?

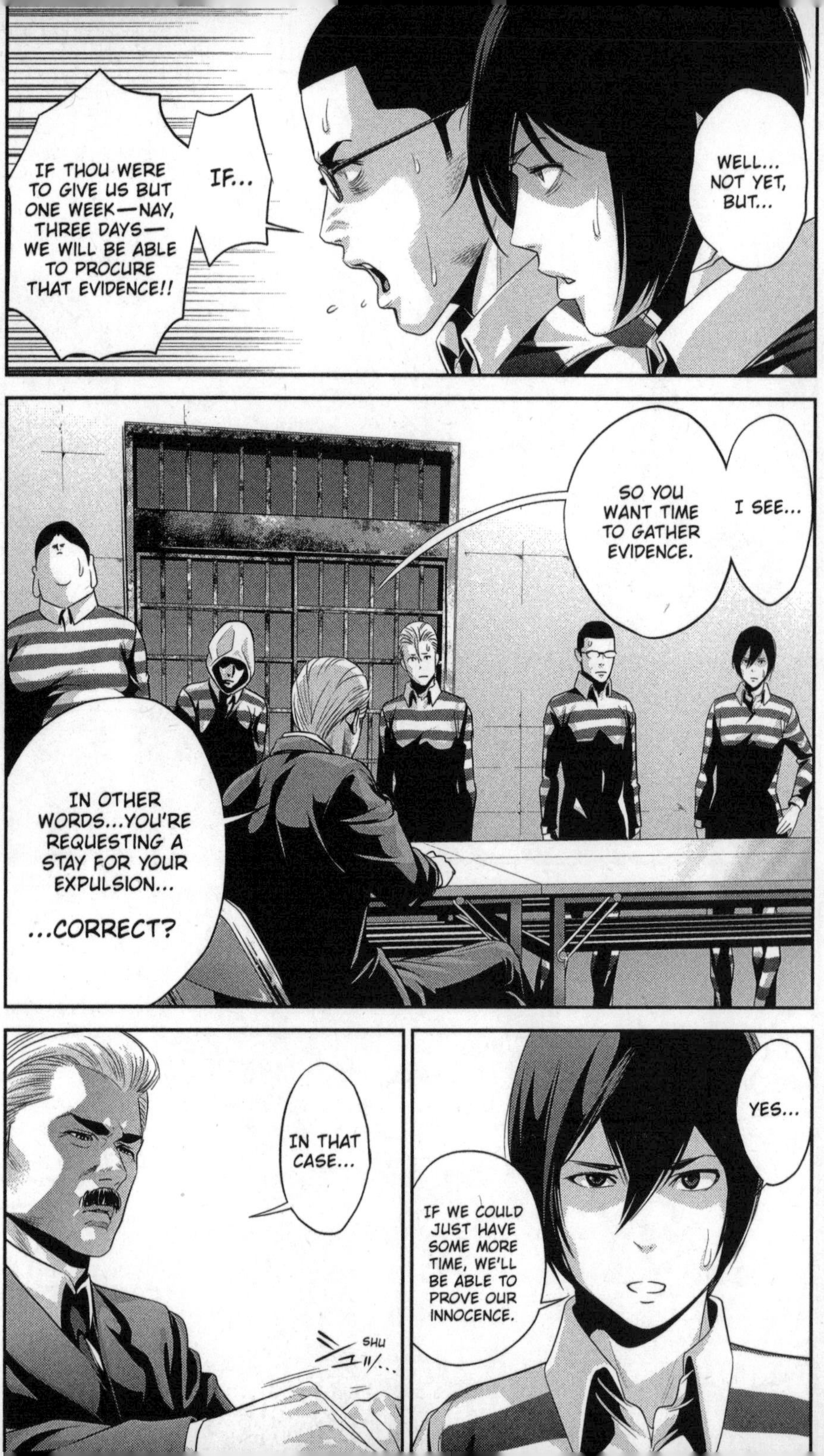
WELL... NOT YET, BUT...
IF...
IF THOU WERE TO GIVE US BUT ONE WEEK—NAY, THREE DAYS—WE WILL BE ABLE TO PROCURE THAT EVIDENCE!!
I SEE...
SO YOU WANT TIME TO GATHER EVIDENCE.
IN OTHER WORDS...YOU'RE REQUESTING A STAY FOR YOUR EXPULSION...
...CORRECT?
YES...
IF WE COULD JUST HAVE SOME MORE TIME, WE'LL BE ABLE TO PROVE OUR INNOCENCE.
IN THAT CASE...
SHU

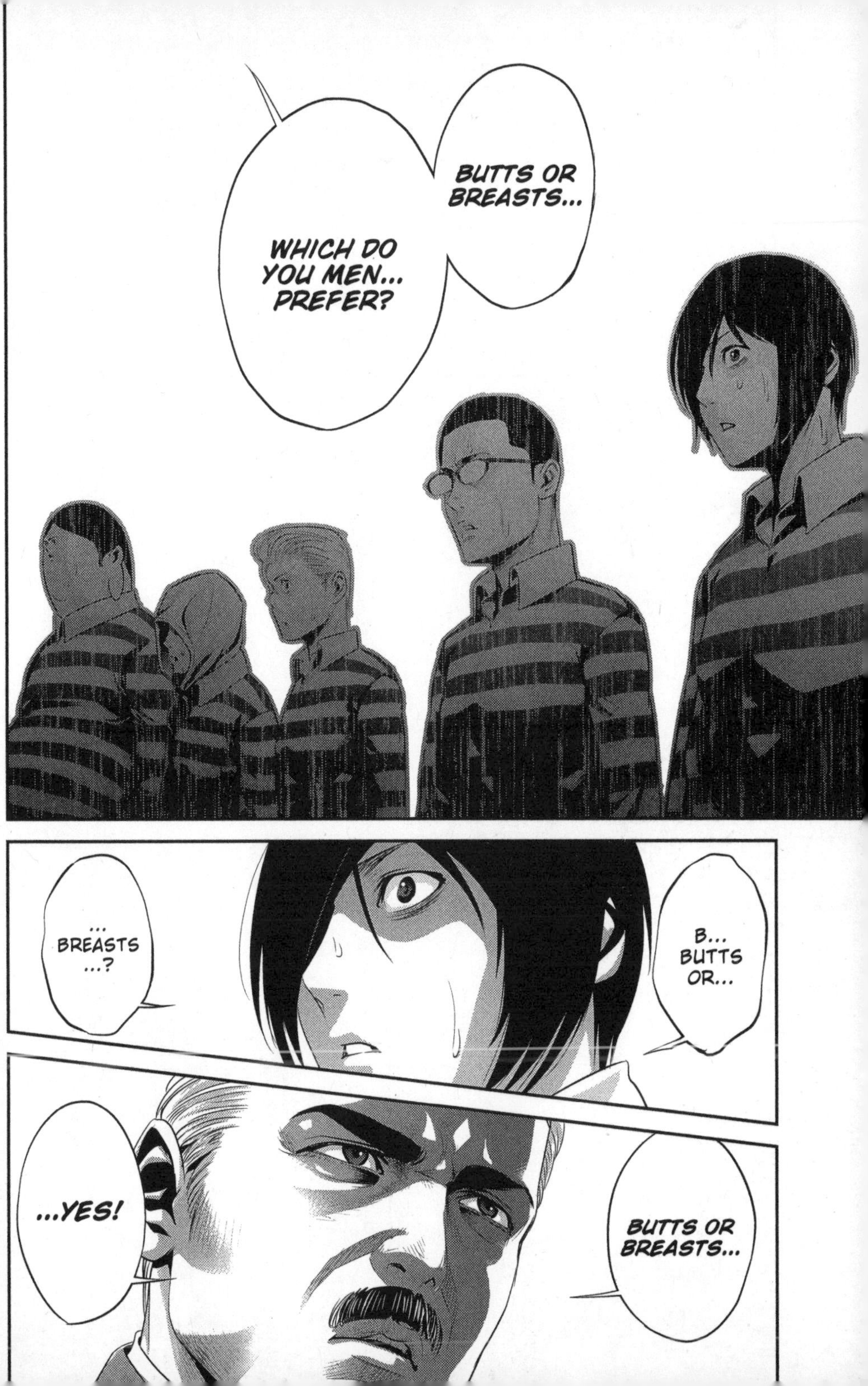
BUTTS OR BREASTS...
WHICH DO YOU MEN... PREFER?
B... BUTTS OR...
... BREASTS ...?
BUTTS OR BREASTS...
...YES!

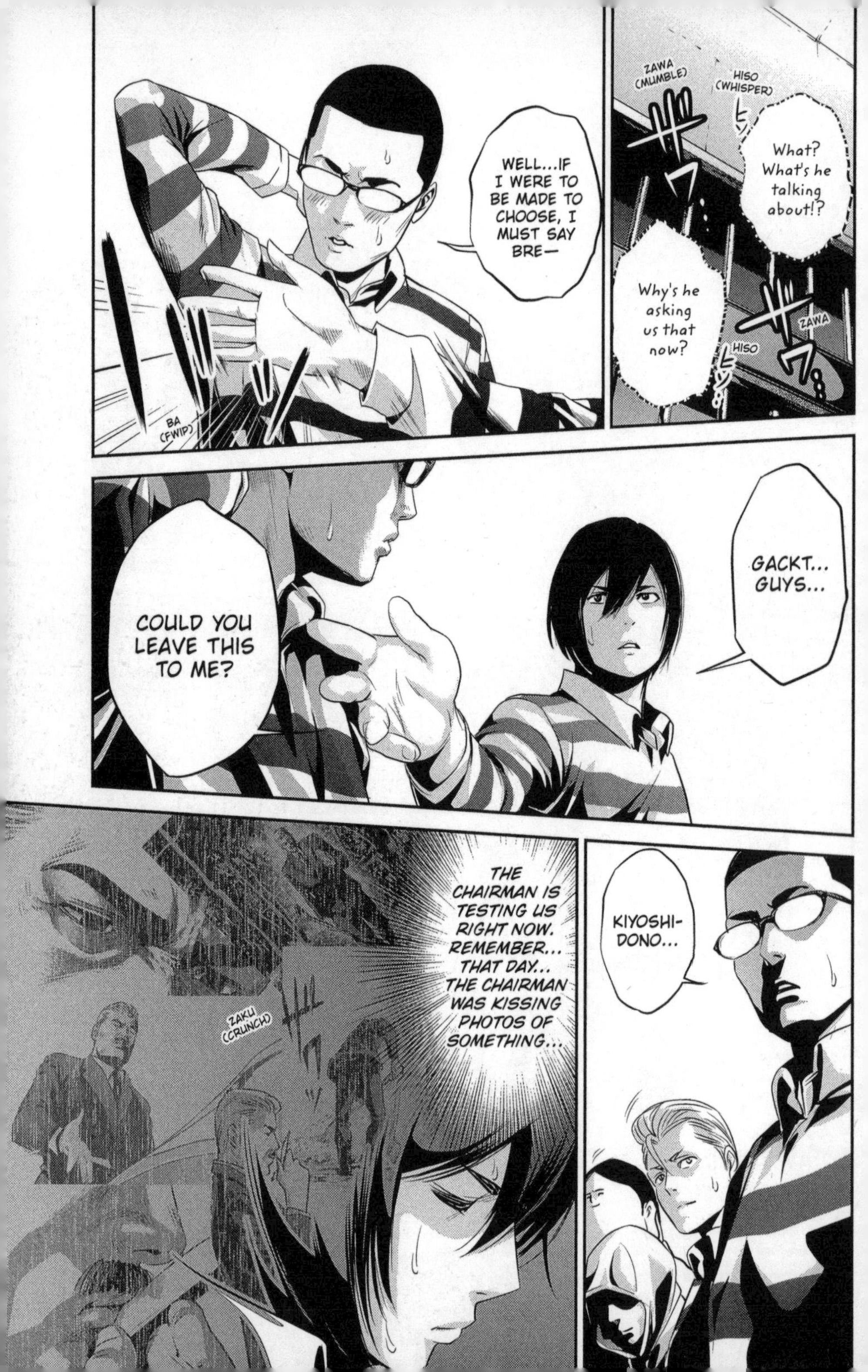
ZAWA (MUMBLE)
HISO (WHISPER)
What? What's he talking about!?
Why's he asking us that now?
ZAWA
HISO
WELL...IF I WERE TO BE MADE TO CHOOSE, I MUST SAY BRE—
BA (FWIP)
GACKT... GUYS...
COULD YOU LEAVE THIS TO ME?
KIYOSHI-DONO...
THE CHAIRMAN IS TESTING US RIGHT NOW. REMEMBER... THAT DAY... THE CHAIRMAN WAS KISSING PHOTOS OF SOMETHING...
ZAKU (CRUNCH)

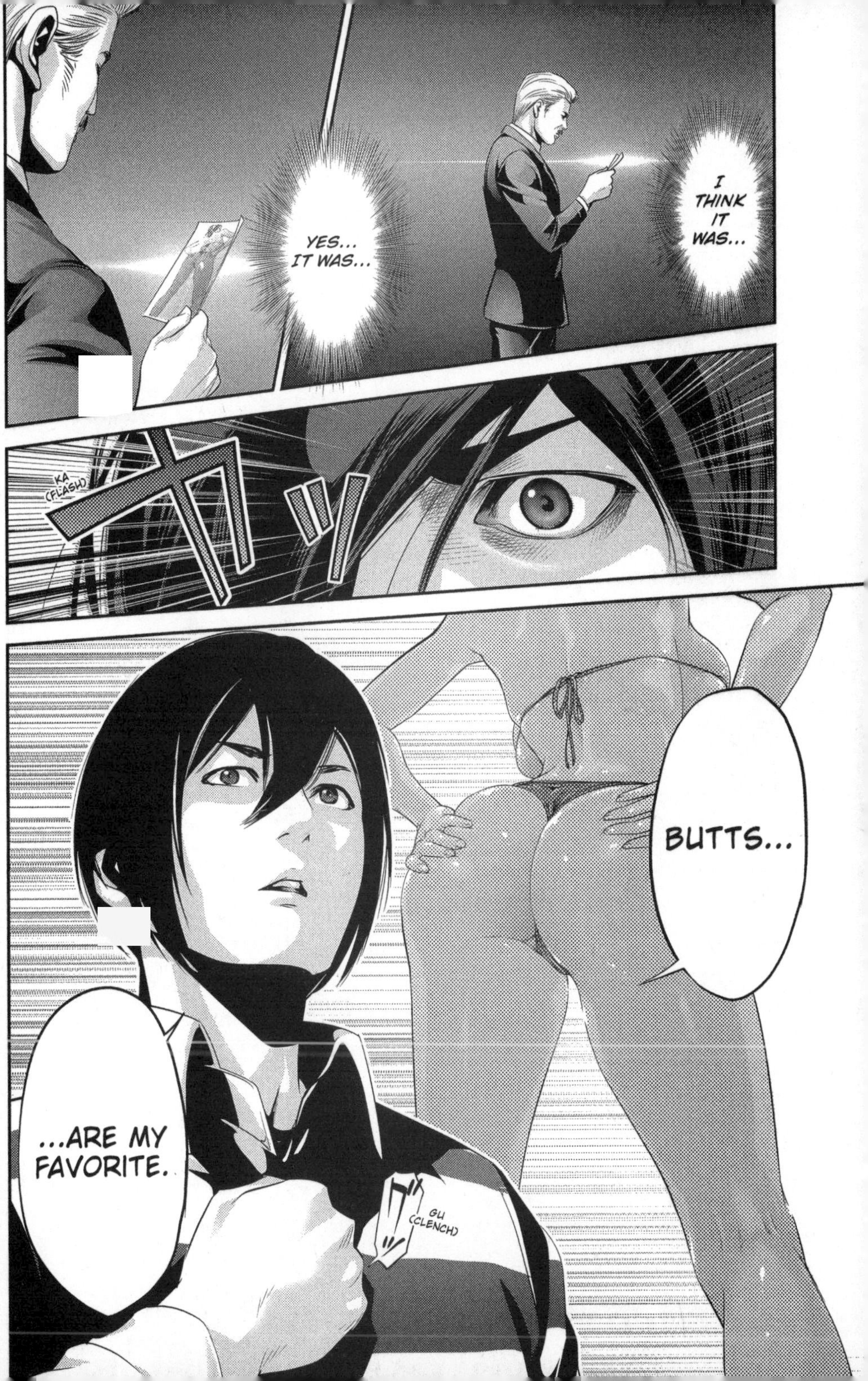
I THINK IT WAS...
YES... IT WAS...
KA (FLASH)
BUTTS...
...ARE MY FAVORITE.
GU (CLENCH)

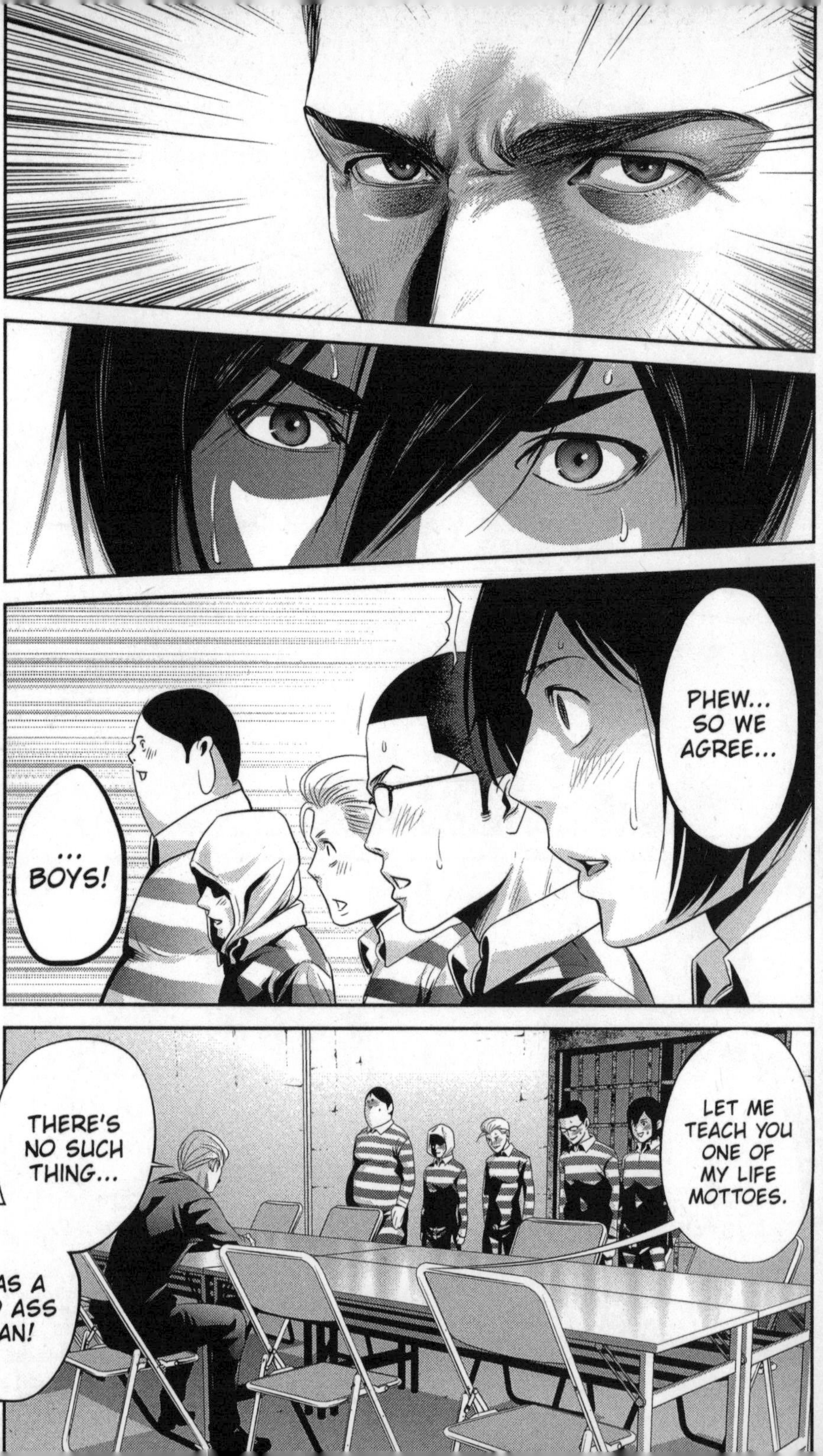
PHEW... SO WE AGREE...
... BOYS!
LET ME TEACH YOU ONE OF MY LIFE MOTTOES.
THERE'S NO SUCH THING...
...AS A BAD ASS MAN!

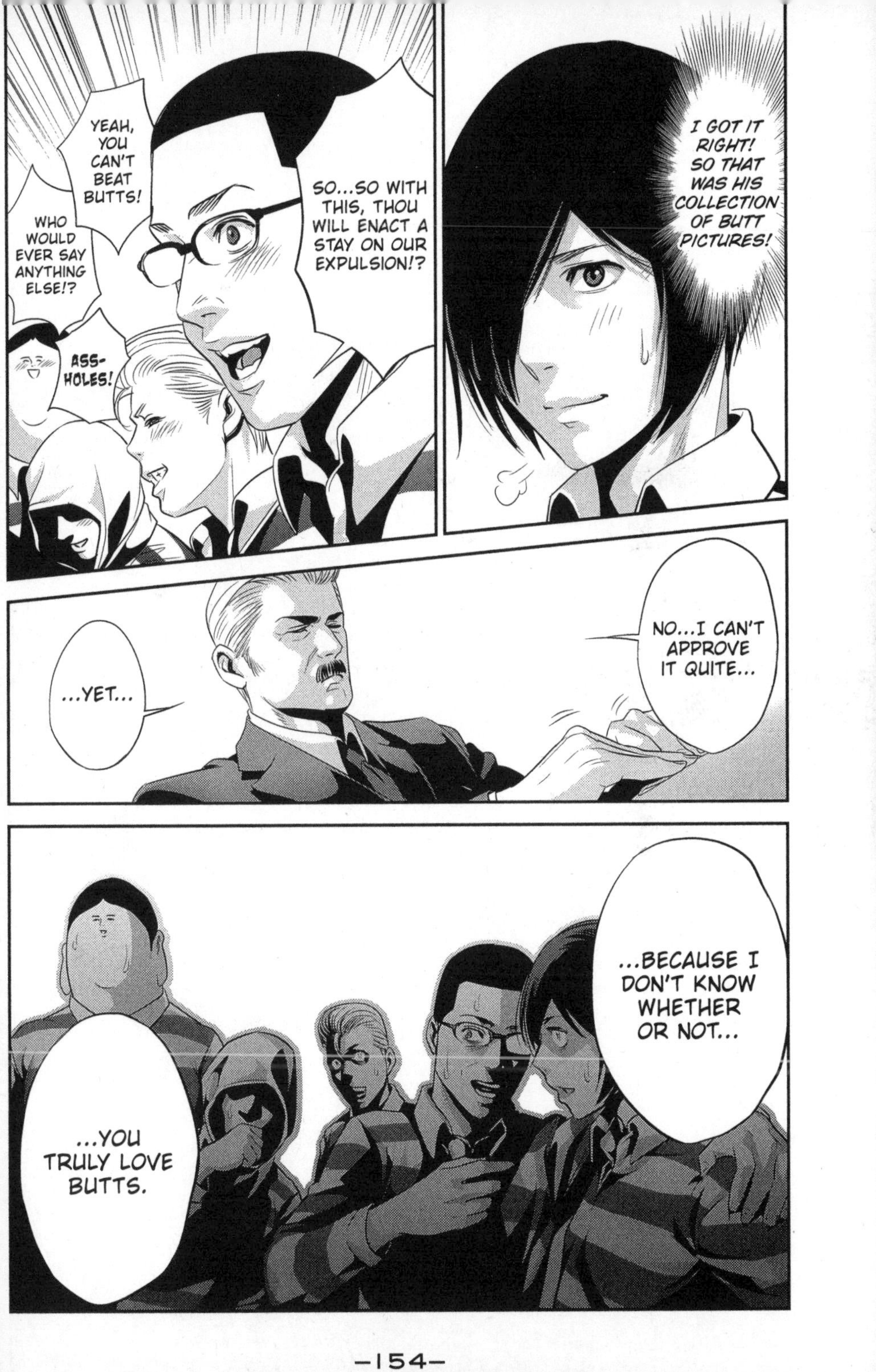
I GOT IT RIGHT! SO THAT WAS HIS COLLECTION OF BUTT PICTURES!
SO...SO WITH THIS, THOU WILL ENACT A STAY ON OUR EXPULSION!?
YEAH, YOU CAN'T BEAT BUTTS!
WHO WOULD EVER SAY ANYTHING ELSE!?
ASS-HOLES!
NO...I CAN'T APPROVE IT QUITE...
...YET...
...BECAUSE I DON'T KNOW WHETHER OR NOT...
...YOU TRULY LOVE BUTTS.

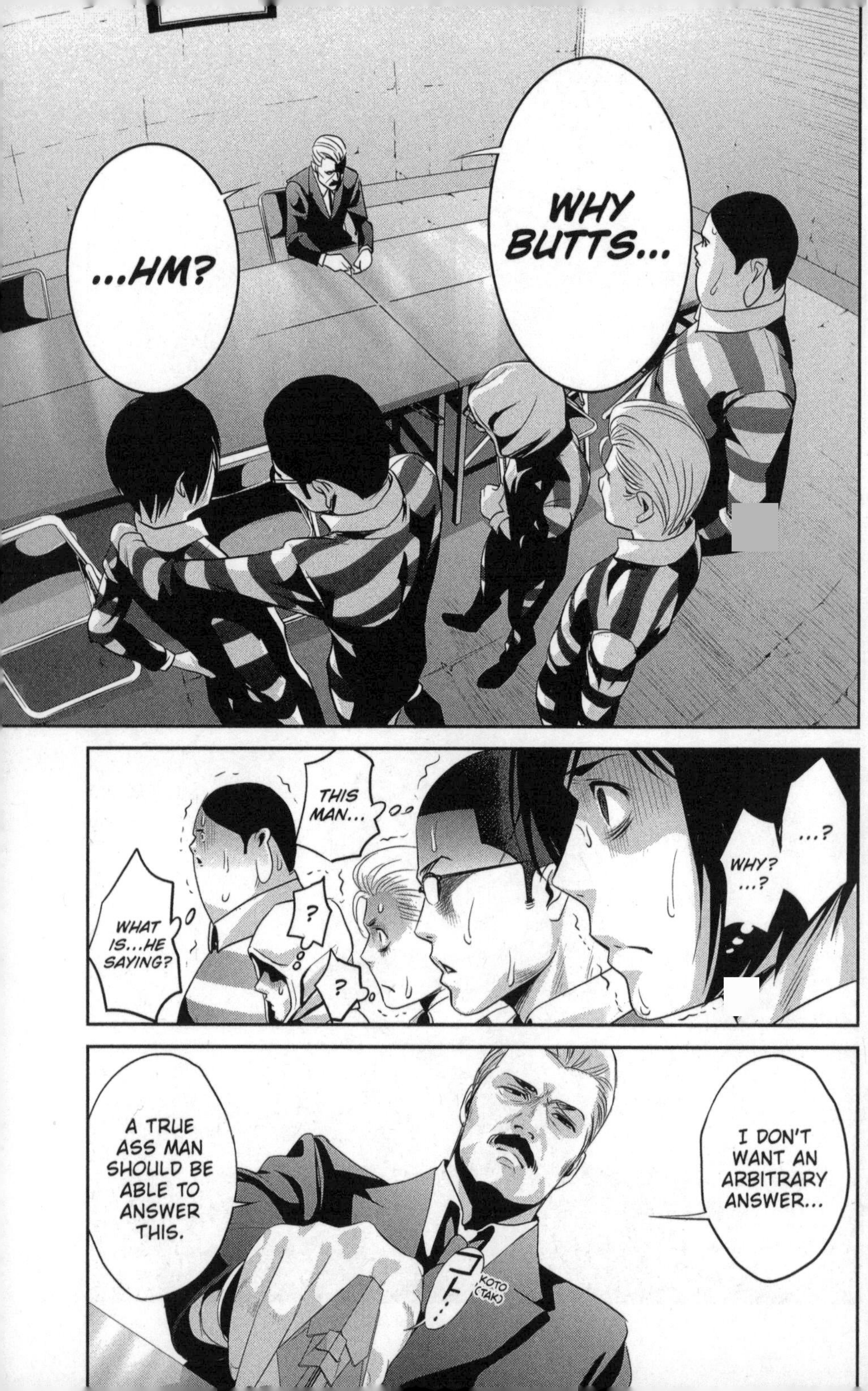
WHY BUTTS...
...HM?
...?
WHY? ...?
THIS MAN...
?
?
WHAT IS...HE SAYING?
I DON'T WANT AN ARBITRARY ANSWER...
A TRUE ASS MAN SHOULD BE ABLE TO ANSWER THIS.
KOTO (TAK)

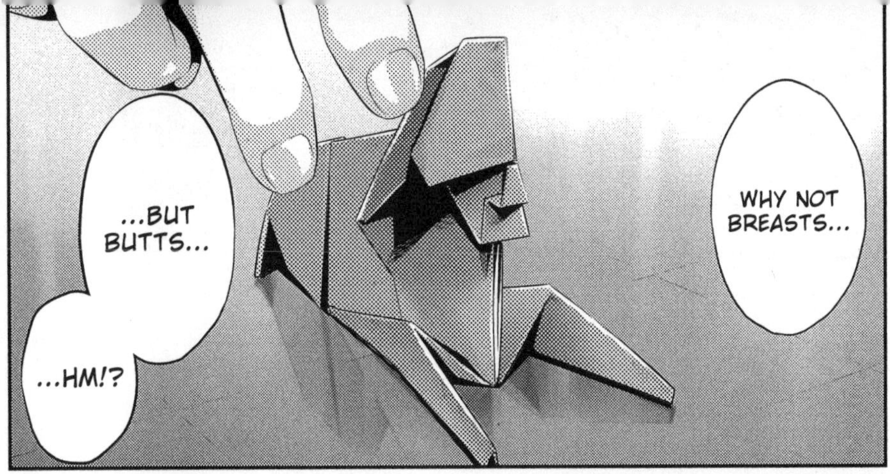
WHY NOT BREASTS...
...BUT BUTTS...
...HM!?

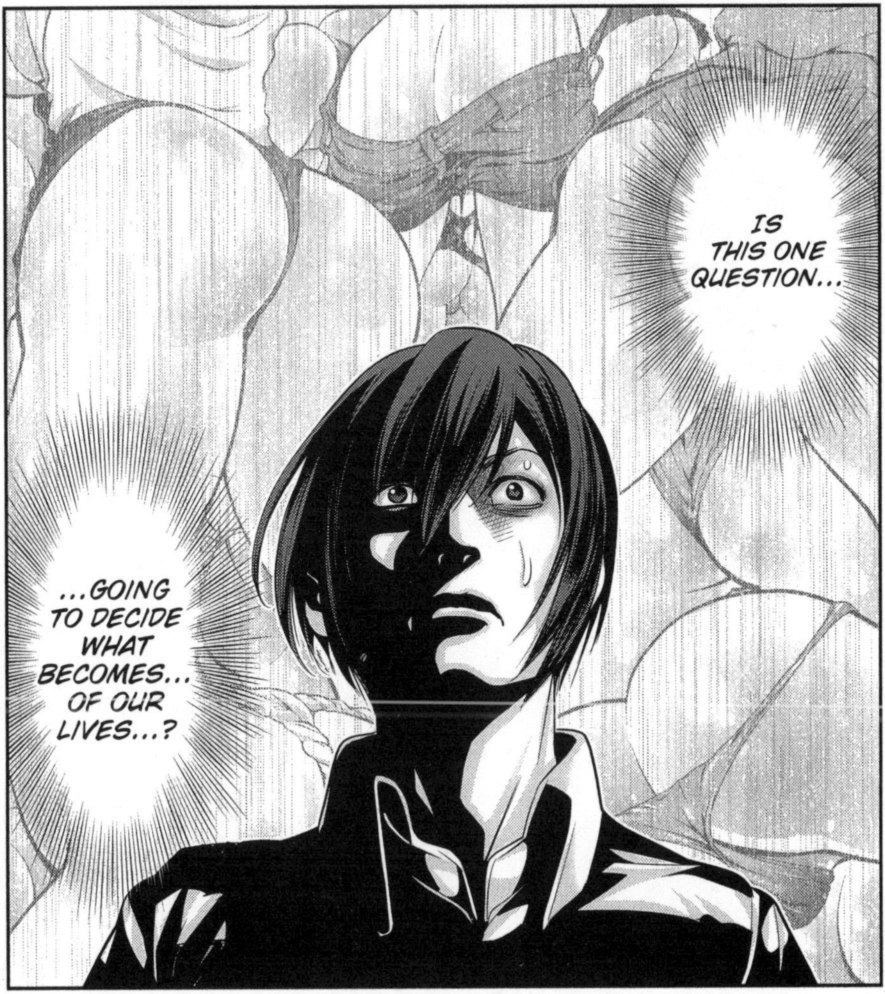
IS THIS ONE QUESTION...
...GOING TO DECIDE WHAT BECOMES... OF OUR LIVES...?

CHAPTER 67: KIYOSHI'S CHOICE

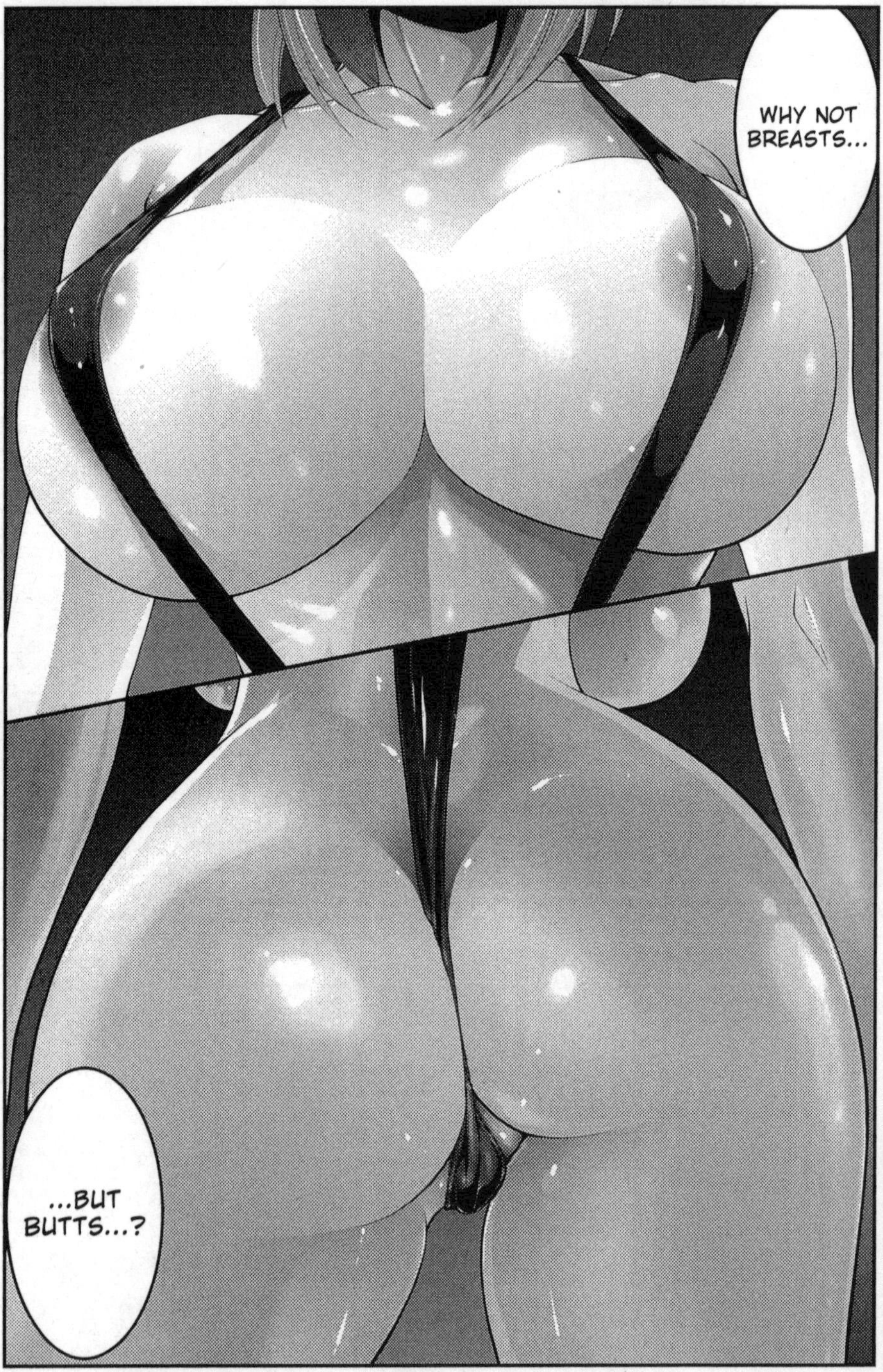
WHY NOT BREASTS...
...BUT BUTTS...?

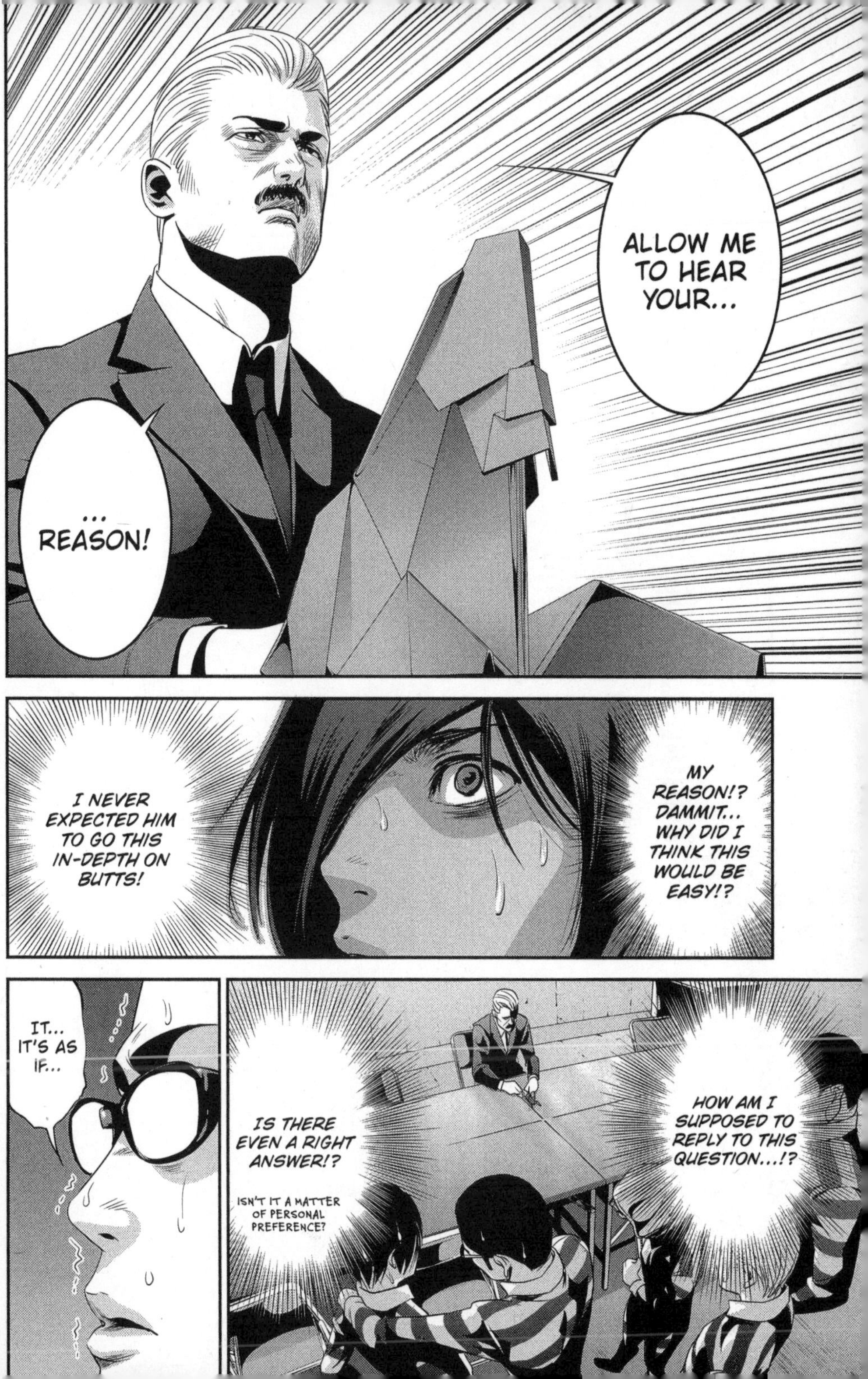
ALLOW ME TO HEAR YOUR...
...REASON!
MY REASON!? DAMMIT... WHY DID I THINK THIS WOULD BE EASY!?
I NEVER EXPECTED HIM TO GO THIS IN-DEPTH ON BUTTS!
HOW AM I SUPPOSED TO REPLY TO THIS QUESTION...!?
IS THERE EVEN A RIGHT ANSWER!?
ISN'T IT A MATTER OF PERSONAL PREFERENCE?
IT... IT'S AS IF...

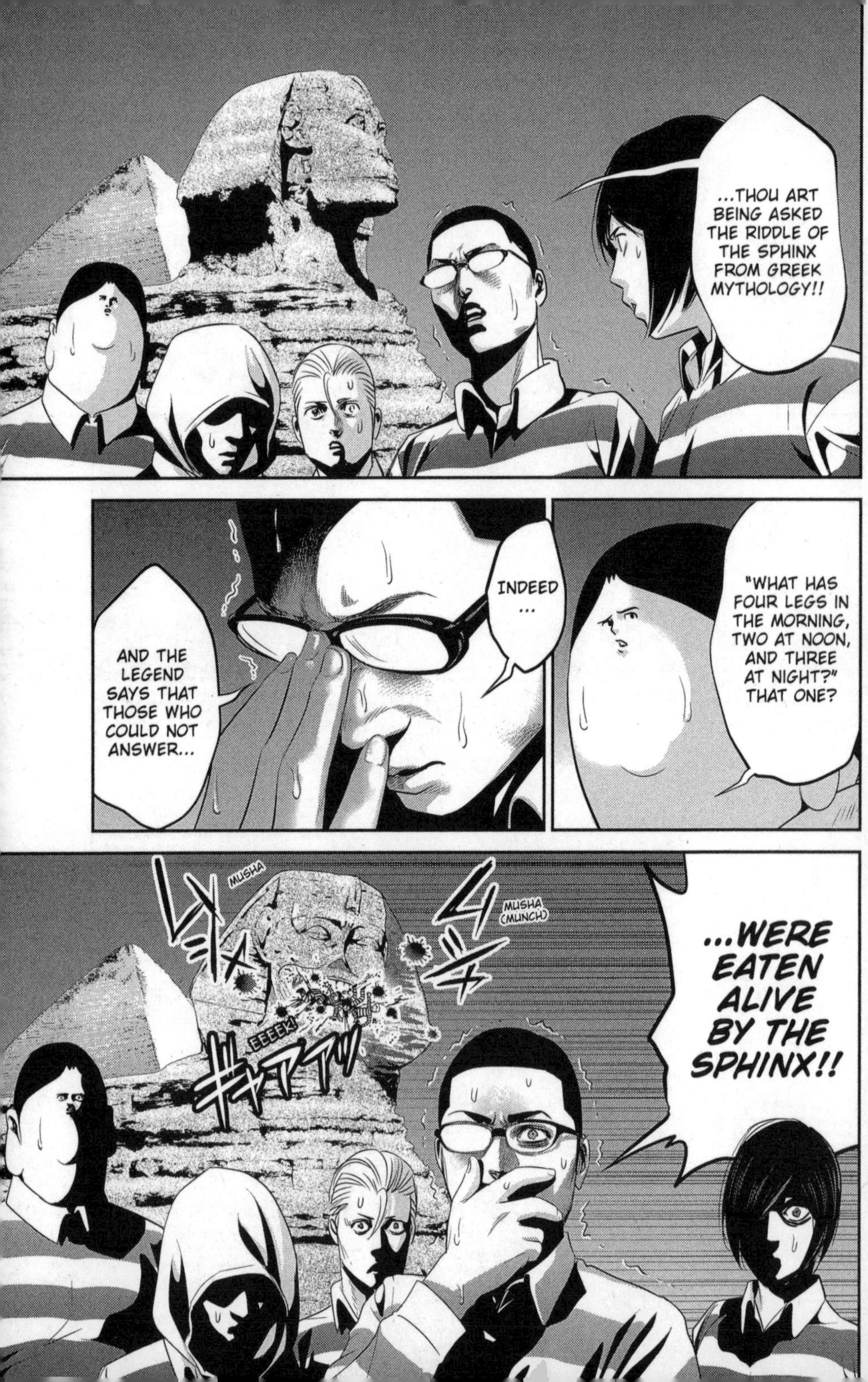
...THOU ART BEING ASKED THE RIDDLE OF THE SPHINX FROM GREEK MYTHOLOGY!!
"WHAT HAS FOUR LEGS IN THE MORNING, TWO AT NOON, AND THREE AT NIGHT?" THAT ONE?
INDEED ...
AND THE LEGEND SAYS THAT THOSE WHO COULD NOT ANSWER...
...WERE EATEN ALIVE BY THE SPHINX!!
MUSHA (MUNCH)
MUSHA
EEEEK!

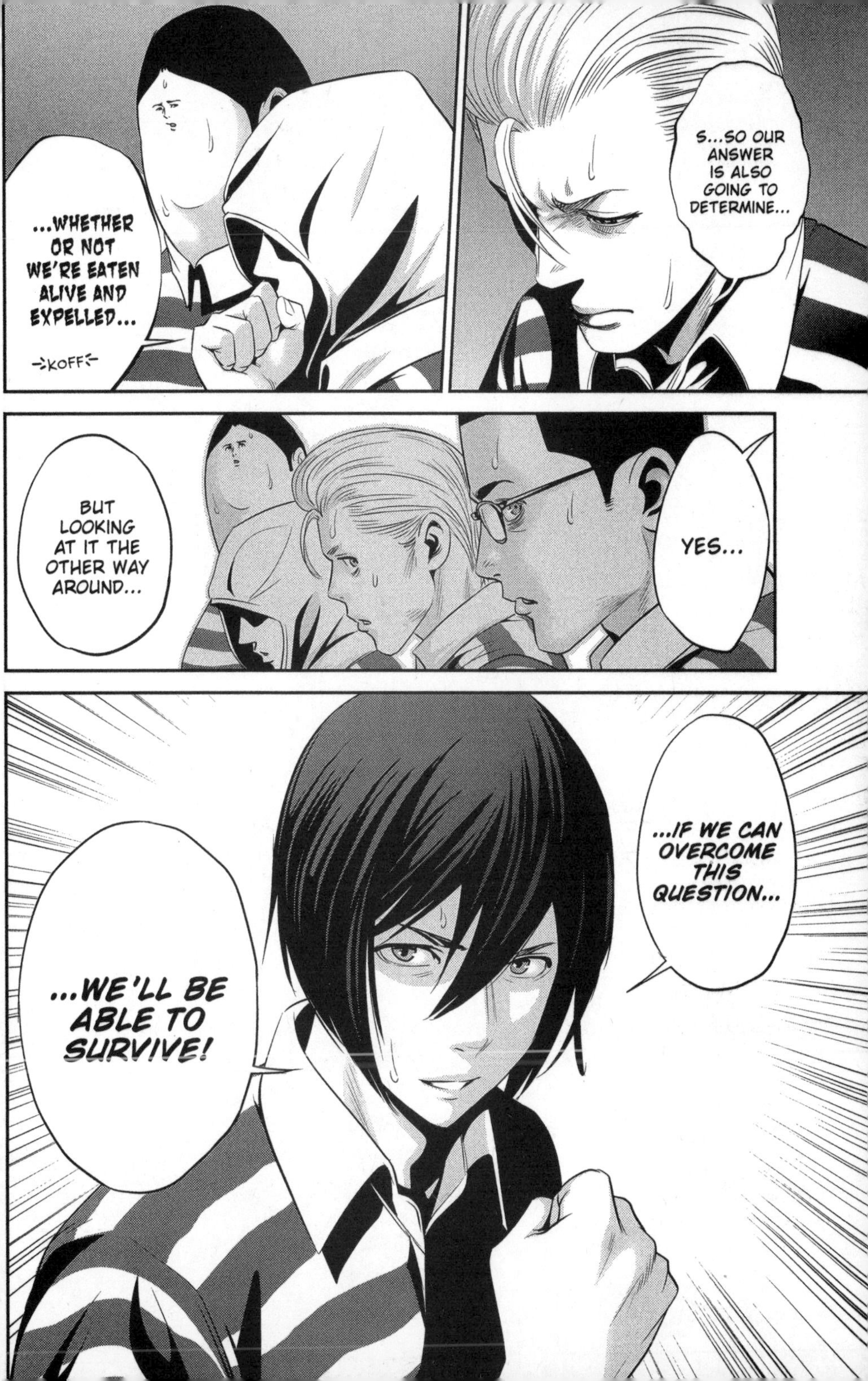
S...SO OUR ANSWER IS ALSO GOING TO DETERMINE...
...WHETHER OR NOT WE'RE EATEN ALIVE AND EXPELLED...
KOFF
YES...
BUT LOOKING AT IT THE OTHER WAY AROUND...
...IF WE CAN OVERCOME THIS QUESTION...
...WE'LL BE ABLE TO SURVIVE!

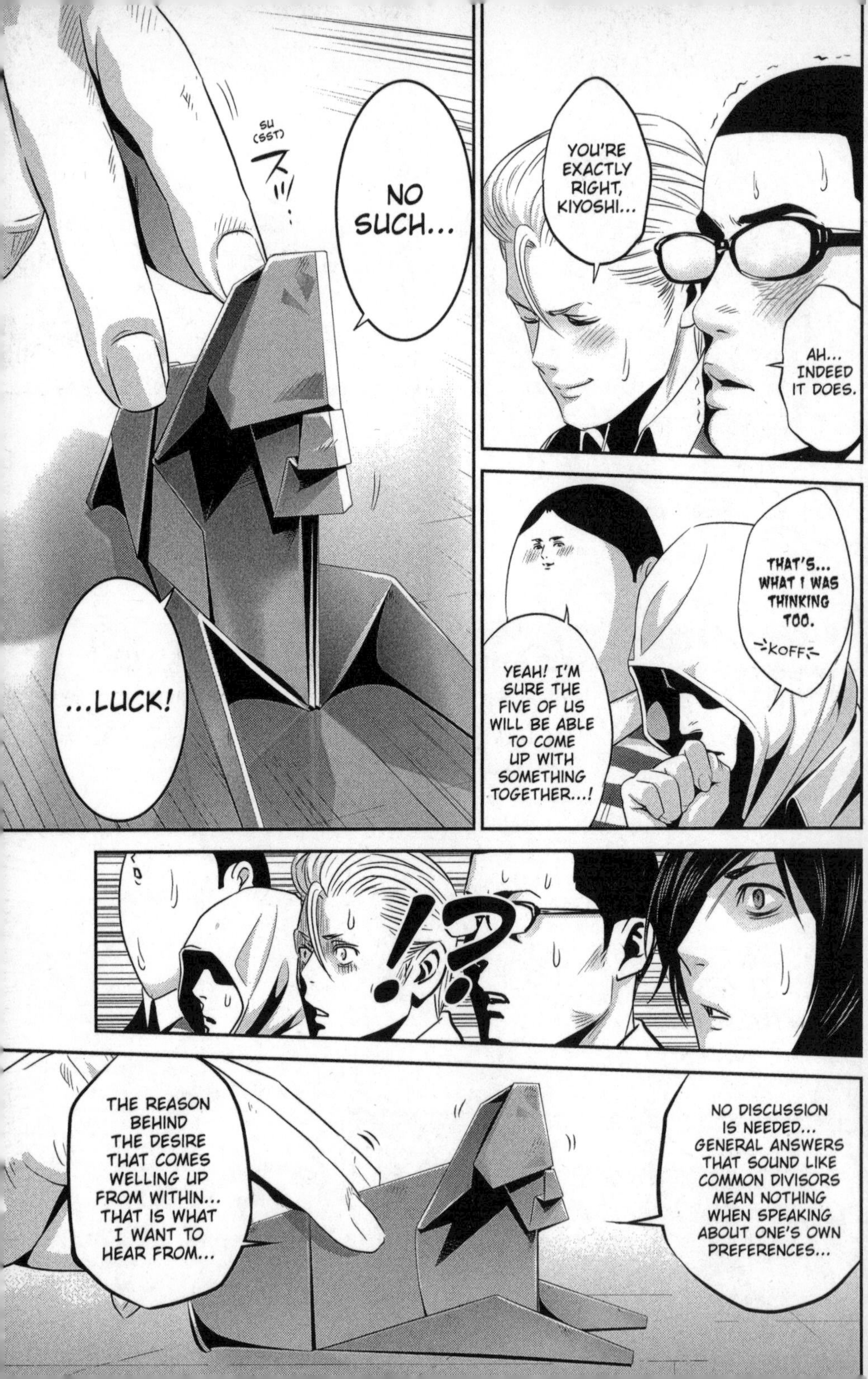
YOU'RE EXACTLY RIGHT, KIYOSHI...
AH... INDEED IT DOES.
THAT'S... WHAT I WAS THINKING TOO.
KOFF
YEAH! I'M SURE THE FIVE OF US WILL BE ABLE TO COME UP WITH SOMETHING TOGETHER...!
SU (SST)
NO SUCH...
...LUCK!
!?
NO DISCUSSION IS NEEDED... GENERAL ANSWERS THAT SOUND LIKE COMMON DIVISORS MEAN NOTHING WHEN SPEAKING ABOUT ONE'S OWN PREFERENCES...
THE REASON BEHIND THE DESIRE THAT COMES WELLING UP FROM WITHIN... THAT IS WHAT I WANT TO HEAR FROM...

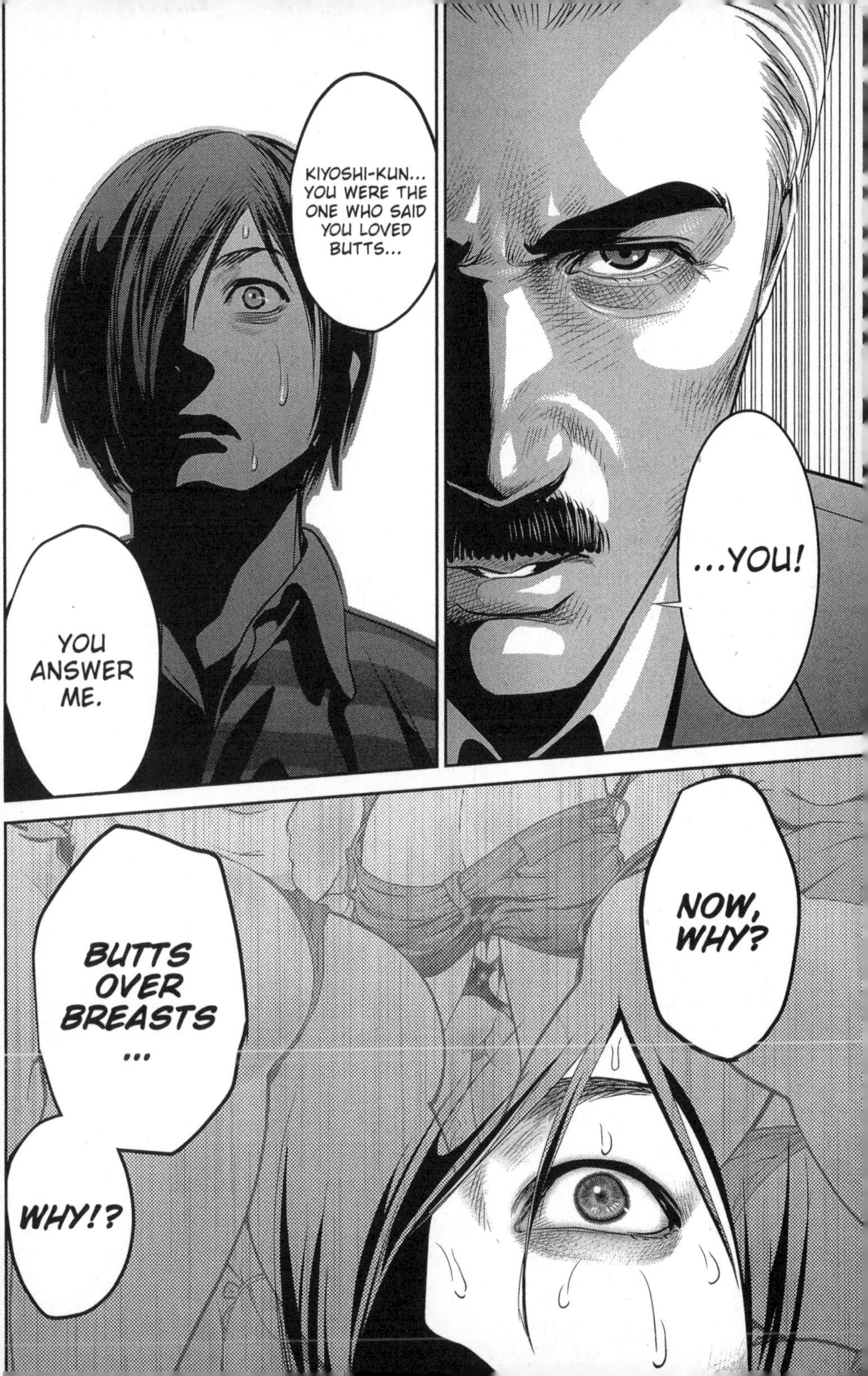
...YOU!
KIYOSHI-KUN... YOU WERE THE ONE WHO SAID YOU LOVED BUTTS...
YOU ANSWER ME.
NOW, WHY?
BUTTS OVER BREASTS...
WHY!?

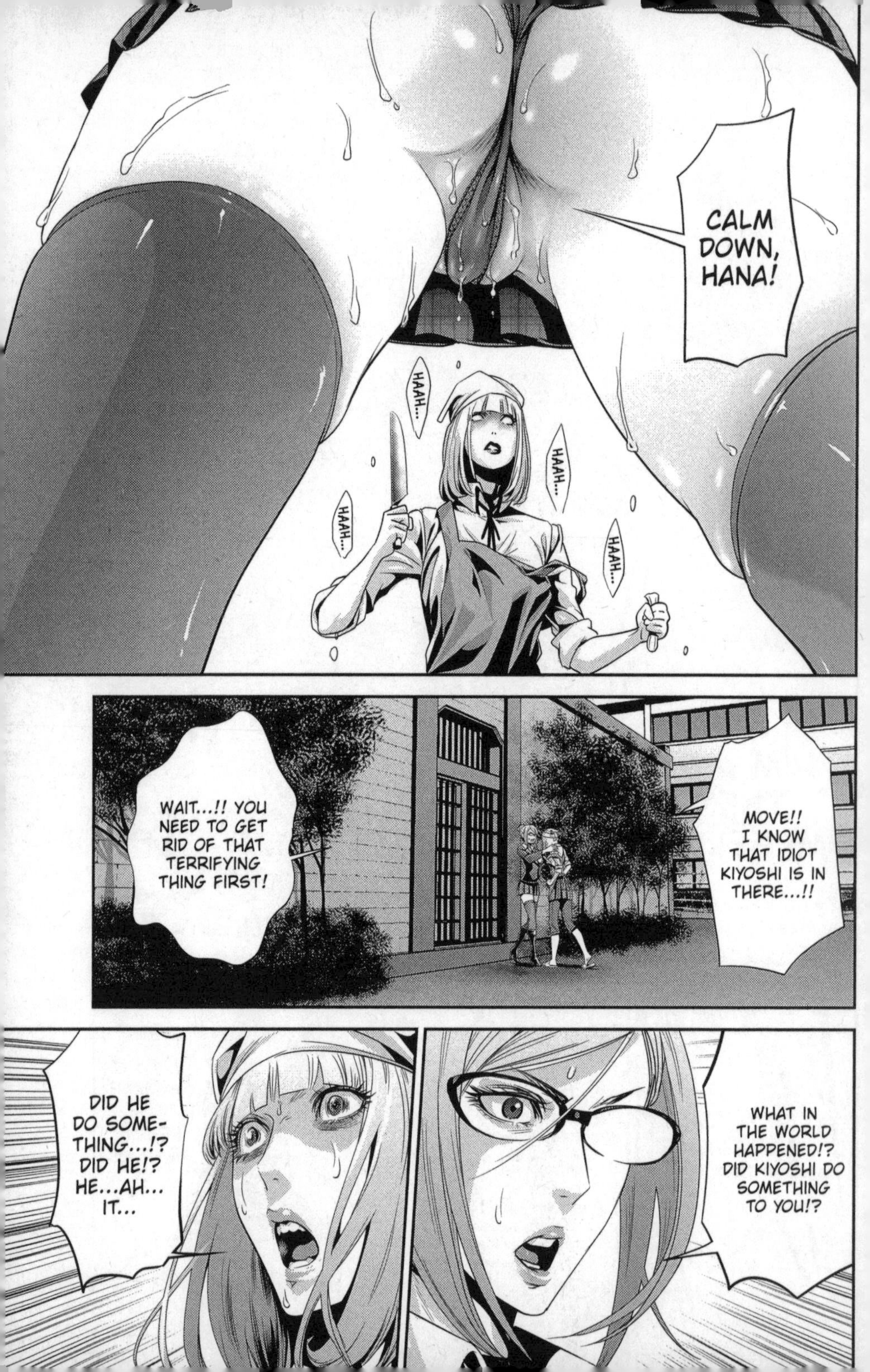
CALM DOWN, HANA!
HAAH...
HAAH...
HAAH...
HAAH...
MOVE!! I KNOW THAT IDIOT KIYOSHI IS IN THERE...!!
WAIT...!! YOU NEED TO GET RID OF THAT TERRIFYING THING FIRST!
WHAT IN THE WORLD HAPPENED!? DID KIYOSHI DO SOMETHING TO YOU!?
DID HE DO SOME-THING...!? DID HE!? HE...AH... IT...

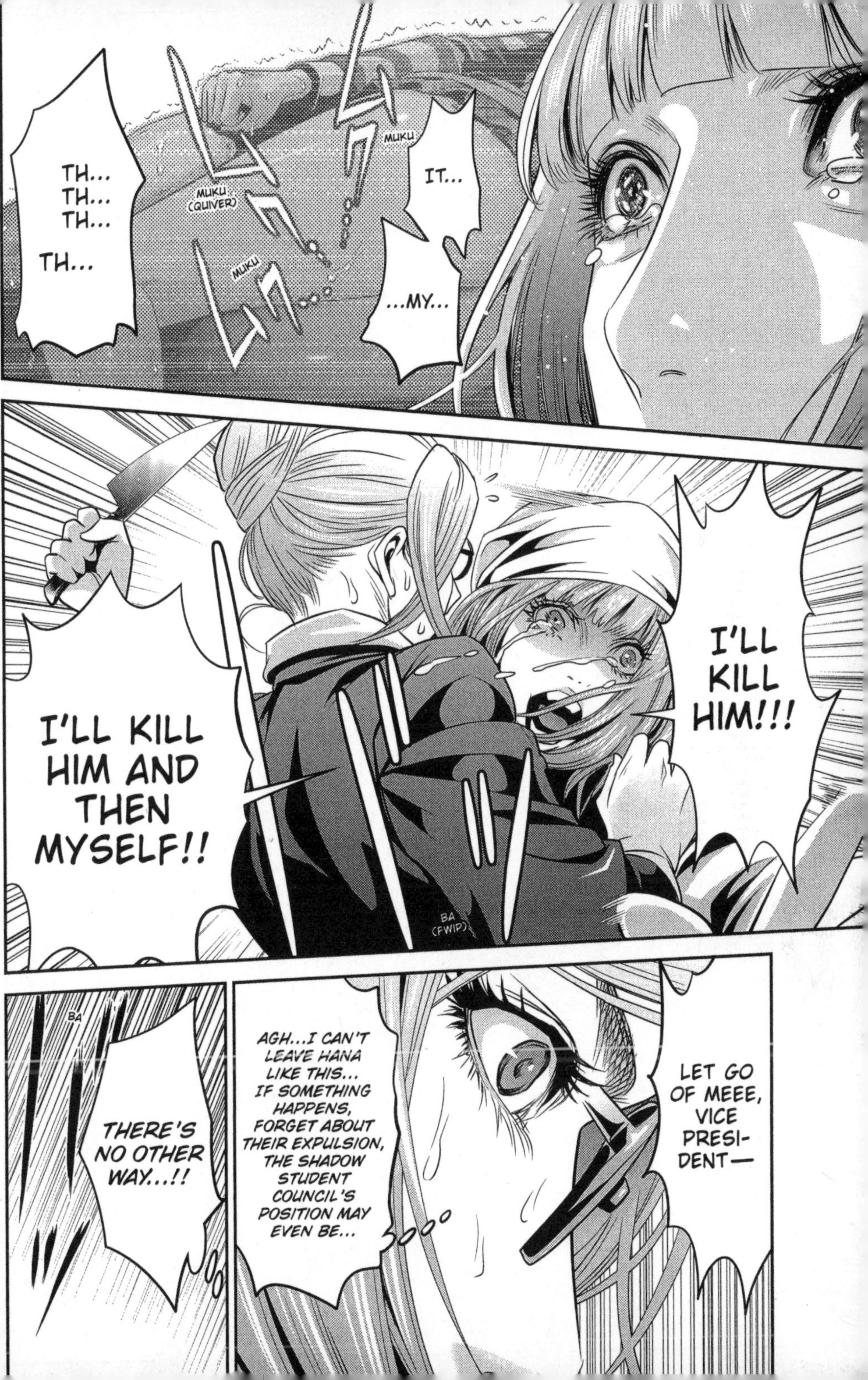
MUKU
IT...
...MY...
MUKU (QUIVER)
MUKU
TH... TH... TH... TH...
I'LL KILL HIM!!!
I'LL KILL HIM AND THEN MYSELF!!
BA (FWIP)
LET GO OF MEEE, VICE PRESIDENT—
AGH...I CAN'T LEAVE HANA LIKE THIS... IF SOMETHING HAPPENS, FORGET ABOUT THEIR EXPULSION, THE SHADOW STUDENT COUNCIL'S POSITION MAY EVEN BE...
BA
THERE'S NO OTHER WAY...!!

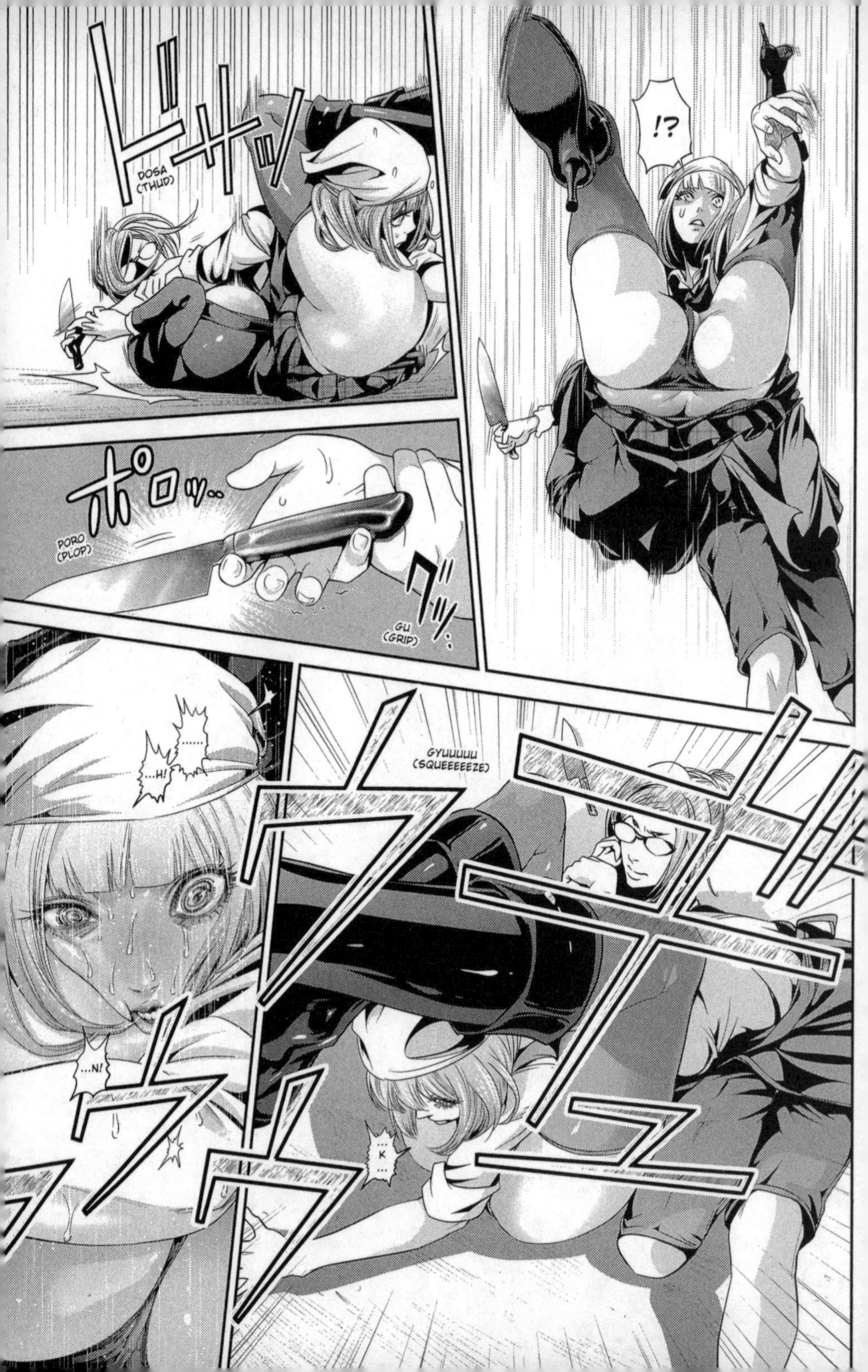
!?
ドサッ
DOSA (THUD)
ポロッ..
PORO (PLOP)
グッ
GU (GRIP)
GYUUUUU (SQUEEEEEZE)
...K
......
...H!
...N!

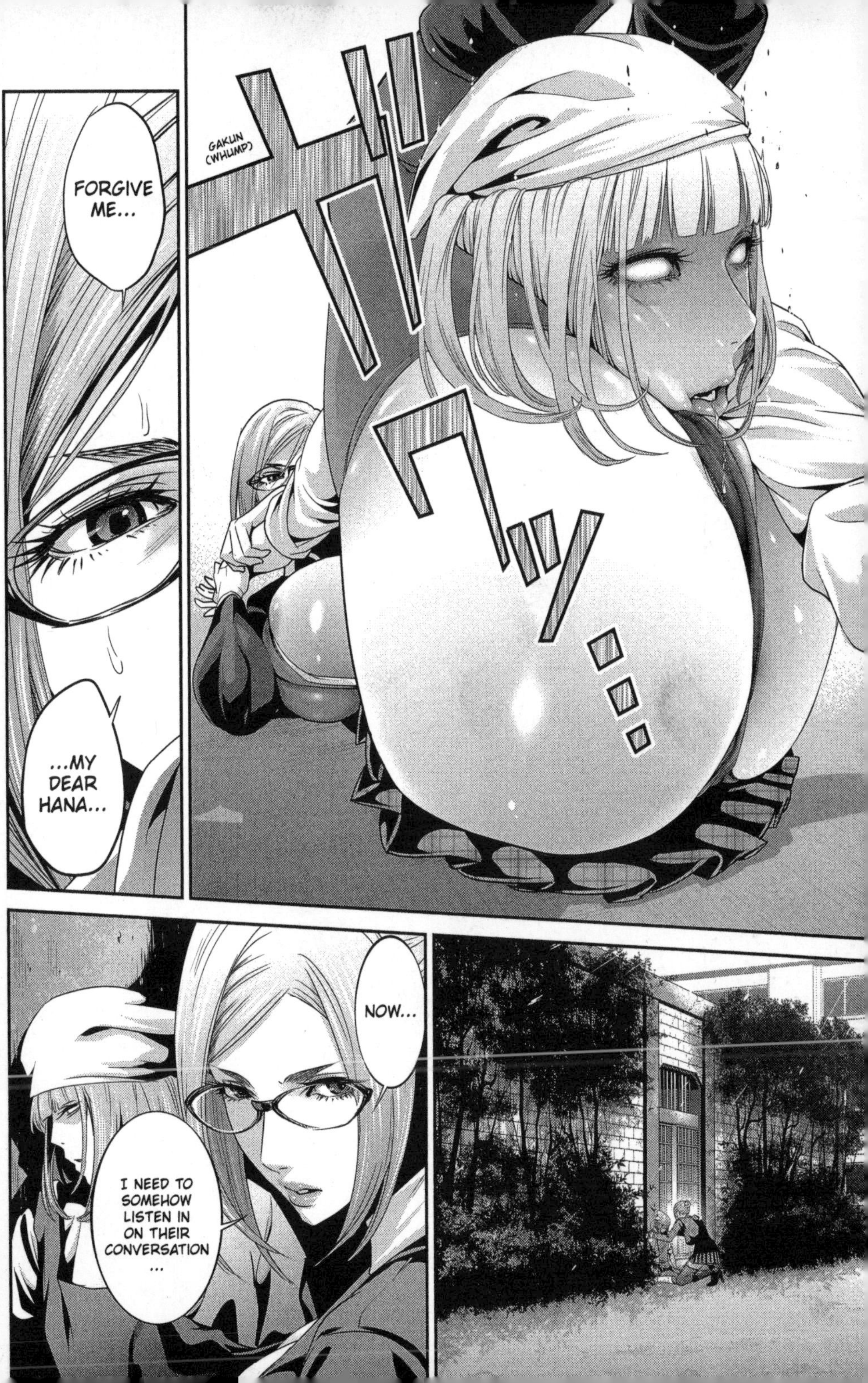
GAKUN (WHUMP)
FORGIVE ME...
...MY DEAR HANA...
NOW...
I NEED TO SOMEHOW LISTEN IN ON THEIR CONVERSATION ...

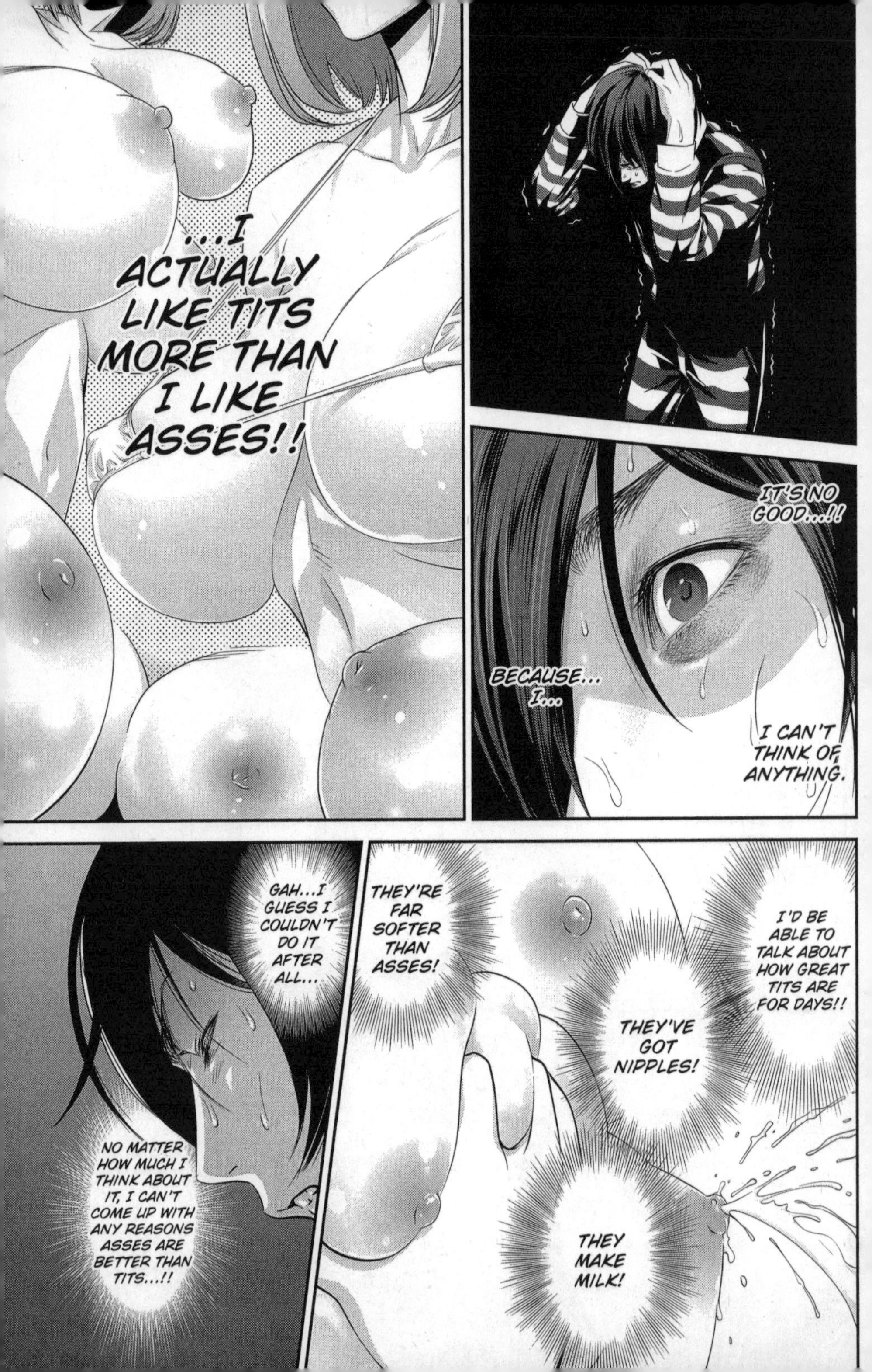
IT'S NO GOOD...!!
BECAUSE... I...
I CAN'T THINK OF ANYTHING.
...I ACTUALLY LIKE TITS MORE THAN I LIKE ASSES!!
I'D BE ABLE TO TALK ABOUT HOW GREAT TITS ARE FOR DAYS!!
THEY'RE FAR SOFTER THAN ASSES!
THEY'VE GOT NIPPLES!
THEY MAKE MILK!
GAH...I GUESS I COULDN'T DO IT AFTER ALL...
NO MATTER HOW MUCH I THINK ABOUT IT, I CAN'T COME UP WITH ANY REASONS ASSES ARE BETTER THAN TITS...!!

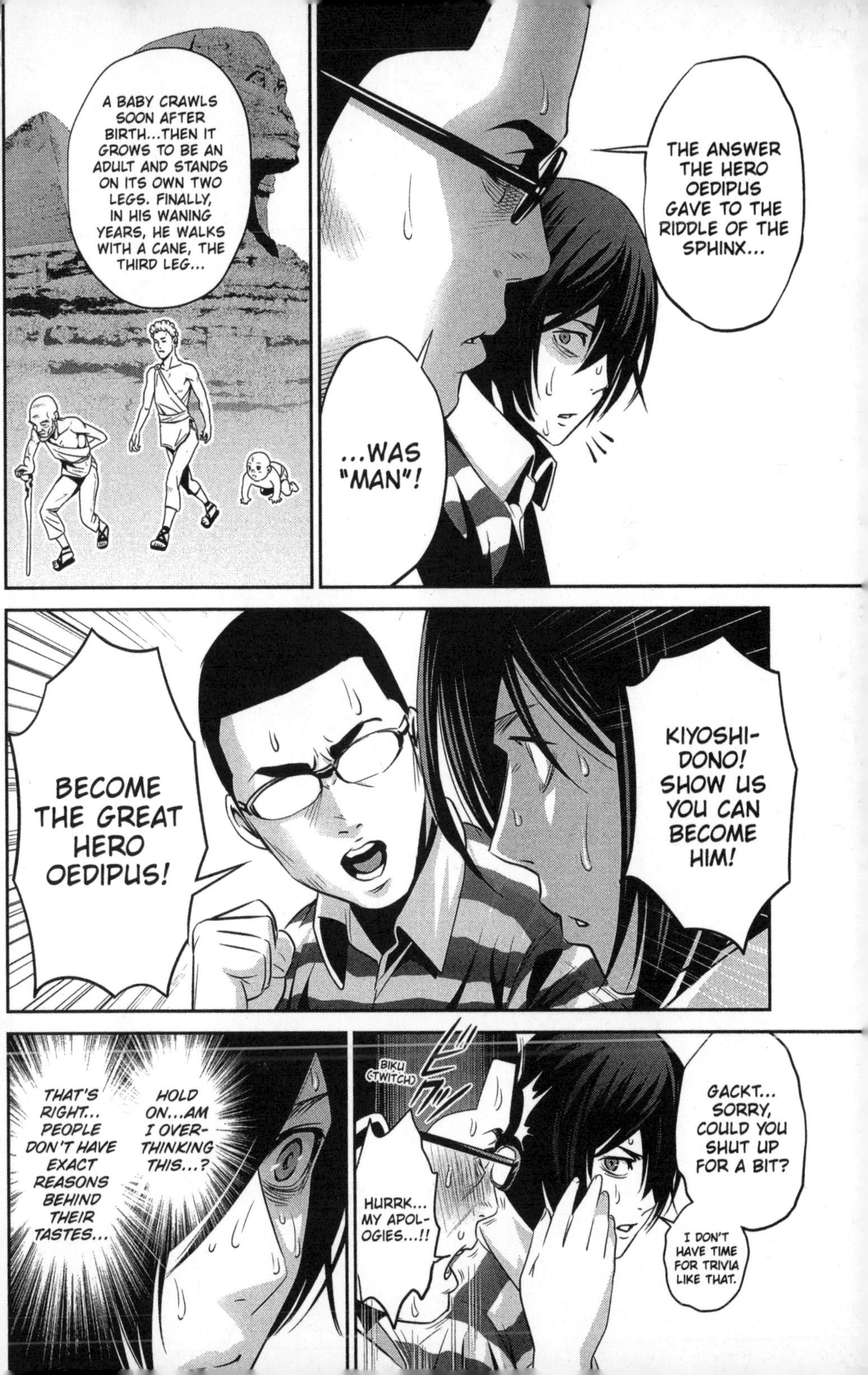
THE ANSWER THE HERO OEDIPUS GAVE TO THE RIDDLE OF THE SPHINX...
...WAS "MAN"!
A BABY CRAWLS SOON AFTER BIRTH...THEN IT GROWS TO BE AN ADULT AND STANDS ON ITS OWN TWO LEGS. FINALLY, IN HIS WANING YEARS, HE WALKS WITH A CANE, THE THIRD LEG...
KIYOSHI-DONO! SHOW US YOU CAN BECOME HIM!
BECOME THE GREAT HERO OEDIPUS!
GACKT... SORRY, COULD YOU SHUT UP FOR A BIT?
I DON'T HAVE TIME FOR TRIVIA LIKE THAT.
BIKU (TWITCH)
HURRK... MY APOLOGIES...!!
HOLD ON...AM I OVER-THINKING THIS...?
THAT'S RIGHT... PEOPLE DON'T HAVE EXACT REASONS BEHIND THEIR TASTES...

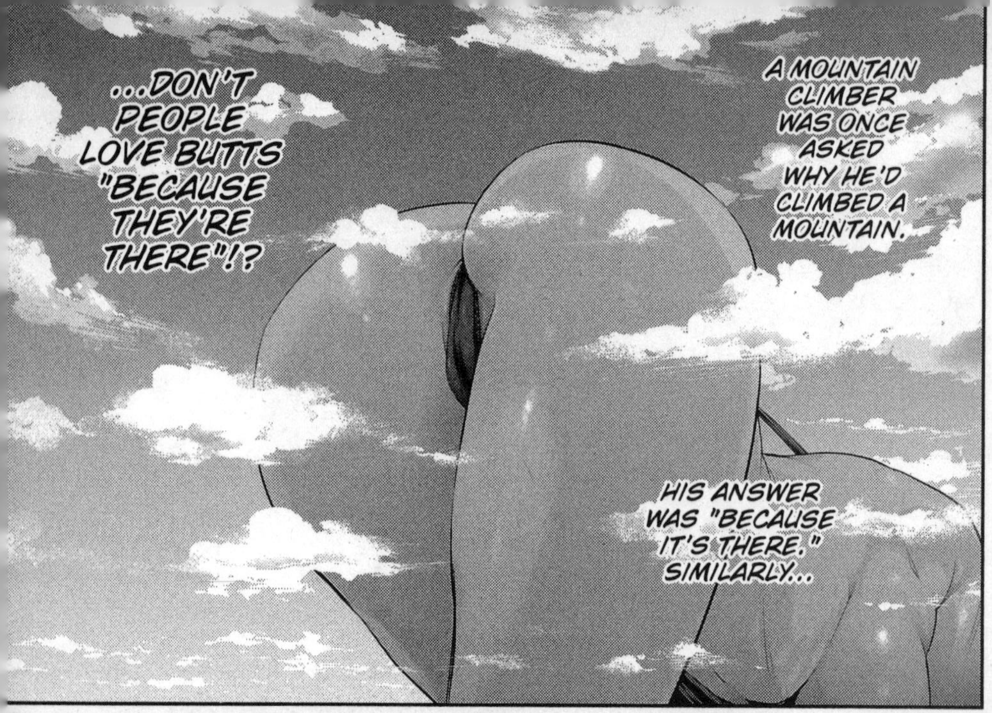
A MOUNTAIN CLIMBER WAS ONCE ASKED WHY HE'D CLIMBED A MOUNTAIN.
HIS ANSWER WAS "BECAUSE IT'S THERE." SIMILARLY...
...DON'T PEOPLE LOVE BUTTS "BECAUSE THEY'RE THERE"!?

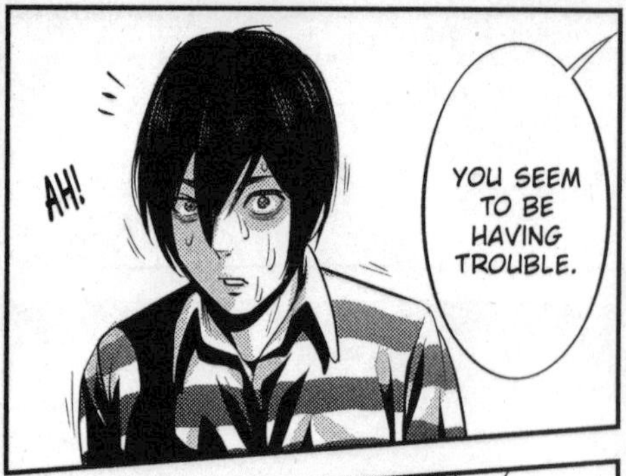
YOU SEEM TO BE HAVING TROUBLE.
AH!

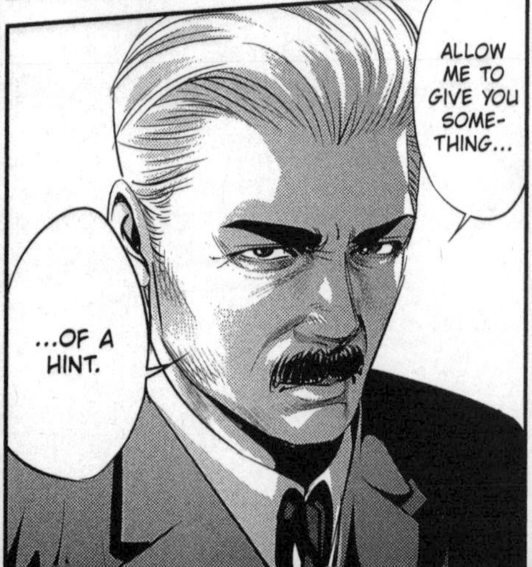
ALLOW ME TO GIVE YOU SOME-THING...
...OF A HINT.

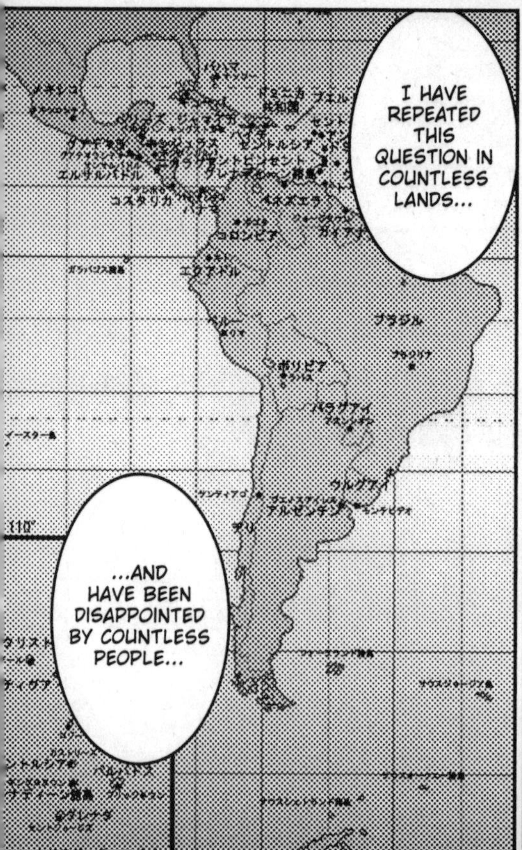
I HAVE REPEATED THIS QUESTION IN COUNTLESS LANDS...
...AND HAVE BEEN DISAPPOINTED BY COUNTLESS PEOPLE...

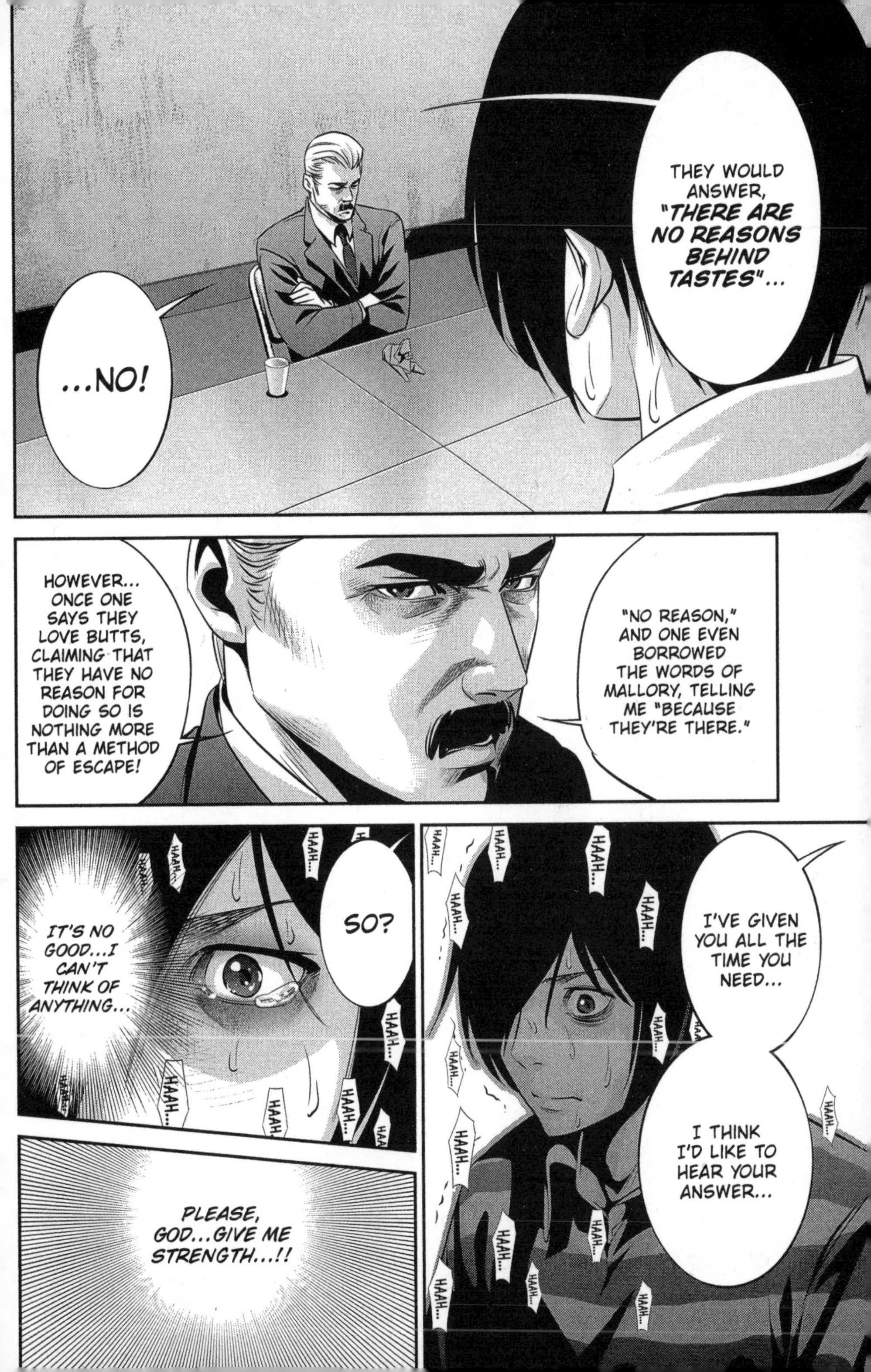
THEY WOULD ANSWER, "THERE ARE NO REASONS BEHIND TASTES"...
...NO!
"NO REASON," AND ONE EVEN BORROWED THE WORDS OF MALLORY, TELLING ME "BECAUSE THEY'RE THERE."
HOWEVER... ONCE ONE SAYS THEY LOVE BUTTS, CLAIMING THAT THEY HAVE NO REASON FOR DOING SO IS NOTHING MORE THAN A METHOD OF ESCAPE!
HAAH... HAAH... HAAH...
I'VE GIVEN YOU ALL THE TIME YOU NEED...
I THINK I'D LIKE TO HEAR YOUR ANSWER...
HAAH... HAAH... HAAH...
SO?
IT'S NO GOOD...I CAN'T THINK OF ANYTHING...
HAAH... HAAH... HAAH...
PLEASE, GOD...GIVE ME STRENGTH...!!

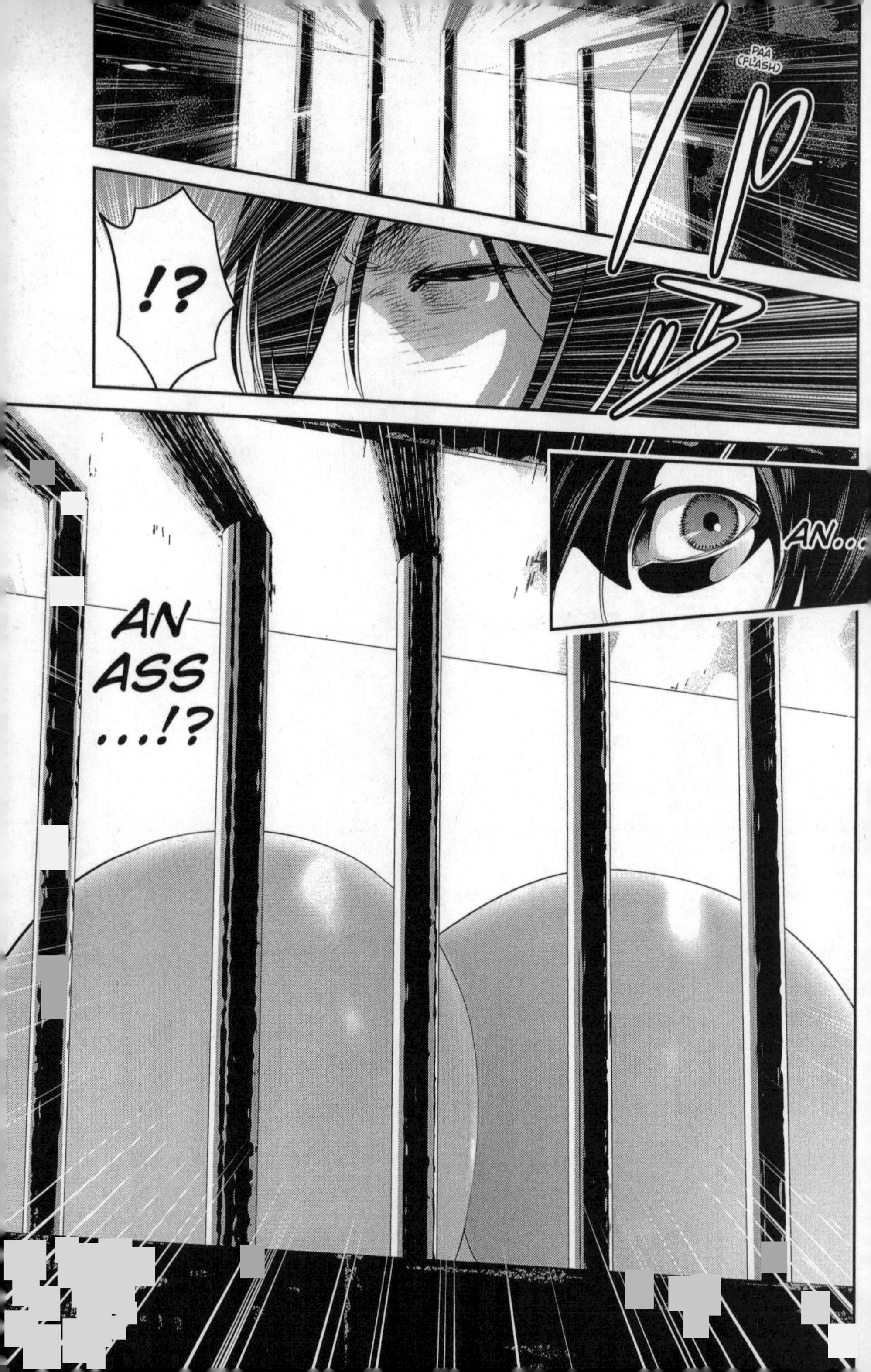
PAA (FLASH)
!?
AN...
AN ASS ...!?

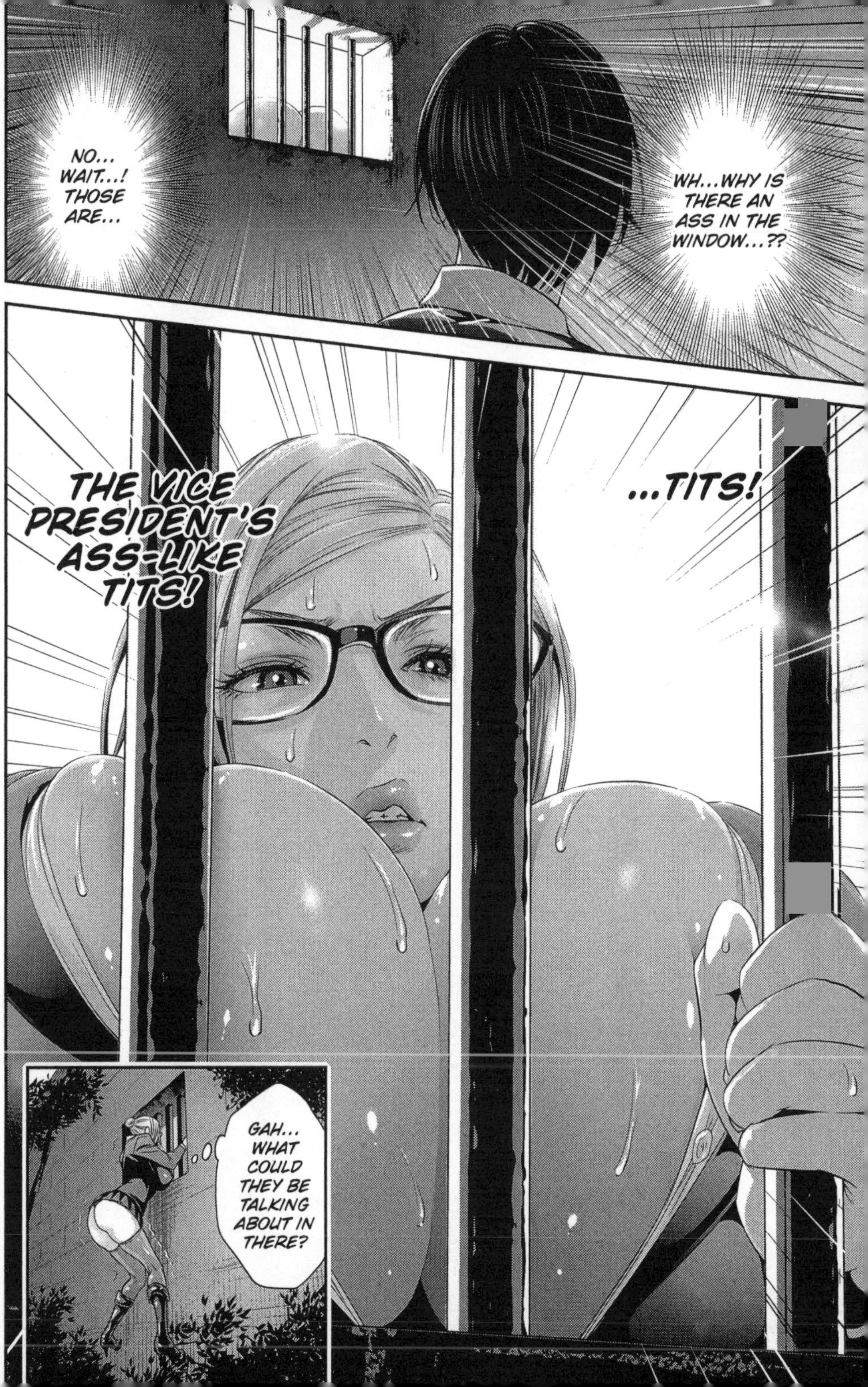
WH...WHY IS THERE AN ASS IN THE WINDOW...??
NO... WAIT...! THOSE ARE...
...TITS!
THE VICE PRESIDENT'S ASS-LIKE TITS!
GAH... WHAT COULD THEY BE TALKING ABOUT IN THERE?

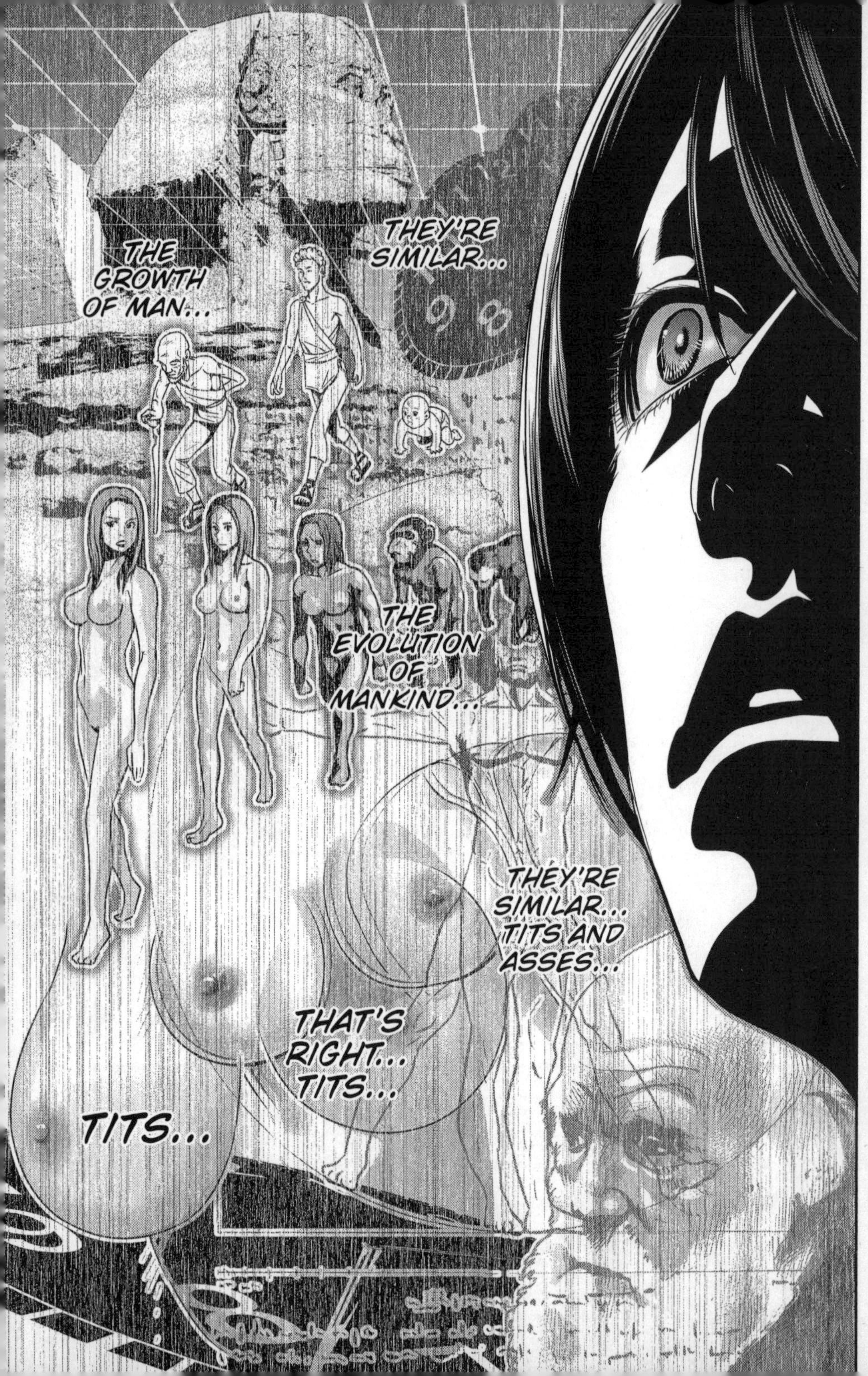
THEY'RE SIMILAR...
THE GROWTH OF MAN...
THE EVOLUTION OF MANKIND...
THEY'RE SIMILAR... TITS AND ASSES...
THAT'S RIGHT... TITS...
TITS...

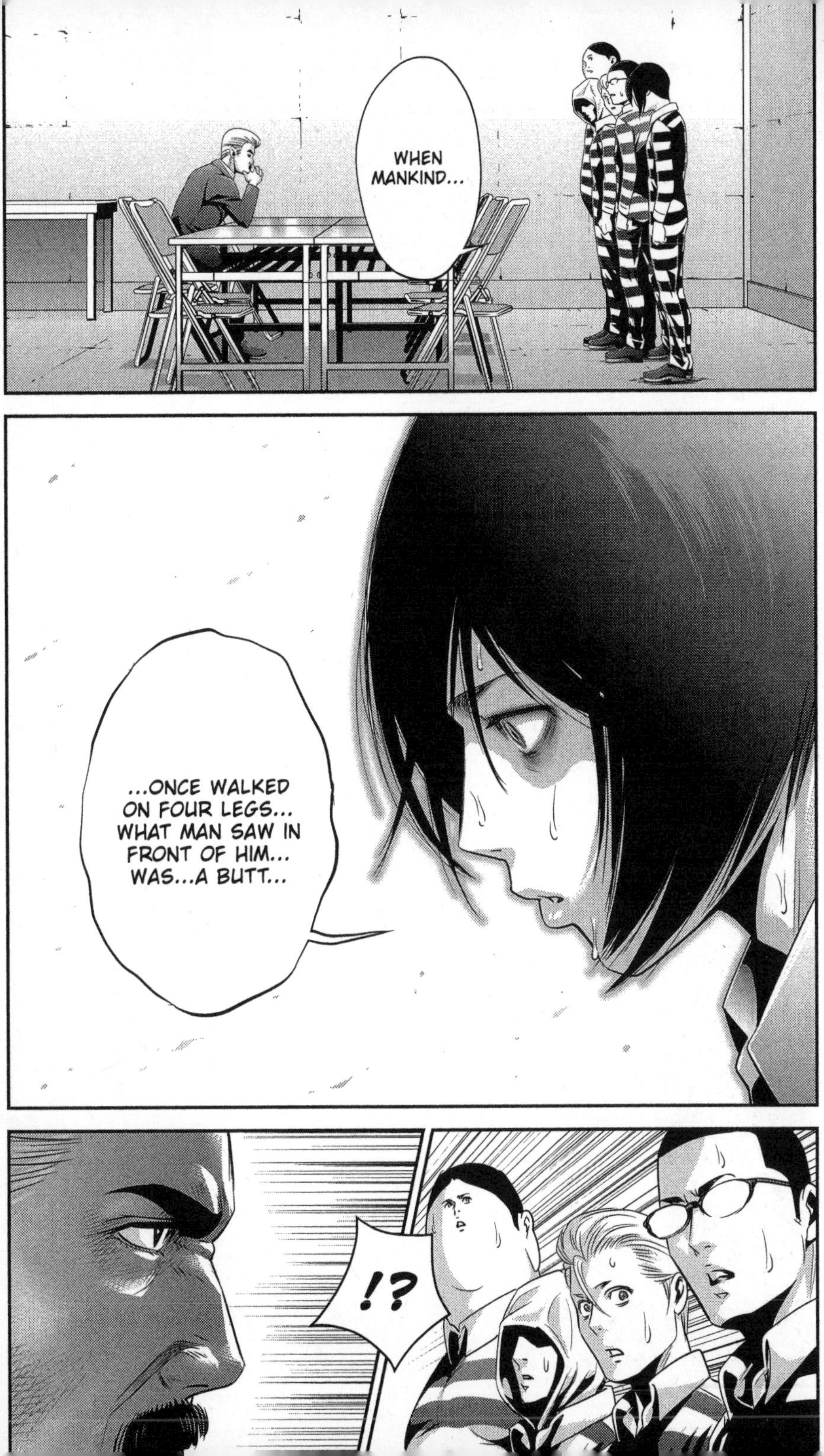
WHEN MANKIND...
...ONCE WALKED ON FOUR LEGS... WHAT MAN SAW IN FRONT OF HIM... WAS...A BUTT...
!?

CHAPTER 68: IT'S A WONDERFUL BUTT

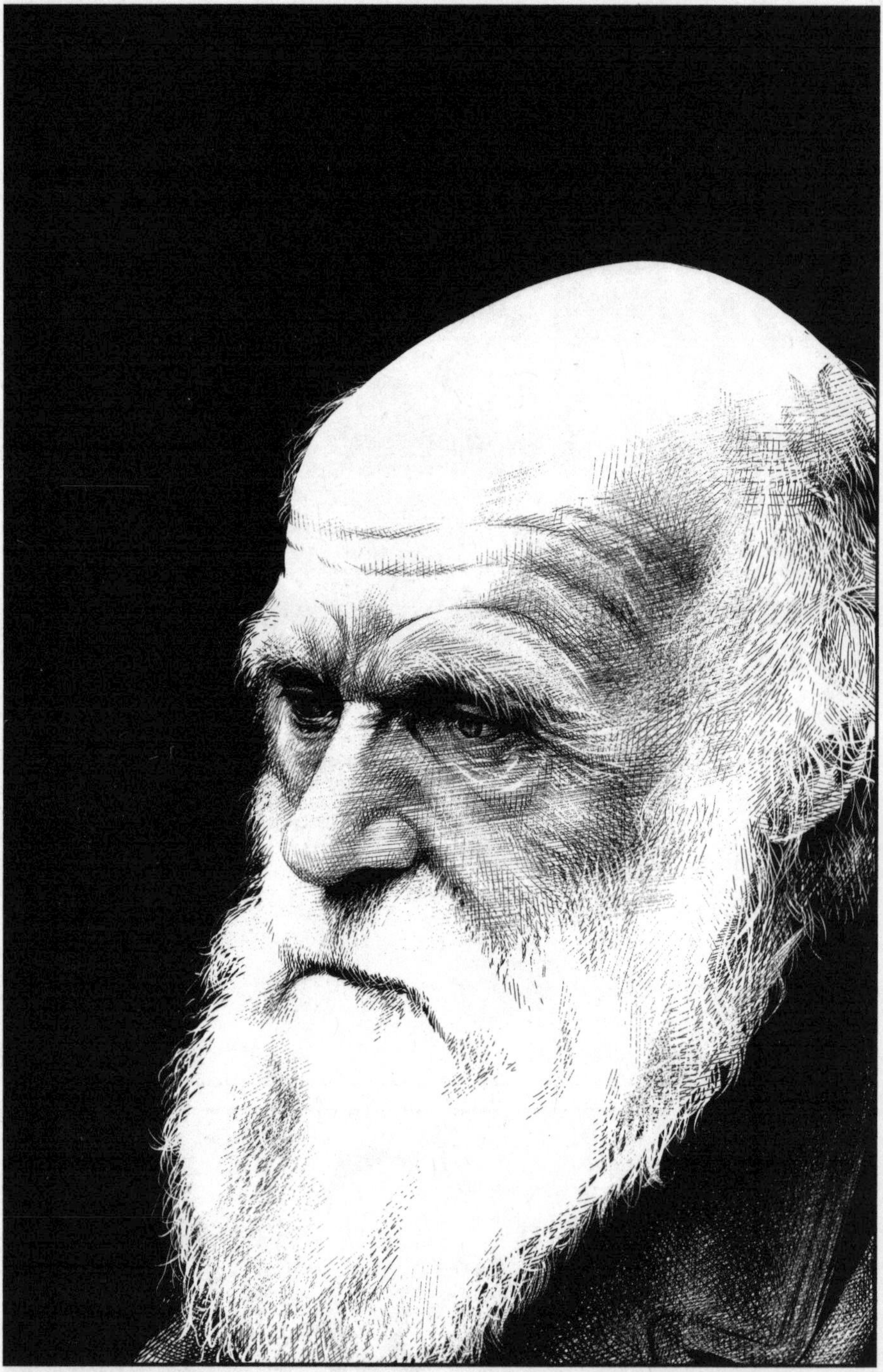

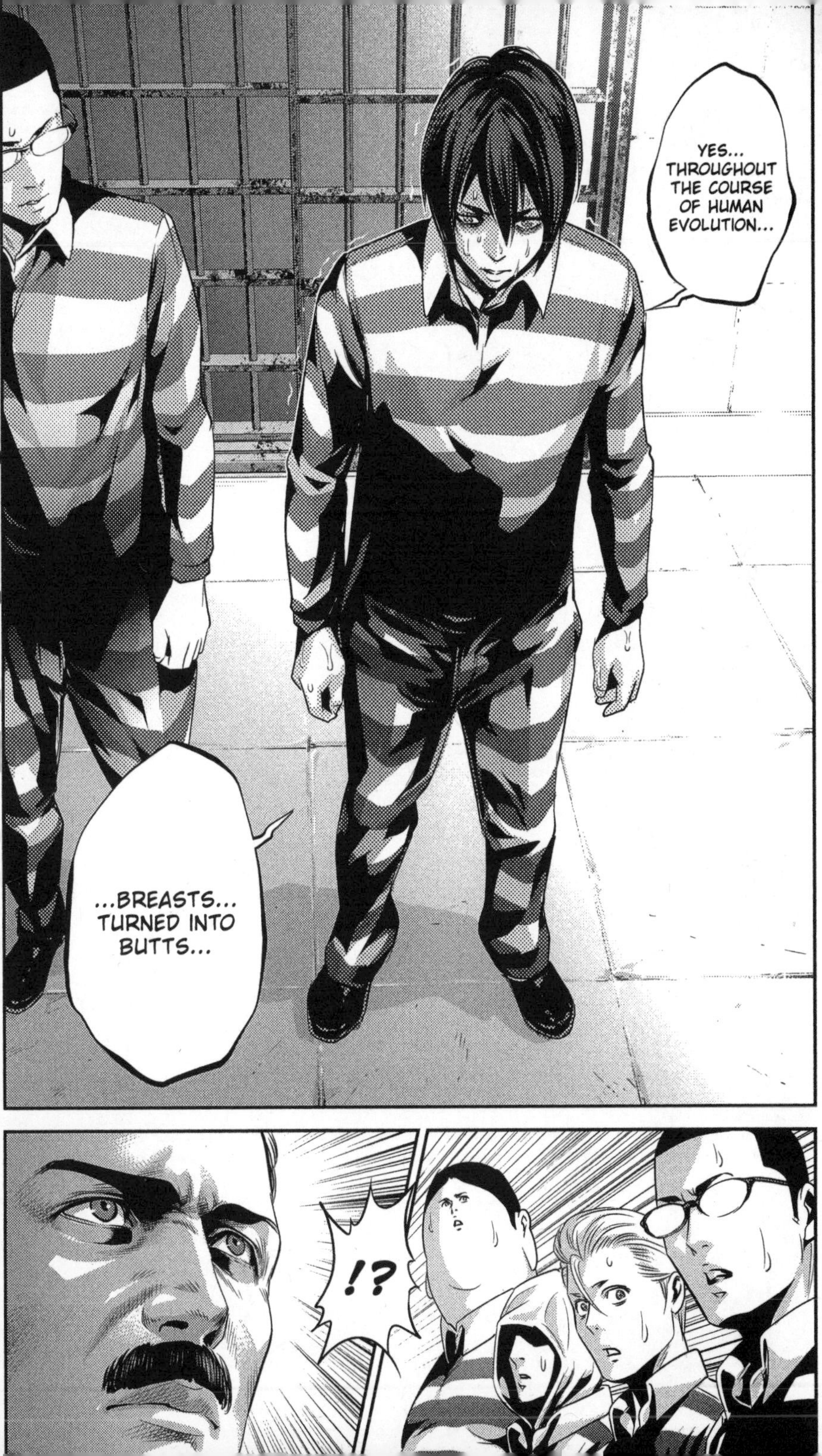
YES... THROUGHOUT THE COURSE OF HUMAN EVOLUTION...
...BREASTS... TURNED INTO BUTTS...
!?

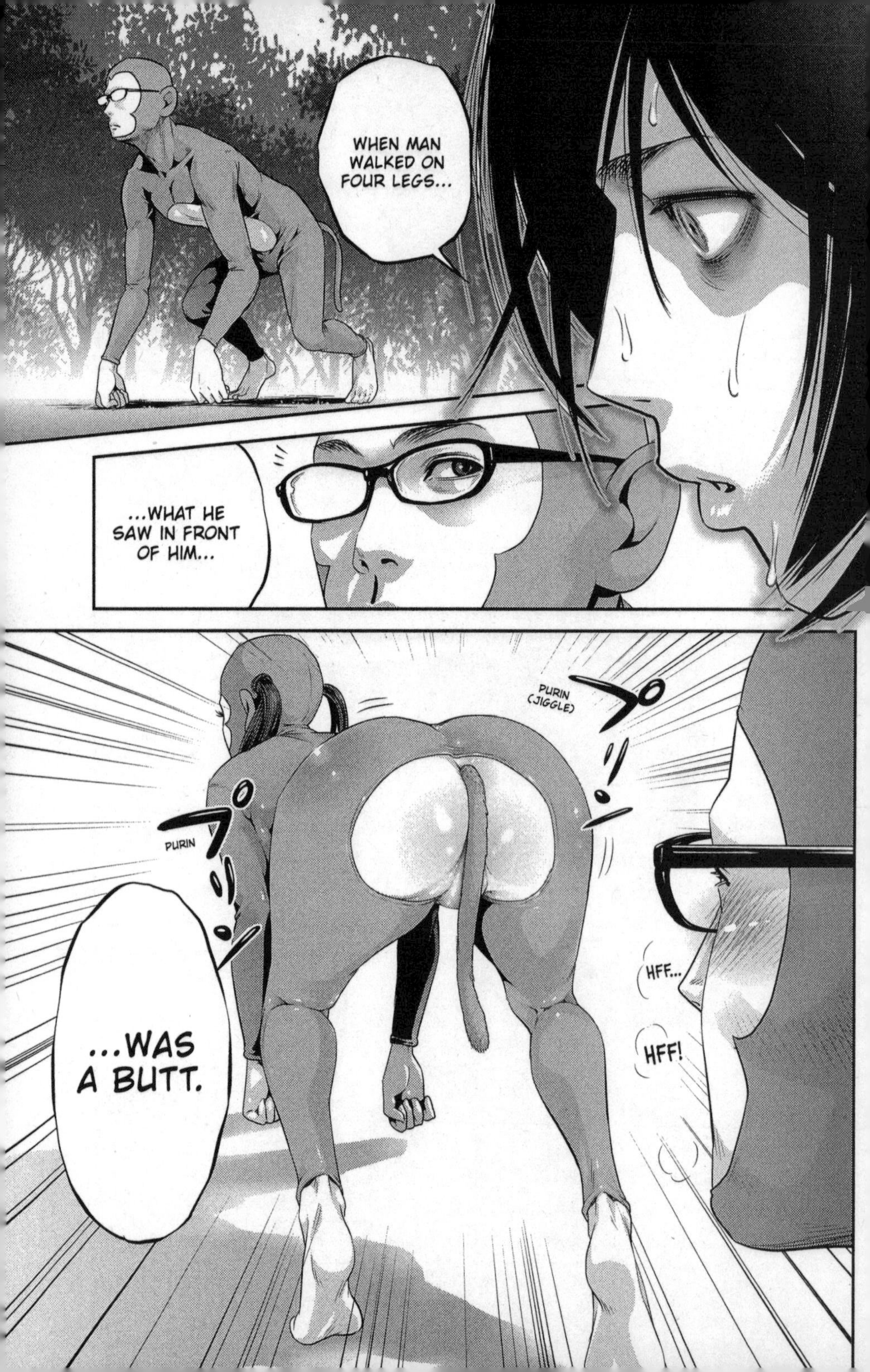
WHEN MAN WALKED ON FOUR LEGS...
...WHAT HE SAW IN FRONT OF HIM...
PURIN (JIGGLE)
HFF...
PURIN
HFF!
...WAS A BUTT.

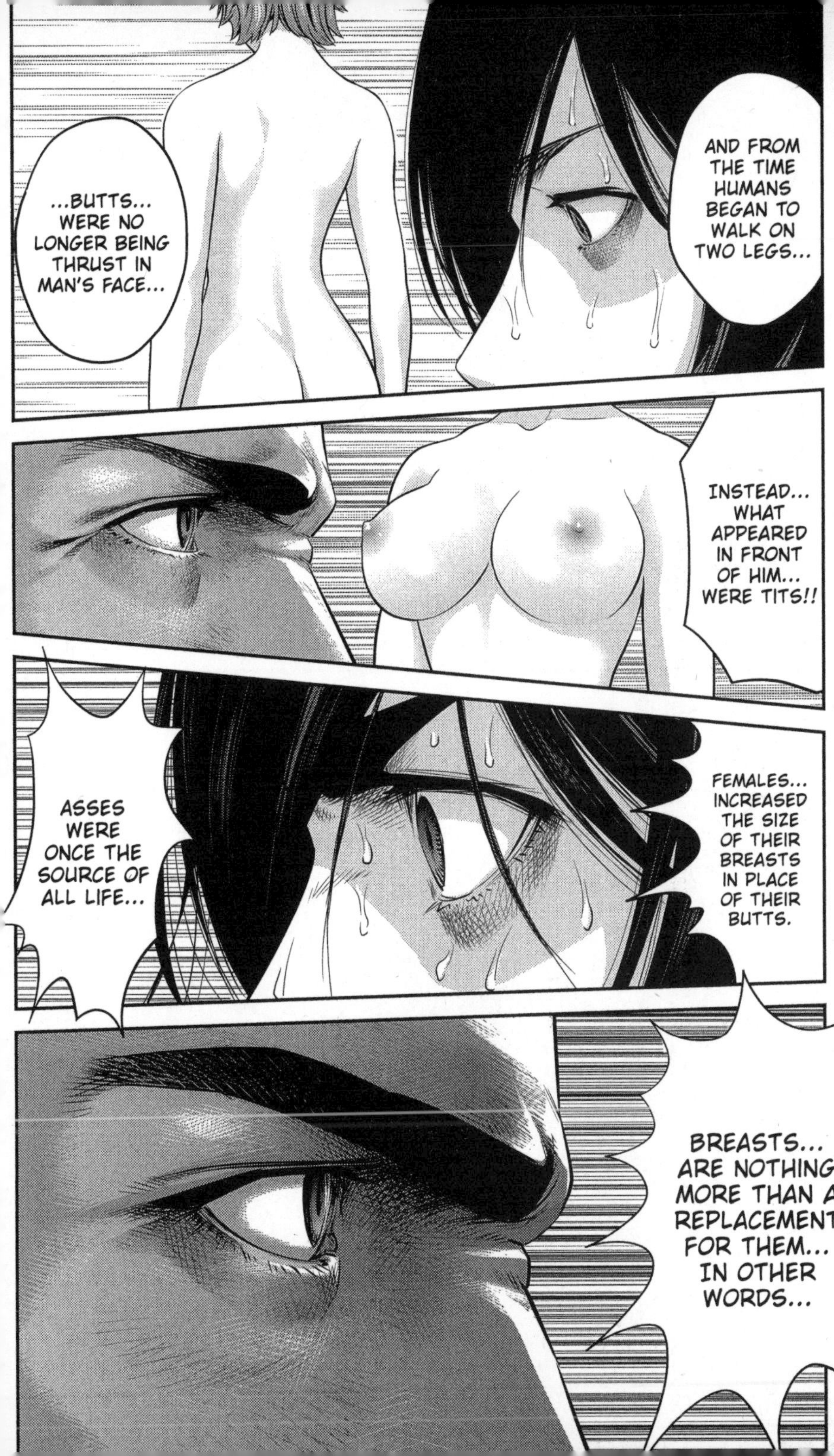
AND FROM THE TIME HUMANS BEGAN TO WALK ON TWO LEGS...
...BUTTS... WERE NO LONGER BEING THRUST IN MAN'S FACE...
INSTEAD... WHAT APPEARED IN FRONT OF HIM... WERE TITS!!
FEMALES... INCREASED THE SIZE OF THEIR BREASTS IN PLACE OF THEIR BUTTS.
ASSES WERE ONCE THE SOURCE OF ALL LIFE...
BREASTS... ARE NOTHING MORE THAN A REPLACEMENT FOR THEM... IN OTHER WORDS...

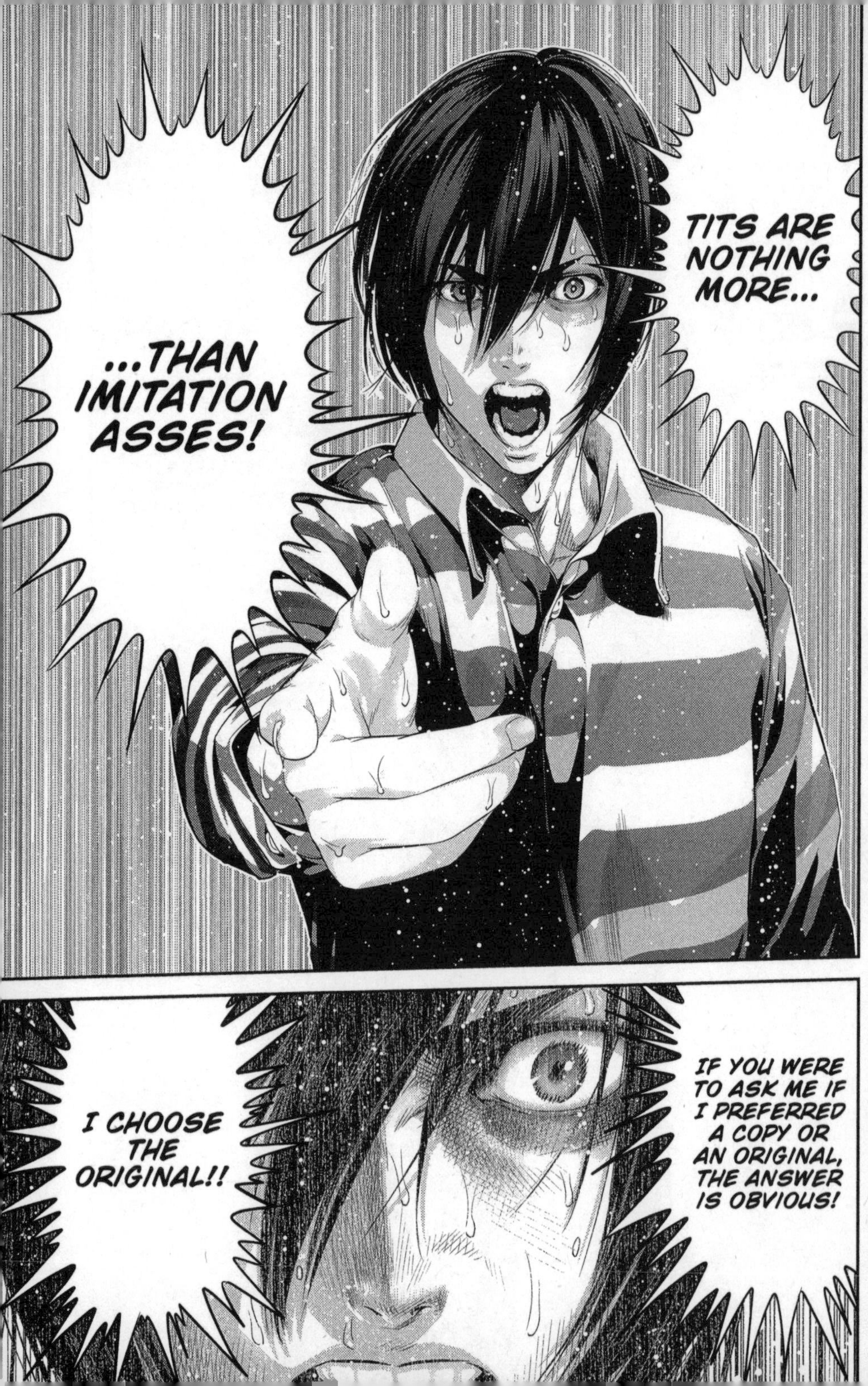
TITS ARE NOTHING MORE...
...THAN IMITATION ASSES!
IF YOU WERE TO ASK ME IF I PREFERRED A COPY OR AN ORIGINAL, THE ANSWER IS OBVIOUS!
I CHOOSE THE ORIGINAL!!

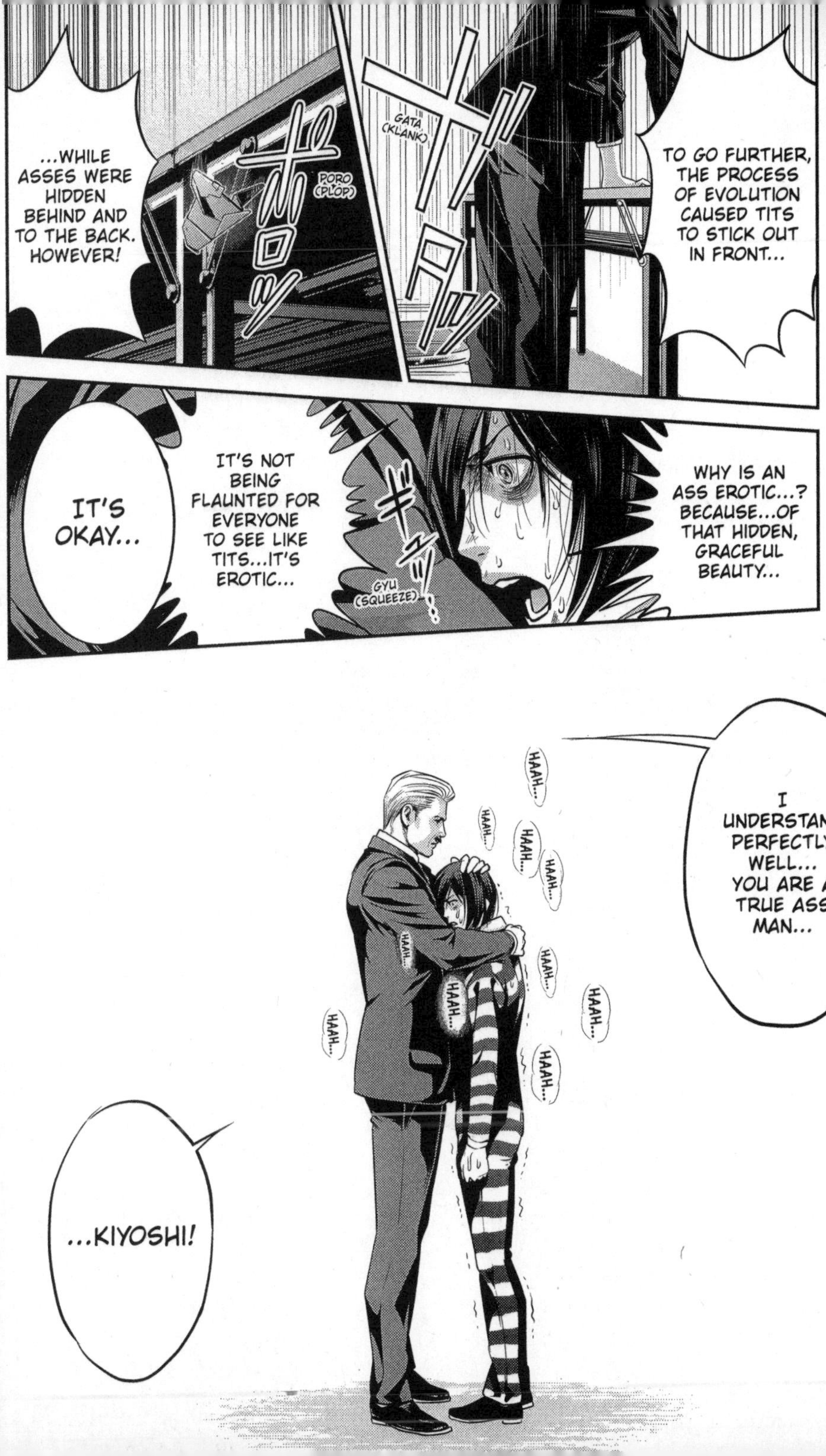
TO GO FURTHER, THE PROCESS OF EVOLUTION CAUSED TITS TO STICK OUT IN FRONT...
GATA (KLANK)
PORO (PLOP)
...WHILE ASSES WERE HIDDEN BEHIND AND TO THE BACK. HOWEVER!
WHY IS AN ASS EROTIC...? BECAUSE...OF THAT HIDDEN, GRACEFUL BEAUTY...
GYU (SQUEEZE)
IT'S NOT BEING FLAUNTED FOR EVERYONE TO SEE LIKE TITS...IT'S EROTIC...
IT'S OKAY...
I UNDERSTAND PERFECTLY WELL... YOU ARE A TRUE ASS MAN...
HAAH...
HAAH...
HAAH...
HAAH...
HAAH...
HAAH...
HAAH...
HAAH...
HAAH...
HAAH...
HAAH...
...KIYOSHI!

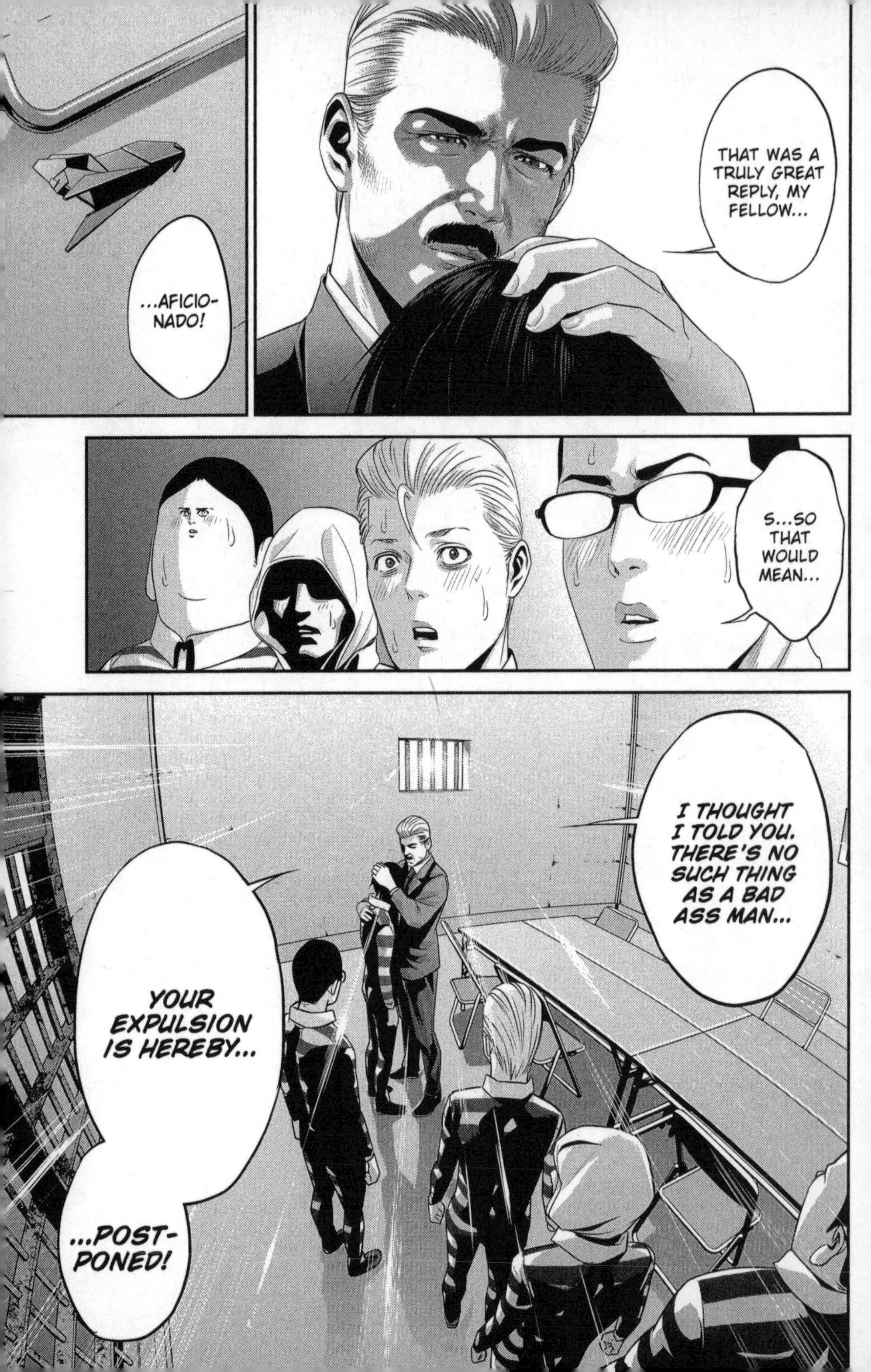
THAT WAS A TRULY GREAT REPLY, MY FELLOW...
...AFICIO-NADO!
S...SO THAT WOULD MEAN...
I THOUGHT I TOLD YOU. THERE'S NO SUCH THING AS A BAD ASS MAN...
YOUR EXPULSION IS HEREBY...
...POST-PONED!

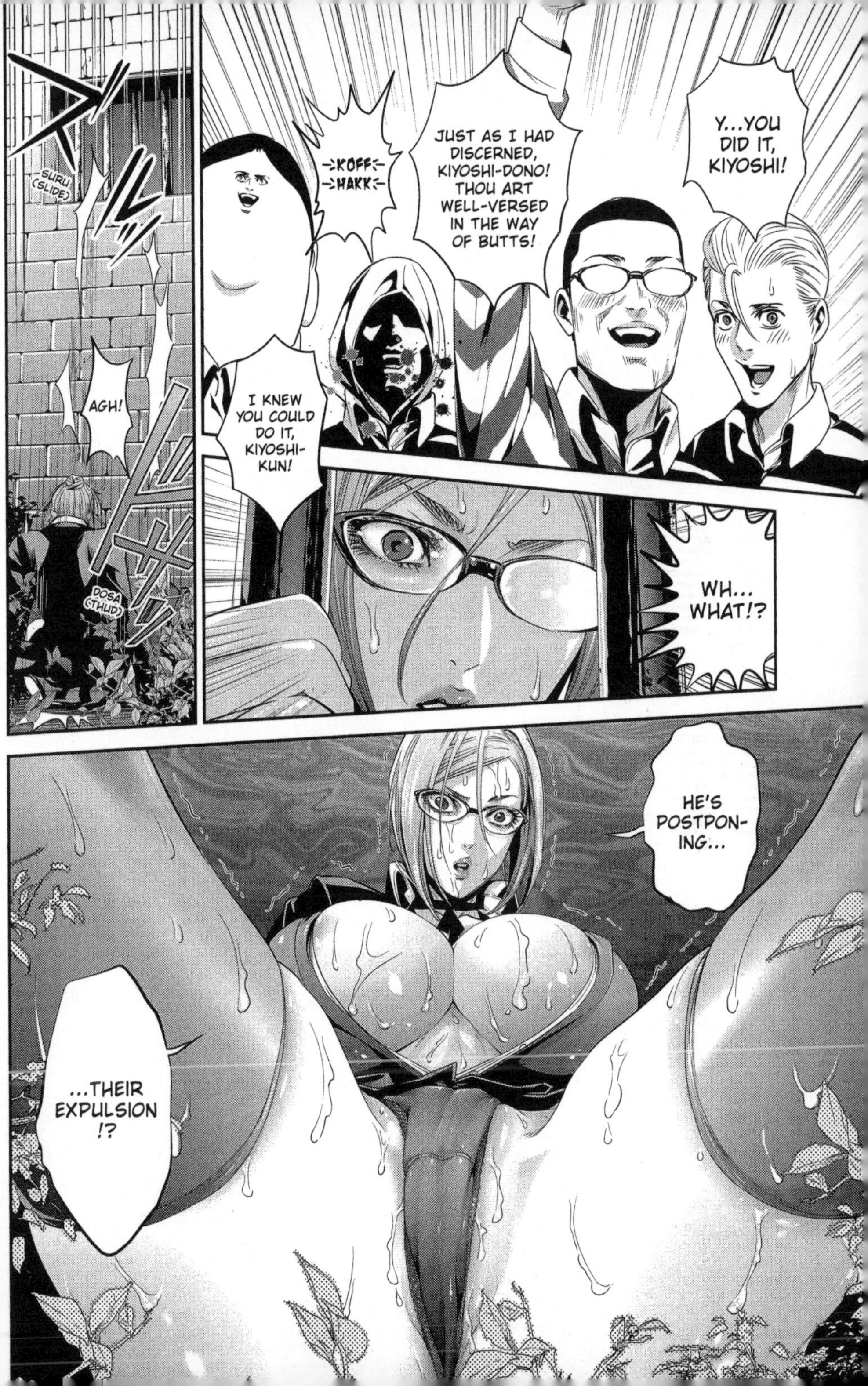
Y…YOU DID IT, KIYOSHI!
JUST AS I HAD DISCERNED, KIYOSHI-DONO! THOU ART WELL-VERSED IN THE WAY OF BUTTS!
KOFF HAKK
I KNEW YOU COULD DO IT, KIYOSHI-KUN!
WH… WHAT!?
SURU (SLIDE)
AGH!
DOSA (THUD)
HE'S POSTPON-ING…
…THEIR EXPULSION !?

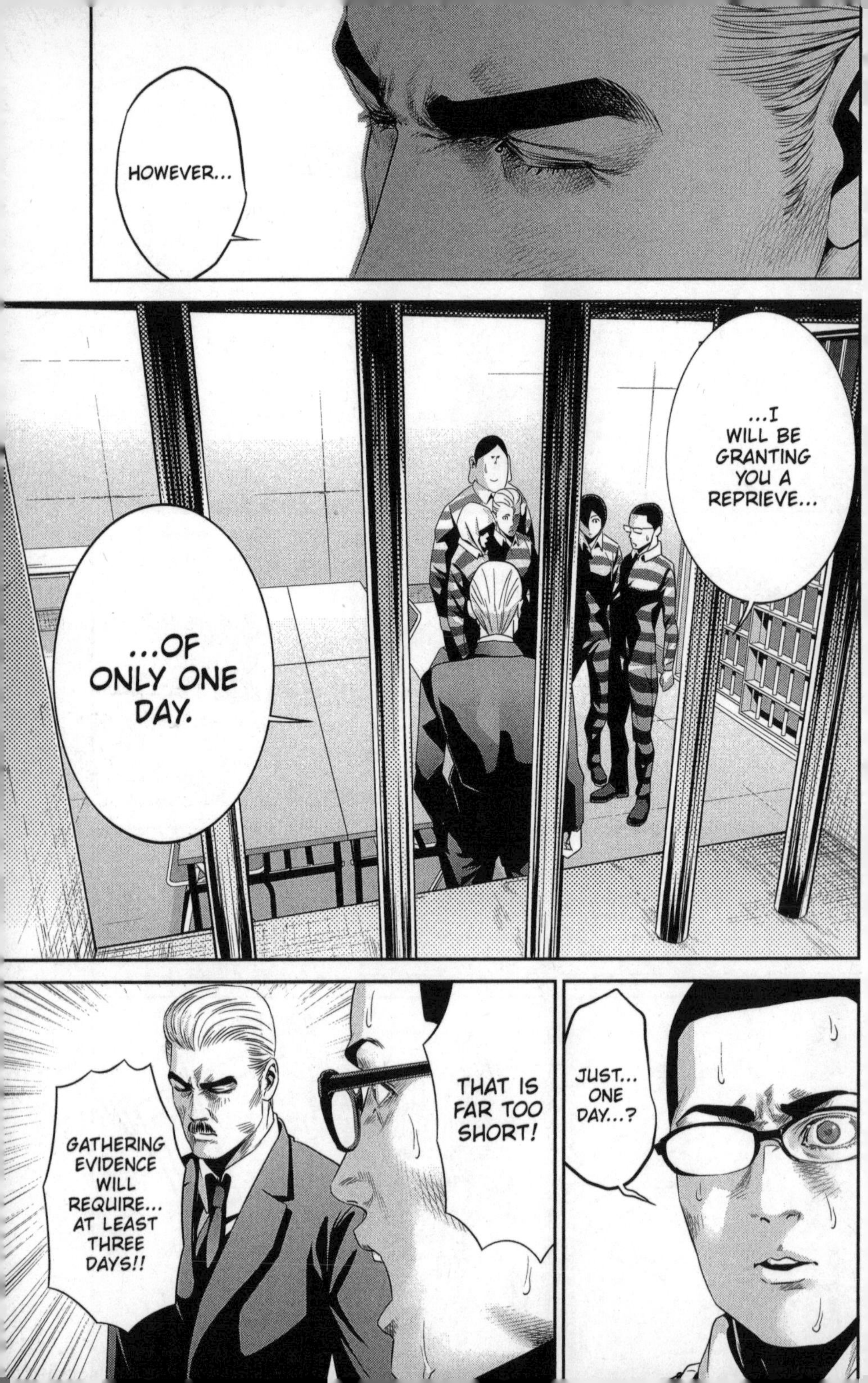
HOWEVER...
...I WILL BE GRANTING YOU A REPRIEVE...
...OF ONLY ONE DAY.
JUST... ONE DAY...?
THAT IS FAR TOO SHORT!
GATHERING EVIDENCE WILL REQUIRE... AT LEAST THREE DAYS!!

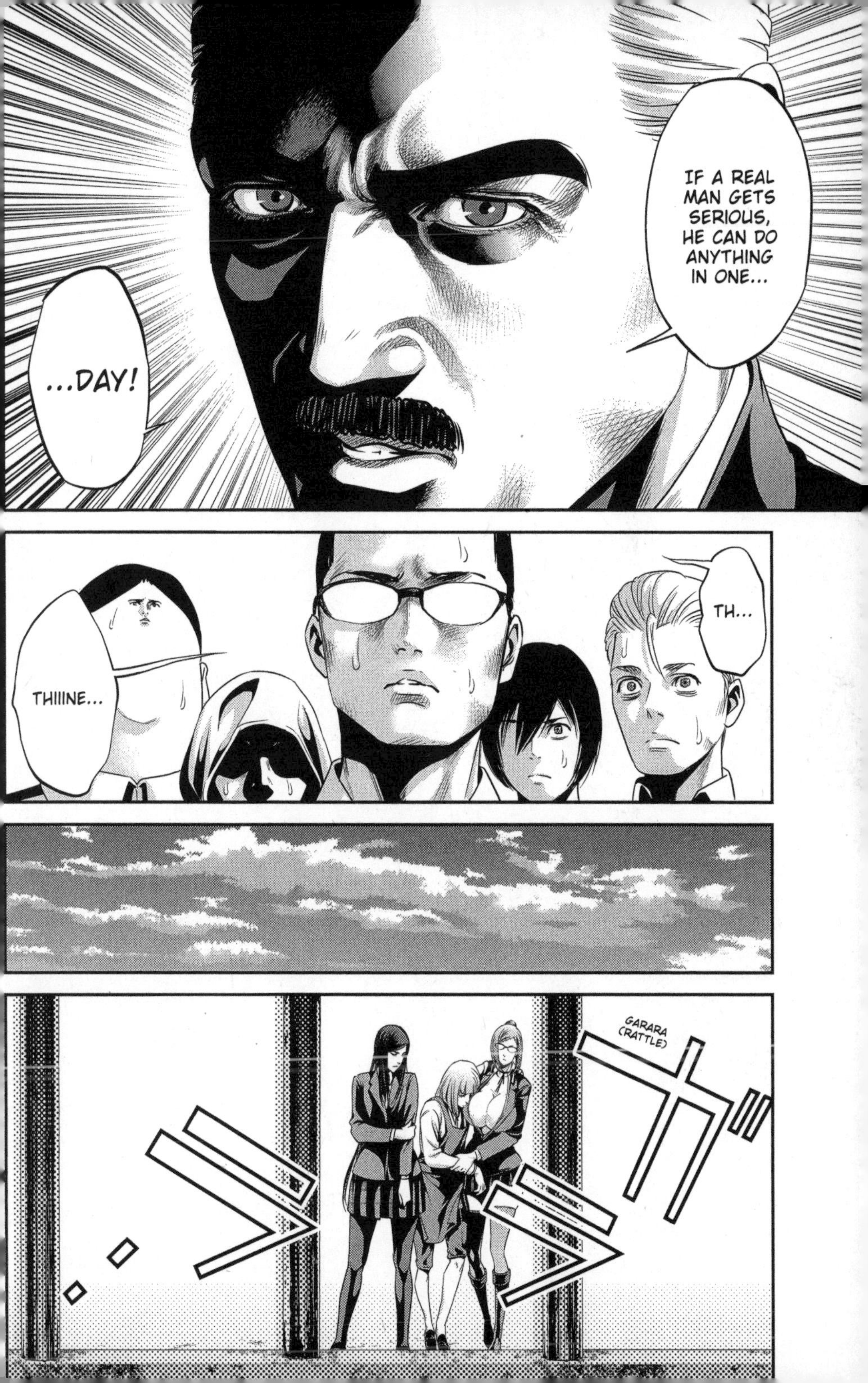
IF A REAL MAN GETS SERIOUS, HE CAN DO ANYTHING IN ONE...
...DAY!
TH...
THIIINE...
GARARA (RATTLE)

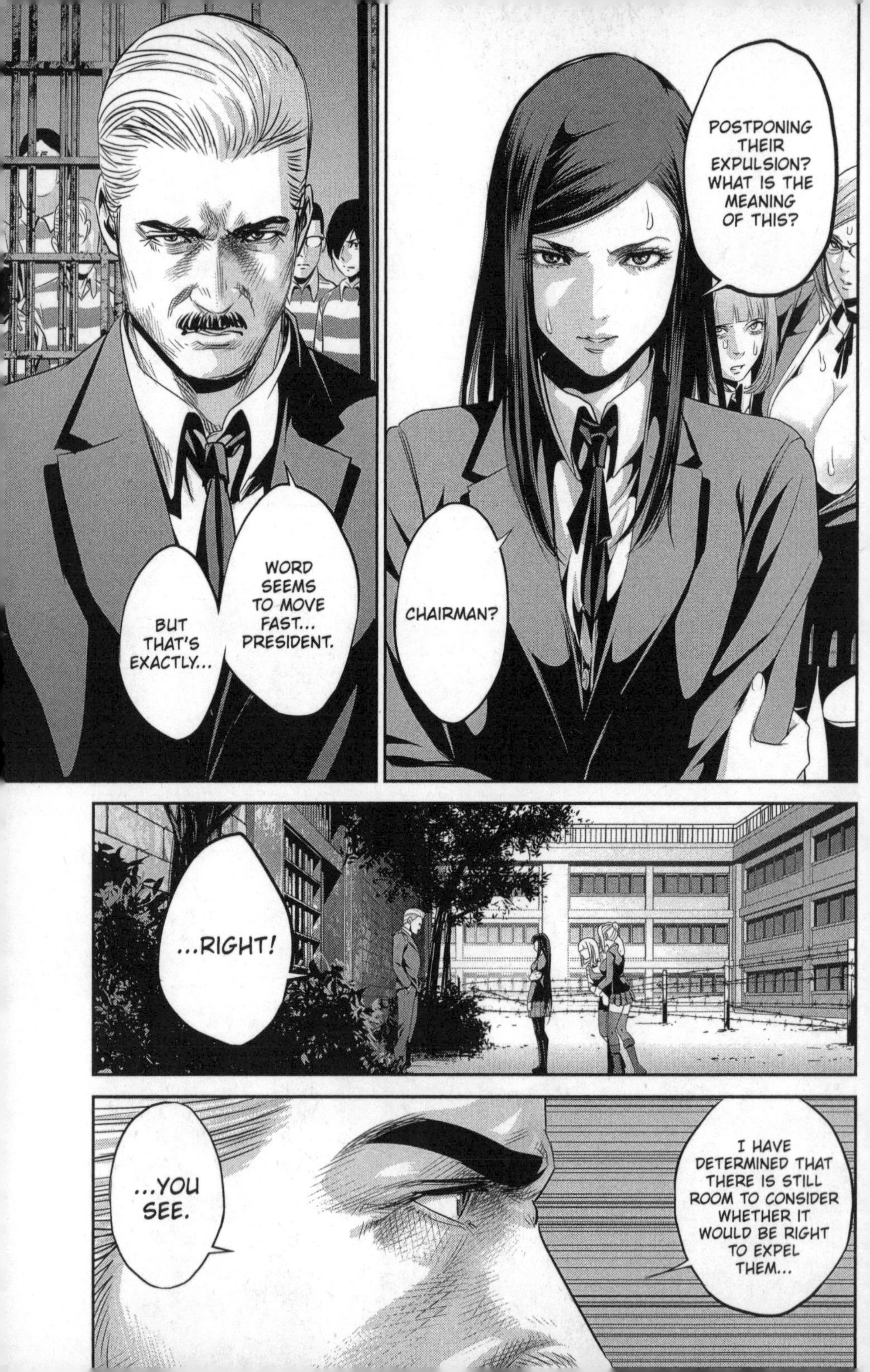
POSTPONING THEIR EXPULSION? WHAT IS THE MEANING OF THIS?
CHAIRMAN?
WORD SEEMS TO MOVE FAST... PRESIDENT.
BUT THAT'S EXACTLY...
...RIGHT!
I HAVE DETERMINED THAT THERE IS STILL ROOM TO CONSIDER WHETHER IT WOULD BE RIGHT TO EXPEL THEM...
...YOU SEE.

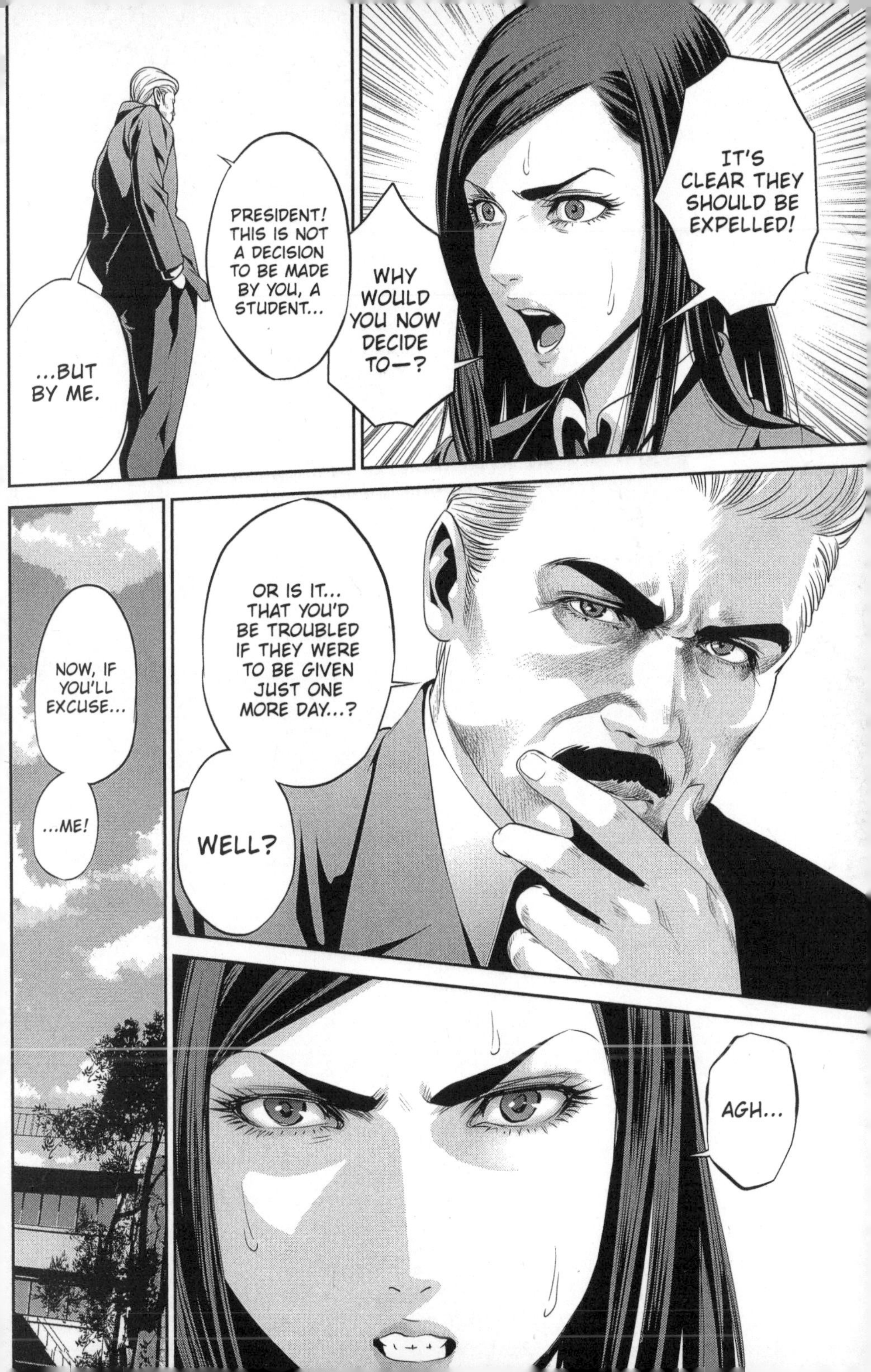
IT'S CLEAR THEY SHOULD BE EXPELLED!
WHY WOULD YOU NOW DECIDE TO—?
PRESIDENT! THIS IS NOT A DECISION TO BE MADE BY YOU, A STUDENT...
...BUT BY ME.
OR IS IT... THAT YOU'D BE TROUBLED IF THEY WERE TO BE GIVEN JUST ONE MORE DAY...?
WELL?
AGH...
NOW, IF YOU'LL EXCUSE...
...ME!

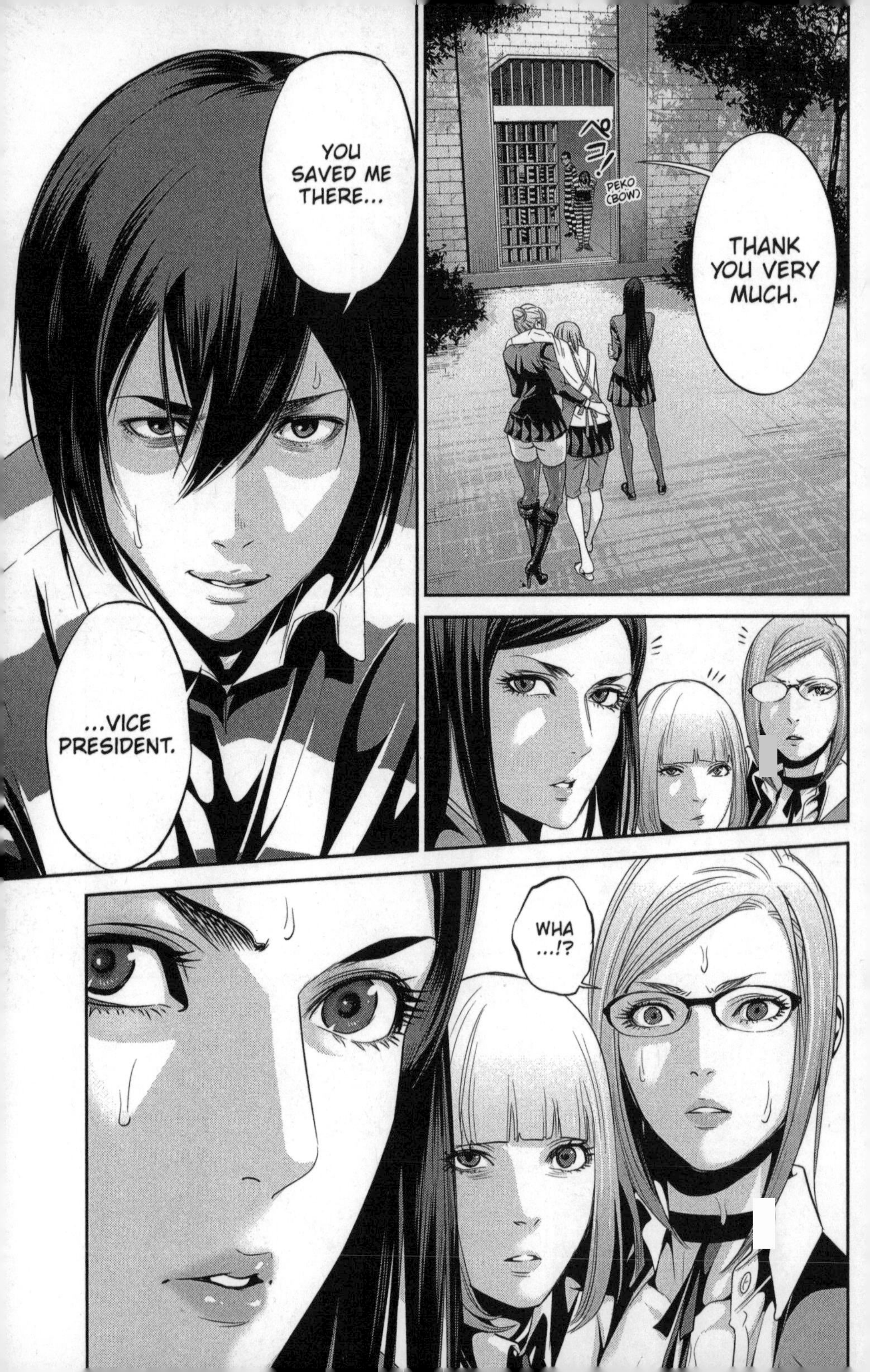
PEKO (BOW)
THANK YOU VERY MUCH.
YOU SAVED ME THERE...
...VICE PRESIDENT.
WHA ...!?

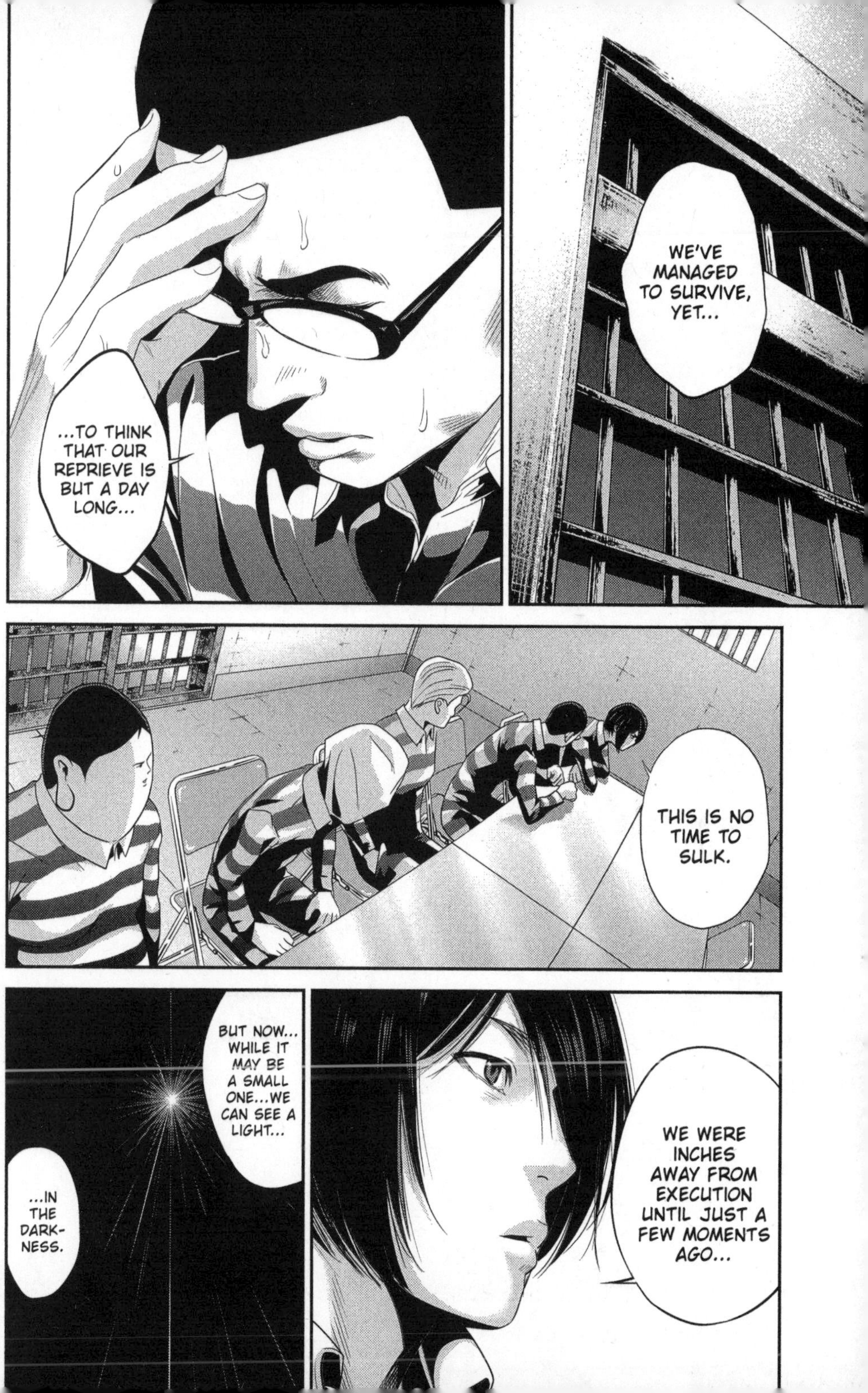
WE'VE MANAGED TO SURVIVE, YET...
...TO THINK THAT OUR REPRIEVE IS BUT A DAY LONG...
THIS IS NO TIME TO SULK.
WE WERE INCHES AWAY FROM EXECUTION UNTIL JUST A FEW MOMENTS AGO...
BUT NOW... WHILE IT MAY BE A SMALL ONE...WE CAN SEE A LIGHT...
...IN THE DARK-NESS.

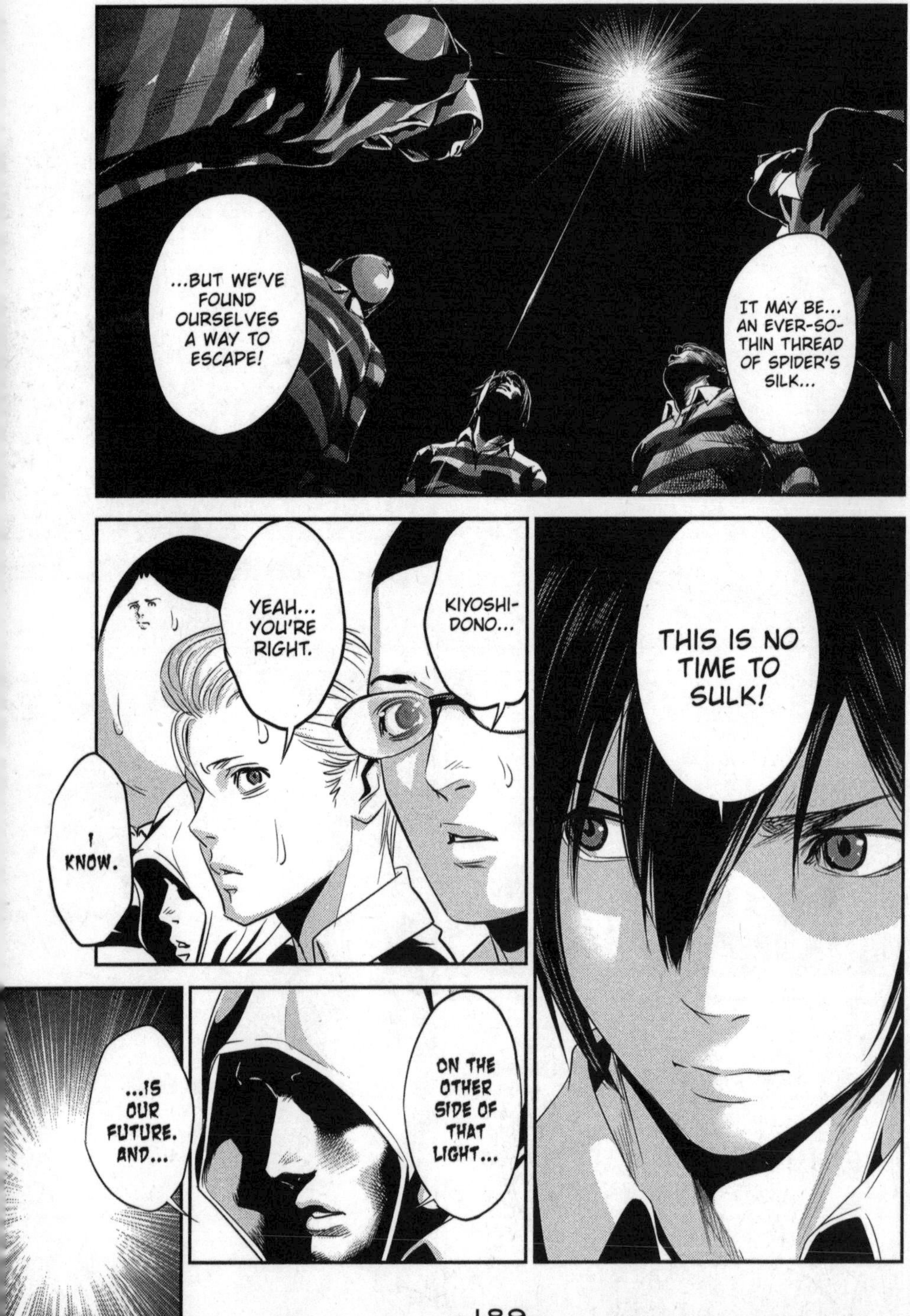
IT MAY BE... AN EVER-SO-THIN THREAD OF SPIDER'S SILK...
...BUT WE'VE FOUND OURSELVES A WAY TO ESCAPE!
THIS IS NO TIME TO SULK!
KIYOSHI-DONO...
YEAH... YOU'RE RIGHT.
I KNOW.
ON THE OTHER SIDE OF THAT LIGHT...
...IS OUR FUTURE. AND...

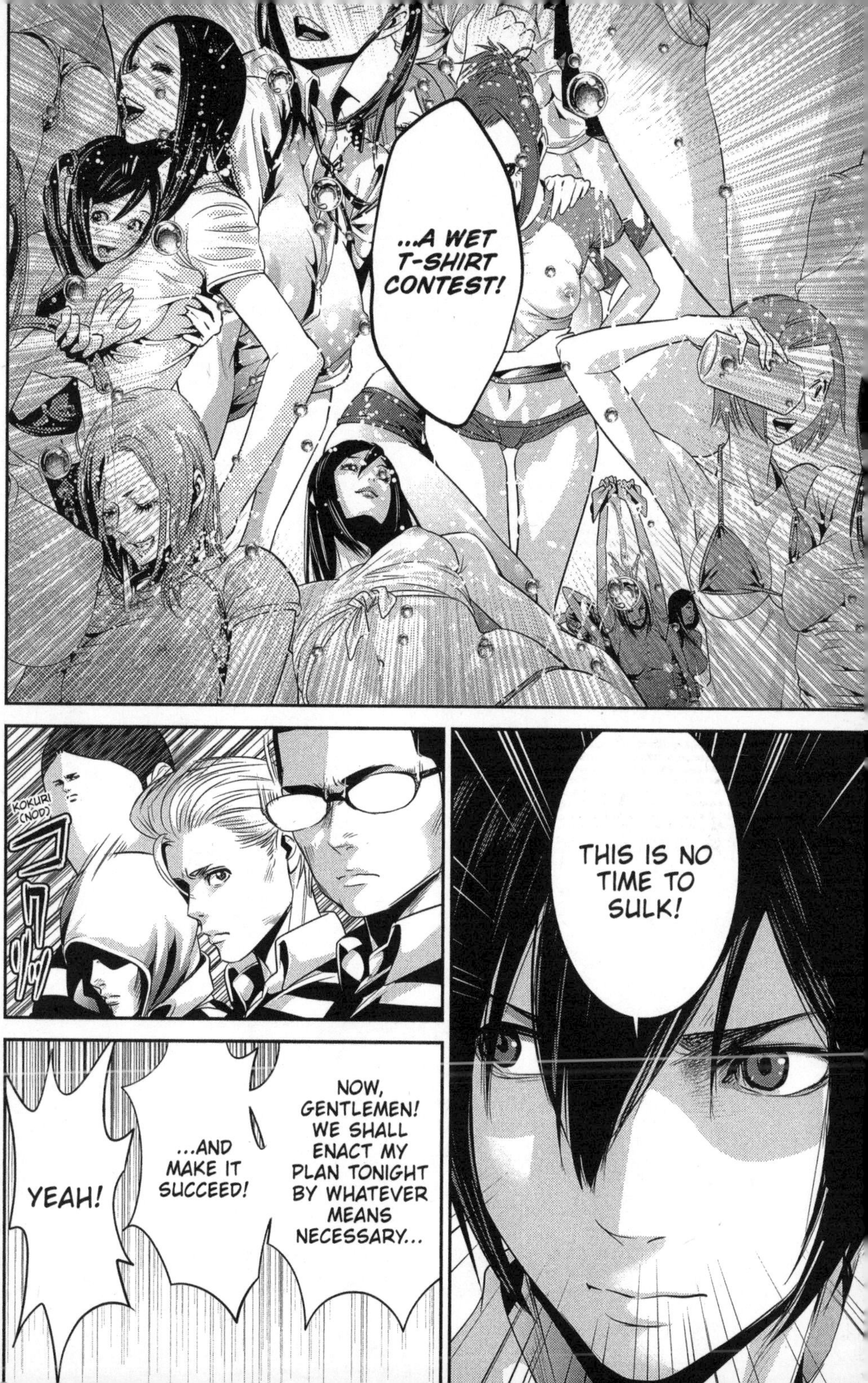
...A WET T-SHIRT CONTEST!
THIS IS NO TIME TO SULK!
KOKURI (NOD)
NOW, GENTLEMEN! WE SHALL ENACT MY PLAN TONIGHT BY WHATEVER MEANS NECESSARY...
...AND MAKE IT SUCCEED!
YEAH!

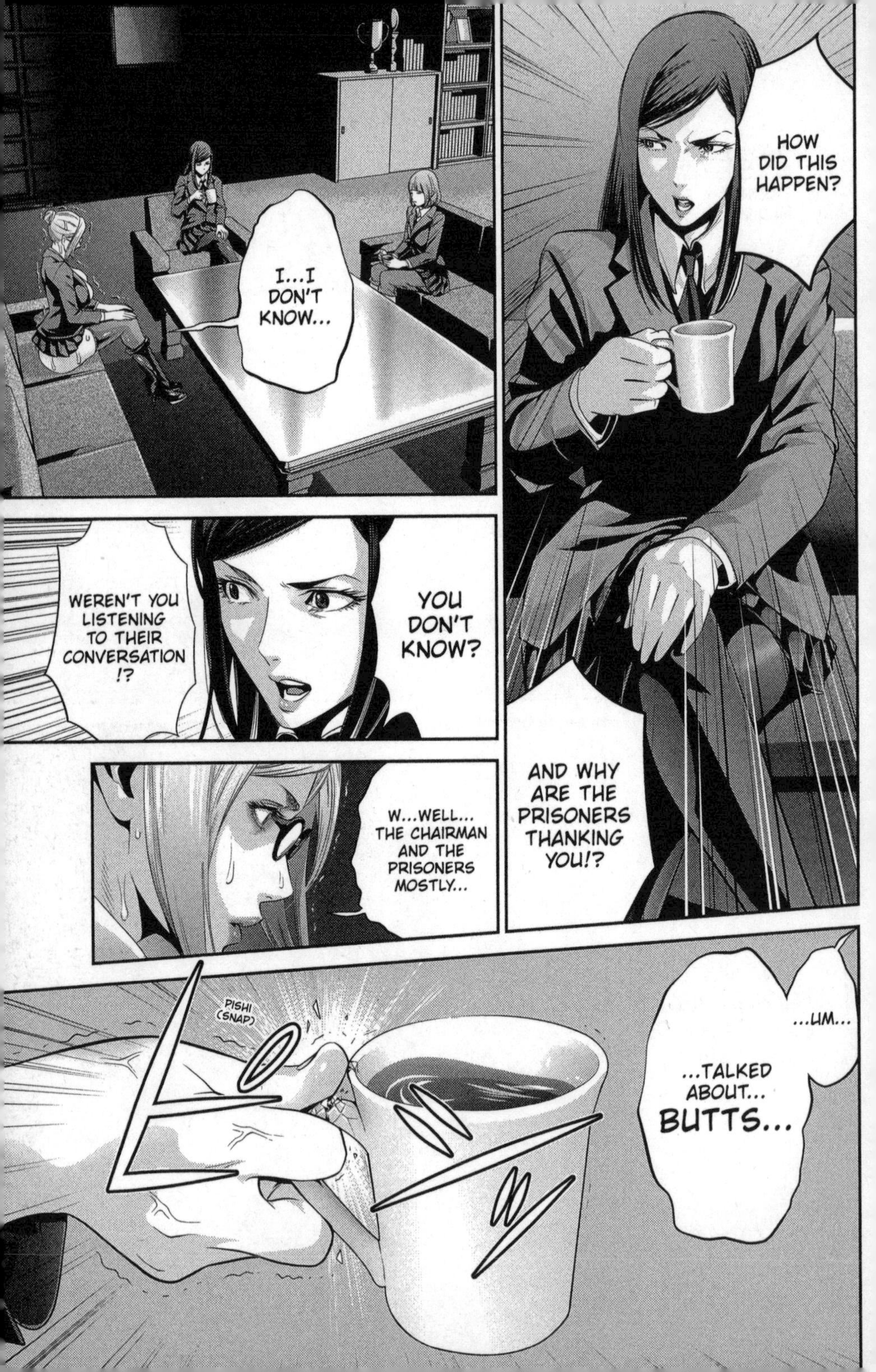
HOW DID THIS HAPPEN?
AND WHY ARE THE PRISONERS THANKING YOU!?
I...I DON'T KNOW...
YOU DON'T KNOW?
WEREN'T YOU LISTENING TO THEIR CONVERSATION!?
W...WELL... THE CHAIRMAN AND THE PRISONERS MOSTLY...
...UM...
...TALKED ABOUT... BUTTS...
PISHI (SNAP)

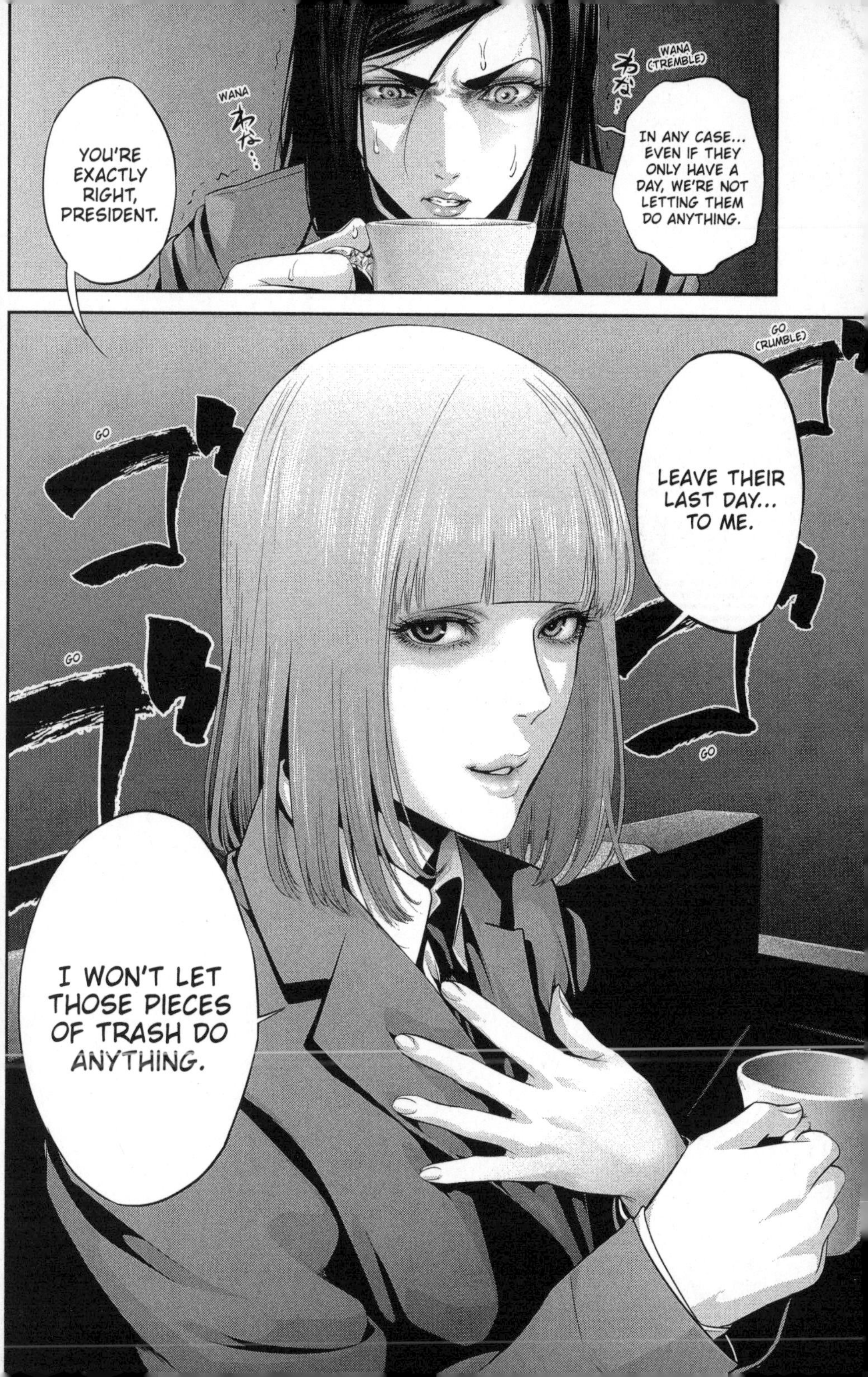

わな…
WANA (TREMBLE)
IN ANY CASE... EVEN IF THEY ONLY HAVE A DAY, WE'RE NOT LETTING THEM DO ANYTHING.
わな…
WANA
YOU'RE EXACTLY RIGHT, PRESIDENT.
GO (RUMBLE)
LEAVE THEIR LAST DAY... TO ME.
GO
GO
GO
I WON'T LET THOSE PIECES OF TRASH DO ANYTHING.

PRISON SCHOOL

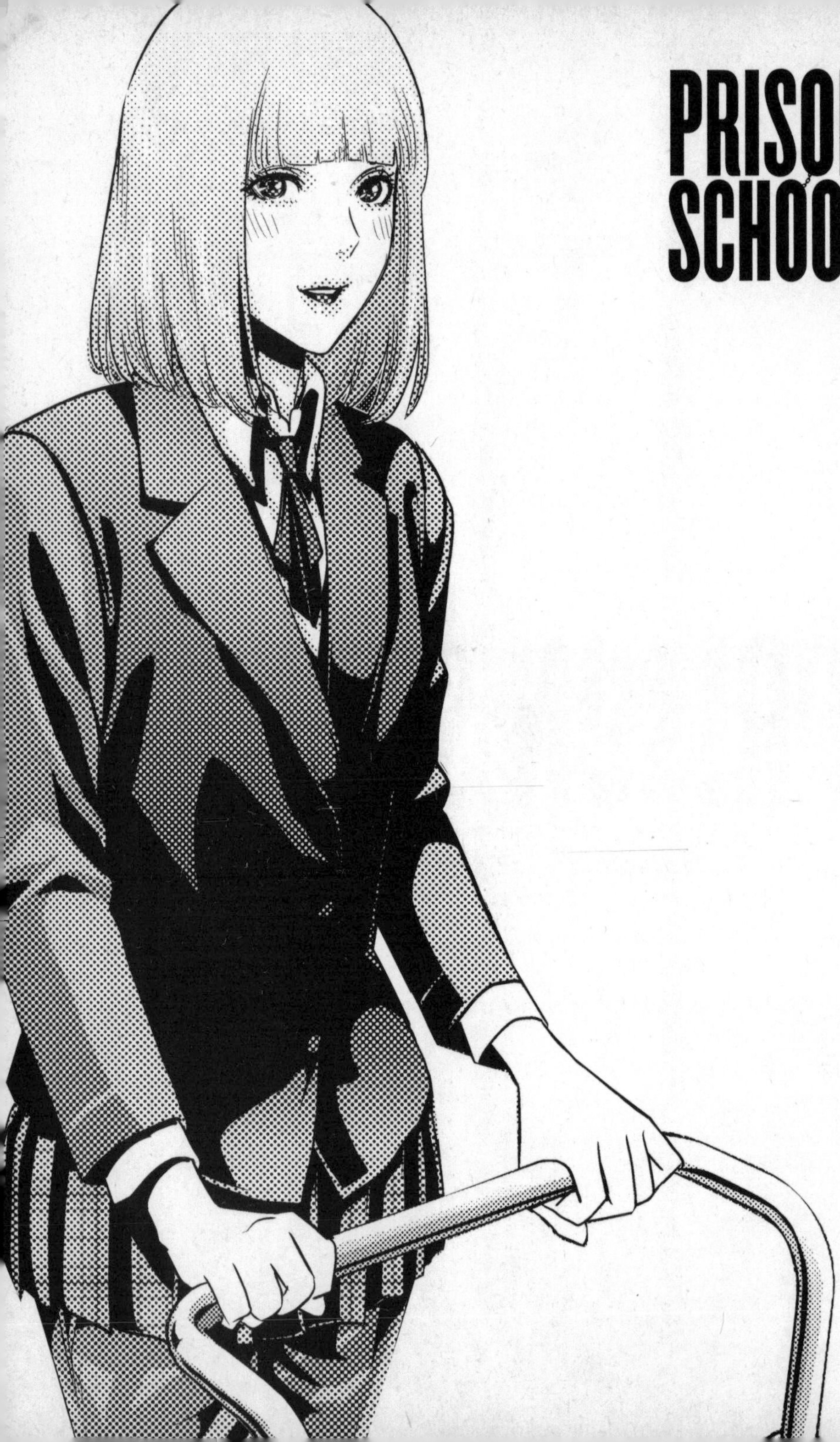

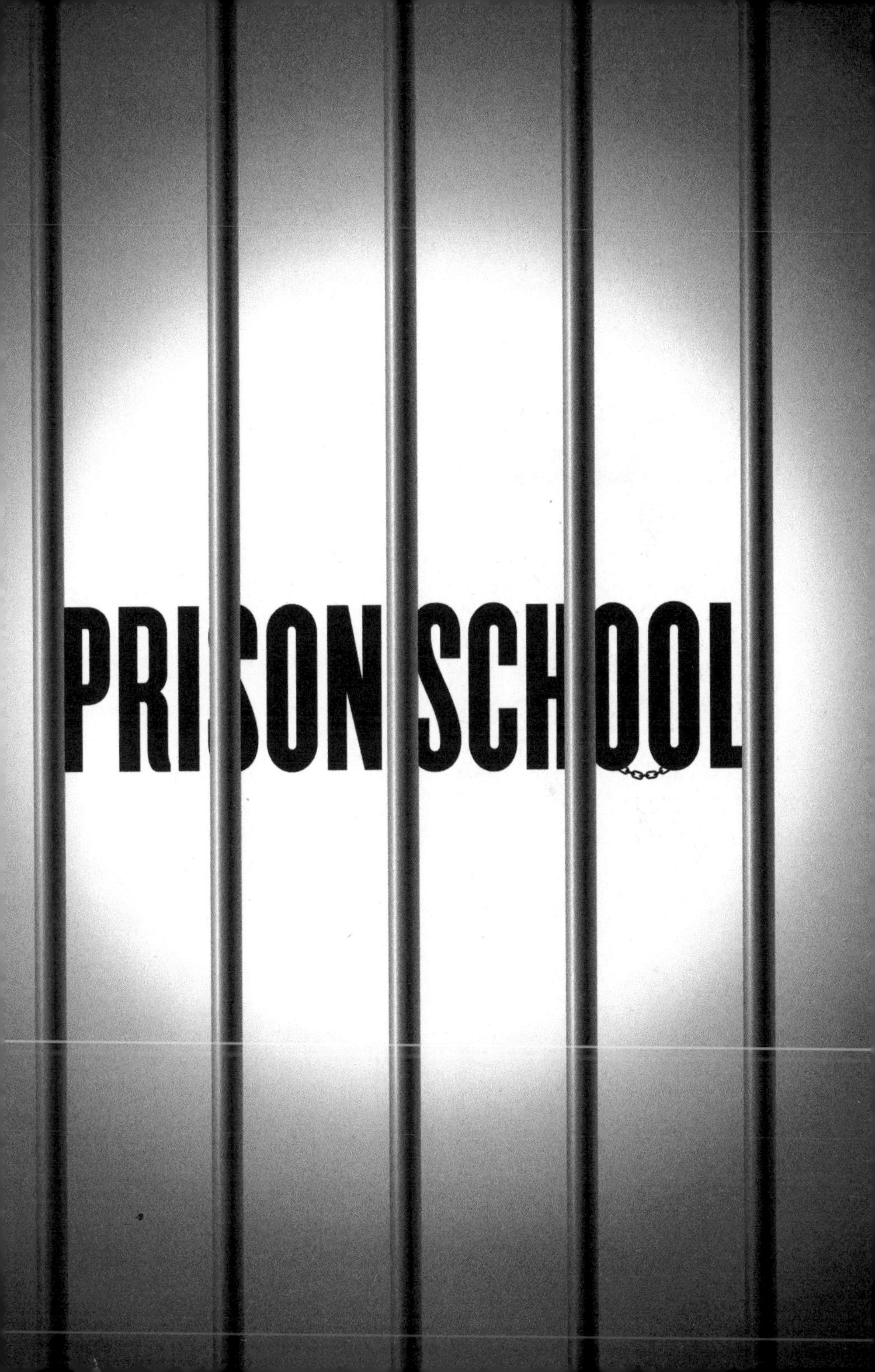
PRISON SCHOOL

CHAPTER 69: ERYNGII BROCKOVICH

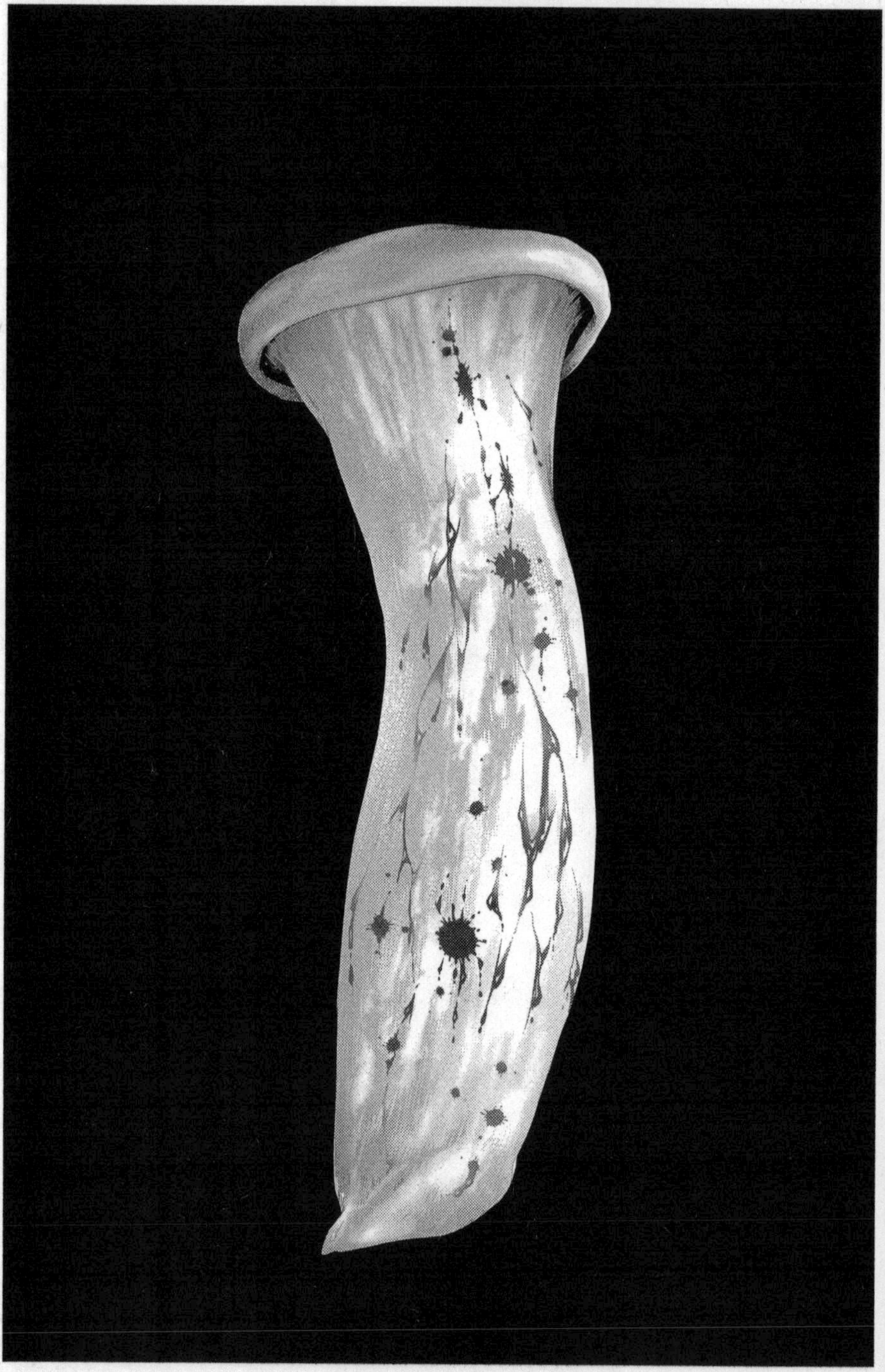

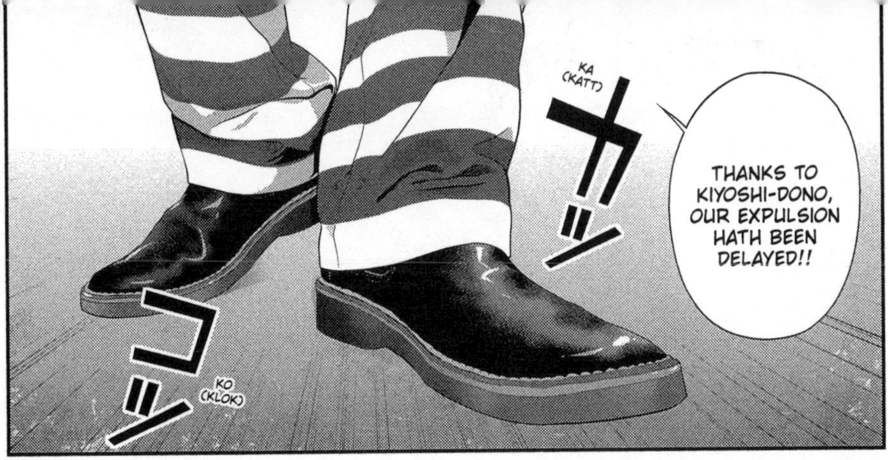
THANKS TO KIYOSHI-DONO, OUR EXPULSION HATH BEEN DELAYED!!
KA (KATT)
KO (KLOK)

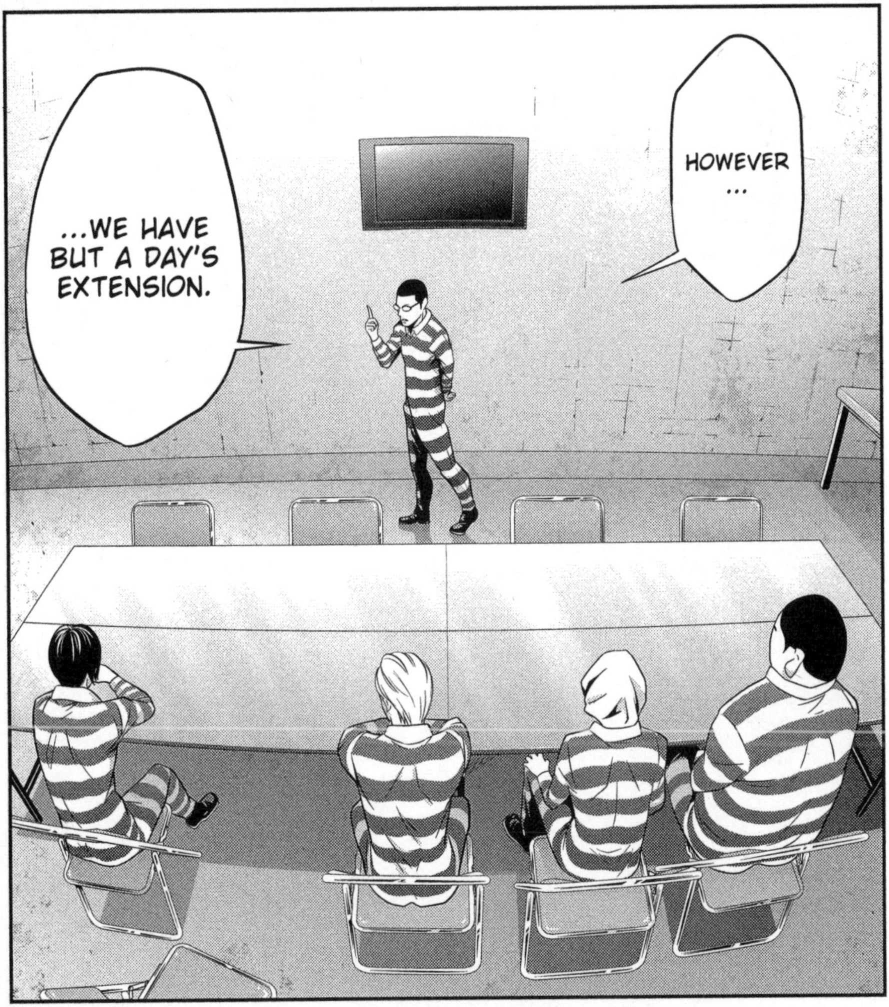
HOWEVER ...
...WE HAVE BUT A DAY'S EXTENSION.

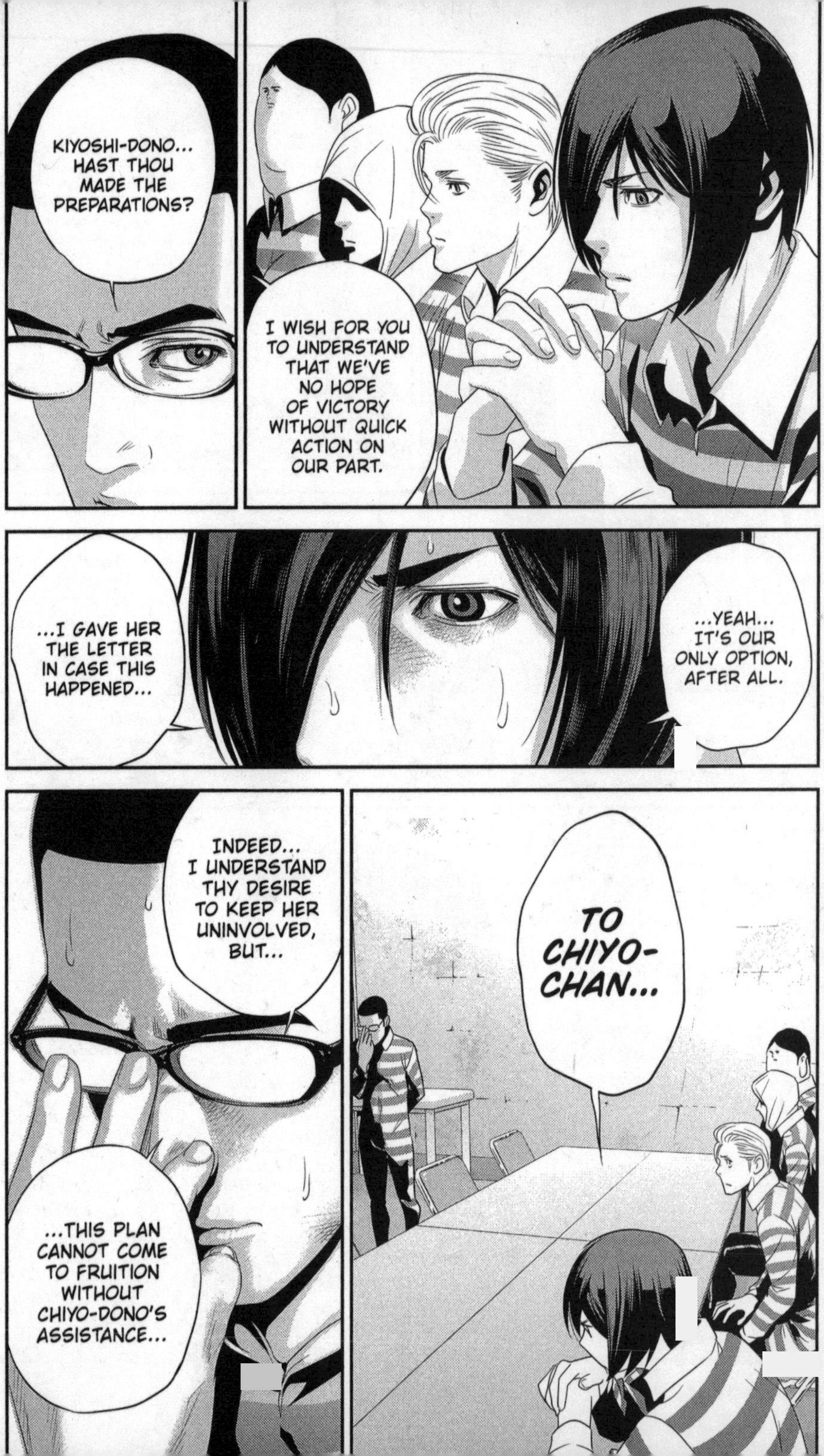
I WISH FOR YOU TO UNDERSTAND THAT WE'VE NO HOPE OF VICTORY WITHOUT QUICK ACTION ON OUR PART.
KIYOSHI-DONO... HAST THOU MADE THE PREPARATIONS?
...YEAH... IT'S OUR ONLY OPTION, AFTER ALL.
...I GAVE HER THE LETTER IN CASE THIS HAPPENED...
TO CHIYO-CHAN...
INDEED... I UNDERSTAND THY DESIRE TO KEEP HER UNINVOLVED, BUT...
...THIS PLAN CANNOT COME TO FRUITION WITHOUT CHIYO-DONO'S ASSISTANCE...

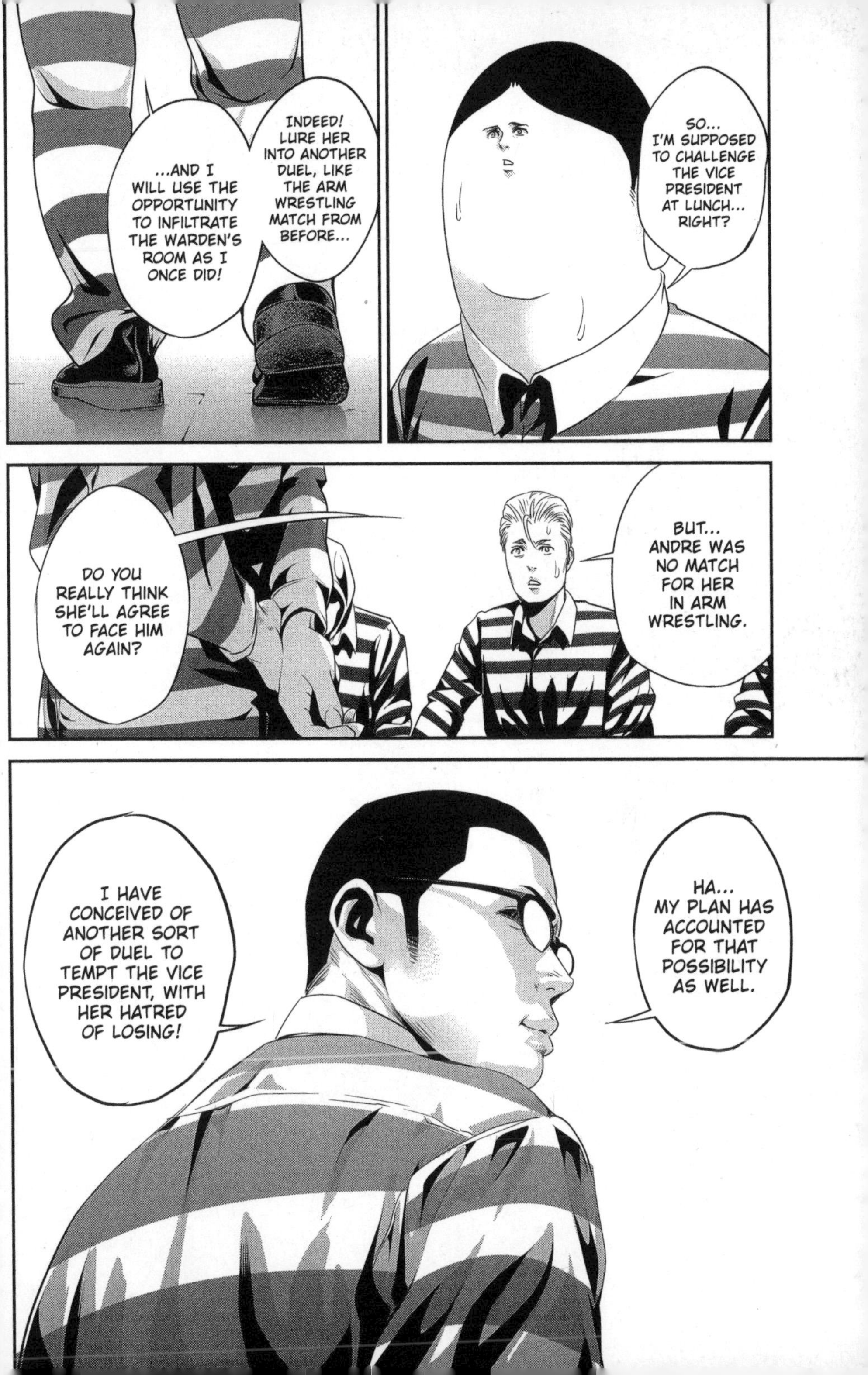
SO... I'M SUPPOSED TO CHALLENGE THE VICE PRESIDENT AT LUNCH... RIGHT?
INDEED! LURE HER INTO ANOTHER DUEL, LIKE THE ARM WRESTLING MATCH FROM BEFORE...
...AND I WILL USE THE OPPORTUNITY TO INFILTRATE THE WARDEN'S ROOM AS I ONCE DID!
BUT... ANDRE WAS NO MATCH FOR HER IN ARM WRESTLING.
DO YOU REALLY THINK SHE'LL AGREE TO FACE HIM AGAIN?
HA... MY PLAN HAS ACCOUNTED FOR THAT POSSIBILITY AS WELL.
I HAVE CONCEIVED OF ANOTHER SORT OF DUEL TO TEMPT THE VICE PRESIDENT, WITH HER HATRED OF LOSING!

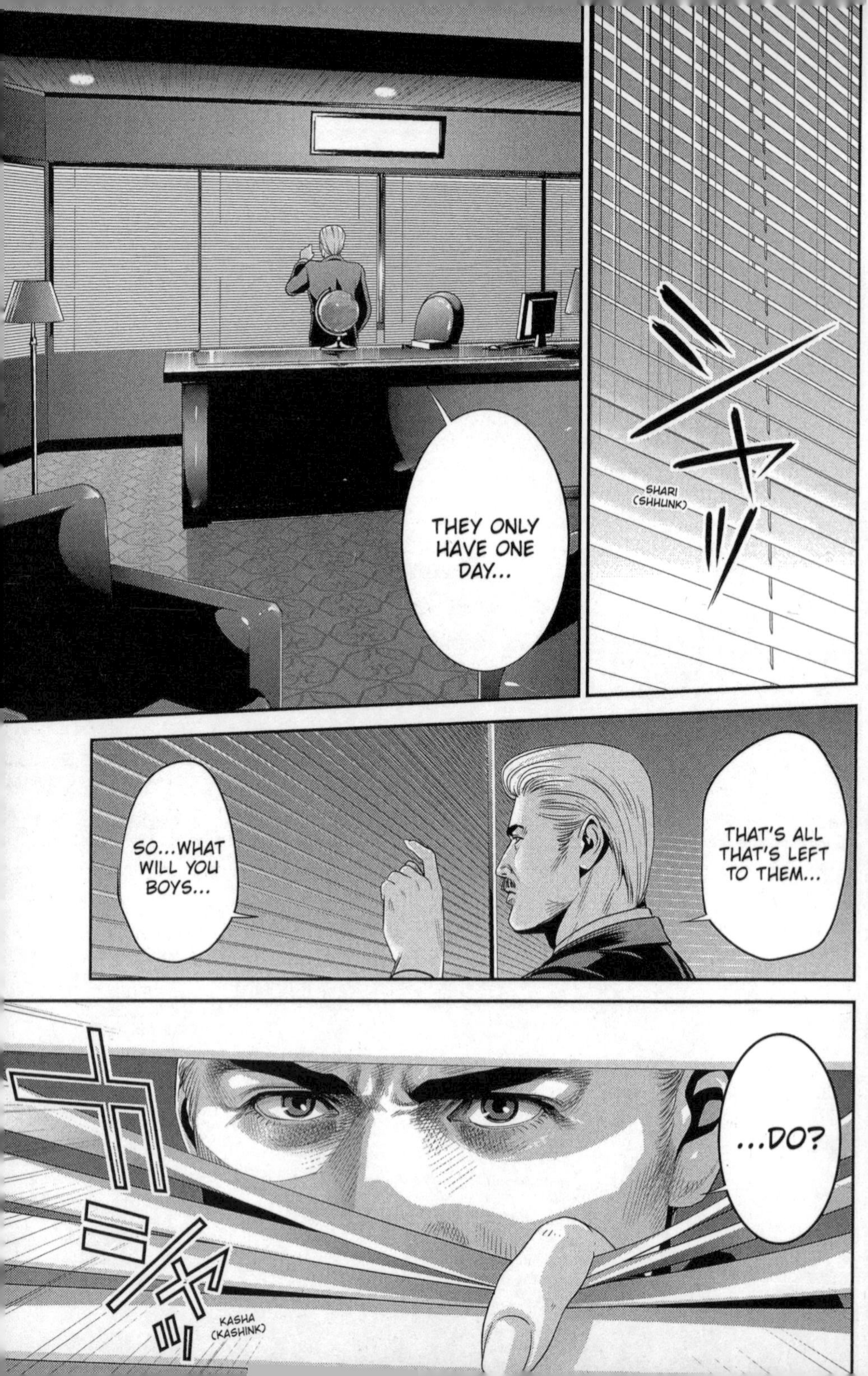
SHARI (SHHUNK)
THEY ONLY HAVE ONE DAY...
THAT'S ALL THAT'S LEFT TO THEM...
SO...WHAT WILL YOU BOYS...
...DO?
KASHA (KASHINK)

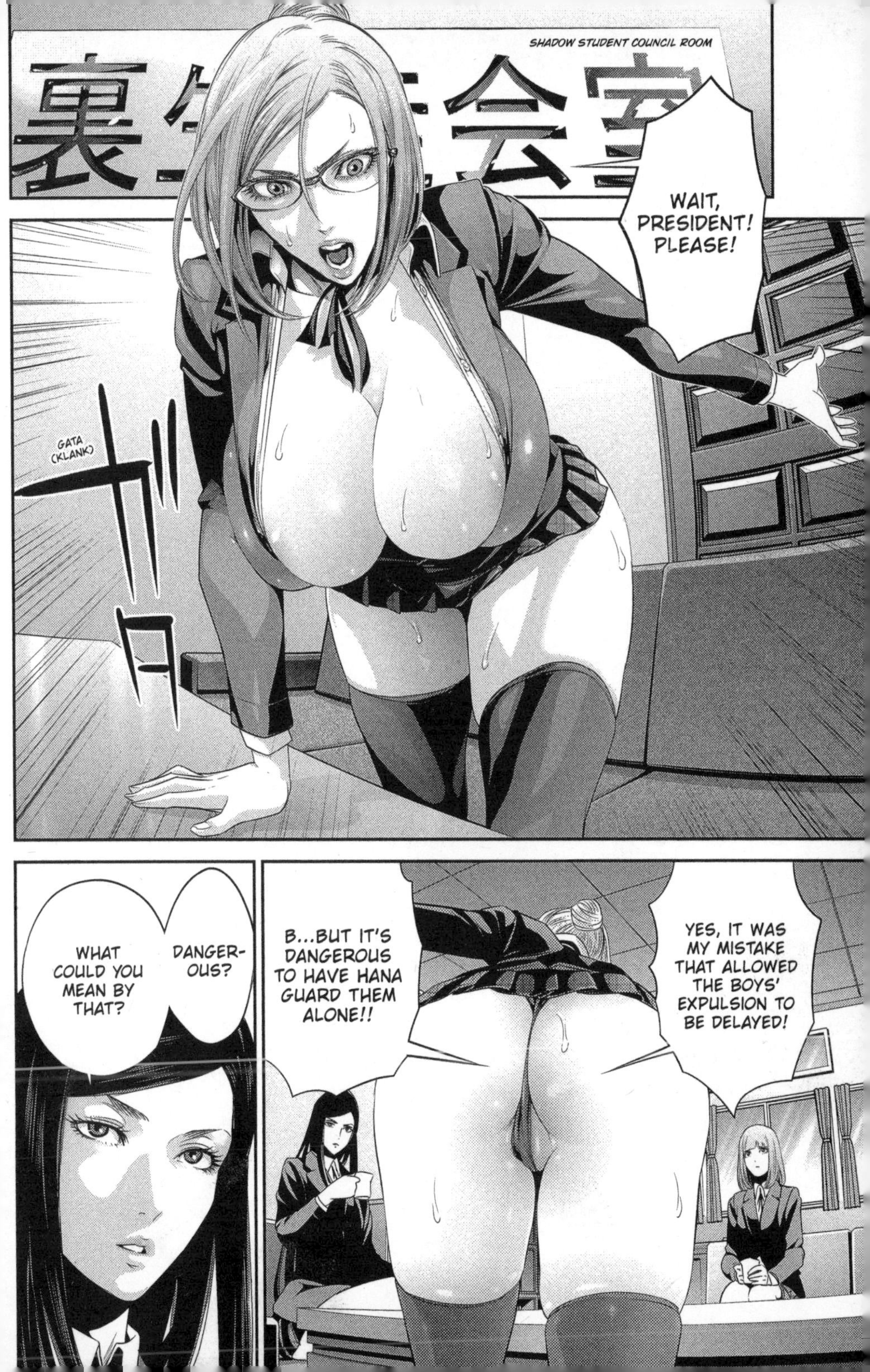
SHADOW STUDENT COUNCIL ROOM
WAIT, PRESIDENT! PLEASE!
GATA (KLANK)
YES, IT WAS MY MISTAKE THAT ALLOWED THE BOYS' EXPULSION TO BE DELAYED!
B...BUT IT'S DANGEROUS TO HAVE HANA GUARD THEM ALONE!!
DANGER-OUS?
WHAT COULD YOU MEAN BY THAT?

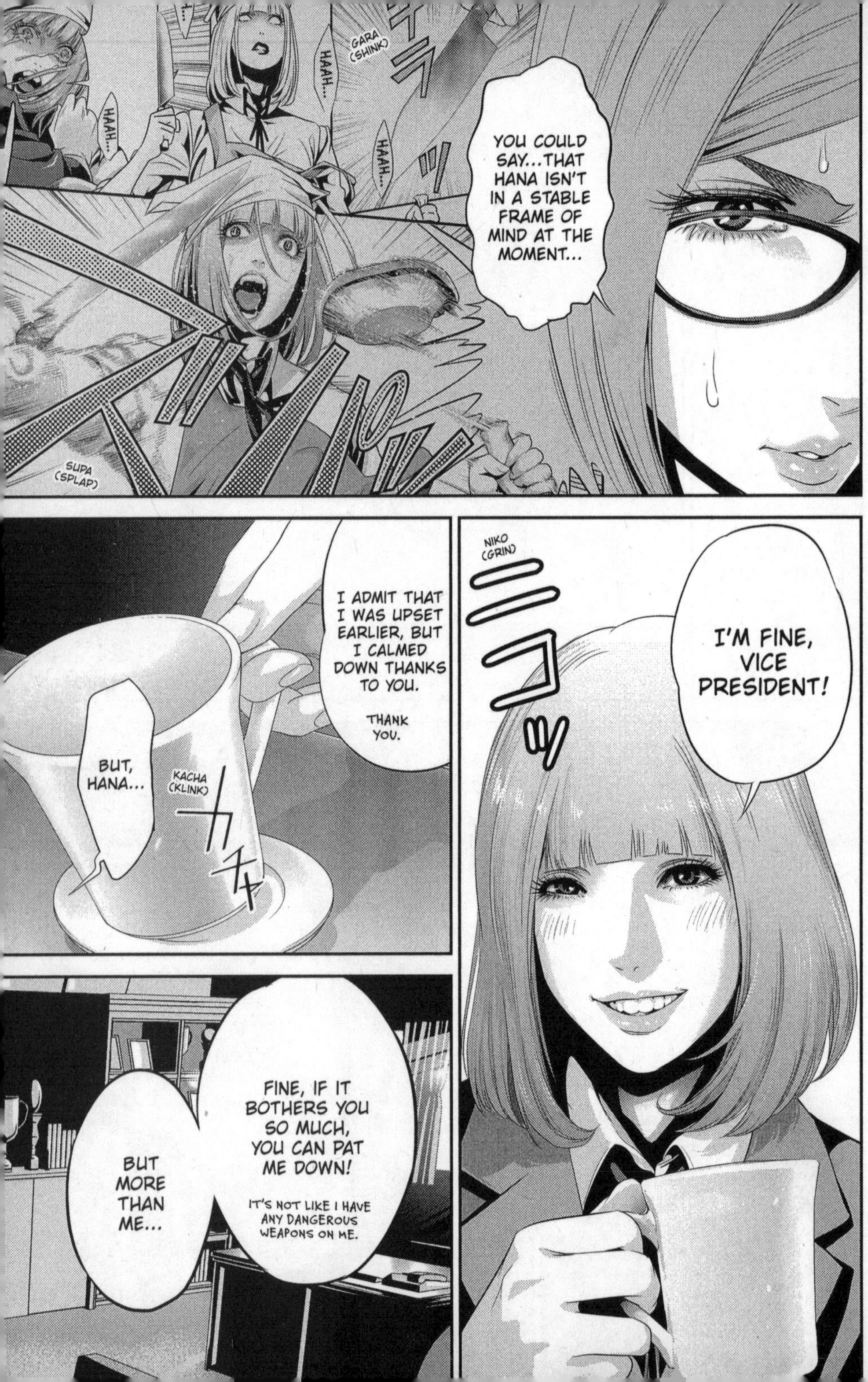
YOU COULD SAY...THAT HANA ISN'T IN A STABLE FRAME OF MIND AT THE MOMENT...
GARA (SHINK)
HAAH...
HAAH...
HAAH...
SUPA (SPLAP)
NIKO (GRIN)
I'M FINE, VICE PRESIDENT!
I ADMIT THAT I WAS UPSET EARLIER, BUT I CALMED DOWN THANKS TO YOU.
THANK YOU.
KACHA (KLINK)
BUT, HANA...
FINE, IF IT BOTHERS YOU SO MUCH, YOU CAN PAT ME DOWN!
IT'S NOT LIKE I HAVE ANY DANGEROUS WEAPONS ON ME.
BUT MORE THAN ME...

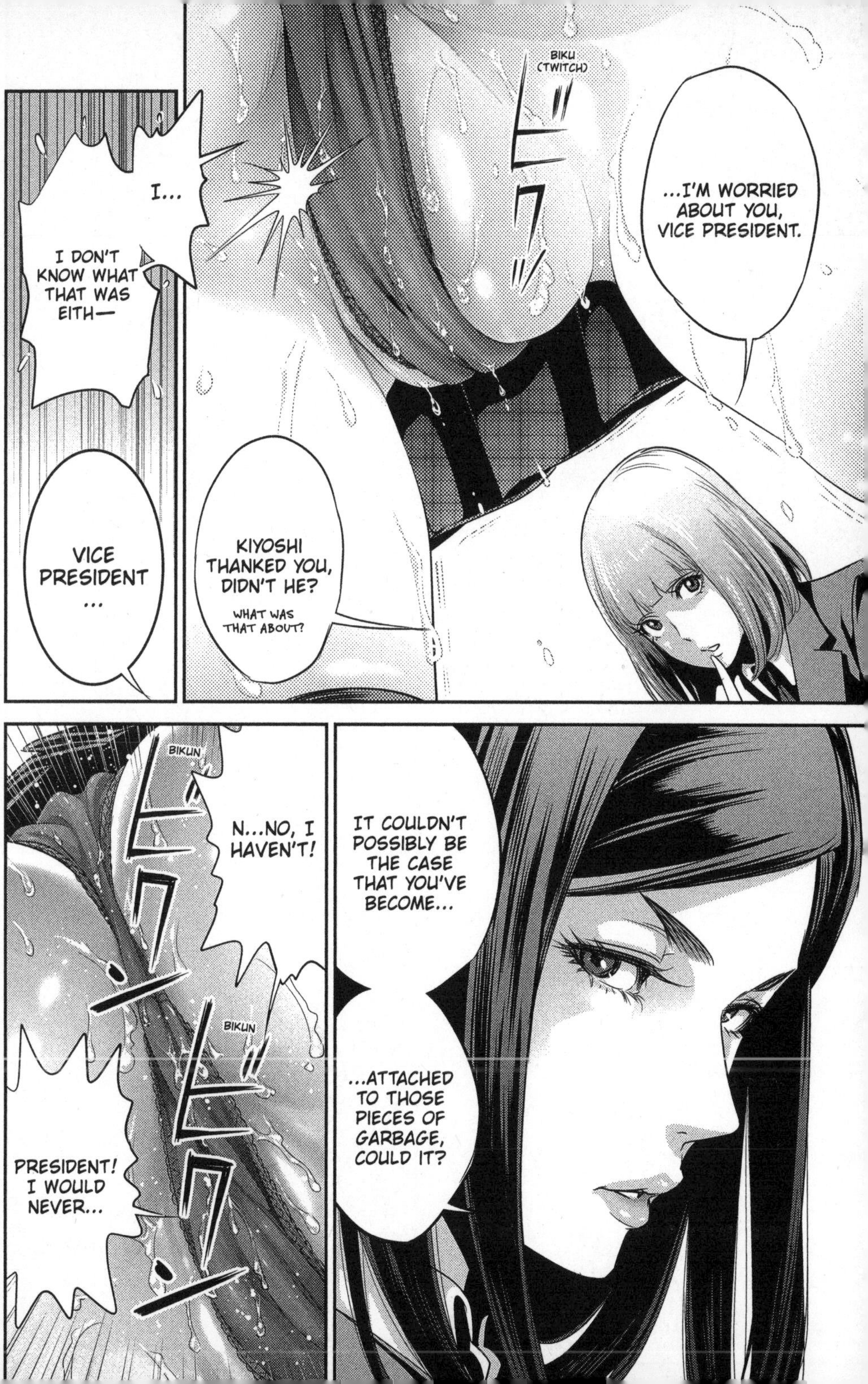
BIKU (TWITCH)
...I'M WORRIED ABOUT YOU, VICE PRESIDENT.
KIYOSHI THANKED YOU, DIDN'T HE?
WHAT WAS THAT ABOUT?
I...
I DON'T KNOW WHAT THAT WAS EITH—
VICE PRESIDENT ...
IT COULDN'T POSSIBLY BE THE CASE THAT YOU'VE BECOME...
...ATTACHED TO THOSE PIECES OF GARBAGE, COULD IT?
BIKUN
N...NO, I HAVEN'T!
BIKUN
PRESIDENT! I WOULD NEVER...

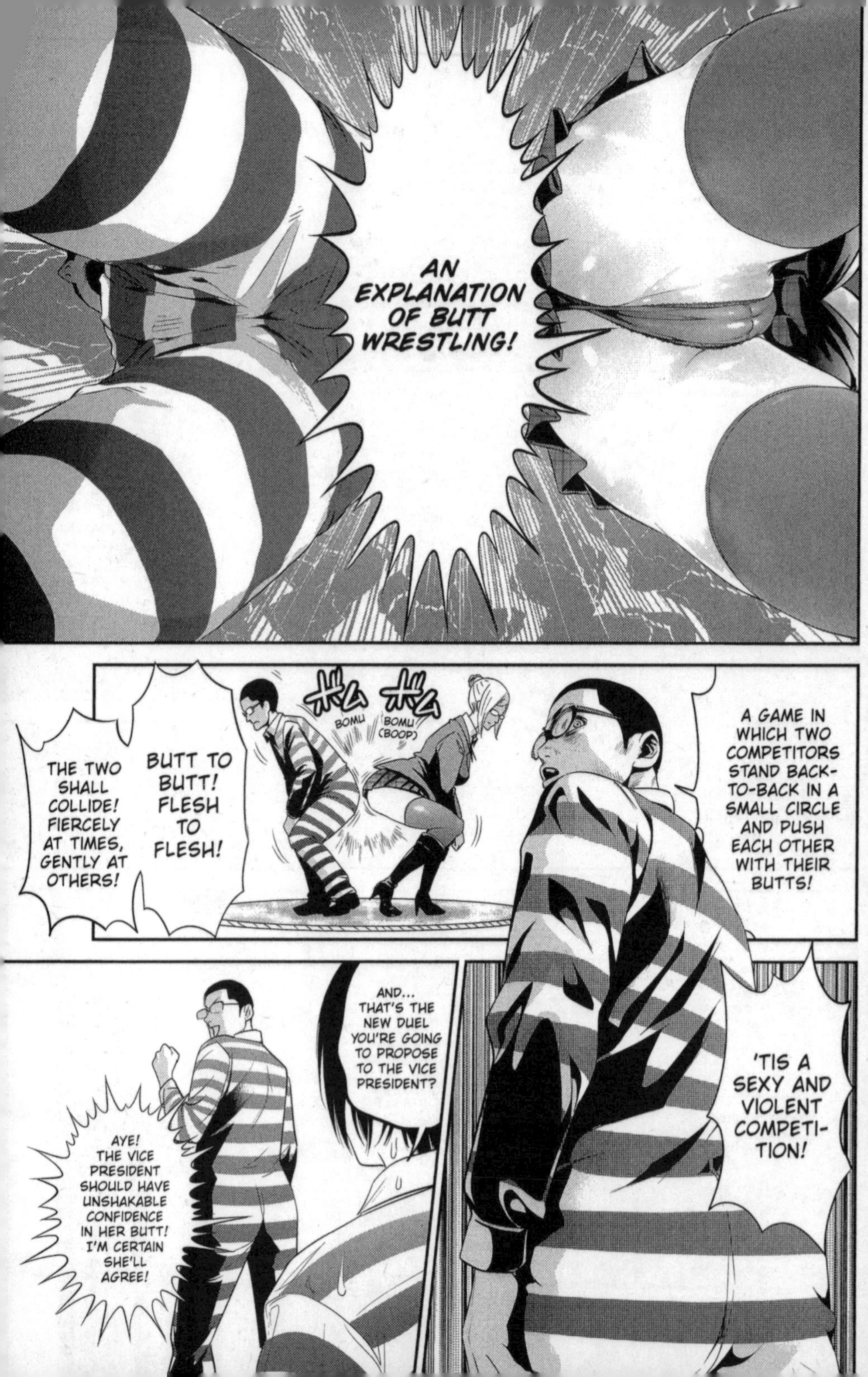
AN EXPLANATION OF BUTT WRESTLING!
A GAME IN WHICH TWO COMPETITORS STAND BACK-TO-BACK IN A SMALL CIRCLE AND PUSH EACH OTHER WITH THEIR BUTTS!
ボム ボム
BOMU BOMU (BOOP)
BUTT TO BUTT! FLESH TO FLESH!
THE TWO SHALL COLLIDE! FIERCELY AT TIMES, GENTLY AT OTHERS!
'TIS A SEXY AND VIOLENT COMPETI-TION!
AND... THAT'S THE NEW DUEL YOU'RE GOING TO PROPOSE TO THE VICE PRESIDENT?
AYE! THE VICE PRESIDENT SHOULD HAVE UNSHAKABLE CONFIDENCE IN HER BUTT! I'M CERTAIN SHE'LL AGREE!

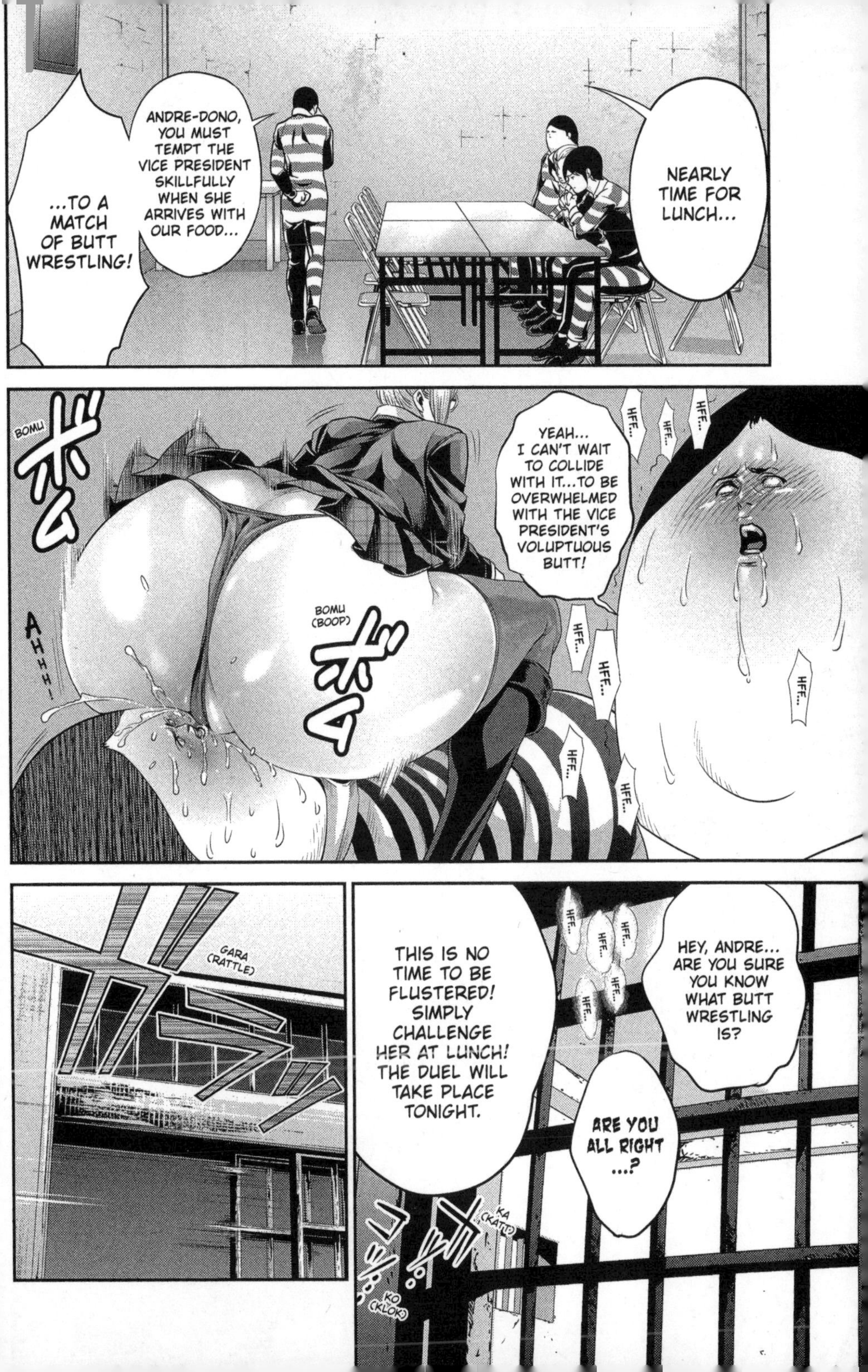

NEARLY TIME FOR LUNCH...
ANDRE-DONO, YOU MUST TEMPT THE VICE PRESIDENT SKILLFULLY WHEN SHE ARRIVES WITH OUR FOOD...
...TO A MATCH OF BUTT WRESTLING!
HFF... HFF... HFF...
YEAH... I CAN'T WAIT TO COLLIDE WITH IT...TO BE OVERWHELMED WITH THE VICE PRESIDENT'S VOLUPTUOUS BUTT!
HFF... HFF... HFF... HFF... HFF...
BOMU (BOOP)
BOMU
AHHH!
HFF... HFF... HFF... HFF... HFF...
HEY, ANDRE... ARE YOU SURE YOU KNOW WHAT BUTT WRESTLING IS?
ARE YOU ALL RIGHT ...?
THIS IS NO TIME TO BE FLUSTERED! SIMPLY CHALLENGE HER AT LUNCH! THE DUEL WILL TAKE PLACE TONIGHT.
KA (KATP)
KO (KLOK)
GARA (RATTLE)

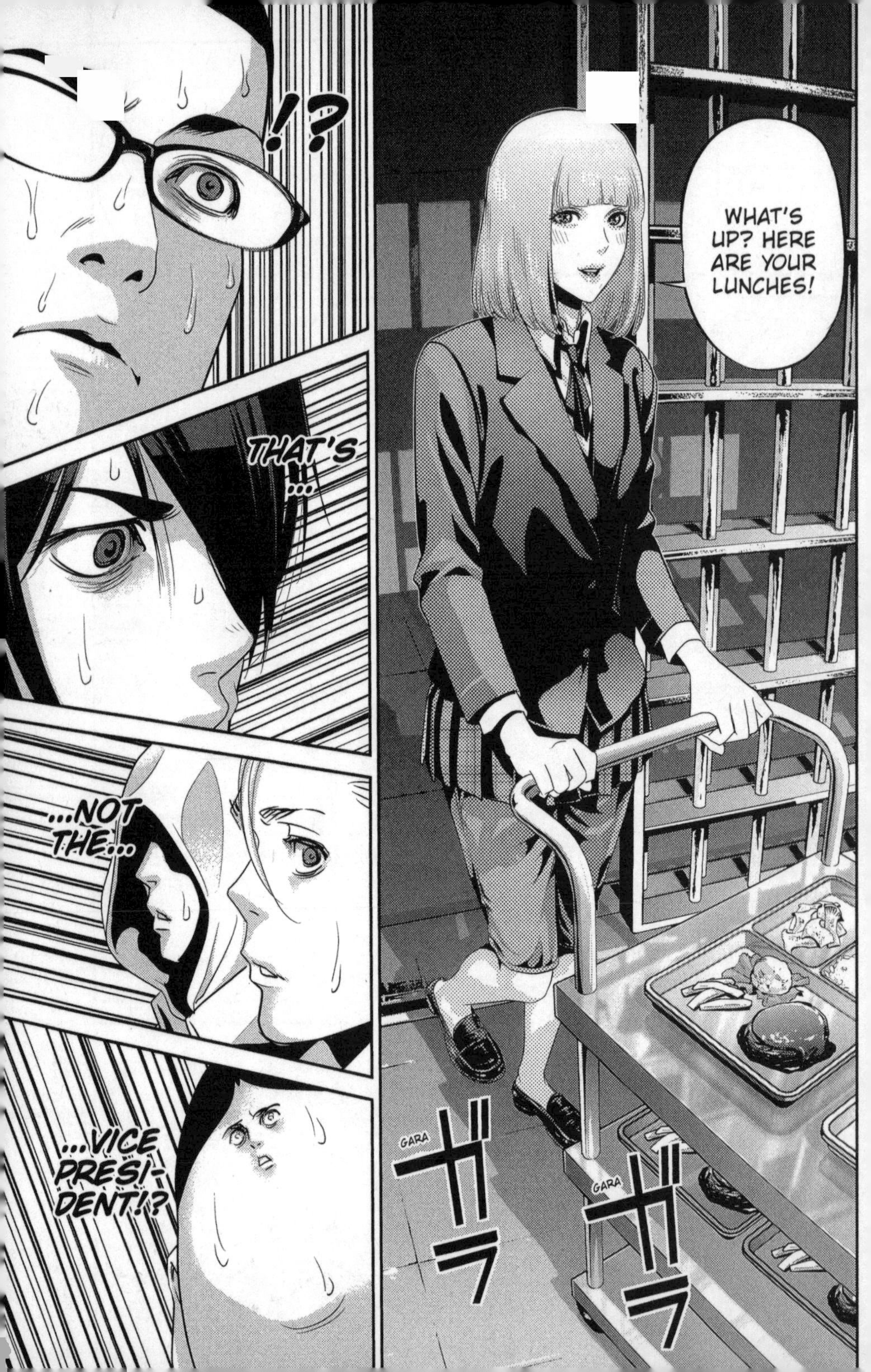
WHAT'S UP? HERE ARE YOUR LUNCHES!
GARA
GARA
!?
THAT'S ...
...NOT THE...
...VICE PRESI-DENT!?

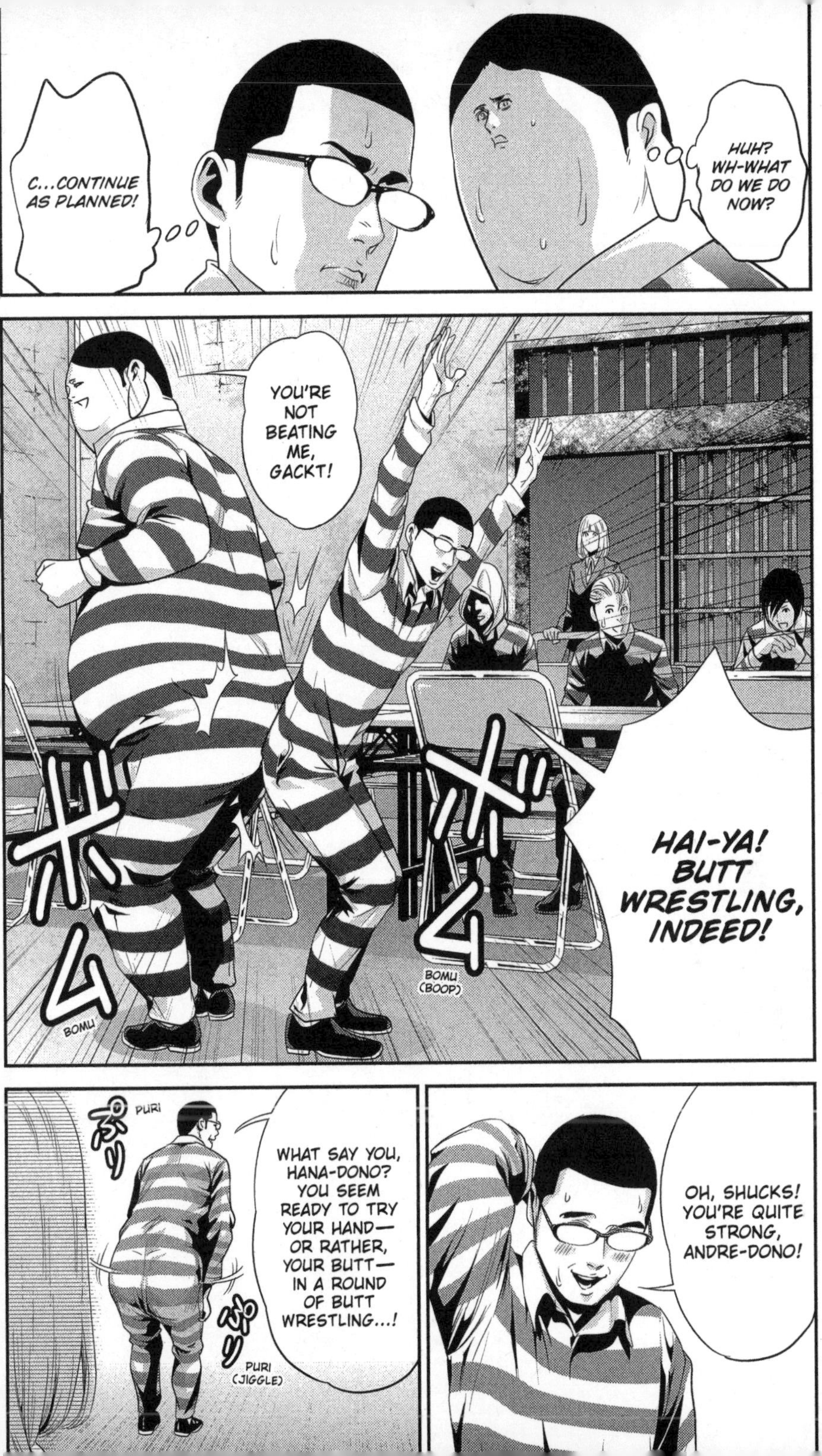
HUH? WH-WHAT DO WE DO NOW?
C...CONTINUE AS PLANNED!
HAI-YA! BUTT WRESTLING, INDEED!
YOU'RE NOT BEATING ME, GACKT!
BOMU (BOOP)
BOMU
OH, SHUCKS! YOU'RE QUITE STRONG, ANDRE-DONO!
WHAT SAY YOU, HANA-DONO? YOU SEEM READY TO TRY YOUR HAND— OR RATHER, YOUR BUTT— IN A ROUND OF BUTT WRESTLING...!
PURI
PURI (JIGGLE)

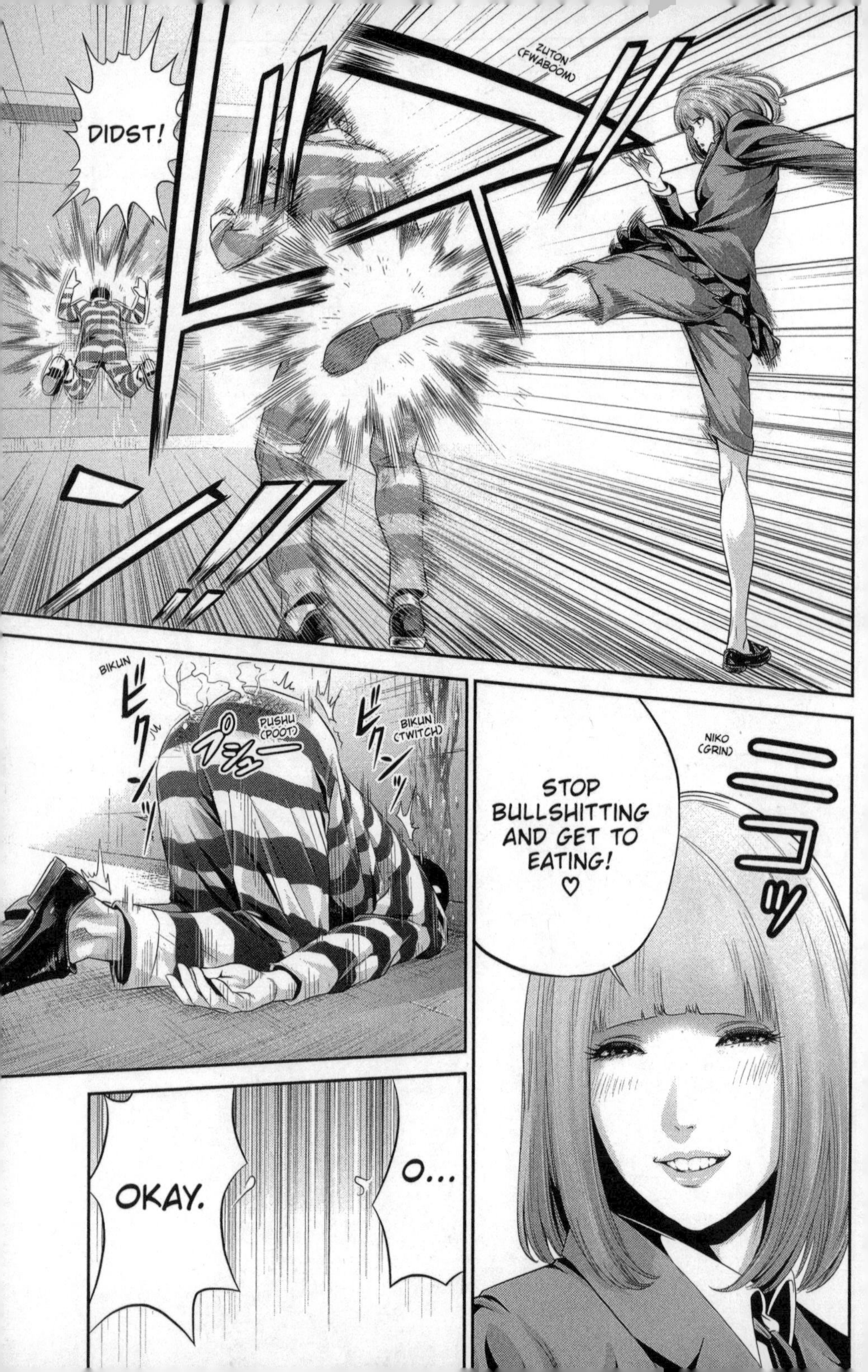
ZUTON (FWABOOM)
DIDST!
NIKO (GRIN)
STOP BULLSHITTING AND GET TO EATING! ♡
BIKUN (TWITCH)
PUSHU (POOT)
BIKUN
O...
OKAY.

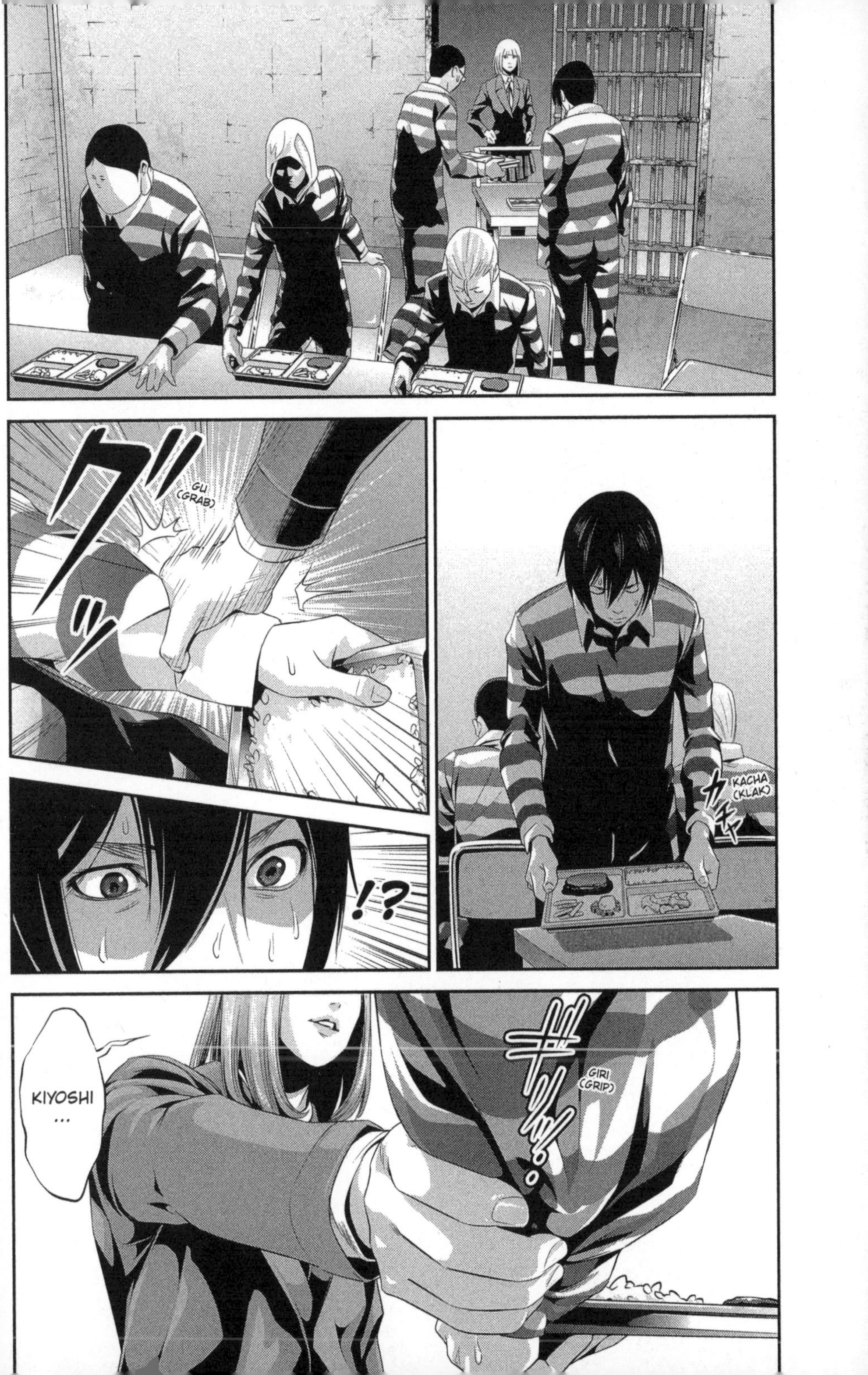
KACHA (KLAK)
GU (GRAB)
!?
GIRI (GRIP)
KIYOSHI ...

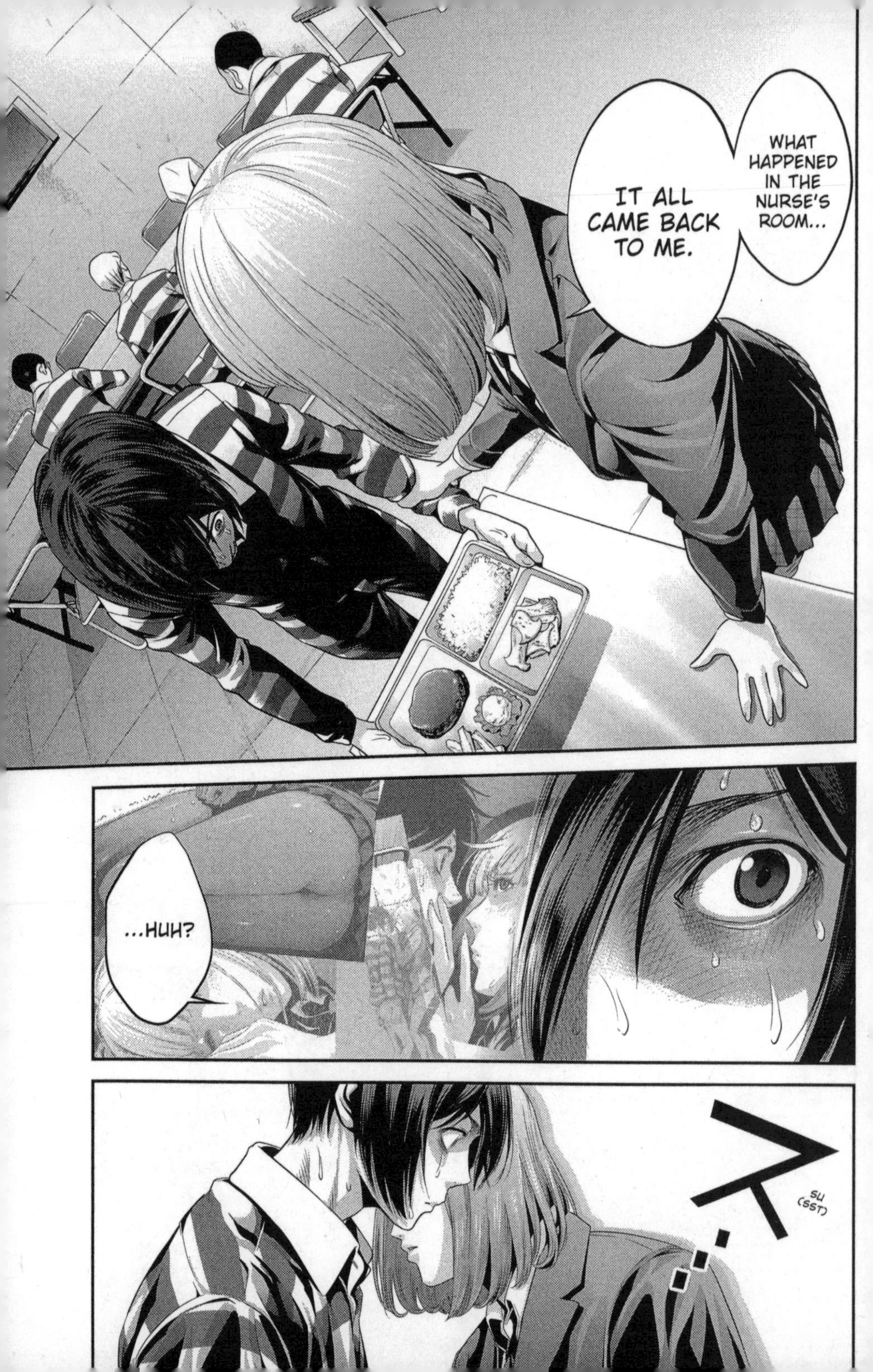
WHAT HAPPENED IN THE NURSE'S ROOM...
IT ALL CAME BACK TO ME.
...HUH?
SU (SST)

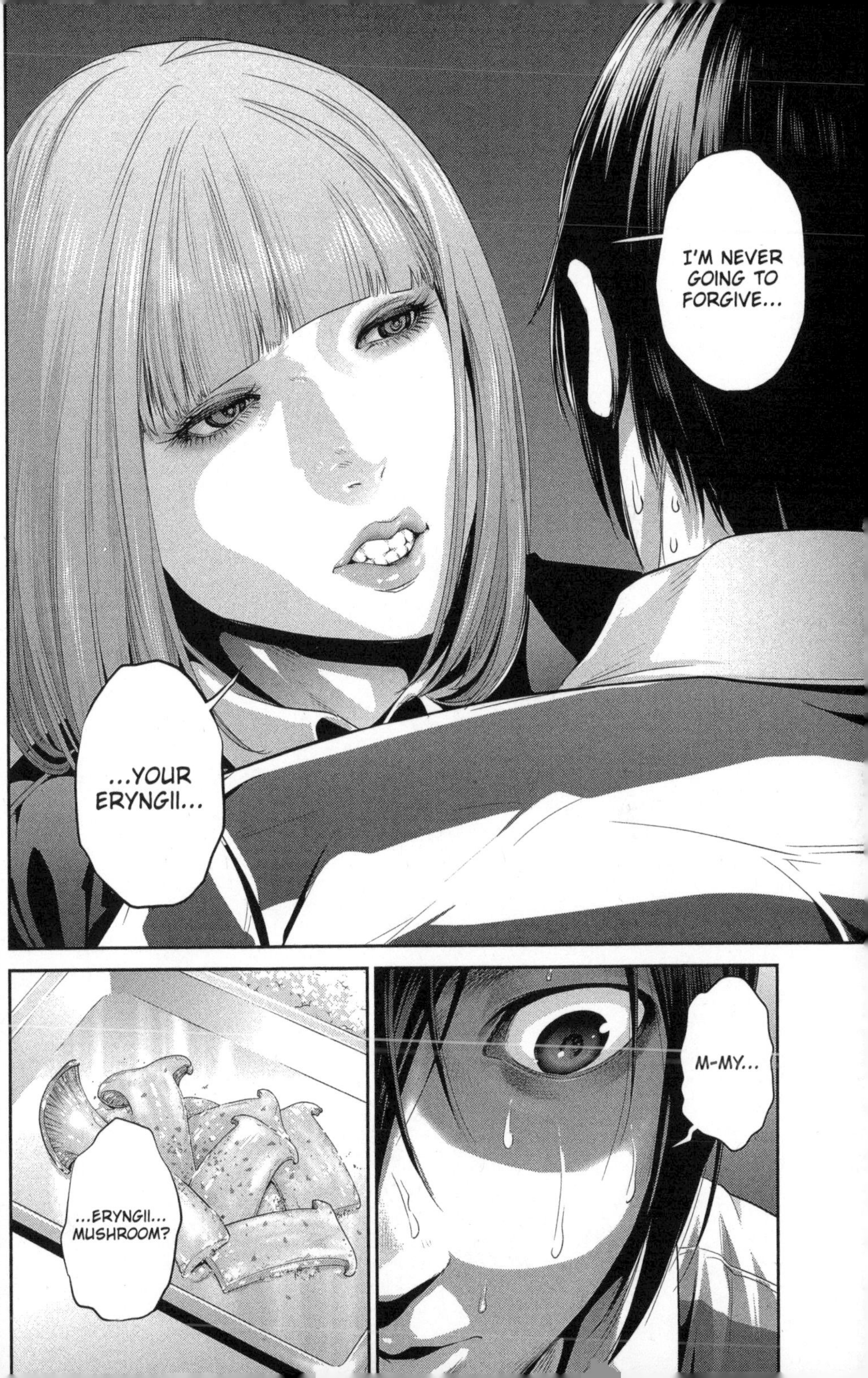
I'M NEVER GOING TO FORGIVE...
...YOUR ERYNGII...
M-MY...
...ERYNGII... MUSHROOM?

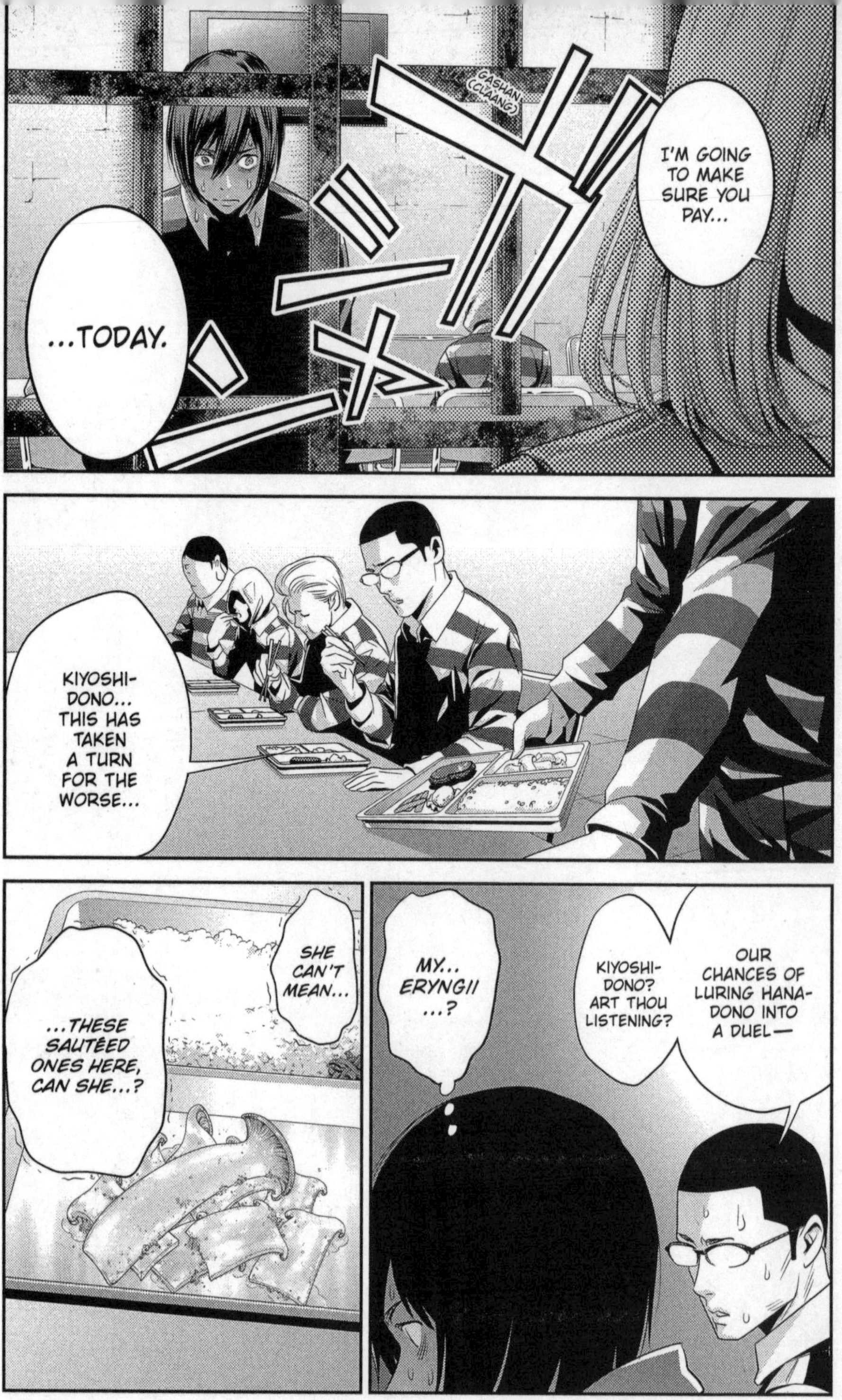
I'M GOING TO MAKE SURE YOU PAY...
GASHAN (CLAANG)
...TODAY.
KIYOSHI-DONO... THIS HAS TAKEN A TURN FOR THE WORSE...
OUR CHANCES OF LURING HANA-DONO INTO A DUEL—
KIYOSHI-DONO? ART THOU LISTENING?
MY... ERYNGII ...?
SHE CAN'T MEAN...
...THESE SAUTÉED ONES HERE, CAN SHE...?

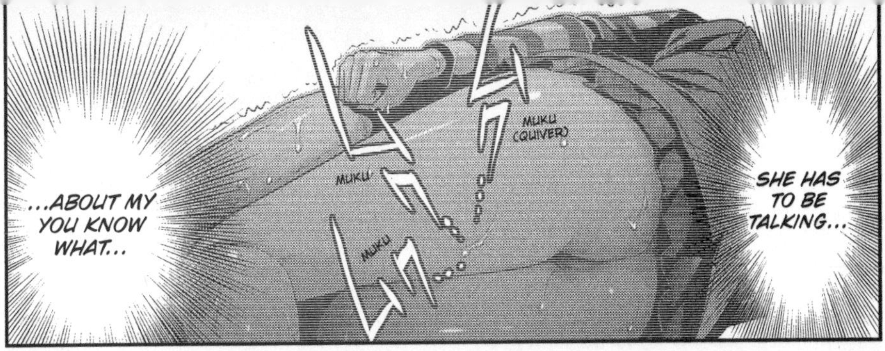
SHE HAS TO BE TALKING...
MUKU (QUIVER)
MUKU
MUKU
...ABOUT MY YOU KNOW WHAT...

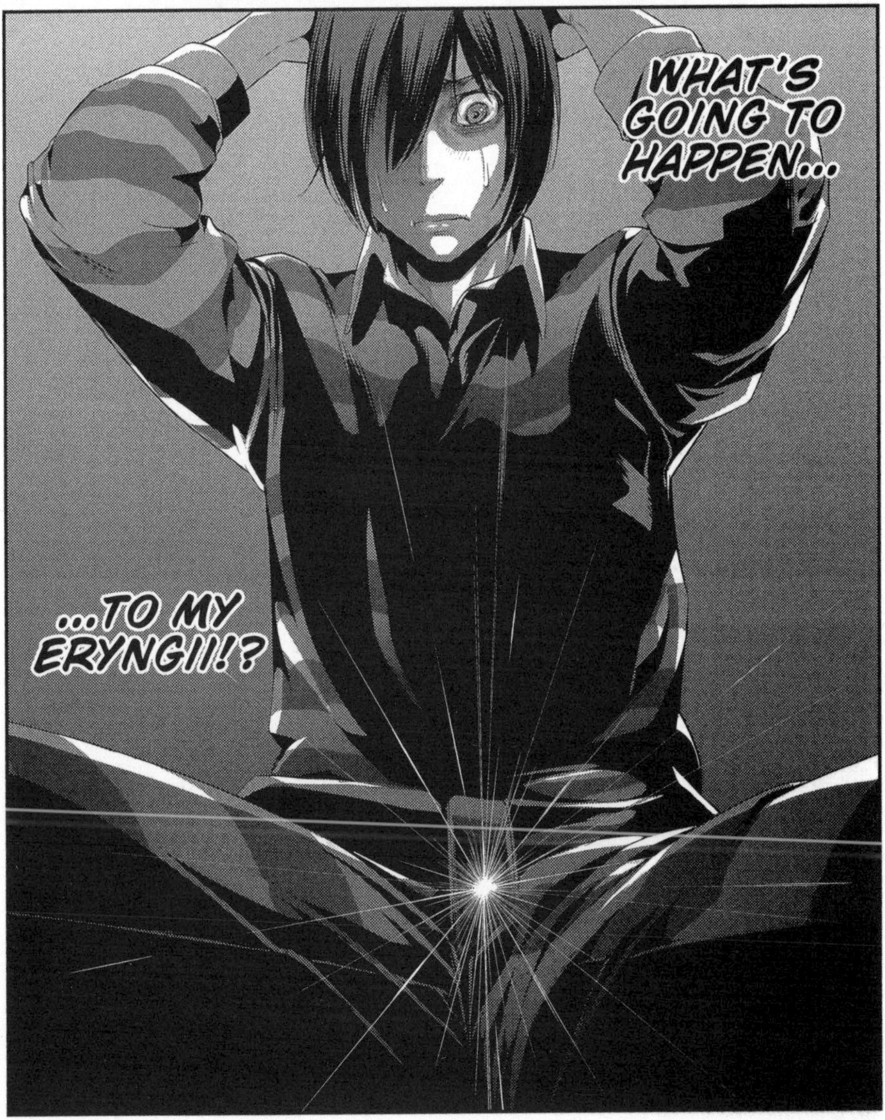
WHAT'S GOING TO HAPPEN...
...TO MY ERYNGII!?

CHAPTER 70: TRAINING DAY

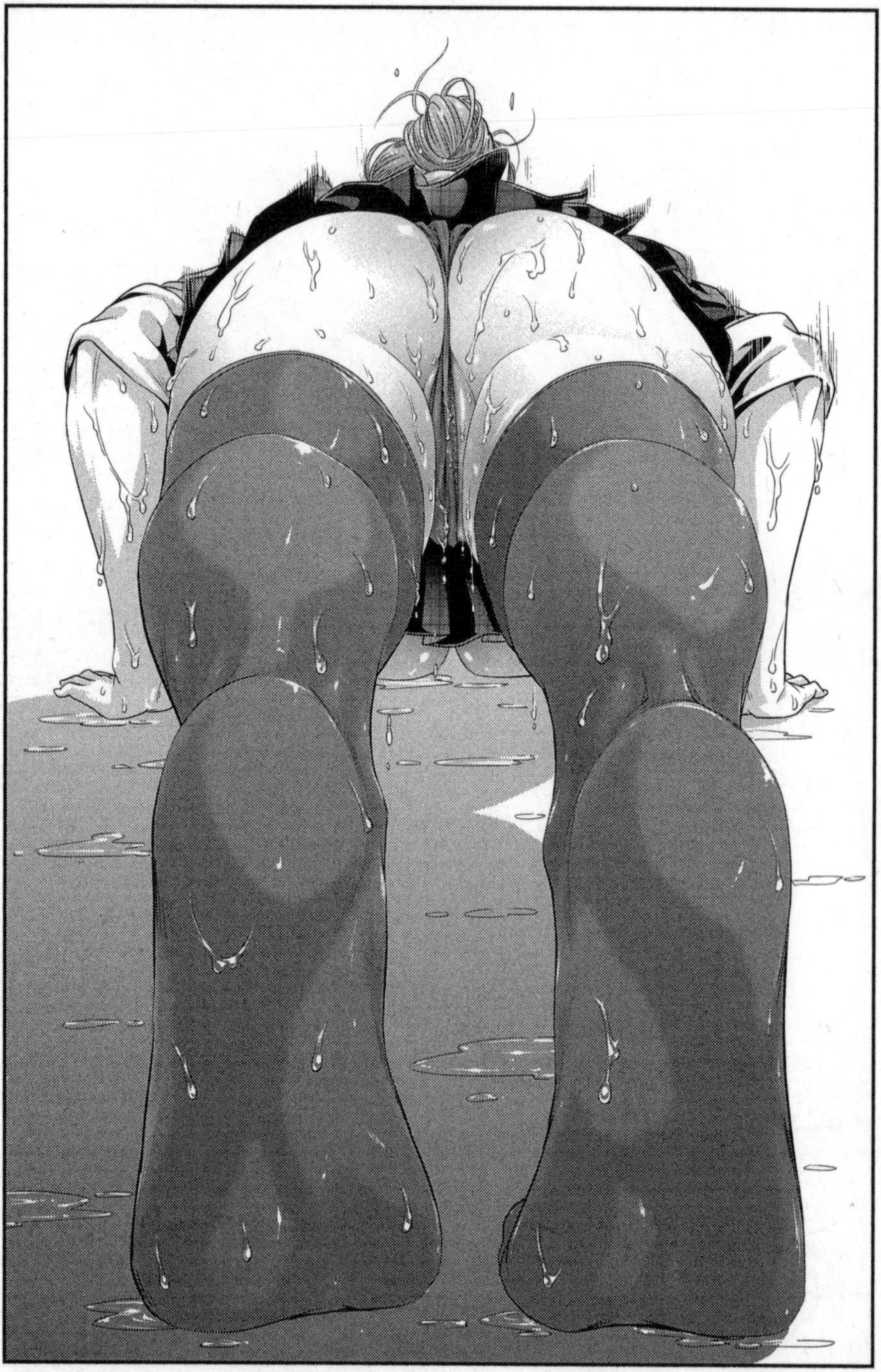

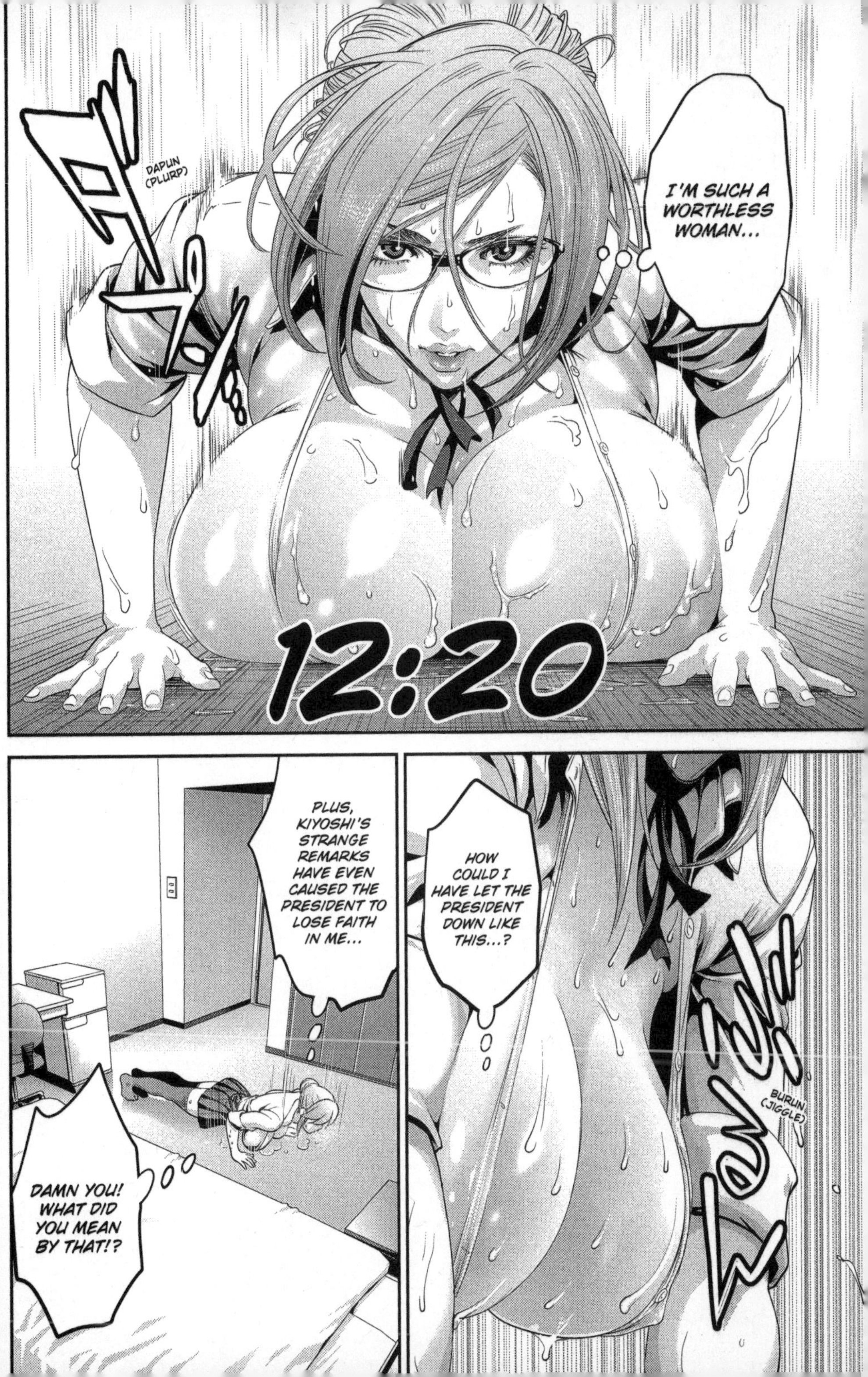
I'M SUCH A WORTHLESS WOMAN...
DAPUN (PLURP)
12:20
HOW COULD I HAVE LET THE PRESIDENT DOWN LIKE THIS...?
BURUN (JIGGLE)
PLUS, KIYOSHI'S STRANGE REMARKS HAVE EVEN CAUSED THE PRESIDENT TO LOSE FAITH IN ME...
DAMN YOU! WHAT DID YOU MEAN BY THAT!?

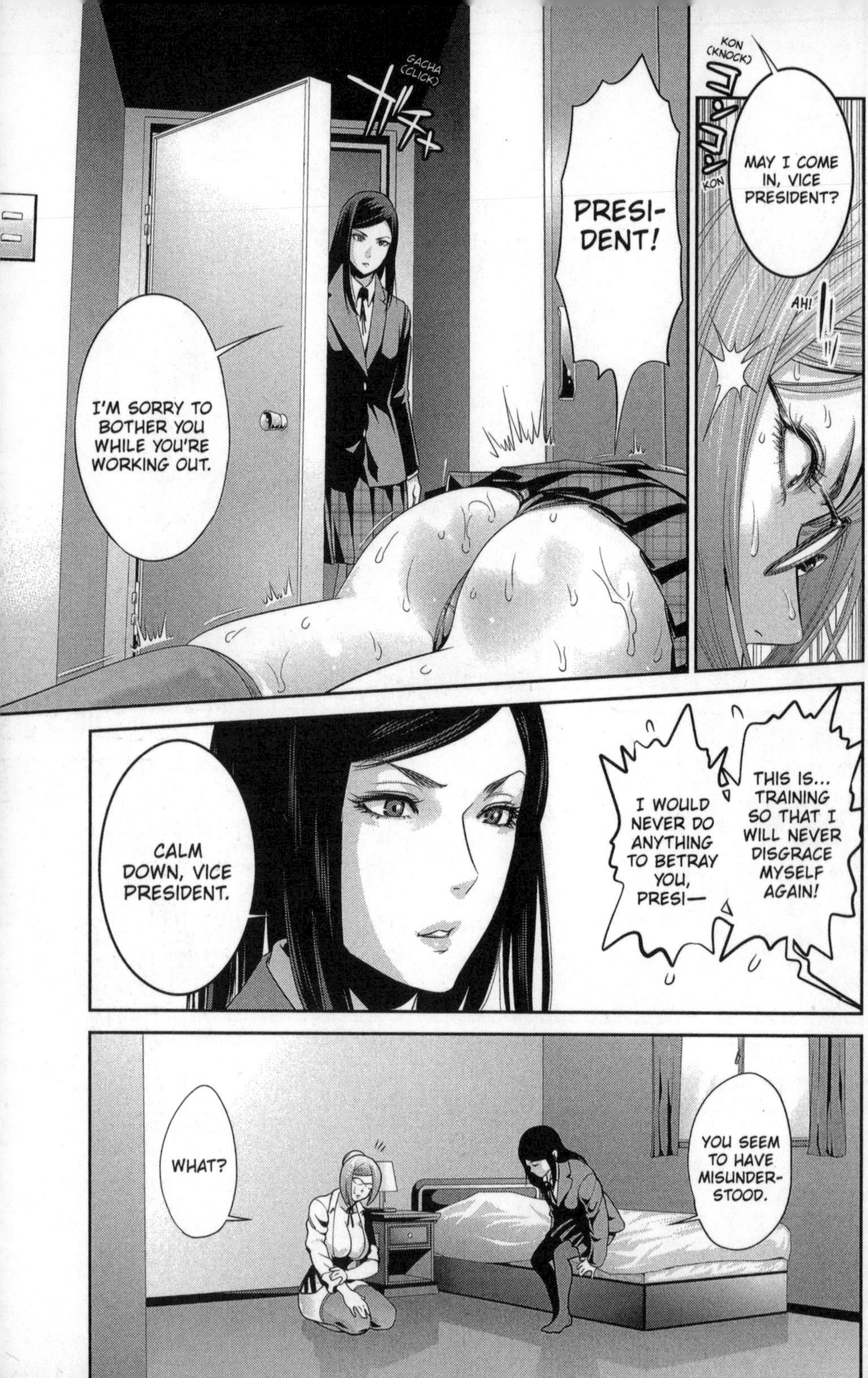
KON (KNOCK)
KON
MAY I COME IN, VICE PRESIDENT?
AH!
PRESI-DENT!
GACHA (CLICK)
I'M SORRY TO BOTHER YOU WHILE YOU'RE WORKING OUT.
THIS IS... TRAINING SO THAT I WILL NEVER DISGRACE MYSELF AGAIN!
I WOULD NEVER DO ANYTHING TO BETRAY YOU, PRESI—
CALM DOWN, VICE PRESIDENT.
YOU SEEM TO HAVE MISUNDER-STOOD.
WHAT?

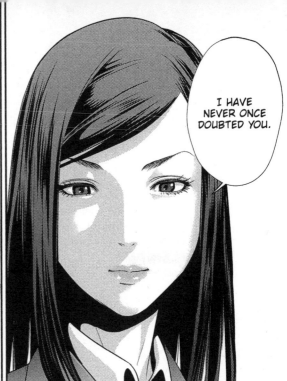

I HAVE NEVER ONCE DOUBTED YOU.

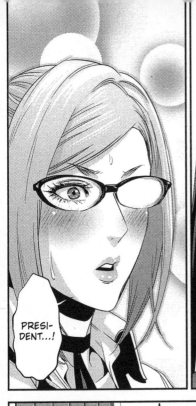

PRESI-DENT...!

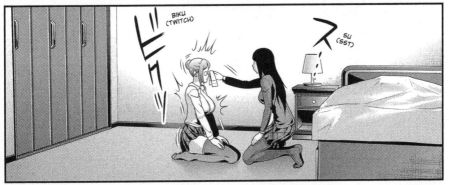

BIKU (TWITCH)

ス SU (SST)

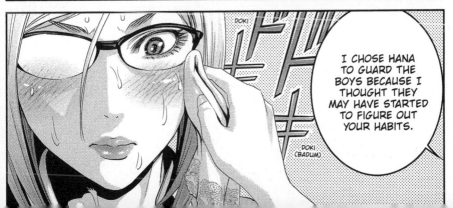

DOKI

I CHOSE HANA TO GUARD THE BOYS BECAUSE I THOUGHT THEY MAY HAVE STARTED TO FIGURE OUT YOUR HABITS.

DOKI (BADUM)

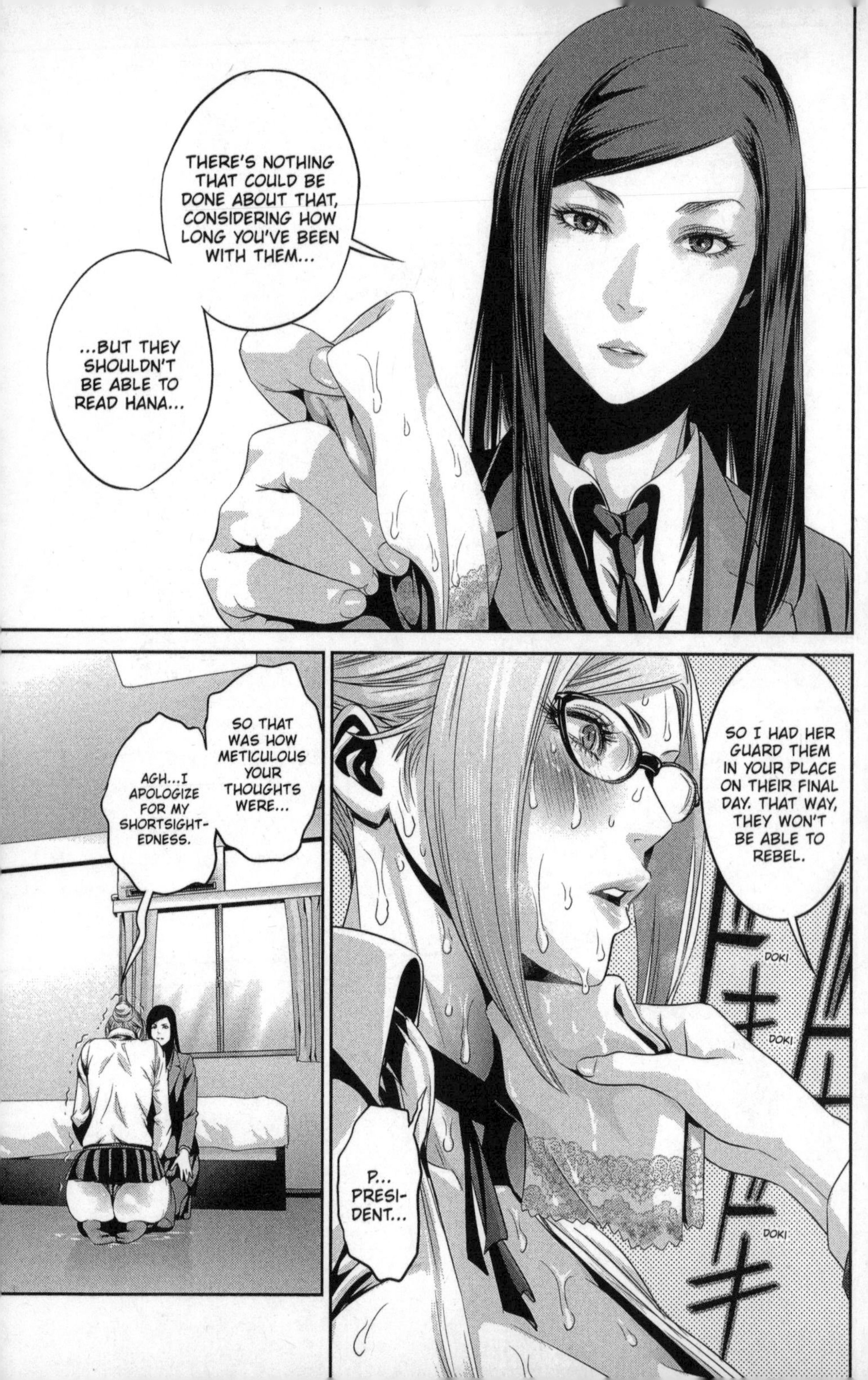
THERE'S NOTHING THAT COULD BE DONE ABOUT THAT, CONSIDERING HOW LONG YOU'VE BEEN WITH THEM...
...BUT THEY SHOULDN'T BE ABLE TO READ HANA...
SO I HAD HER GUARD THEM IN YOUR PLACE ON THEIR FINAL DAY. THAT WAY, THEY WON'T BE ABLE TO REBEL.
DOKI
DOKI
DOKI
P... PRESI-DENT...
SO THAT WAS HOW METICULOUS YOUR THOUGHTS WERE...
AGH...I APOLOGIZE FOR MY SHORTSIGHT-EDNESS.

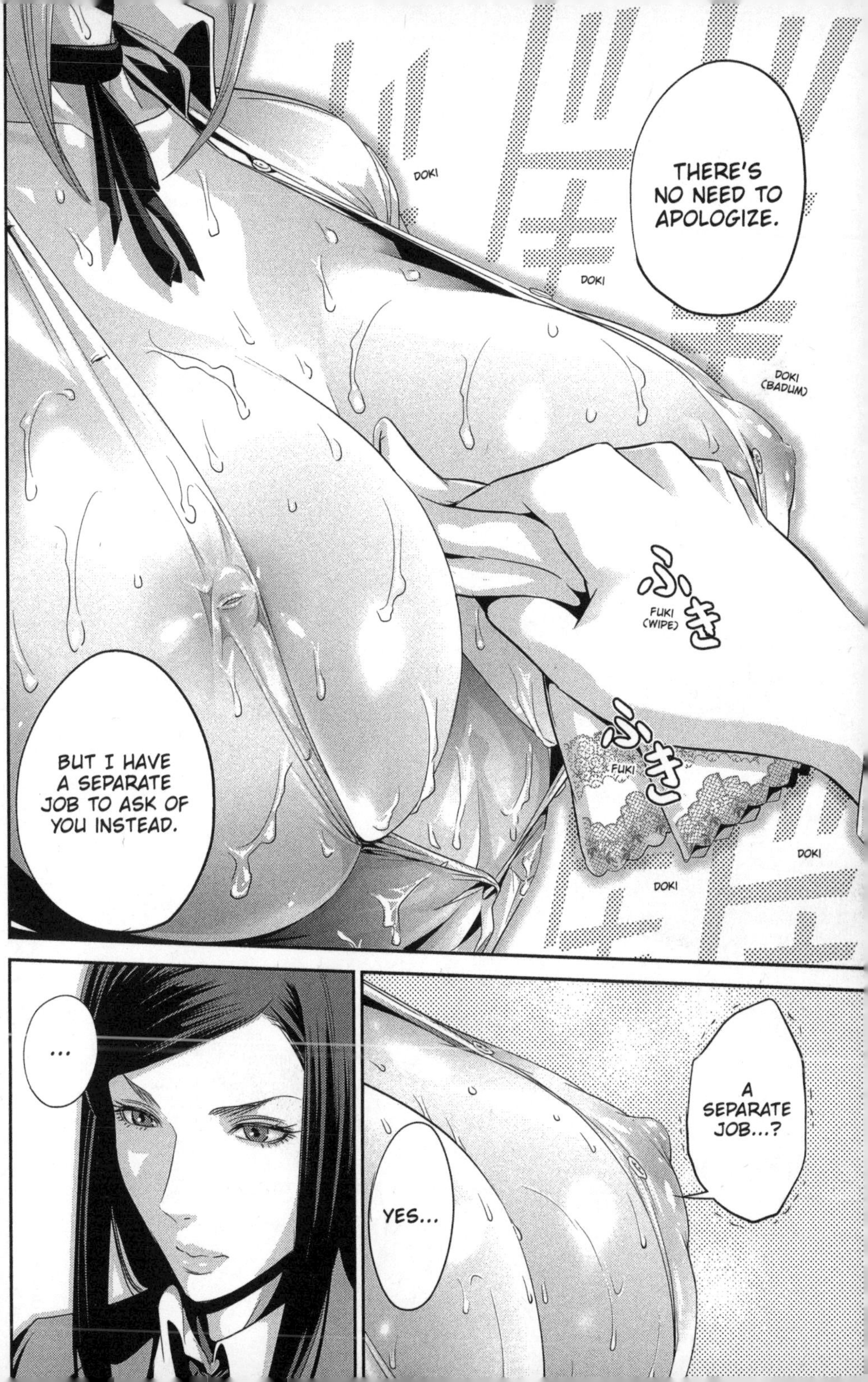
THERE'S NO NEED TO APOLOGIZE.
DOKI
DOKI
DOKI (BADUM)
ふき
FUKI (WIPE)
ふき
FUKI
DOKI
DOKI
BUT I HAVE A SEPARATE JOB TO ASK OF YOU INSTEAD.
A SEPARATE JOB...?
YES...
...

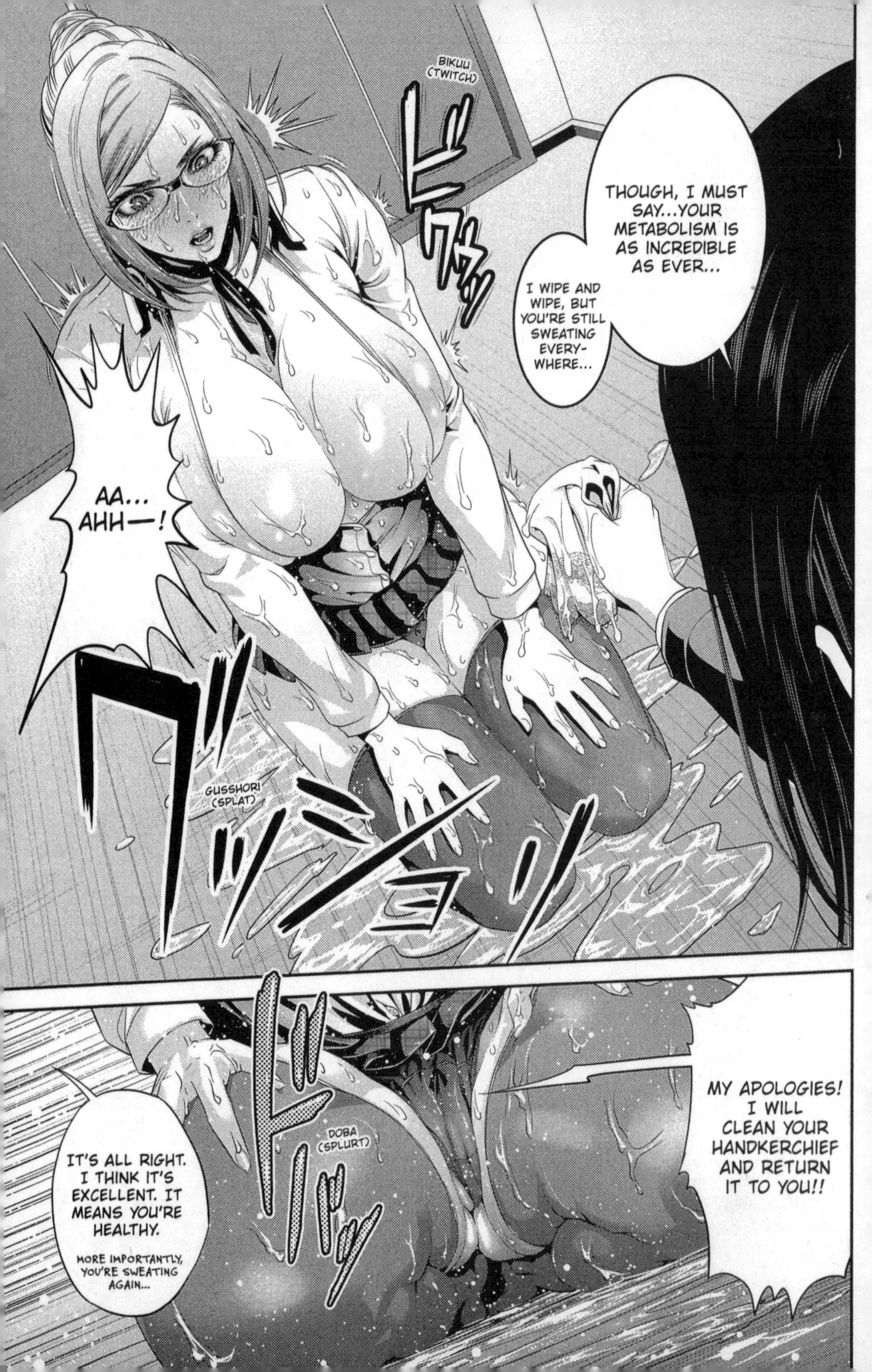
THOUGH, I MUST SAY...YOUR METABOLISM IS AS INCREDIBLE AS EVER...
I WIPE AND WIPE, BUT YOU'RE STILL SWEATING EVERY-WHERE...
BIKUU (TWITCH)
AA... AHH—!
GUSSHORI (SPLAT)
MY APOLOGIES! I WILL CLEAN YOUR HANDKERCHIEF AND RETURN IT TO YOU!!
DOBA (SPLURT)
IT'S ALL RIGHT. I THINK IT'S EXCELLENT. IT MEANS YOU'RE HEALTHY.
MORE IMPORTANTLY, YOU'RE SWEATING AGAIN...

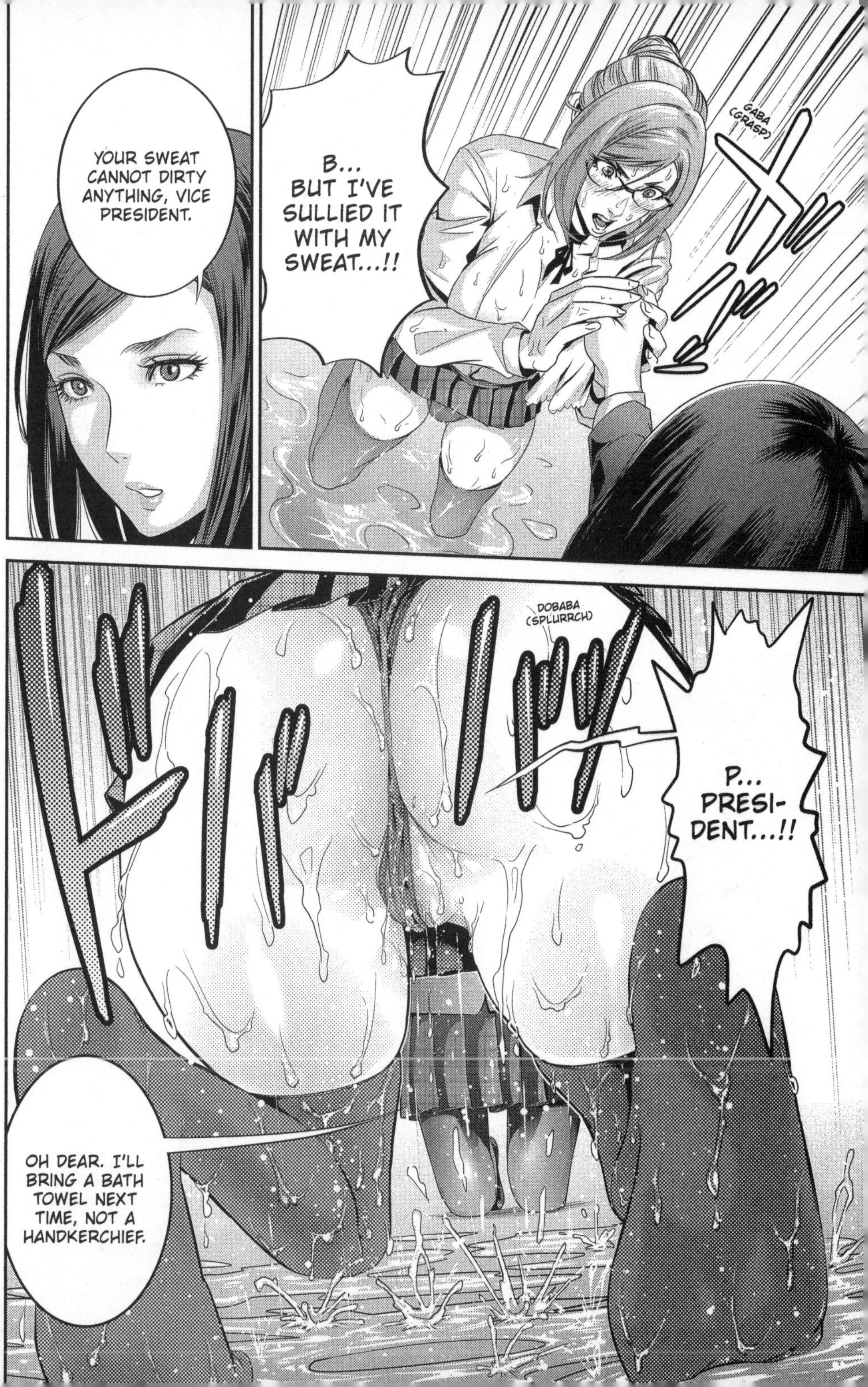
GABA (GRASP)
B... BUT I'VE SULLIED IT WITH MY SWEAT...!!
YOUR SWEAT CANNOT DIRTY ANYTHING, VICE PRESIDENT.
P... PRESIDENT...!!
DOBABA (SPLURRCH)
OH DEAR. I'LL BRING A BATH TOWEL NEXT TIME, NOT A HANDKERCHIEF.

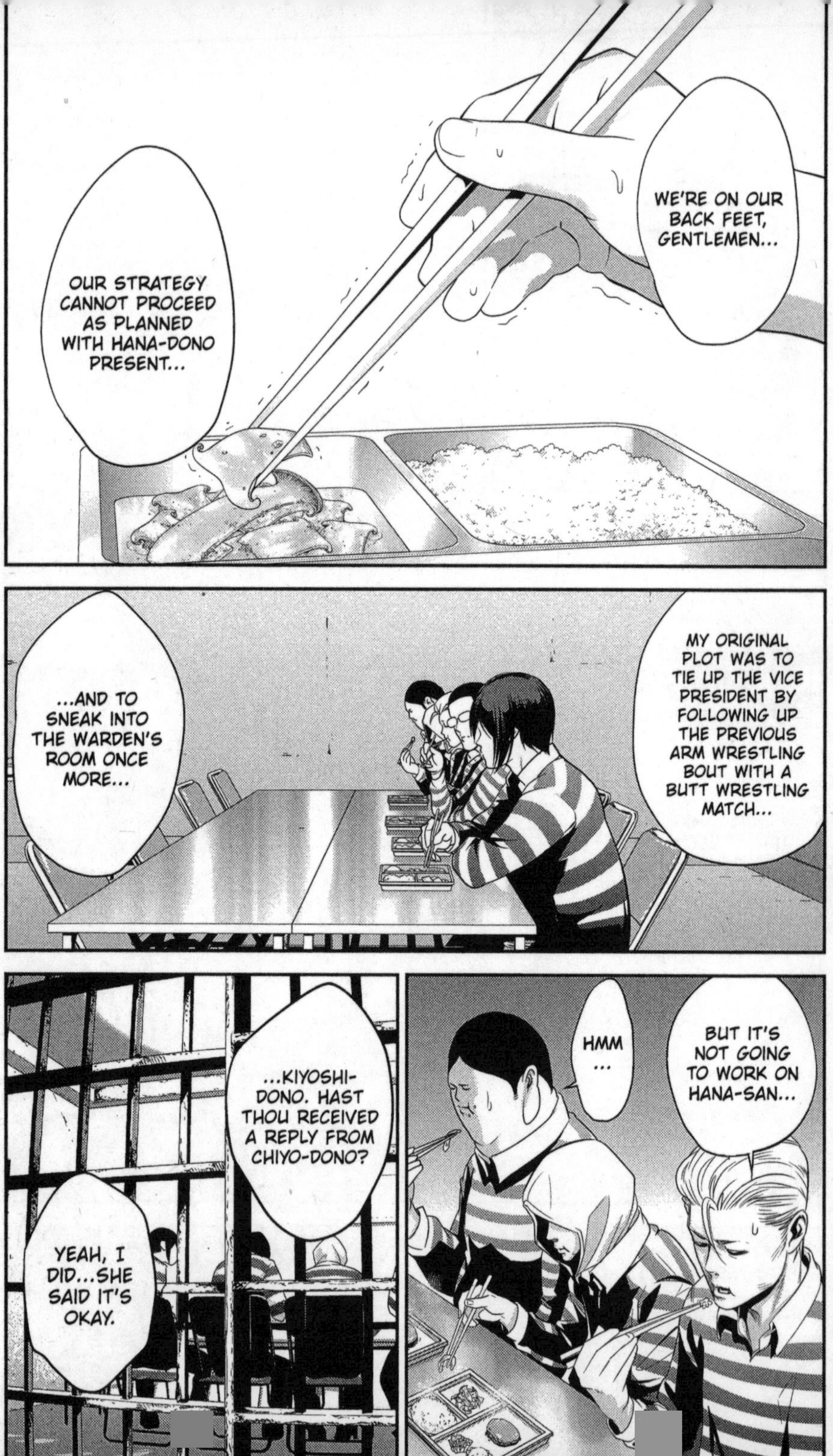
WE'RE ON OUR BACK FEET, GENTLEMEN...
OUR STRATEGY CANNOT PROCEED AS PLANNED WITH HANA-DONO PRESENT...
MY ORIGINAL PLOT WAS TO TIE UP THE VICE PRESIDENT BY FOLLOWING UP THE PREVIOUS ARM WRESTLING BOUT WITH A BUTT WRESTLING MATCH...
...AND TO SNEAK INTO THE WARDEN'S ROOM ONCE MORE...
BUT IT'S NOT GOING TO WORK ON HANA-SAN...
HMM ...
...KIYOSHI-DONO. HAST THOU RECEIVED A REPLY FROM CHIYO-DONO?
YEAH, I DID...SHE SAID IT'S OKAY.

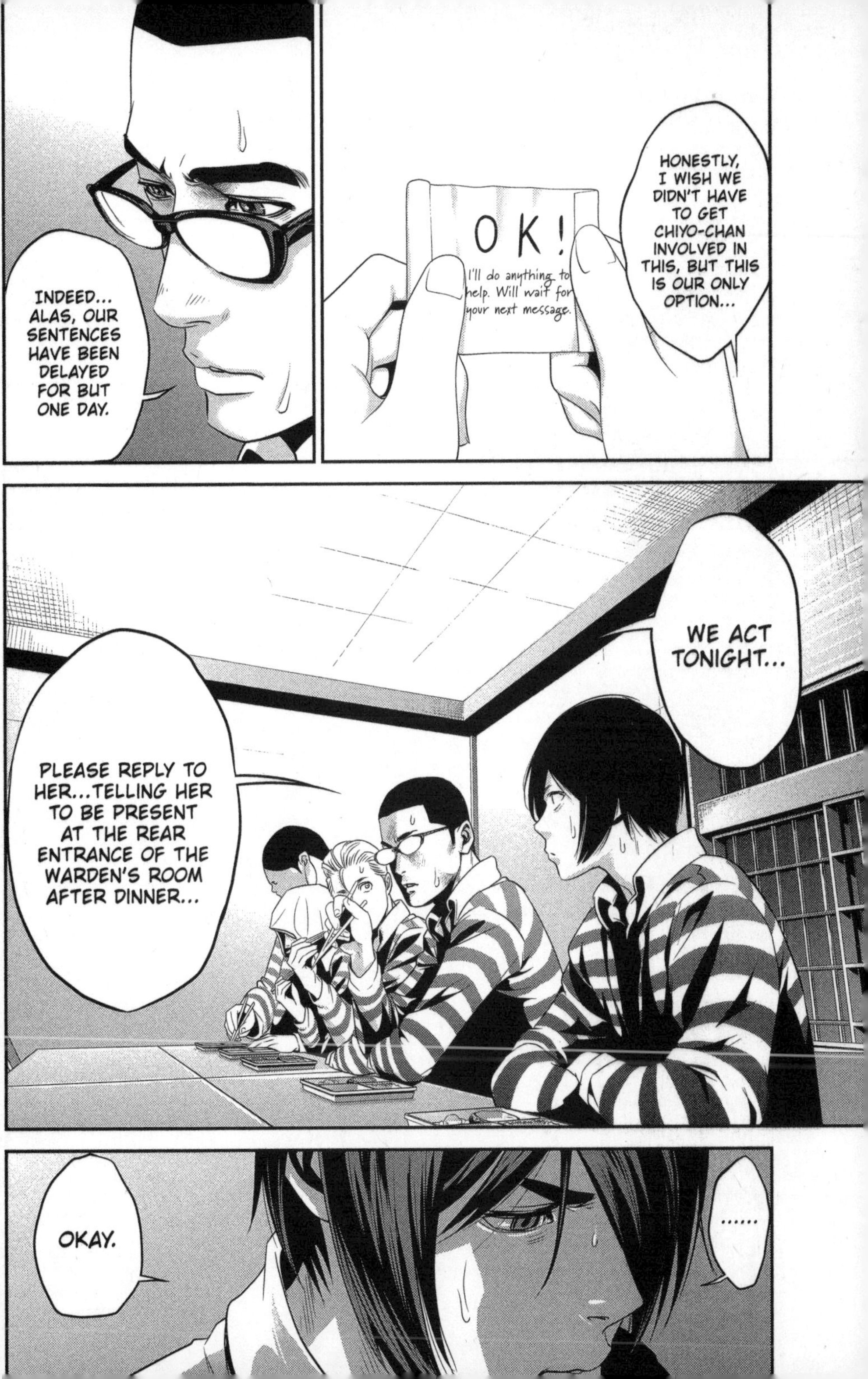
OK!
I'll do anything to help. Will wait for your next message.
HONESTLY, I WISH WE DIDN'T HAVE TO GET CHIYO-CHAN INVOLVED IN THIS, BUT THIS IS OUR ONLY OPTION...
INDEED... ALAS, OUR SENTENCES HAVE BEEN DELAYED FOR BUT ONE DAY.
WE ACT TONIGHT...
PLEASE REPLY TO HER...TELLING HER TO BE PRESENT AT THE REAR ENTRANCE OF THE WARDEN'S ROOM AFTER DINNER...
......
OKAY.

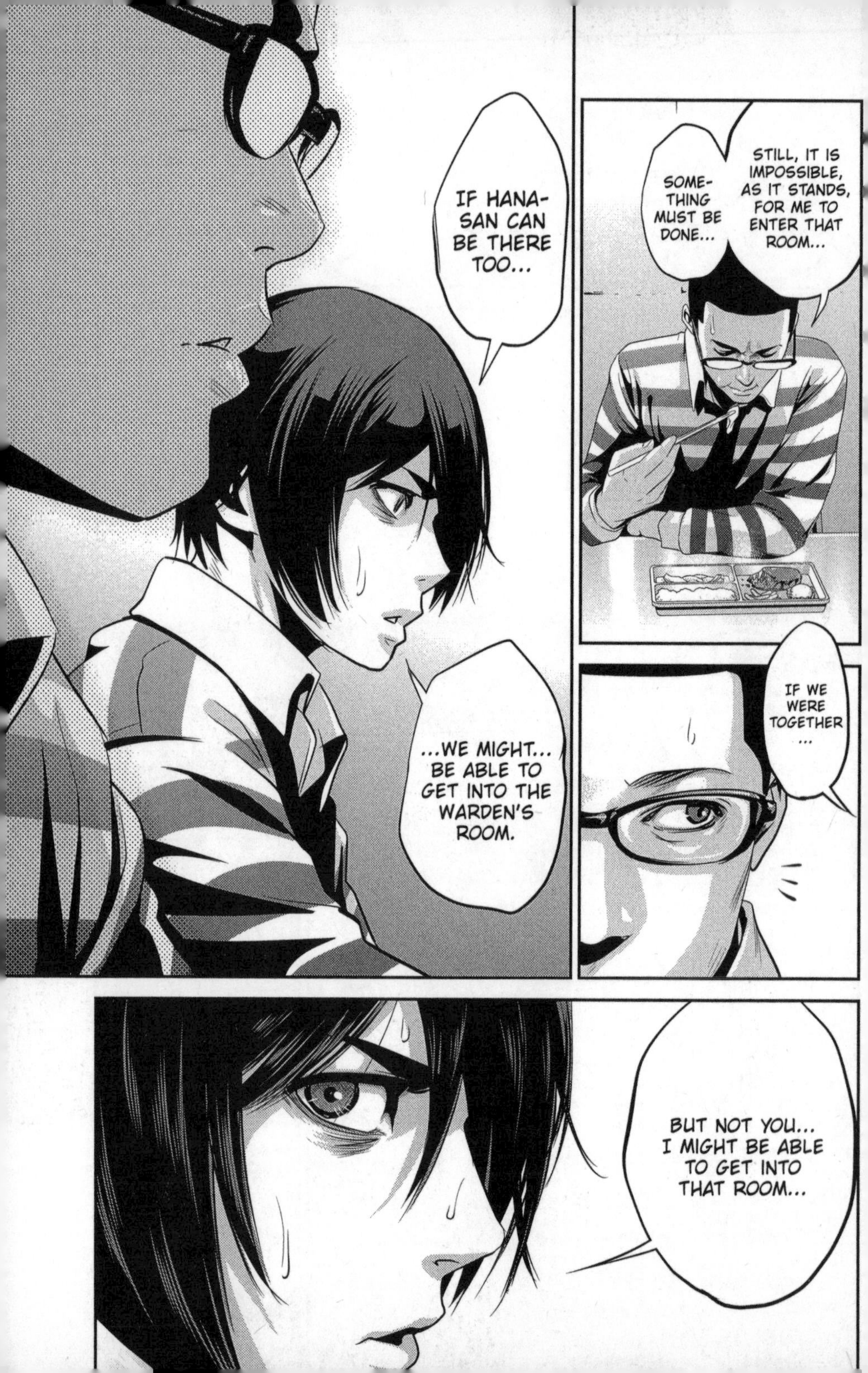
STILL, IT IS IMPOSSIBLE, AS IT STANDS, FOR ME TO ENTER THAT ROOM...
SOME-THING MUST BE DONE...
IF WE WERE TOGETHER ...
IF HANA-SAN CAN BE THERE TOO...
...WE MIGHT... BE ABLE TO GET INTO THE WARDEN'S ROOM.
BUT NOT YOU... I MIGHT BE ABLE TO GET INTO THAT ROOM...

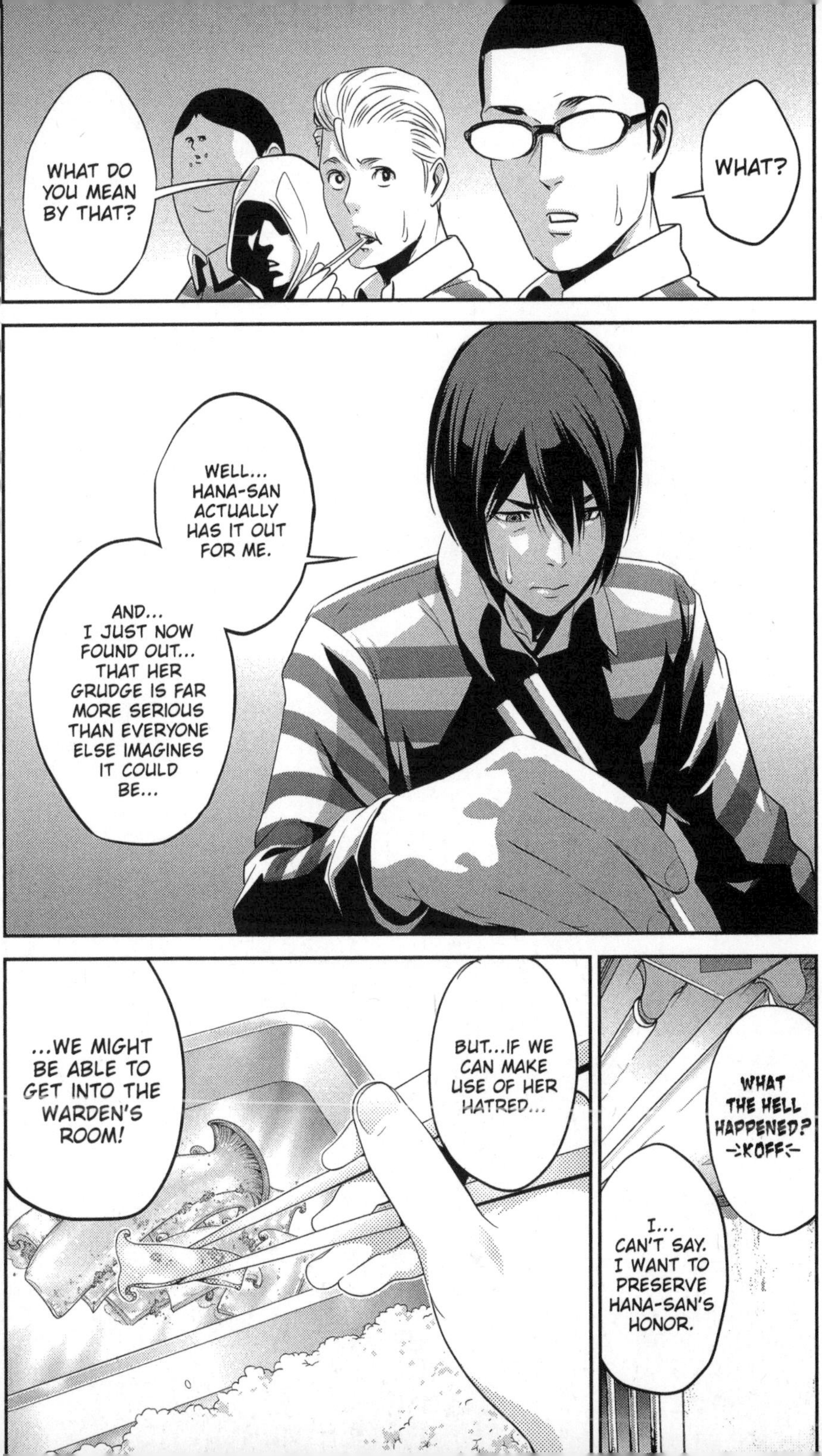
WHAT?
WHAT DO YOU MEAN BY THAT?
WELL... HANA-SAN ACTUALLY HAS IT OUT FOR ME.
AND... I JUST NOW FOUND OUT... THAT HER GRUDGE IS FAR MORE SERIOUS THAN EVERYONE ELSE IMAGINES IT COULD BE...
WHAT THE HELL HAPPENED? -KOFF-
I... CAN'T SAY. I WANT TO PRESERVE HANA-SAN'S HONOR.
BUT...IF WE CAN MAKE USE OF HER HATRED...
...WE MIGHT BE ABLE TO GET INTO THE WARDEN'S ROOM!

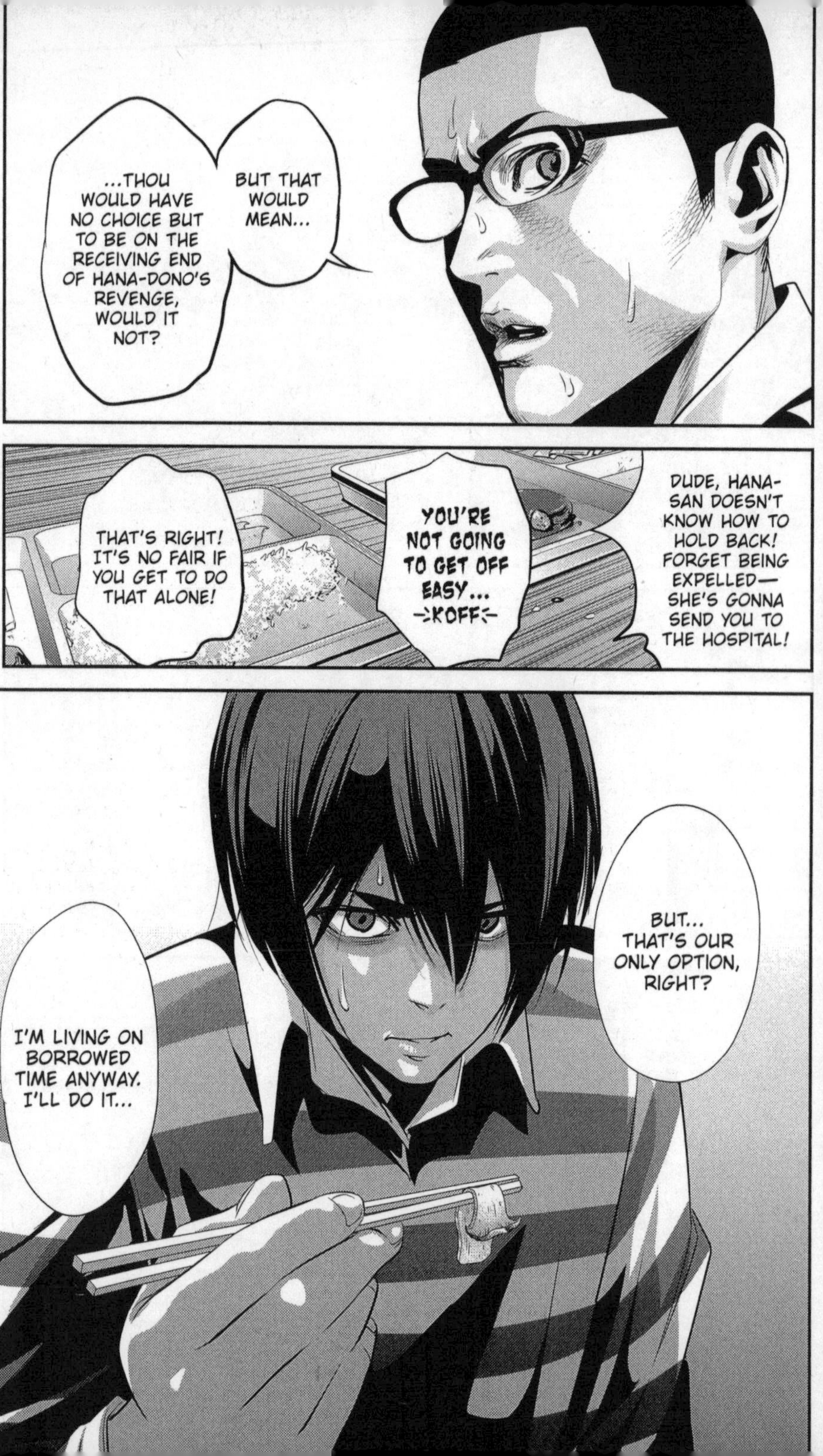
BUT THAT WOULD MEAN...
...THOU WOULD HAVE NO CHOICE BUT TO BE ON THE RECEIVING END OF HANA-DONO'S REVENGE, WOULD IT NOT?
DUDE, HANA-SAN DOESN'T KNOW HOW TO HOLD BACK! FORGET BEING EXPELLED—SHE'S GONNA SEND YOU TO THE HOSPITAL!
YOU'RE NOT GOING TO GET OFF EASY... *KOFF*
THAT'S RIGHT! IT'S NO FAIR IF YOU GET TO DO THAT ALONE!
BUT... THAT'S OUR ONLY OPTION, RIGHT?
I'M LIVING ON BORROWED TIME ANYWAY. I'LL DO IT...

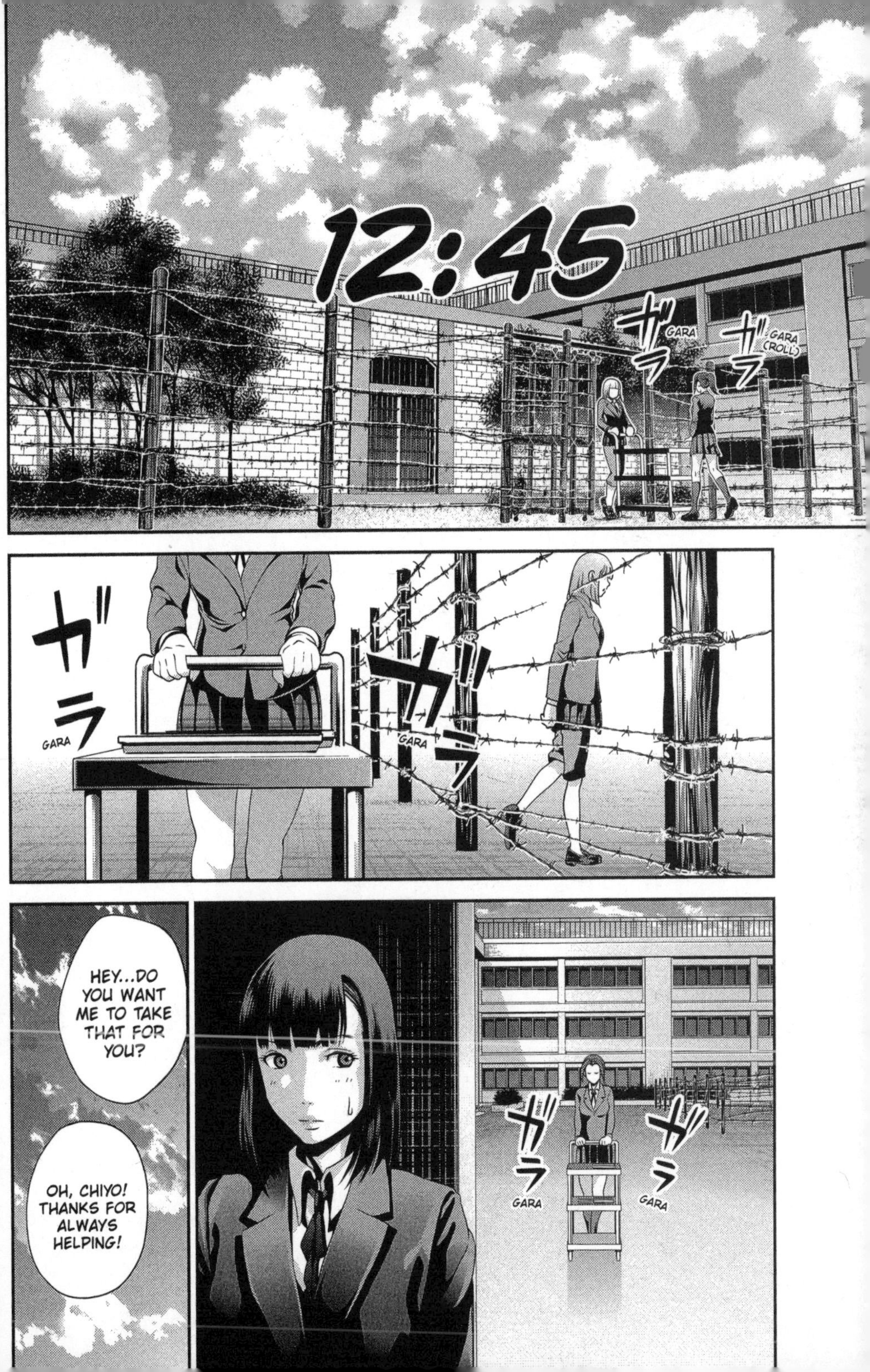
12:45
ガラ
GARA (ROLL)
ガラ
GARA
ガラ
GARA
ガラ
GARA
ガラ
GARA
ガラ
GARA
HEY...DO YOU WANT ME TO TAKE THAT FOR YOU?
OH, CHIYO! THANKS FOR ALWAYS HELPING!

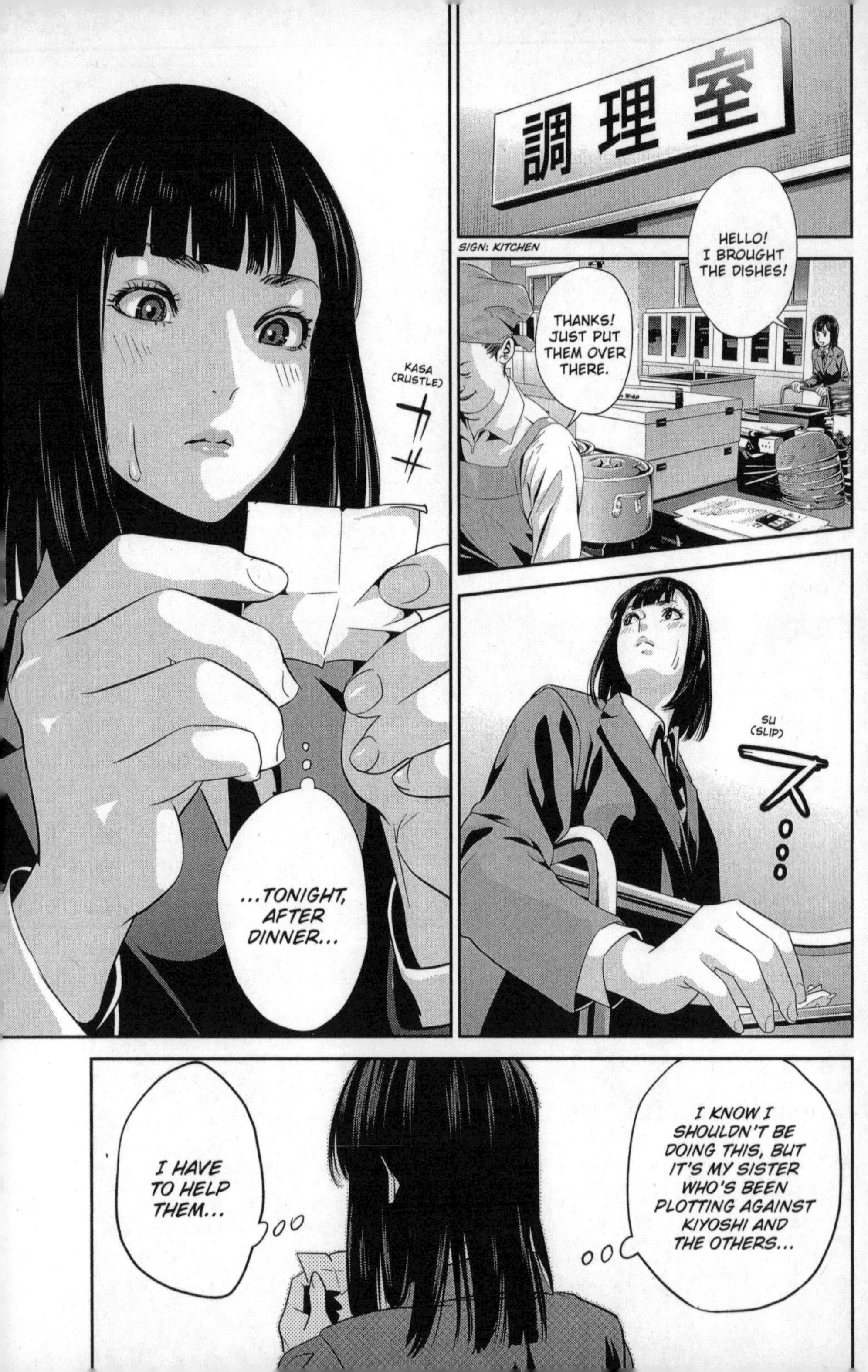
調理室
SIGN: KITCHEN
HELLO! I BROUGHT THE DISHES!
THANKS! JUST PUT THEM OVER THERE.
SU (SLIP)
ス
KASA (RUSTLE)
カサ
...TONIGHT, AFTER DINNER...
I KNOW I SHOULDN'T BE DOING THIS, BUT IT'S MY SISTER WHO'S BEEN PLOTTING AGAINST KIYOSHI AND THE OTHERS...
I HAVE TO HELP THEM...

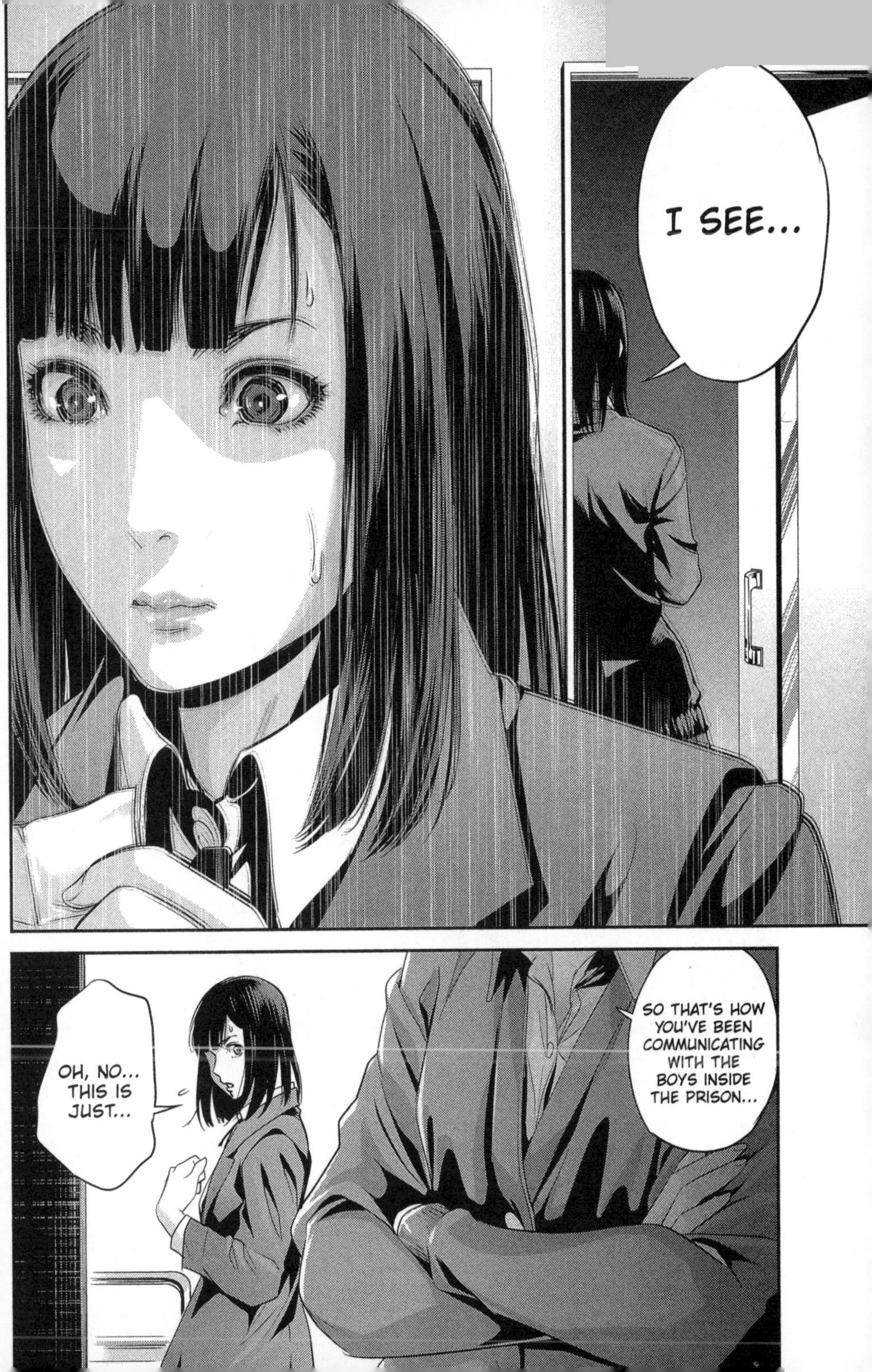
I SEE...
SO THAT'S HOW YOU'VE BEEN COMMUNICATING WITH THE BOYS INSIDE THE PRISON...
OH, NO... THIS IS JUST...

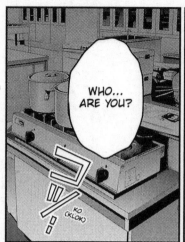

WHO... ARE YOU?

KO (KLOK)

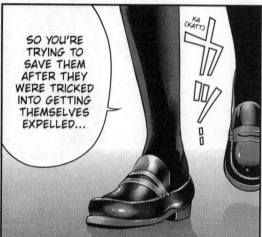

SO YOU'RE TRYING TO SAVE THEM AFTER THEY WERE TRICKED INTO GETTING THEMSELVES EXPELLED...

KA (KATT)

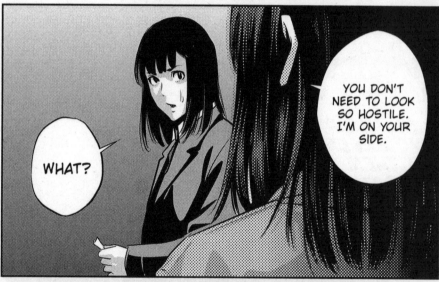

WHAT?

YOU DON'T NEED TO LOOK SO HOSTILE. I'M ON YOUR SIDE.

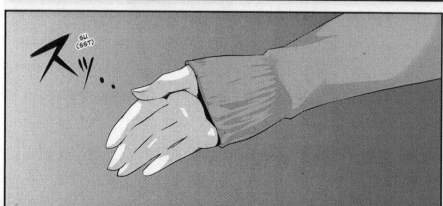

SU (SST)

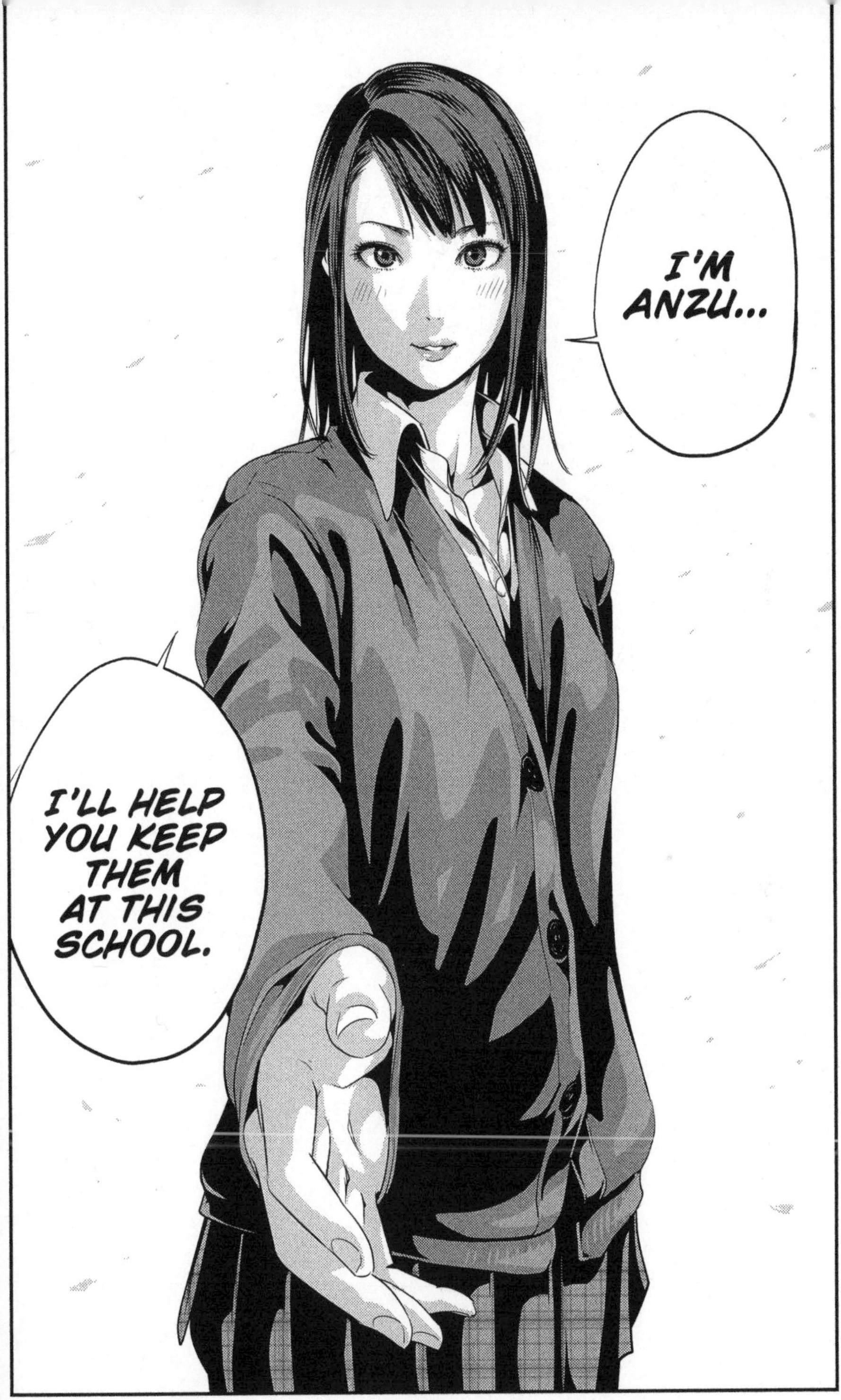
I'M ANZU...
I'LL HELP YOU KEEP THEM AT THIS SCHOOL.

CHAPTER 71: BLOOD DIAMOND

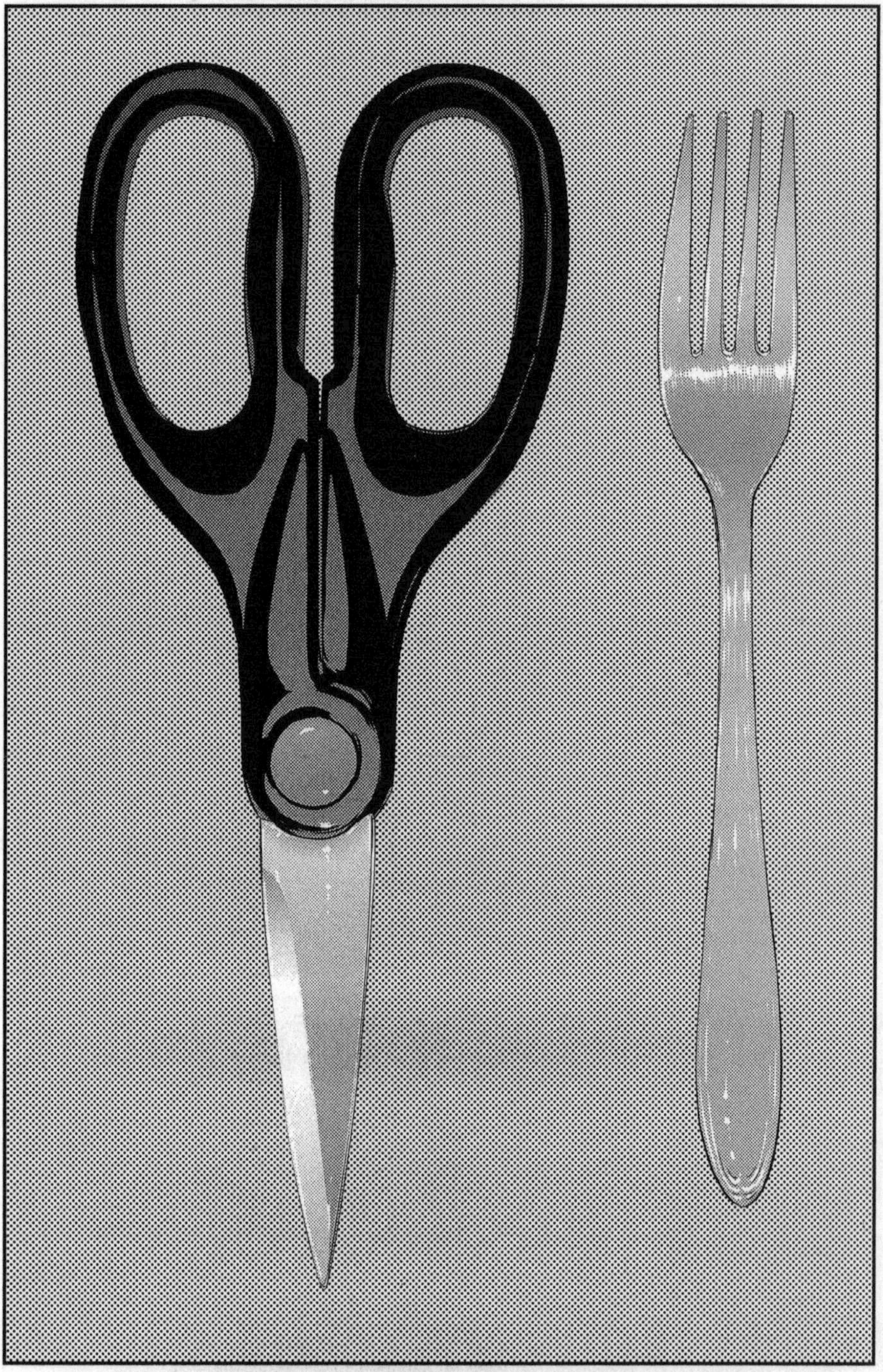

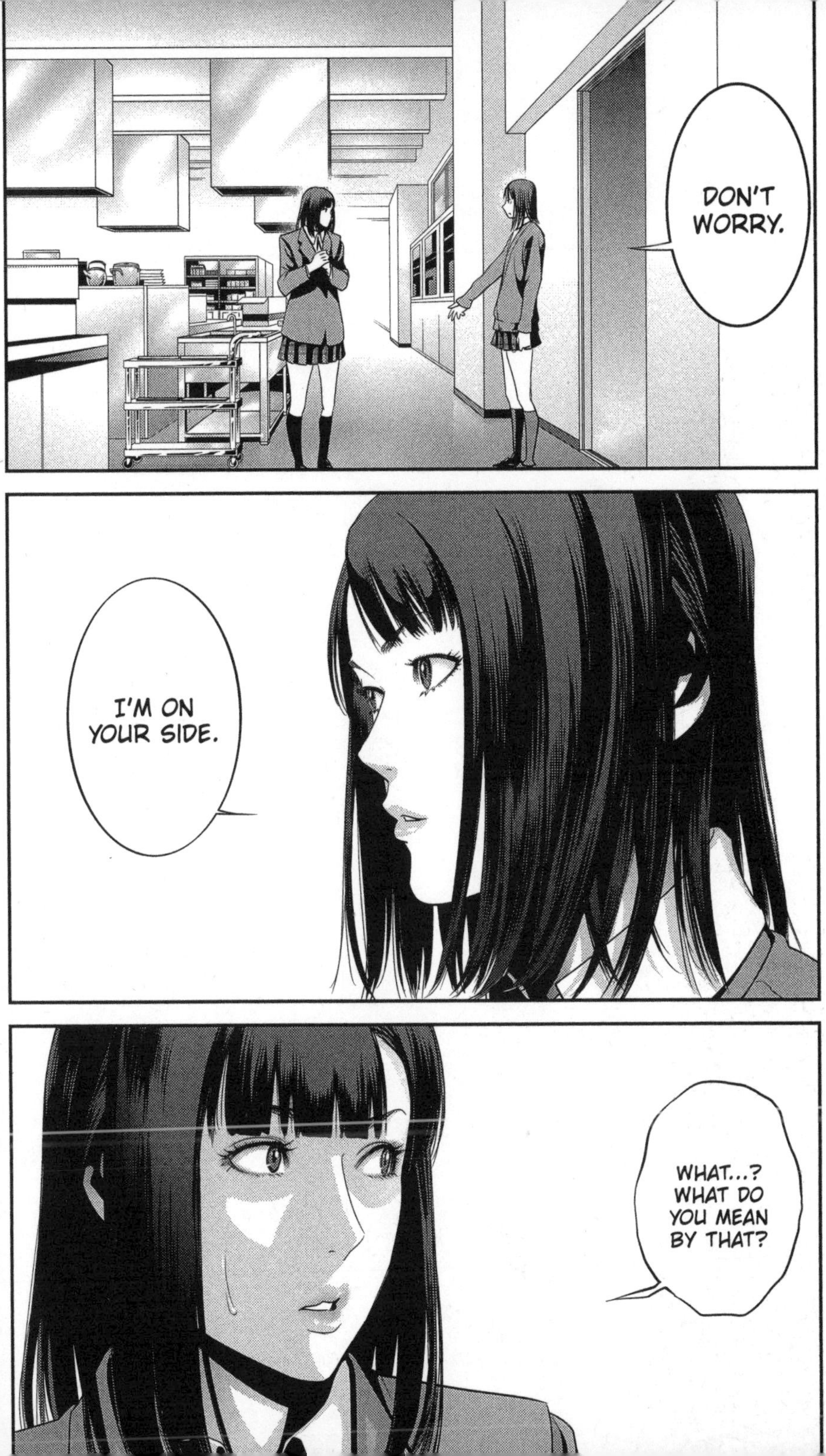
DON'T WORRY.
I'M ON YOUR SIDE.
WHAT...? WHAT DO YOU MEAN BY THAT?

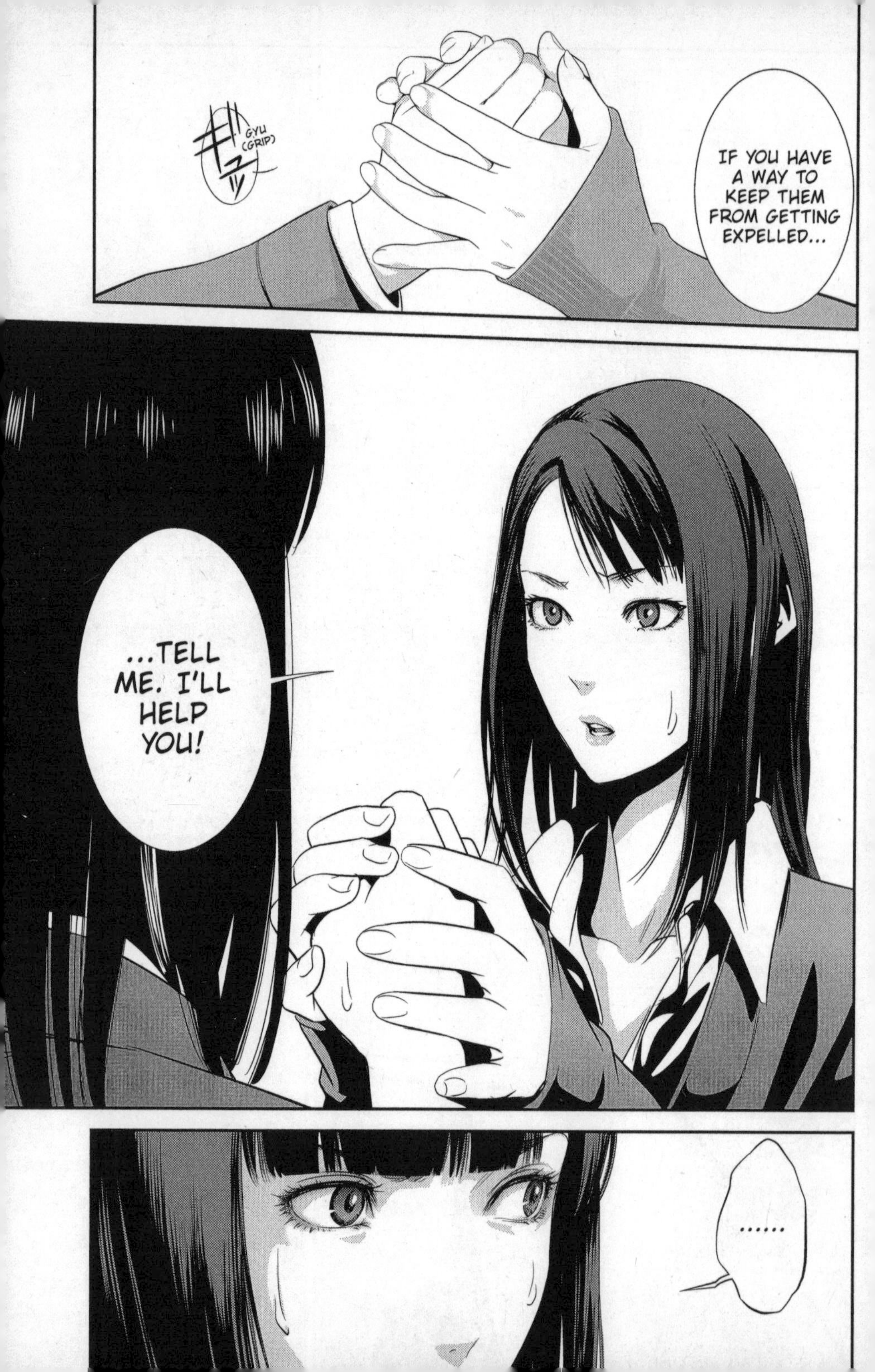
IF YOU HAVE A WAY TO KEEP THEM FROM GETTING EXPELLED...
GYU (GRIP)
...TELL ME. I'LL HELP YOU!
......

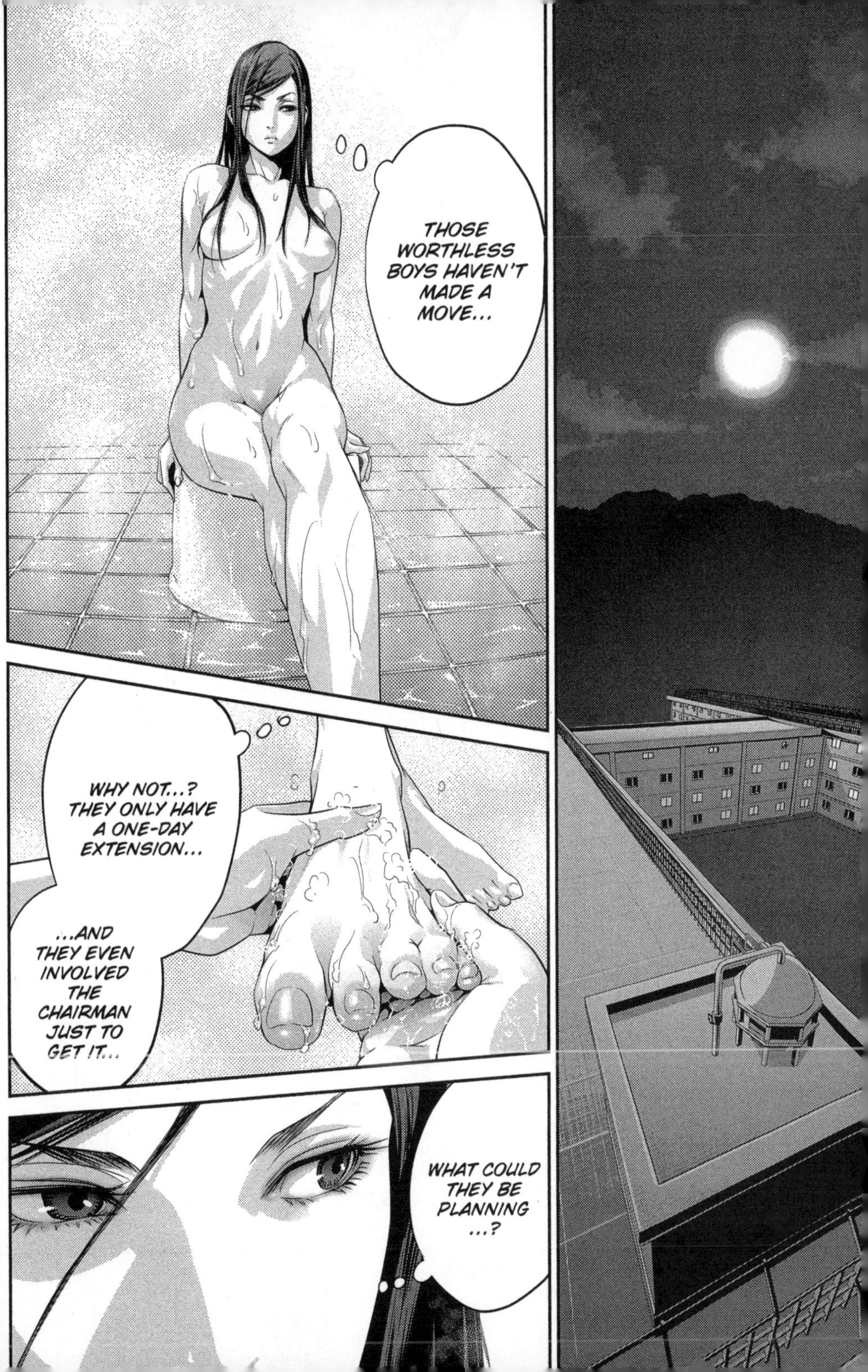
THOSE WORTHLESS BOYS HAVEN'T MADE A MOVE...
WHY NOT...? THEY ONLY HAVE A ONE-DAY EXTENSION...
...AND THEY EVEN INVOLVED THE CHAIRMAN JUST TO GET IT...
WHAT COULD THEY BE PLANNING ...?

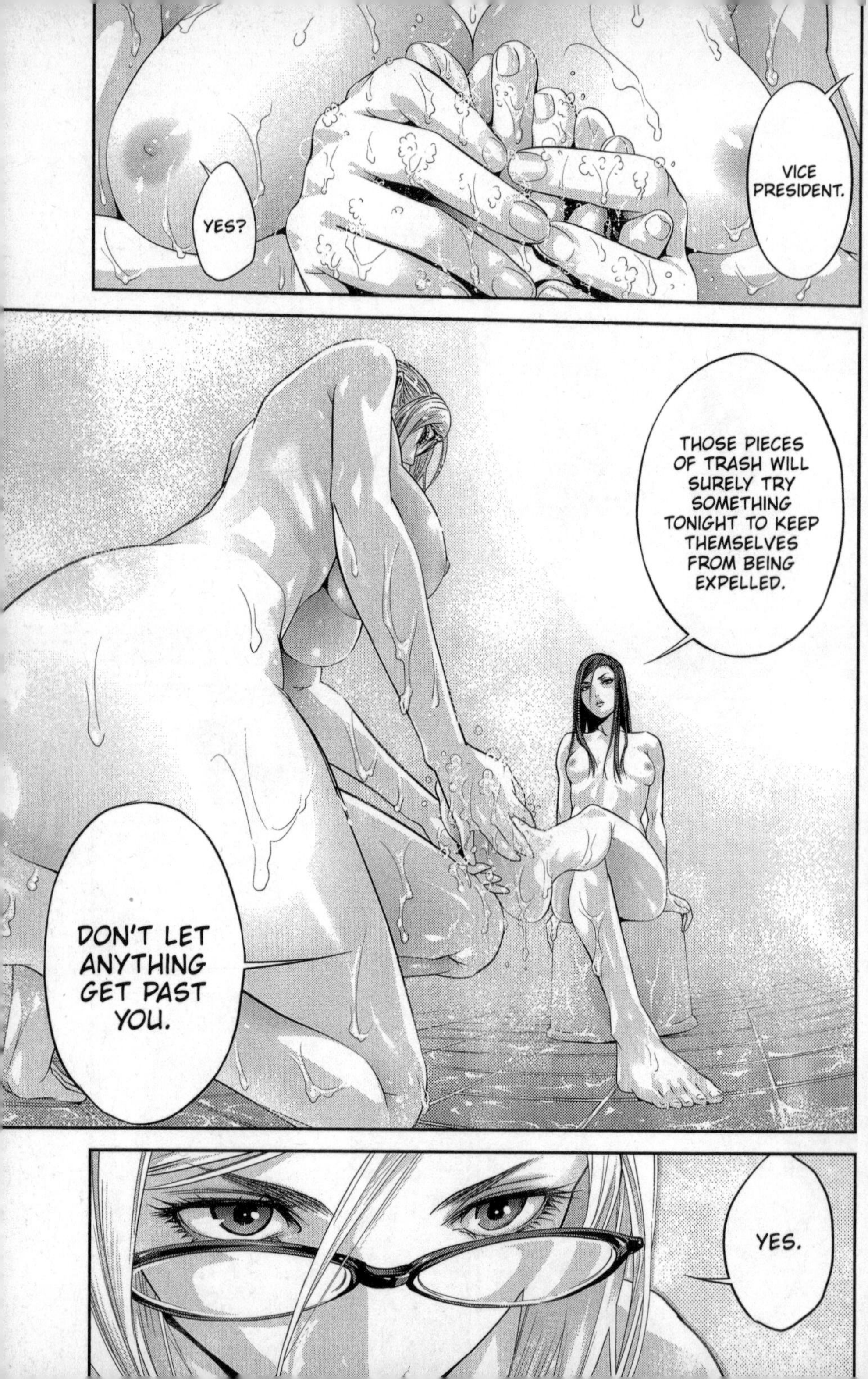
VICE PRESIDENT.
YES?
THOSE PIECES OF TRASH WILL SURELY TRY SOMETHING TONIGHT TO KEEP THEMSELVES FROM BEING EXPELLED.
DON'T LET ANYTHING GET PAST YOU.
YES.

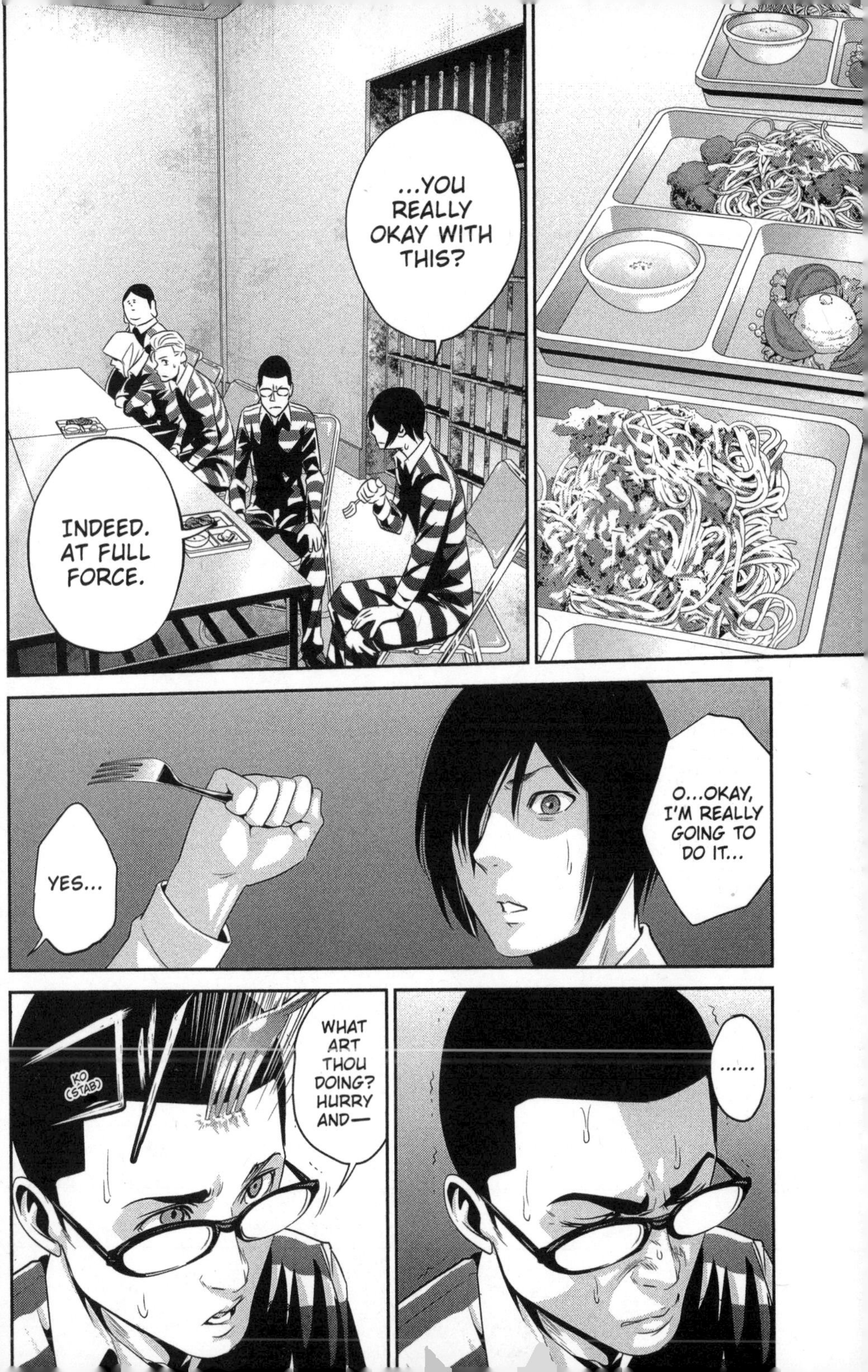
...YOU REALLY OKAY WITH THIS?
INDEED. AT FULL FORCE.
O...OKAY, I'M REALLY GOING TO DO IT...
YES...
......
WHAT ART THOU DOING? HURRY AND—
KO (STAB)

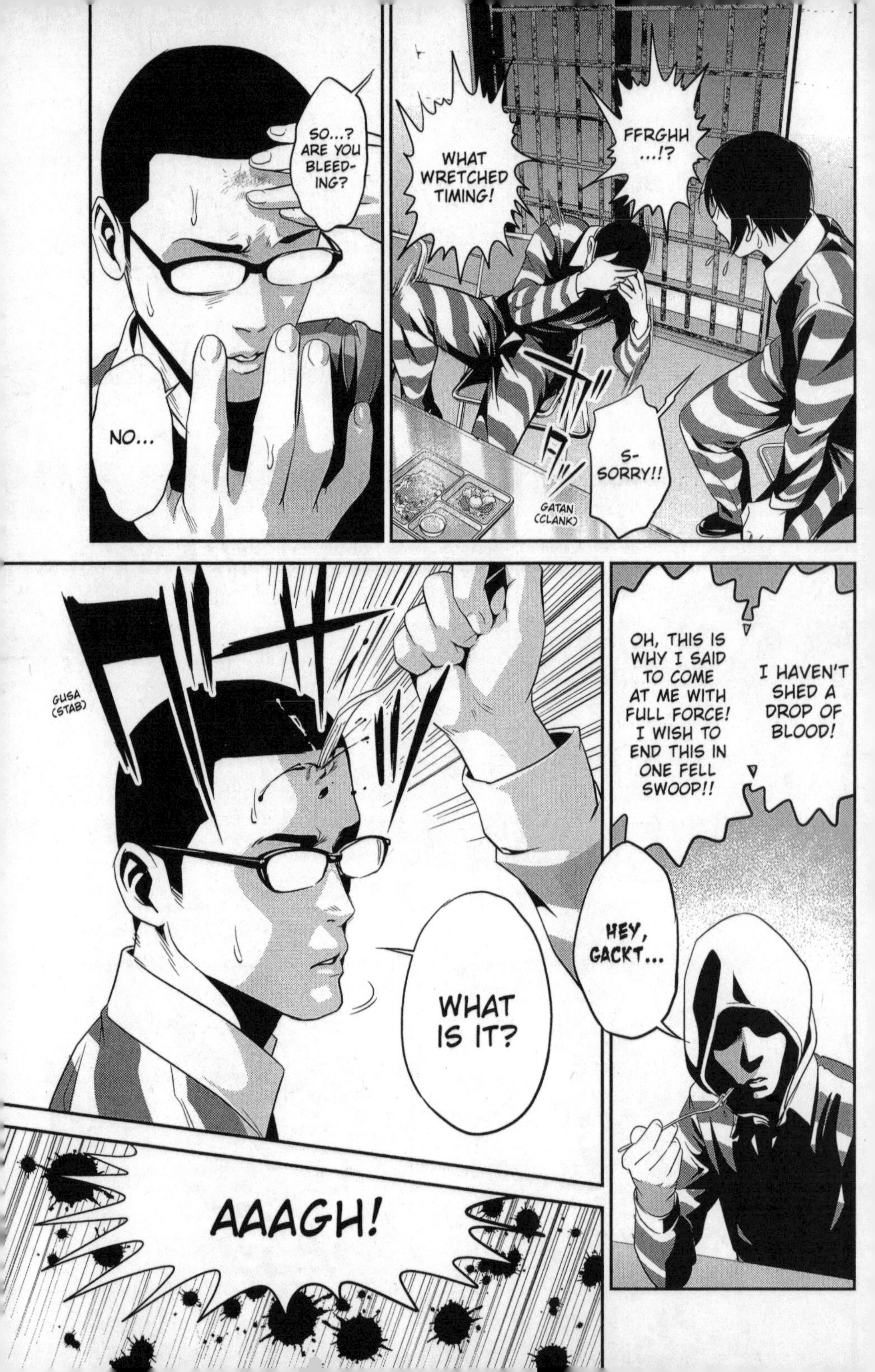
FFRGHH ...!?
WHAT WRETCHED TIMING!
S-SORRY!!
GATAN (CLANK)
SO...? ARE YOU BLEED-ING?
NO...
I HAVEN'T SHED A DROP OF BLOOD!
OH, THIS IS WHY I SAID TO COME AT ME WITH FULL FORCE! I WISH TO END THIS IN ONE FELL SWOOP!!
HEY, GACKT...
GUSA (STAB)
WHAT IS IT?
AAAGH!

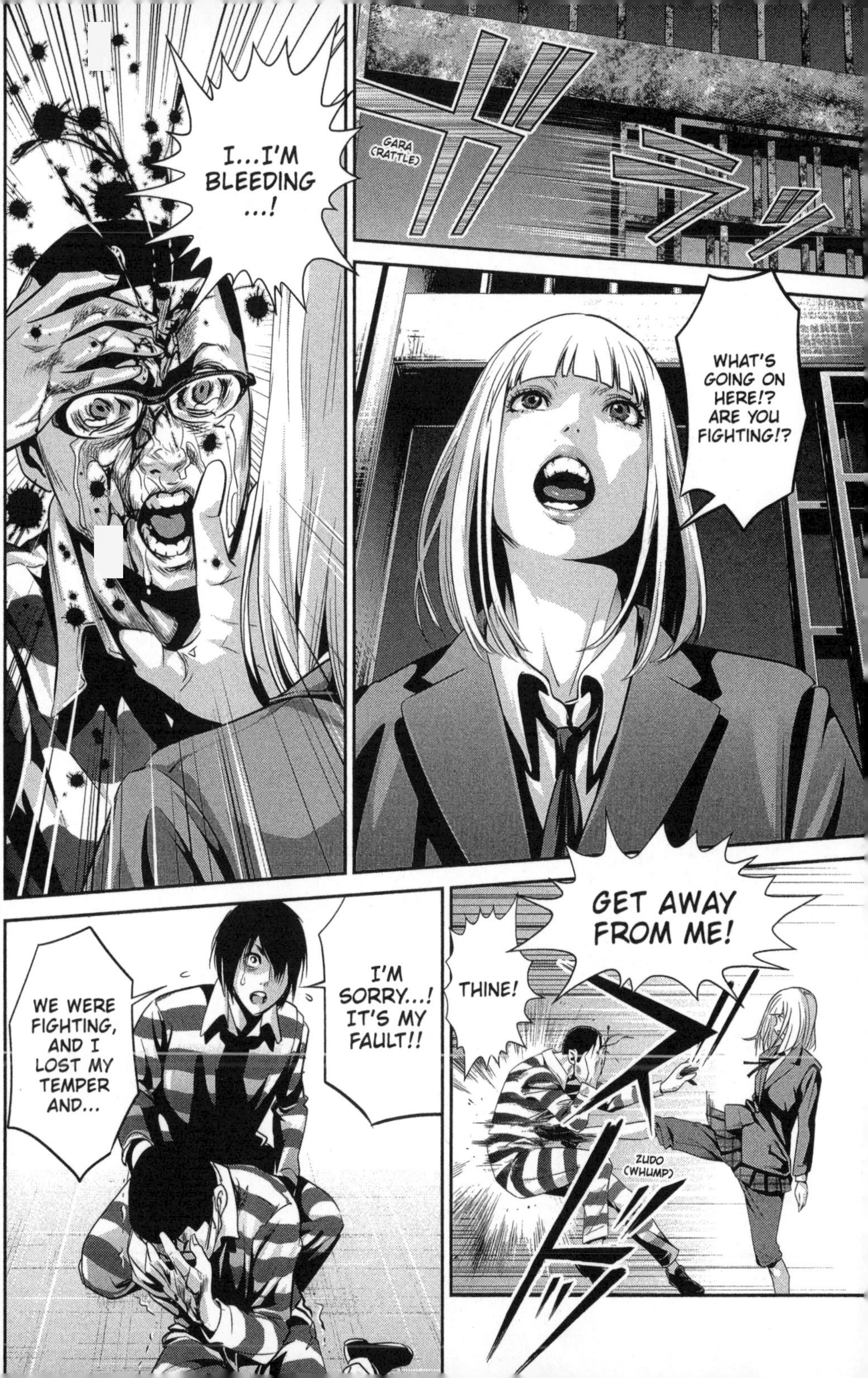
GARA (RATTLE)
WHAT'S GOING ON HERE!? ARE YOU FIGHTING!?
I...I'M BLEEDING ...!
GET AWAY FROM ME!
THINE!
ZUDO (WHUMP)
I'M SORRY...! IT'S MY FAULT!!
WE WERE FIGHTING, AND I LOST MY TEMPER AND...

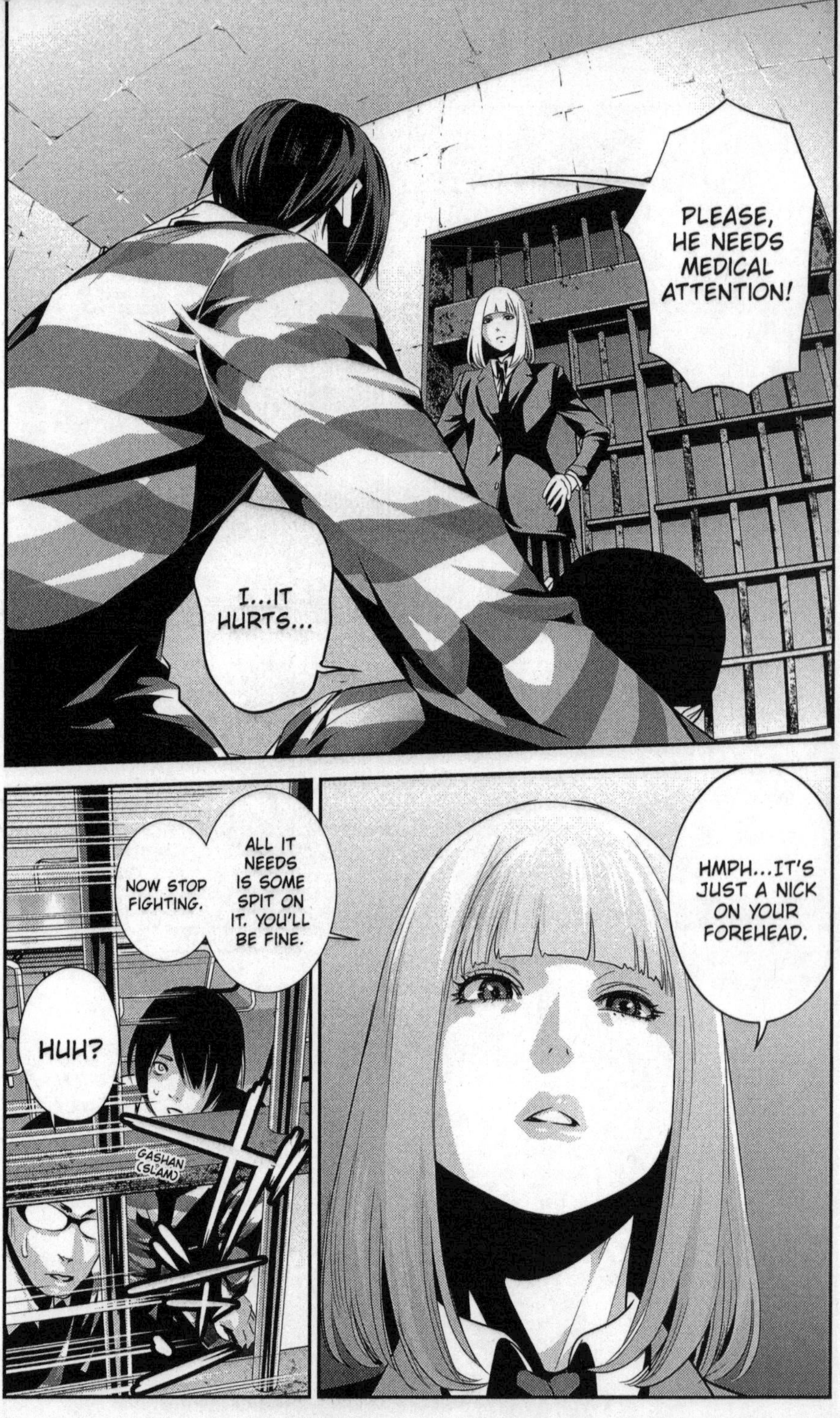
PLEASE, HE NEEDS MEDICAL ATTENTION!
I...IT HURTS...
HMPH...IT'S JUST A NICK ON YOUR FOREHEAD.
ALL IT NEEDS IS SOME SPIT ON IT. YOU'LL BE FINE.
NOW STOP FIGHTING.
HUH?
GASHAN (SLAM)

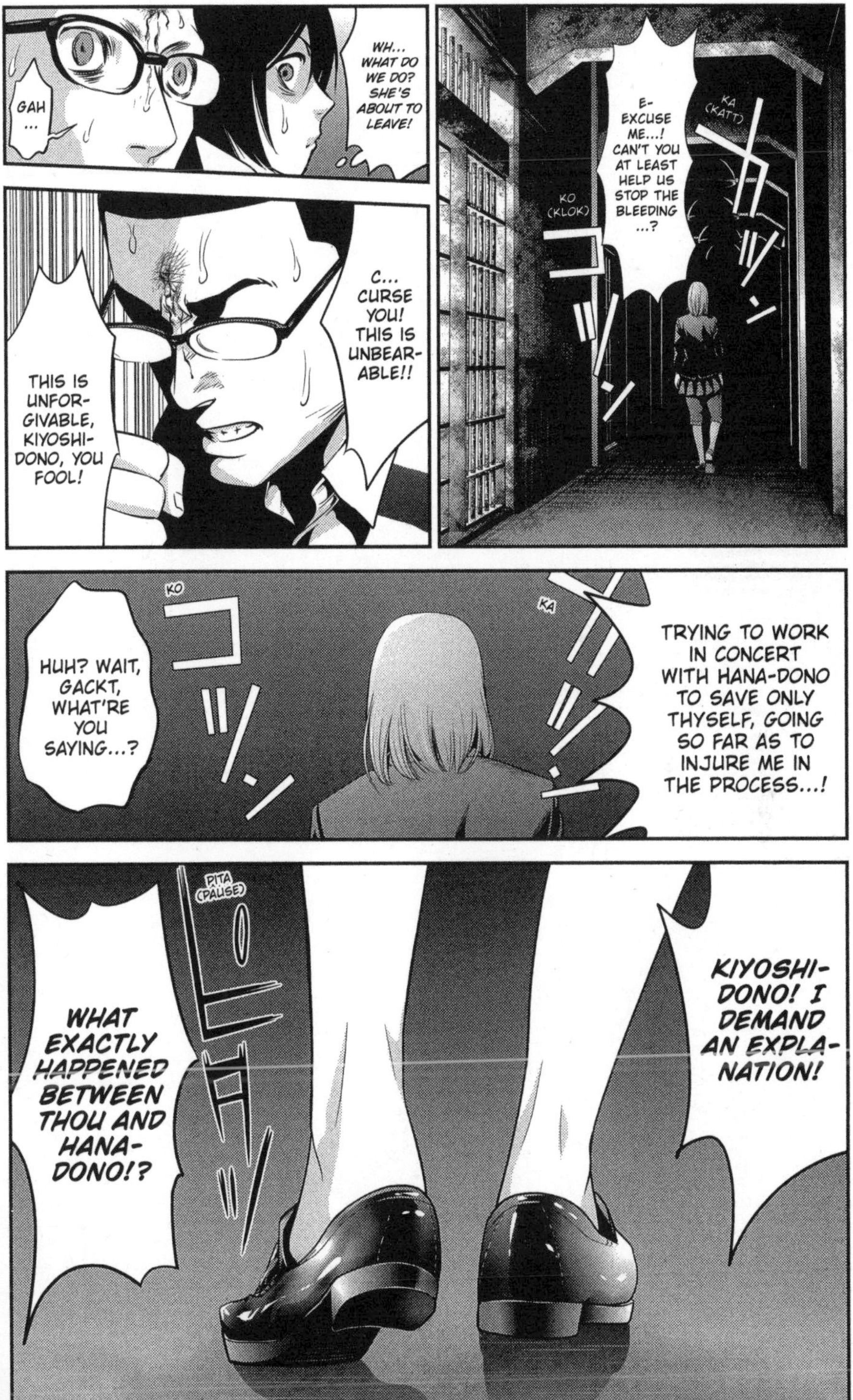
KA (KATT)
E-EXCUSE ME...! CAN'T YOU AT LEAST HELP US STOP THE BLEEDING ...?
KO (KLOK)
WH... WHAT DO WE DO? SHE'S ABOUT TO LEAVE!
GAH ...
C... CURSE YOU! THIS IS UNBEARABLE!!
THIS IS UNFORGIVABLE, KIYOSHI-DONO, YOU FOOL!
TRYING TO WORK IN CONCERT WITH HANA-DONO TO SAVE ONLY THYSELF, GOING SO FAR AS TO INJURE ME IN THE PROCESS...!
KA
KO
HUH? WAIT, GACKT, WHAT'RE YOU SAYING...?
KIYOSHI-DONO! I DEMAND AN EXPLANATION!
PITA (PAUSE)
WHAT EXACTLY HAPPENED BETWEEN THOU AND HANA-DONO!?

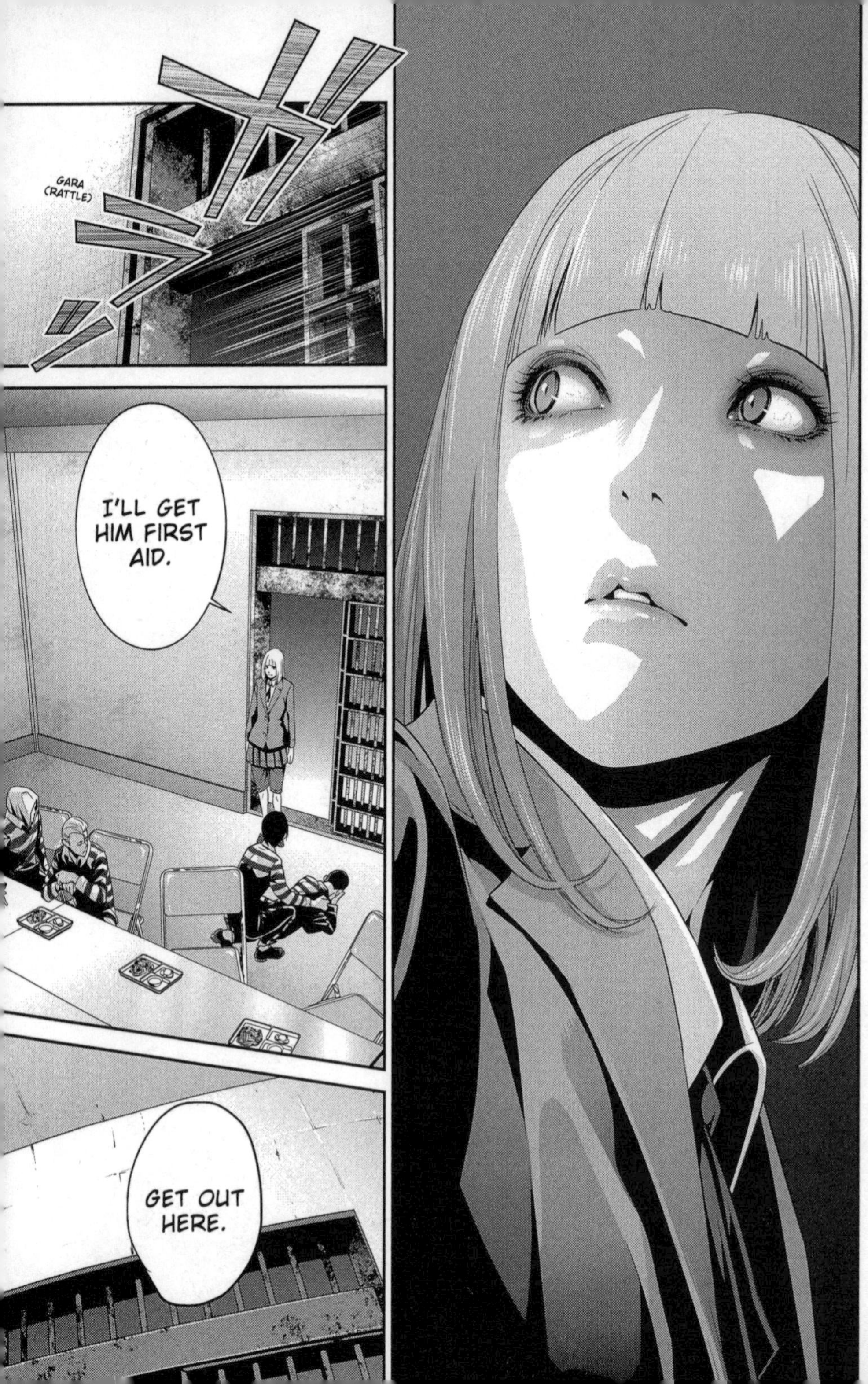

GARA (RATTLE)
I'LL GET HIM FIRST AID.
GET OUT HERE.

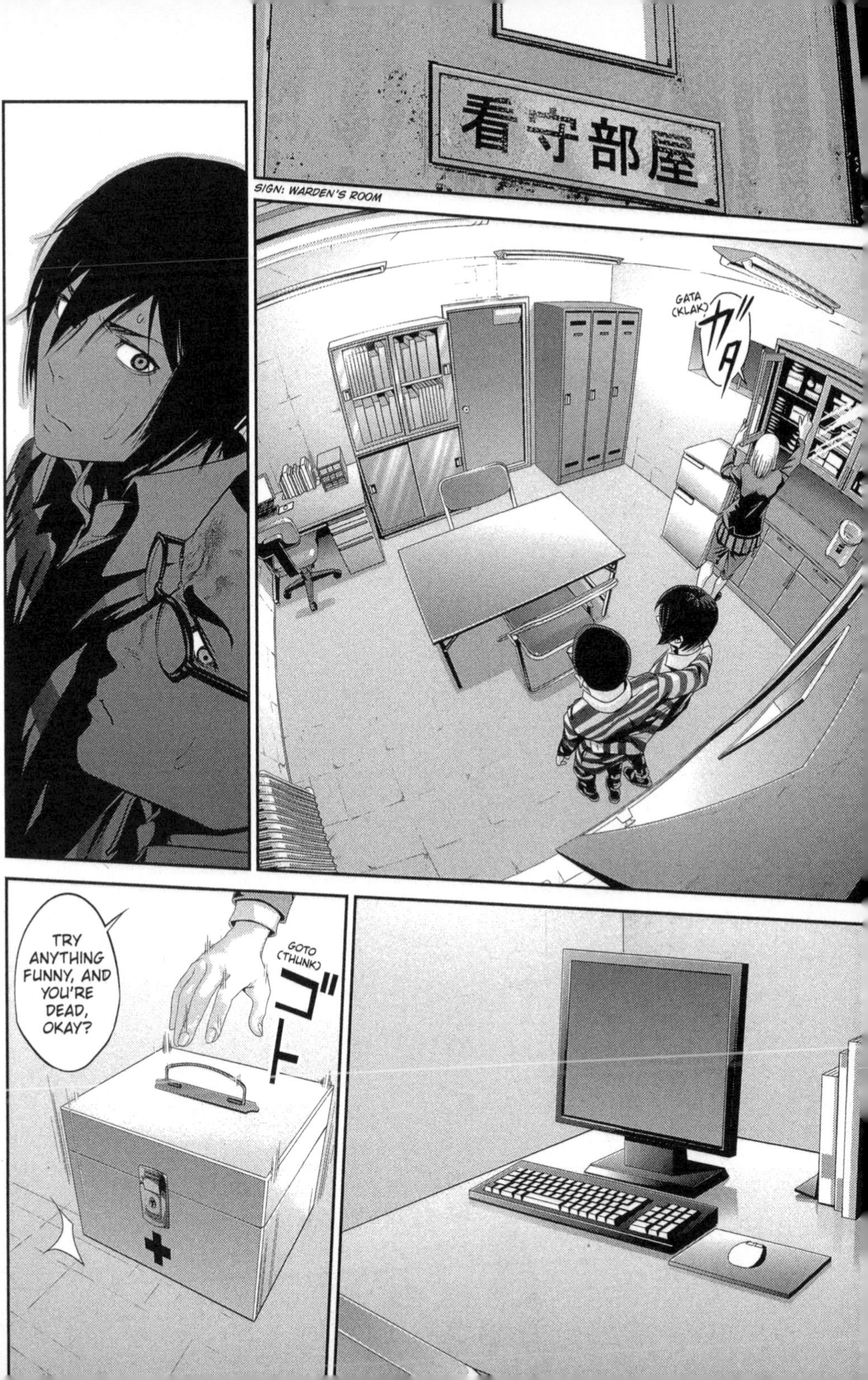
看守部屋
SIGN: WARDEN'S ROOM
ガタ
GATA (KLAK)
ゴト
GOTO (THUNK)
TRY ANYTHING FUNNY, AND YOU'RE DEAD, OKAY?

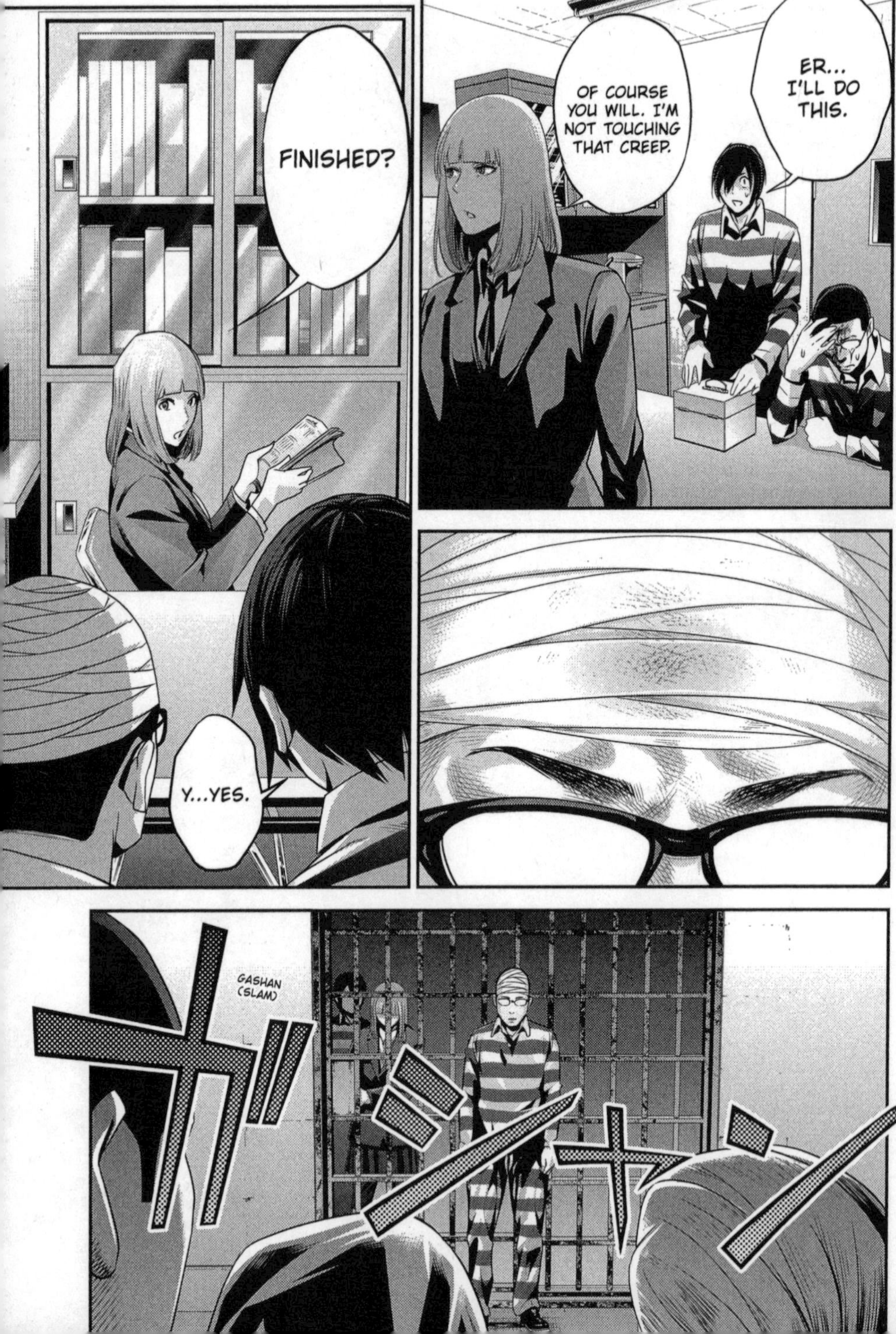
ER... I'LL DO THIS.
OF COURSE YOU WILL. I'M NOT TOUCHING THAT CREEP.
FINISHED?
Y...YES.
GASHAN (SLAM)

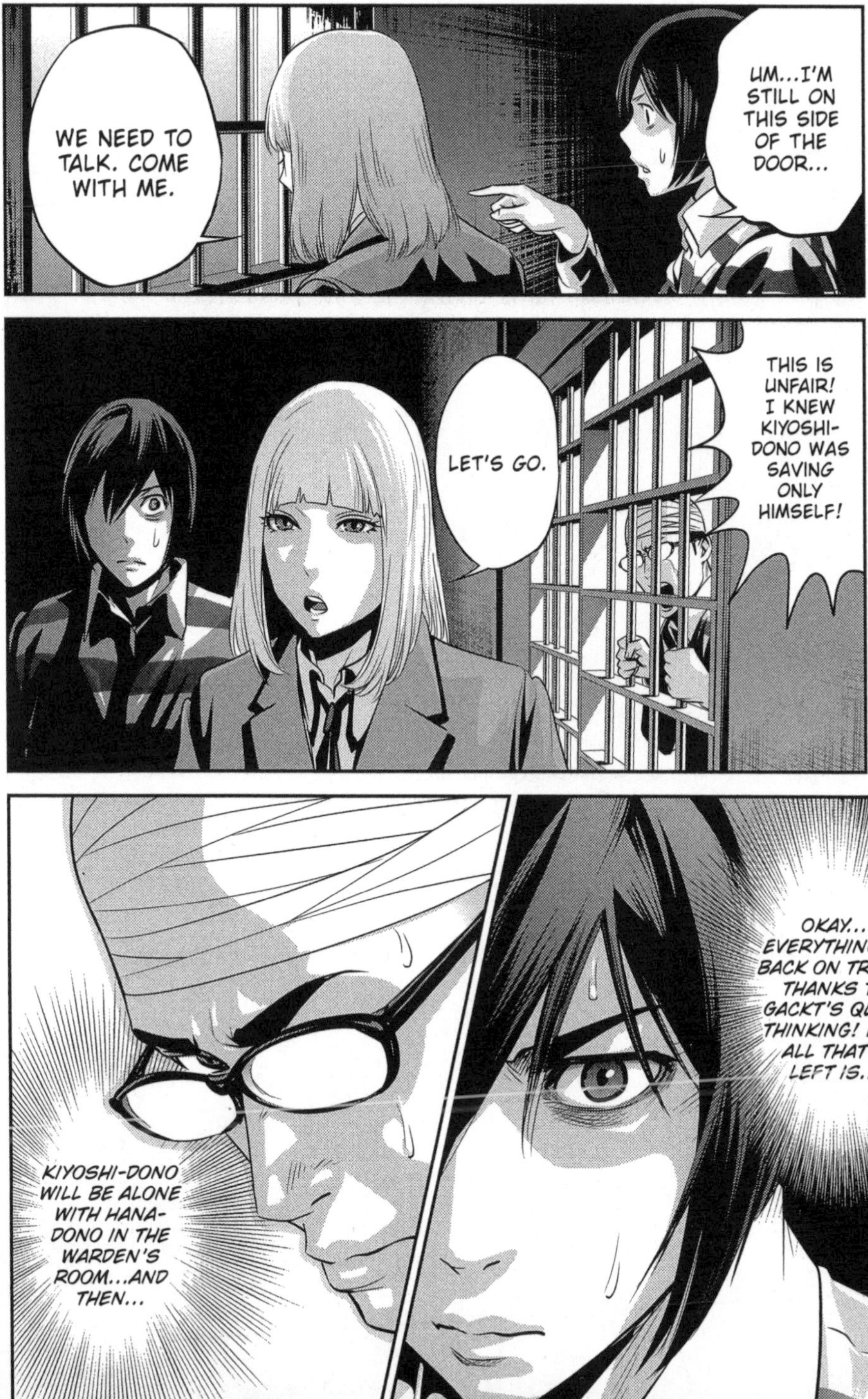
UM...I'M STILL ON THIS SIDE OF THE DOOR...
WE NEED TO TALK. COME WITH ME.
THIS IS UNFAIR! I KNEW KIYOSHI-DONO WAS SAVING ONLY HIMSELF!
LET'S GO.
OKAY... EVERYTHING IS BACK ON TRACK, THANKS TO GACKT'S QUICK THINKING! NOW ALL THAT'S LEFT IS...
KIYOSHI-DONO WILL BE ALONE WITH HANA-DONO IN THE WARDEN'S ROOM...AND THEN...

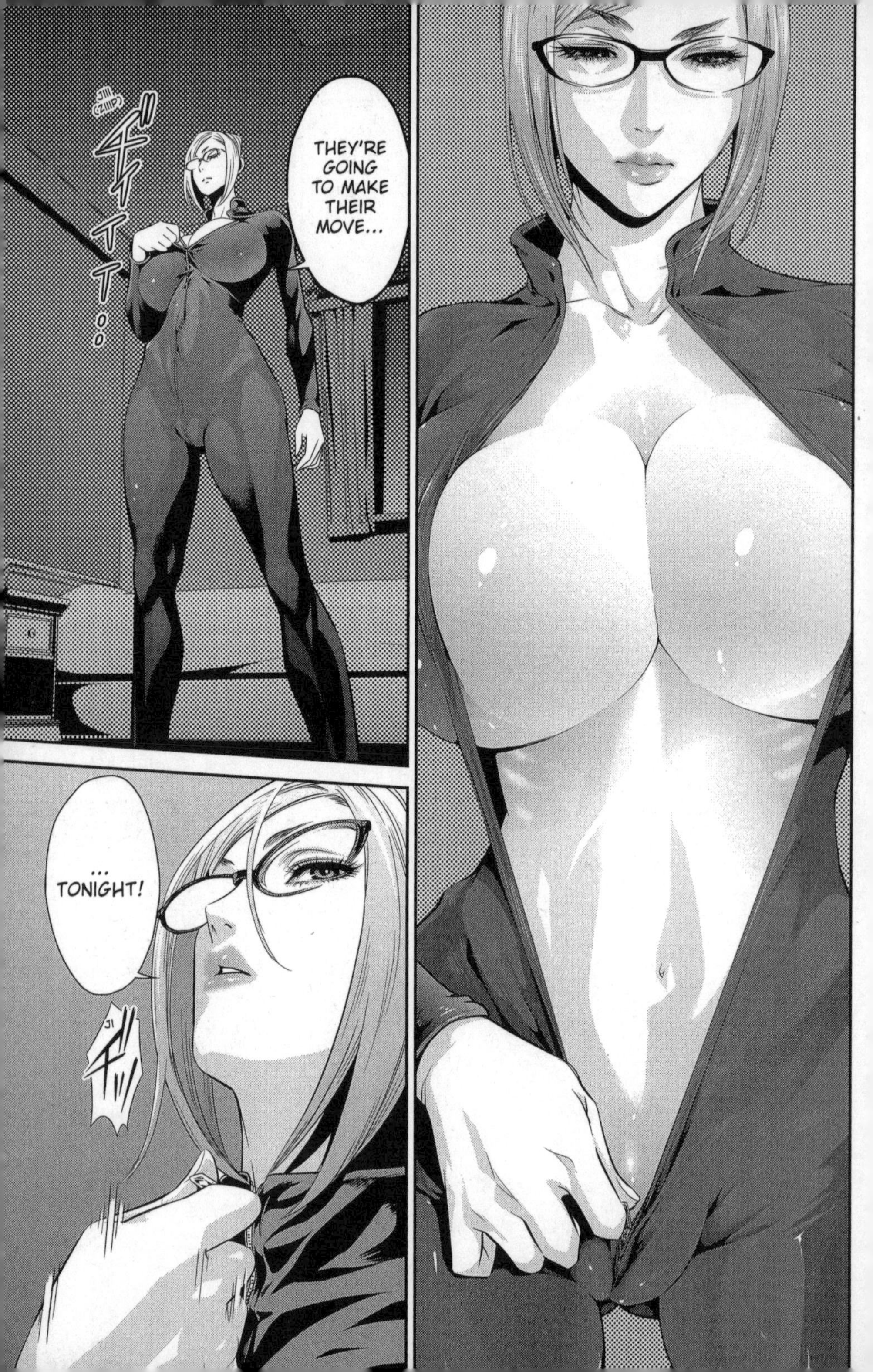
THEY'RE GOING TO MAKE THEIR MOVE...
JIII (ZIIIP)
... TONIGHT!
JI

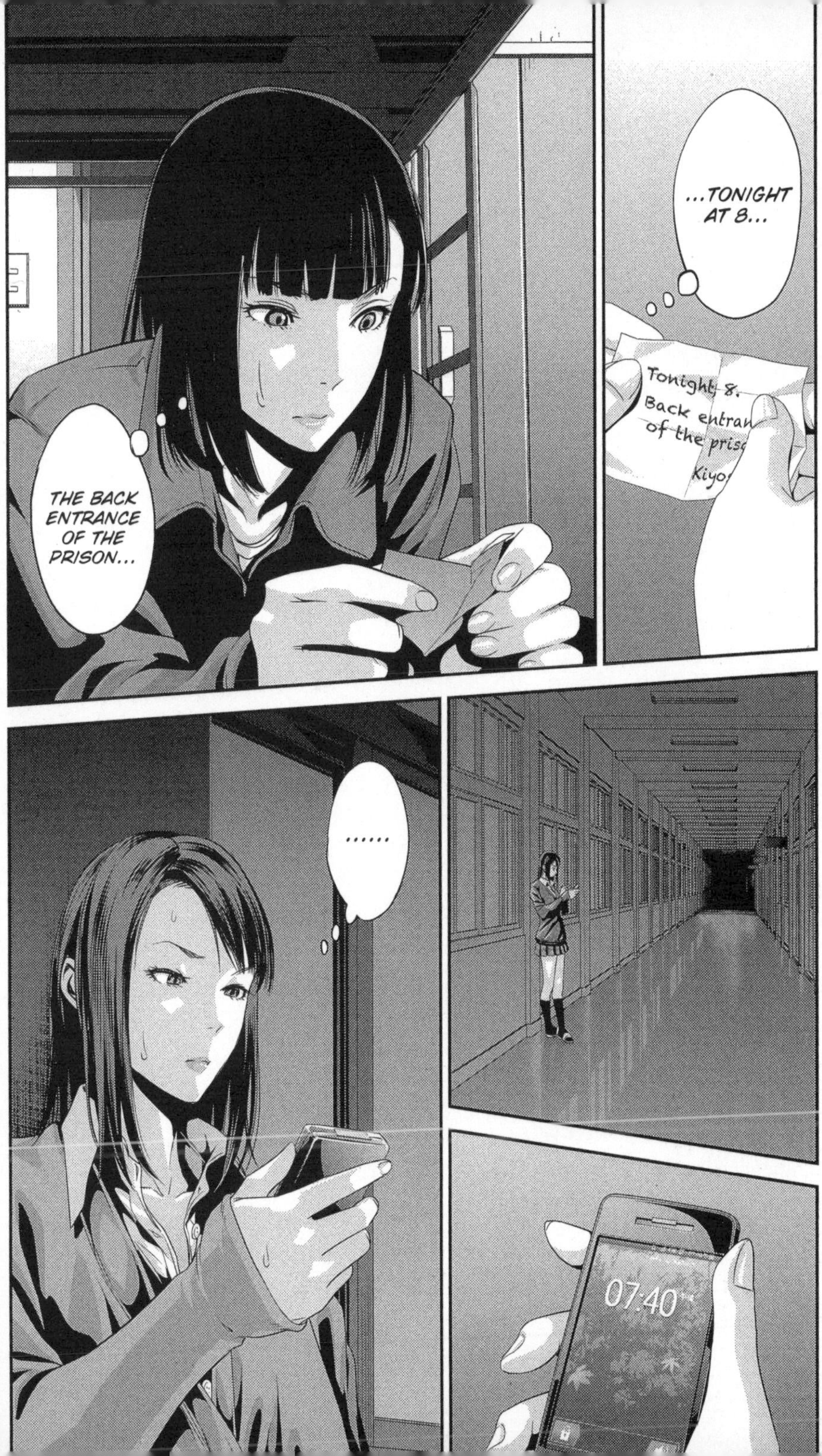
...TONIGHT AT 8...
Tonight 8.
Back entran
of the priso
Kiyo
THE BACK ENTRANCE OF THE PRISON...
07:40
......

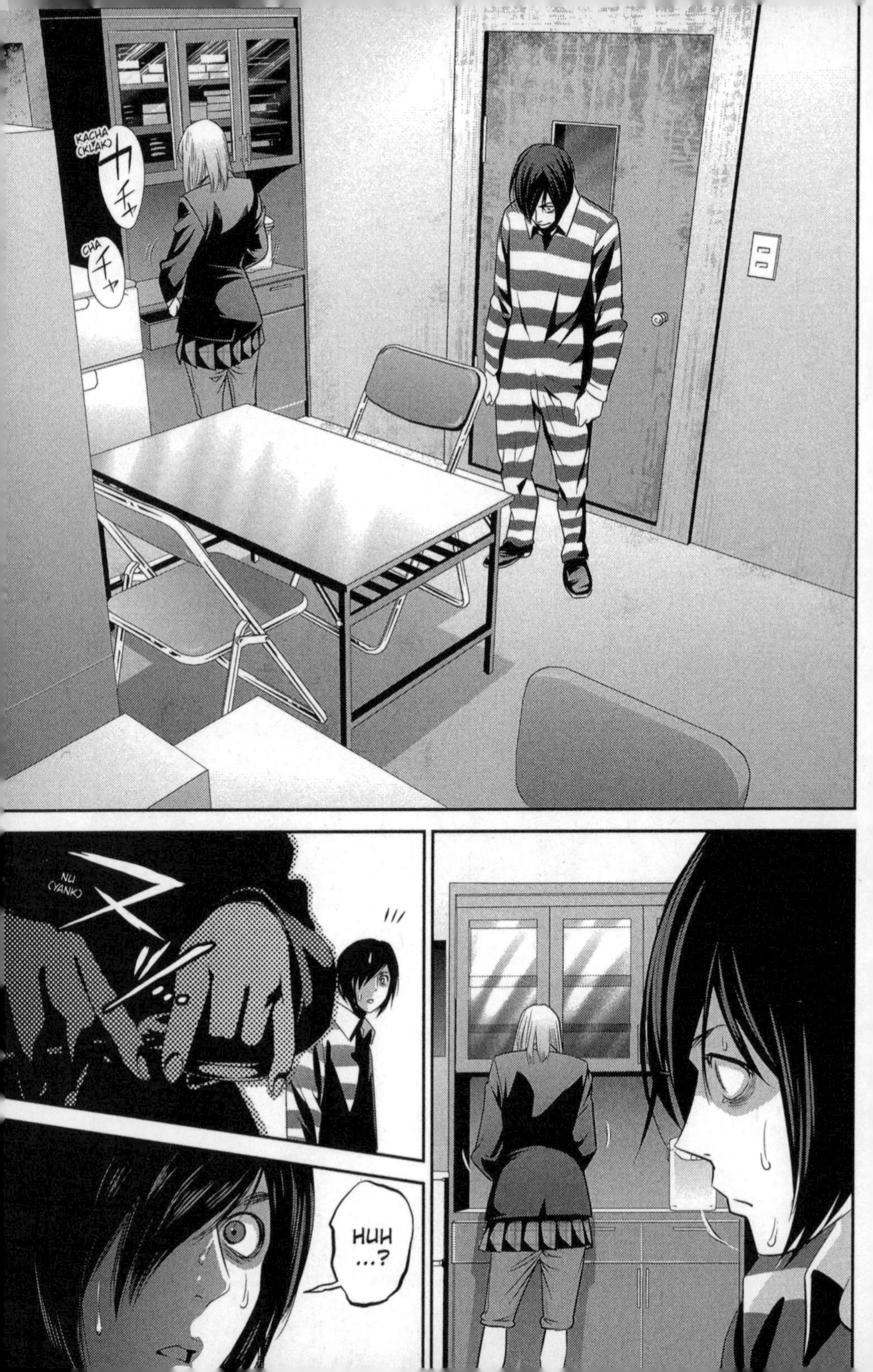
KACHA (KLAK)
カチャ
CHA
チャ
NU (YANK)
ヌッ
HUH ...?

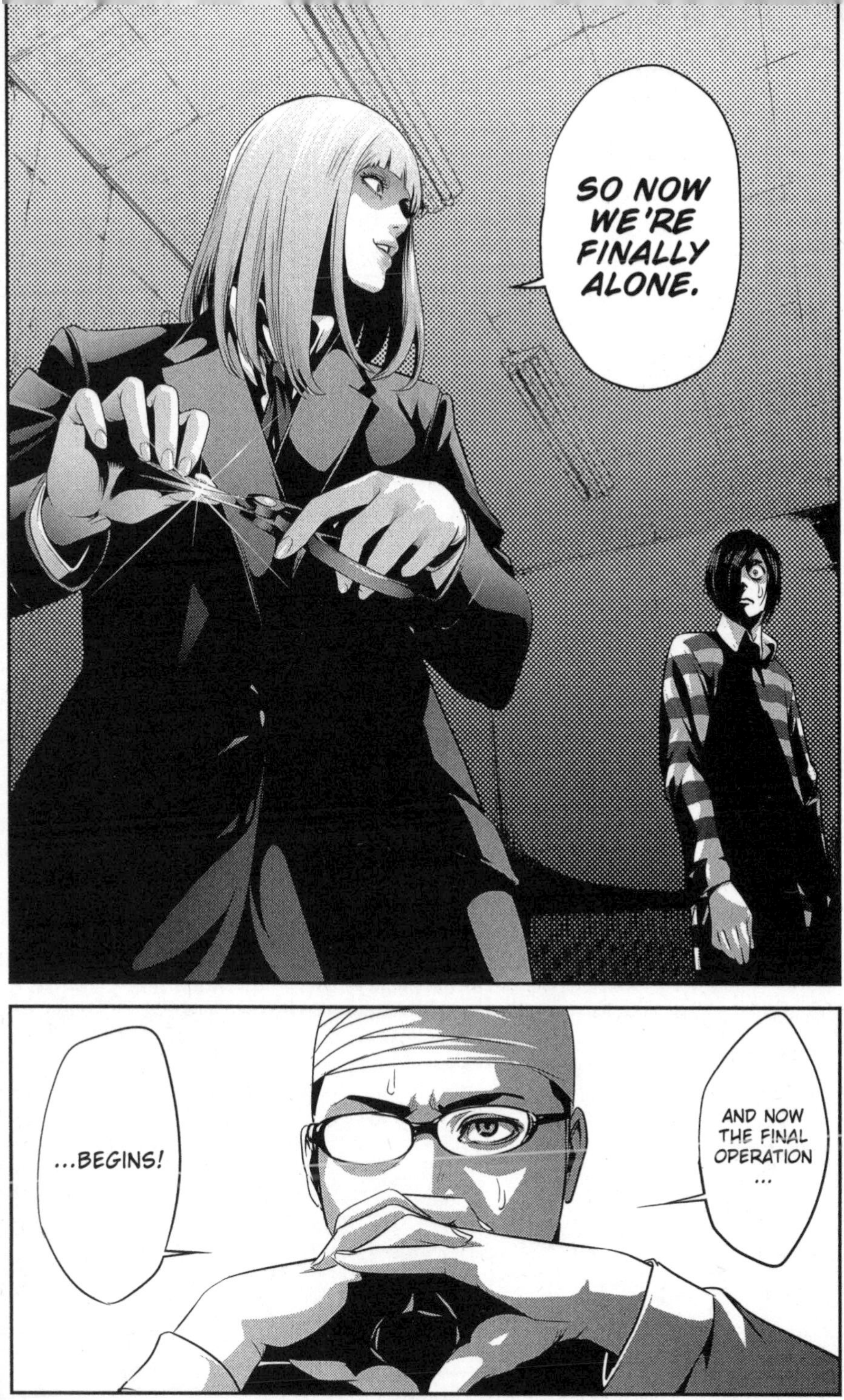
SO NOW WE'RE FINALLY ALONE.
AND NOW THE FINAL OPERATION ...
...BEGINS!

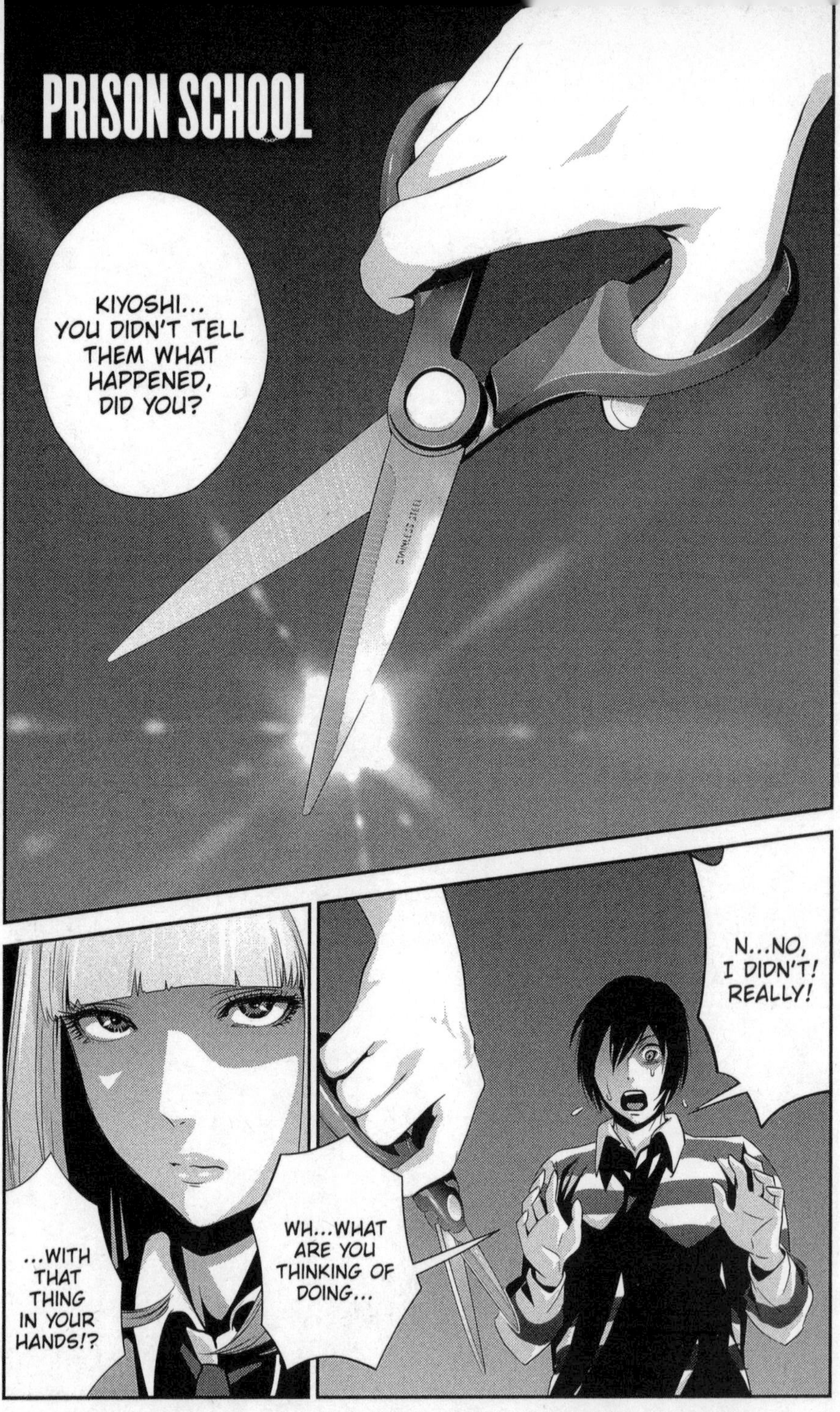
PRISON SCHOOL
KIYOSHI... YOU DIDN'T TELL THEM WHAT HAPPENED, DID YOU?
N...NO, I DIDN'T! REALLY!
WH...WHAT ARE YOU THINKING OF DOING...
...WITH THAT THING IN YOUR HANDS!?

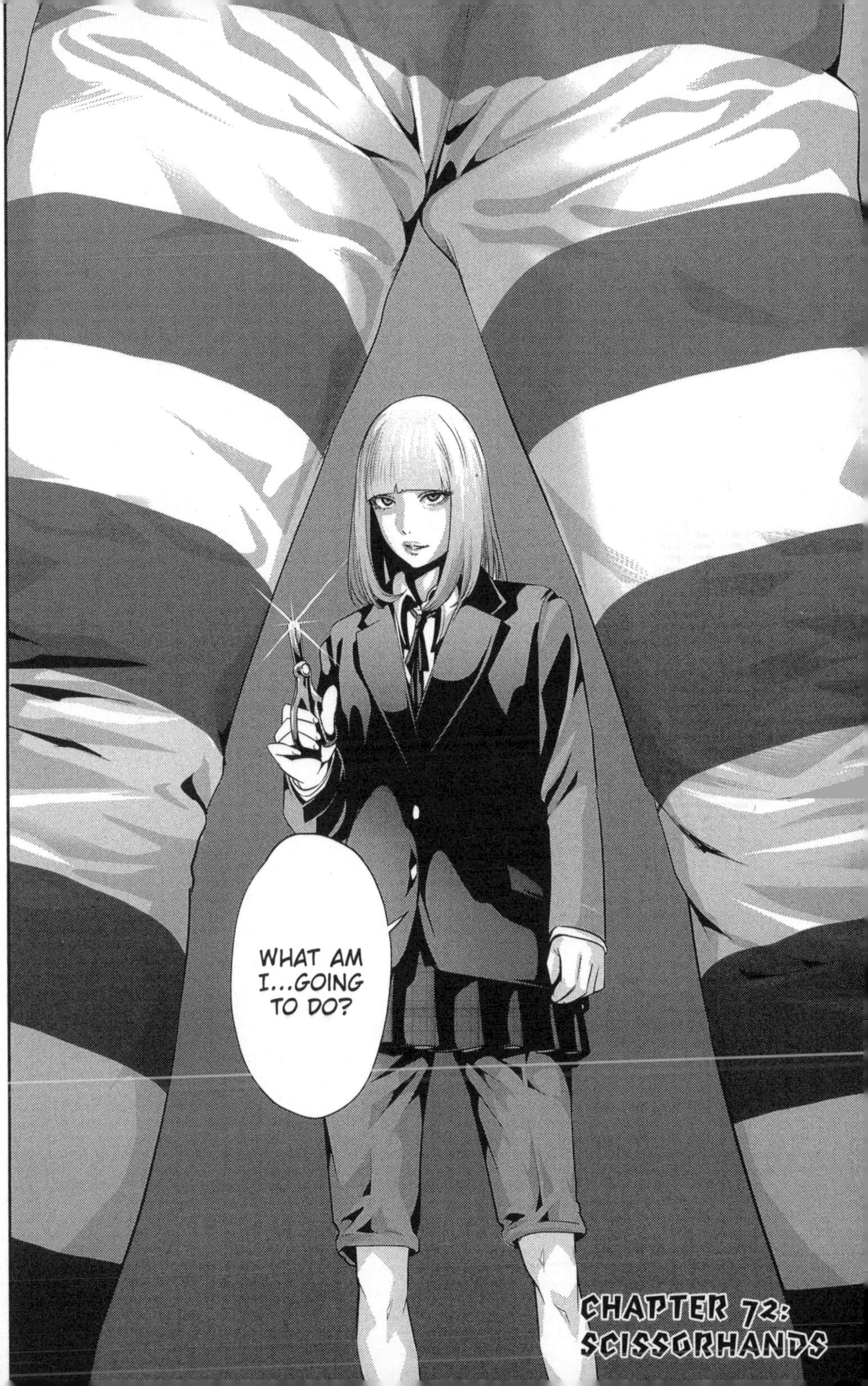
WHAT AM I...GOING TO DO?
CHAPTER 72: SCISSORHANDS

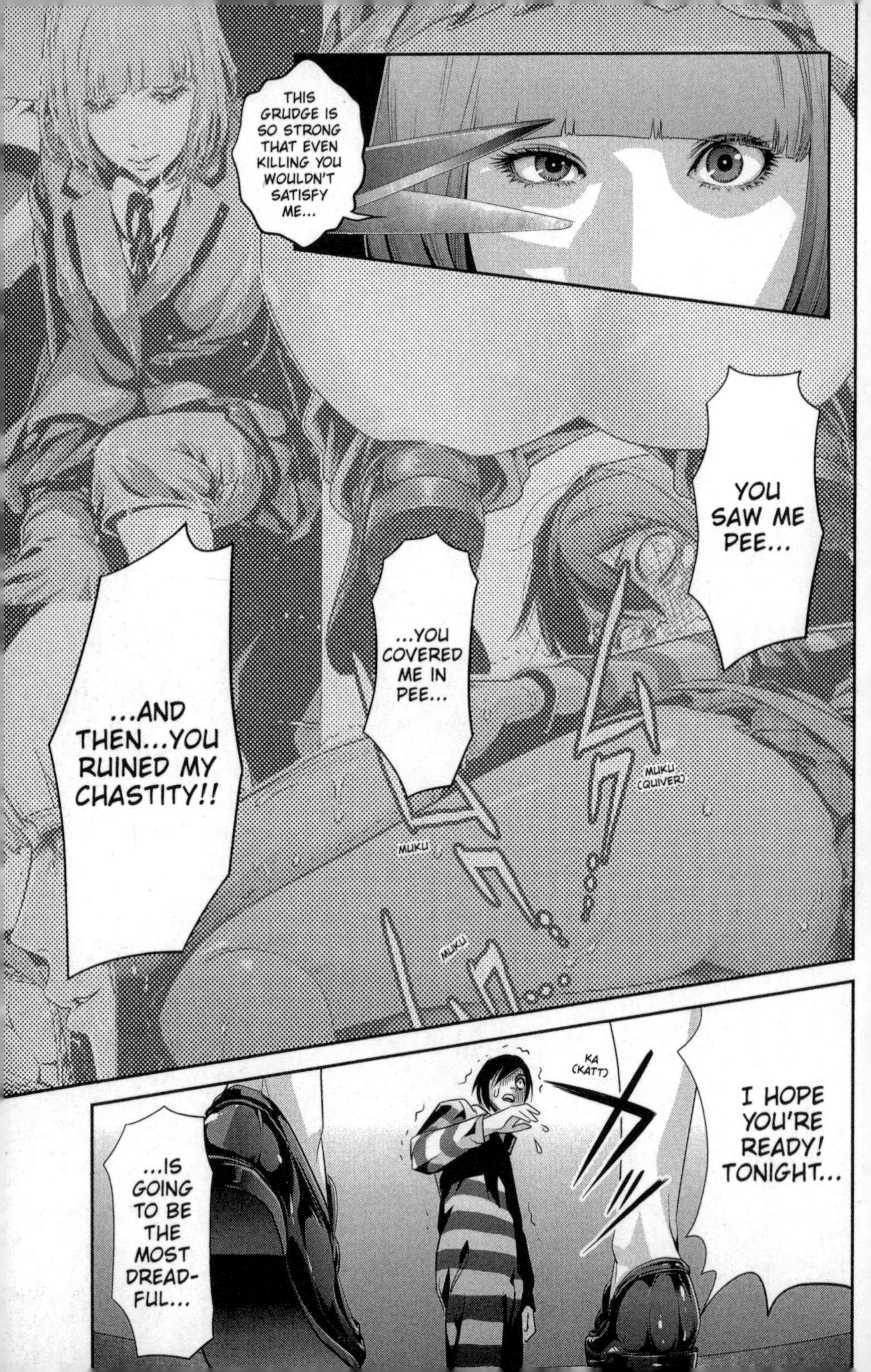
THIS GRUDGE IS SO STRONG THAT EVEN KILLING YOU WOULDN'T SATISFY ME...
YOU SAW ME PEE...
MUKU (QUIVER)
...YOU COVERED ME IN PEE...
MUKU
MUKU
...AND THEN...YOU RUINED MY CHASTITY!!
I HOPE YOU'RE READY! TONIGHT...
KA (KATT)
...IS GOING TO BE THE MOST DREAD-FUL...

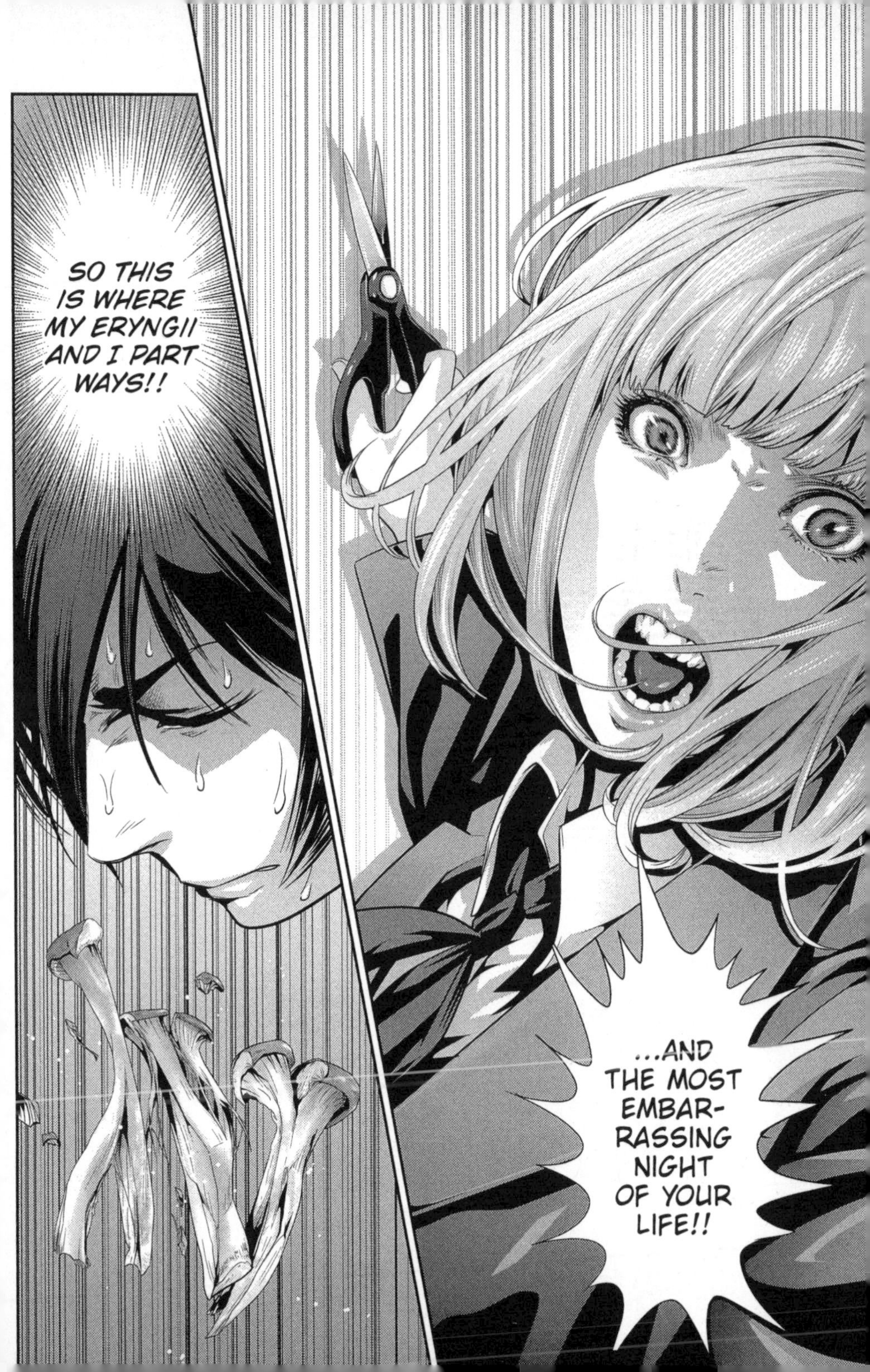
...AND THE MOST EMBARRASSING NIGHT OF YOUR LIFE!!
SO THIS IS WHERE MY ERYNGII AND I PART WAYS!!

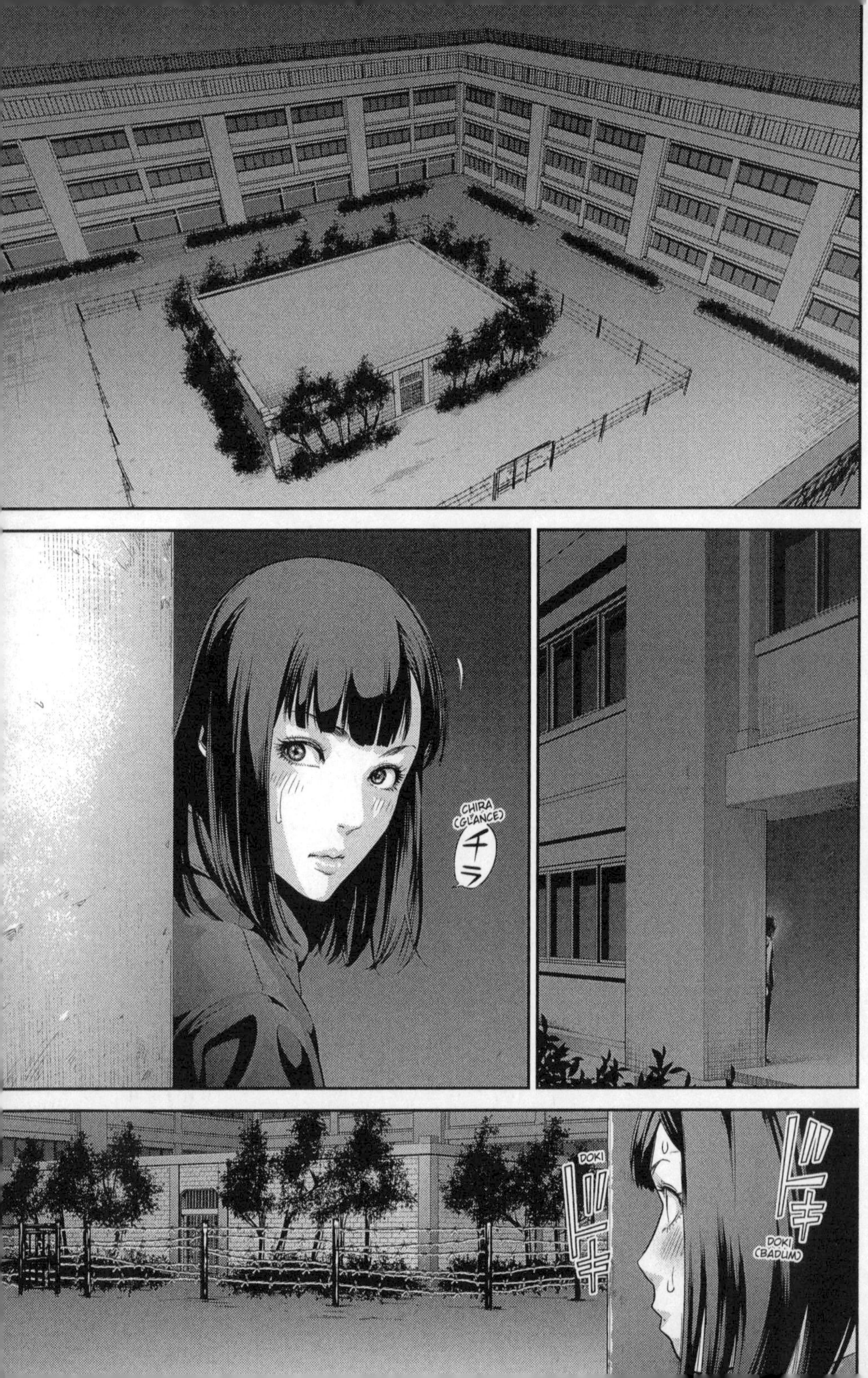
CHIRA (GLANCE)
チラ
ドキ
DOKI (BADUM)
DOKI
ドキ

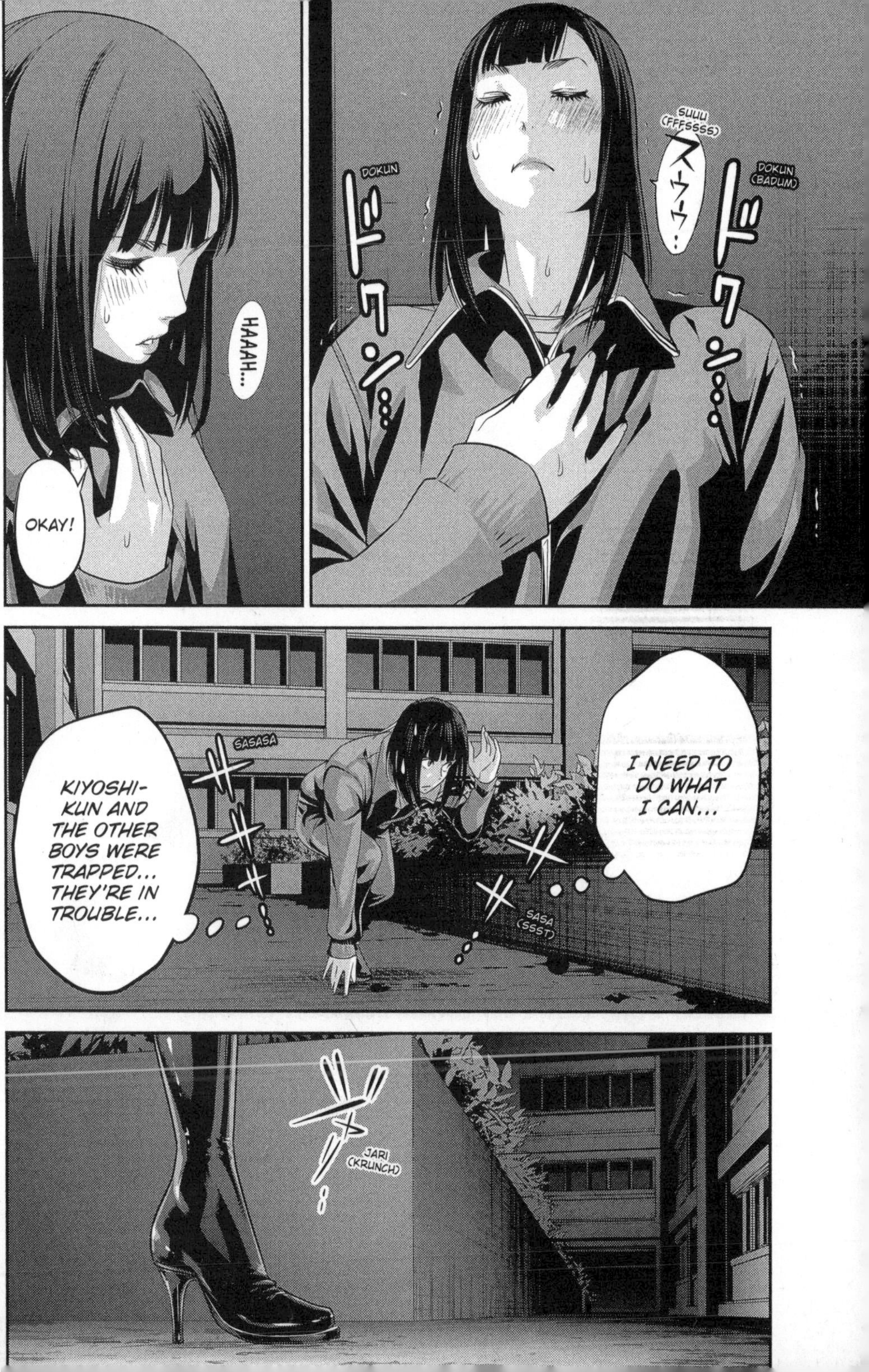
DOKUN (BADUM)
ドクン…
SUUU (FFFSSSS)
スゥゥ…
DOKUN
ドクン…
HAAAH...
OKAY!
I NEED TO DO WHAT I CAN...
SASA (SSST)
SASASA
KIYOSHI-KUN AND THE OTHER BOYS WERE TRAPPED... THEY'RE IN TROUBLE...
JARI (KRUNCH)

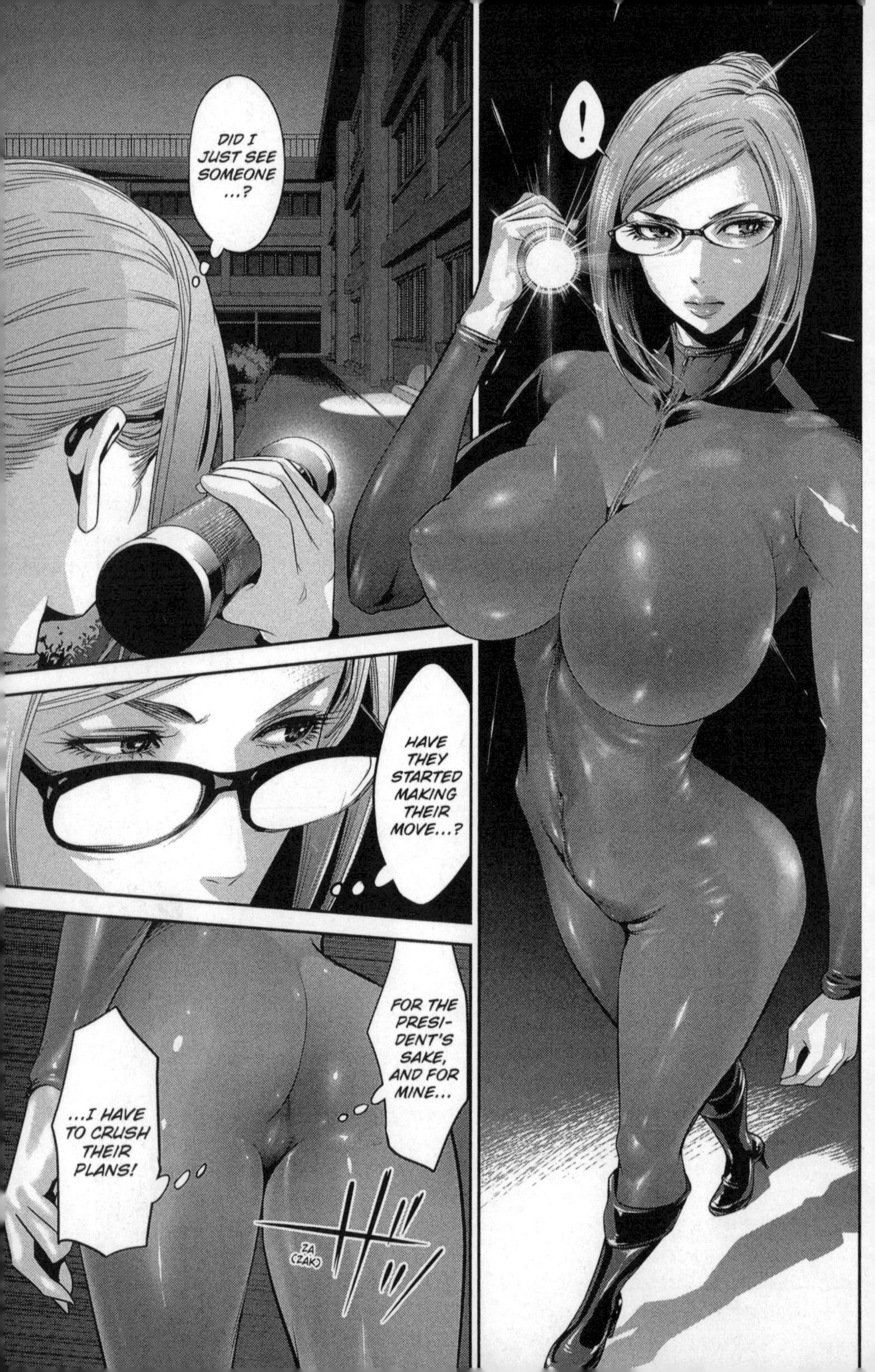
!
DID I JUST SEE SOMEONE ...?
HAVE THEY STARTED MAKING THEIR MOVE...?
FOR THE PRESI-DENT'S SAKE, AND FOR MINE...
...I HAVE TO CRUSH THEIR PLANS!
ZA (ZAK)

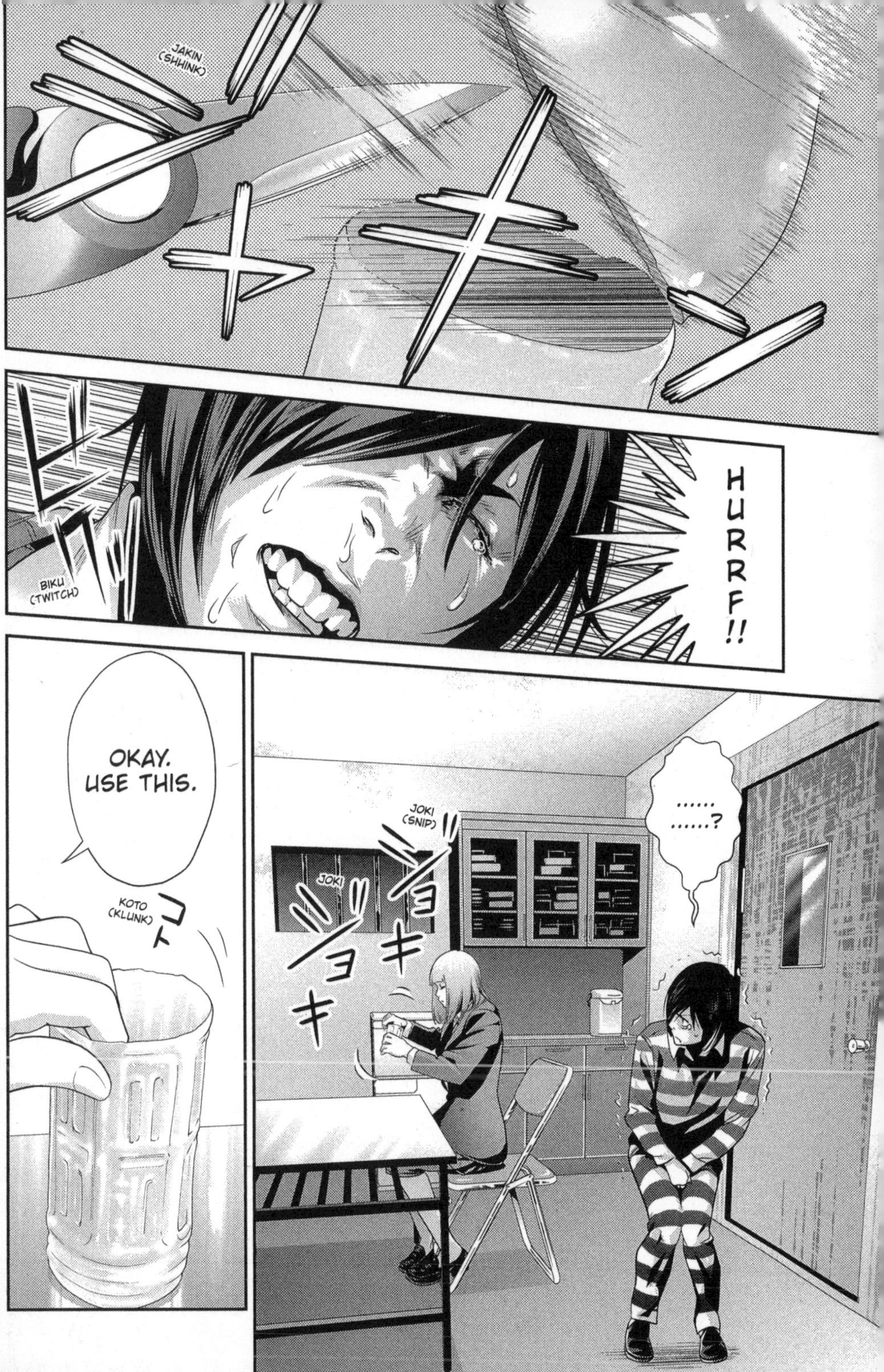
JAKIN (SHHINK)
BIKU (TWITCH)
HURRF!!
......
......?
JOKI (SNIP)
JOKI
OKAY. USE THIS.
KOTO (KLUNK)

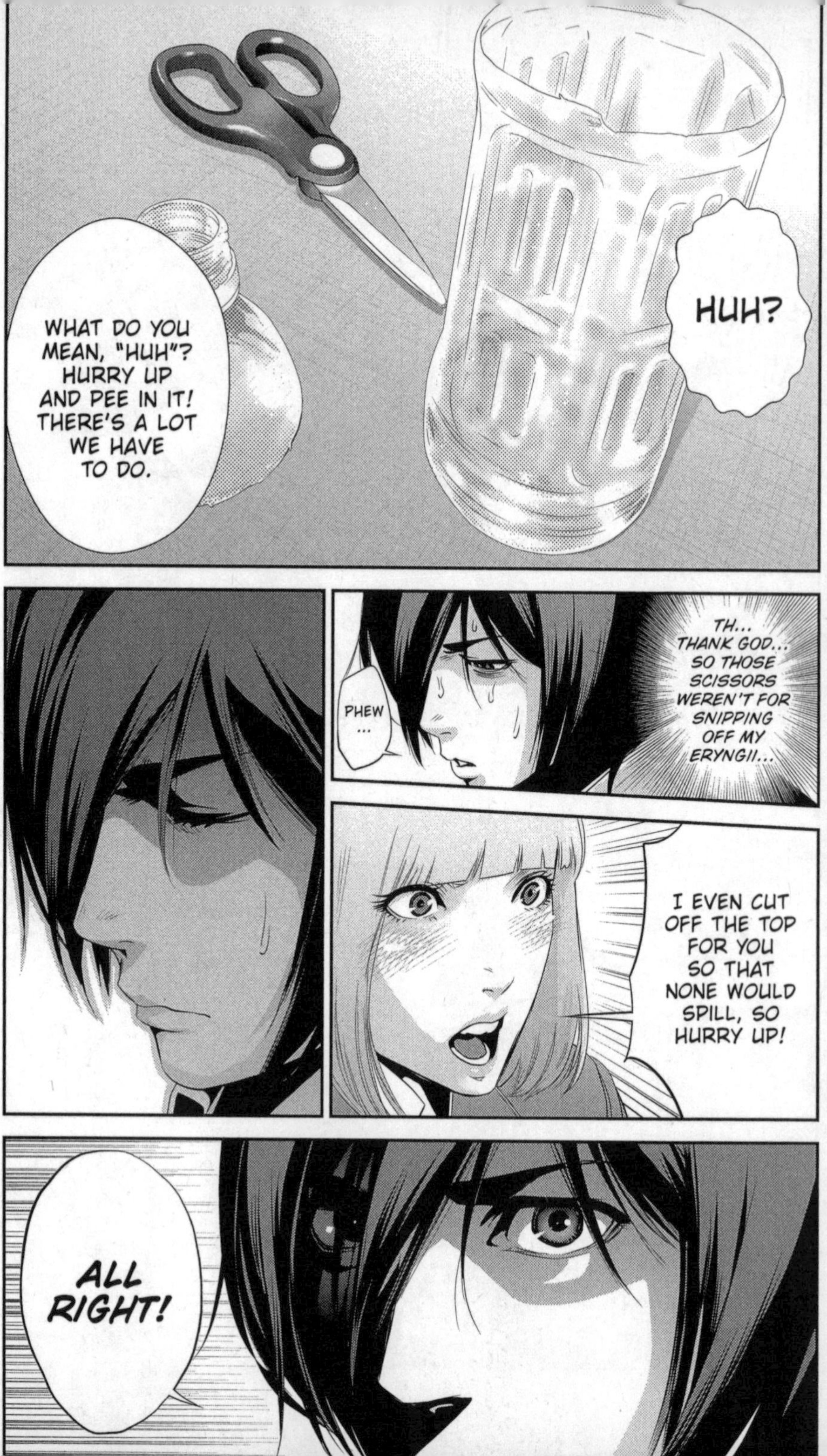

HUH?
WHAT DO YOU MEAN, "HUH"? HURRY UP AND PEE IN IT! THERE'S A LOT WE HAVE TO DO.
TH... THANK GOD... SO THOSE SCISSORS WEREN'T FOR SNIPPING OFF MY ERYNGII...
PHEW...
I EVEN CUT OFF THE TOP FOR YOU SO THAT NONE WOULD SPILL, SO HURRY UP!
ALL RIGHT!

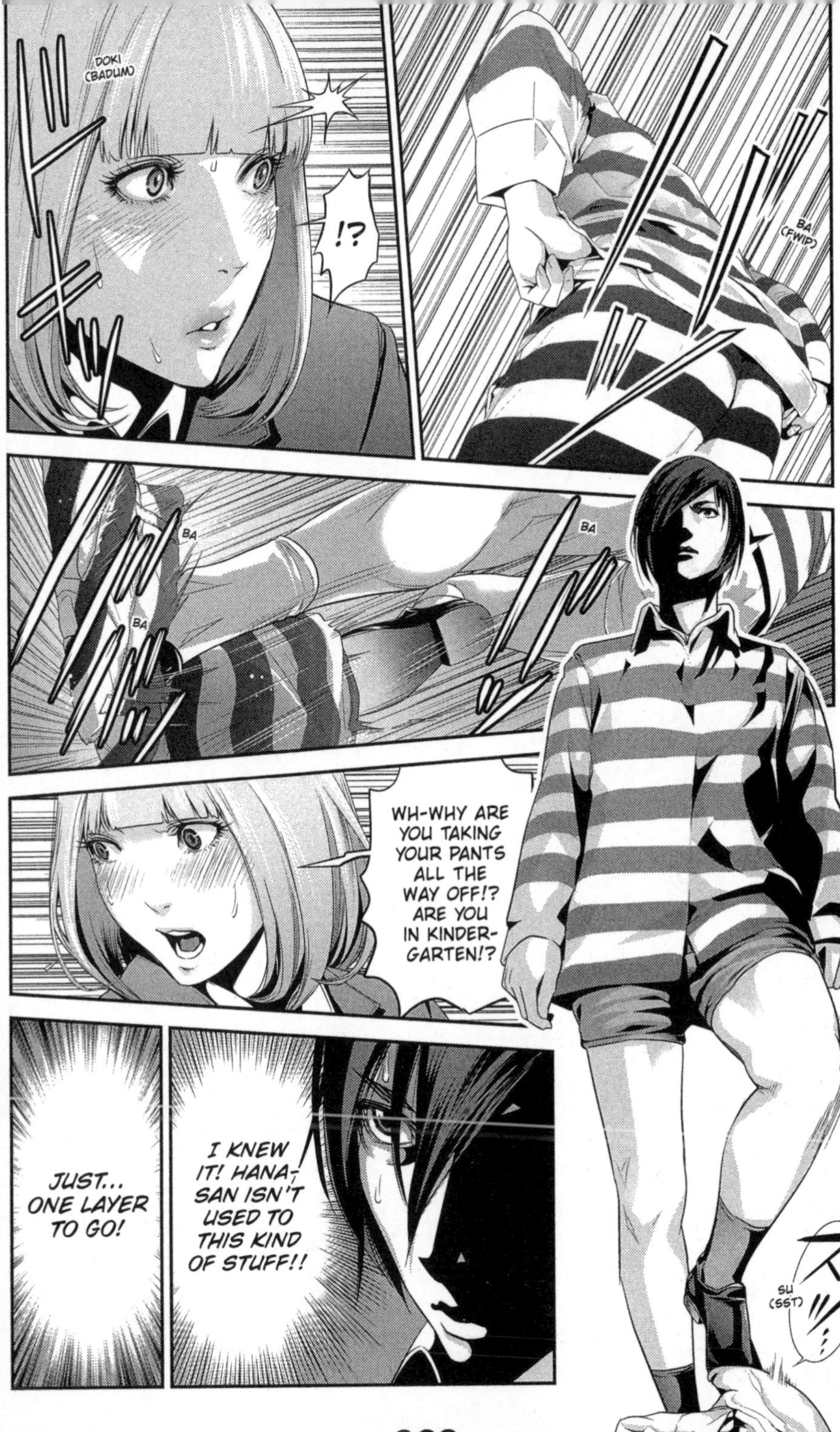
BA (FWIP)
DOKI (BADUM)
!?
SU (SST)
BA
BA
BA
WH-WHY ARE YOU TAKING YOUR PANTS ALL THE WAY OFF!? ARE YOU IN KINDER-GARTEN!?
I KNEW IT! HANA-SAN ISN'T USED TO THIS KIND OF STUFF!!
JUST... ONE LAYER TO GO!

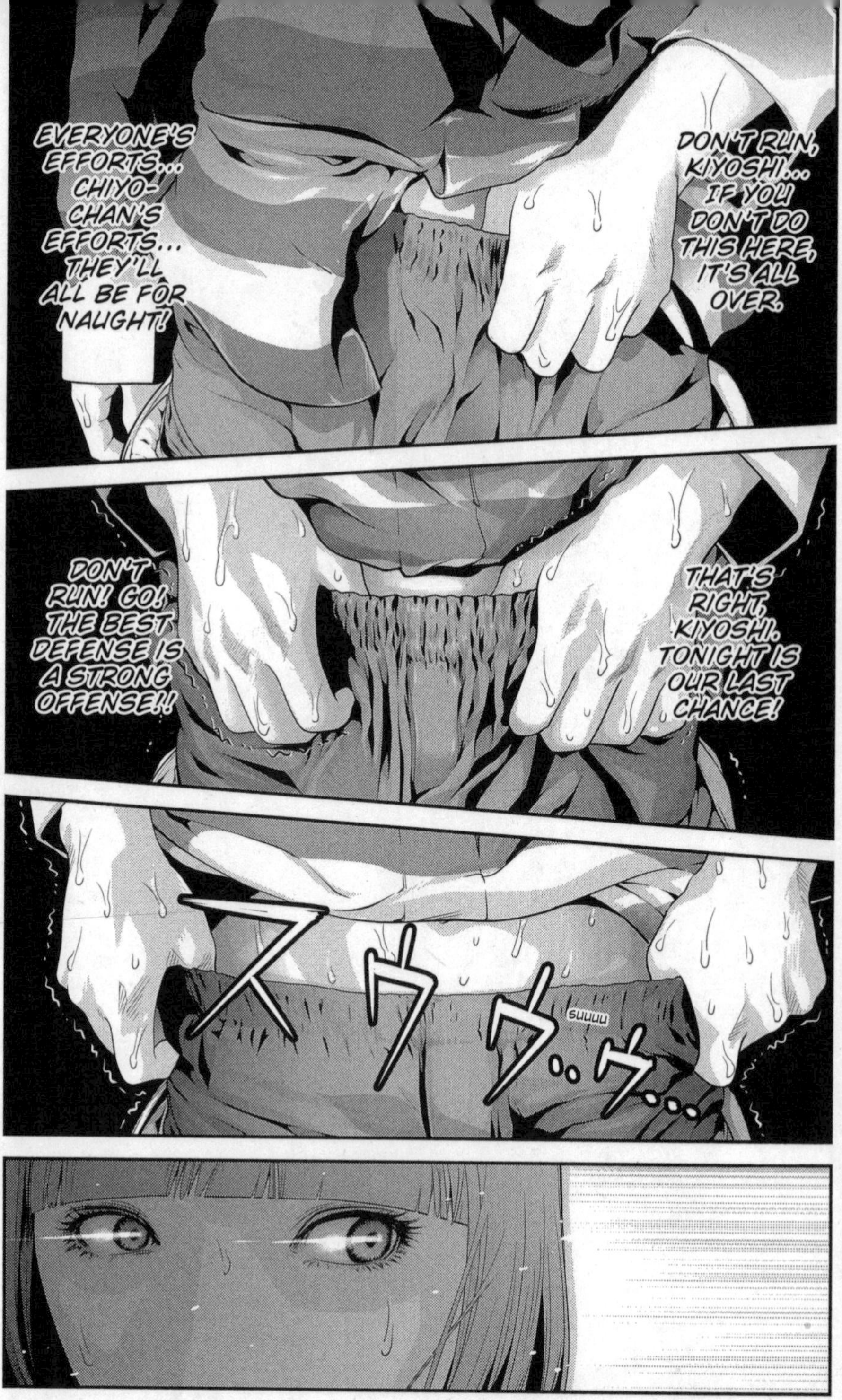
DON'T RUN, KIYOSHI... IF YOU DON'T DO THIS HERE, IT'S ALL OVER.
EVERYONE'S EFFORTS... CHIYO-CHAN'S EFFORTS... THEY'LL ALL BE FOR NAUGHT!
THAT'S RIGHT, KIYOSHI. TONIGHT IS OUR LAST CHANCE!
DON'T RUN! GO! THE BEST DEFENSE IS A STRONG OFFENSE!!
suuuu

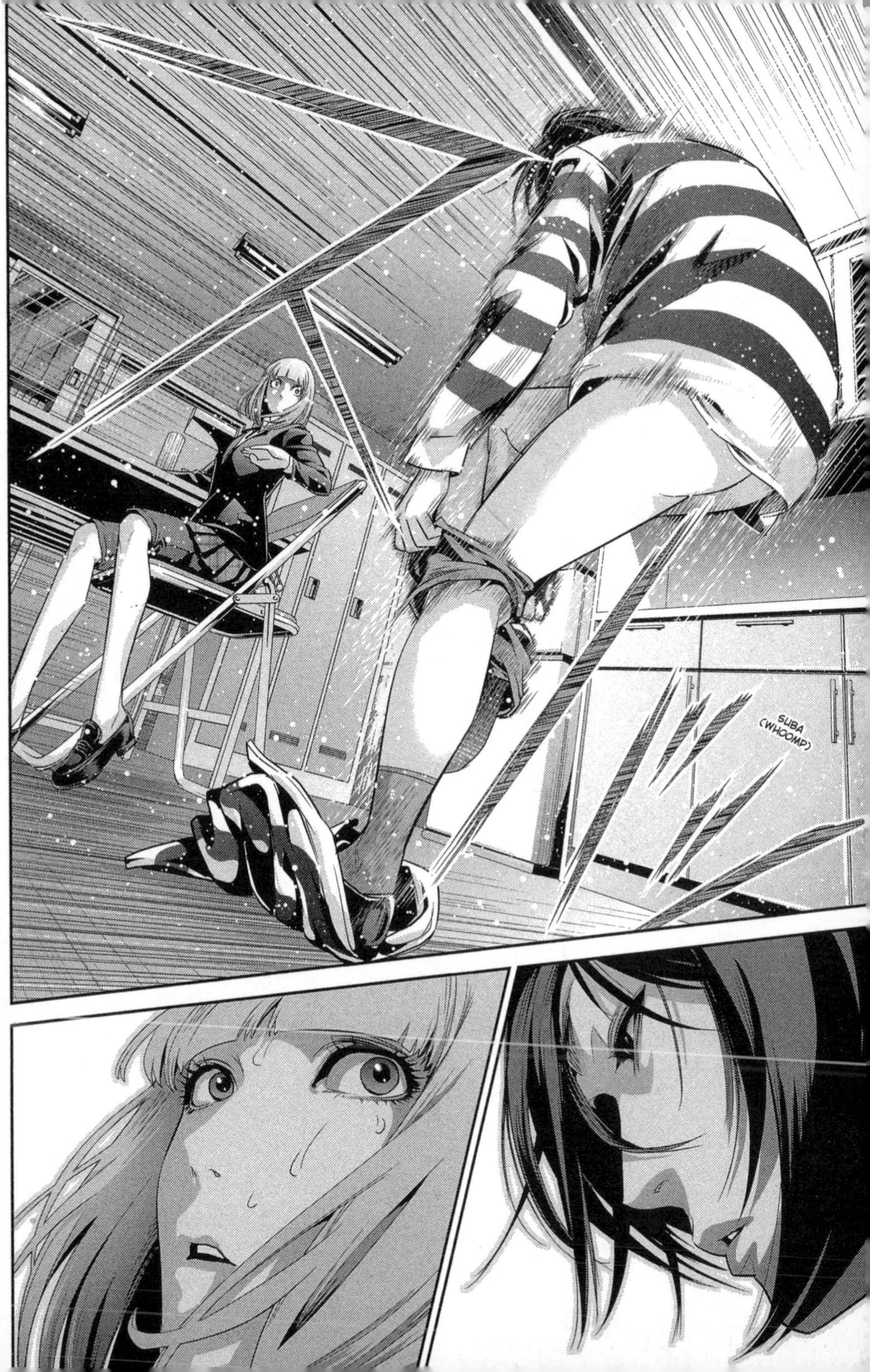
SUBA
(WHOOMP)

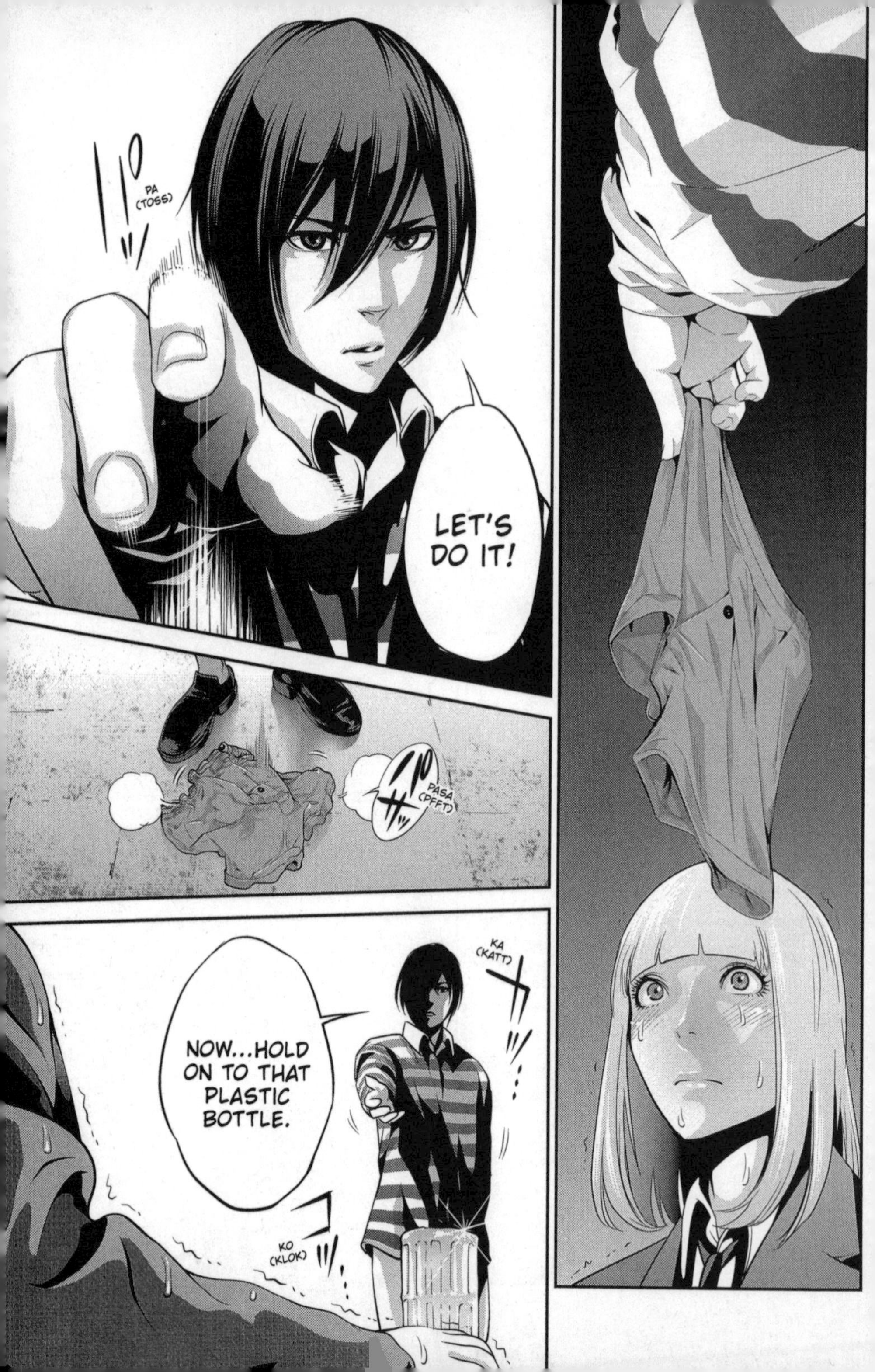
PA (TOSS)
LET'S DO IT!
PASA (PFFT)
KA (KATT)
NOW...HOLD ON TO THAT PLASTIC BOTTLE.
KO (KLOK)

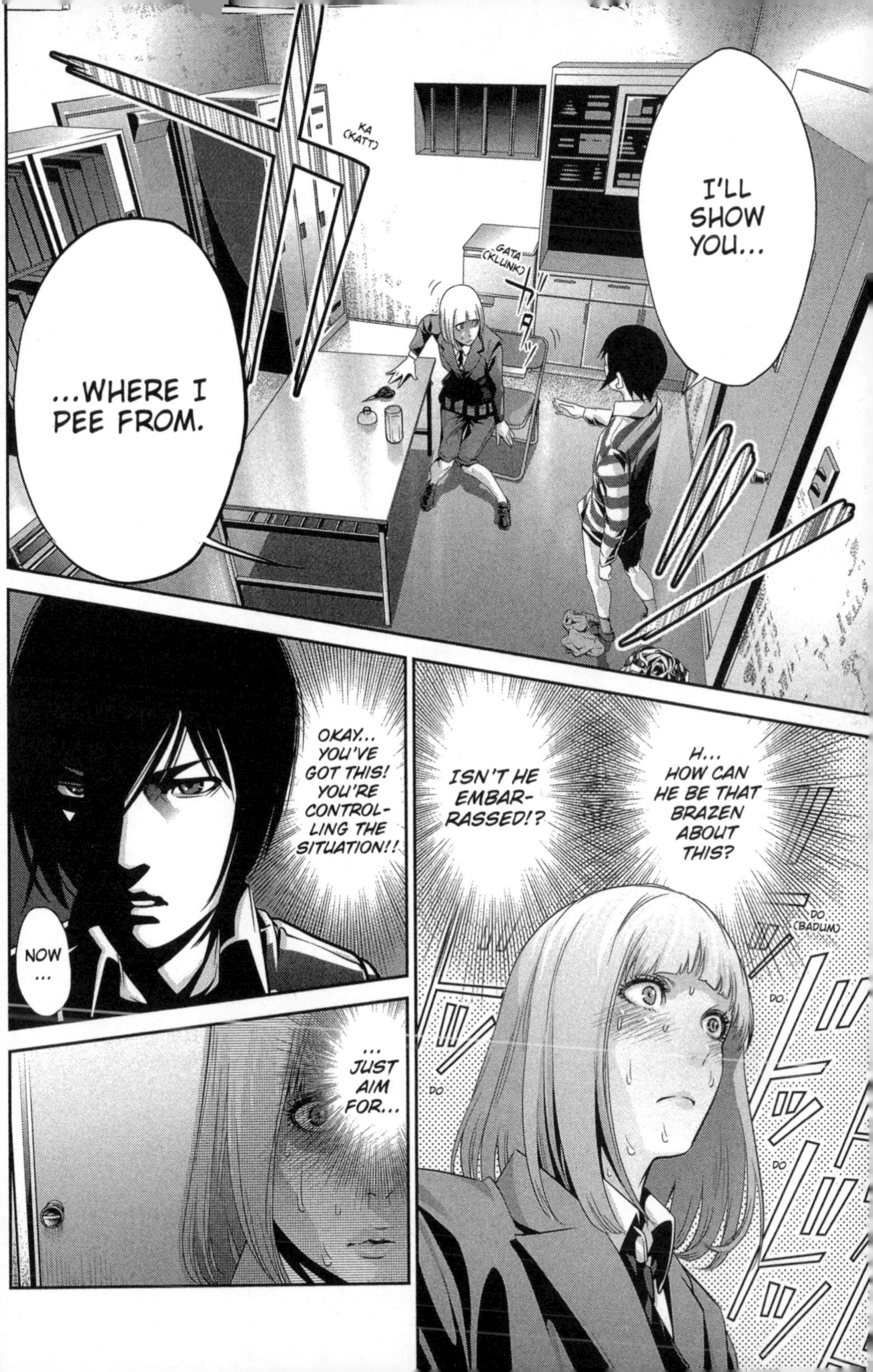
I'LL SHOW YOU...
KA (KATT)
GATA (KLUNK)
...WHERE I PEE FROM.
H... HOW CAN HE BE THAT BRAZEN ABOUT THIS?
ISN'T HE EMBARRASSED!?
DO (BADUM)
DO
DO
DO
OKAY... YOU'VE GOT THIS! YOU'RE CONTROLLING THE SITUATION!!
NOW...
...JUST AIM FOR...

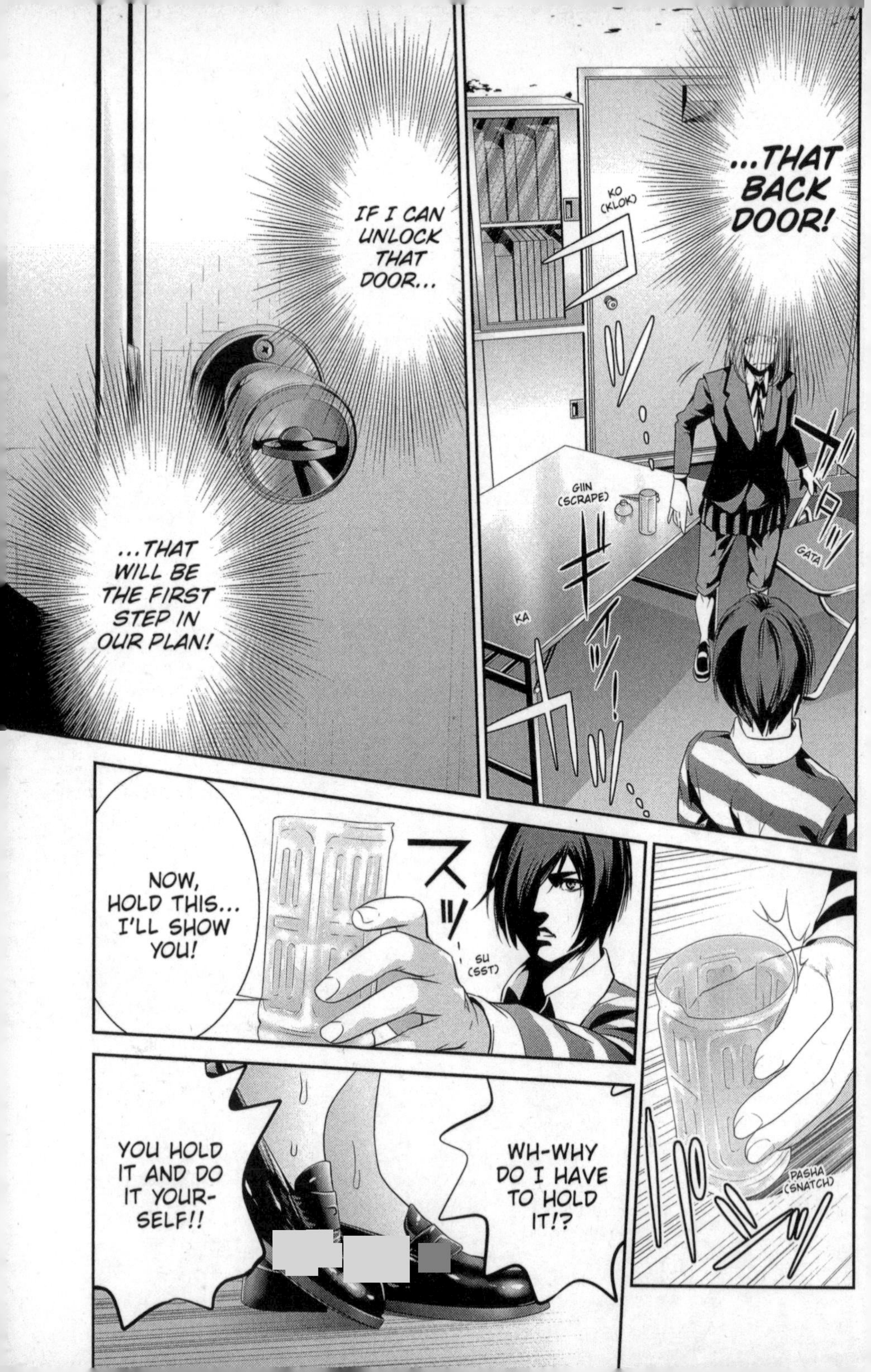
...THAT BACK DOOR!
KO (KLOK)
GIIN (SCRAPE)
GATA
KA
IF I CAN UNLOCK THAT DOOR...
...THAT WILL BE THE FIRST STEP IN OUR PLAN!
PASHA (SNATCH)
NOW, HOLD THIS... I'LL SHOW YOU!
SU (SST)
WH-WHY DO I HAVE TO HOLD IT!?
YOU HOLD IT AND DO IT YOUR-SELF!!

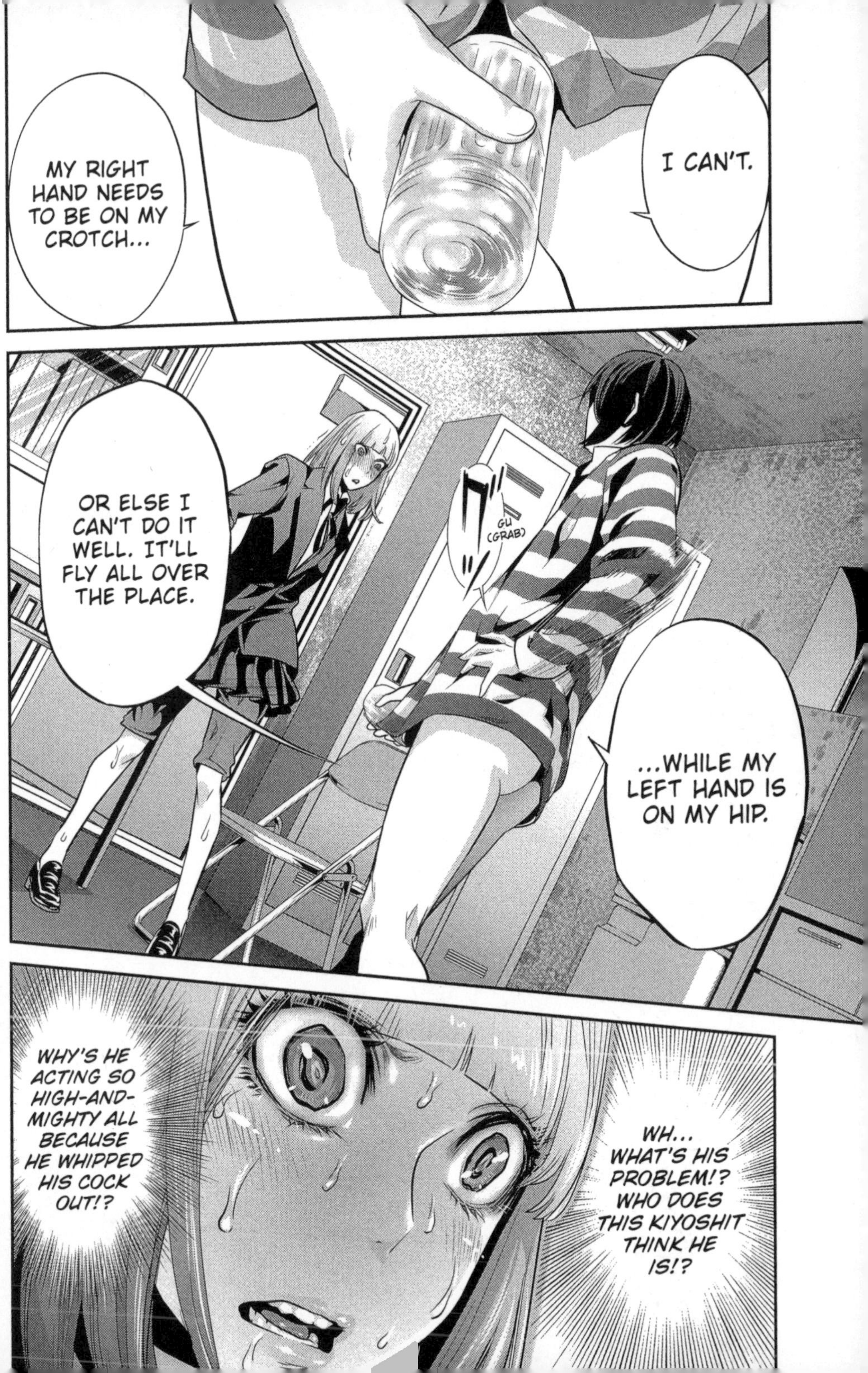
I CAN'T.
MY RIGHT HAND NEEDS TO BE ON MY CROTCH...
GU (GRAB)
...WHILE MY LEFT HAND IS ON MY HIP.
OR ELSE I CAN'T DO IT WELL. IT'LL FLY ALL OVER THE PLACE.
WH... WHAT'S HIS PROBLEM!? WHO DOES THIS KIYOSHIT THINK HE IS!?
WHY'S HE ACTING SO HIGH-AND-MIGHTY ALL BECAUSE HE WHIPPED HIS COCK OUT!?

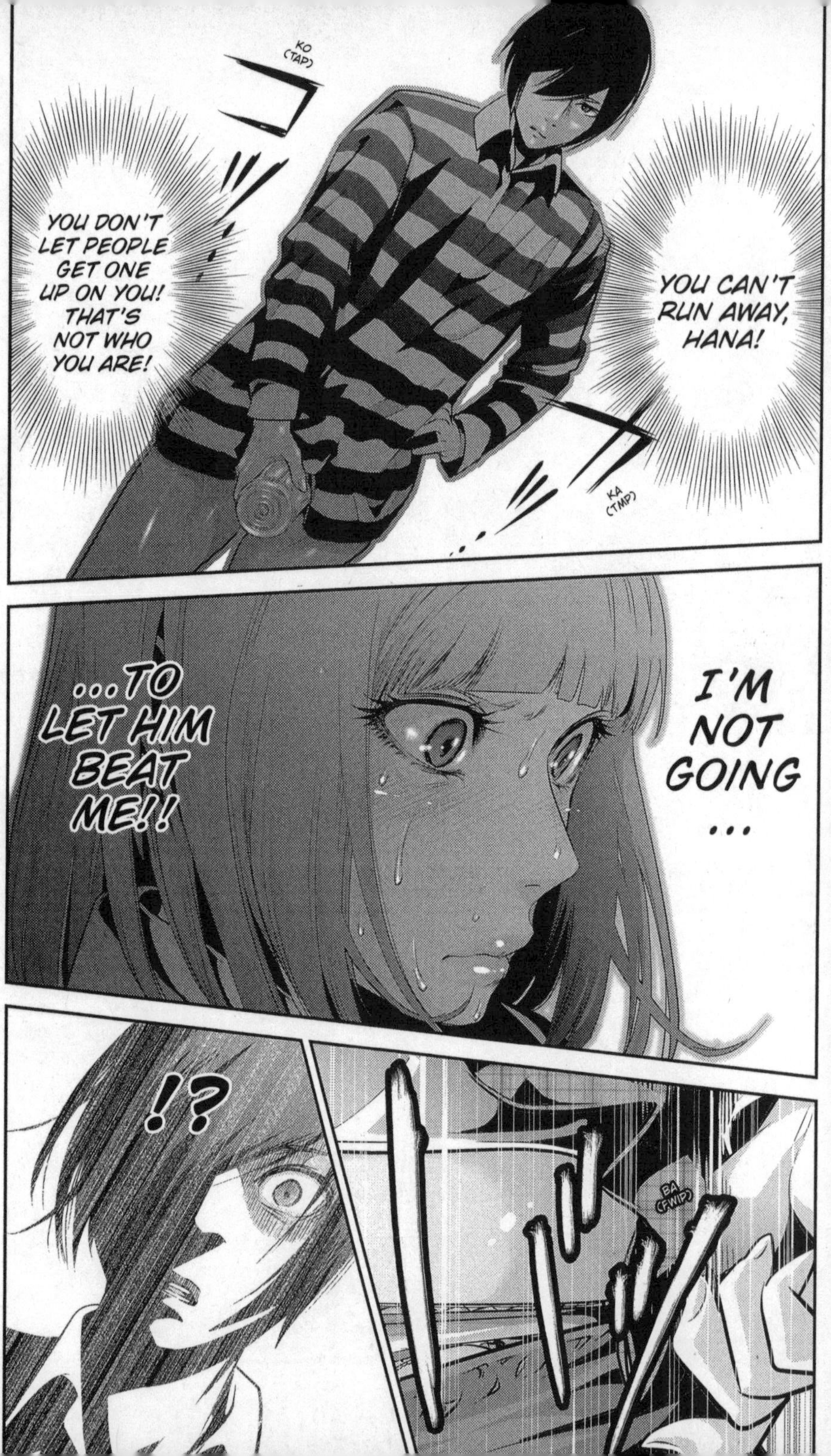
KO (TAP)
YOU CAN'T RUN AWAY, HANA!
YOU DON'T LET PEOPLE GET ONE UP ON YOU! THAT'S NOT WHO YOU ARE!
KA (TMP)
I'M NOT GOING...
...TO LET HIM BEAT ME!!
BA (FWIP)
!?

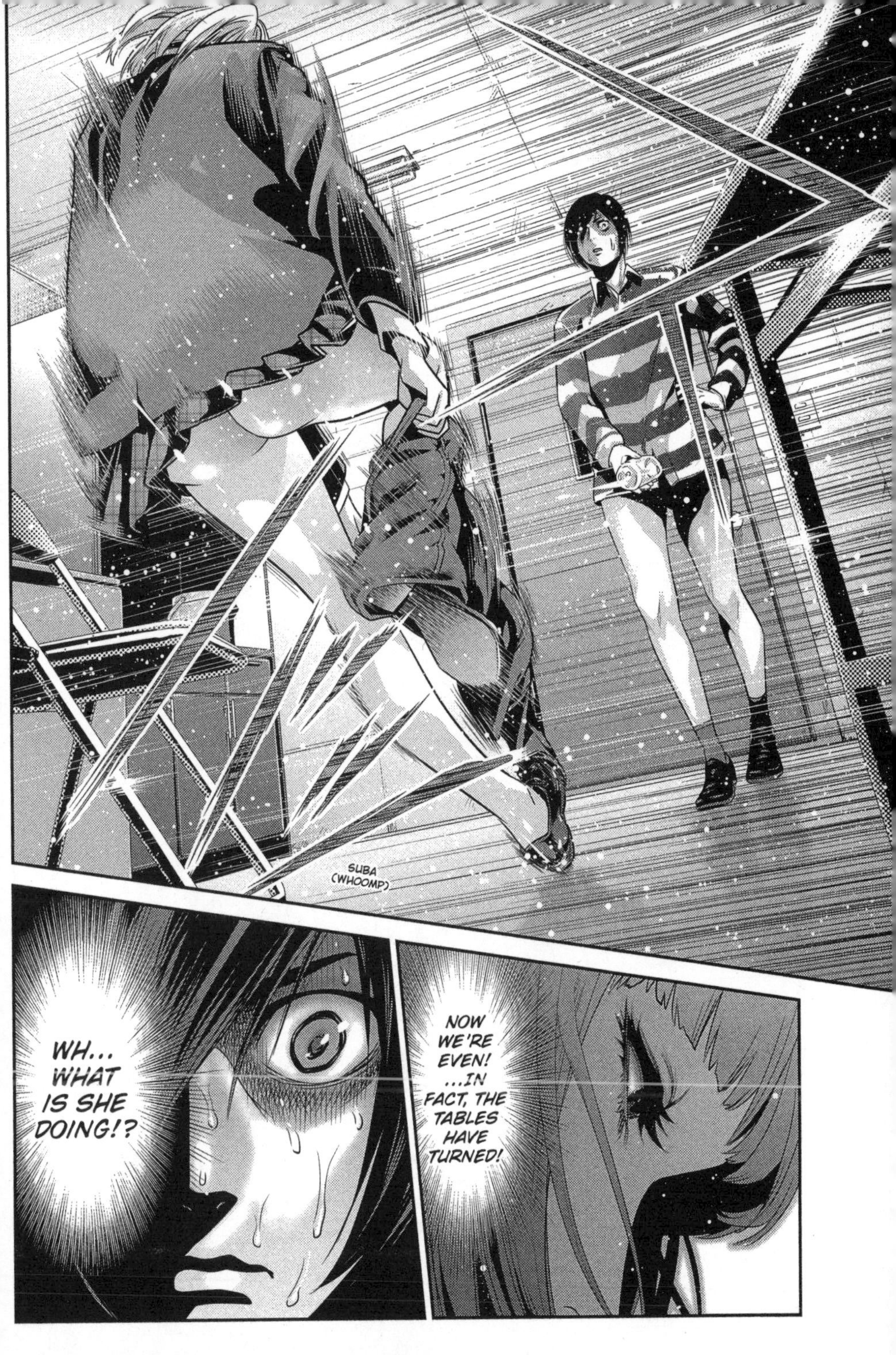
SUBA (WHOOMP)
NOW WE'RE EVEN! ...IN FACT, THE TABLES HAVE TURNED!
WH... WHAT IS SHE DOING!?

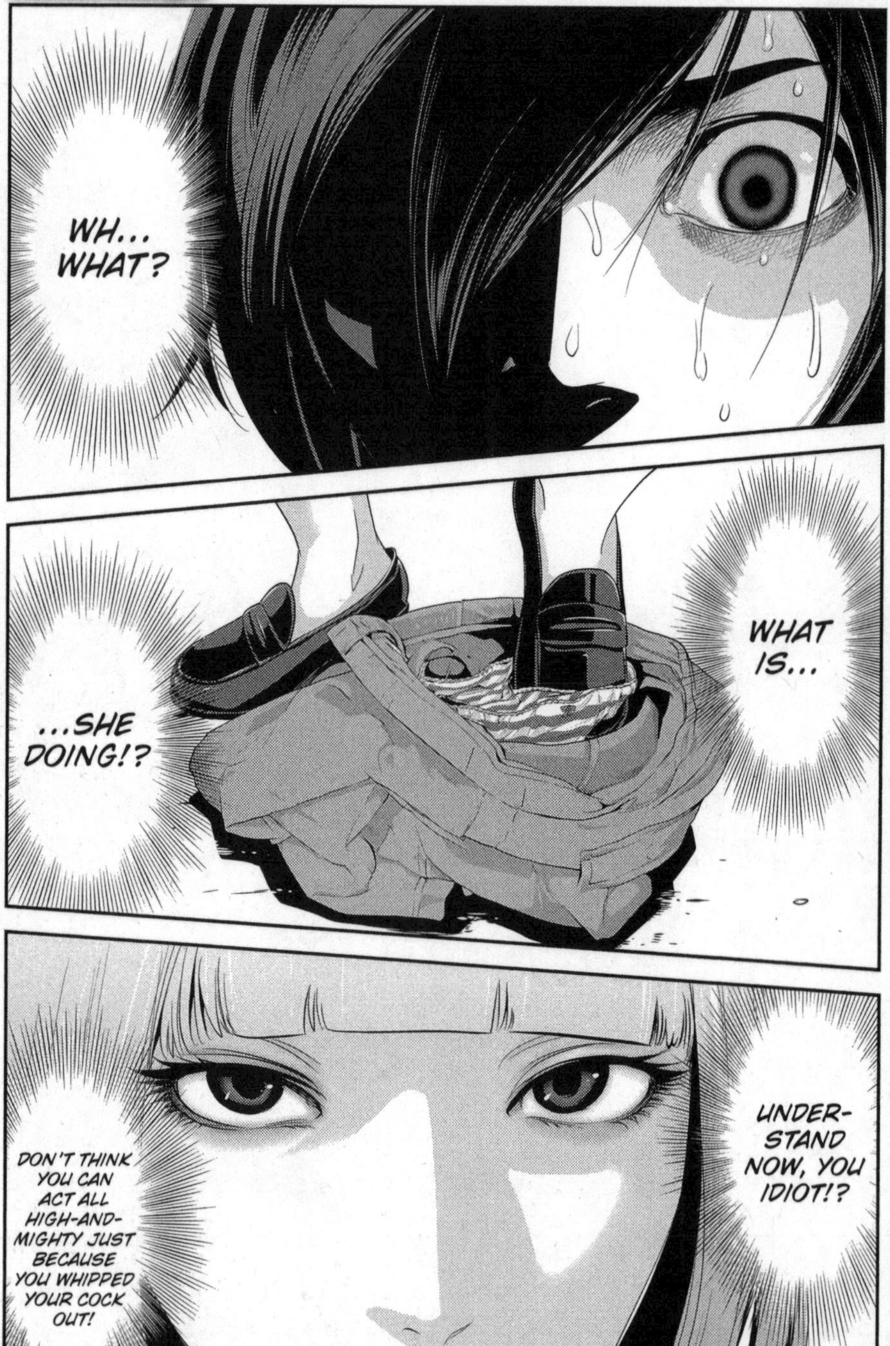
WH... WHAT?
WHAT IS...
...SHE DOING!?
UNDER-STAND NOW, YOU IDIOT!?
DON'T THINK YOU CAN ACT ALL HIGH-AND-MIGHTY JUST BECAUSE YOU WHIPPED YOUR COCK OUT!

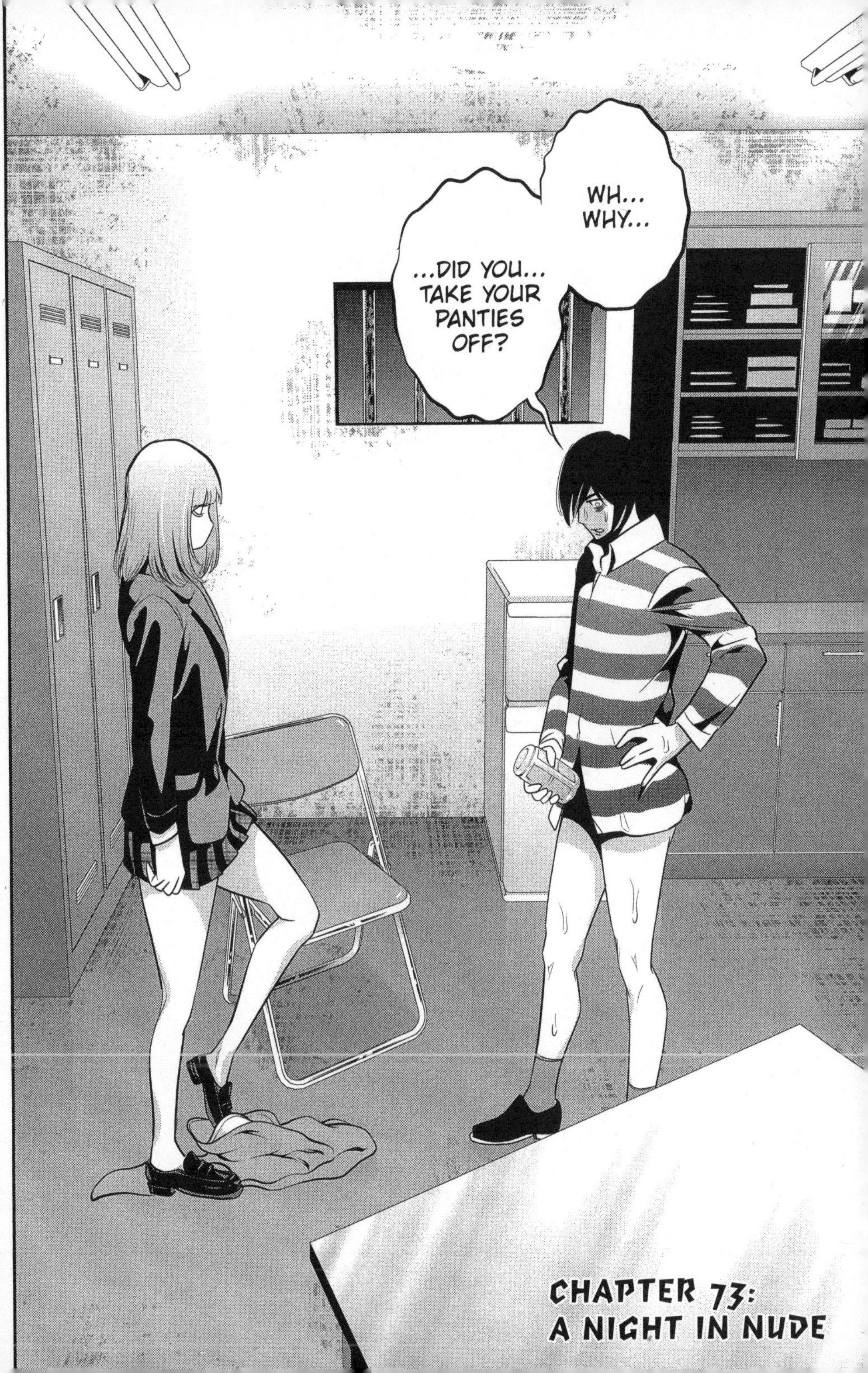
WH... WHY...
...DID YOU... TAKE YOUR PANTIES OFF?
CHAPTER 73: A NIGHT IN NUDE

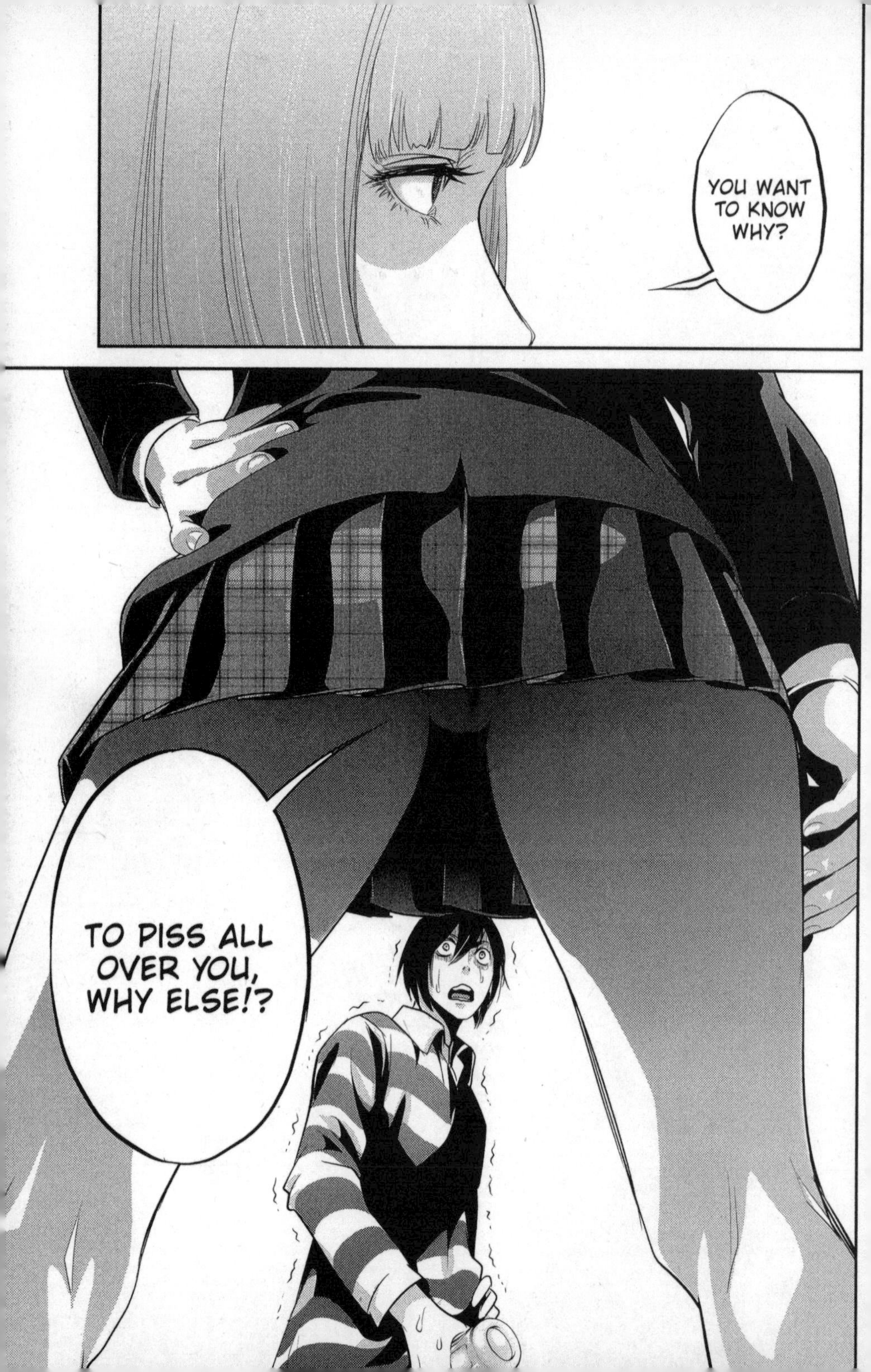
YOU WANT TO KNOW WHY?
TO PISS ALL OVER YOU, WHY ELSE!?

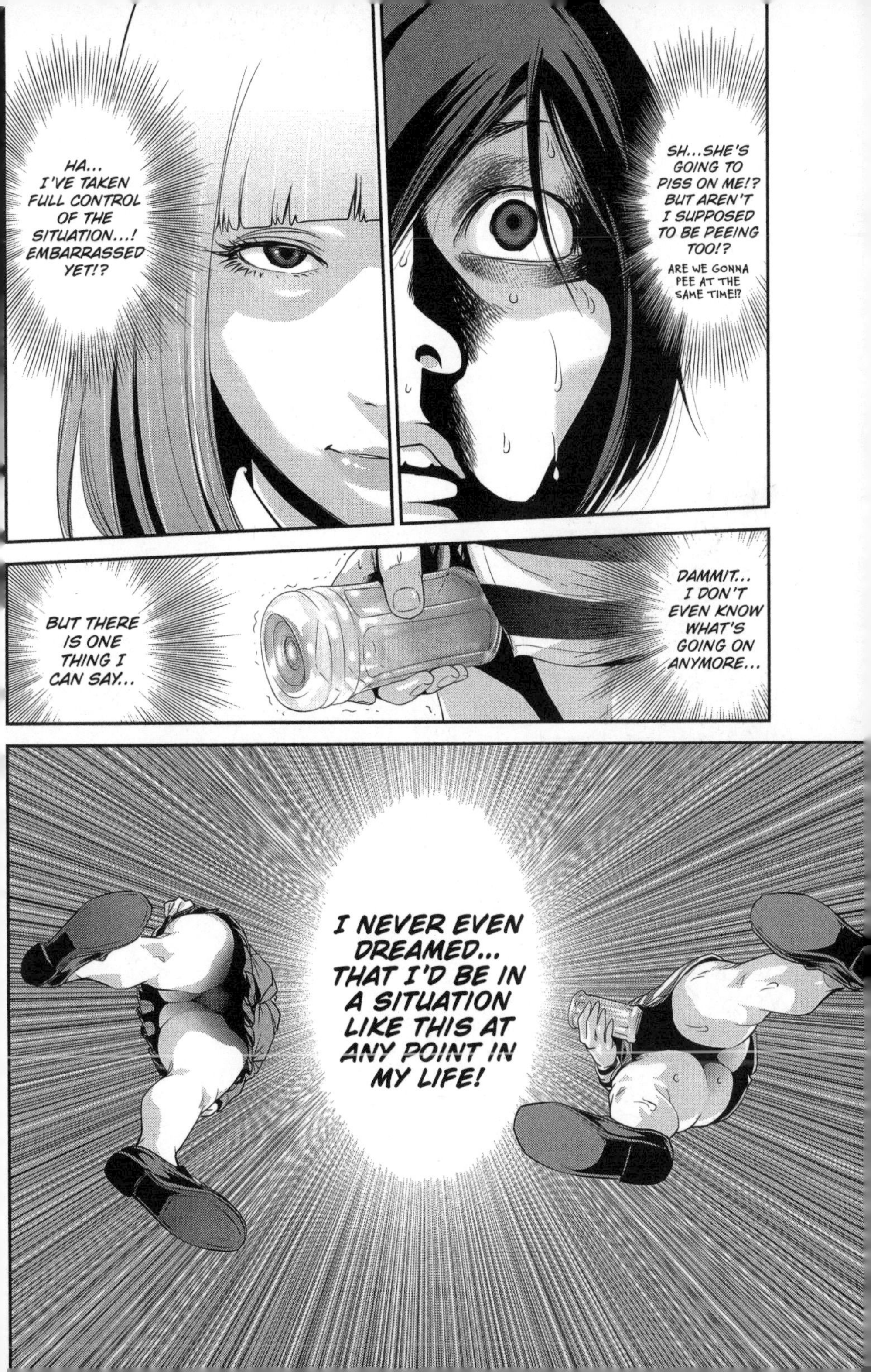
SH...SHE'S GOING TO PISS ON ME!? BUT AREN'T I SUPPOSED TO BE PEEING TOO!?
ARE WE GONNA PEE AT THE SAME TIME!?
HA... I'VE TAKEN FULL CONTROL OF THE SITUATION...! EMBARRASSED YET!?
DAMMIT... I DON'T EVEN KNOW WHAT'S GOING ON ANYMORE...
BUT THERE IS ONE THING I CAN SAY...
I NEVER EVEN DREAMED... THAT I'D BE IN A SITUATION LIKE THIS AT ANY POINT IN MY LIFE!

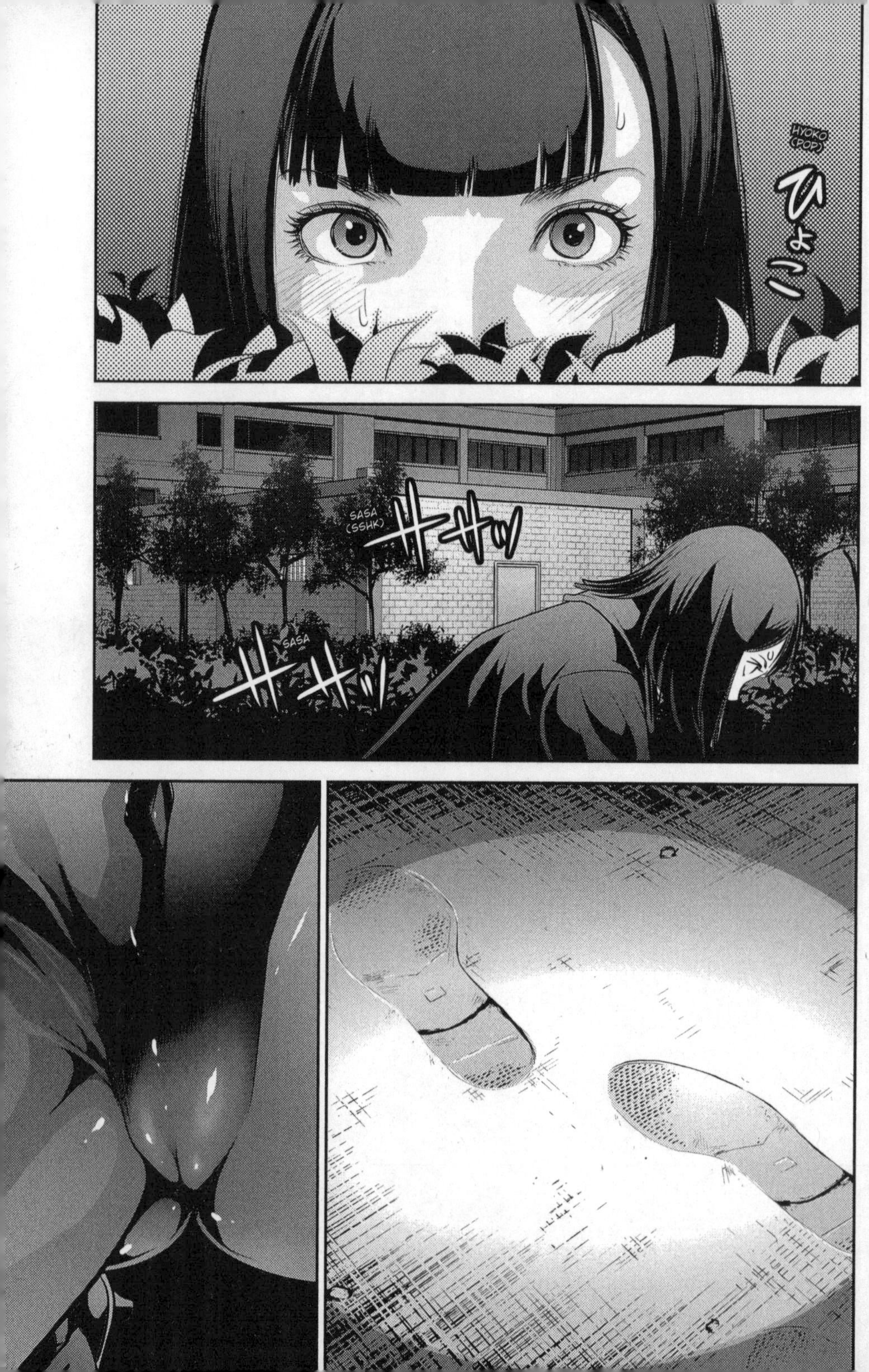
HYOKO (POP)
ひょこ
SASA (SSHK)
SASA

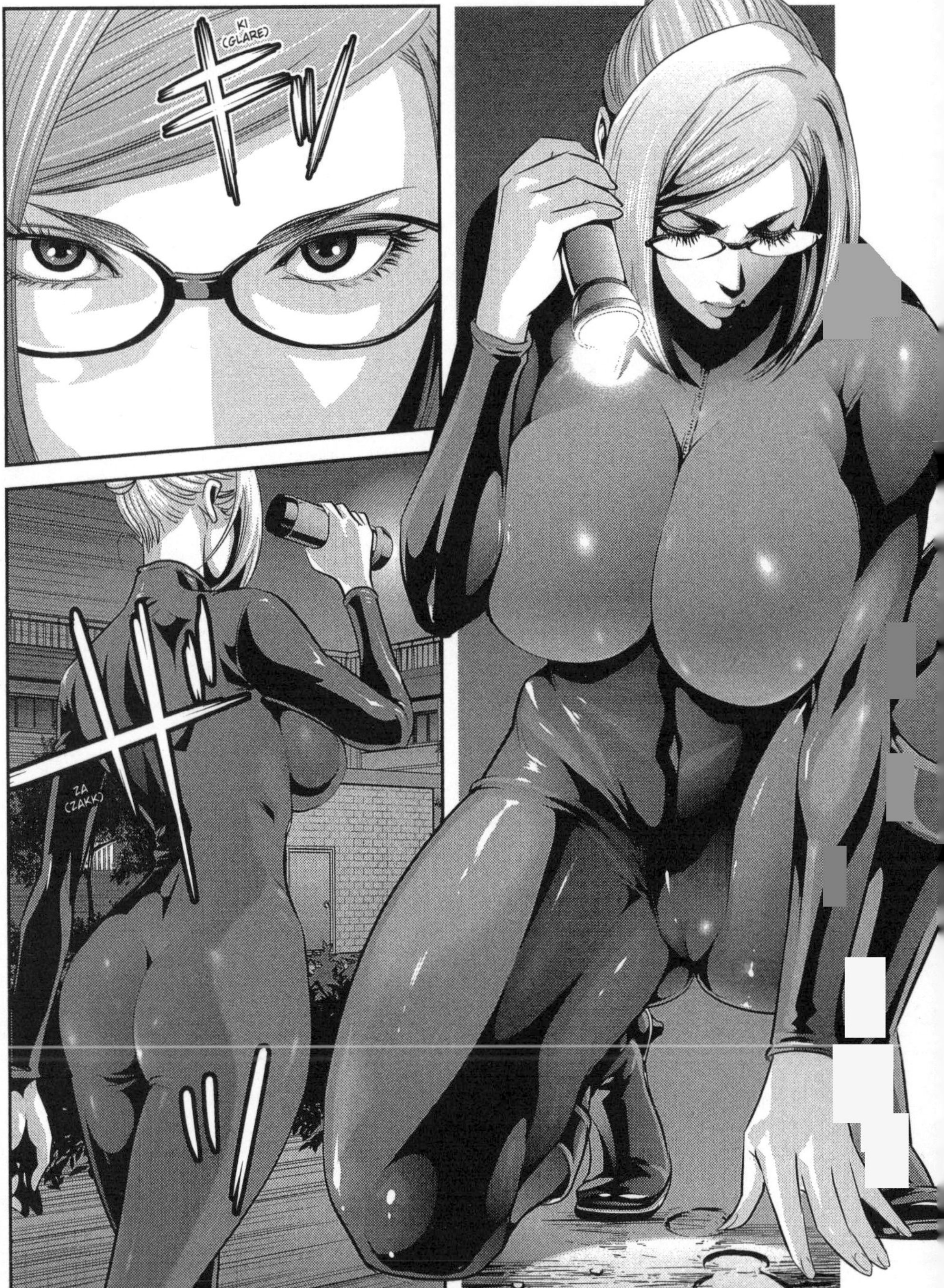
KI (GLARE)
ZA (ZAKK)

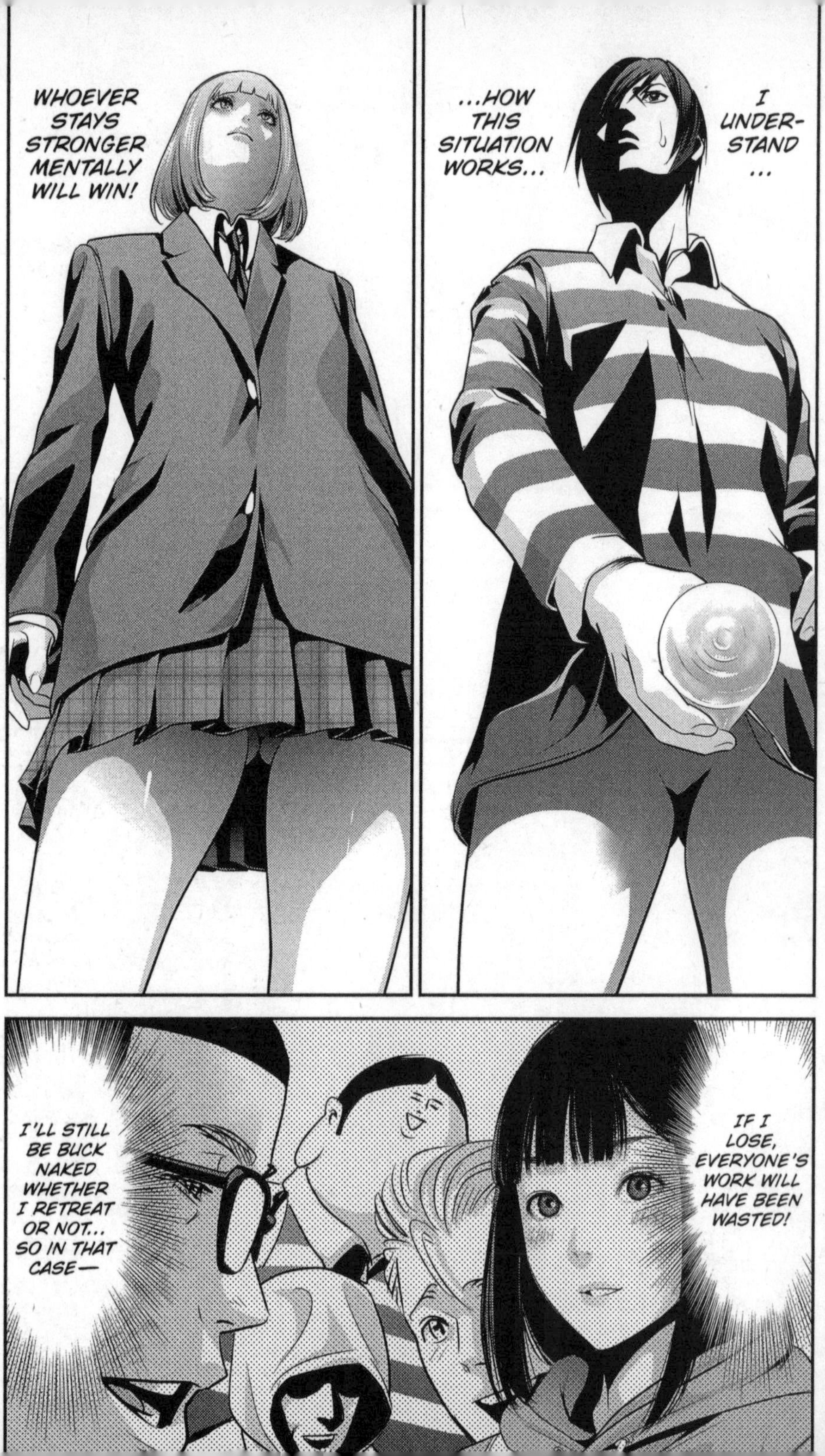
I UNDER-STAND...
...HOW THIS SITUATION WORKS...
WHOEVER STAYS STRONGER MENTALLY WILL WIN!
IF I LOSE, EVERYONE'S WORK WILL HAVE BEEN WASTED!
I'LL STILL BE BUCK NAKED WHETHER I RETREAT OR NOT... SO IN THAT CASE—

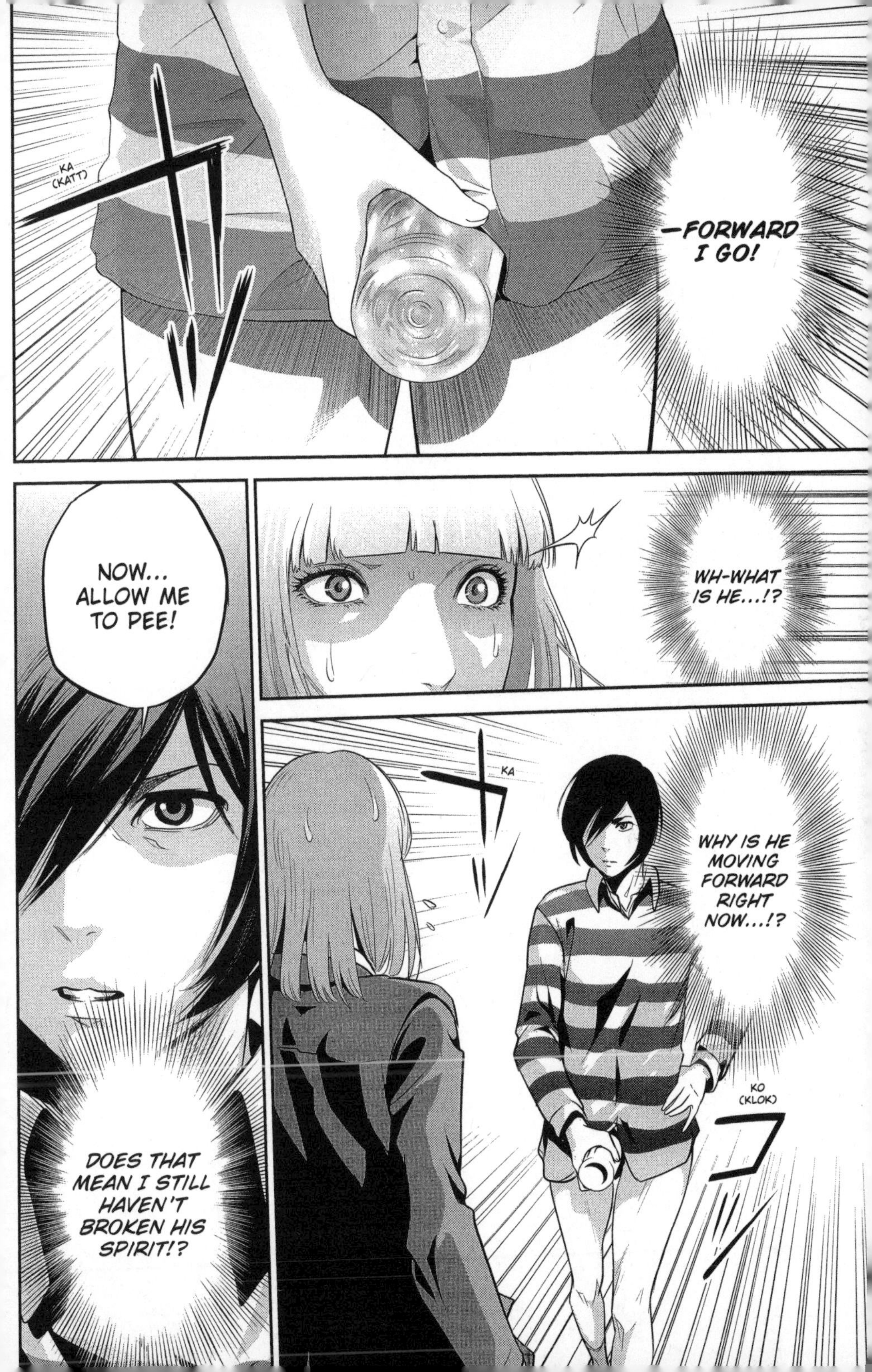
—FORWARD I GO!
KA (KATT)
WH-WHAT IS HE...!?
WHY IS HE MOVING FORWARD RIGHT NOW...!?
KA
KO (KLOK)
NOW... ALLOW ME TO PEE!
DOES THAT MEAN I STILL HAVEN'T BROKEN HIS SPIRIT!?

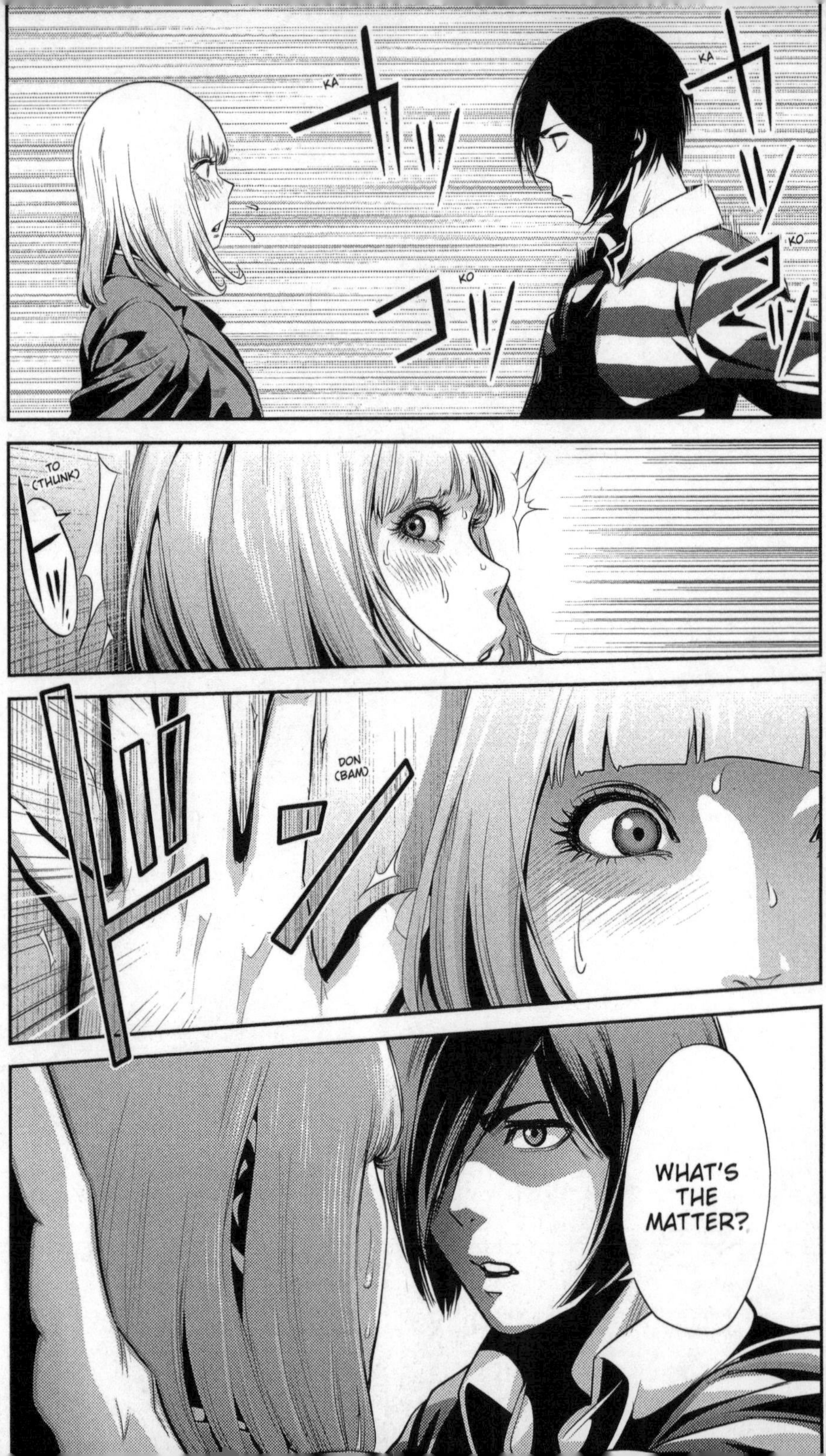
KA
KO
KA
KO
TO (THUNK)
DON (BAM)
WHAT'S THE MATTER?

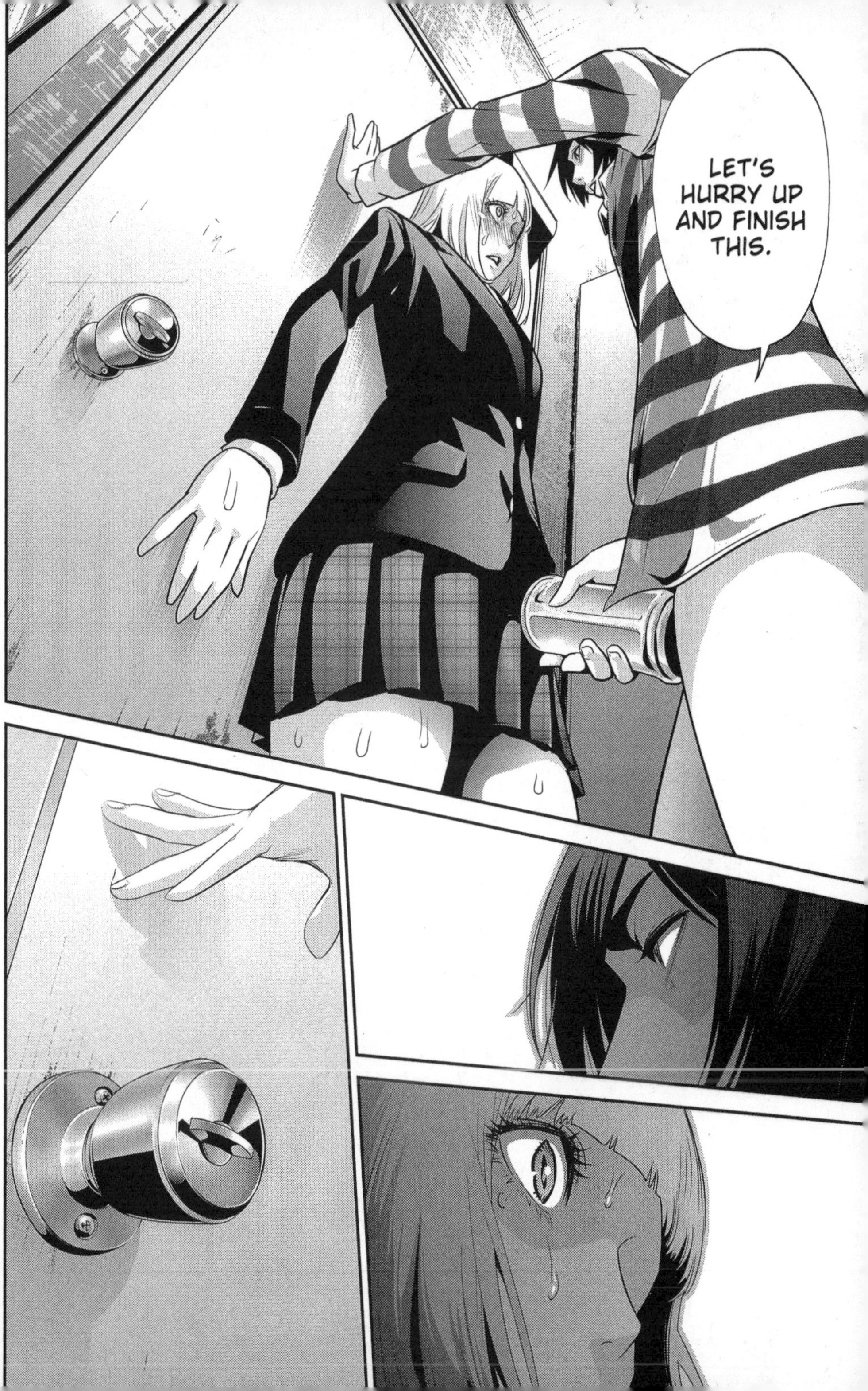
LET'S HURRY UP AND FINISH THIS.

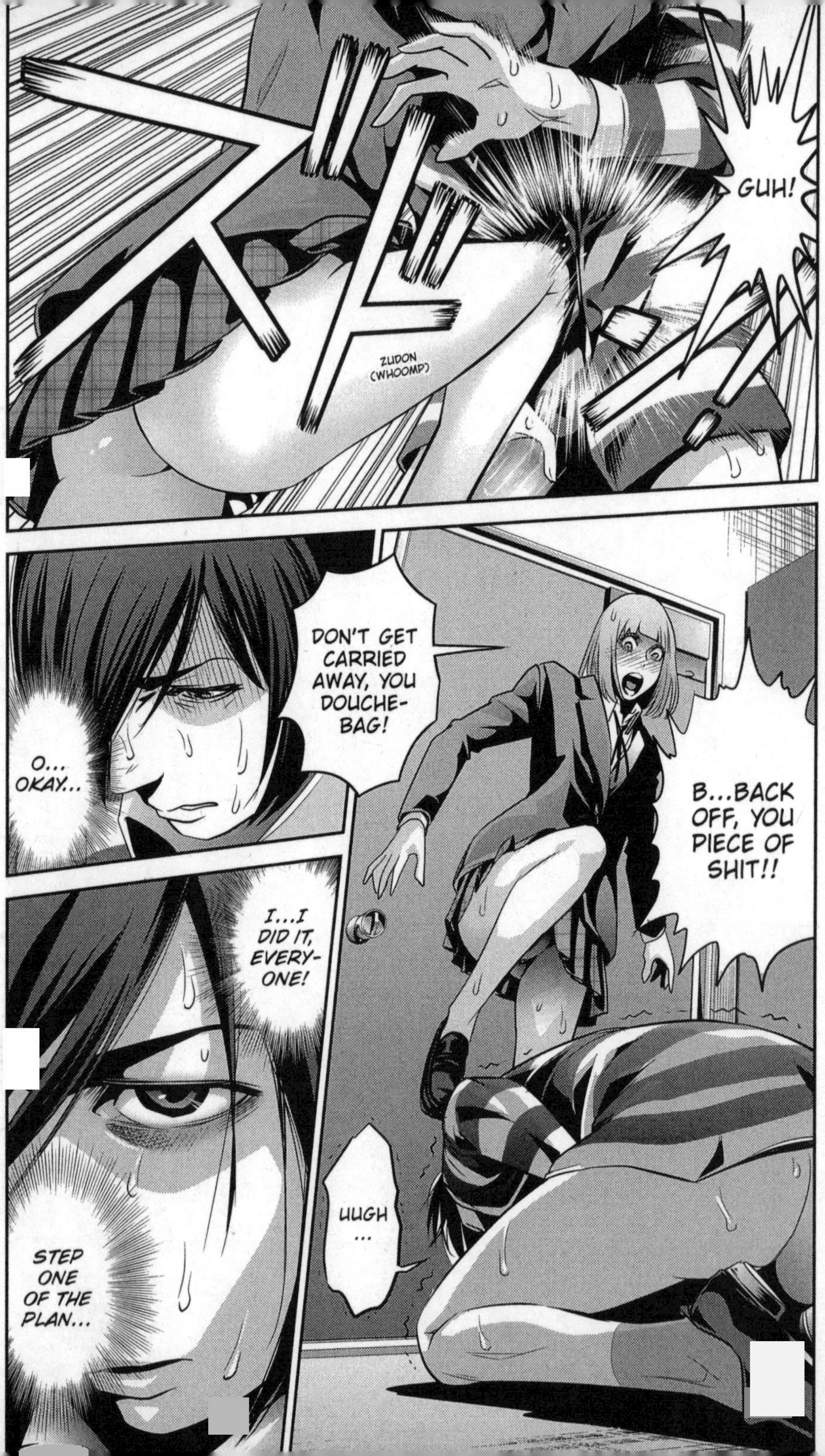
GUH!
ZUDON (WHOOMP)
DON'T GET CARRIED AWAY, YOU DOUCHE-BAG!
B...BACK OFF, YOU PIECE OF SHIT!!
UUGH ...
O... OKAY...
I...I DID IT, EVERY-ONE!
STEP ONE OF THE PLAN...

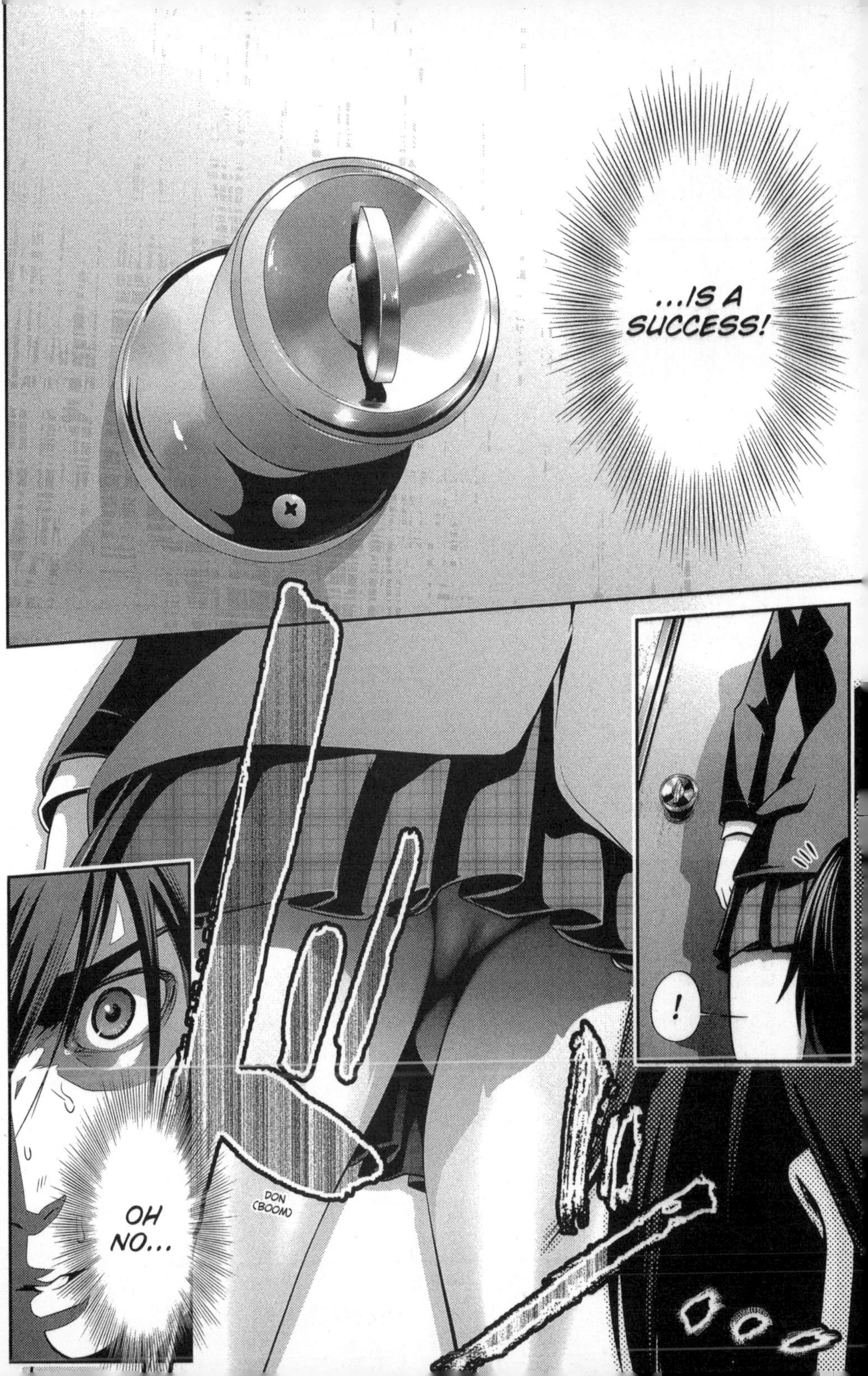
...IS A SUCCESS!
!
DON (BOOM)
OH NO...

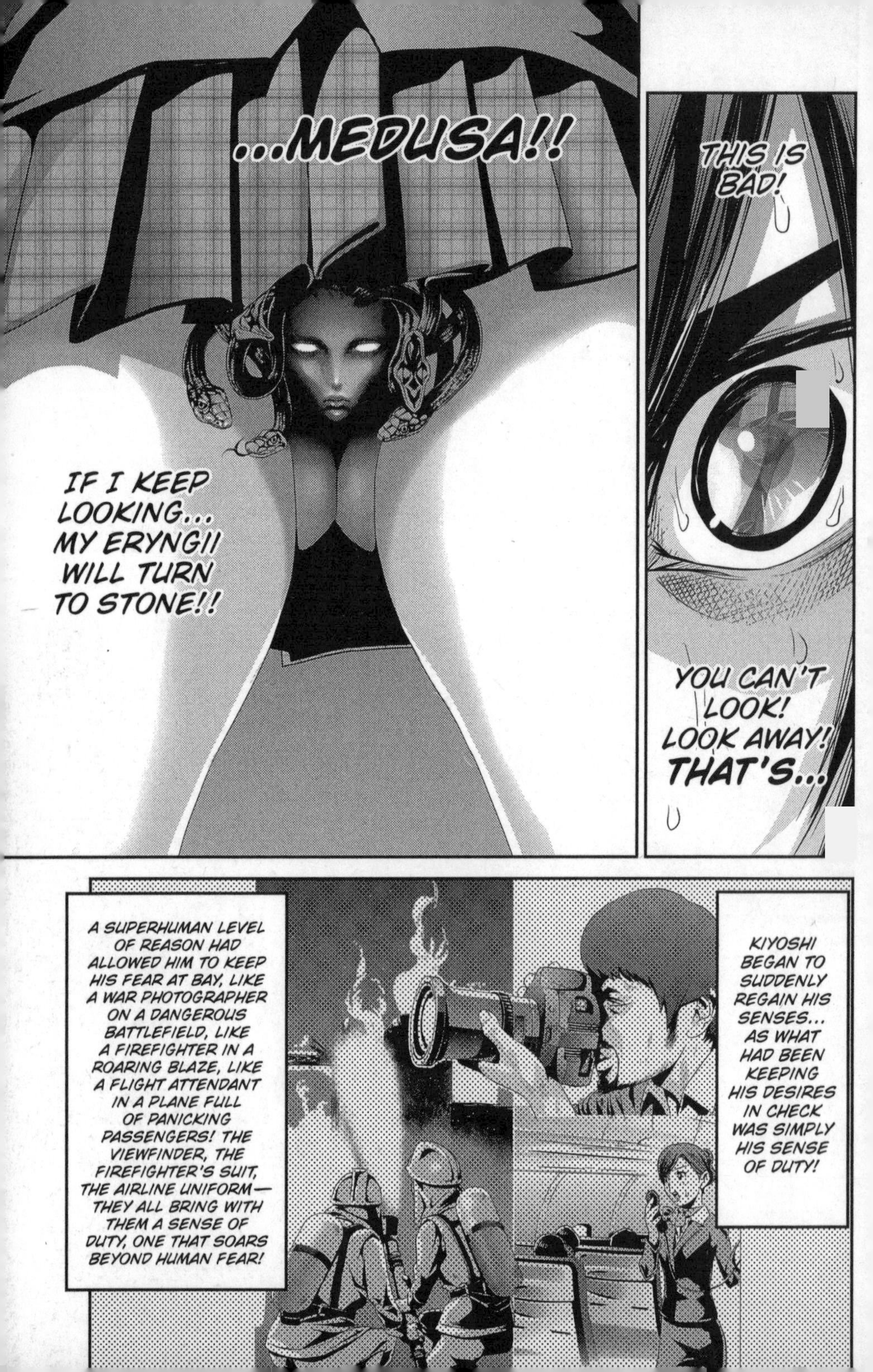
THIS IS BAD!
YOU CAN'T LOOK! LOOK AWAY! THAT'S...
...MEDUSA!!
IF I KEEP LOOKING... MY ERYNGII WILL TURN TO STONE!!
KIYOSHI BEGAN TO SUDDENLY REGAIN HIS SENSES... AS WHAT HAD BEEN KEEPING HIS DESIRES IN CHECK WAS SIMPLY HIS SENSE OF DUTY!
A SUPERHUMAN LEVEL OF REASON HAD ALLOWED HIM TO KEEP HIS FEAR AT BAY, LIKE A WAR PHOTOGRAPHER ON A DANGEROUS BATTLEFIELD, LIKE A FIREFIGHTER IN A ROARING BLAZE, LIKE A FLIGHT ATTENDANT IN A PLANE FULL OF PANICKING PASSENGERS! THE VIEWFINDER, THE FIREFIGHTER'S SUIT, THE AIRLINE UNIFORM—THEY ALL BRING WITH THEM A SENSE OF DUTY, ONE THAT SOARS BEYOND HUMAN FEAR!

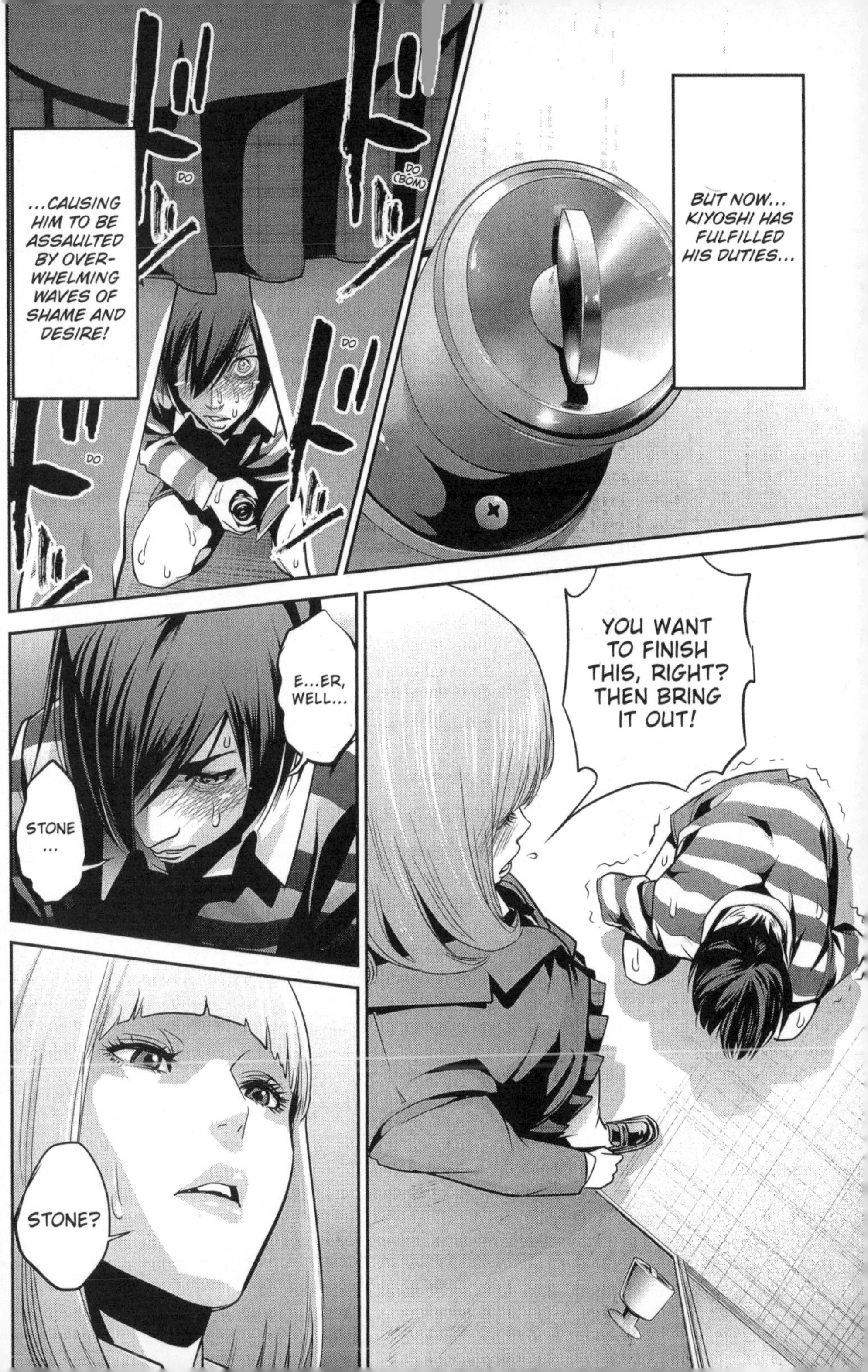
BUT NOW... KIYOSHI HAS FULFILLED HIS DUTIES...
DO (BOM)
DO
...CAUSING HIM TO BE ASSAULTED BY OVER-WHELMING WAVES OF SHAME AND DESIRE!
DO
DO
YOU WANT TO FINISH THIS, RIGHT? THEN BRING IT OUT!
E...ER, WELL...
STONE ...
STONE?

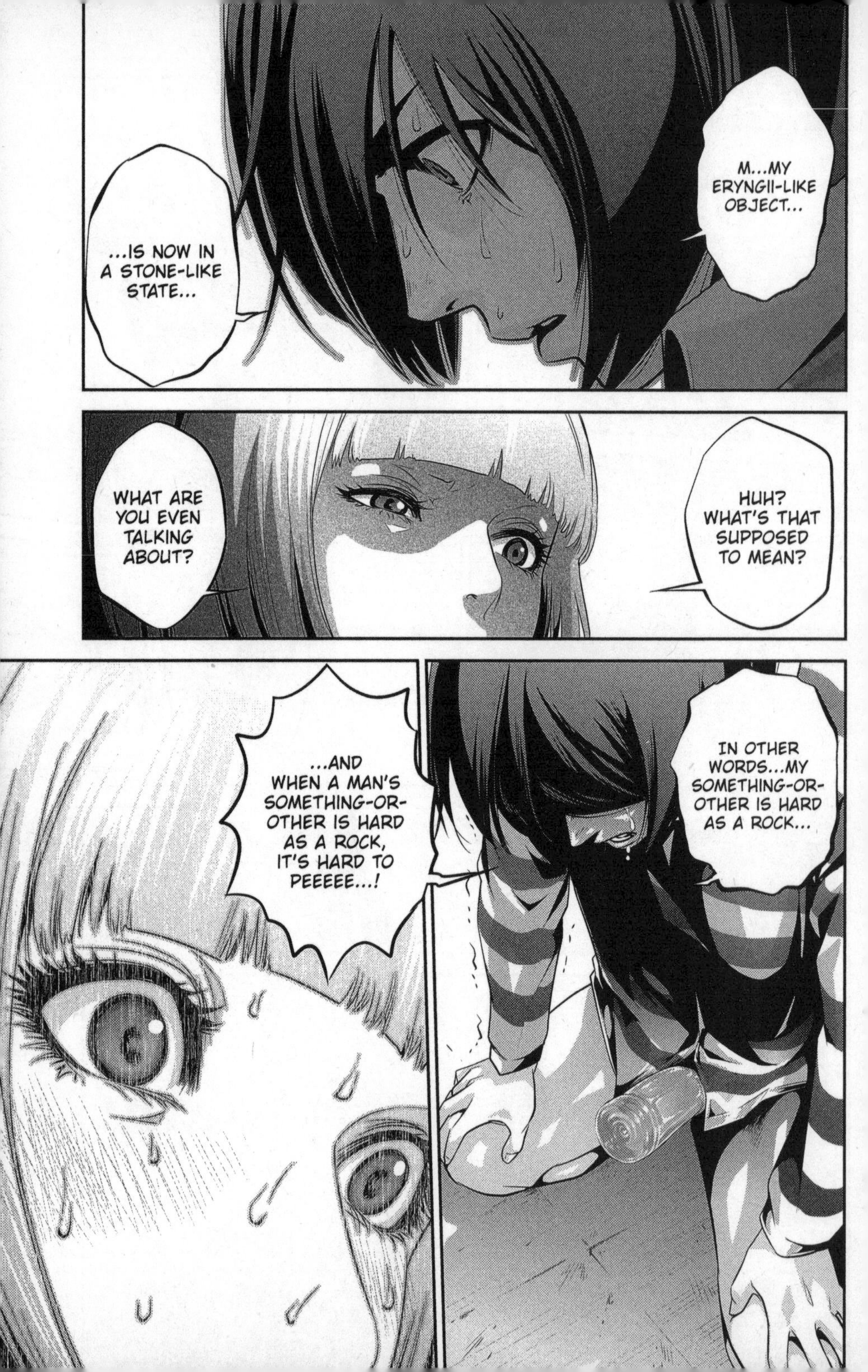
M...MY ERYNGII-LIKE OBJECT...
...IS NOW IN A STONE-LIKE STATE...
HUH? WHAT'S THAT SUPPOSED TO MEAN?
WHAT ARE YOU EVEN TALKING ABOUT?
IN OTHER WORDS...MY SOMETHING-OR-OTHER IS HARD AS A ROCK...
...AND WHEN A MAN'S SOMETHING-OR-OTHER IS HARD AS A ROCK, IT'S HARD TO PEEEEE...!

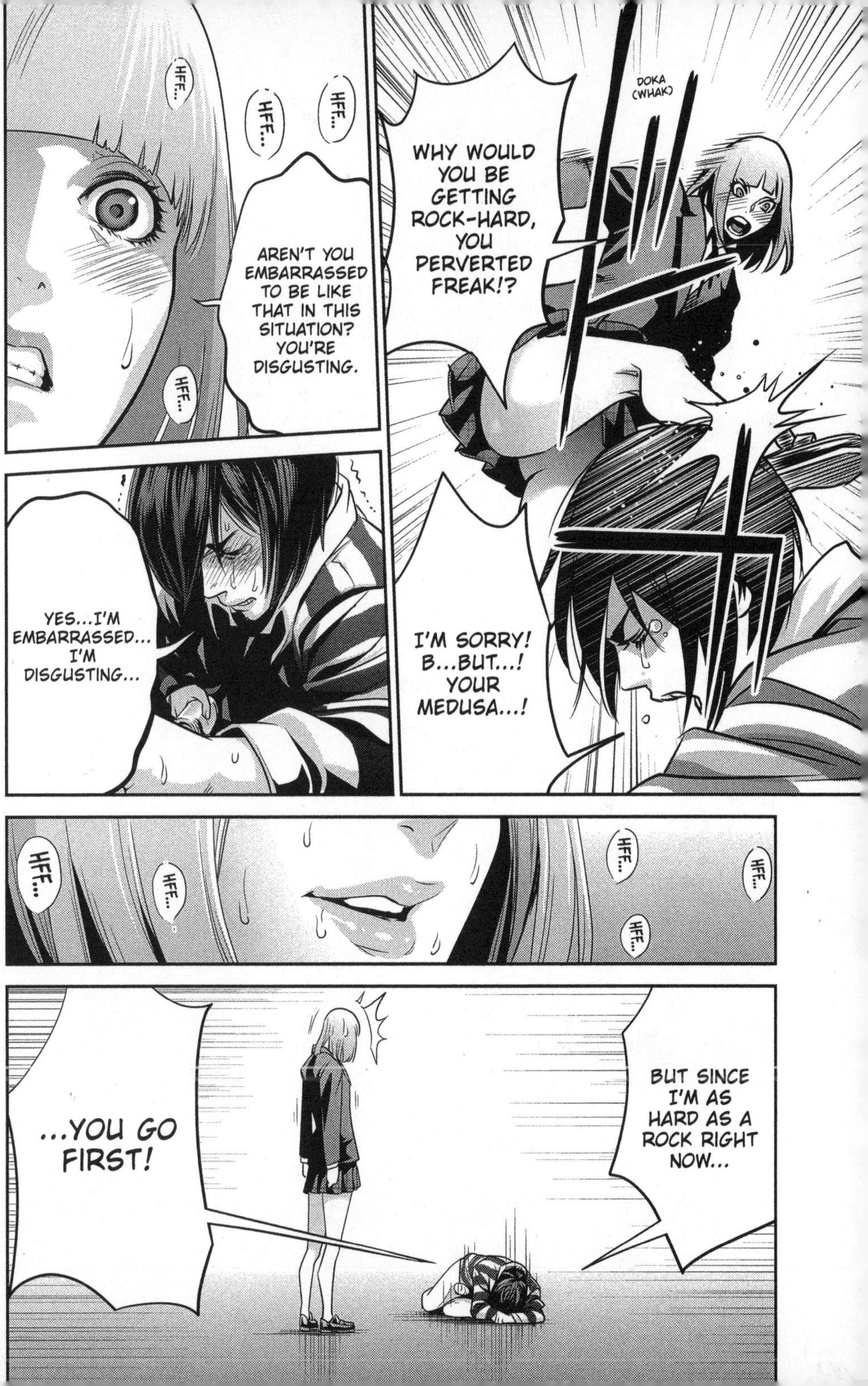
DOKA (WHAK)
WHY WOULD YOU BE GETTING ROCK-HARD, YOU PERVERTED FREAK!?
I'M SORRY! B...BUT...! YOUR MEDUSA...!
HFF...
HFF...
HFF...
AREN'T YOU EMBARRASSED TO BE LIKE THAT IN THIS SITUATION? YOU'RE DISGUSTING.
HFF...
YES...I'M EMBARRASSED... I'M DISGUSTING...
HFF...
HFF...
HFF...
HFF...
HFF...
BUT SINCE I'M AS HARD AS A ROCK RIGHT NOW...
...YOU GO FIRST!

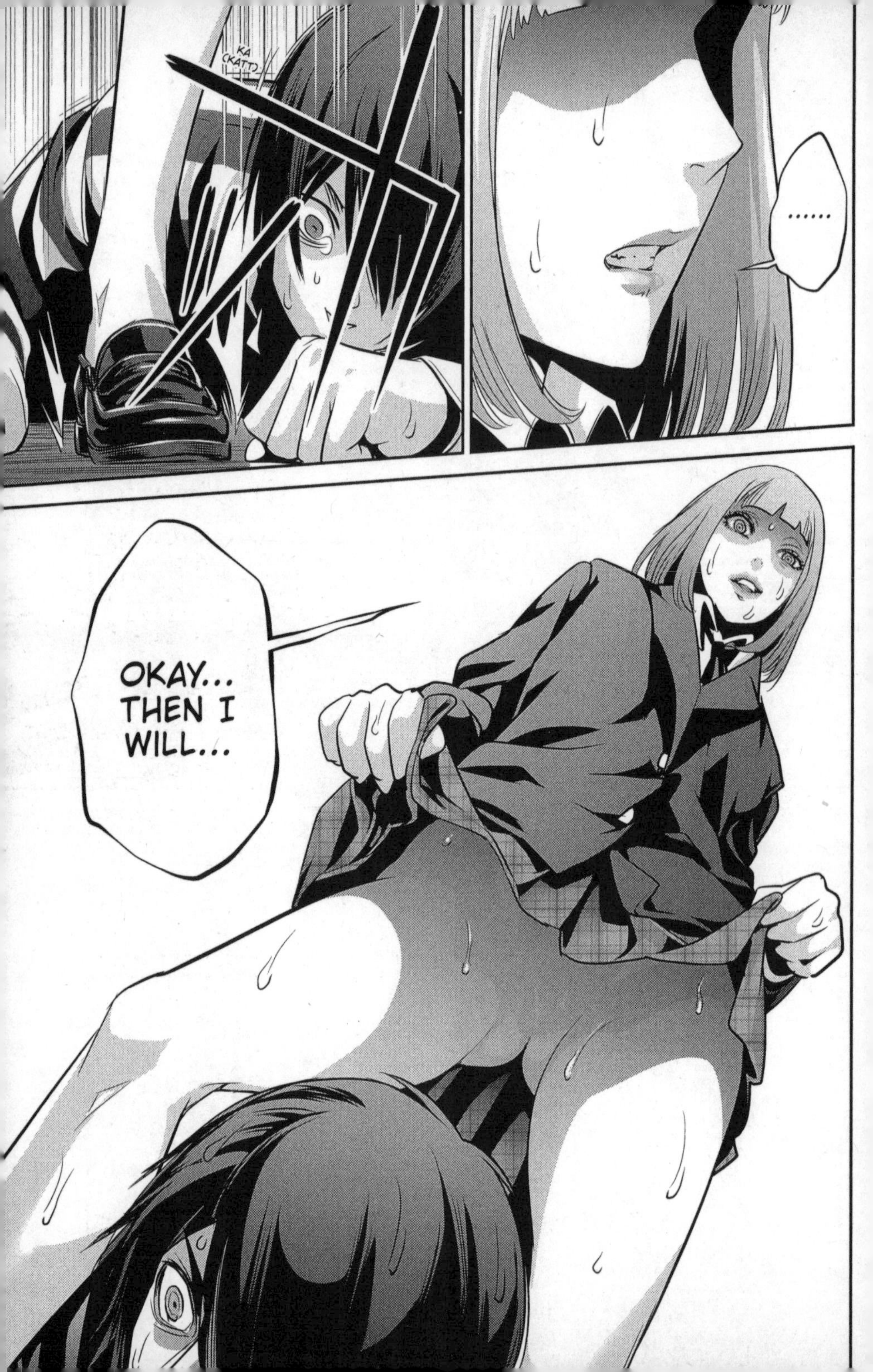
......
KA (KATT)
OKAY... THEN I WILL...

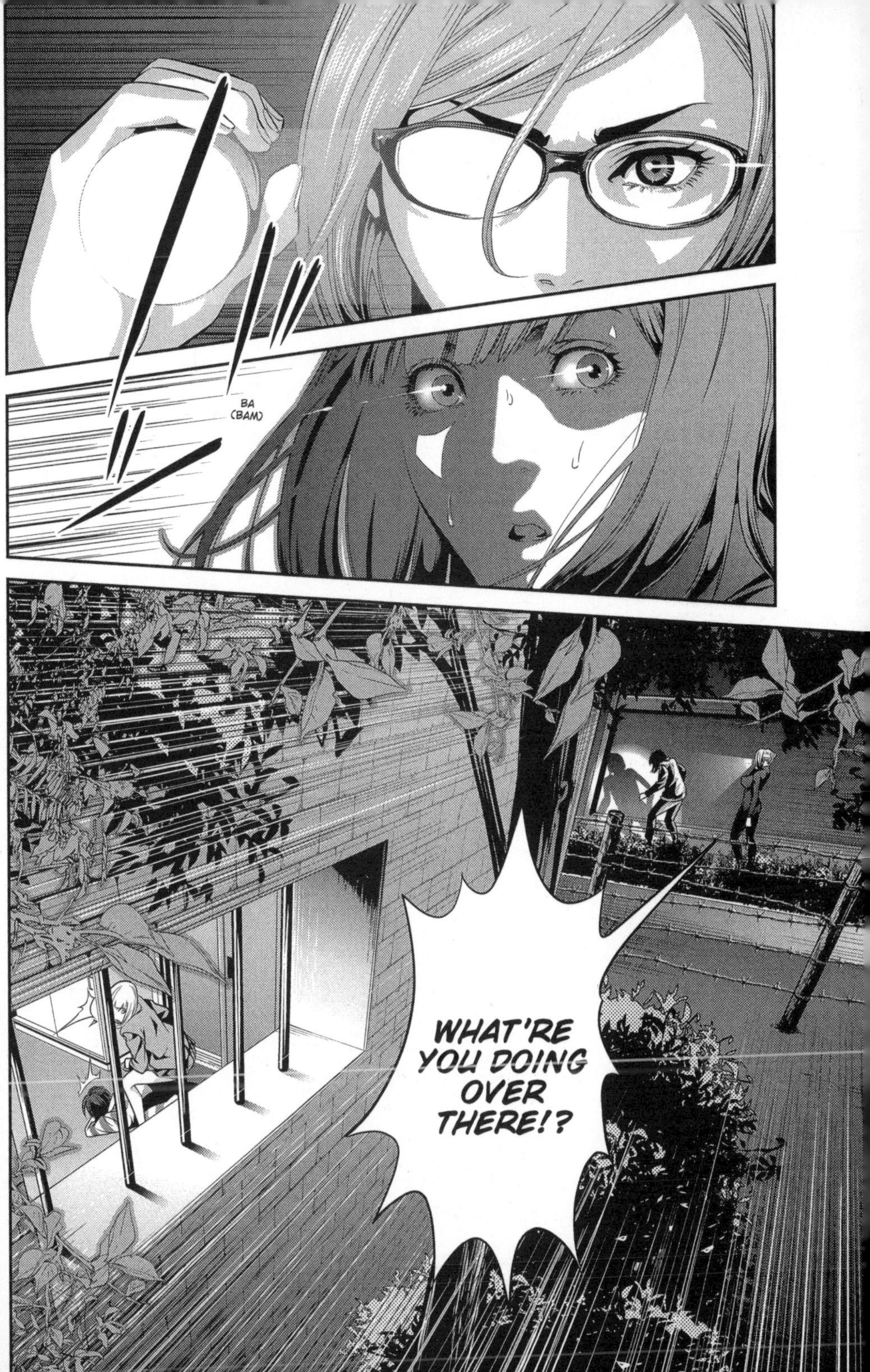
BA (BAM)
WHAT'RE YOU DOING OVER THERE!?

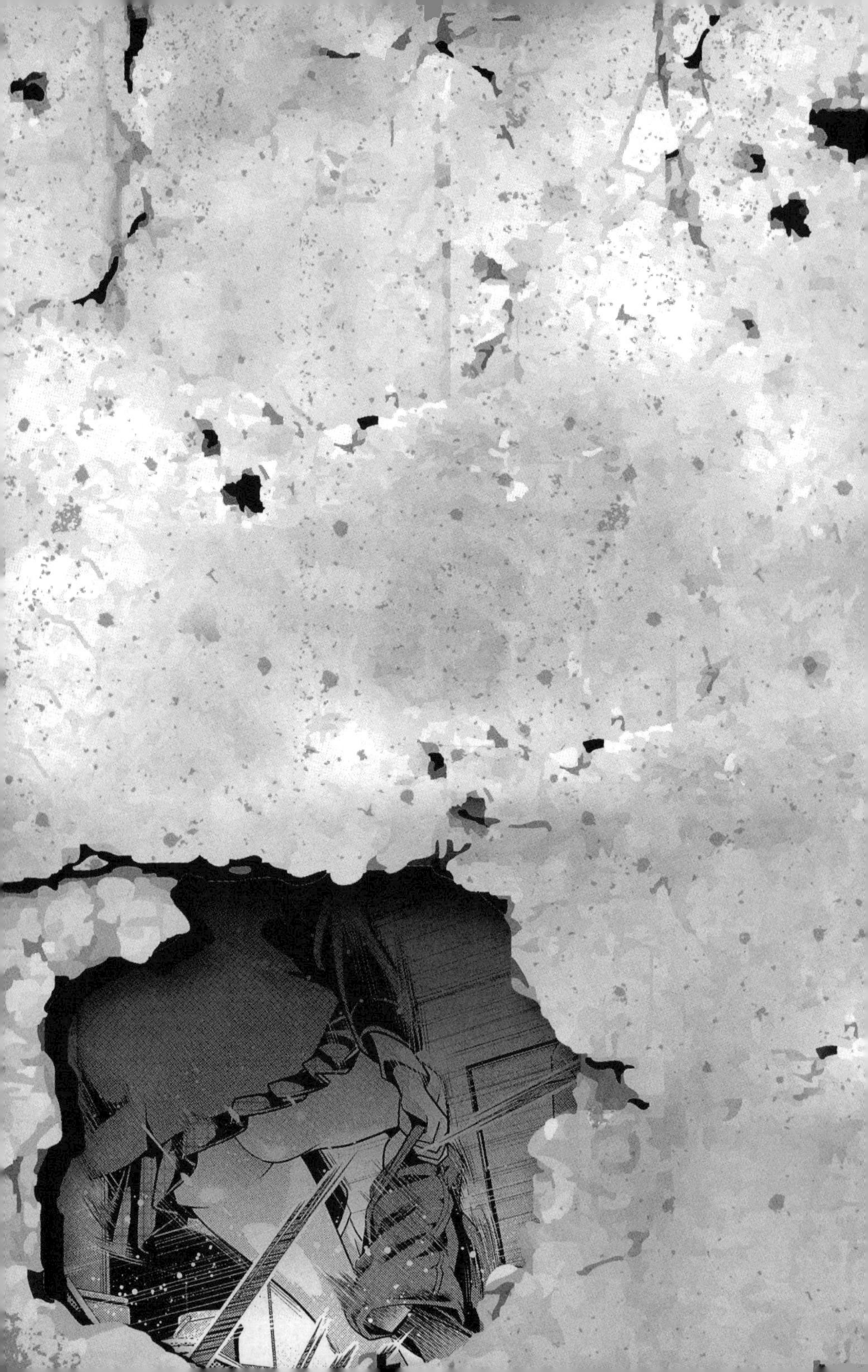

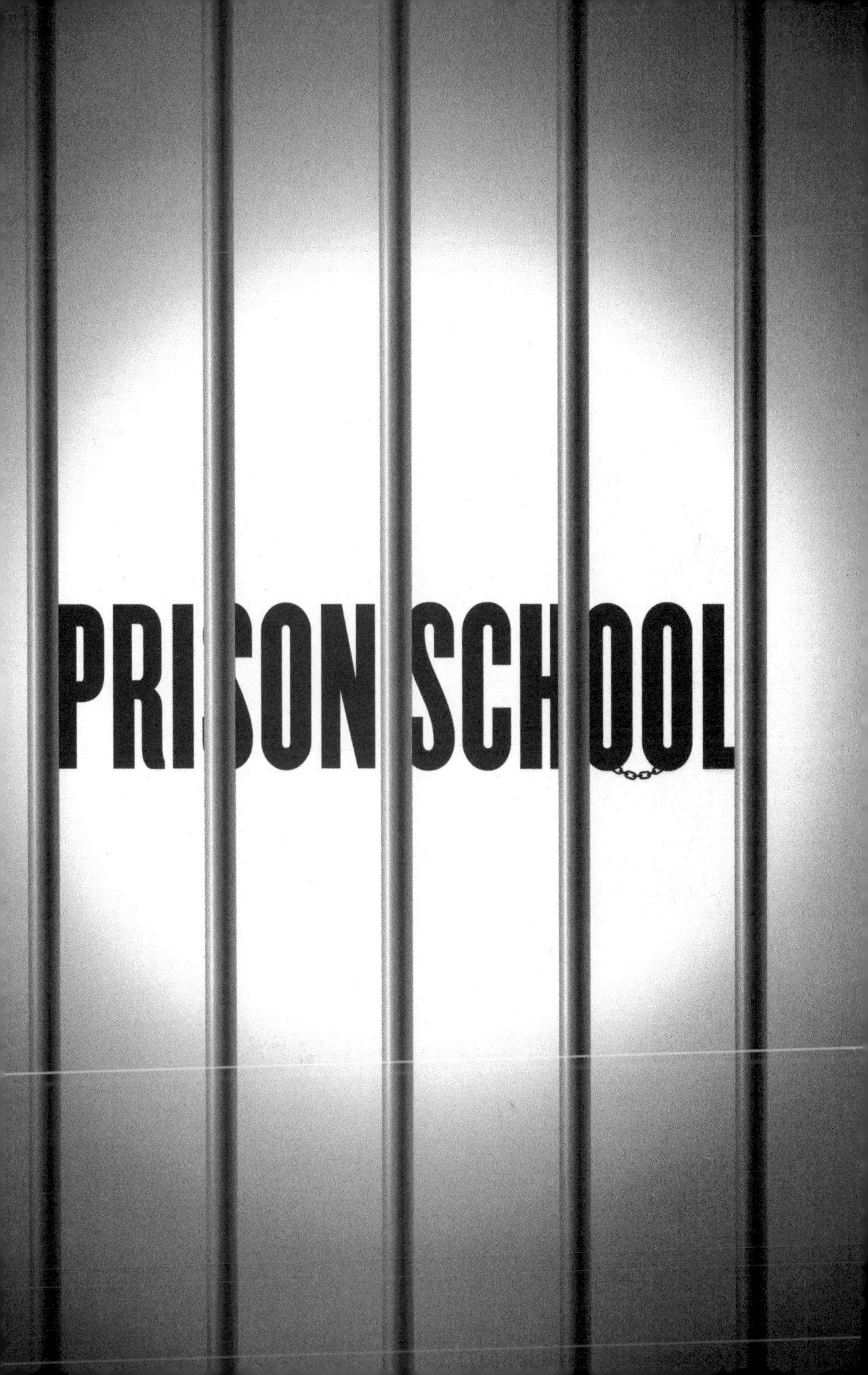
PRISON SCHOOL

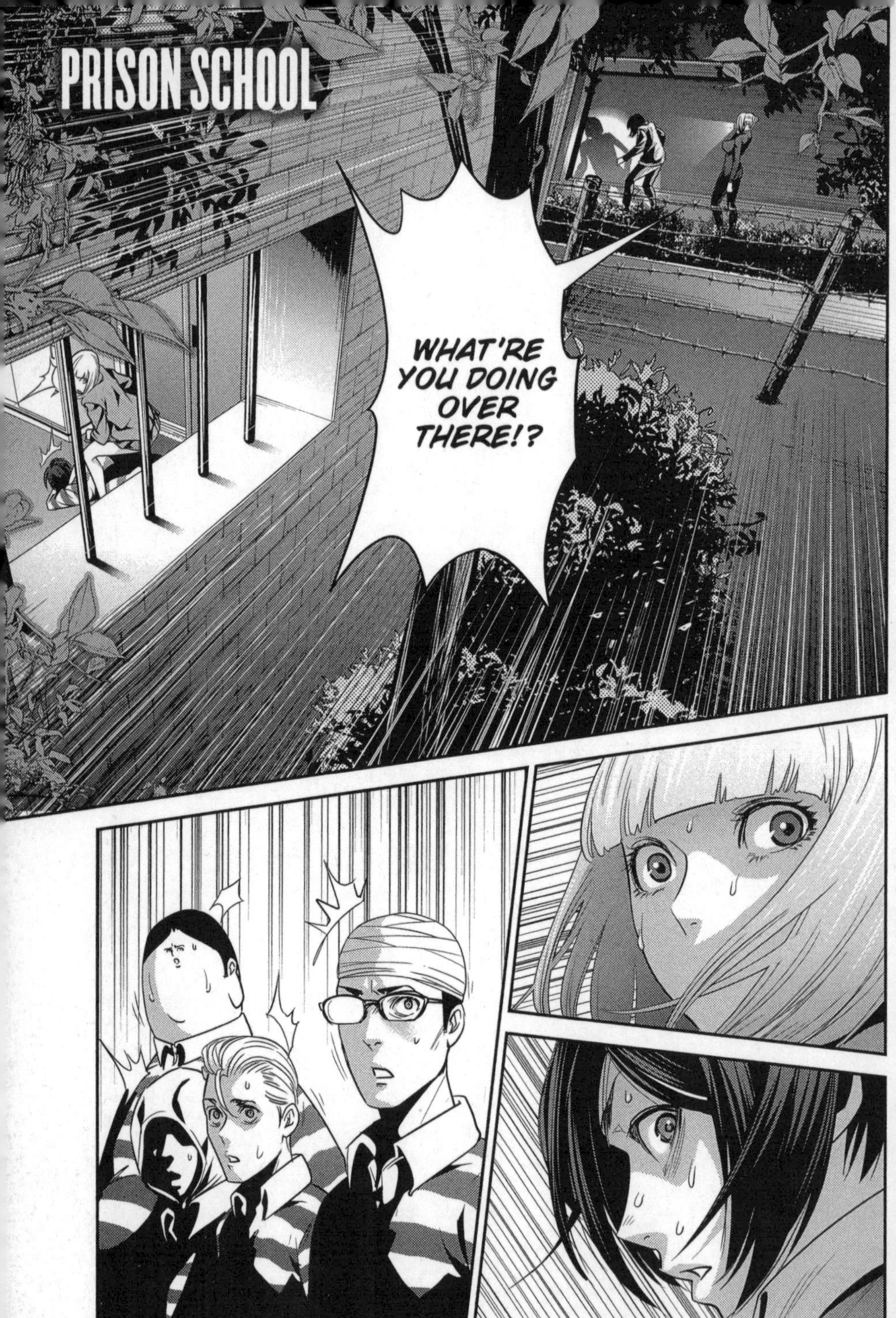
PRISON SCHOOL
WHAT'RE YOU DOING OVER THERE!?

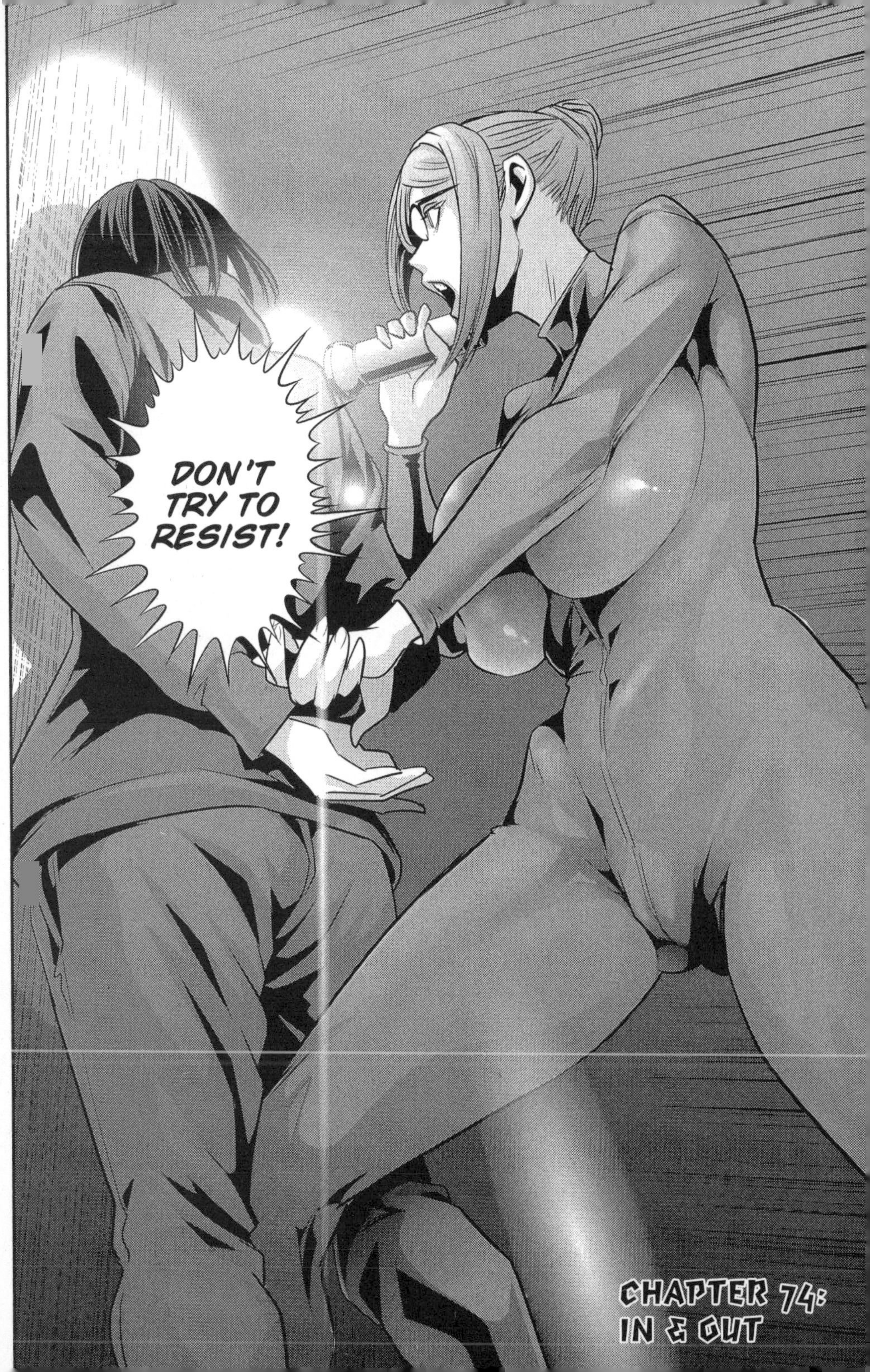
DON'T TRY TO RESIST!
CHAPTER 74: IN & OUT

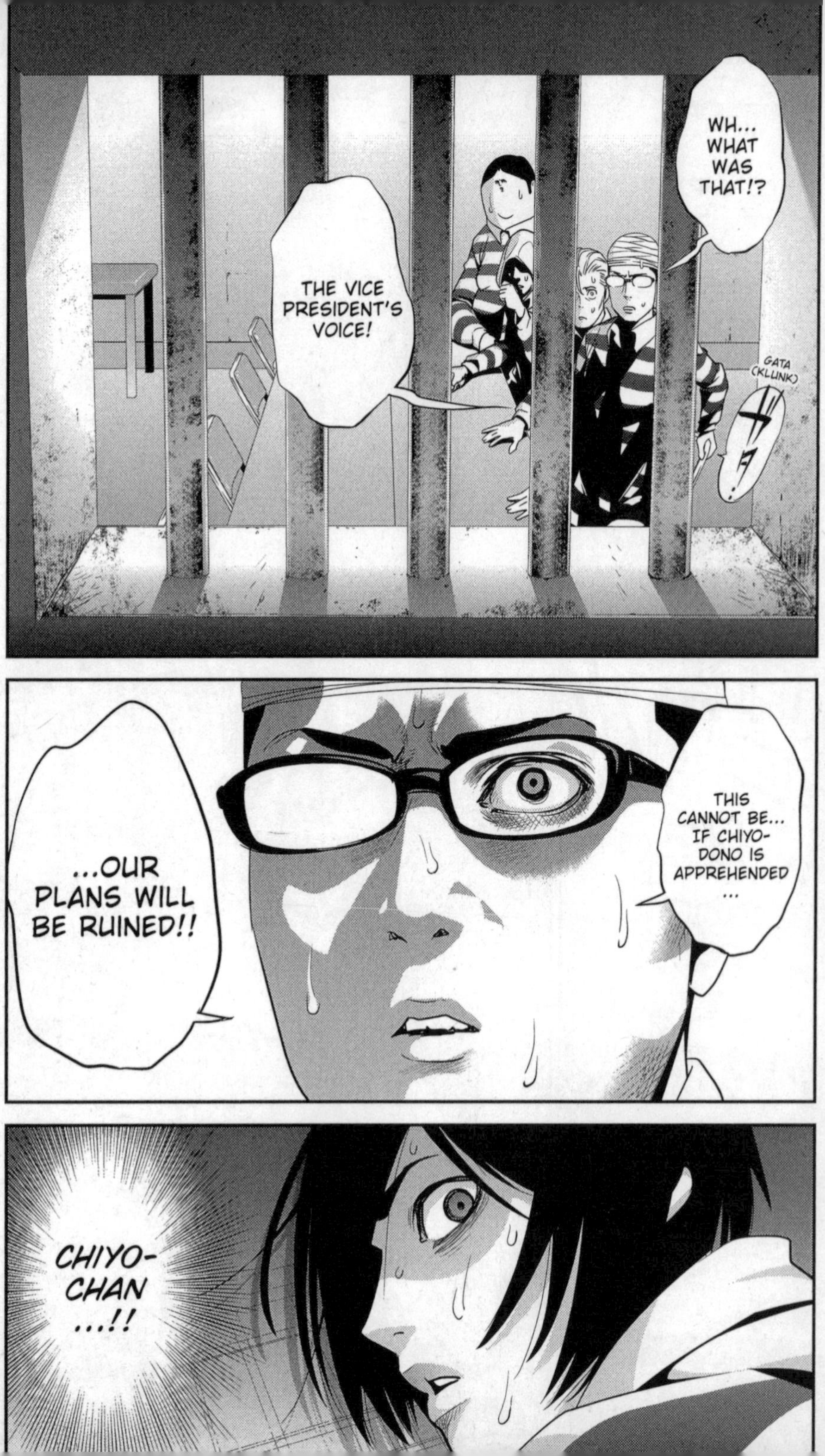
WH... WHAT WAS THAT!?
THE VICE PRESIDENT'S VOICE!
GATA (KLUNK)
THIS CANNOT BE... IF CHIYO-DONO IS APPREHENDED ...
...OUR PLANS WILL BE RUINED!!
CHIYO-CHAN ...!!

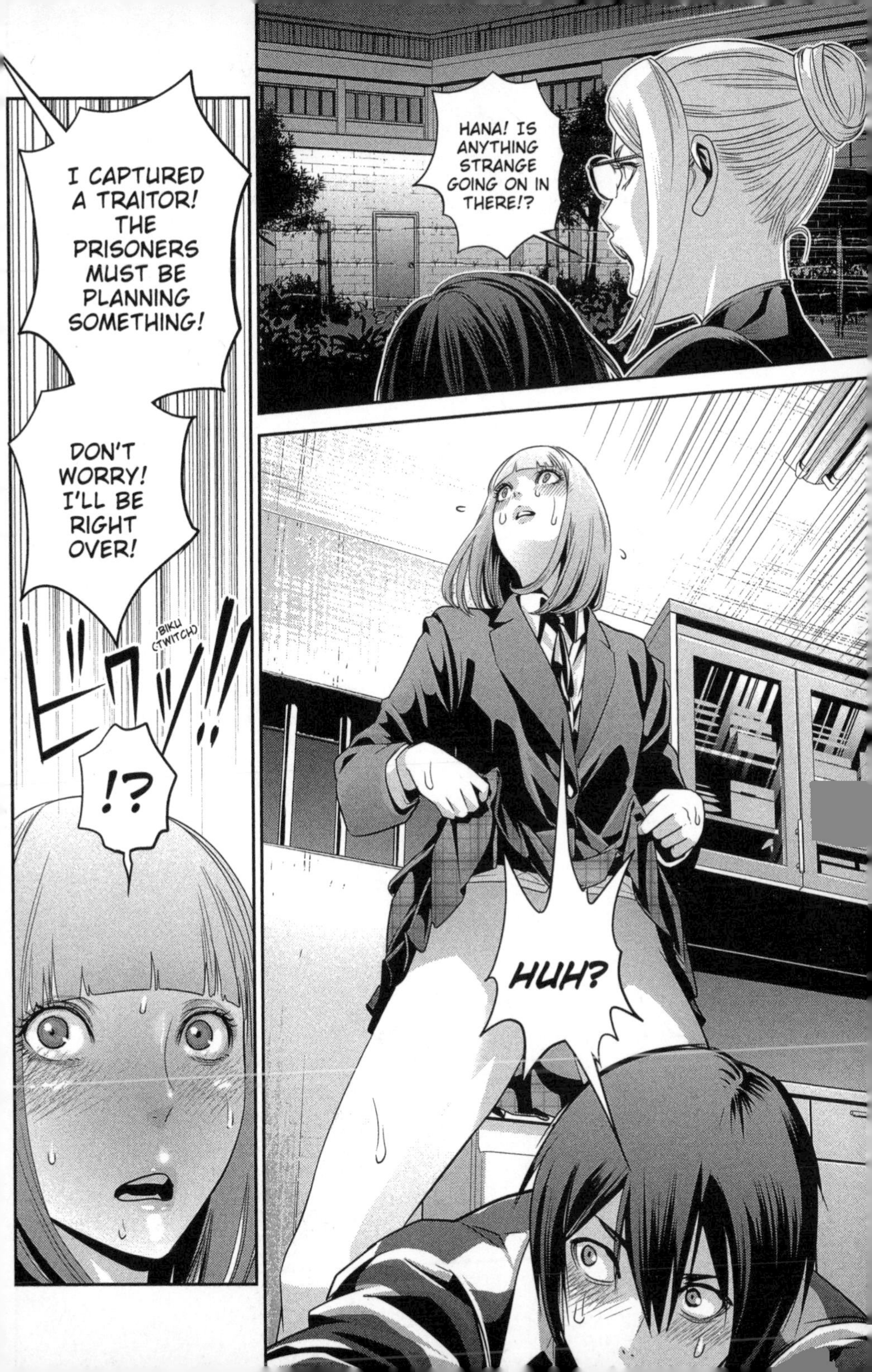
HANA! IS ANYTHING STRANGE GOING ON IN THERE!?
HUH?
I CAPTURED A TRAITOR! THE PRISONERS MUST BE PLANNING SOMETHING!
DON'T WORRY! I'LL BE RIGHT OVER!
BIKU (TWITCH)
!?

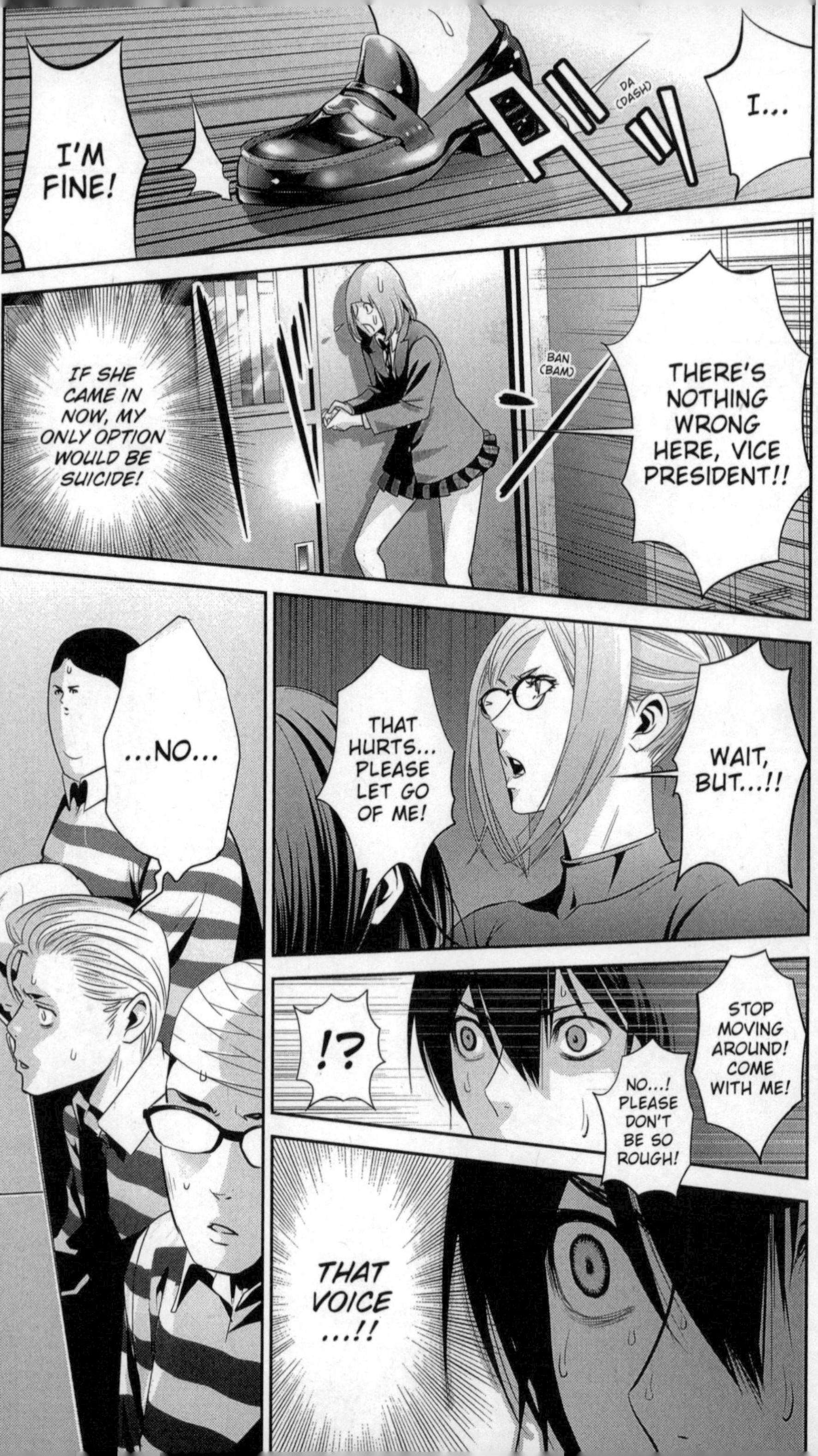
I...
DA (DASH)
I'M FINE!
THERE'S NOTHING WRONG HERE, VICE PRESIDENT!!
BAN (BAM)
IF SHE CAME IN NOW, MY ONLY OPTION WOULD BE SUICIDE!
WAIT, BUT...!!
THAT HURTS... PLEASE LET GO OF ME!
STOP MOVING AROUND! COME WITH ME!
NO...! PLEASE DON'T BE SO ROUGH!
!?
THAT VOICE ...!!
...NO...

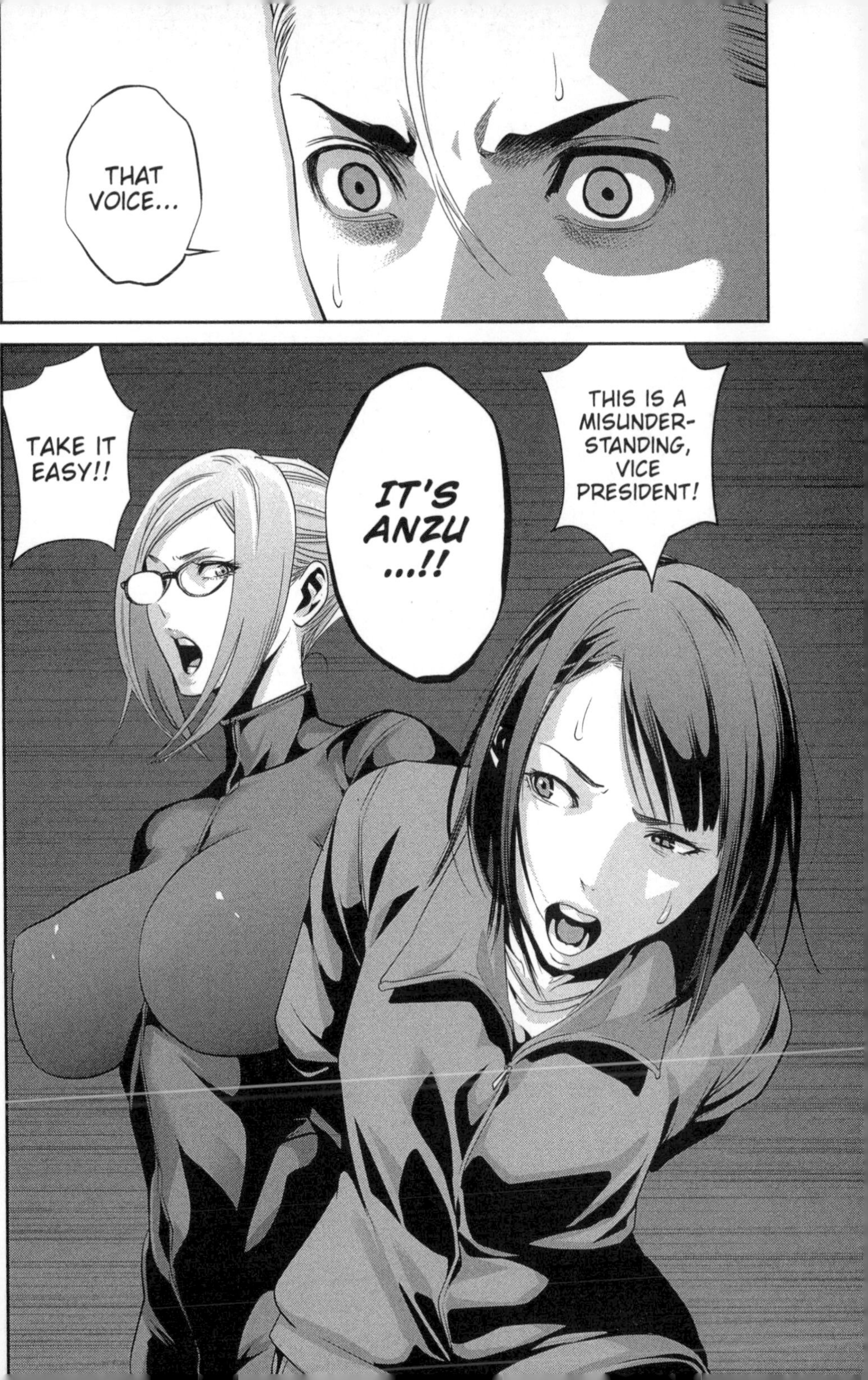
THAT VOICE...
THIS IS A MISUNDERSTANDING, VICE PRESIDENT!
IT'S ANZU ...!!
TAKE IT EASY!!

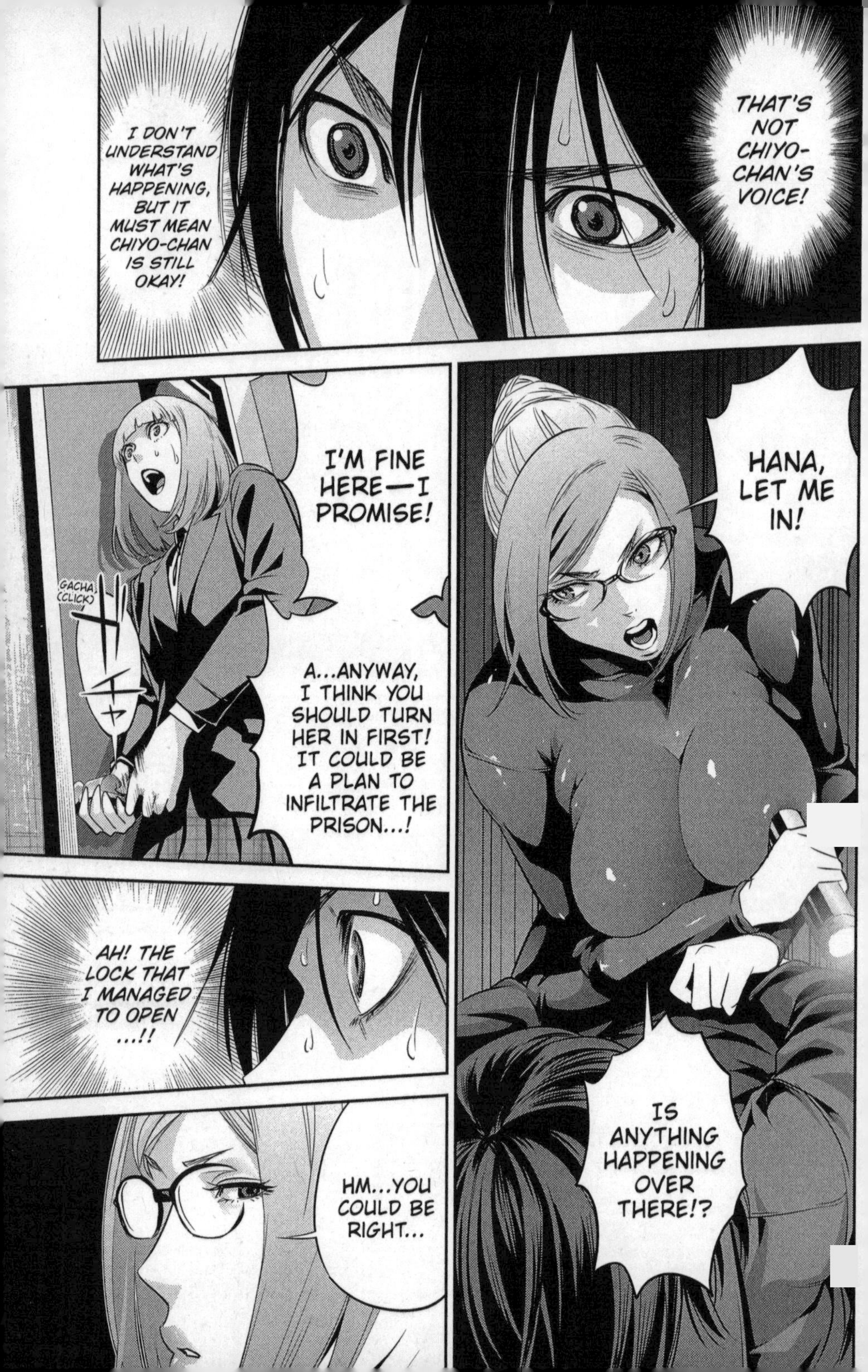
THAT'S NOT CHIYO-CHAN'S VOICE!
I DON'T UNDERSTAND WHAT'S HAPPENING, BUT IT MUST MEAN CHIYO-CHAN IS STILL OKAY!
HANA, LET ME IN!
IS ANYTHING HAPPENING OVER THERE!?
I'M FINE HERE—I PROMISE!
A...ANYWAY, I THINK YOU SHOULD TURN HER IN FIRST! IT COULD BE A PLAN TO INFILTRATE THE PRISON...!
GACHA (CLICK)
AH! THE LOCK THAT I MANAGED TO OPEN ...!!
HM...YOU COULD BE RIGHT...

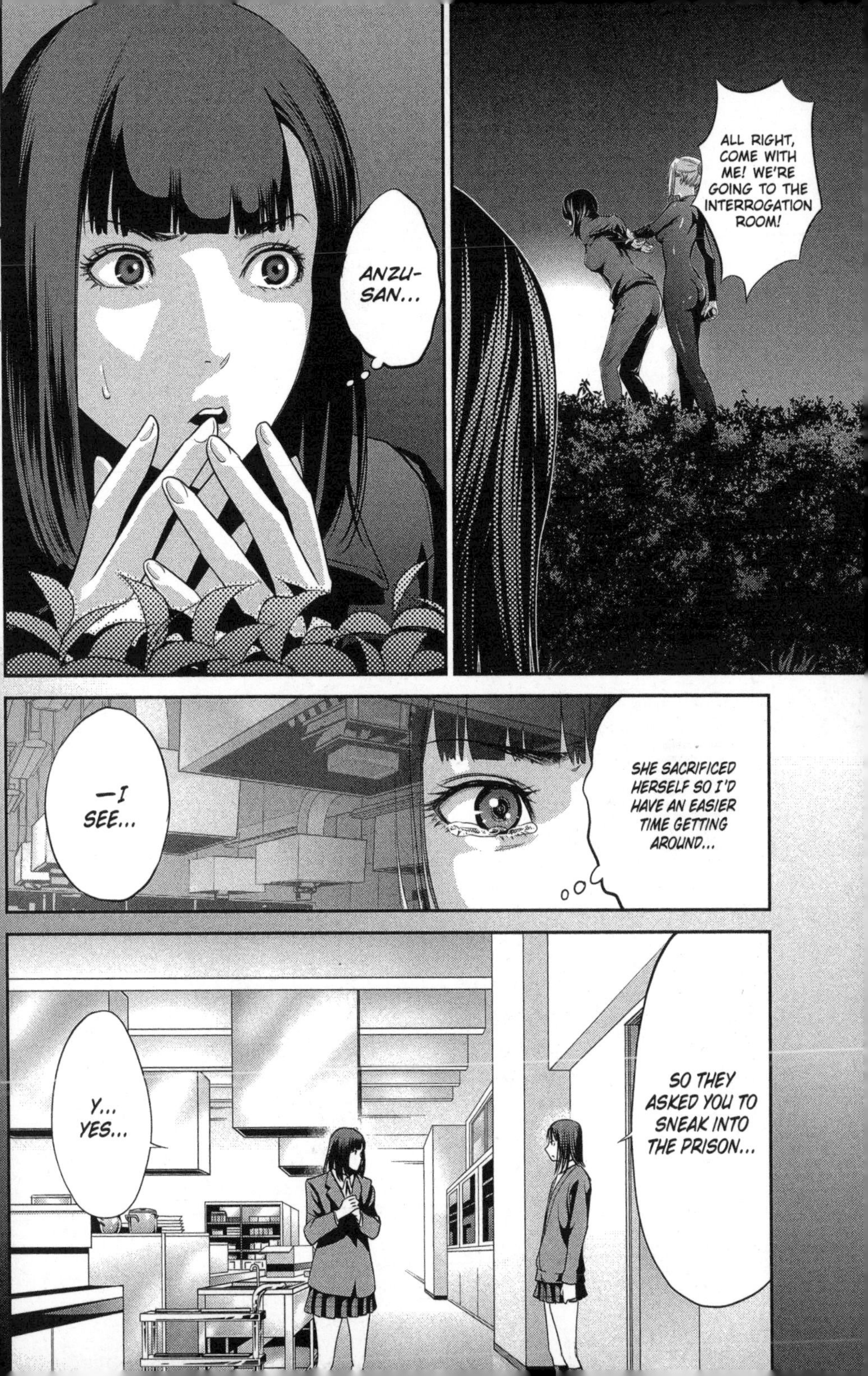
ALL RIGHT, COME WITH ME! WE'RE GOING TO THE INTERROGATION ROOM!
ANZU-SAN...
SHE SACRIFICED HERSELF SO I'D HAVE AN EASIER TIME GETTING AROUND...
—I SEE...
SO THEY ASKED YOU TO SNEAK INTO THE PRISON...
Y... YES...

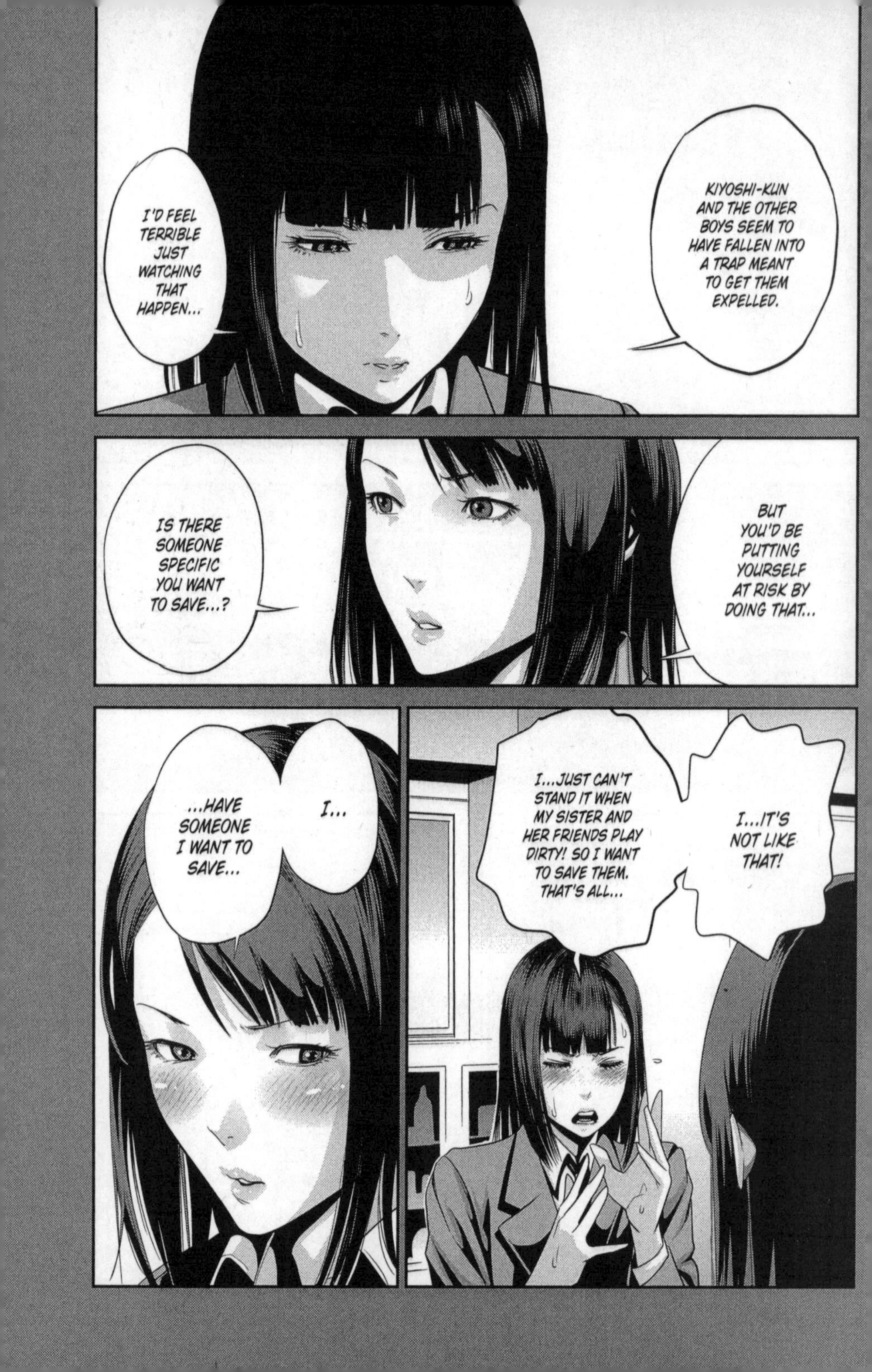

KIYOSHI-KUN AND THE OTHER BOYS SEEM TO HAVE FALLEN INTO A TRAP MEANT TO GET THEM EXPELLED.
I'D FEEL TERRIBLE JUST WATCHING THAT HAPPEN...
BUT YOU'D BE PUTTING YOURSELF AT RISK BY DOING THAT...
IS THERE SOMEONE SPECIFIC YOU WANT TO SAVE...?
I...IT'S NOT LIKE THAT!
I...JUST CAN'T STAND IT WHEN MY SISTER AND HER FRIENDS PLAY DIRTY! SO I WANT TO SAVE THEM. THAT'S ALL...
I...
...HAVE SOMEONE I WANT TO SAVE...

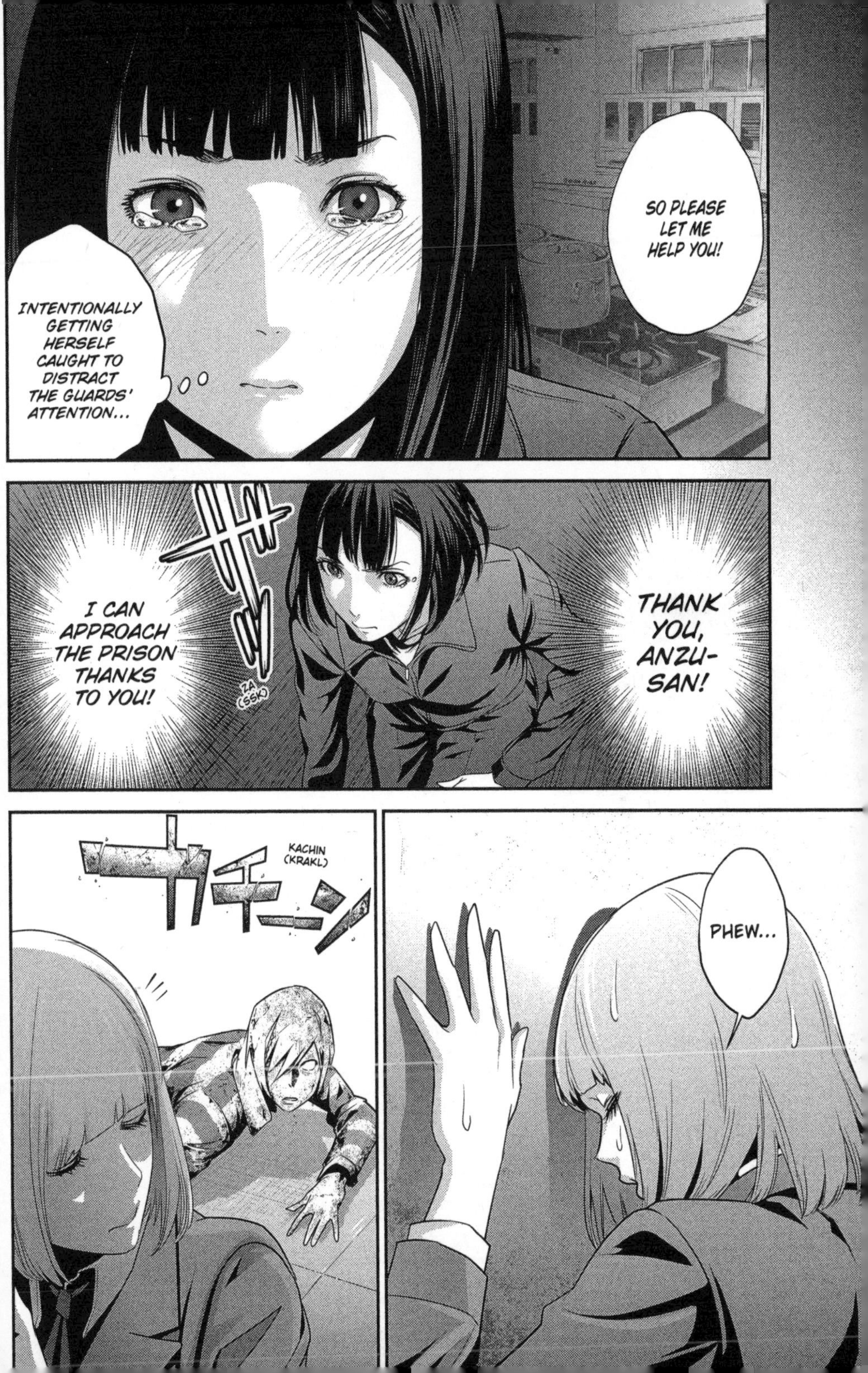
SO PLEASE LET ME HELP YOU!
INTENTIONALLY GETTING HERSELF CAUGHT TO DISTRACT THE GUARDS' ATTENTION...
THANK YOU, ANZU-SAN!
ZA (SSK)
I CAN APPROACH THE PRISON THANKS TO YOU!
PHEW...
KACHIN (KRAKL)

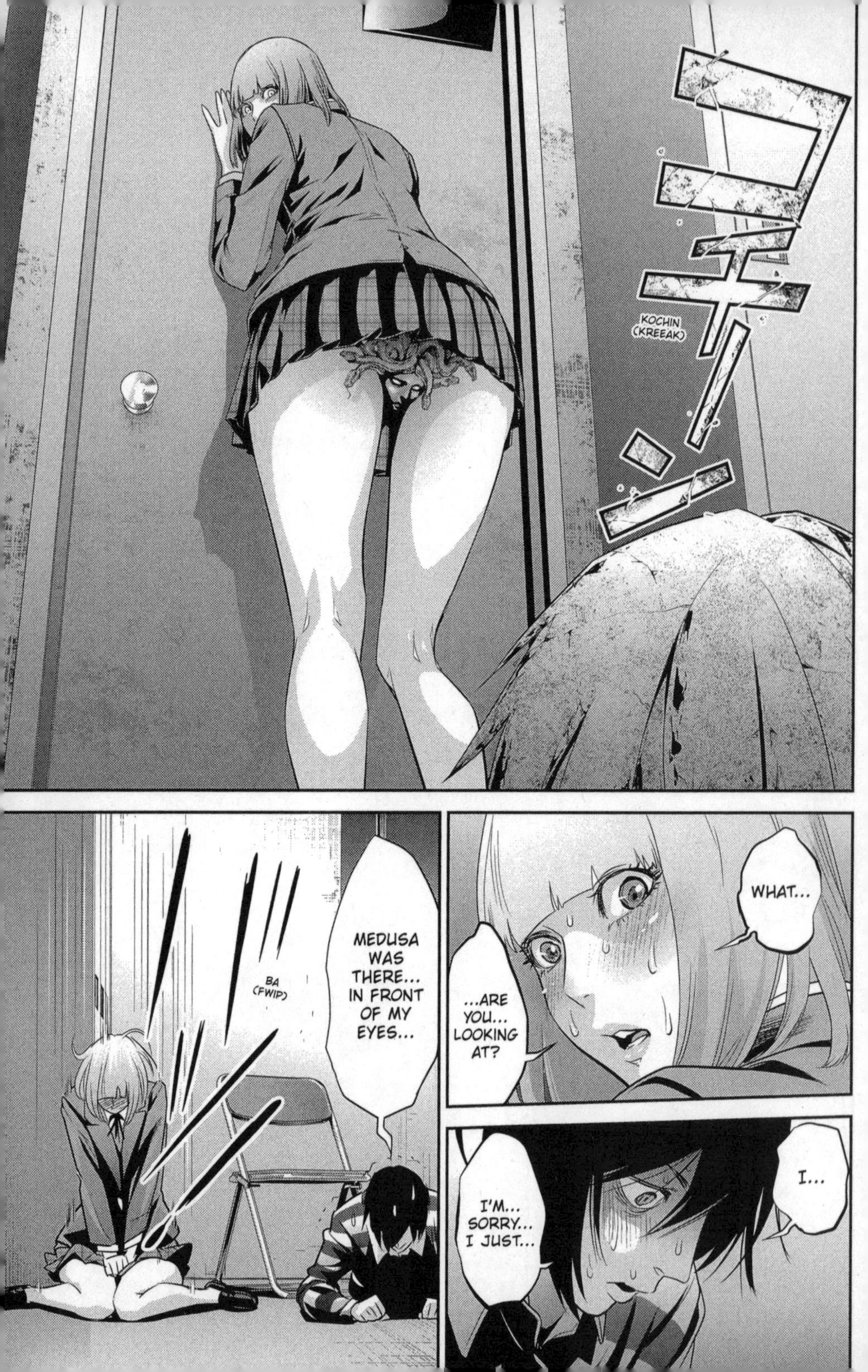
KOCHIN
(KREEAK)
WHAT...
...ARE YOU... LOOKING AT?
I...
I'M... SORRY... I JUST...
MEDUSA WAS THERE... IN FRONT OF MY EYES...
BA
(FWIP)

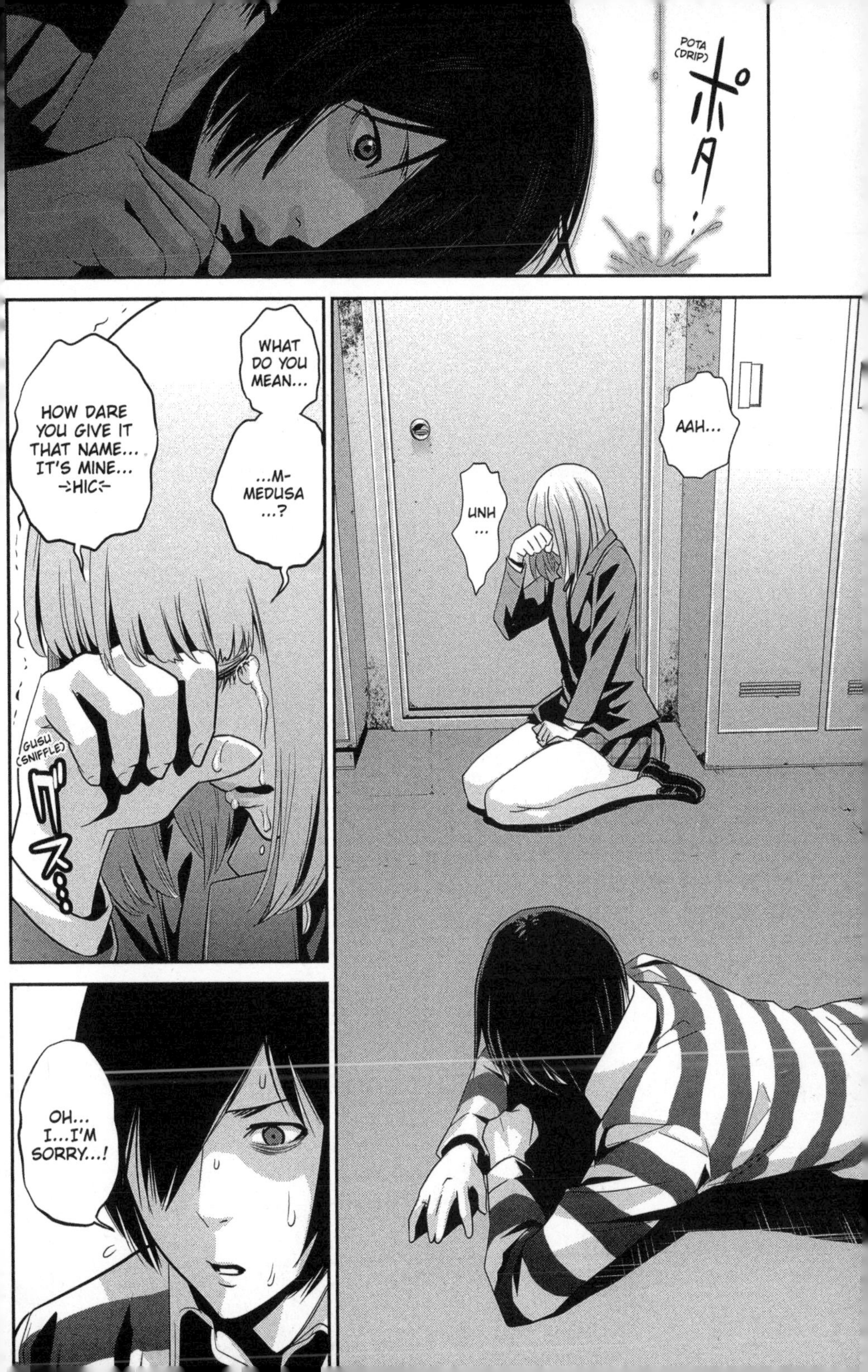
POTA (DRIP)
ポタ!
AAH...
UNH...
WHAT DO YOU MEAN...
...M-MEDUSA...?
HOW DARE YOU GIVE IT THAT NAME... IT'S MINE... HIC
GUSU (SNIFFLE)
OH... I...I'M SORRY...!

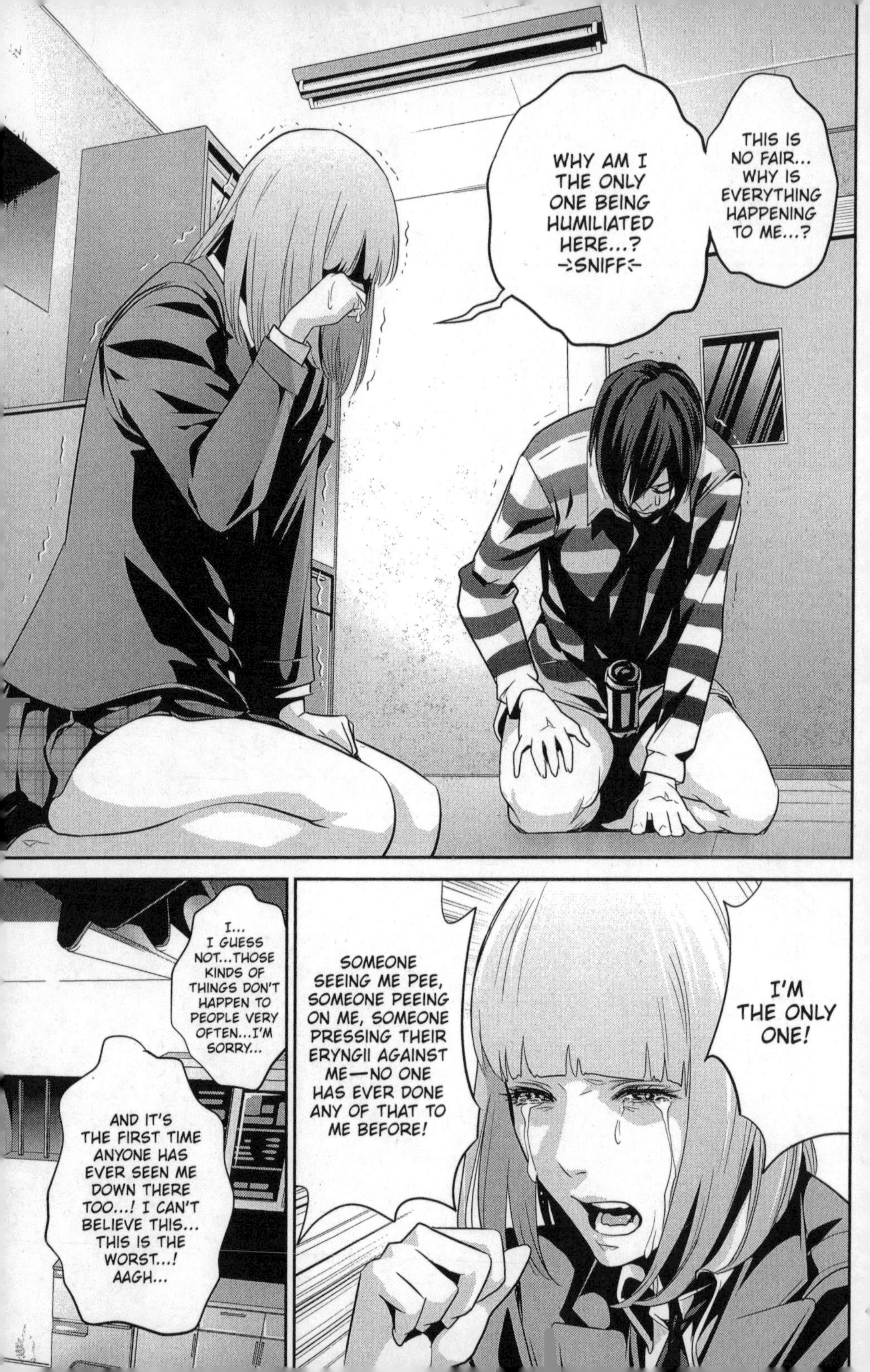
THIS IS NO FAIR... WHY IS EVERYTHING HAPPENING TO ME...?
WHY AM I THE ONLY ONE BEING HUMILIATED HERE...? -SNIFF-
I'M THE ONLY ONE!
SOMEONE SEEING ME PEE, SOMEONE PEEING ON ME, SOMEONE PRESSING THEIR ERYNGII AGAINST ME—NO ONE HAS EVER DONE ANY OF THAT TO ME BEFORE!
I... I GUESS NOT...THOSE KINDS OF THINGS DON'T HAPPEN TO PEOPLE VERY OFTEN...I'M SORRY...
AND IT'S THE FIRST TIME ANYONE HAS EVER SEEN ME DOWN THERE TOO...! I CAN'T BELIEVE THIS... THIS IS THE WORST...! AAGH...

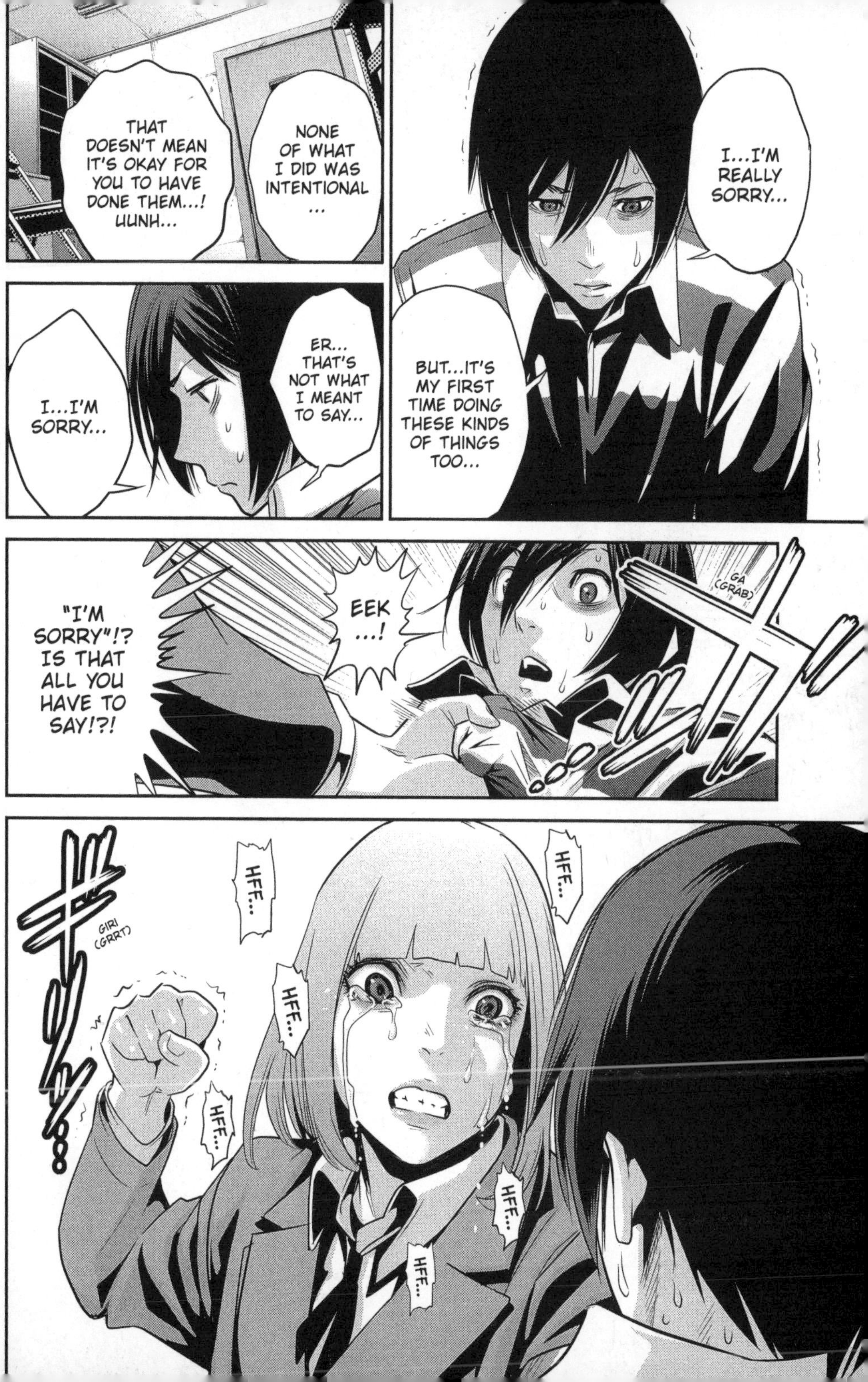
I...I'M REALLY SORRY...
BUT...IT'S MY FIRST TIME DOING THESE KINDS OF THINGS TOO...
NONE OF WHAT I DID WAS INTENTIONAL...
THAT DOESN'T MEAN IT'S OKAY FOR YOU TO HAVE DONE THEM...! UUNH...
ER... THAT'S NOT WHAT I MEANT TO SAY...
I...I'M SORRY...
GA (GRAB)
EEK...!
"I'M SORRY"!? IS THAT ALL YOU HAVE TO SAY!?!
HFF...
HFF...
HFF...
HFF...
HFF...
HFF...
GIRI (GRRT)

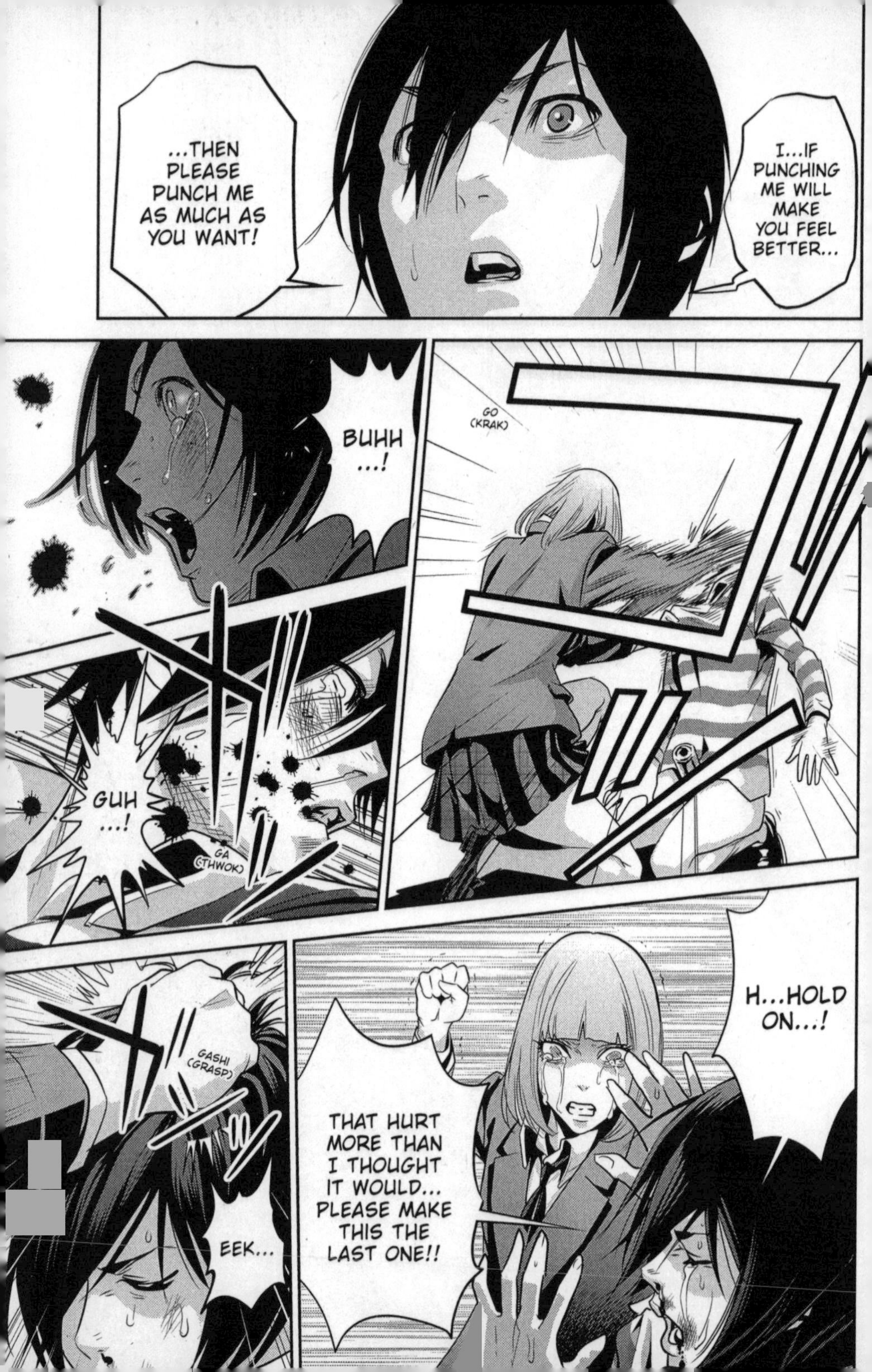
I...IF PUNCHING ME WILL MAKE YOU FEEL BETTER...
...THEN PLEASE PUNCH ME AS MUCH AS YOU WANT!
GO (KRAK)
BUHH ...!
GUH ...!
GA (THWOK)
H...HOLD ON...!
THAT HURT MORE THAN I THOUGHT IT WOULD... PLEASE MAKE THIS THE LAST ONE!!
GASHI (GRASP)
EEK...

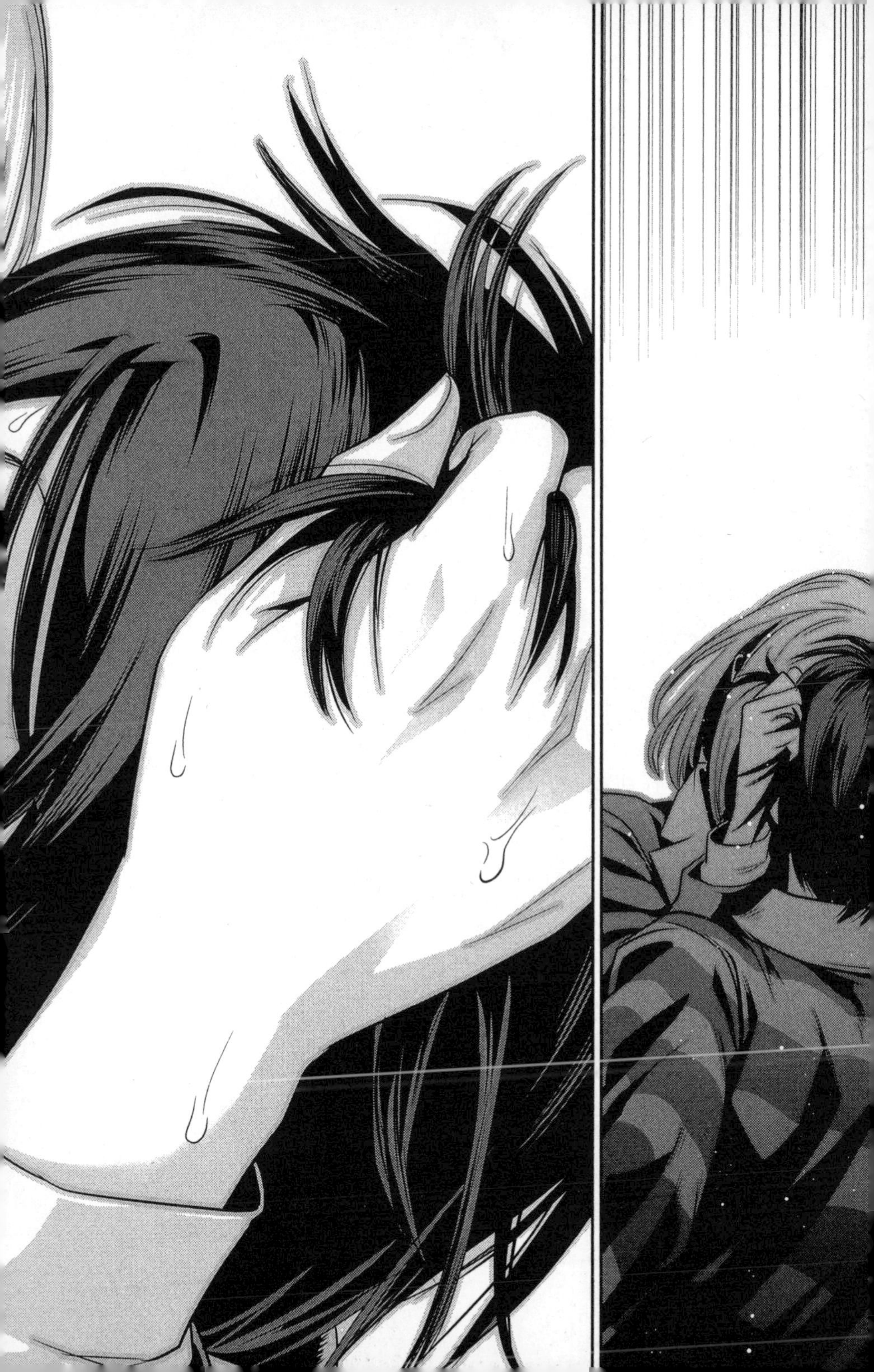

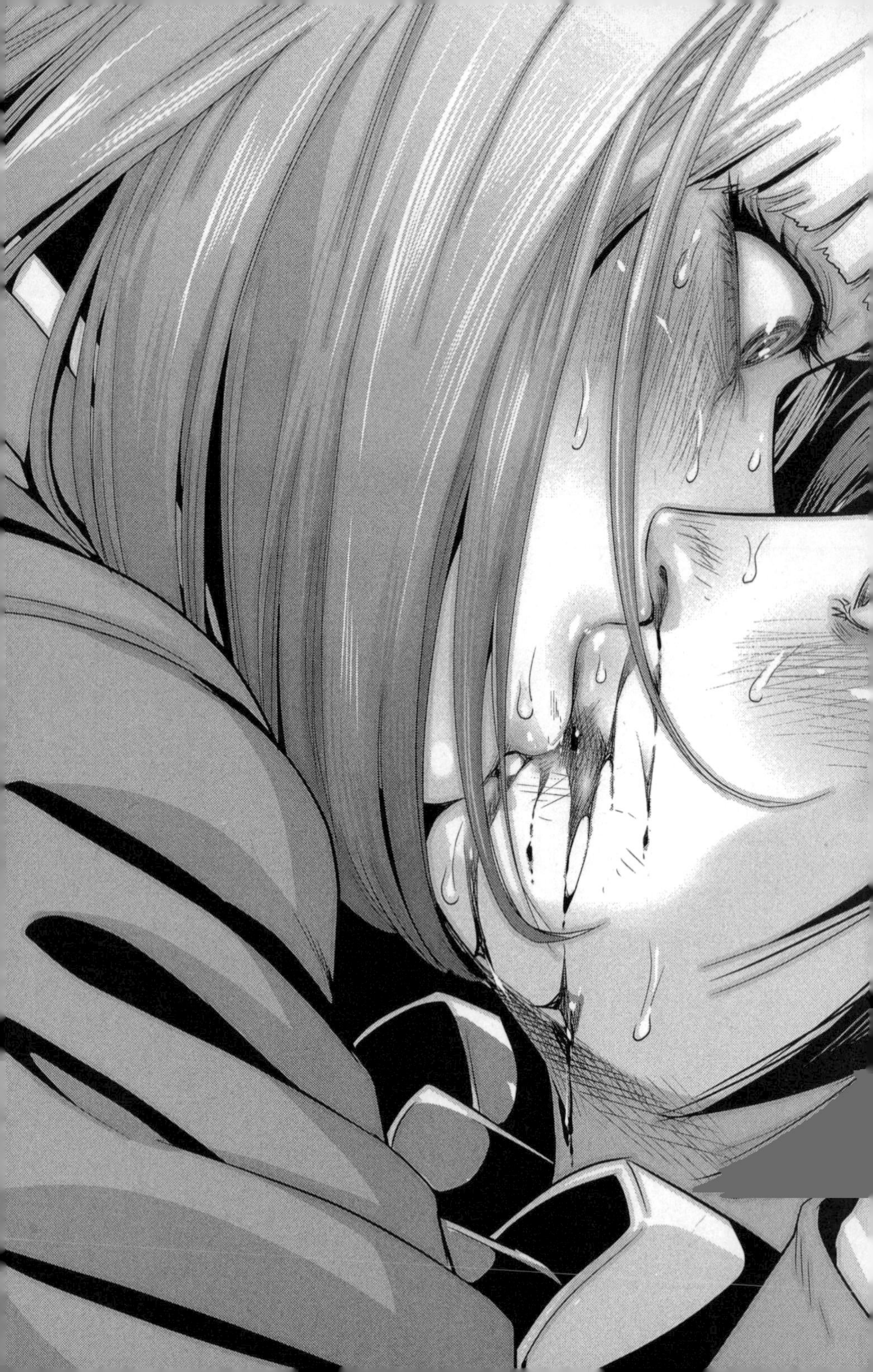

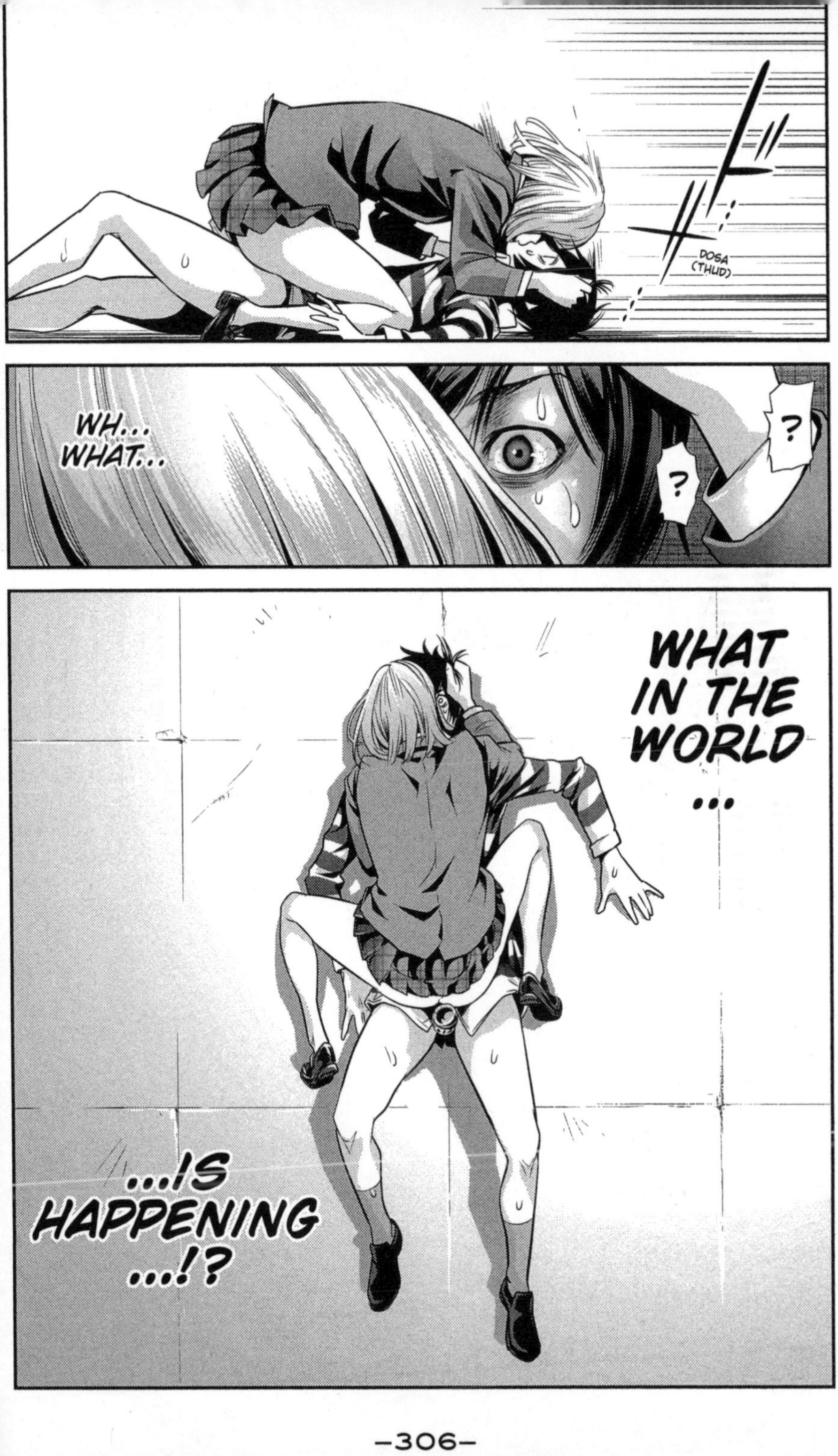
DOSA (THUD)
?
?
WH... WHAT...
WHAT IN THE WORLD ...
...IS HAPPENING ...!?

CHAPTER 75: KISS KISS BANG BANG

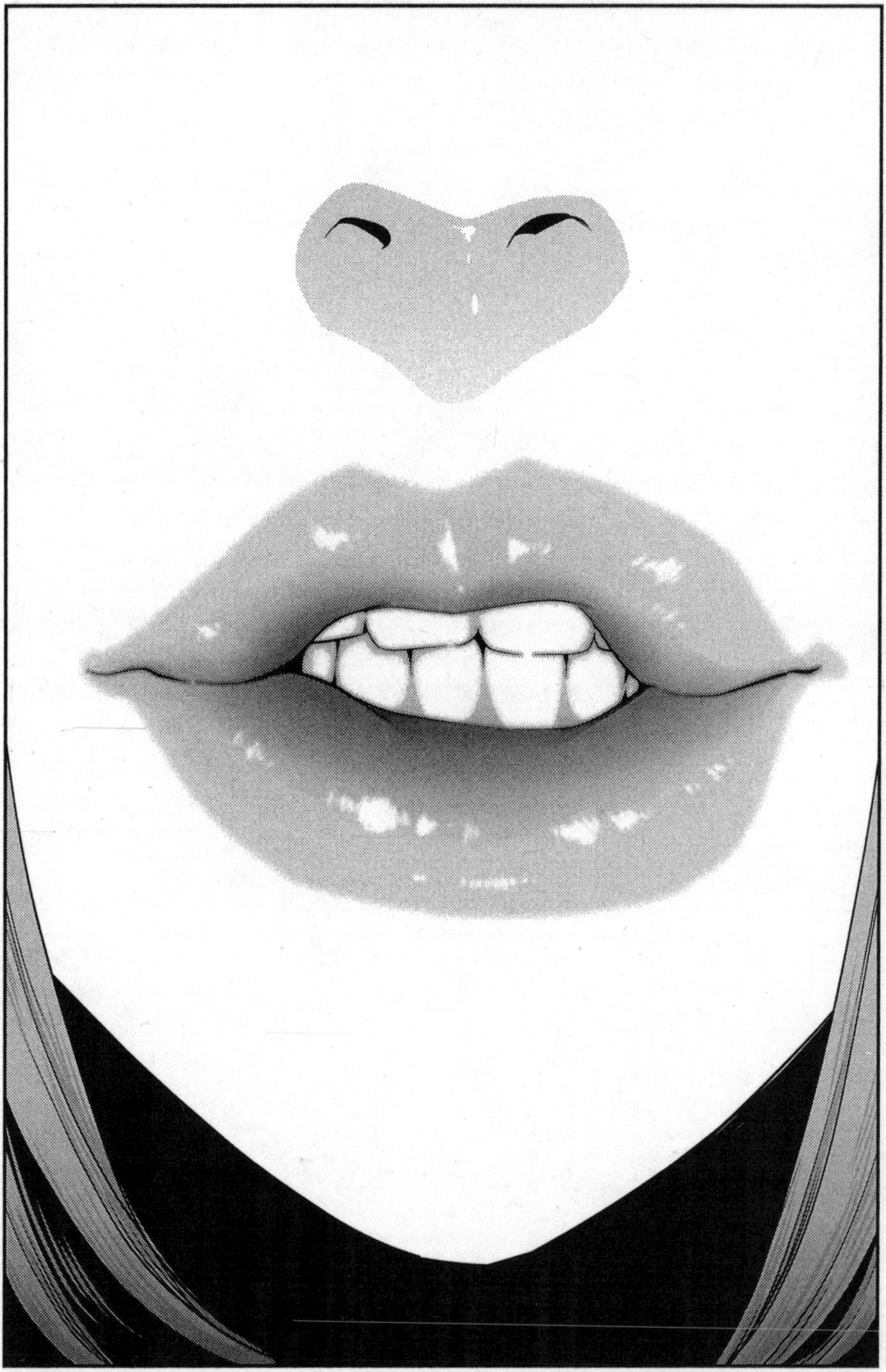

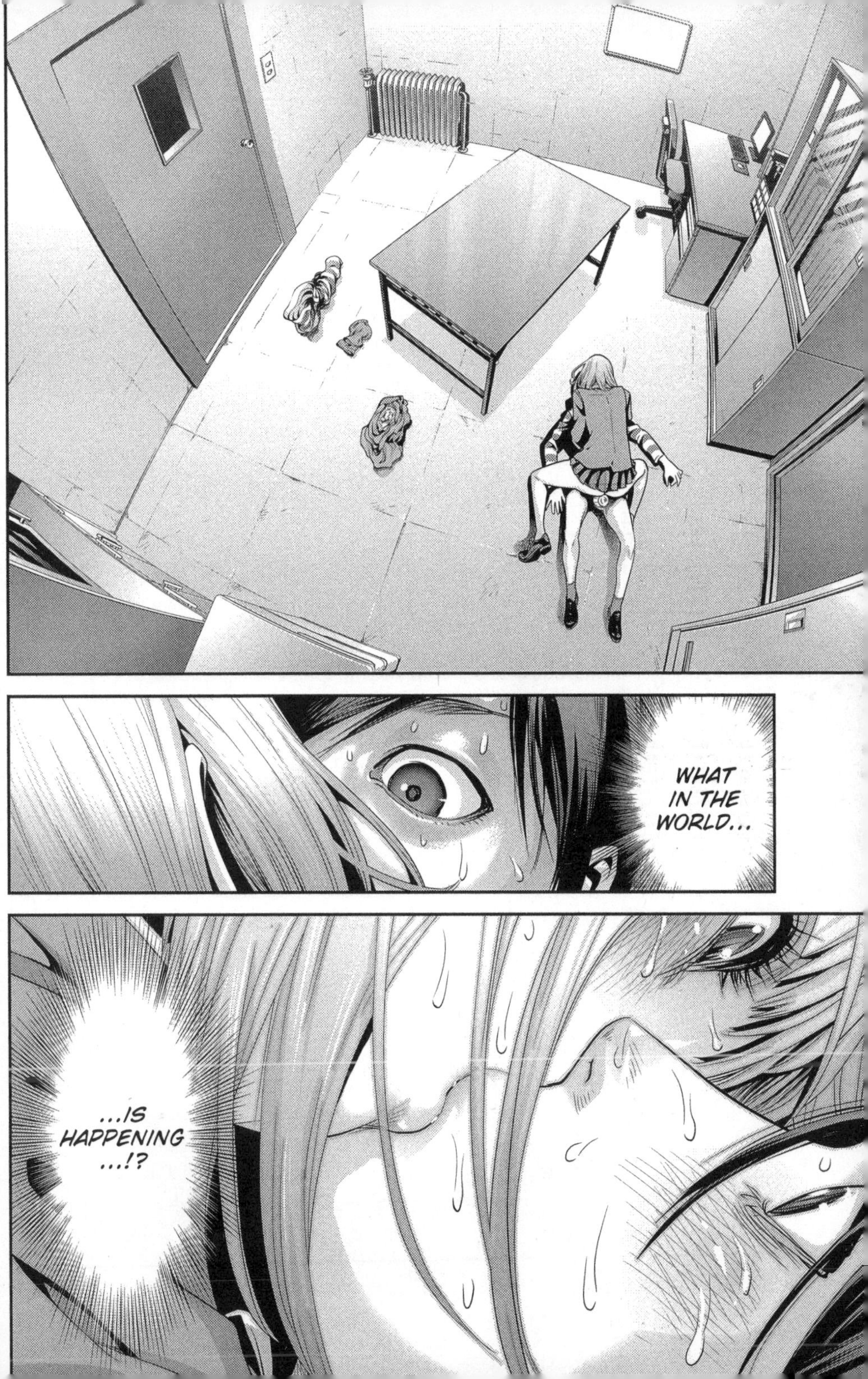
WHAT IN THE WORLD...
...IS HAPPENING ...!?

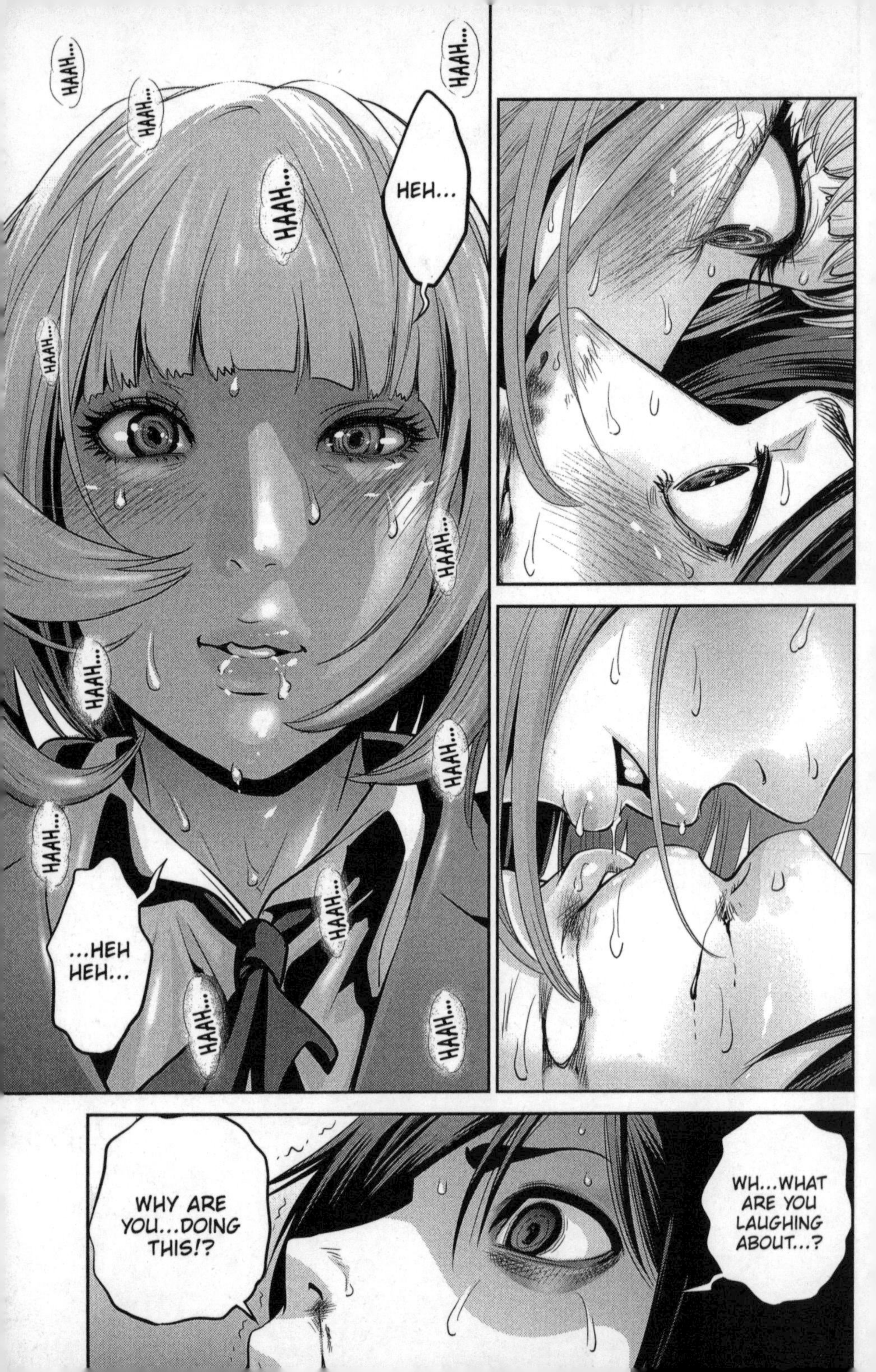
HAAH...
HEH...
HAAH...
HAAH...
HAAH...
HAAH...
HAAH...
HAAH...
HAAH...
HAAH...
HAAH...
HAAH...
...HEH HEH...
WH...WHAT ARE YOU LAUGHING ABOUT...?
WHY ARE YOU...DOING THIS!?

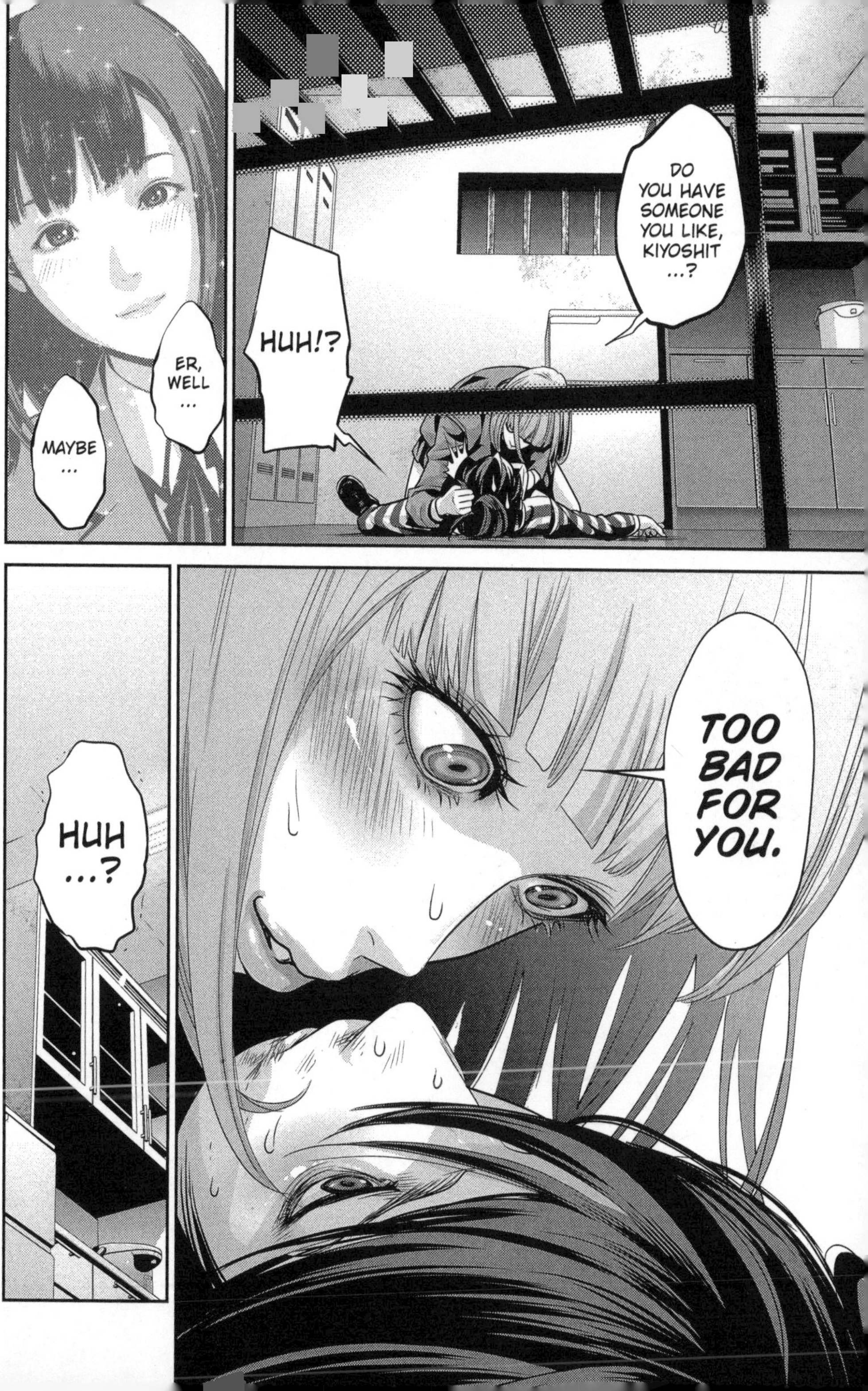
DO YOU HAVE SOMEONE YOU LIKE, KIYOSHIT ...?
HUH!?
ER, WELL ...
MAYBE ...
TOO BAD FOR YOU.
HUH ...?

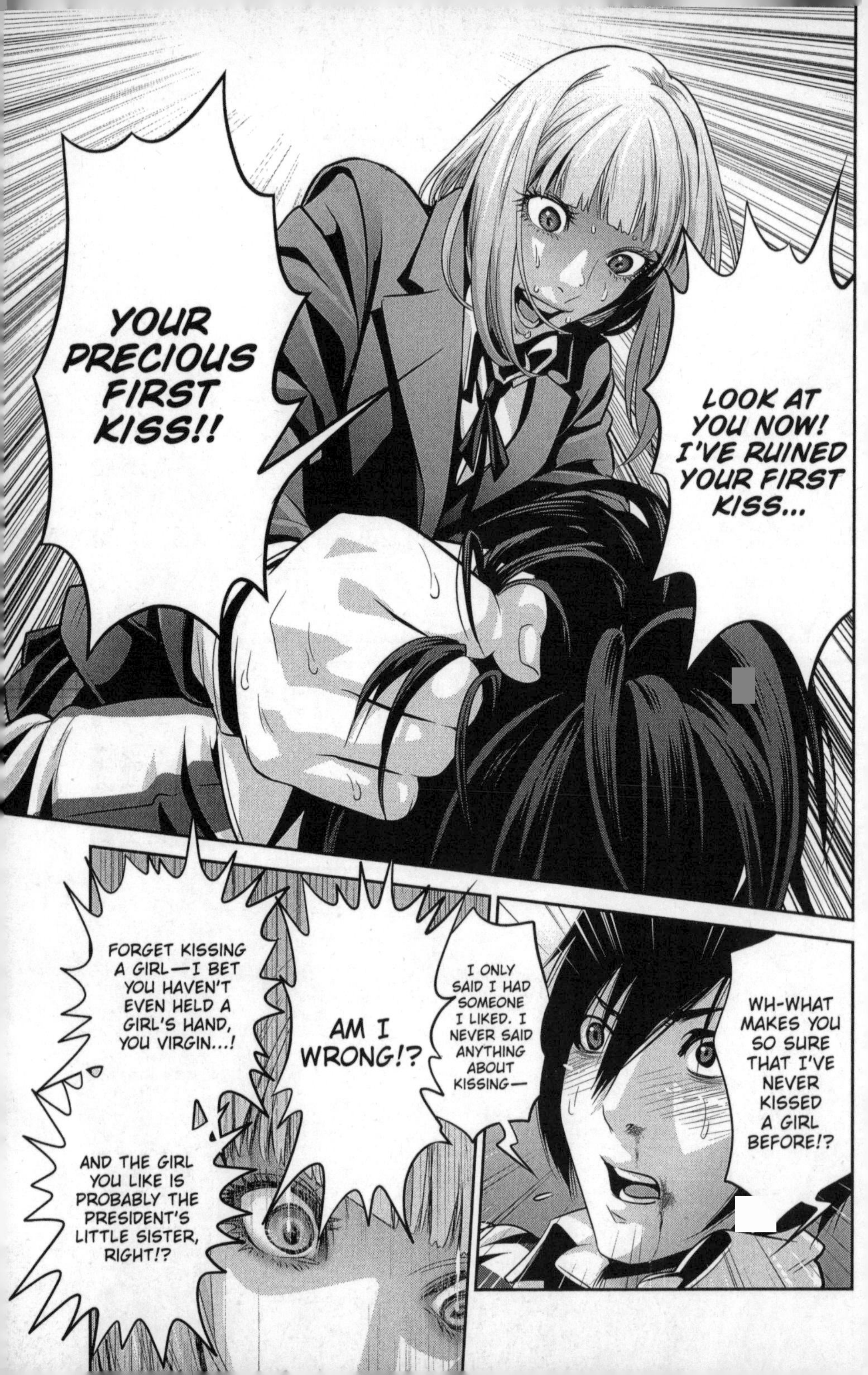
LOOK AT YOU NOW! I'VE RUINED YOUR FIRST KISS...
YOUR PRECIOUS FIRST KISS!!
WH-WHAT MAKES YOU SO SURE THAT I'VE NEVER KISSED A GIRL BEFORE!?
I ONLY SAID I HAD SOMEONE I LIKED. I NEVER SAID ANYTHING ABOUT KISSING—
FORGET KISSING A GIRL—I BET YOU HAVEN'T EVEN HELD A GIRL'S HAND, YOU VIRGIN...!
AM I WRONG!?
AND THE GIRL YOU LIKE IS PROBABLY THE PRESIDENT'S LITTLE SISTER, RIGHT!?

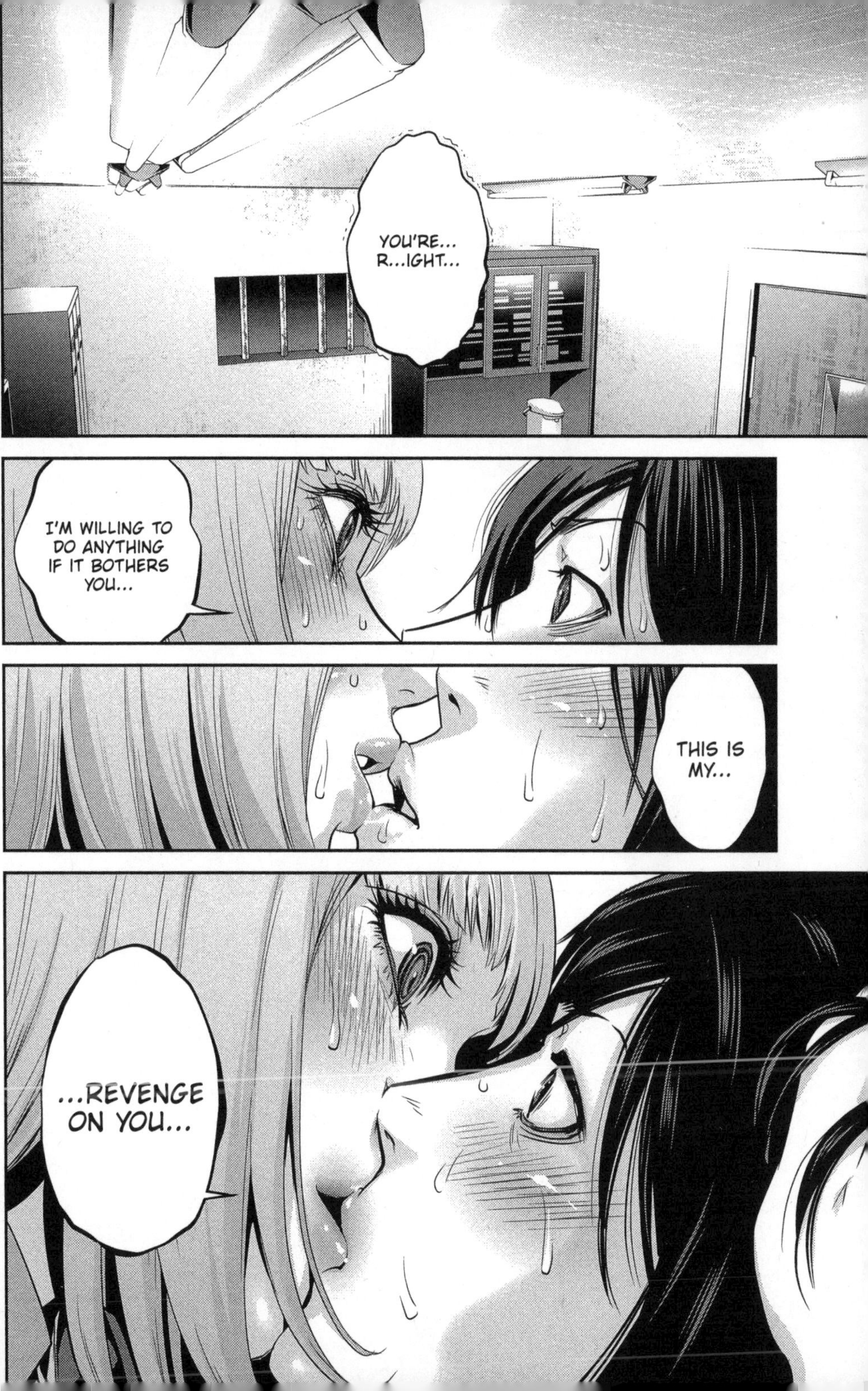
YOU'RE... R...IGHT...
I'M WILLING TO DO ANYTHING IF IT BOTHERS YOU...
THIS IS MY...
...REVENGE ON YOU...

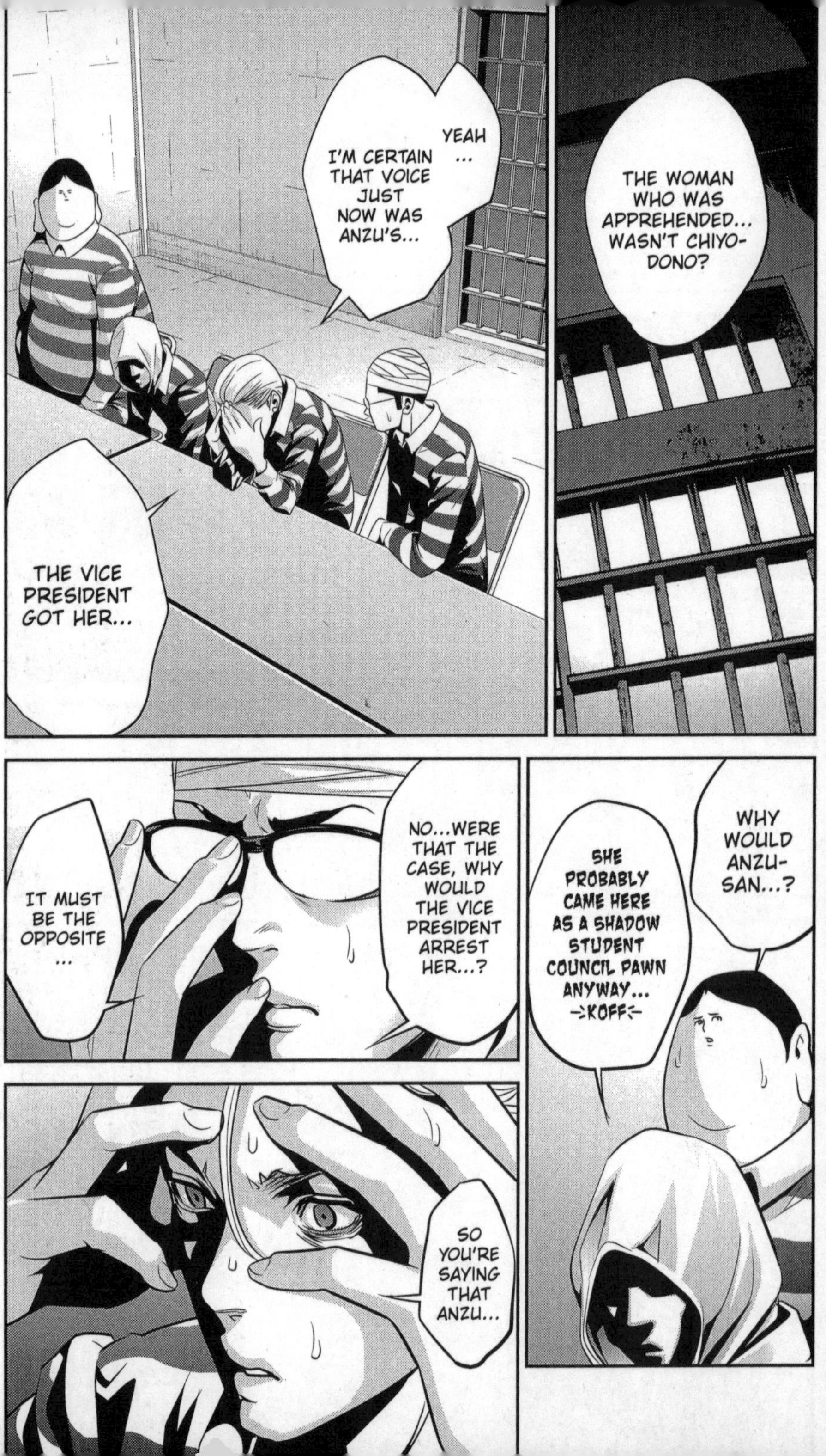
THE WOMAN WHO WAS APPREHENDED... WASN'T CHIYO-DONO?
YEAH ...
I'M CERTAIN THAT VOICE JUST NOW WAS ANZU'S...
THE VICE PRESIDENT GOT HER...
WHY WOULD ANZU-SAN...?
SHE PROBABLY CAME HERE AS A SHADOW STUDENT COUNCIL PAWN ANYWAY... -KOFF-
NO...WERE THAT THE CASE, WHY WOULD THE VICE PRESIDENT ARREST HER...?
IT MUST BE THE OPPOSITE ...
SO YOU'RE SAYING THAT ANZU...

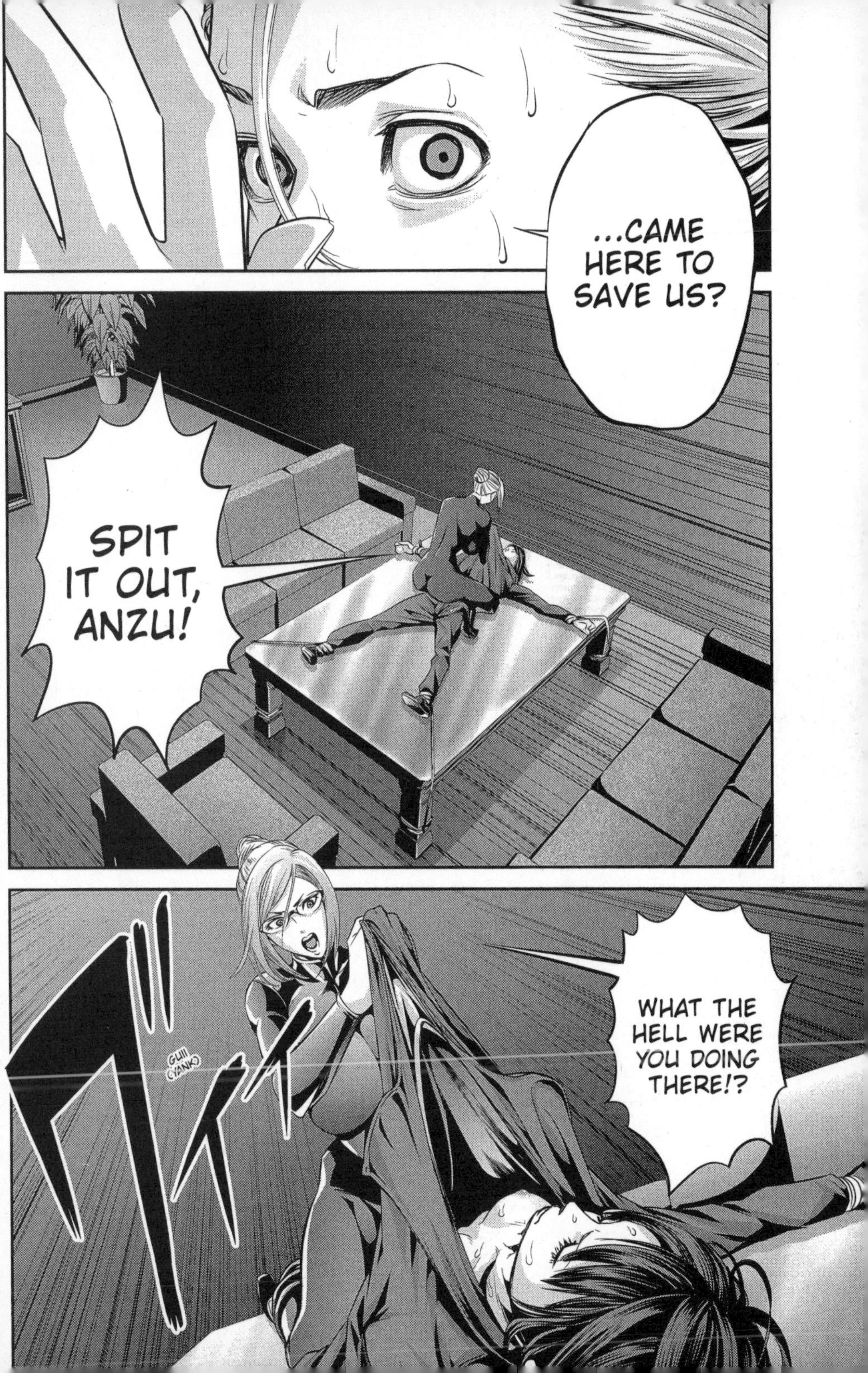
...CAME HERE TO SAVE US?
SPIT IT OUT, ANZU!
WHAT THE HELL WERE YOU DOING THERE!?
GUII (YANK)

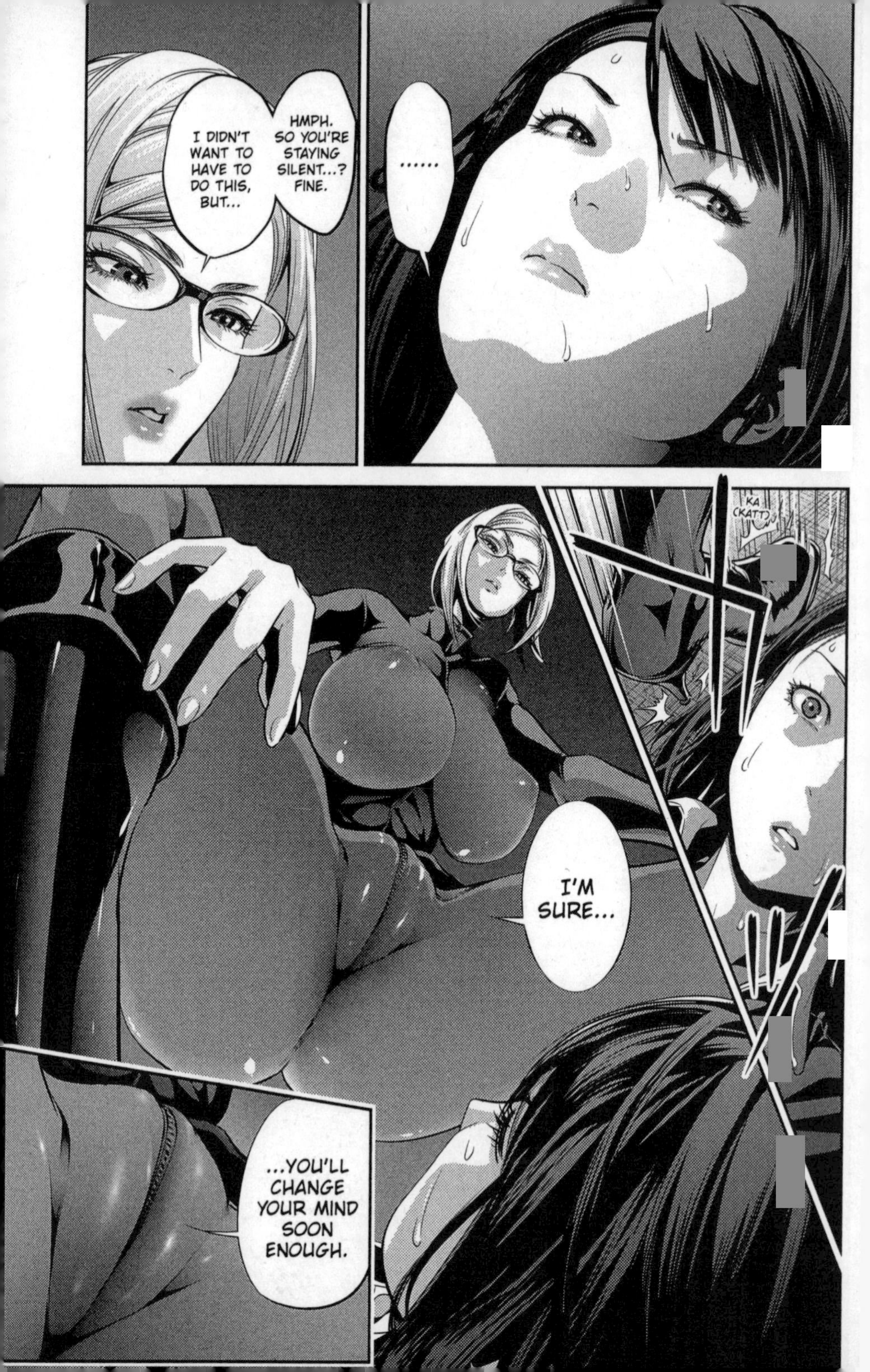
......
HMPH. SO YOU'RE STAYING SILENT...? FINE.
I DIDN'T WANT TO HAVE TO DO THIS, BUT...
KA CKATT
I'M SURE...
...YOU'LL CHANGE YOUR MIND SOON ENOUGH.

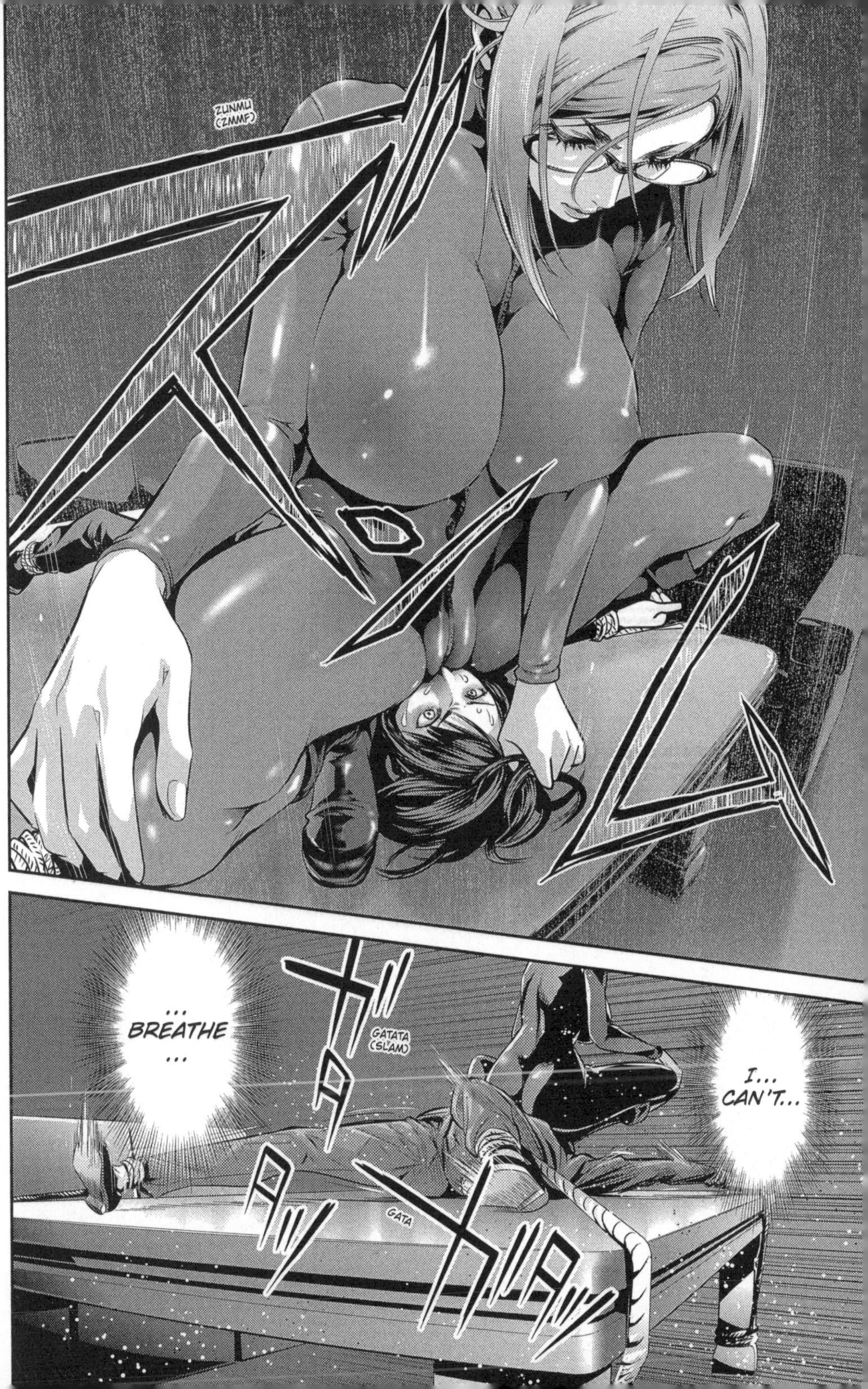
ZUNMU (ZMMF)
I... CAN'T...
GATATA (SLAM)
... BREATHE ...
GATA

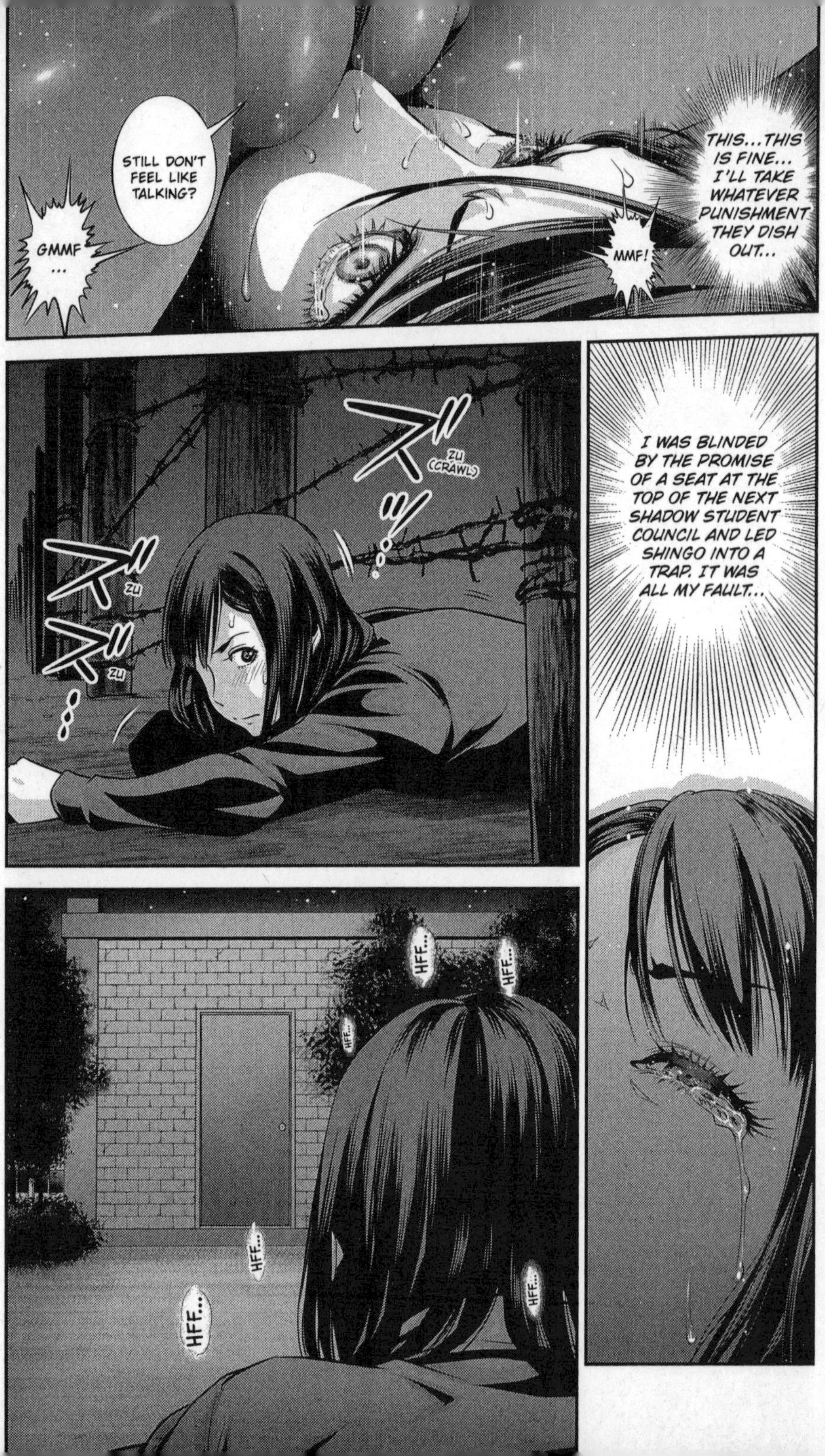
THIS...THIS IS FINE... I'LL TAKE WHATEVER PUNISHMENT THEY DISH OUT...
MMF!
STILL DON'T FEEL LIKE TALKING?
GMMF ...
I WAS BLINDED BY THE PROMISE OF A SEAT AT THE TOP OF THE NEXT SHADOW STUDENT COUNCIL AND LED SHINGO INTO A TRAP. IT WAS ALL MY FAULT...
ZU (CRAWL)
ZU
ZU
HFF...
HFF...
HFF...
HFF...
HFF...
HFF...

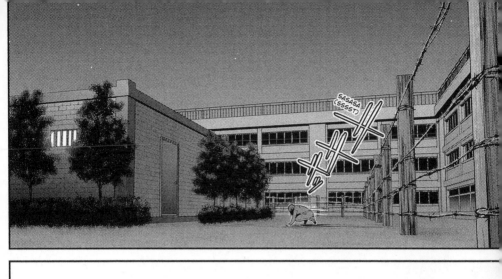

SASASA
(SSSST)

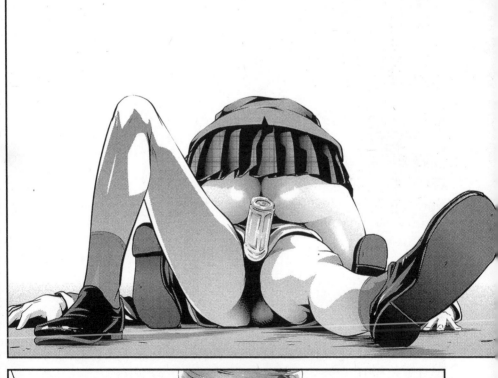

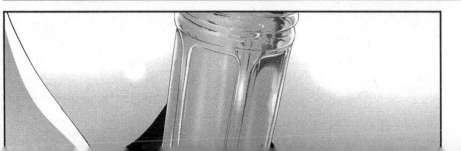

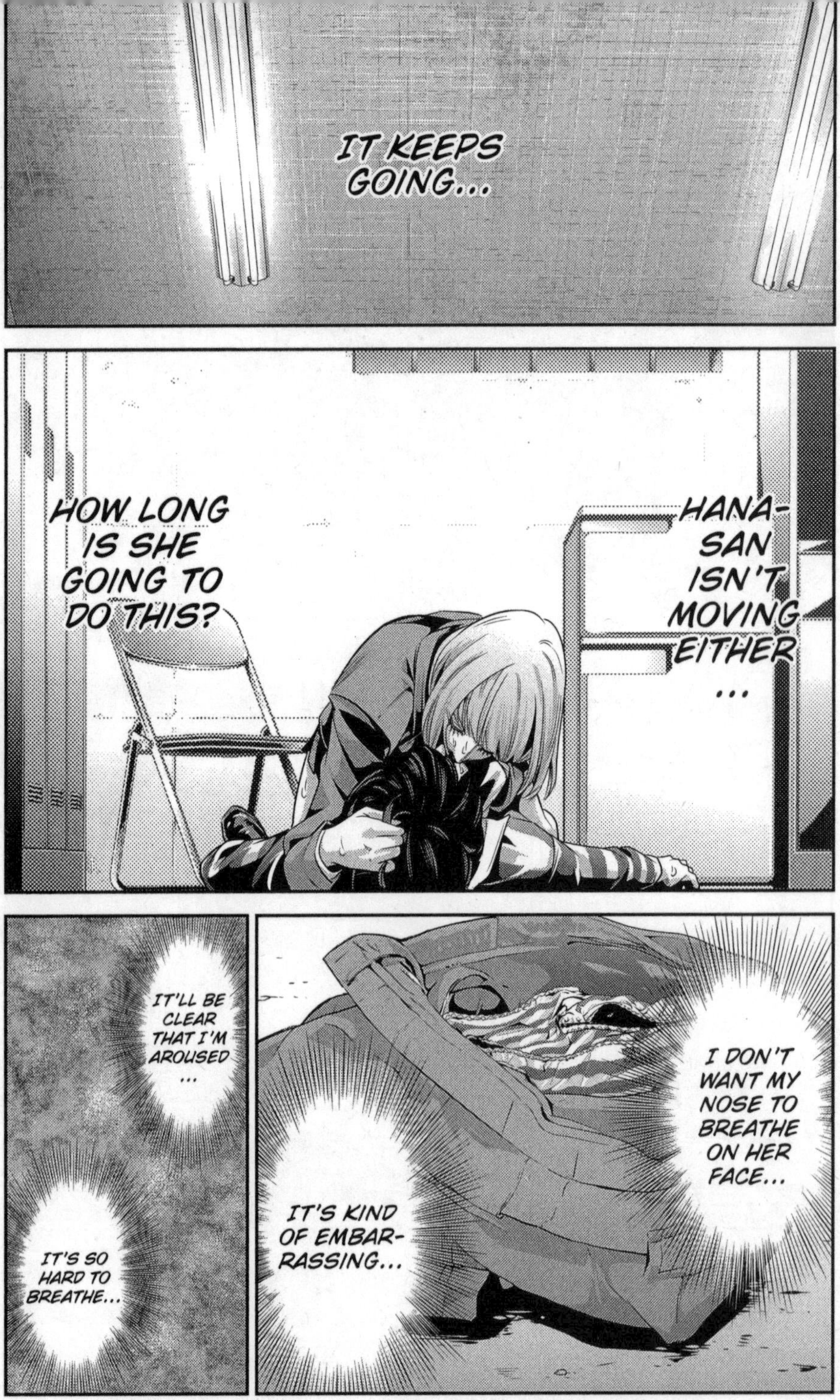
IT KEEPS GOING...
HANA-SAN ISN'T MOVING EITHER...
HOW LONG IS SHE GOING TO DO THIS?
I DON'T WANT MY NOSE TO BREATHE ON HER FACE...
IT'S KIND OF EMBARRASSING...
IT'LL BE CLEAR THAT I'M AROUSED...
IT'S SO HARD TO BREATHE...

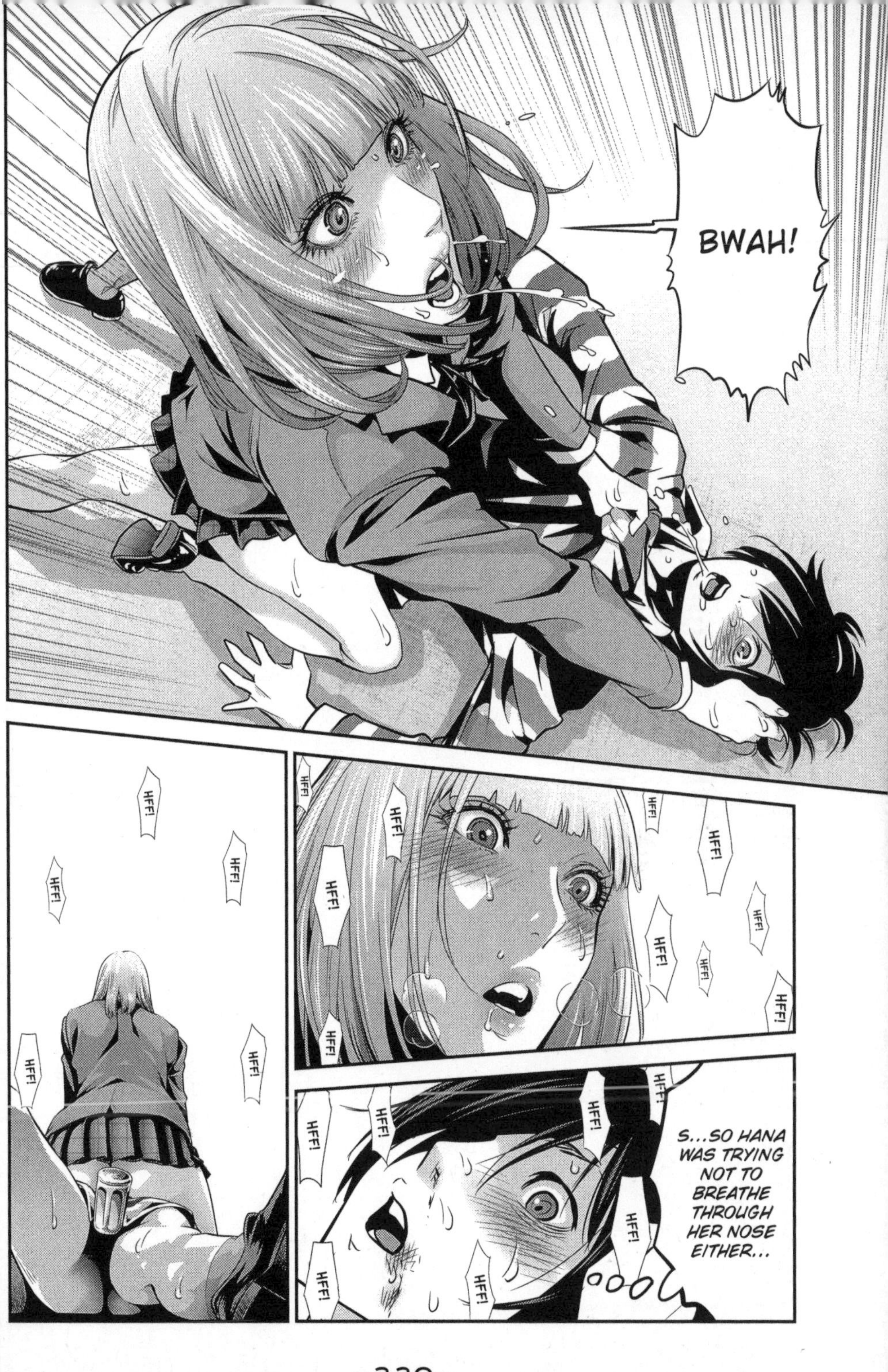
BWAH!
HFF!
HFF!
HFF!
HFF!
HFF!
HFF!
HFF!
HFF!
HFF!
HFF!
HFF!
HFF!
HFF!
S...SO HANA WAS TRYING NOT TO BREATHE THROUGH HER NOSE EITHER...
HFF!
HFF!
HFF!
HFF!
HFF!
HFF!
HFF!
HFF!
HFF!

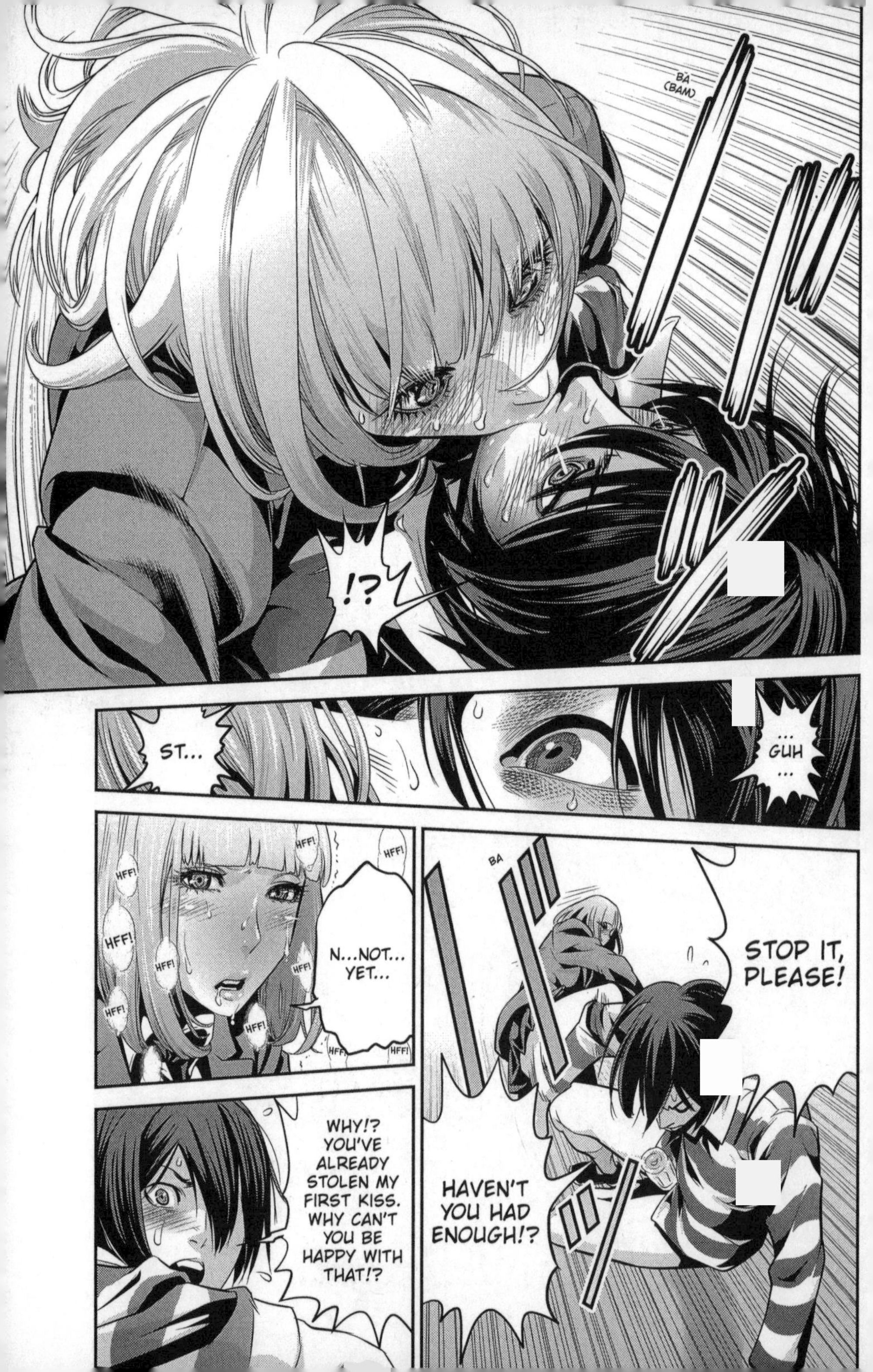
BA (BAM)
!?
...GUH...
ST...
BA
STOP IT, PLEASE!
HAVEN'T YOU HAD ENOUGH!?
HFF! HFF! HFF! HFF! HFF! HFF! HFF! HFF! HFF!
N...NOT... YET...
WHY!? YOU'VE ALREADY STOLEN MY FIRST KISS. WHY CAN'T YOU BE HAPPY WITH THAT!?

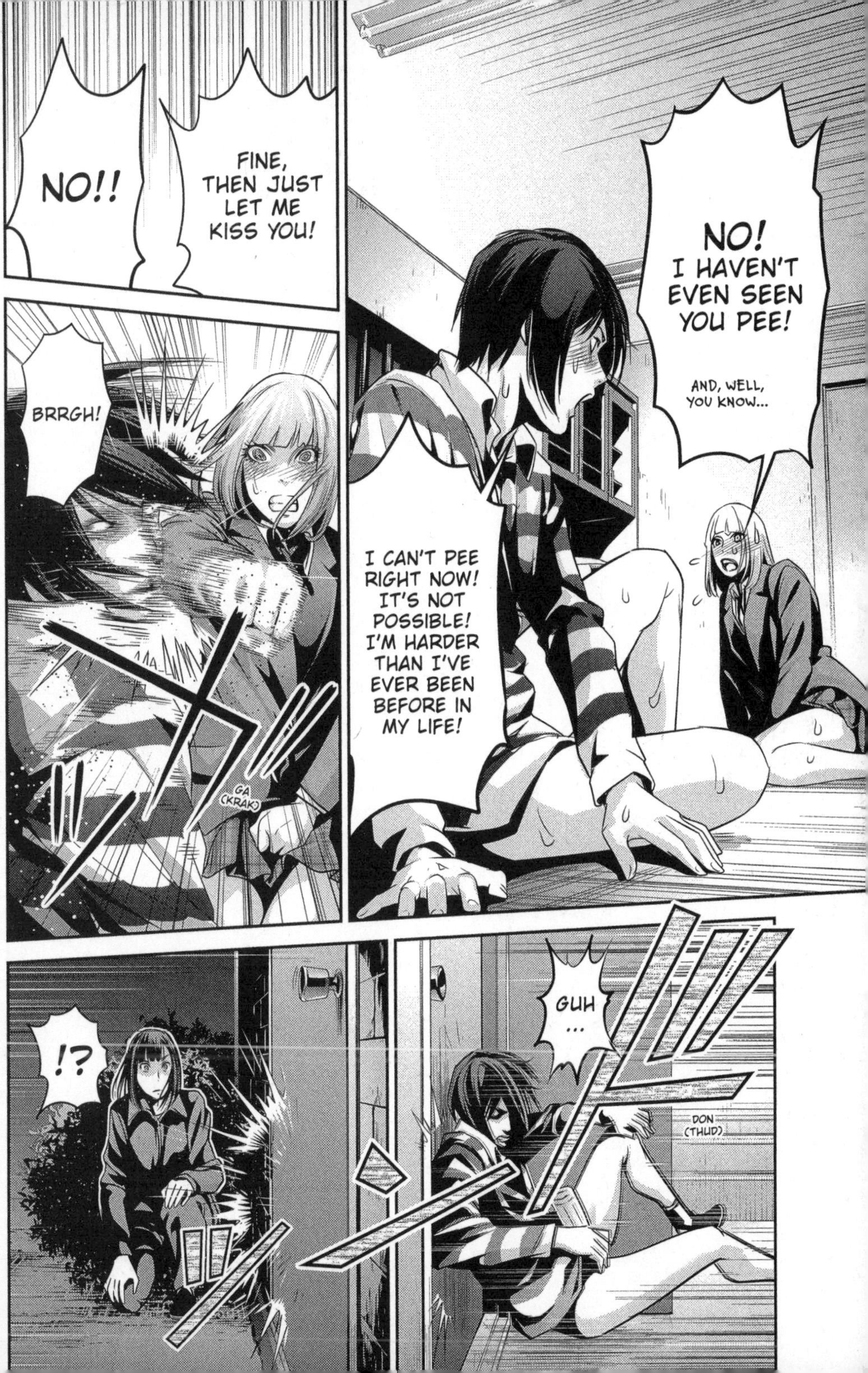
NO! I HAVEN'T EVEN SEEN YOU PEE!
AND, WELL, YOU KNOW...
I CAN'T PEE RIGHT NOW! IT'S NOT POSSIBLE! I'M HARDER THAN I'VE EVER BEEN BEFORE IN MY LIFE!
FINE, THEN JUST LET ME KISS YOU!
NO!!
BRRGH!
GA (KRAK)
GUH ...
DON (THUD)
!?

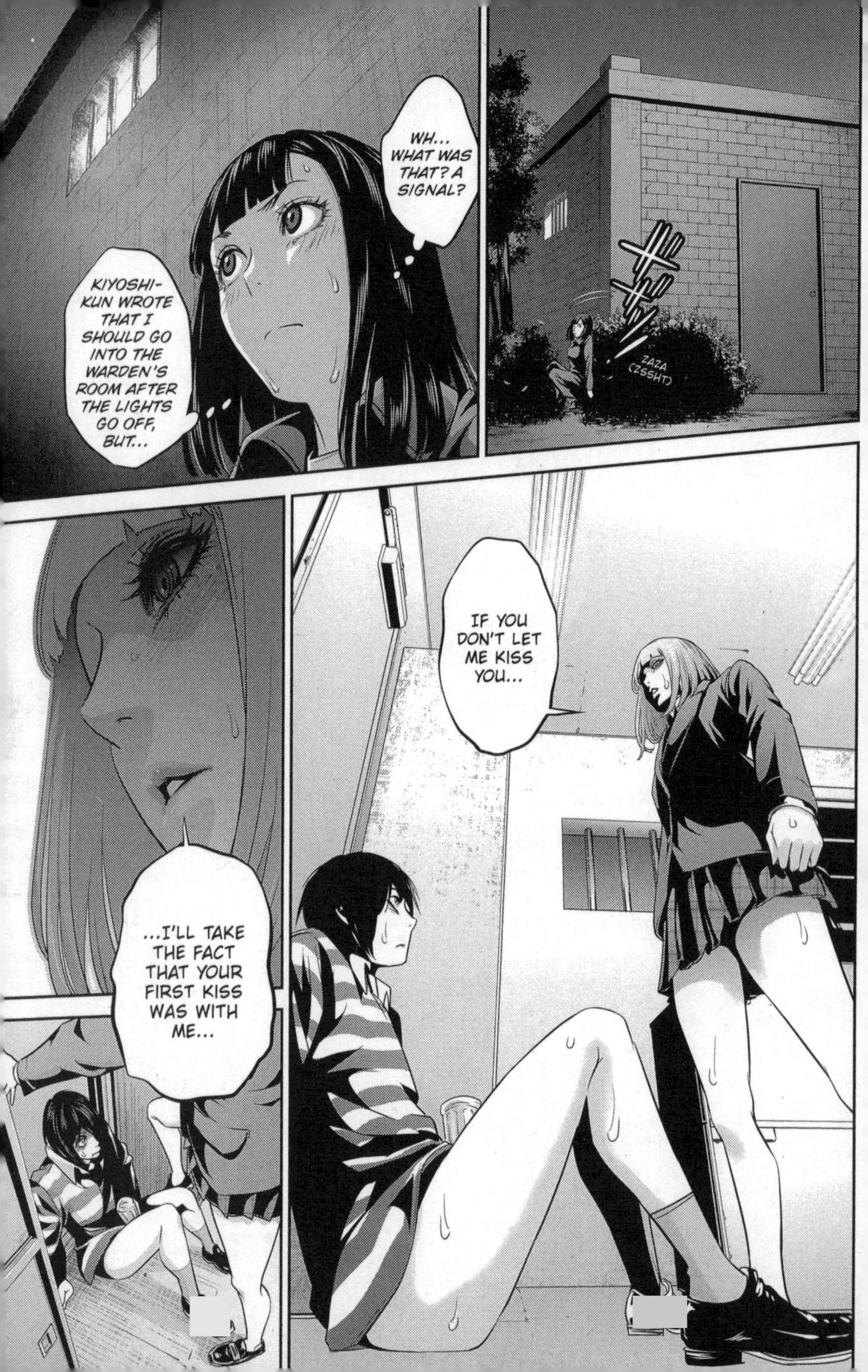
ZAZA (ZSSHT)
WH... WHAT WAS THAT? A SIGNAL?
KIYOSHI-KUN WROTE THAT I SHOULD GO INTO THE WARDEN'S ROOM AFTER THE LIGHTS GO OFF, BUT...
IF YOU DON'T LET ME KISS YOU...
...I'LL TAKE THE FACT THAT YOUR FIRST KISS WAS WITH ME...

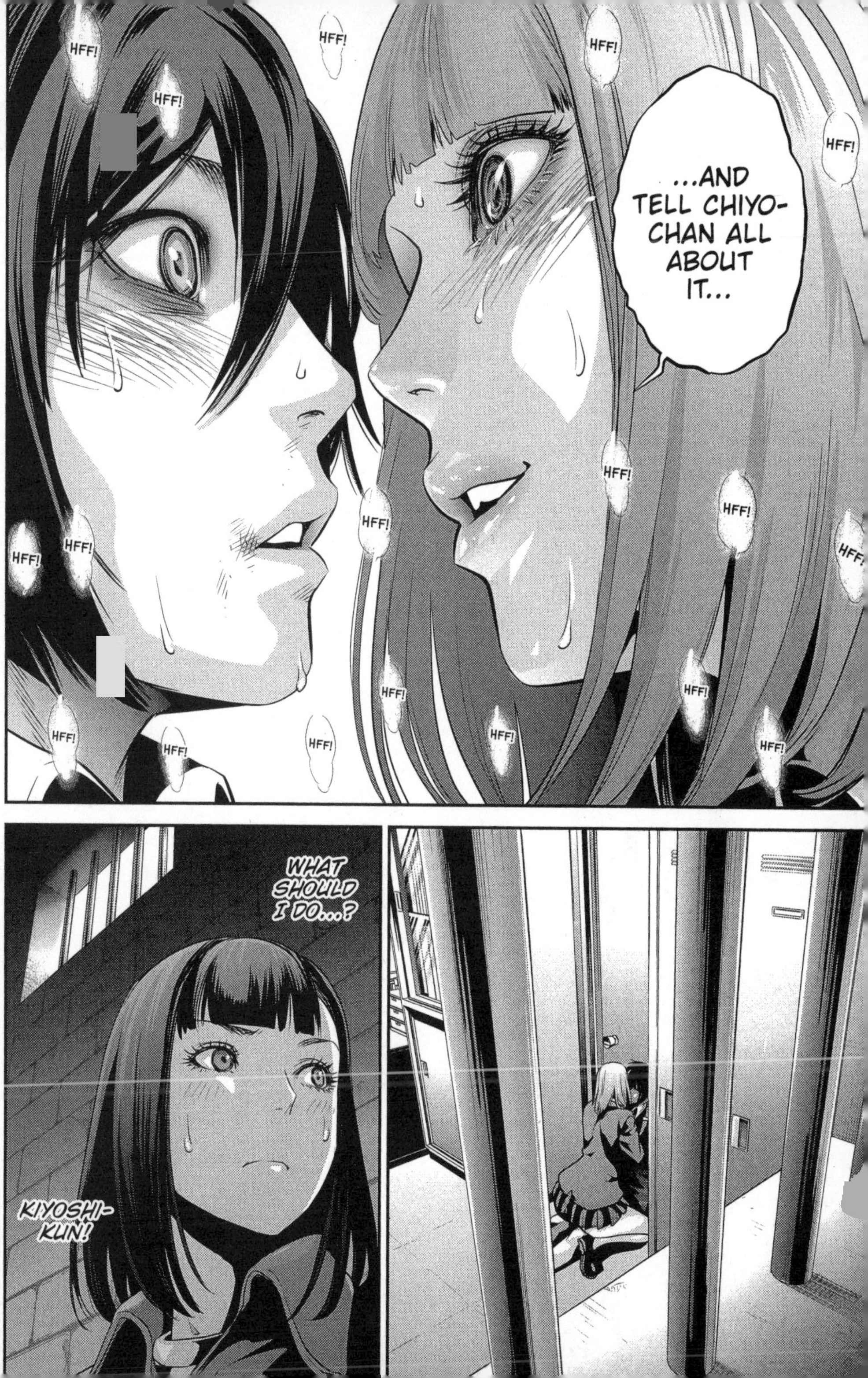
HFF!
HFF!
HFF!
...AND TELL CHIYO-CHAN ALL ABOUT IT...
HFF!
HFF!
HFF!
HFF!
HFF!
HFF!
HFF!
HFF!
HFF!
HFF!
HFF!
HFF!
HFF!
HFF!
HFF!
WHAT SHOULD I DO...?
KIYOSHI-KUN!

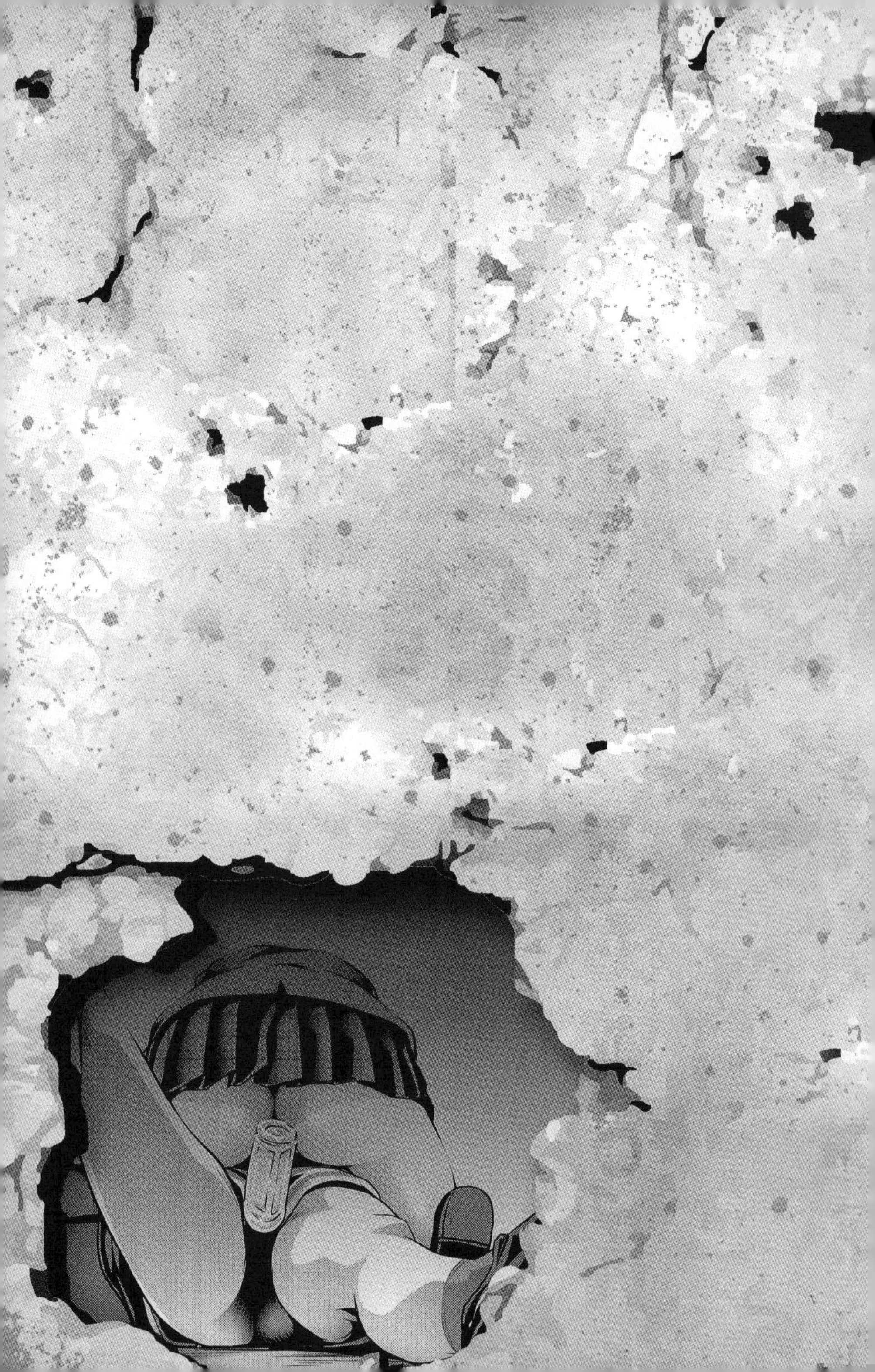

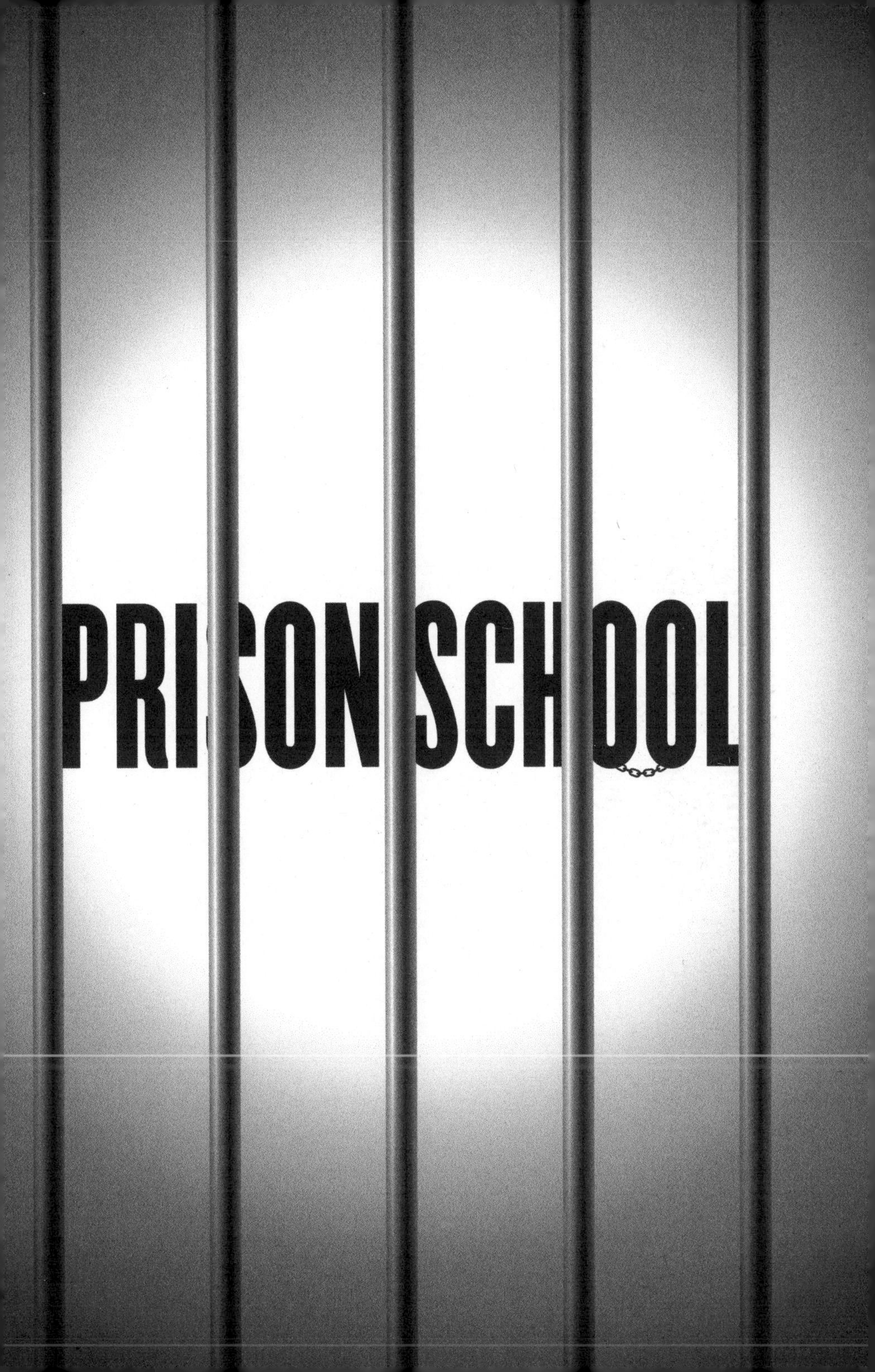
PRISON SCHOOL

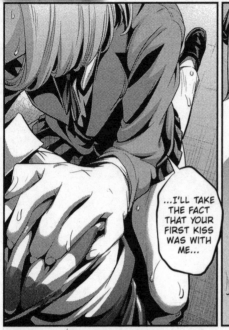

...I'LL TAKE THE FACT THAT YOUR FIRST KISS WAS WITH ME...

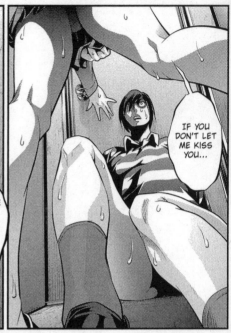

IF YOU DON'T LET ME KISS YOU...

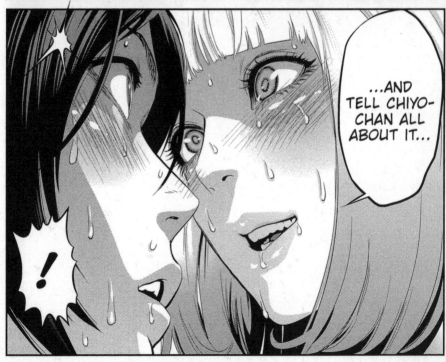

...AND TELL CHIYO-CHAN ALL ABOUT IT...

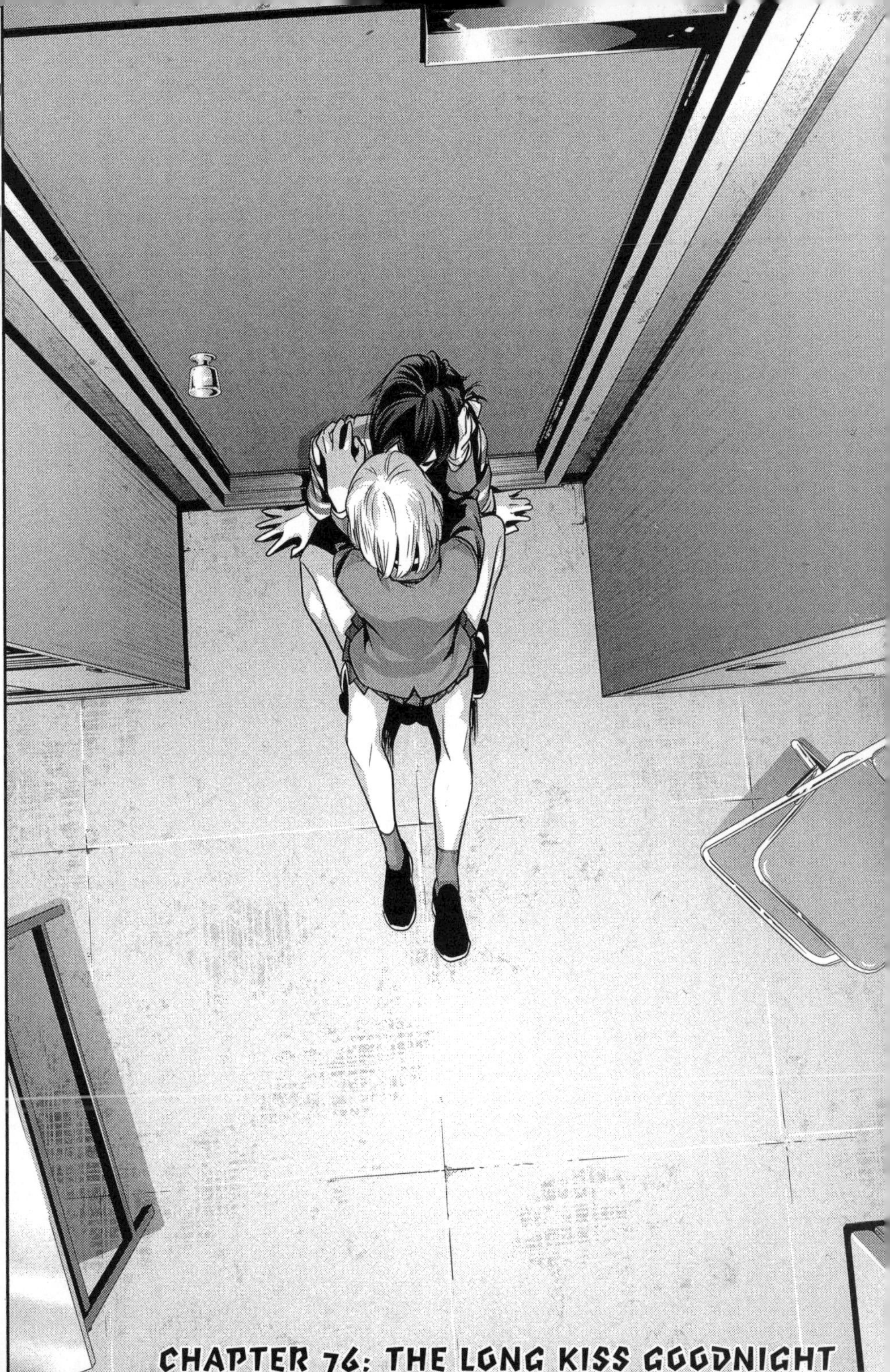

CHAPTER 76: THE LONG KISS GOODNIGHT

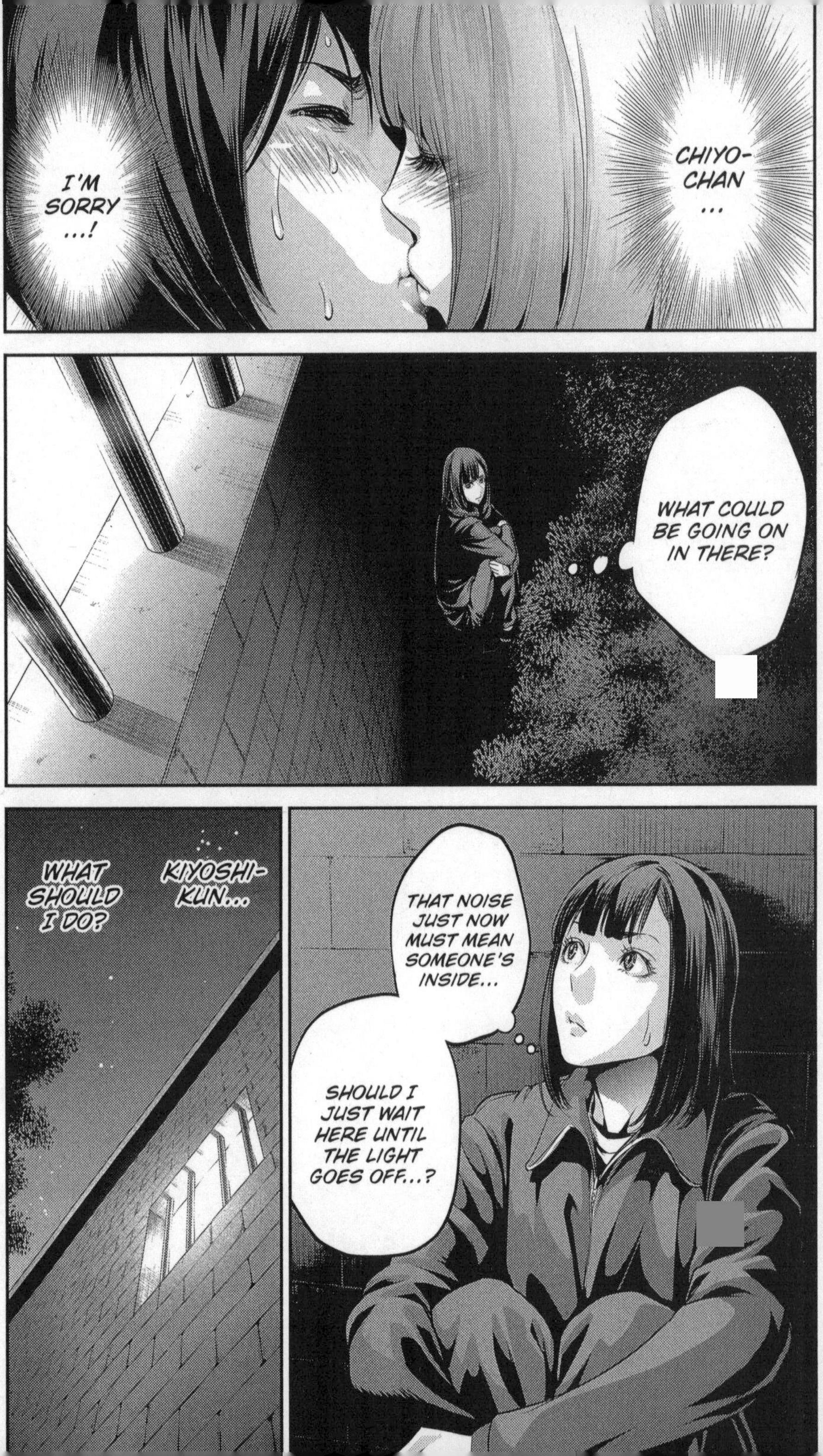
CHIYO-CHAN...
I'M SORRY...!
WHAT COULD BE GOING ON IN THERE?
THAT NOISE JUST NOW MUST MEAN SOMEONE'S INSIDE...
SHOULD I JUST WAIT HERE UNTIL THE LIGHT GOES OFF...?
KIYOSHI-KUN...
WHAT SHOULD I DO?

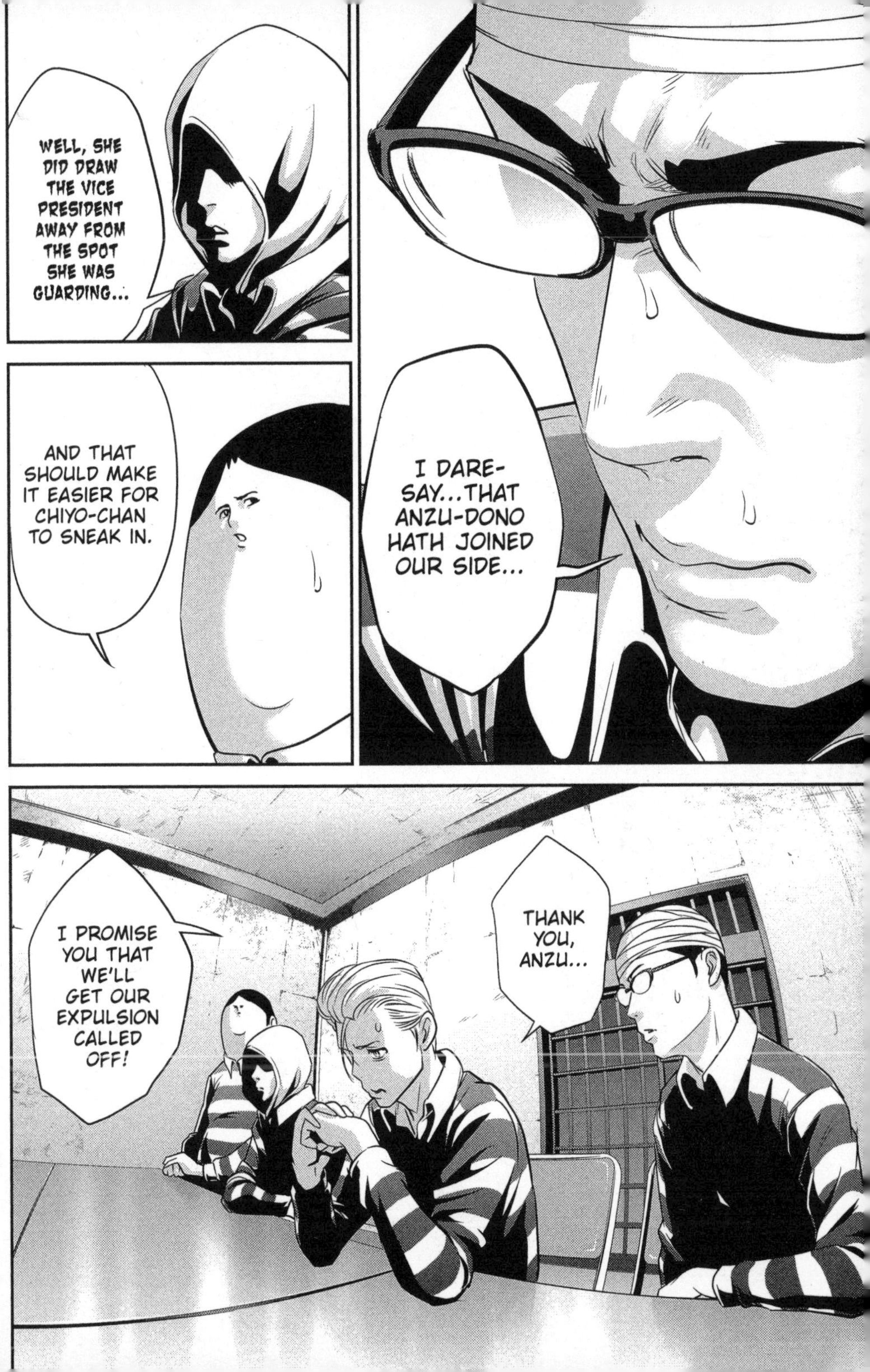
I DARE-SAY...THAT ANZU-DONO HATH JOINED OUR SIDE...
WELL, SHE DID DRAW THE VICE PRESIDENT AWAY FROM THE SPOT SHE WAS GUARDING...
AND THAT SHOULD MAKE IT EASIER FOR CHIYO-CHAN TO SNEAK IN.
THANK YOU, ANZU...
I PROMISE YOU THAT WE'LL GET OUR EXPULSION CALLED OFF!

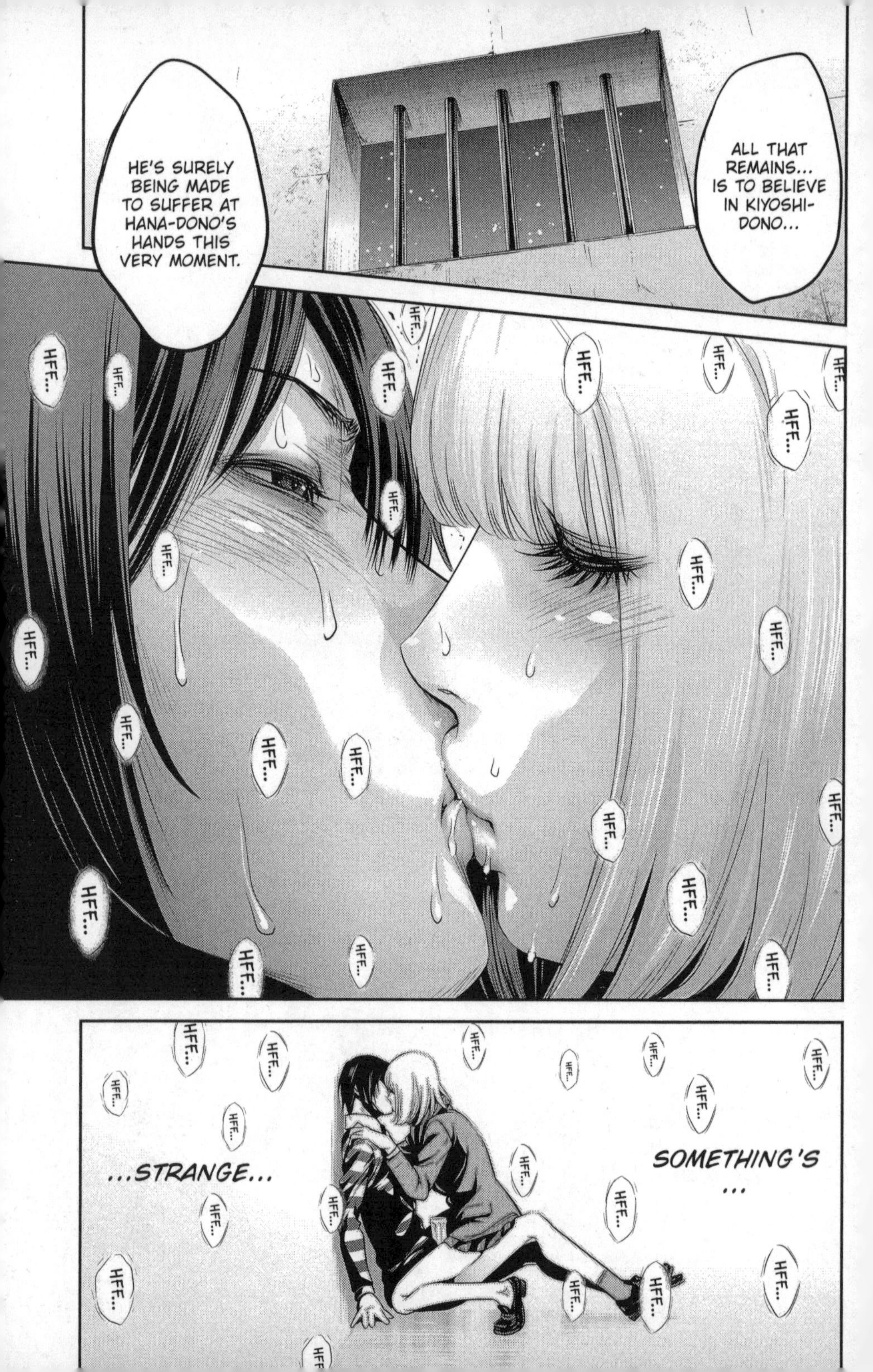
ALL THAT REMAINS... IS TO BELIEVE IN KIYOSHI-DONO...
HE'S SURELY BEING MADE TO SUFFER AT HANA-DONO'S HANDS THIS VERY MOMENT.
HFF...
HFF...
HFF...
HFF...
HFF...
HFF...
HFF...
HFF...
HFF...
HFF...
HFF...
HFF...
HFF...
HFF...
HFF...
HFF...
HFF...
HFF...
HFF...
HFF...
HFF...
HFF...
HFF...
SOMETHING'S ...
...STRANGE...
HFF...
HFF...
HFF...
HFF...
HFF...
HFF...
HFF...
HFF...
HFF...
HFF...
HFF...
HFF...
HFF...
HFF...
HFF...
HFF...
HFF...
HFF...

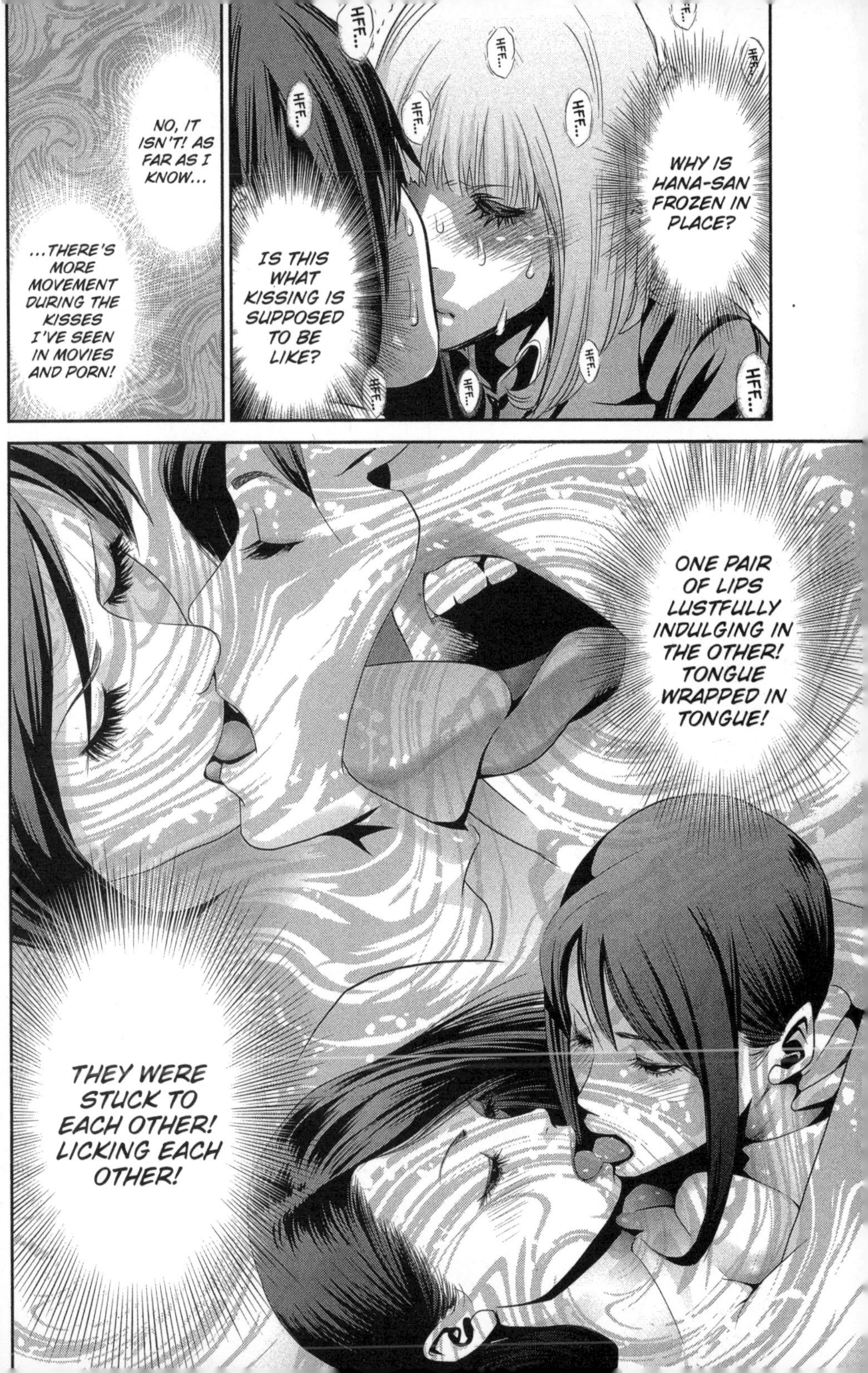
HFF...
HFF...
HFF...
WHY IS HANA-SAN FROZEN IN PLACE?
HFF...
HFF...
HFF...
IS THIS WHAT KISSING IS SUPPOSED TO BE LIKE?
HFF...
HFF...
HFF...
HFF...
NO, IT ISN'T! AS FAR AS I KNOW...
...THERE'S MORE MOVEMENT DURING THE KISSES I'VE SEEN IN MOVIES AND PORN!
ONE PAIR OF LIPS LUSTFULLY INDULGING IN THE OTHER! TONGUE WRAPPED IN TONGUE!
THEY WERE STUCK TO EACH OTHER! LICKING EACH OTHER!

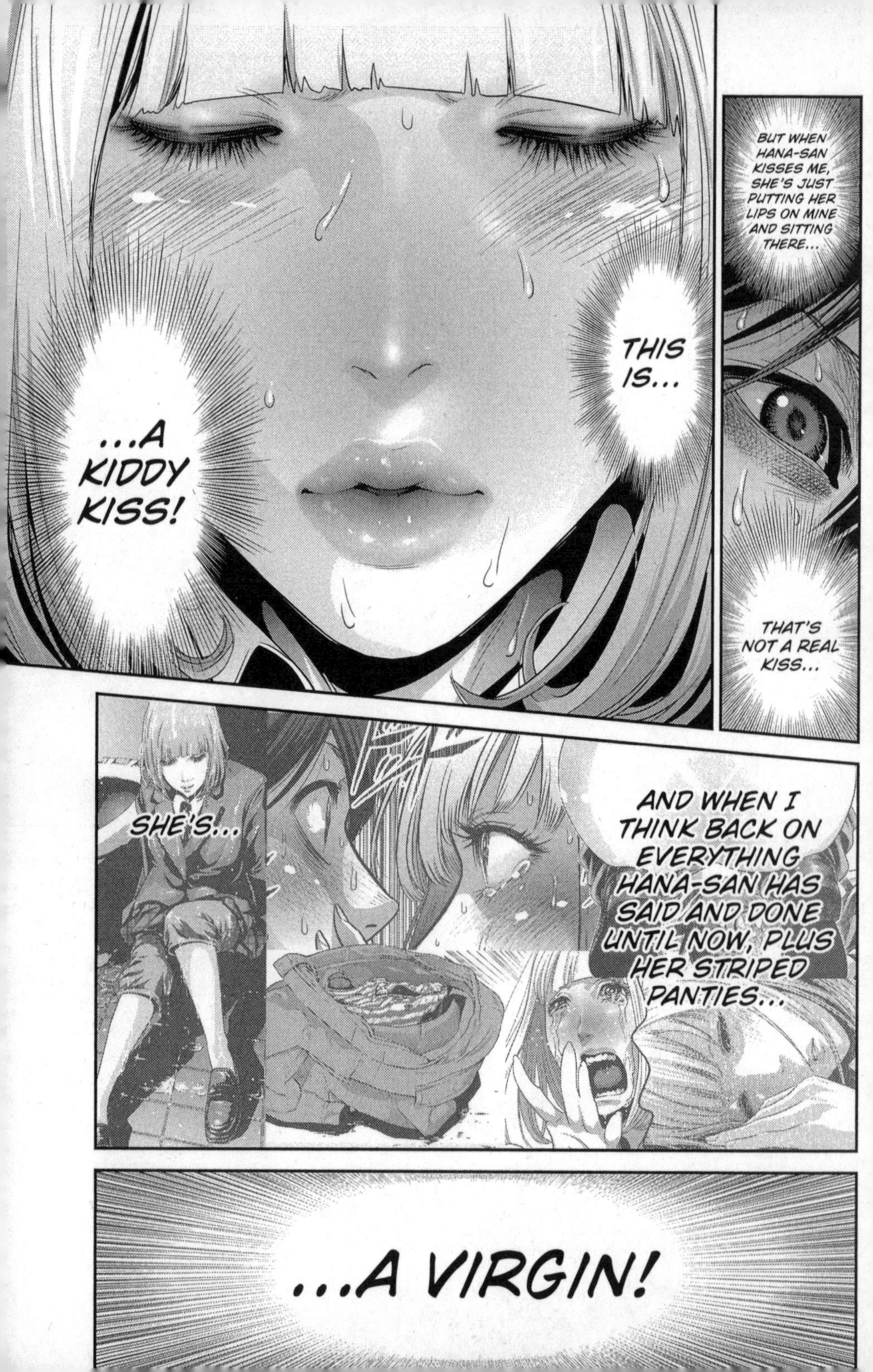
BUT WHEN HANA-SAN KISSES ME, SHE'S JUST PUTTING HER LIPS ON MINE AND SITTING THERE...
THAT'S NOT A REAL KISS...
THIS IS...
...A KIDDY KISS!
AND WHEN I THINK BACK ON EVERYTHING HANA-SAN HAS SAID AND DONE UNTIL NOW, PLUS HER STRIPED PANTIES...
SHE'S...
...A VIRGIN!

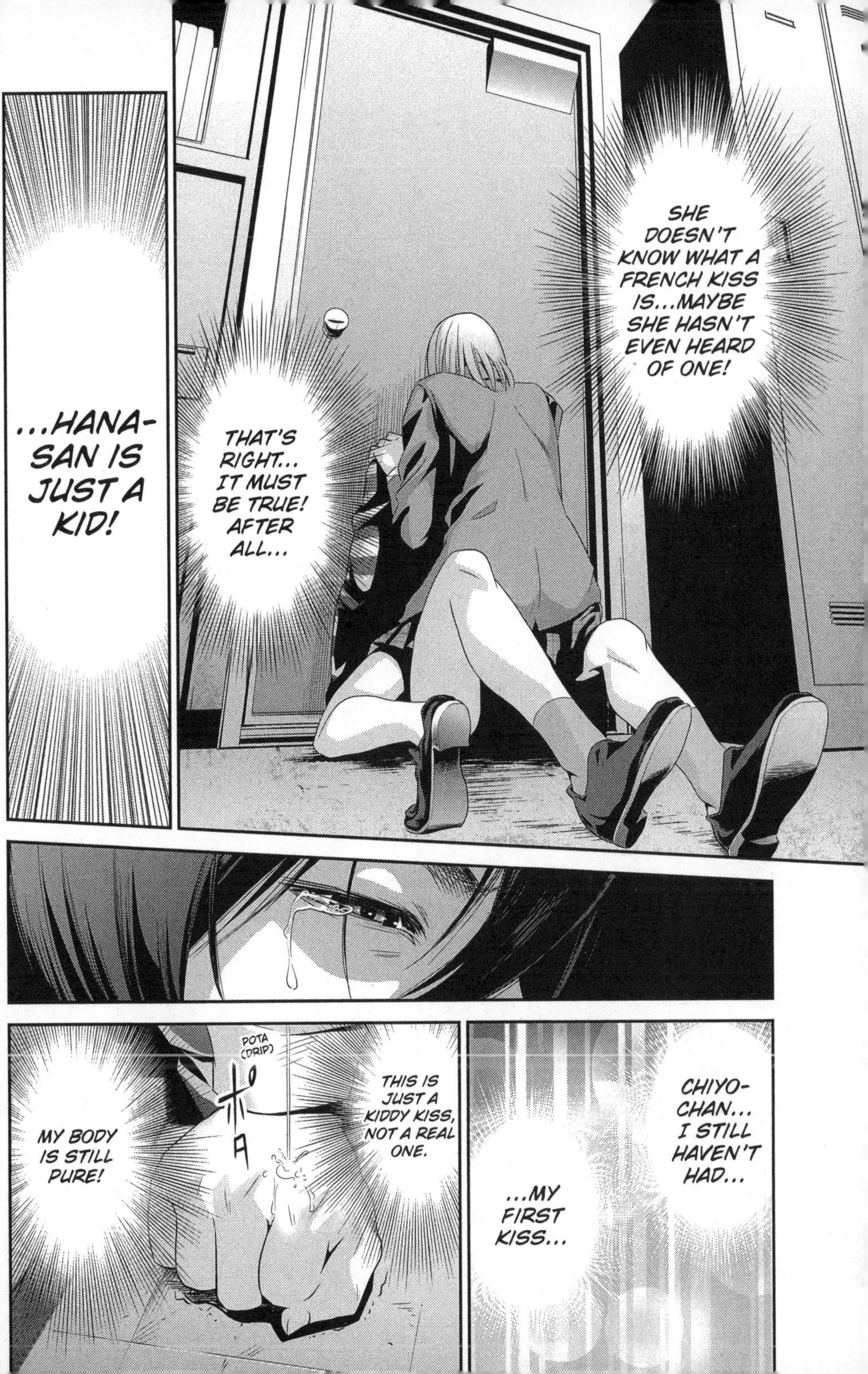
SHE DOESN'T KNOW WHAT A FRENCH KISS IS...MAYBE SHE HASN'T EVEN HEARD OF ONE!
THAT'S RIGHT... IT MUST BE TRUE! AFTER ALL...
...HANA-SAN IS JUST A KID!
CHIYO-CHAN... I STILL HAVEN'T HAD...
...MY FIRST KISS...
POTA (DRIP)
THIS IS JUST A KIDDY KISS, NOT A REAL ONE.
MY BODY IS STILL PURE!

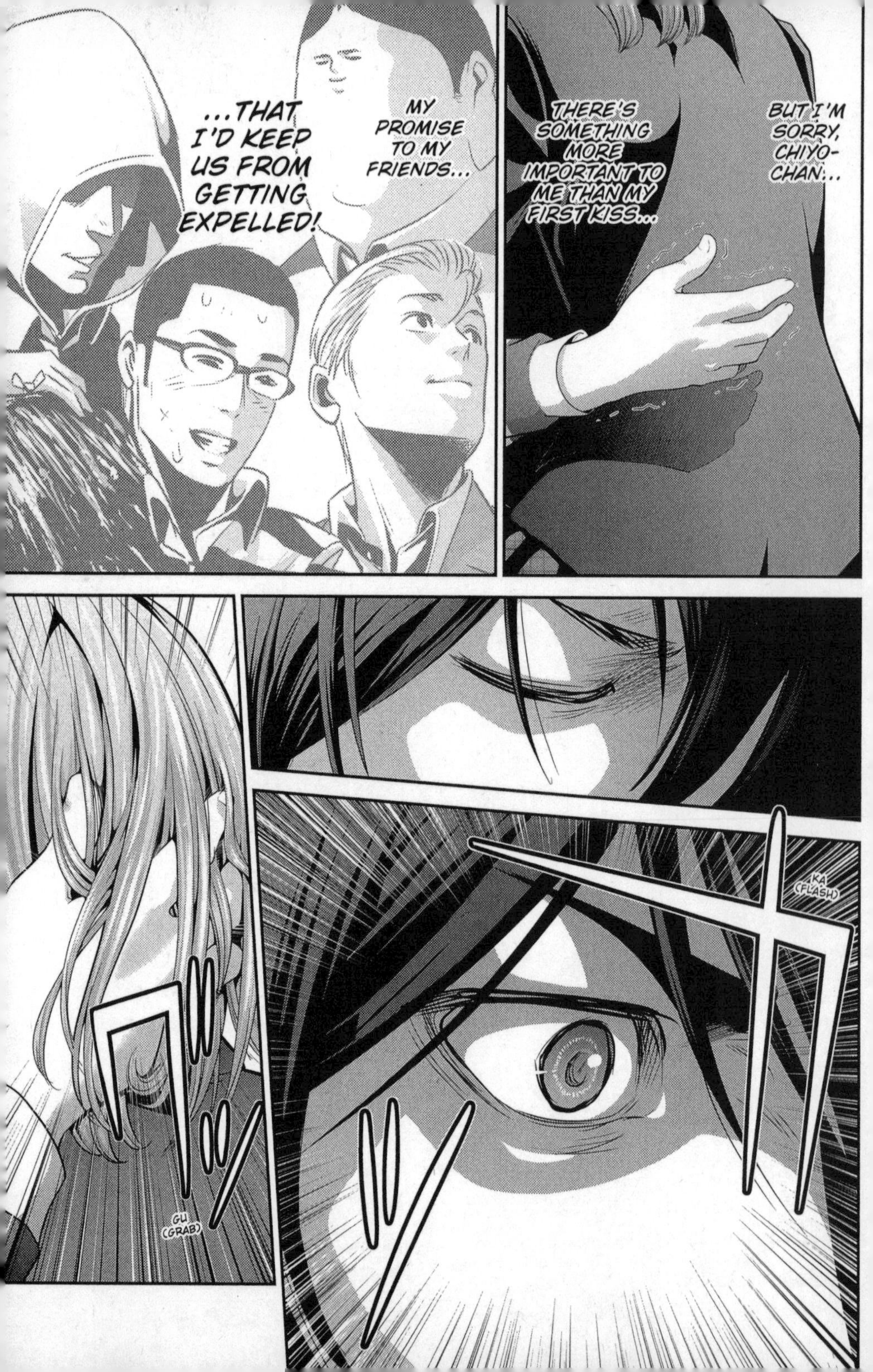
BUT I'M SORRY, CHIYO-CHAN...
THERE'S SOMETHING MORE IMPORTANT TO ME THAN MY FIRST KISS...
MY PROMISE TO MY FRIENDS...
...THAT I'D KEEP US FROM GETTING EXPELLED!
KA (FLASH)
GU (GRAB)

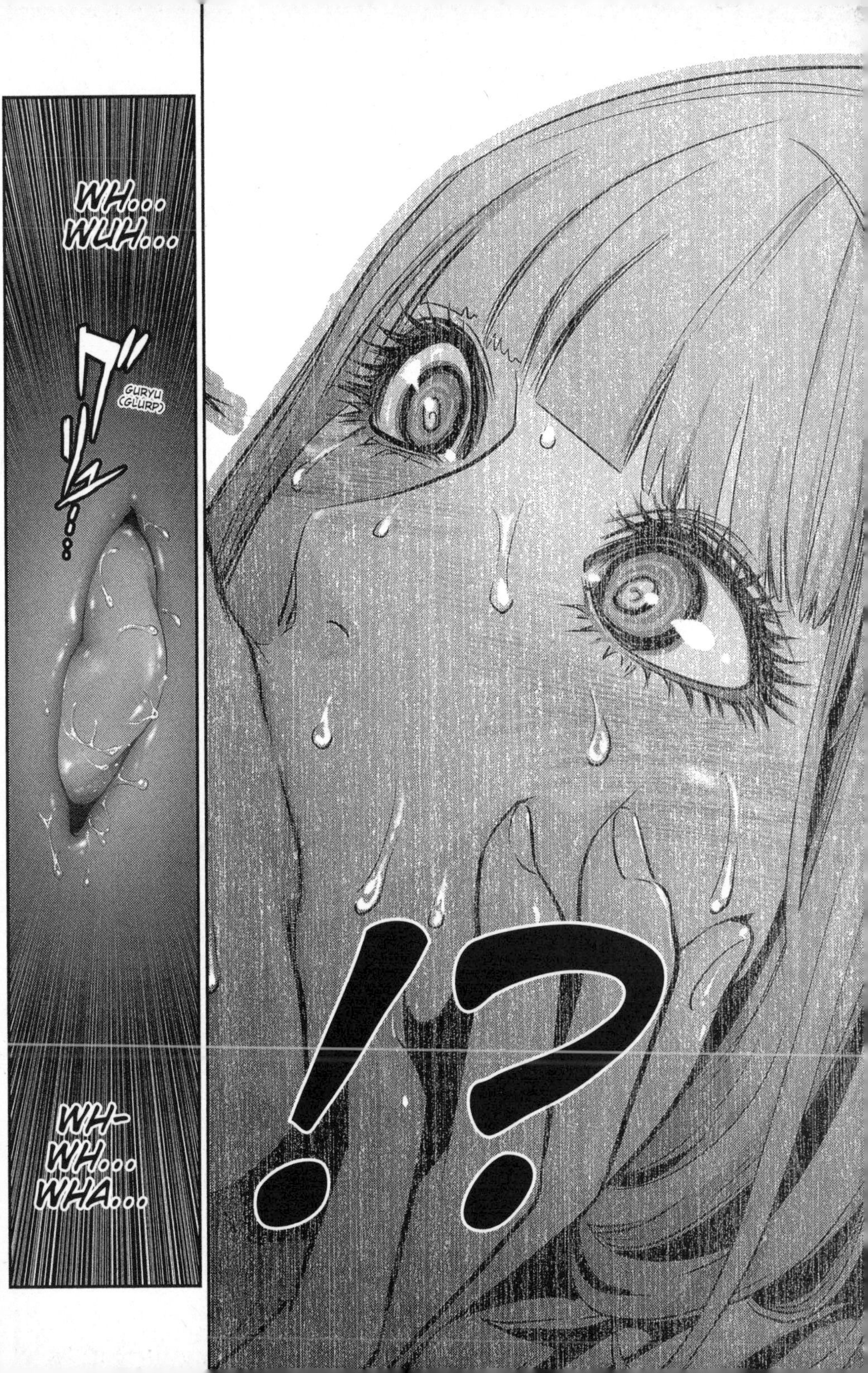
!?
WH... WUH...
GURYU (GLURP)
WH- WH... WHA...

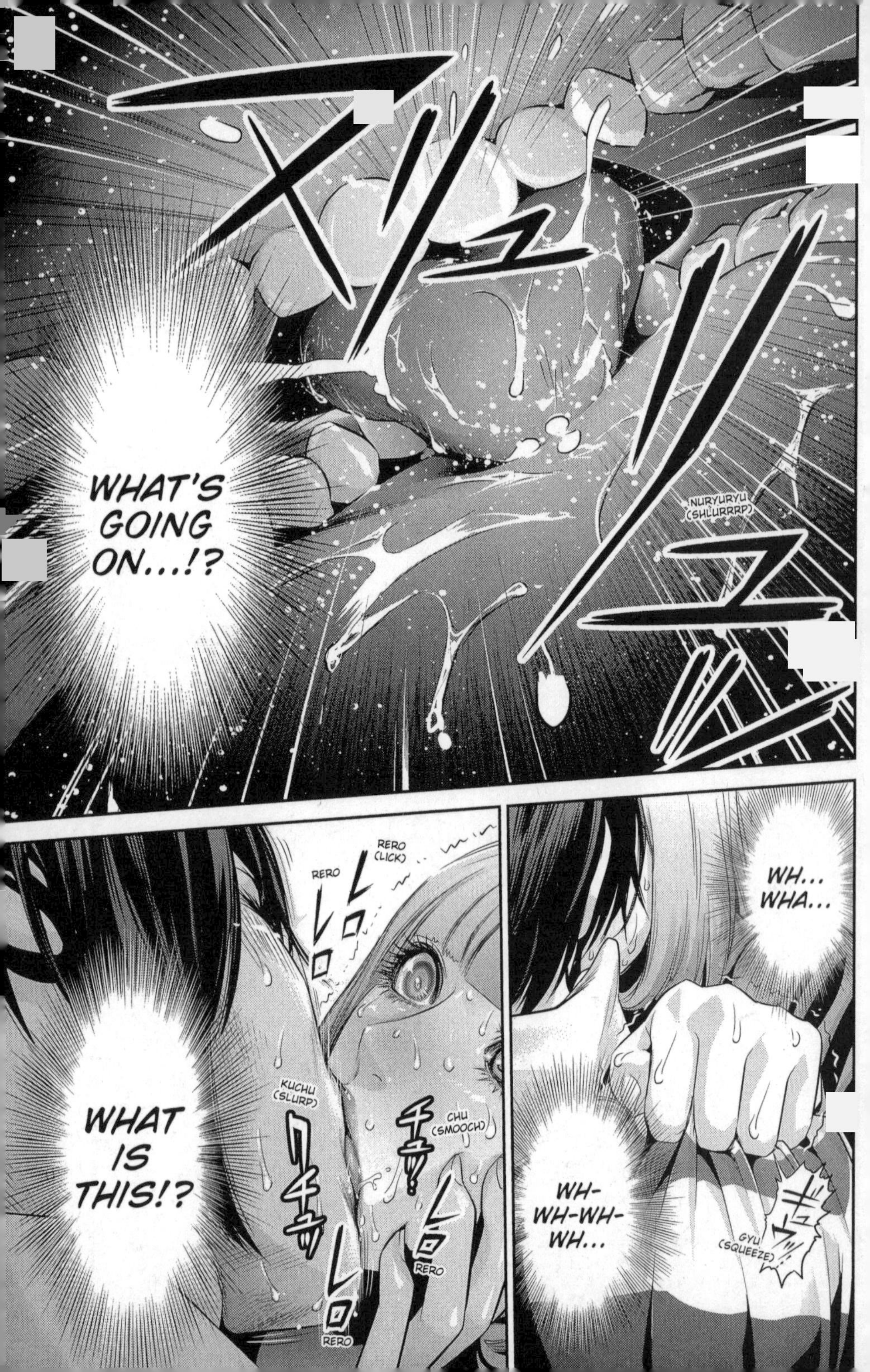
NURYURYU (SHLURRRP)
WHAT'S GOING ON...!?
WH... WHA...
WH-WH-WH-WH...
GYU (SQUEEZE)
RERO (LICK)
RERO
CHU (SMOOCH)
KUCHU (SLURP)
WHAT IS THIS!?
RERO
RERO

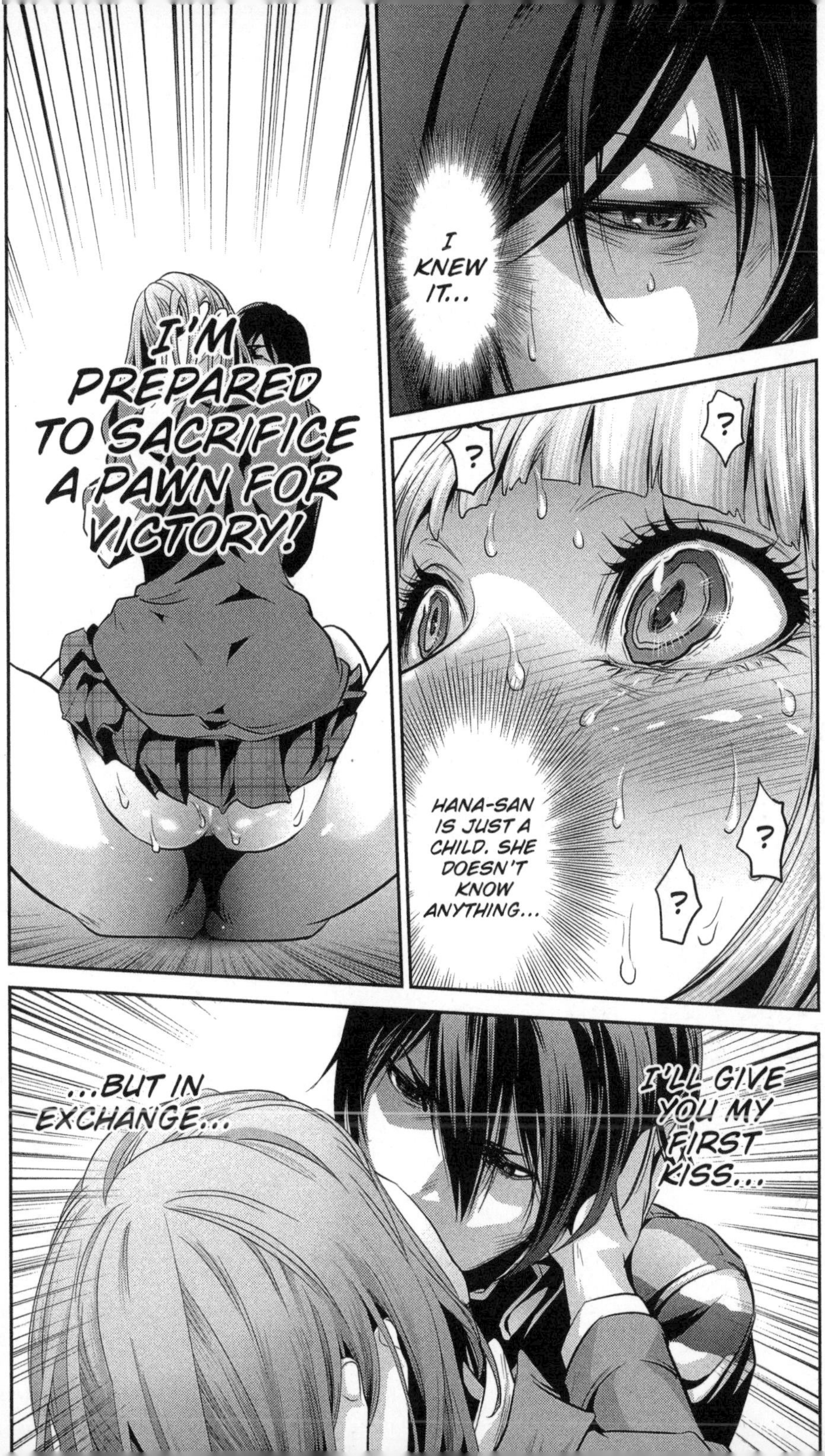
I KNEW IT...
?
?
HANA-SAN IS JUST A CHILD. SHE DOESN'T KNOW ANYTHING...
?
?
I'M PREPARED TO SACRIFICE A PAWN FOR VICTORY!
I'LL GIVE YOU MY FIRST KISS...
...BUT IN EXCHANGE...

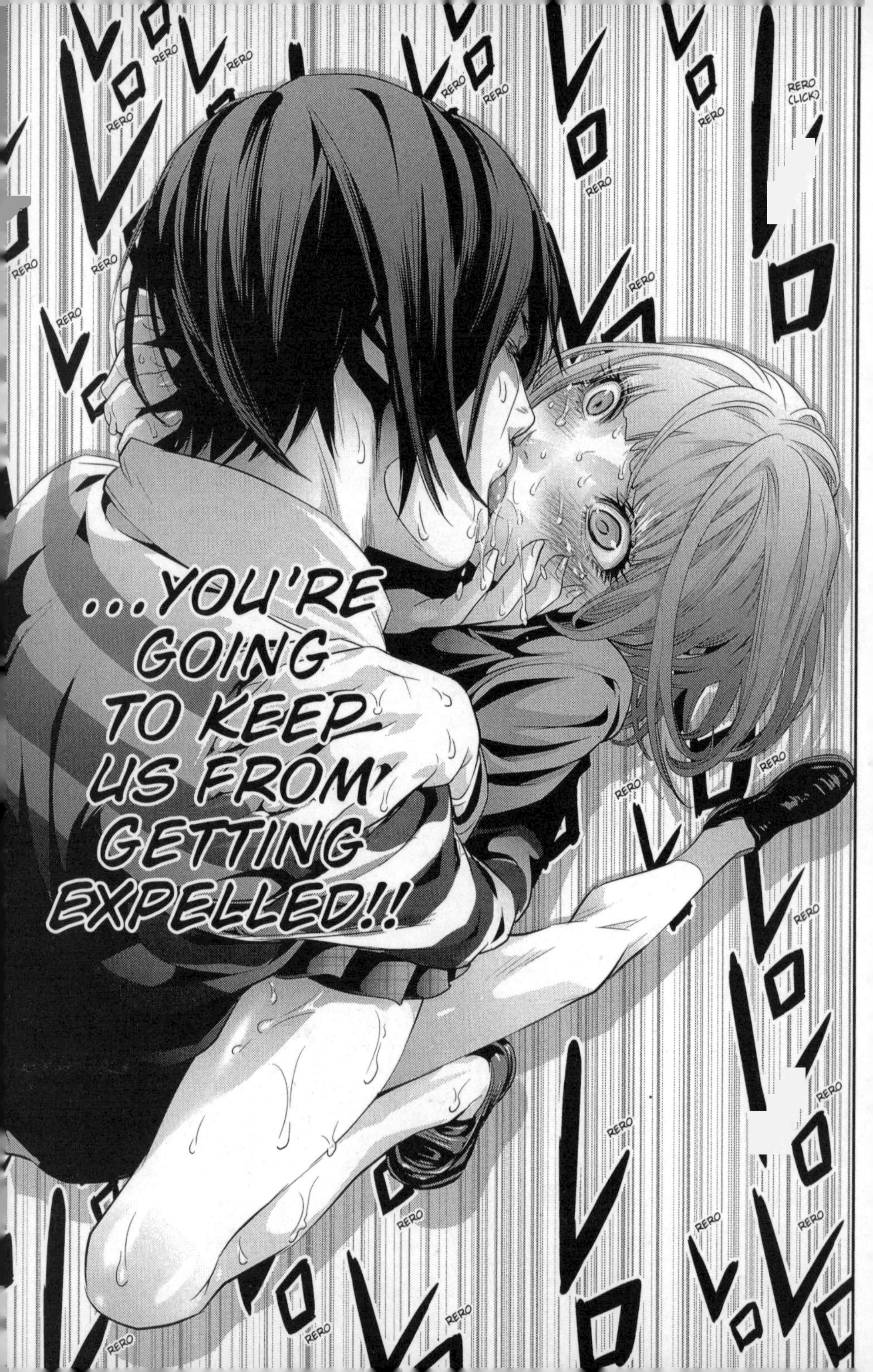
RERO (LICK)
RERO
...YOU'RE GOING TO KEEP US FROM GETTING EXPELLED!!
RERO

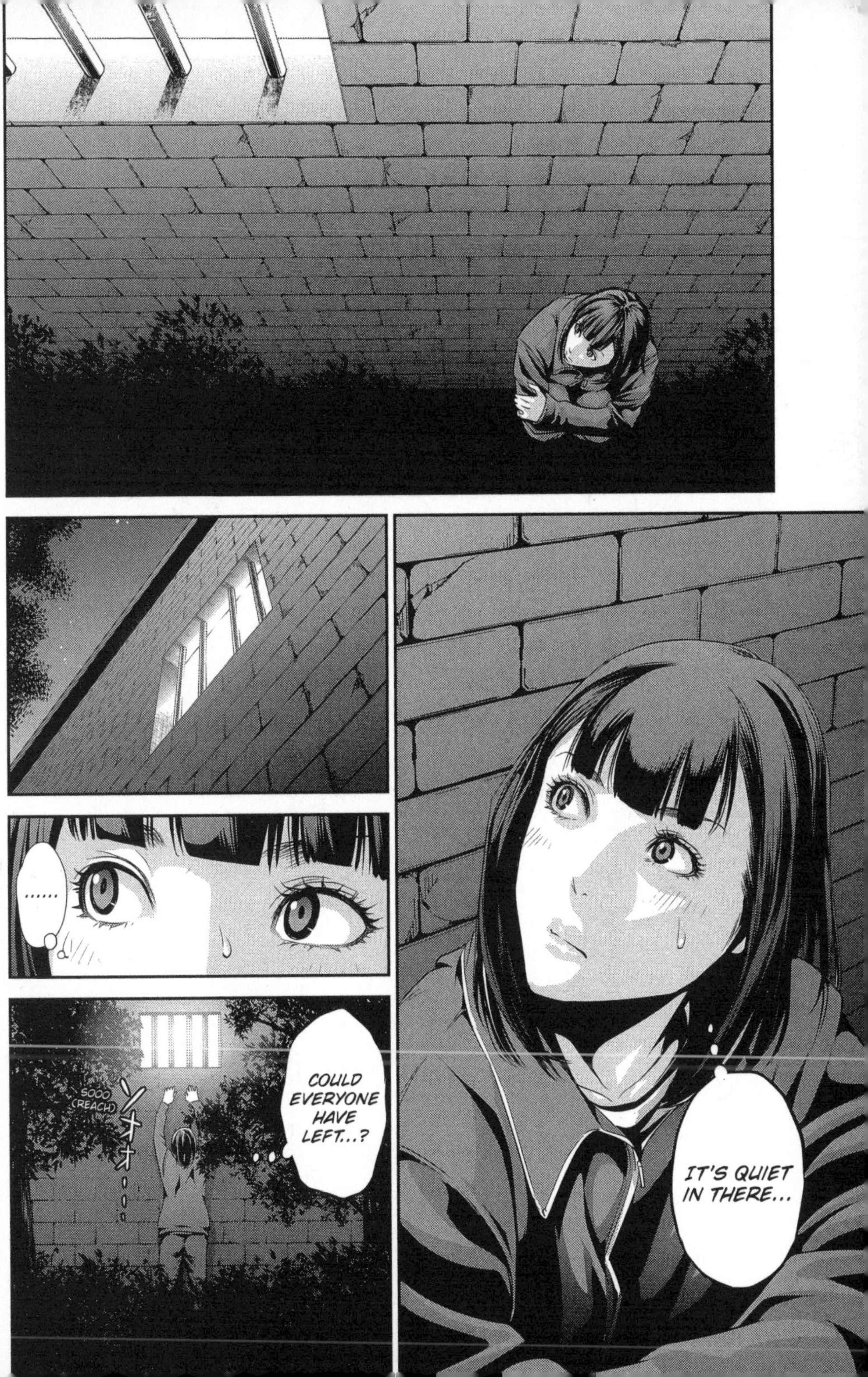
IT'S QUIET IN THERE...
......
COULD EVERYONE HAVE LEFT...?
SOOO (REACH)

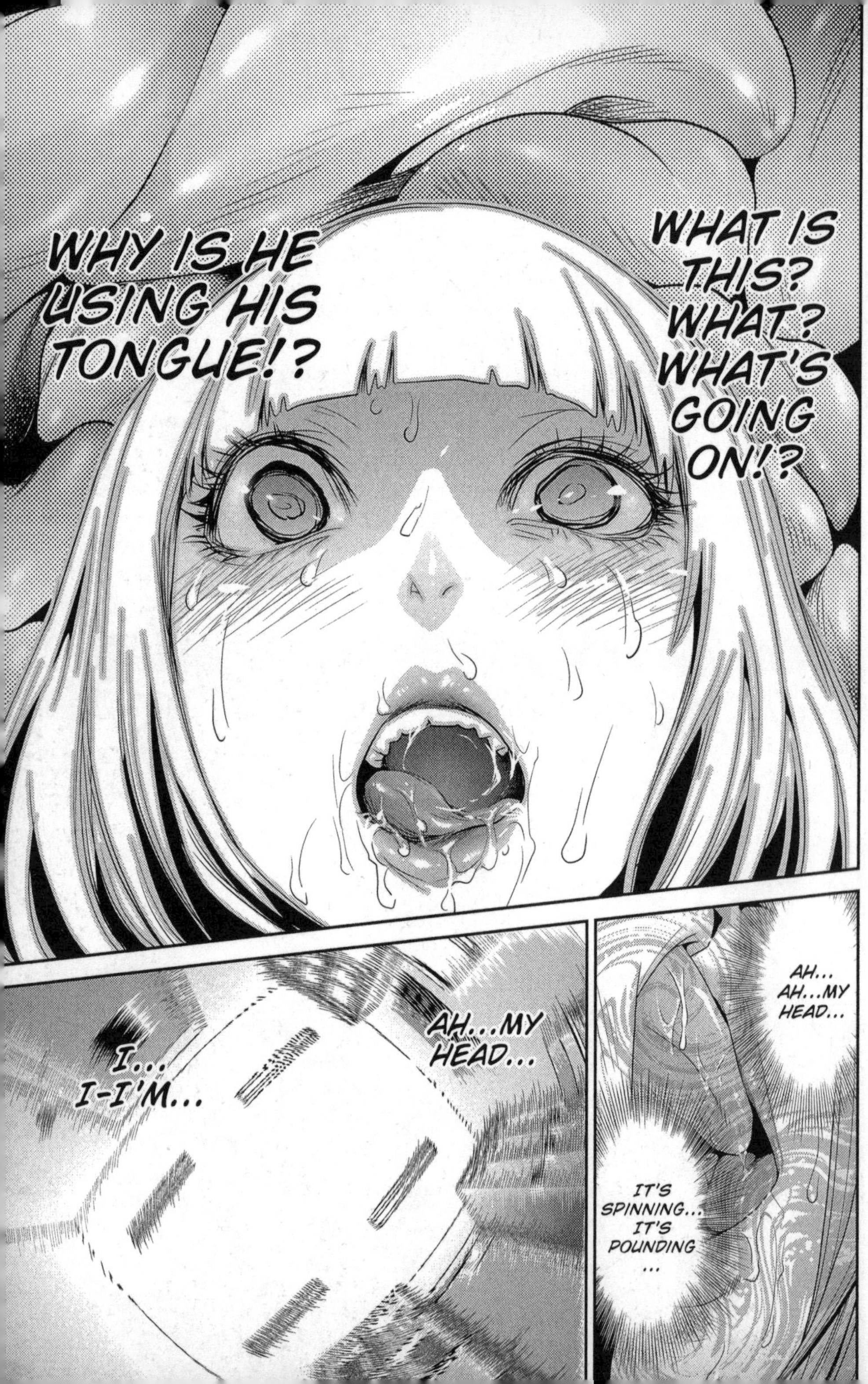
WHAT IS THIS? WHAT? WHAT'S GOING ON!?
WHY IS HE USING HIS TONGUE!?
AH... AH...MY HEAD...
IT'S SPINNING... IT'S POUNDING ...
AH...MY HEAD...
I... I-I'M...

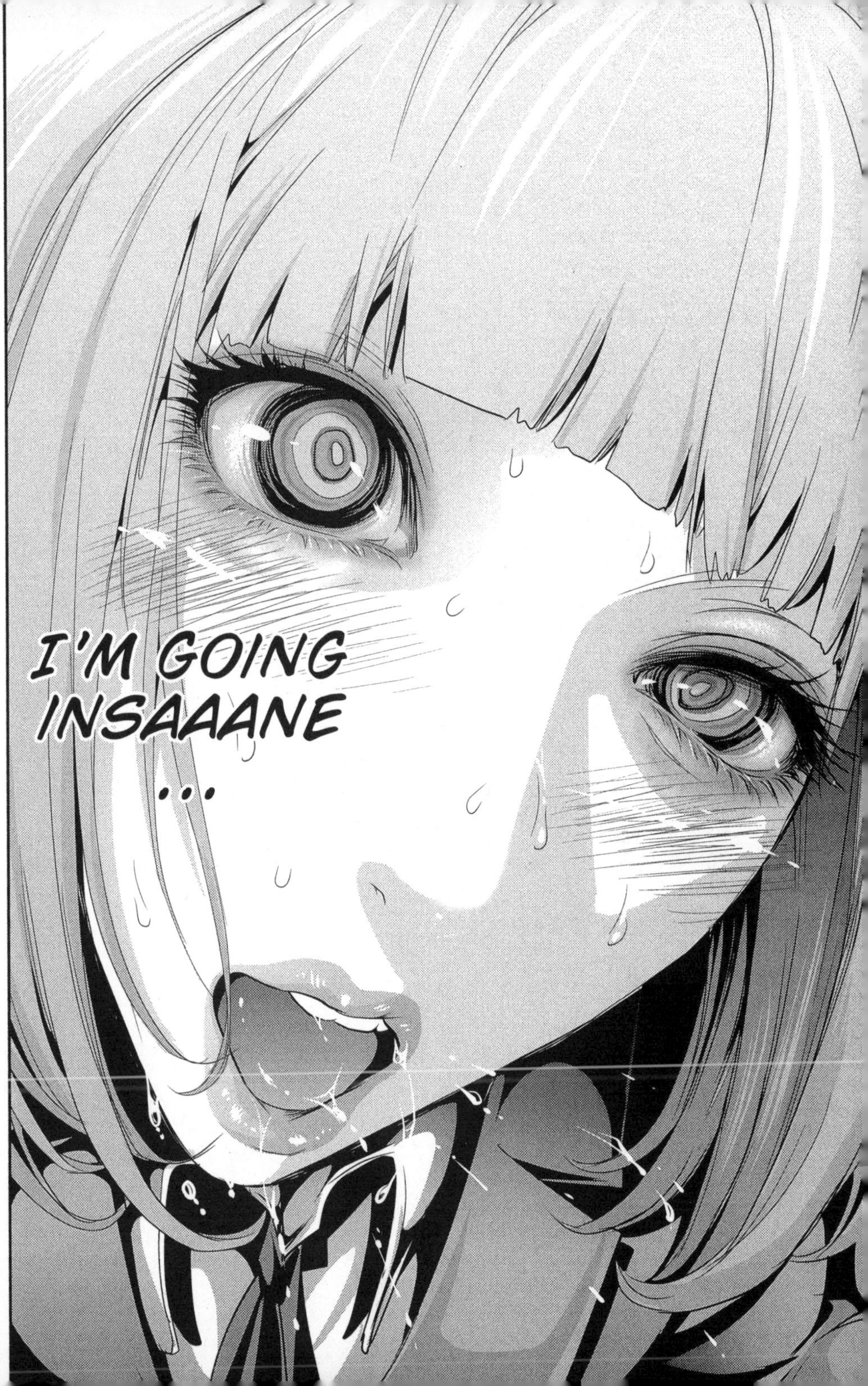
I'M GOING INSAAANE
...

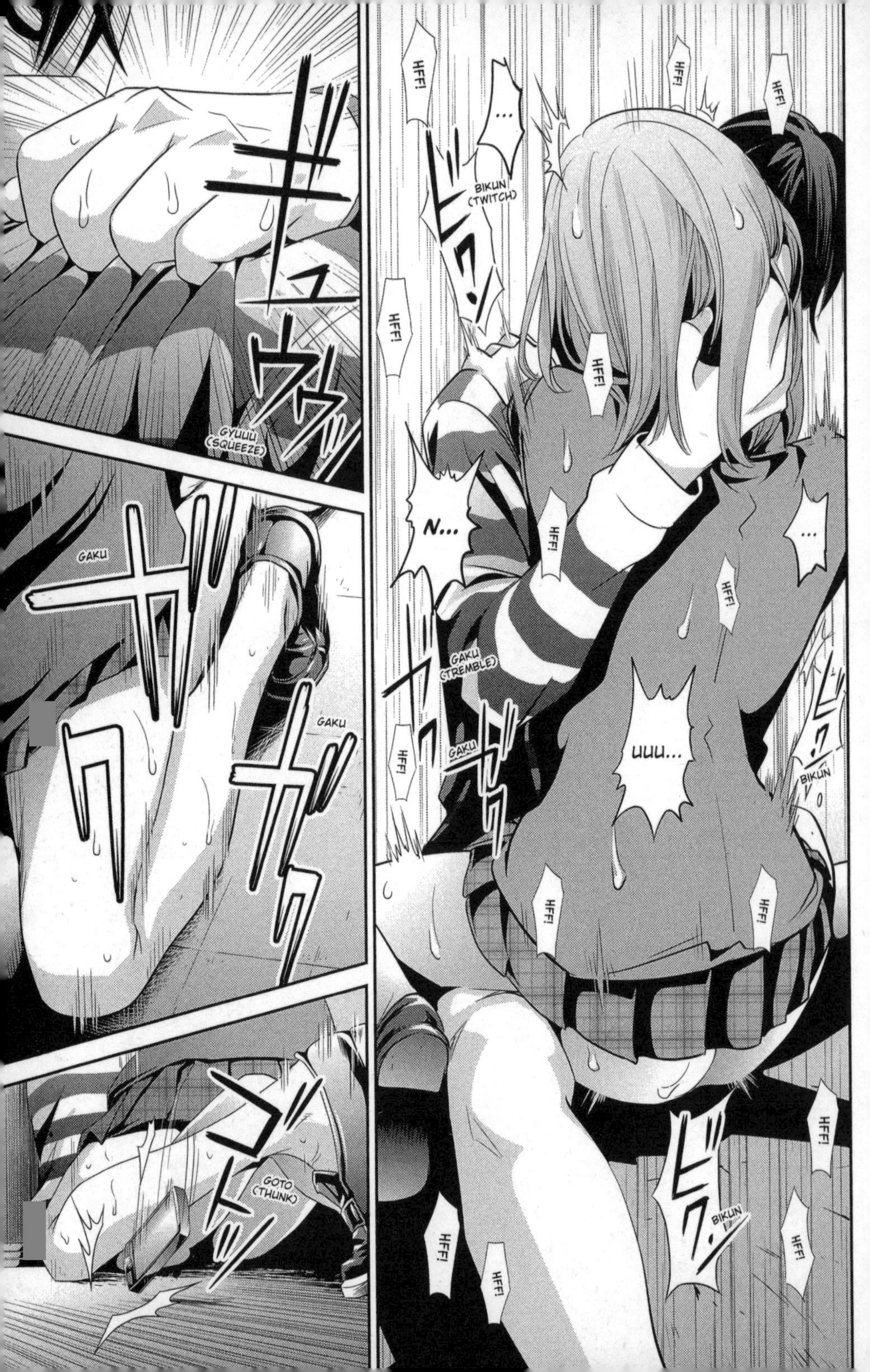
HFF!
HFF!
...
HFF!
BIKUN (TWITCH)
HFF!
HFF!
...
N...
HFF!
HFF!
GAKU (TREMBLE)
uuu...
BIKUN
GAKU
HFF!
HFF!
HFF!
HFF!
BIKUN
HFF!
HFF!
HFF!
GYUUU (SQUEEZE)
GAKU
GAKU
GOTO (THUNK)

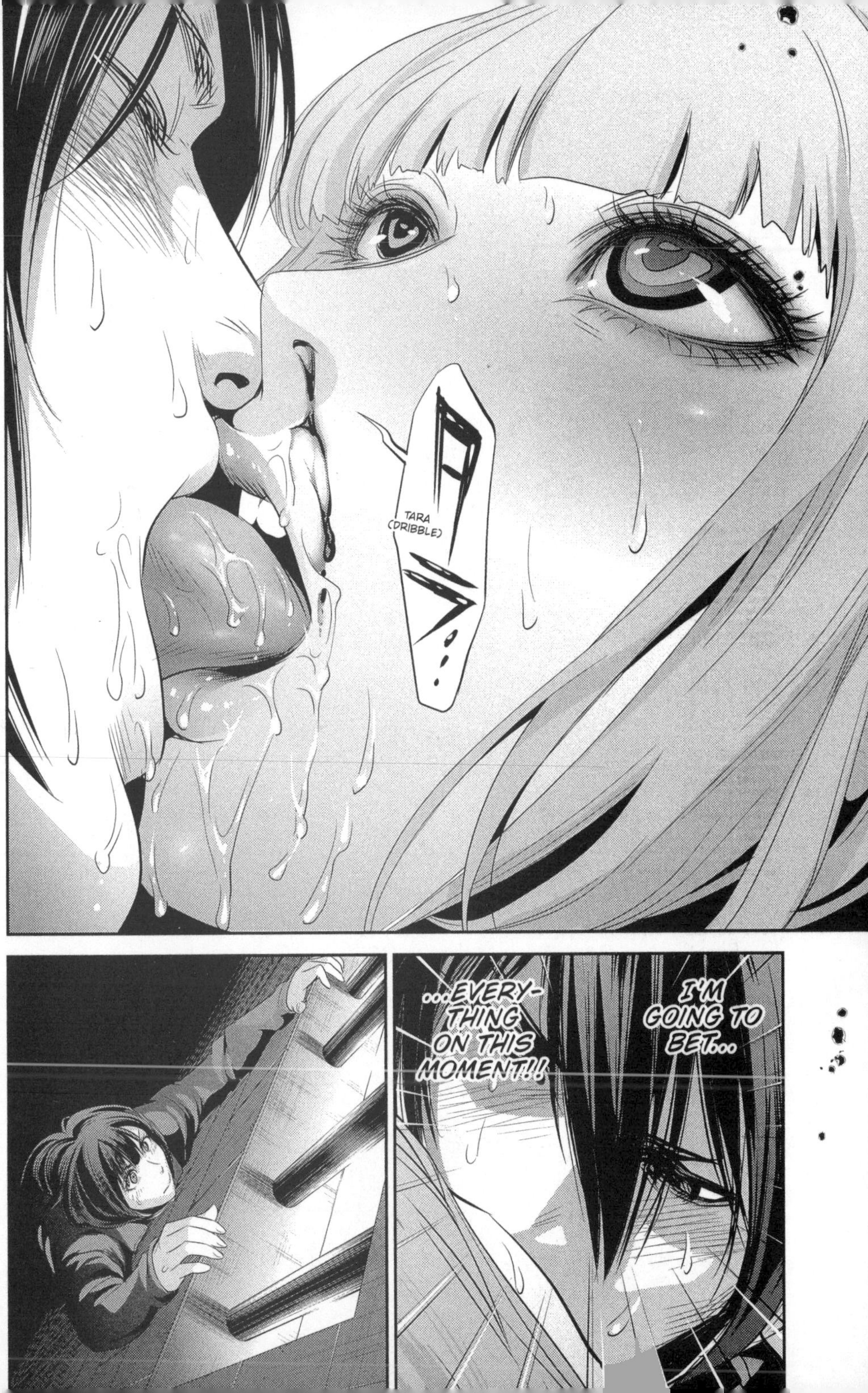
TARA (DRIBBLE)
I'M GOING TO BET...
...EVERY-THING ON THIS MOMENT!!

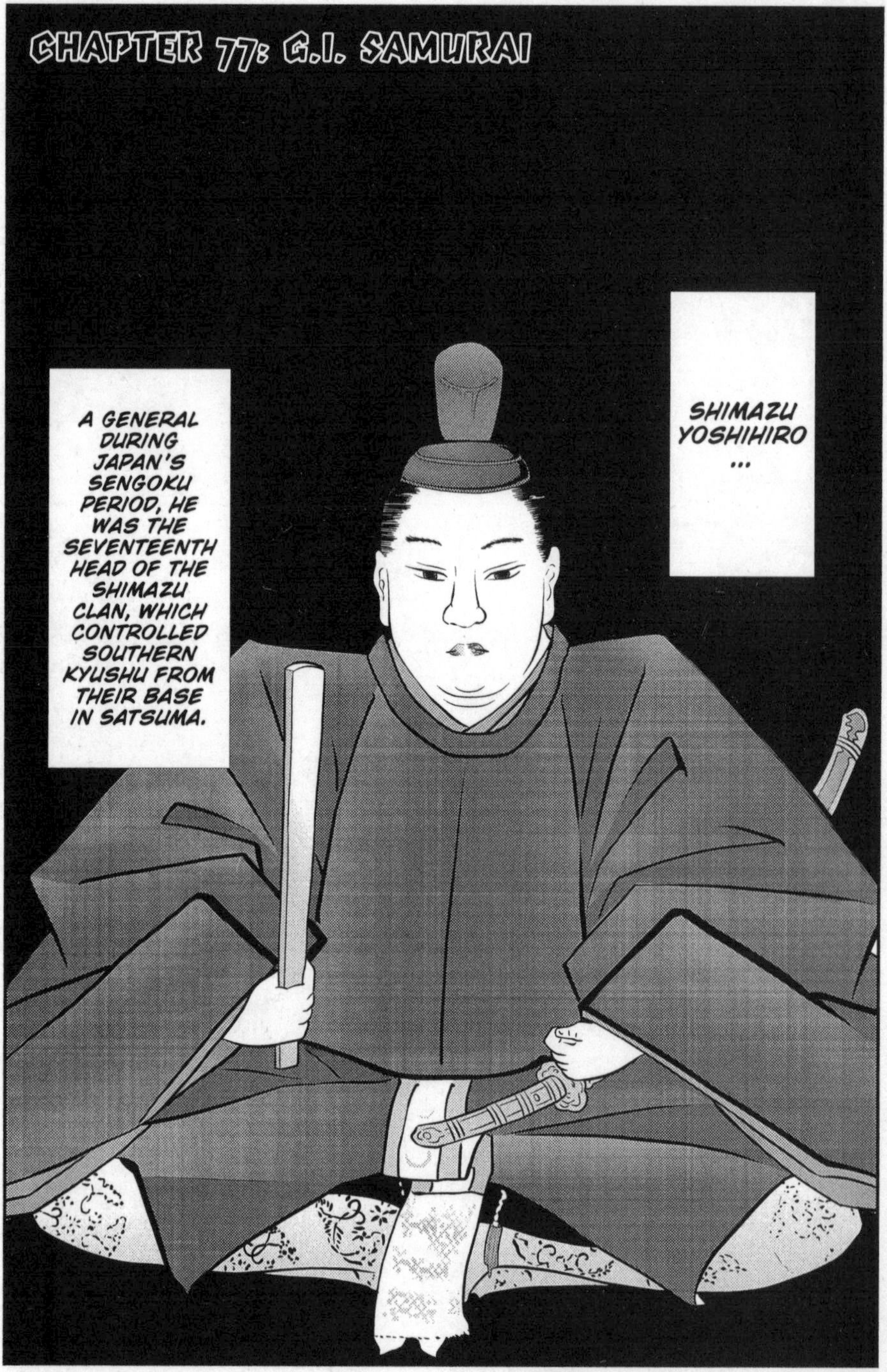
CHAPTER 77: G.I. SAMURAI
SHIMAZU YOSHIHIRO ...
A GENERAL DURING JAPAN'S SENGOKU PERIOD, HE WAS THE SEVENTEENTH HEAD OF THE SHIMAZU CLAN, WHICH CONTROLLED SOUTHERN KYUSHU FROM THEIR BASE IN SATSUMA.

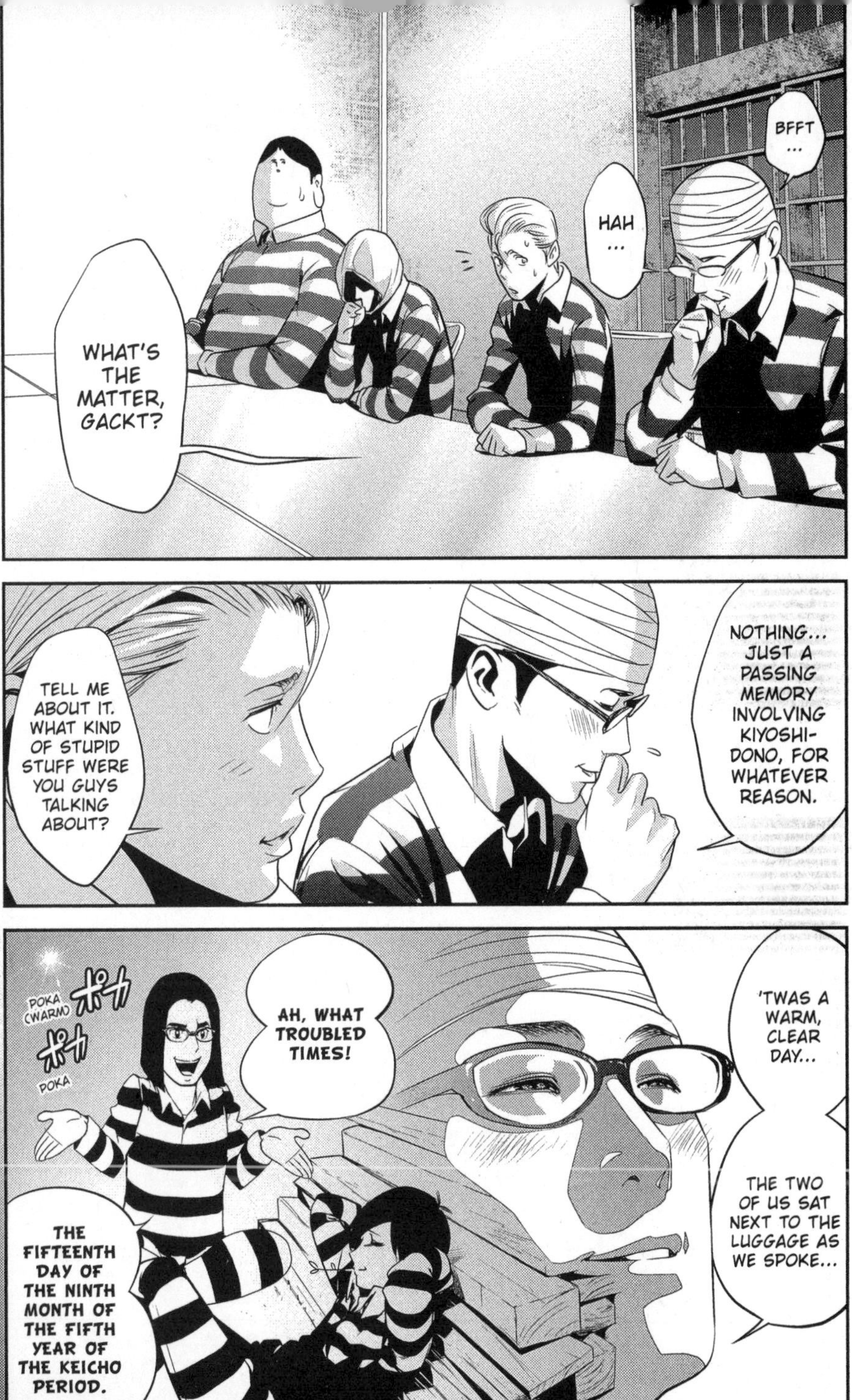
BFFT ...
HAH ...
WHAT'S THE MATTER, GACKT?
NOTHING... JUST A PASSING MEMORY INVOLVING KIYOSHI-DONO, FOR WHATEVER REASON.
TELL ME ABOUT IT. WHAT KIND OF STUPID STUFF WERE YOU GUYS TALKING ABOUT?
'TWAS A WARM, CLEAR DAY...
THE TWO OF US SAT NEXT TO THE LUGGAGE AS WE SPOKE...
AH, WHAT TROUBLED TIMES!
ポカ
POKA (WARM)
ポカ
POKA
THE FIFTEENTH DAY OF THE NINTH MONTH OF THE FIFTH YEAR OF THE KEICHO PERIOD.

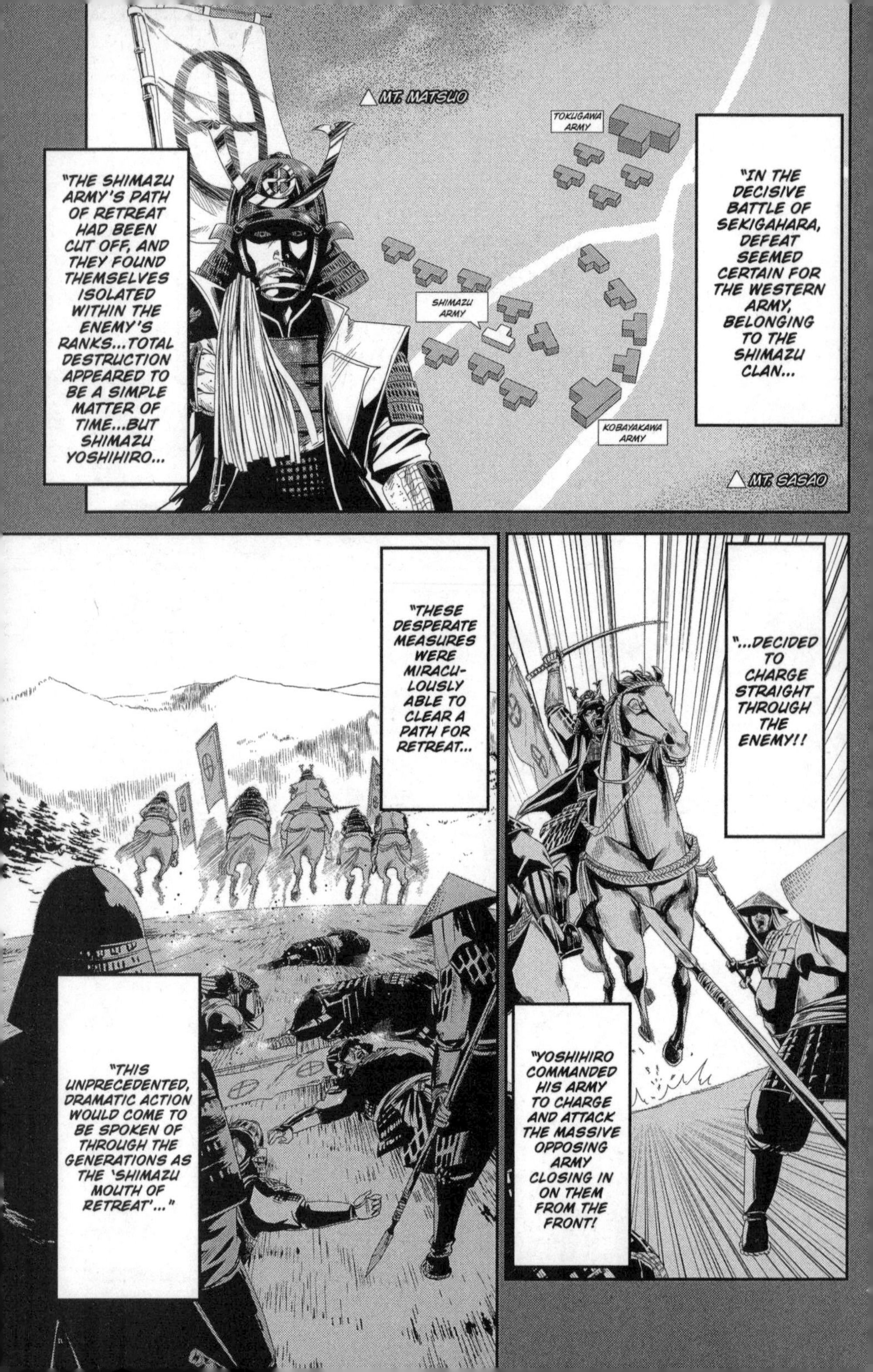
"IN THE DECISIVE BATTLE OF SEKIGAHARA, DEFEAT SEEMED CERTAIN FOR THE WESTERN ARMY, BELONGING TO THE SHIMAZU CLAN...
MT. MATSUO
TOKUGAWA ARMY
SHIMAZU ARMY
KOBAYAKAWA ARMY
MT. SASAO
"THE SHIMAZU ARMY'S PATH OF RETREAT HAD BEEN CUT OFF, AND THEY FOUND THEMSELVES ISOLATED WITHIN THE ENEMY'S RANKS...TOTAL DESTRUCTION APPEARED TO BE A SIMPLE MATTER OF TIME...BUT SHIMAZU YOSHIHIRO...
"...DECIDED TO CHARGE STRAIGHT THROUGH THE ENEMY!!
"YOSHIHIRO COMMANDED HIS ARMY TO CHARGE AND ATTACK THE MASSIVE OPPOSING ARMY CLOSING IN ON THEM FROM THE FRONT!
"THESE DESPERATE MEASURES WERE MIRACU-LOUSLY ABLE TO CLEAR A PATH FOR RETREAT...
"THIS UNPRECEDENTED, DRAMATIC ACTION WOULD COME TO BE SPOKEN OF THROUGH THE GENERATIONS AS THE 'SHIMAZU MOUTH OF RETREAT'..."

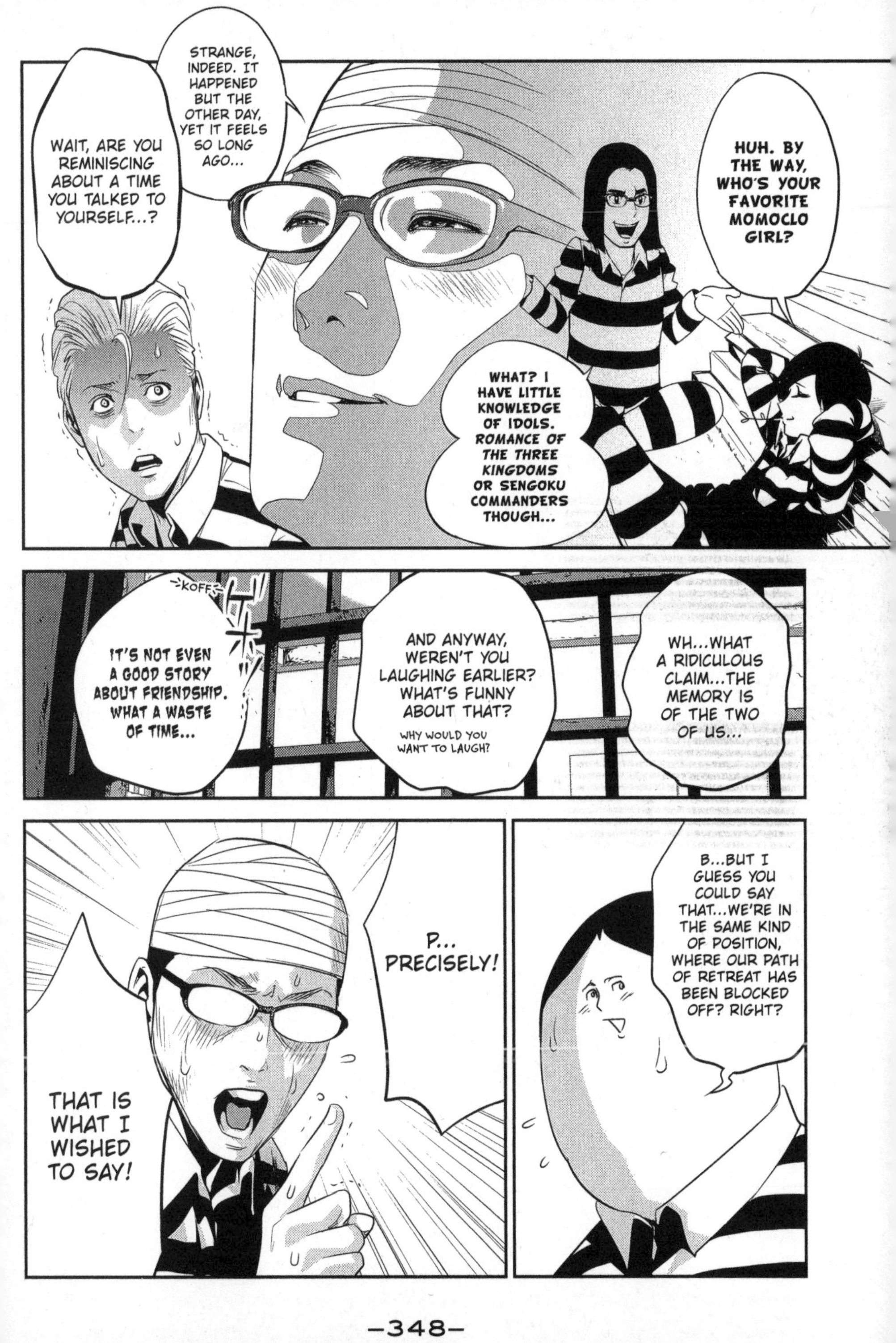
HUH. BY THE WAY, WHO'S YOUR FAVORITE MOMOCLO GIRL?
STRANGE, INDEED. IT HAPPENED BUT THE OTHER DAY, YET IT FEELS SO LONG AGO...
WAIT, ARE YOU REMINISCING ABOUT A TIME YOU TALKED TO YOURSELF...?
WHAT? I HAVE LITTLE KNOWLEDGE OF IDOLS. ROMANCE OF THE THREE KINGDOMS OR SENGOKU COMMANDERS THOUGH...
WH...WHAT A RIDICULOUS CLAIM...THE MEMORY IS OF THE TWO OF US...
AND ANYWAY, WEREN'T YOU LAUGHING EARLIER? WHAT'S FUNNY ABOUT THAT?
WHY WOULD YOU WANT TO LAUGH?
KOFF
IT'S NOT EVEN A GOOD STORY ABOUT FRIENDSHIP. WHAT A WASTE OF TIME...
B...BUT I GUESS YOU COULD SAY THAT...WE'RE IN THE SAME KIND OF POSITION, WHERE OUR PATH OF RETREAT HAS BEEN BLOCKED OFF? RIGHT?
P... PRECISELY!
THAT IS WHAT I WISHED TO SAY!

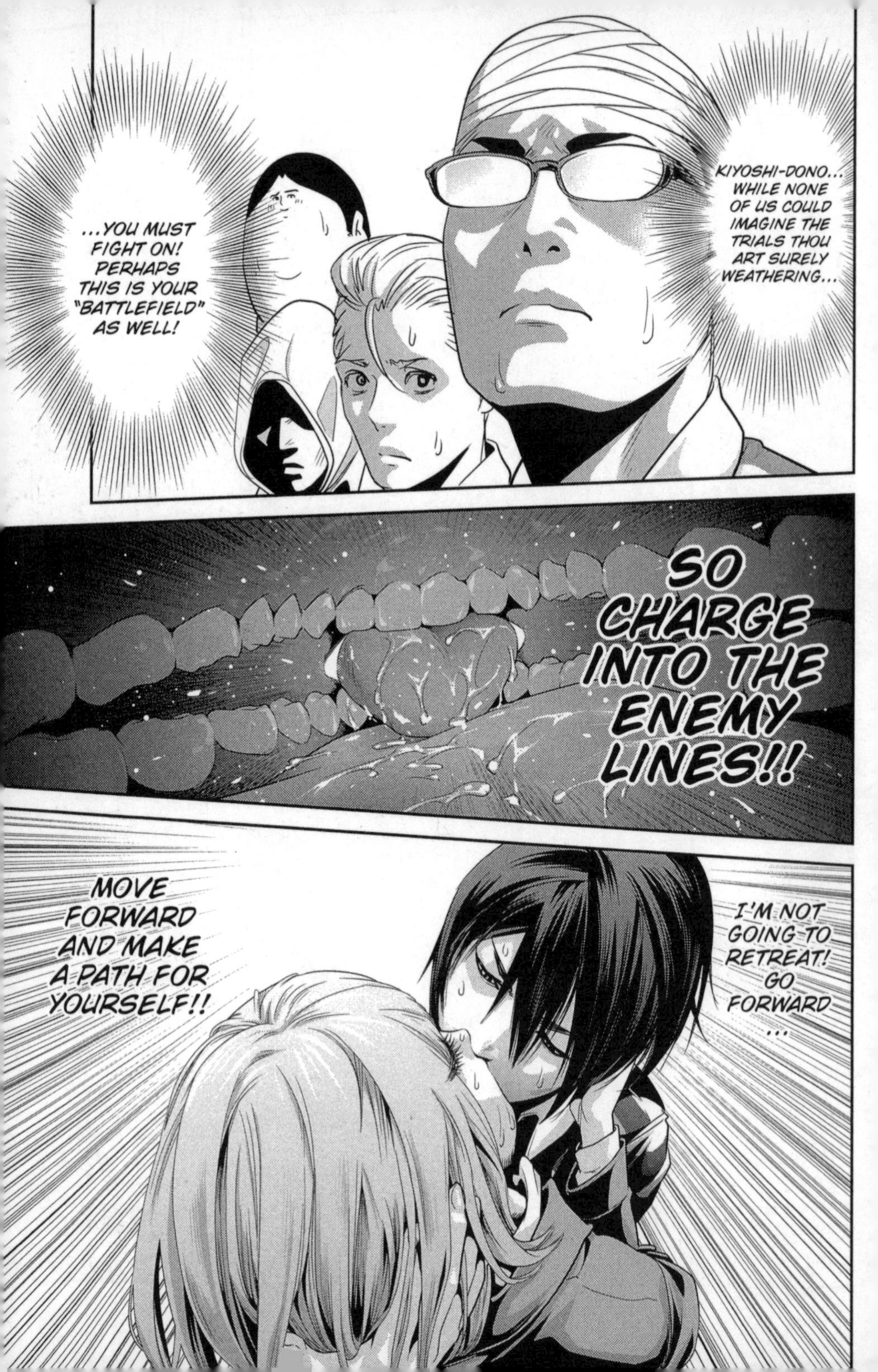
KIYOSHI-DONO... WHILE NONE OF US COULD IMAGINE THE TRIALS THOU ART SURELY WEATHERING...
...YOU MUST FIGHT ON! PERHAPS THIS IS YOUR "BATTLEFIELD" AS WELL!
SO CHARGE INTO THE ENEMY LINES!!
I'M NOT GOING TO RETREAT! GO FORWARD...
MOVE FORWARD AND MAKE A PATH FOR YOURSELF!!

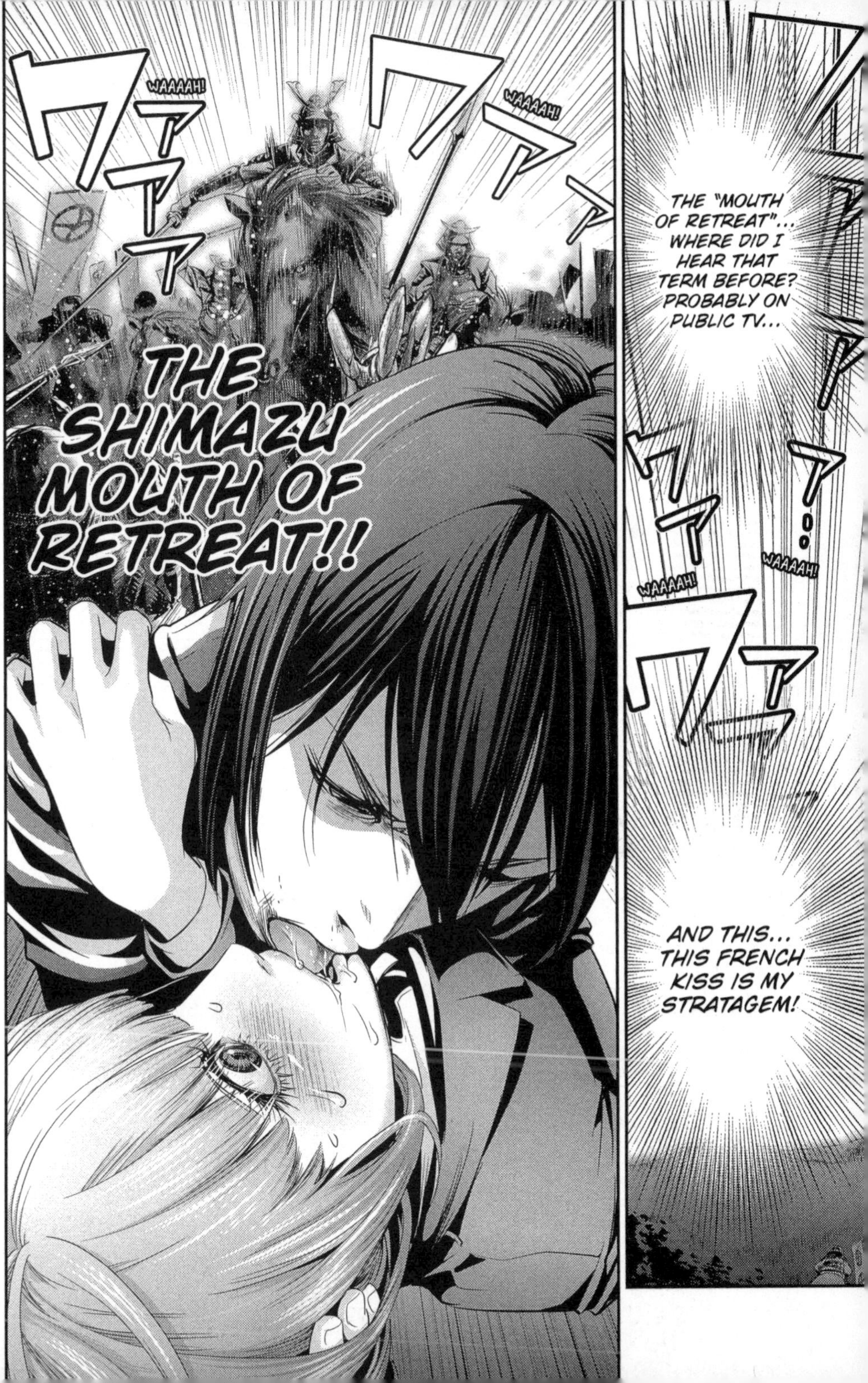
THE "MOUTH OF RETREAT"... WHERE DID I HEAR THAT TERM BEFORE? PROBABLY ON PUBLIC TV...
WAAAAH!
WAAAAH!
AND THIS... THIS FRENCH KISS IS MY STRATAGEM!
WAAAAH!
WAAAAH!
THE SHIMAZU MOUTH OF RETREAT!!

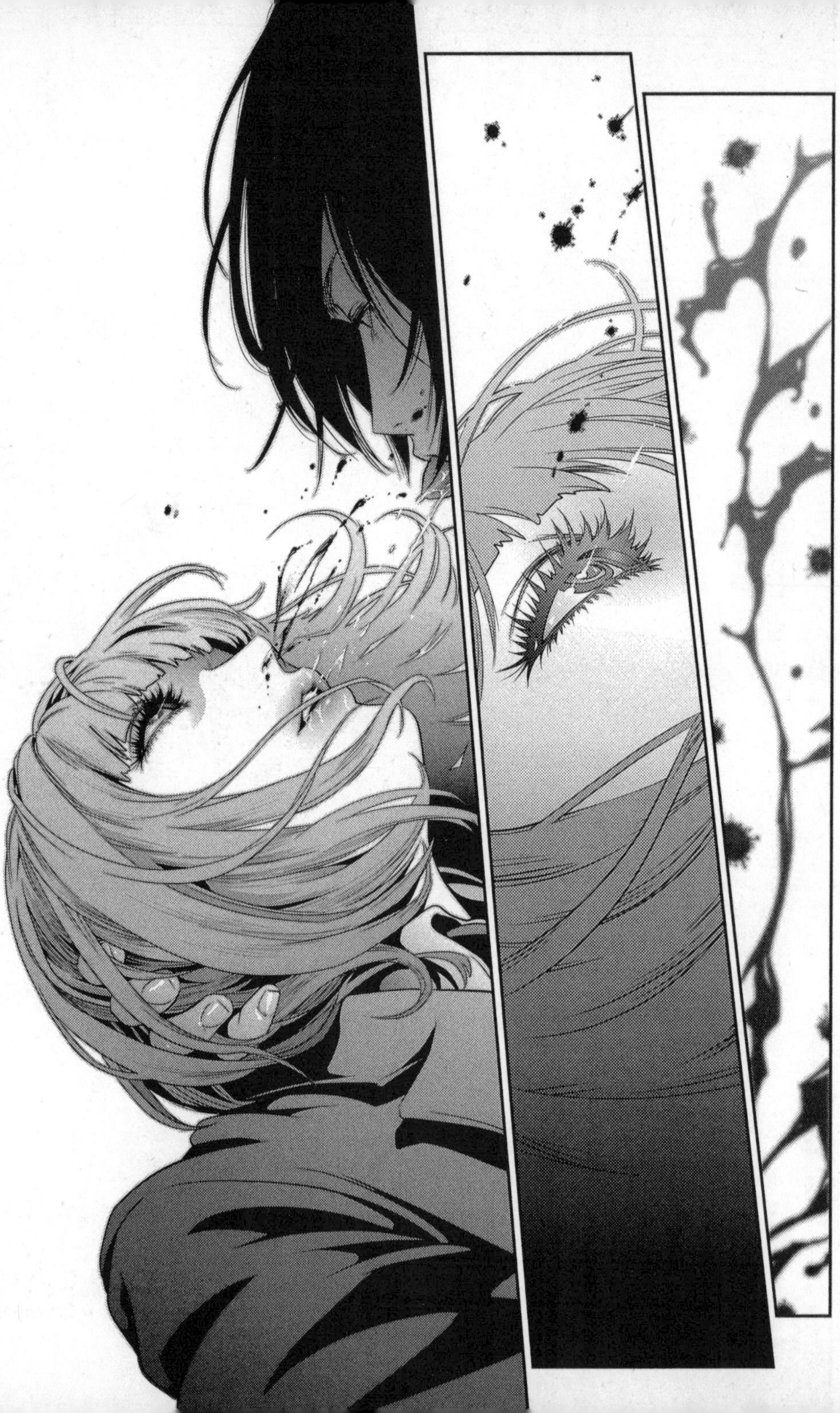

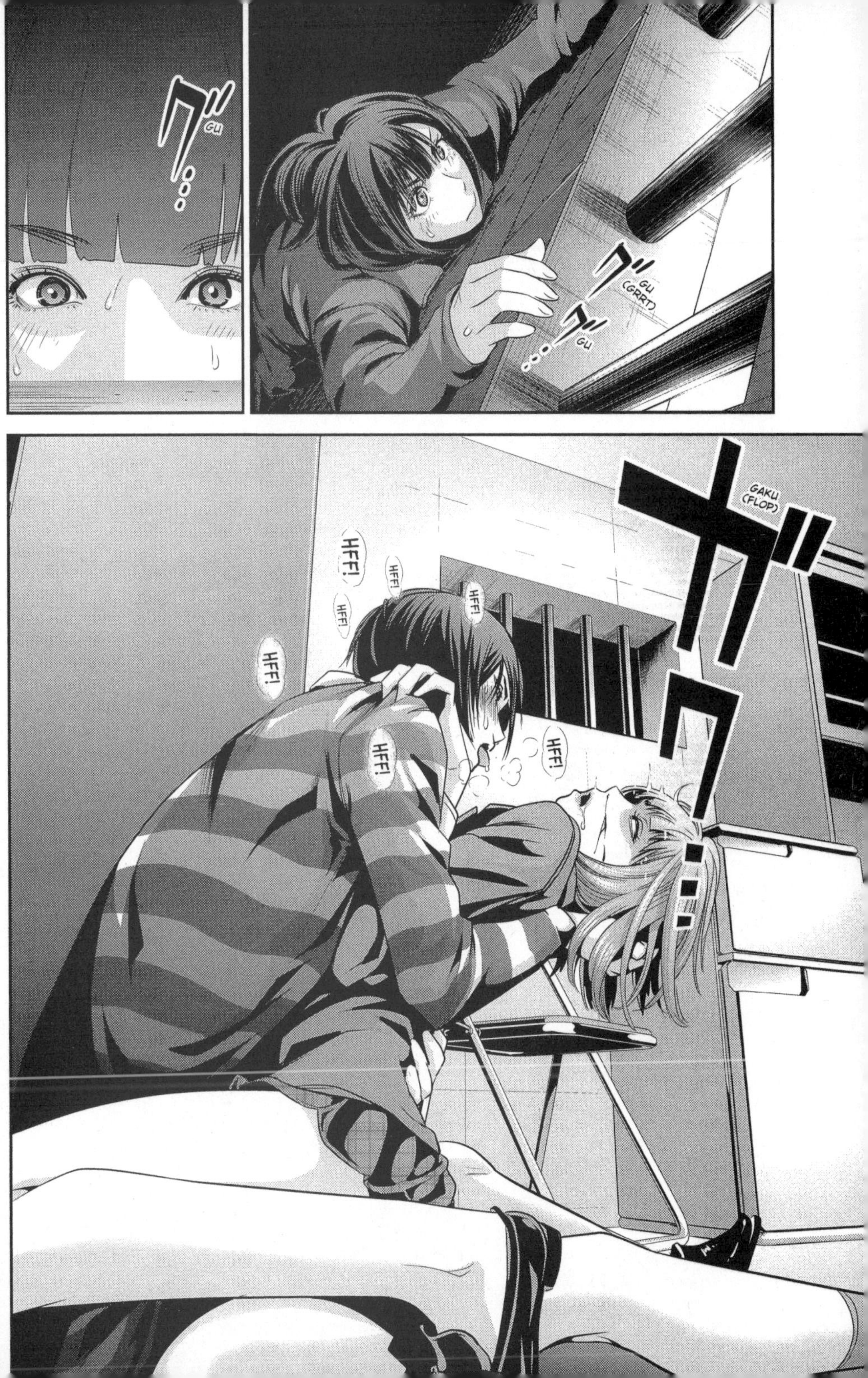
GU (GRRT)
GU
GU
GAKU (FLOP)
HFF!
HFF!
HFF!
HFF!
HFF!
HFF!
HFF!

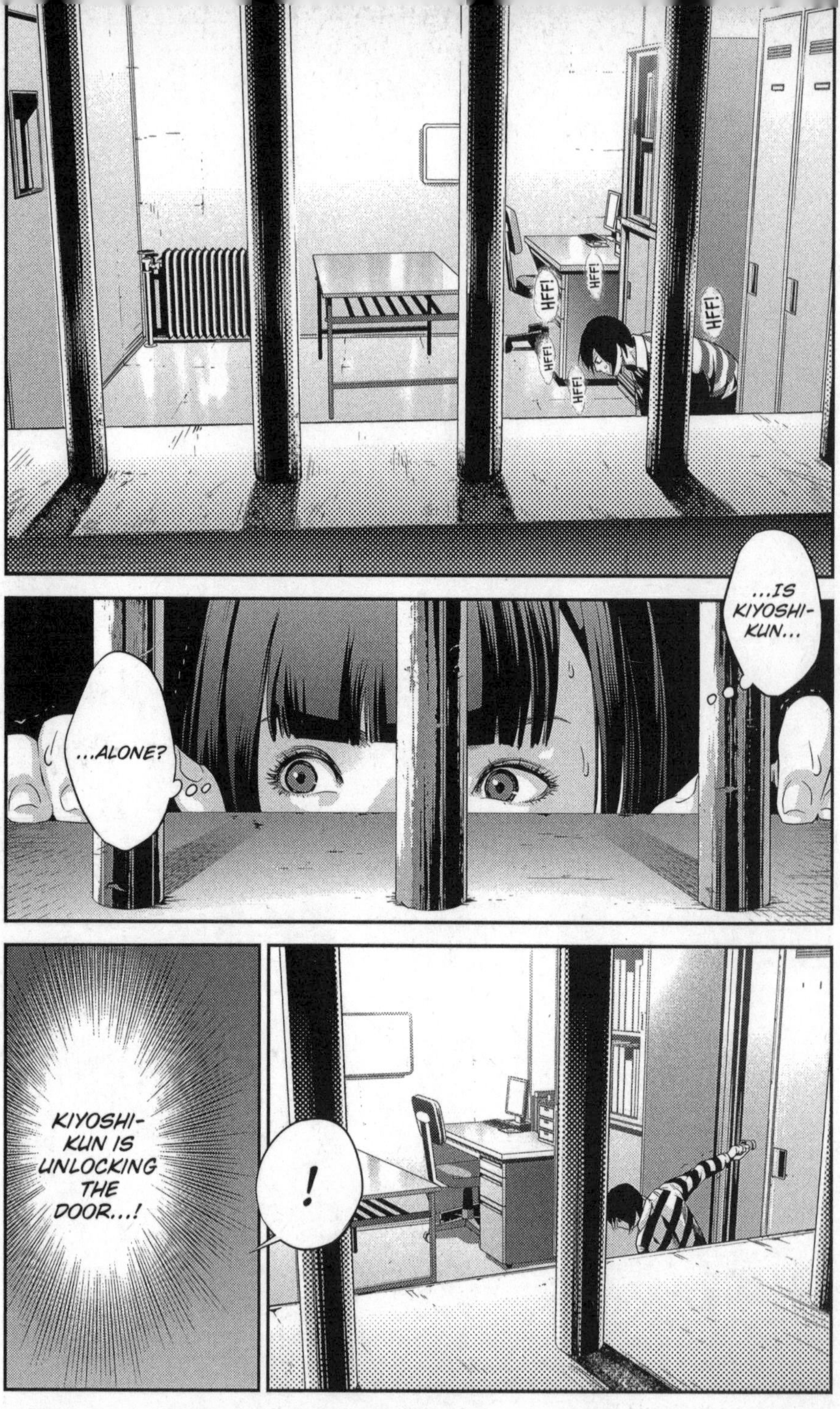
HFF!
HFF!
HFF!
HFF!
HFF!
...IS KIYOSHI-KUN...
...ALONE?
!
KIYOSHI-KUN IS UNLOCKING THE DOOR...!

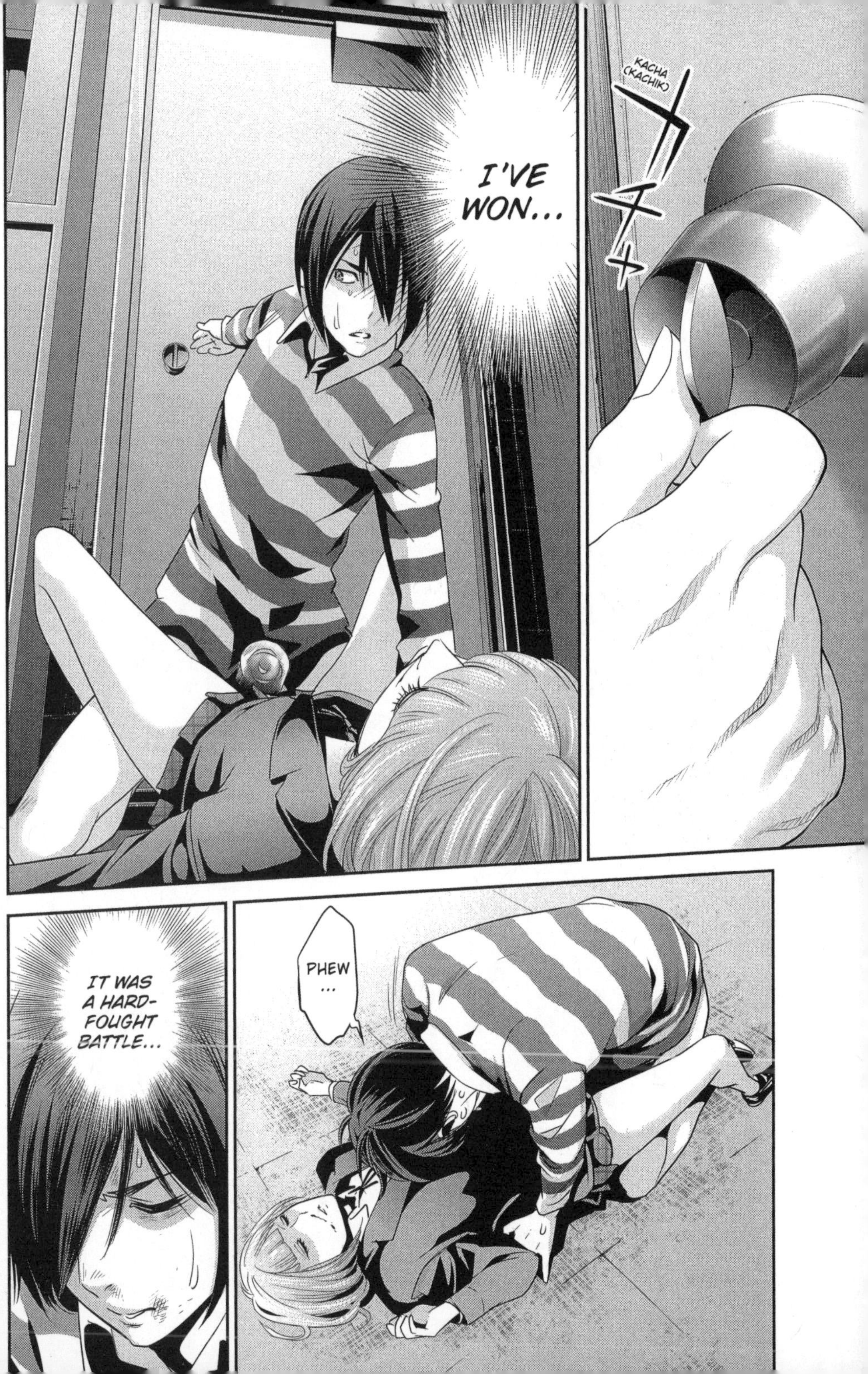
KACHA (KACHIK)
I'VE WON...
PHEW ...
IT WAS A HARD-FOUGHT BATTLE...

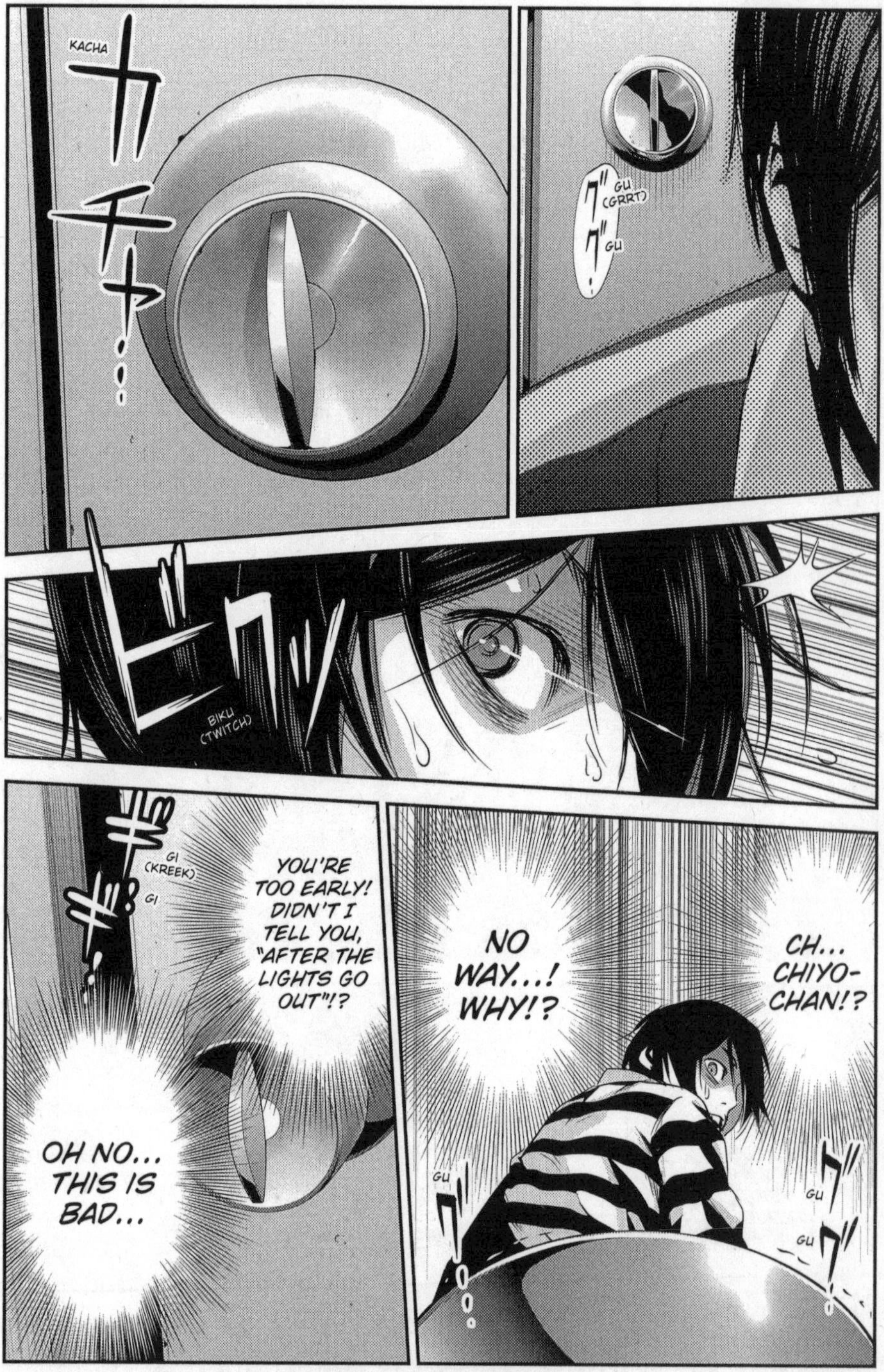
GU (GRRT)
GU
KACHA
BIKU (TWITCH)
CH... CHIYO-CHAN!?
NO WAY...! WHY!?
GU
GU
GU
YOU'RE TOO EARLY! DIDN'T I TELL YOU, "AFTER THE LIGHTS GO OUT"!?
GI (KREEK)
GI
OH NO... THIS IS BAD...

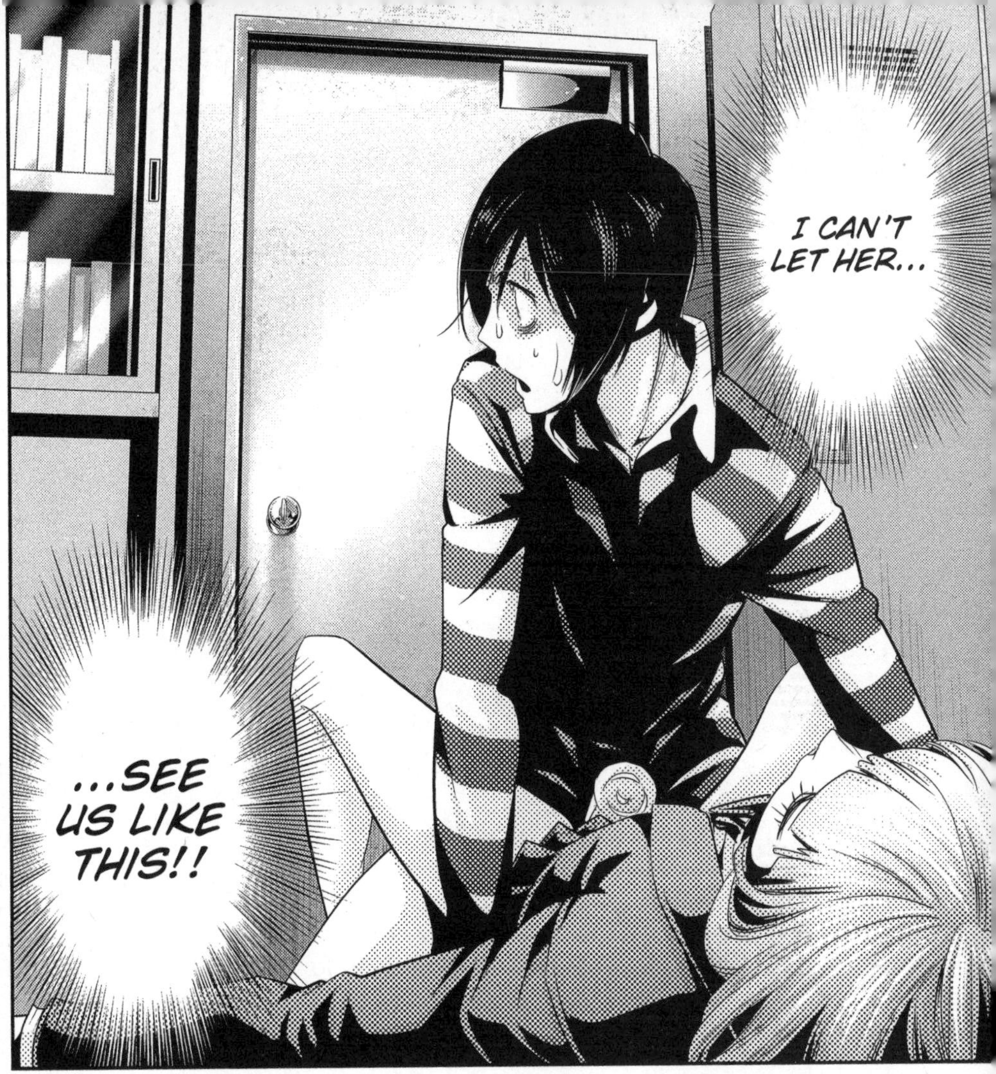
I CAN'T LET HER...
...SEE US LIKE THIS!!
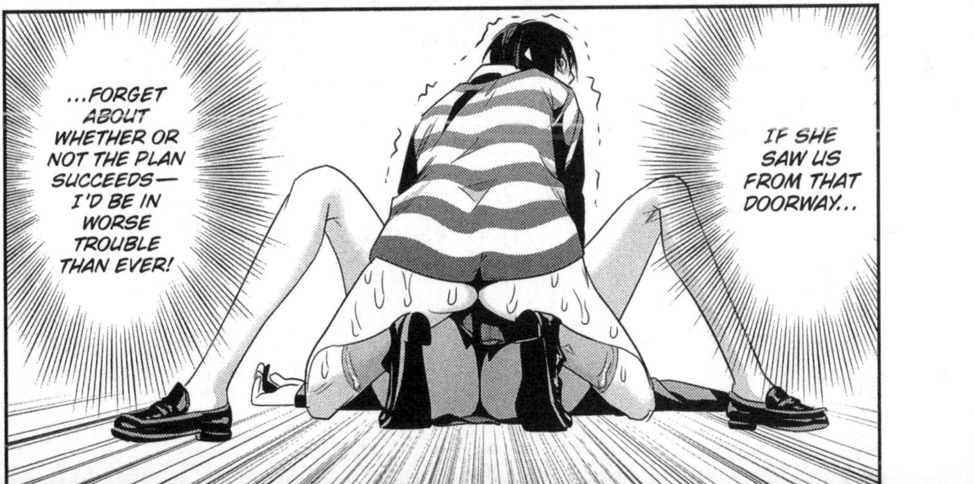
IF SHE SAW US FROM THAT DOORWAY...
...FORGET ABOUT WHETHER OR NOT THE PLAN SUCCEEDS—I'D BE IN WORSE TROUBLE THAN EVER!

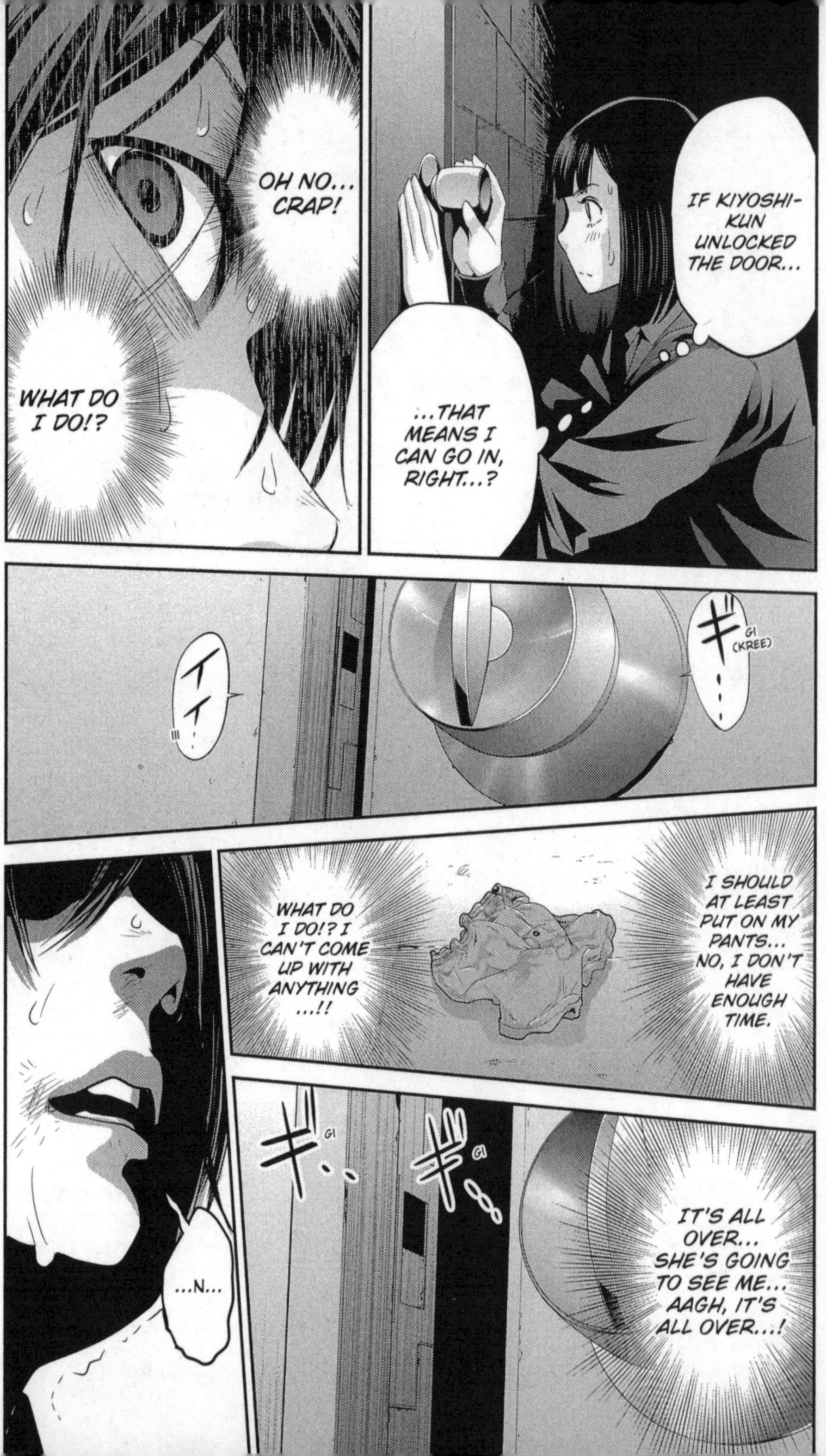
IF KIYOSHI-KUN UNLOCKED THE DOOR...
...THAT MEANS I CAN GO IN, RIGHT...?
OH NO... CRAP!
WHAT DO I DO!?
GI (KREE)
I SHOULD AT LEAST PUT ON MY PANTS... NO, I DON'T HAVE ENOUGH TIME.
WHAT DO I DO!? I CAN'T COME UP WITH ANYTHING ...!!
IT'S ALL OVER... SHE'S GOING TO SEE ME... AAGH, IT'S ALL OVER...!
GI
GI
...N...

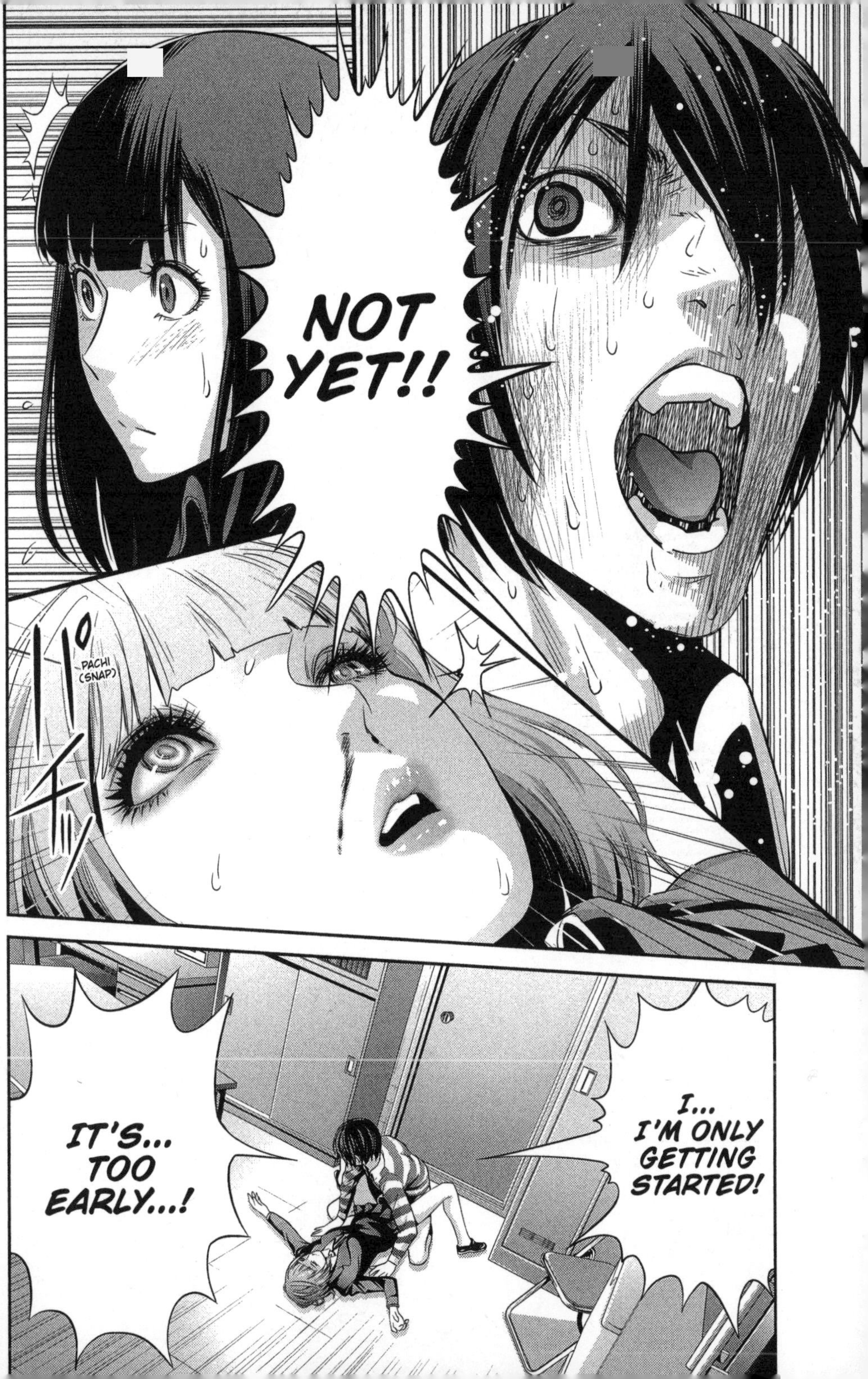
NOT YET!!
PACHI (SNAP)
I... I'M ONLY GETTING STARTED!
IT'S... TOO EARLY...!

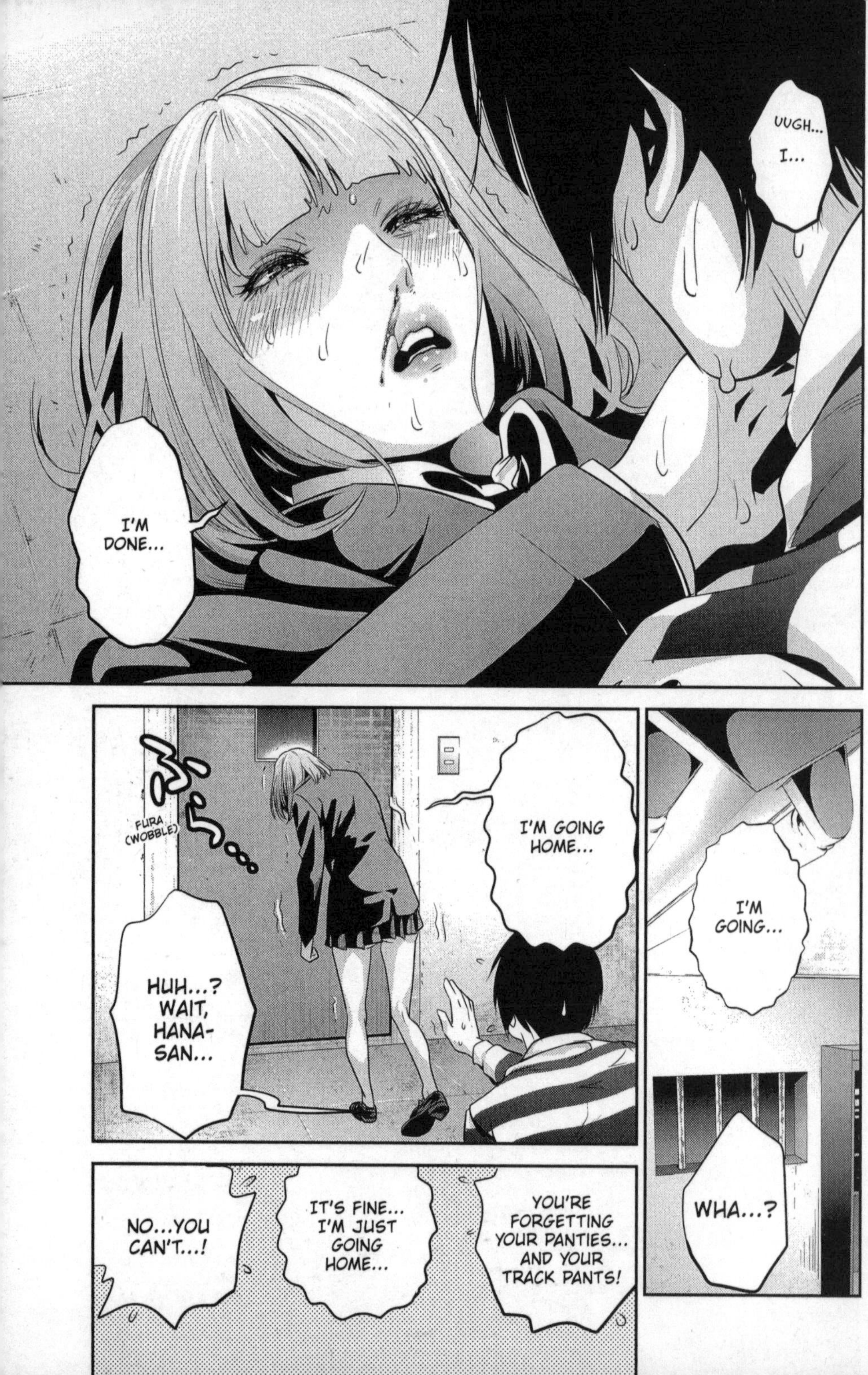
UUGH... I...
I'M DONE...
I'M GOING...
WHA...?
I'M GOING HOME...
ふら…
FURA (WOBBLE)
HUH...? WAIT, HANA-SAN...
YOU'RE FORGETTING YOUR PANTIES... AND YOUR TRACK PANTS!
IT'S FINE... I'M JUST GOING HOME...
NO...YOU CAN'T...!

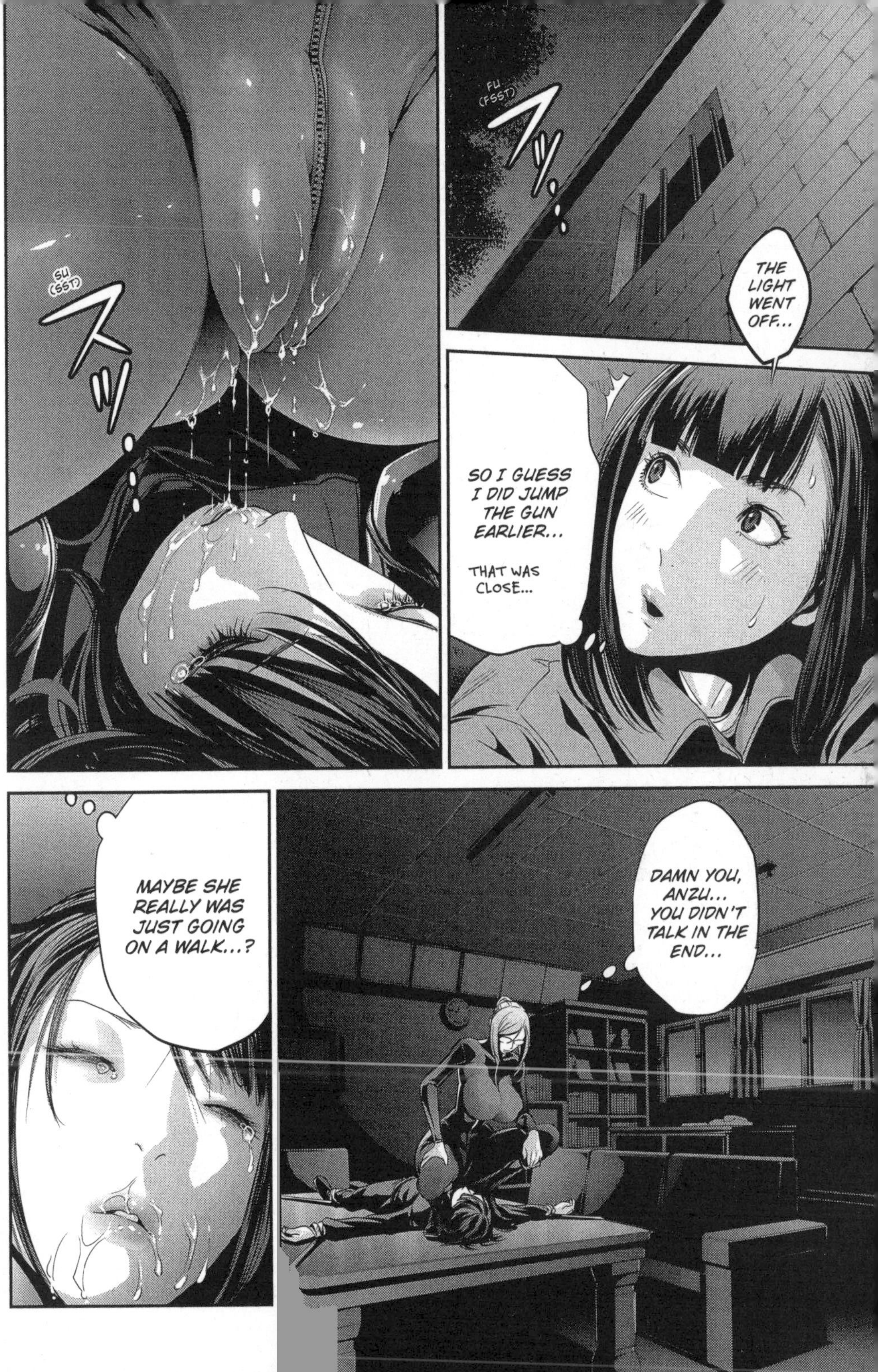
FU (FSST)
THE LIGHT WENT OFF...
SO I GUESS I DID JUMP THE GUN EARLIER...
THAT WAS CLOSE...
SU (SSST)
DAMN YOU, ANZU... YOU DIDN'T TALK IN THE END...
MAYBE SHE REALLY WAS JUST GOING ON A WALK...?

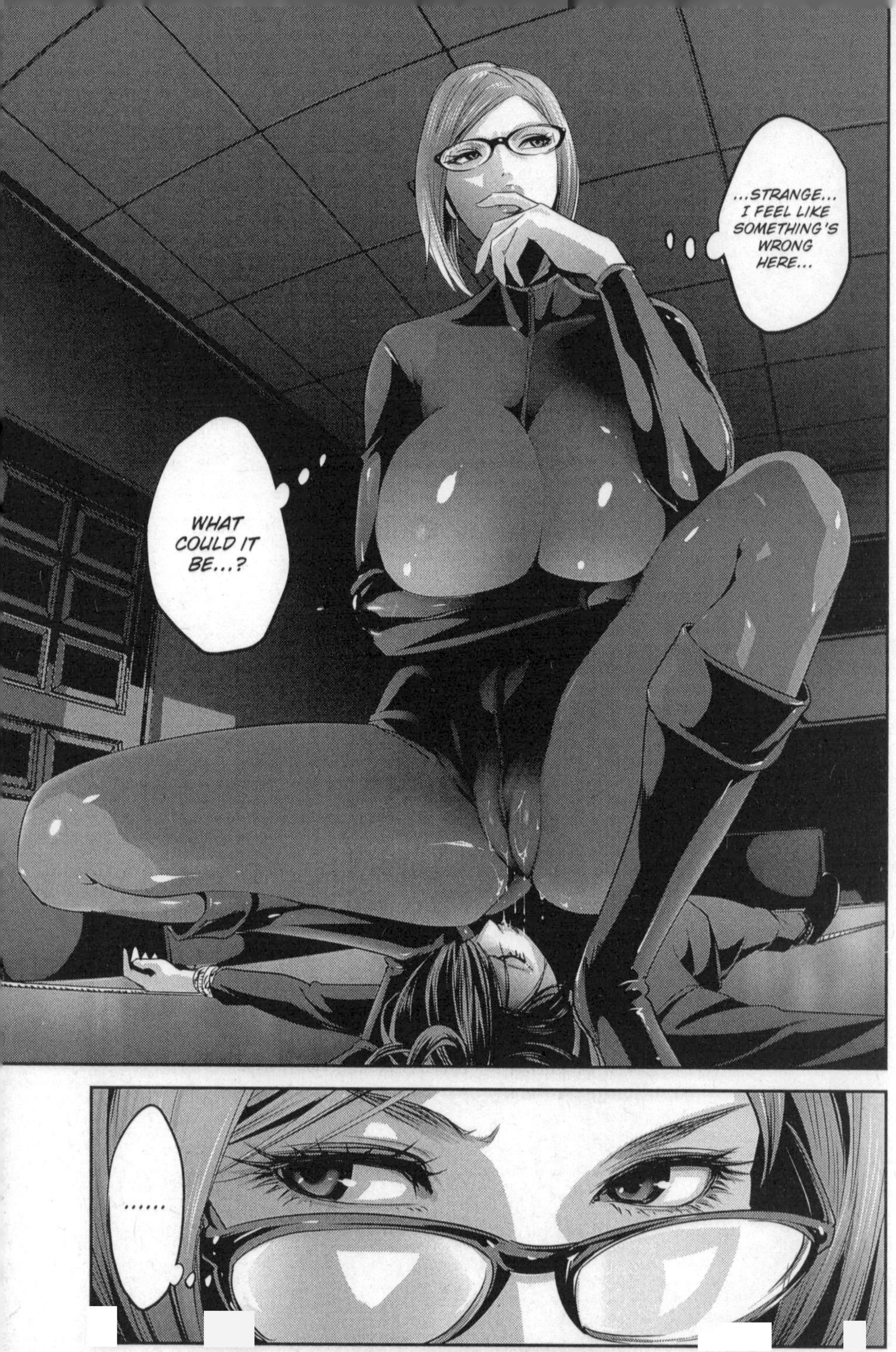
...STRANGE... I FEEL LIKE SOMETHING'S WRONG HERE...
WHAT COULD IT BE...?
......

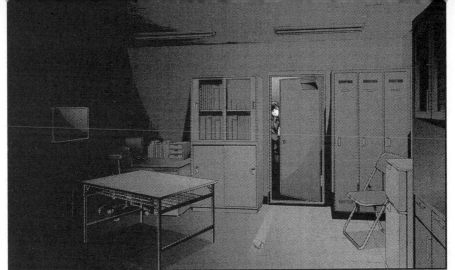

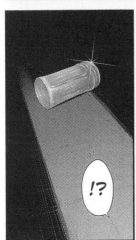

!?

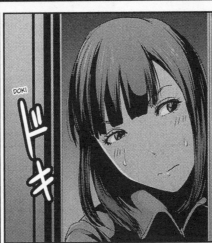

DOKI
(SNEAK)

DOKI!
(BADUM)

SOOOO
(SNEAK)

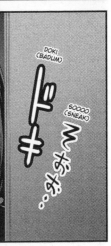

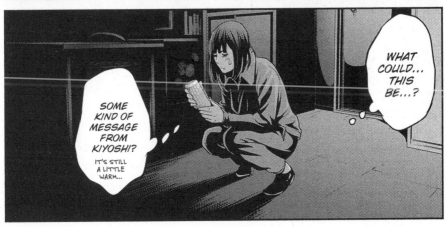

WHAT
COULD...
THIS
BE...?

SOME
KIND OF
MESSAGE
FROM
KIYOSHI?

IT'S STILL
A LITTLE
WARM...

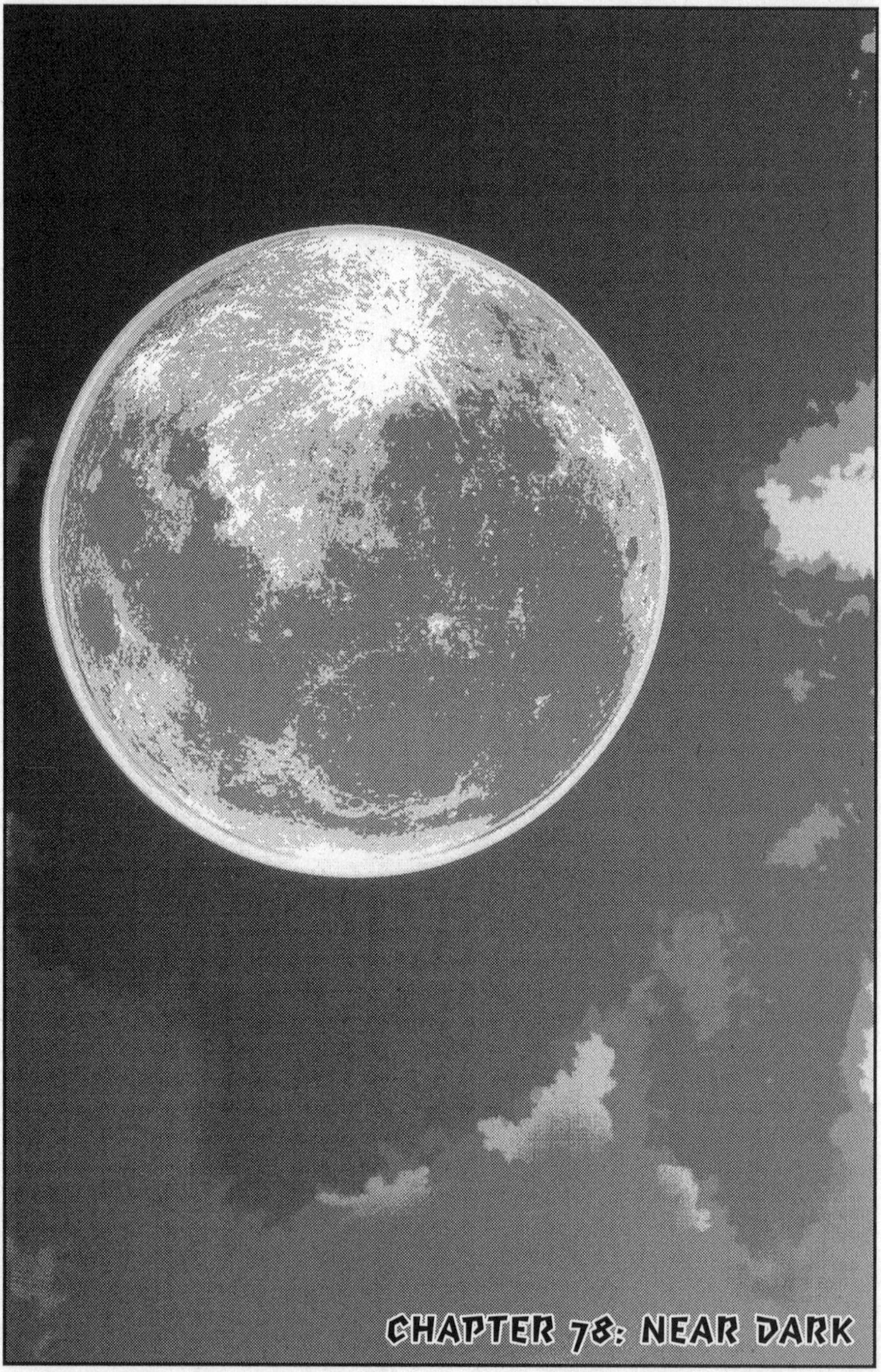
CHAPTER 78: NEAR DARK

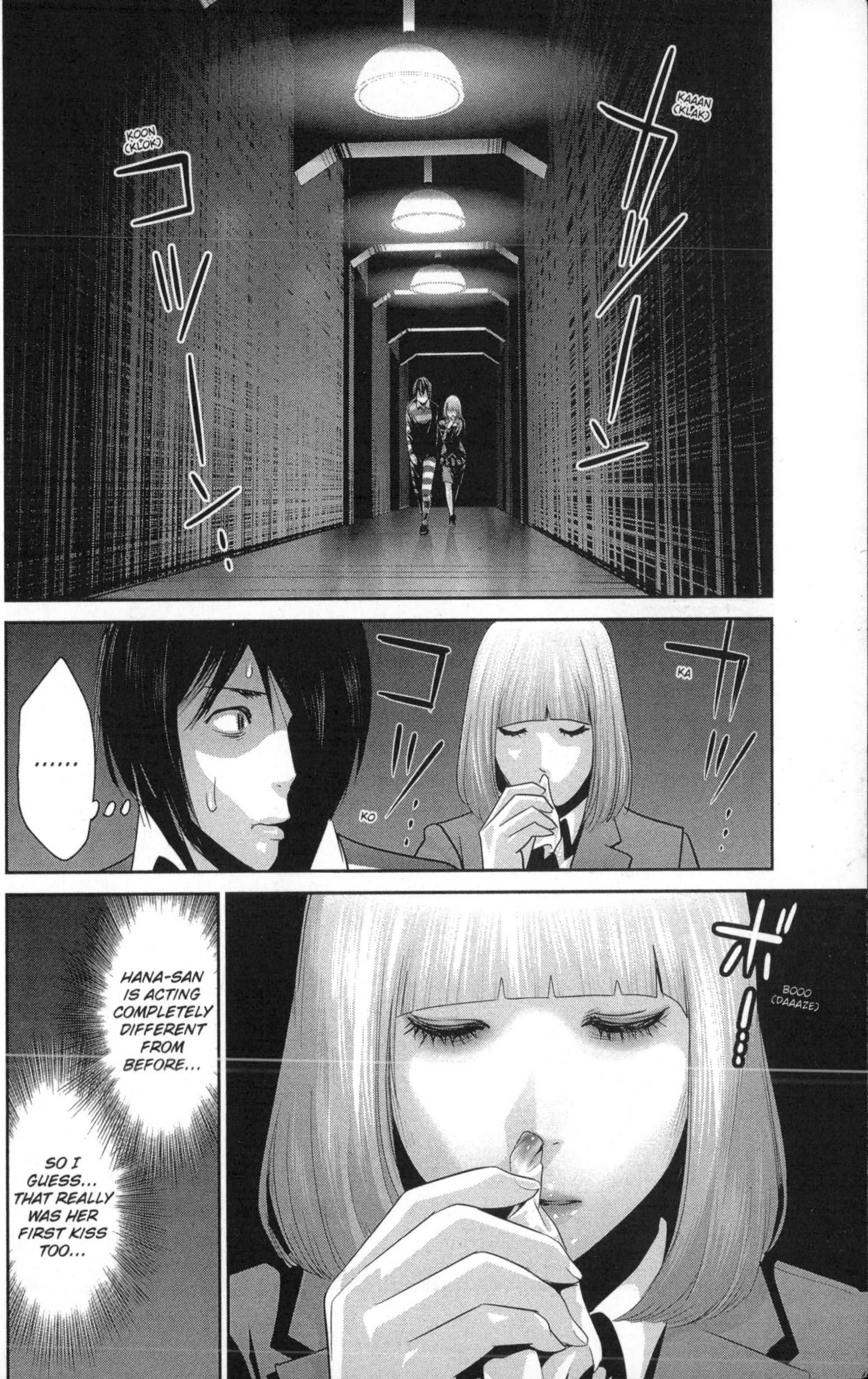
KAAAN (KLAK)
KOON (KLOK)
KA
KO
......
BOOO (DAAAZE)
HANA-SAN IS ACTING COMPLETELY DIFFERENT FROM BEFORE...
SO I GUESS... THAT REALLY WAS HER FIRST KISS TOO...

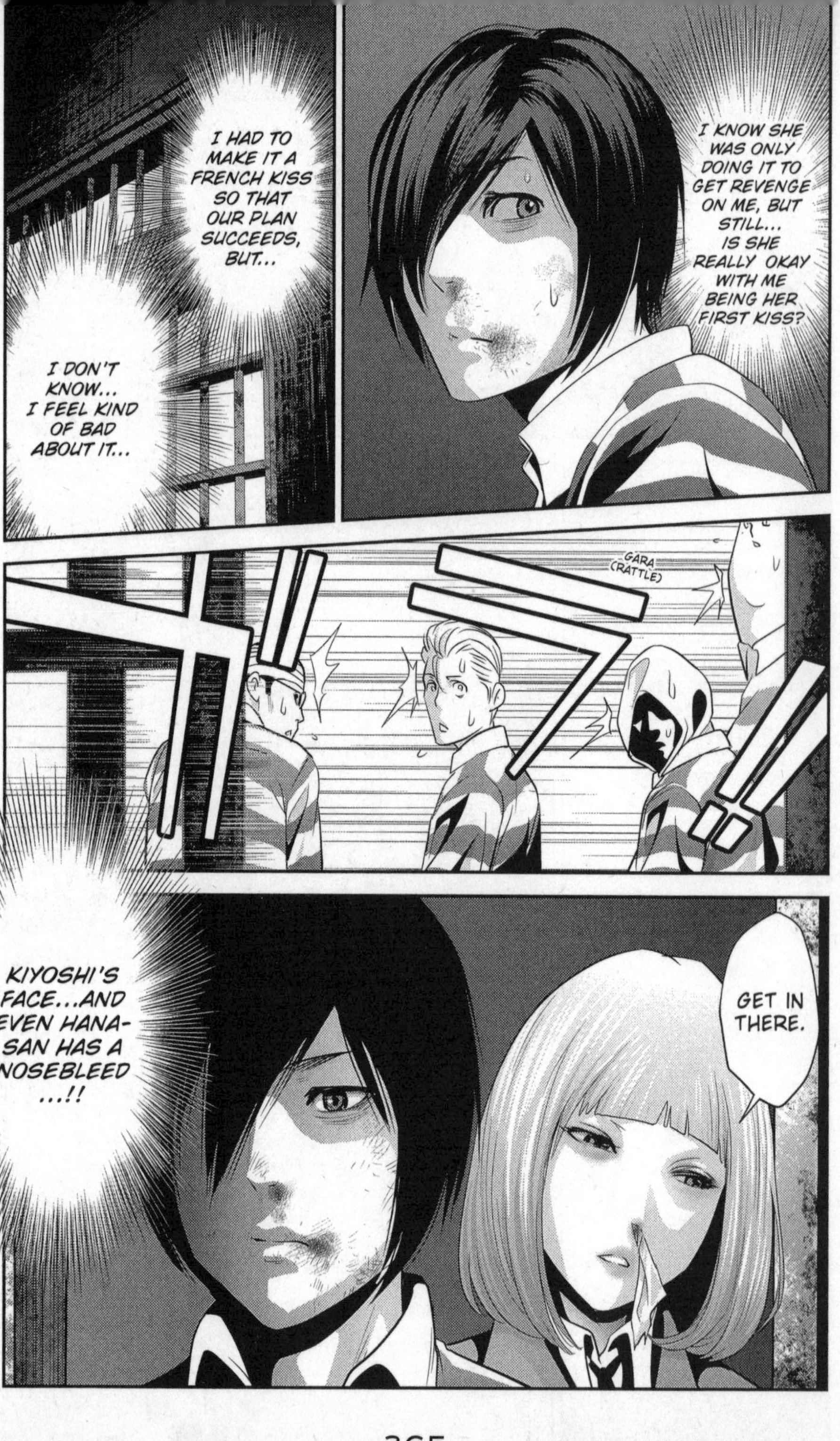
I KNOW SHE WAS ONLY DOING IT TO GET REVENGE ON ME, BUT STILL... IS SHE REALLY OKAY WITH ME BEING HER FIRST KISS?
I HAD TO MAKE IT A FRENCH KISS SO THAT OUR PLAN SUCCEEDS, BUT...
I DON'T KNOW... I FEEL KIND OF BAD ABOUT IT...
GARA (RATTLE)
GET IN THERE.
KIYOSHI'S FACE...AND EVEN HANA-SAN HAS A NOSEBLEED ...!!

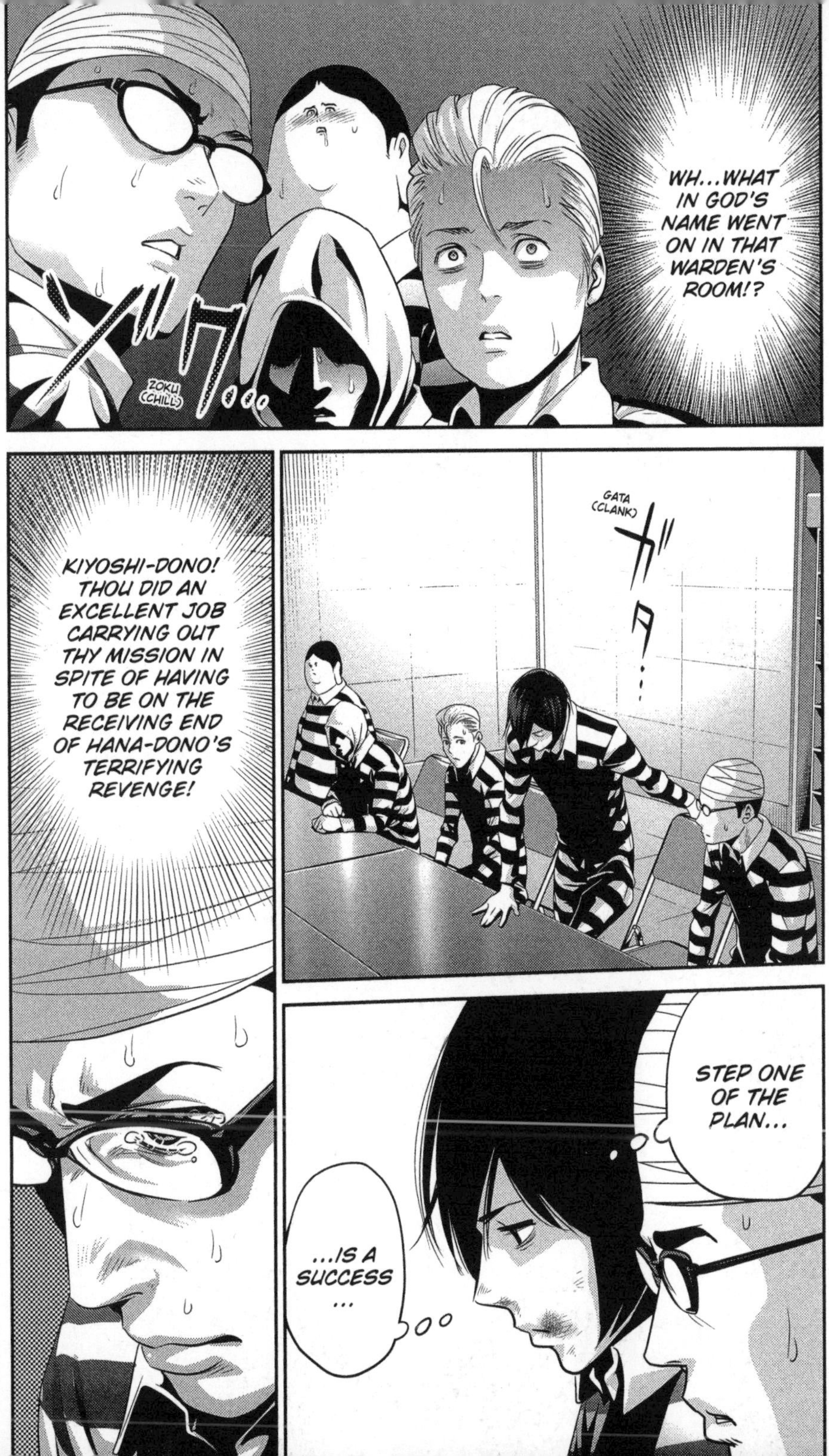
ZOKU (CHILL)
WH...WHAT IN GOD'S NAME WENT ON IN THAT WARDEN'S ROOM!?
GATA (CLANK)
STEP ONE OF THE PLAN...
...IS A SUCCESS ...
KIYOSHI-DONO! THOU DID AN EXCELLENT JOB CARRYING OUT THY MISSION IN SPITE OF HAVING TO BE ON THE RECEIVING END OF HANA-DONO'S TERRIFYING REVENGE!

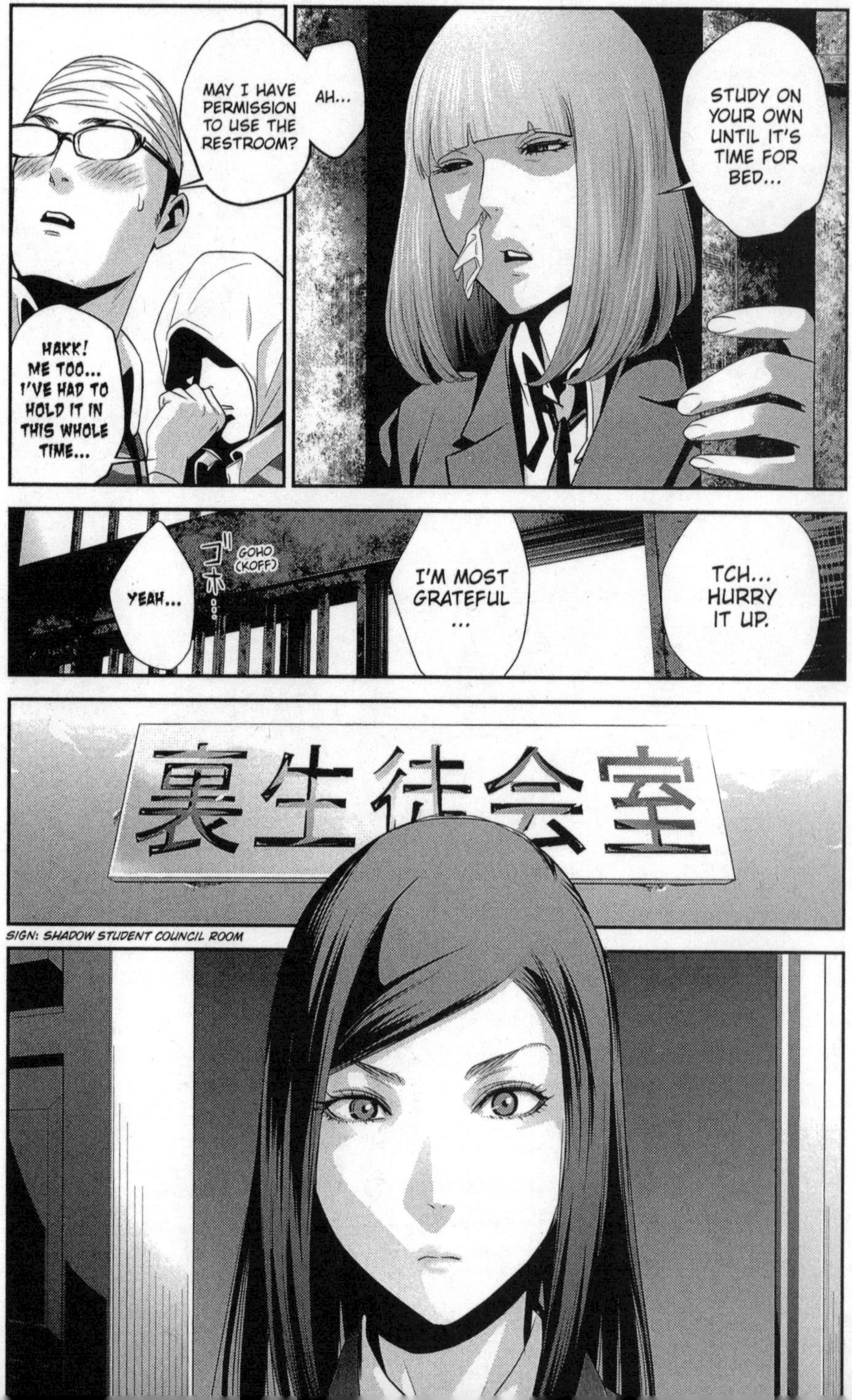
STUDY ON YOUR OWN UNTIL IT'S TIME FOR BED...
AH...
MAY I HAVE PERMISSION TO USE THE RESTROOM?
HAKK! ME TOO... I'VE HAD TO HOLD IT IN THIS WHOLE TIME...
TCH... HURRY IT UP.
I'M MOST GRATEFUL ...
ゴホ...
GOHO (KOFF)
YEAH...
裏生徒会室
SIGN: SHADOW STUDENT COUNCIL ROOM

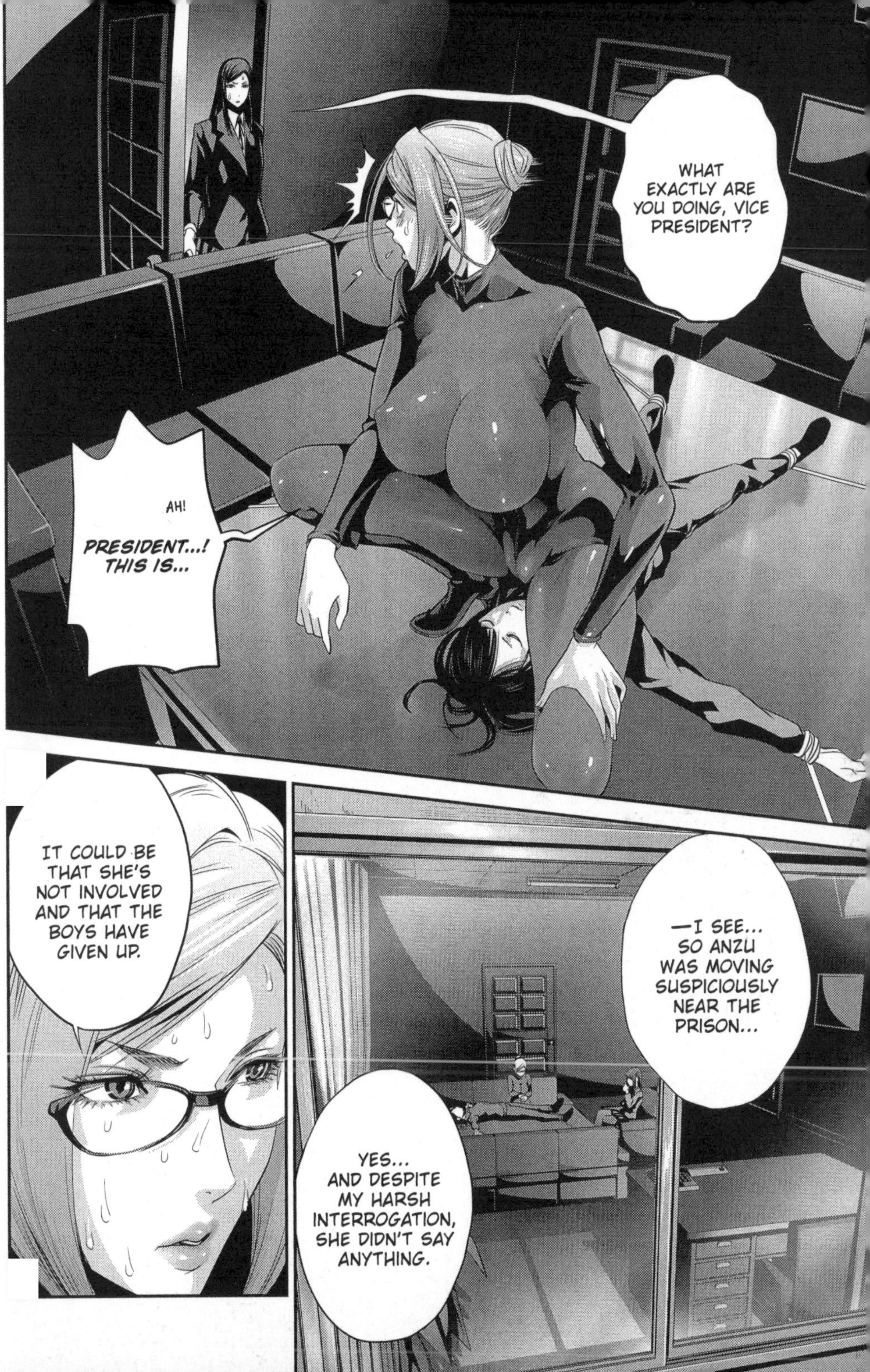
WHAT EXACTLY ARE YOU DOING, VICE PRESIDENT?
AH!
PRESIDENT...! THIS IS...
—I SEE... SO ANZU WAS MOVING SUSPICIOUSLY NEAR THE PRISON...
YES... AND DESPITE MY HARSH INTERROGATION, SHE DIDN'T SAY ANYTHING.
IT COULD BE THAT SHE'S NOT INVOLVED AND THAT THE BOYS HAVE GIVEN UP.

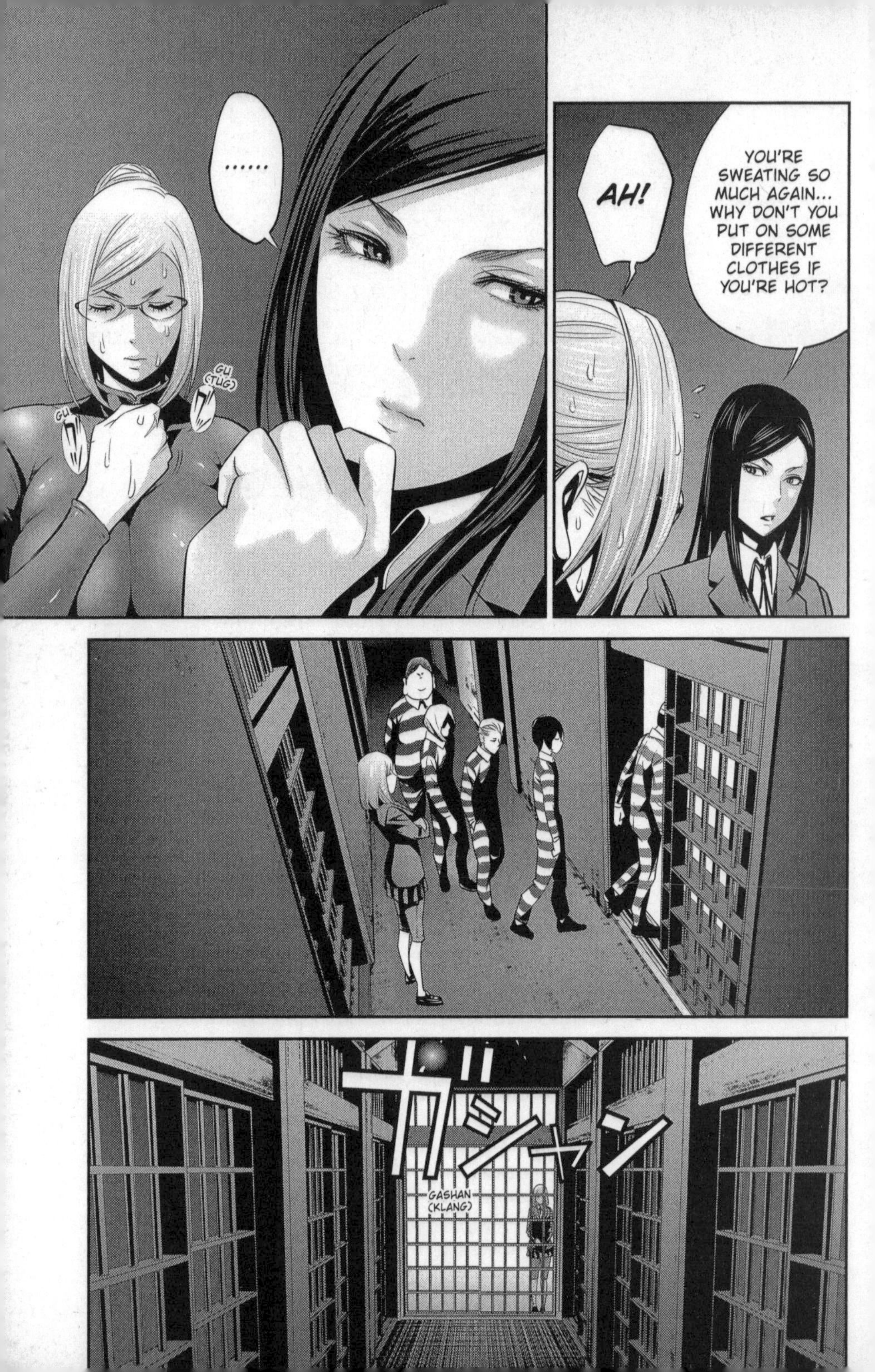
YOU'RE SWEATING SO MUCH AGAIN... WHY DON'T YOU PUT ON SOME DIFFERENT CLOTHES IF YOU'RE HOT?
AH!
......
GU (TUG)
GU
GASHAN (KLANG)

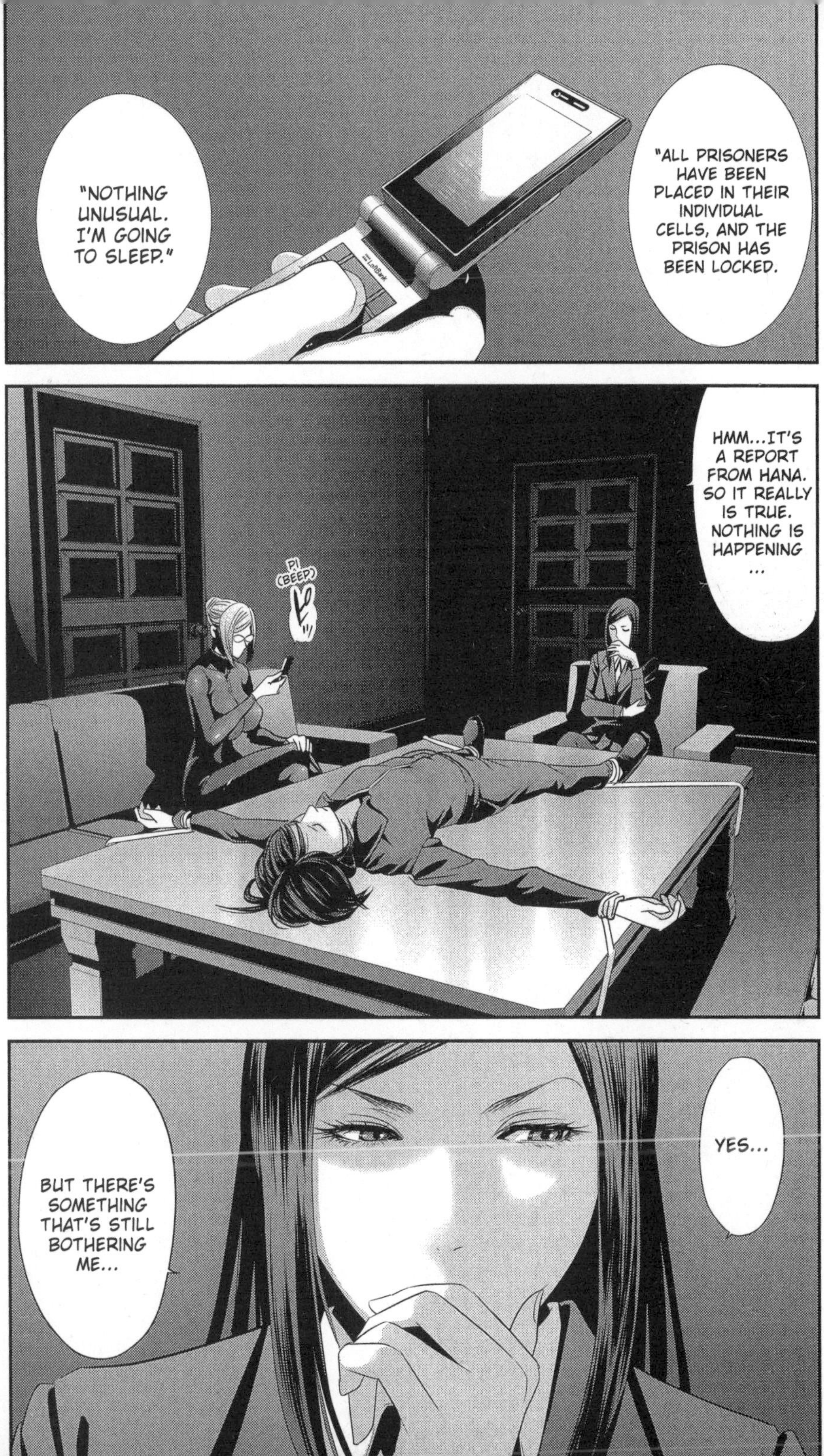
"ALL PRISONERS HAVE BEEN PLACED IN THEIR INDIVIDUAL CELLS, AND THE PRISON HAS BEEN LOCKED.
"NOTHING UNUSUAL. I'M GOING TO SLEEP."
HMM...IT'S A REPORT FROM HANA. SO IT REALLY IS TRUE. NOTHING IS HAPPENING ...
PI (BEEP)
YES...
BUT THERE'S SOMETHING THAT'S STILL BOTHERING ME...

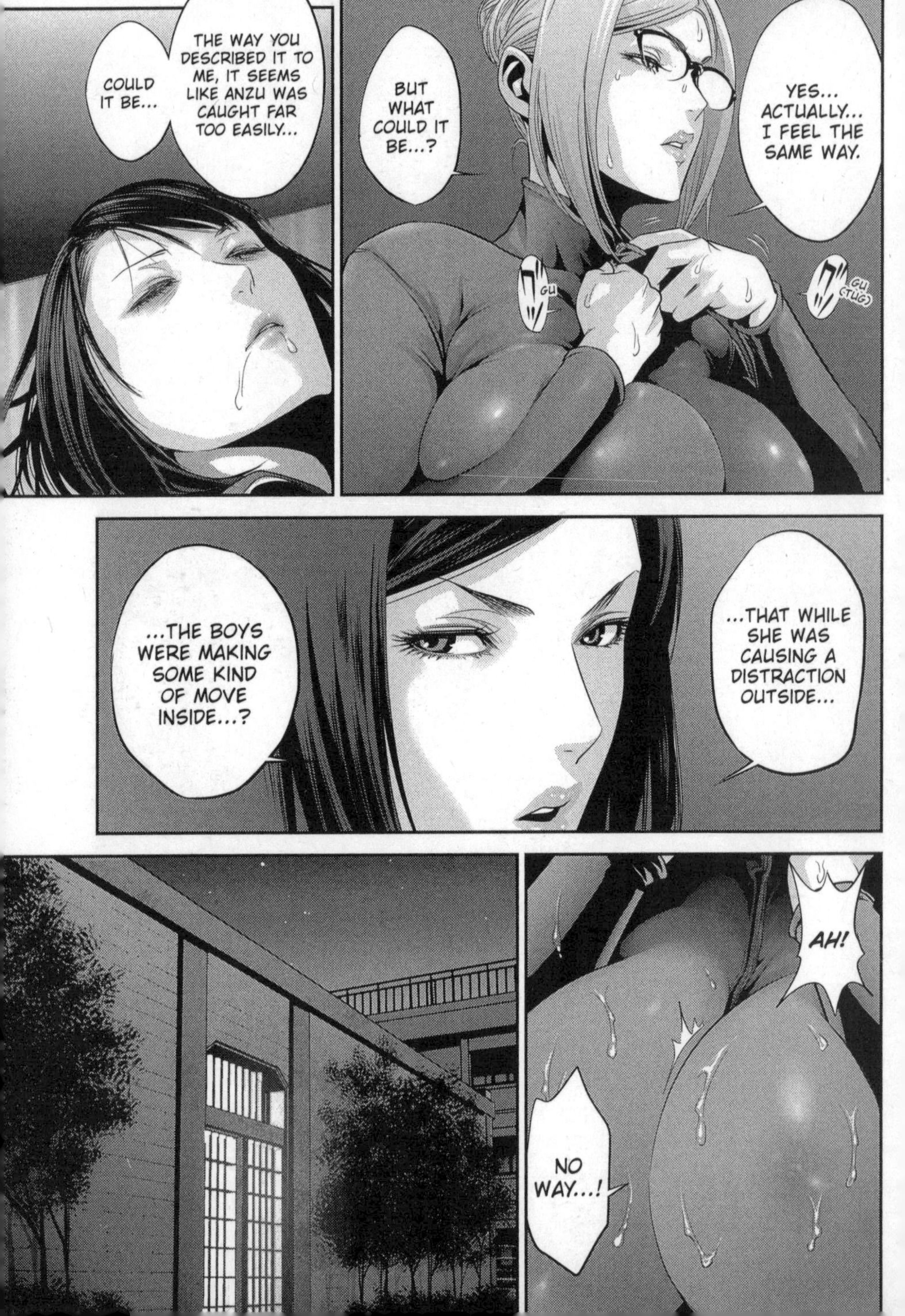
YES... ACTUALLY... I FEEL THE SAME WAY.
BUT WHAT COULD IT BE...?
GU (TUG)
GU
THE WAY YOU DESCRIBED IT TO ME, IT SEEMS LIKE ANZU WAS CAUGHT FAR TOO EASILY...
COULD IT BE...
...THAT WHILE SHE WAS CAUSING A DISTRACTION OUTSIDE...
...THE BOYS WERE MAKING SOME KIND OF MOVE INSIDE...?
AH!
NO WAY...!

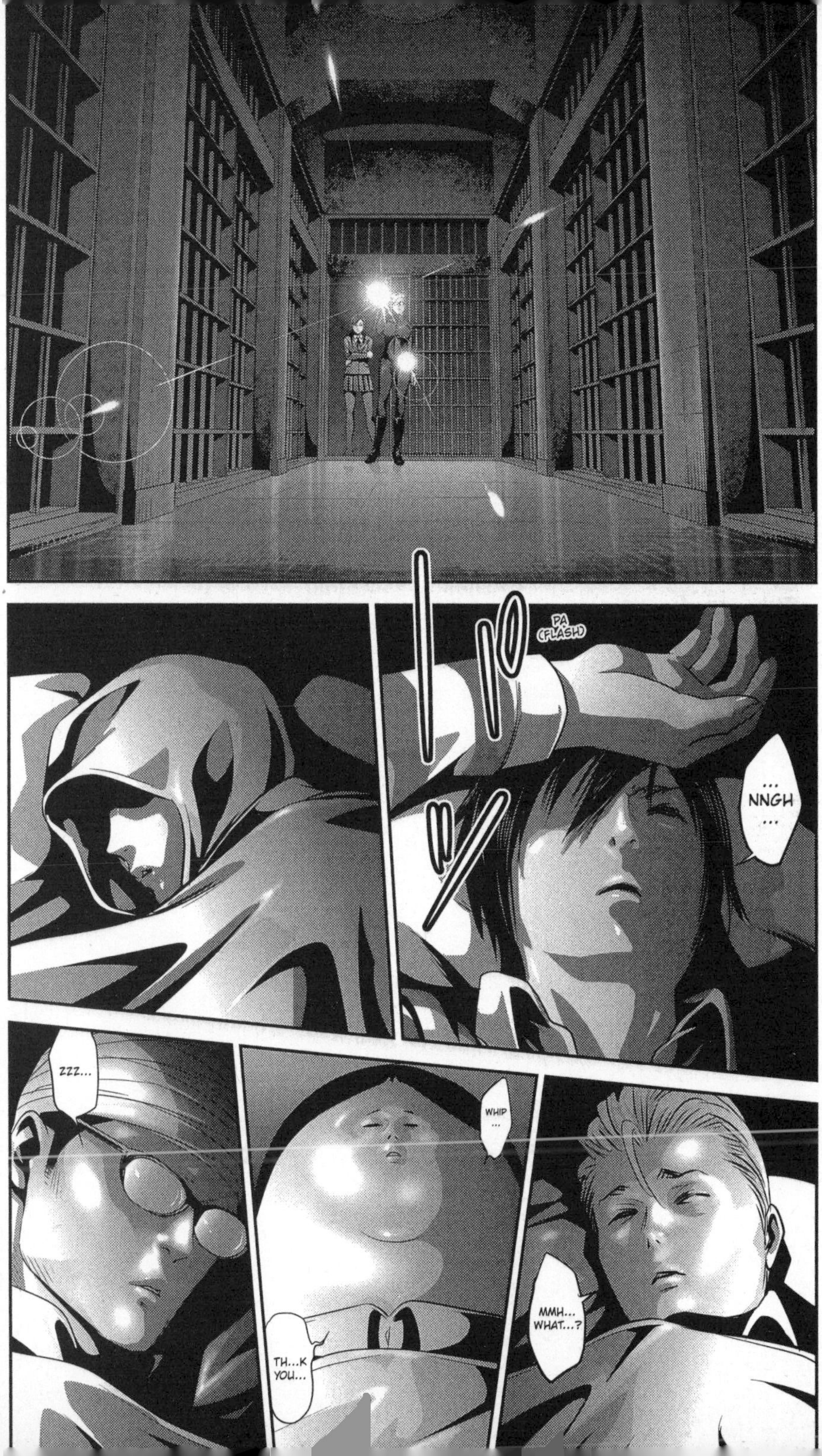
PA
(FLASH)
...NNGH...
MMH... WHAT...?
WHIP...
TH...K YOU...
ZZZ...

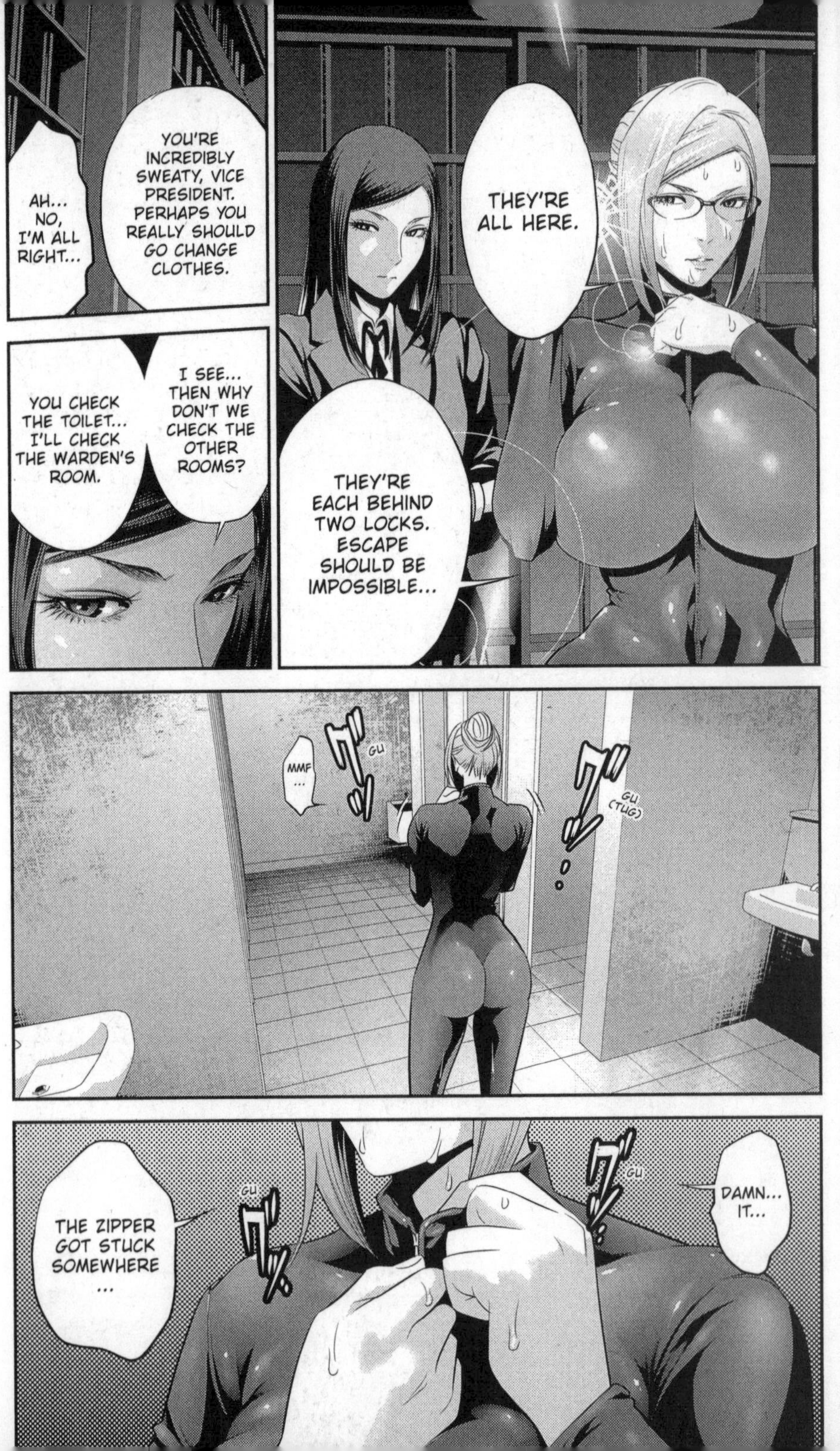
THEY'RE ALL HERE.
THEY'RE EACH BEHIND TWO LOCKS. ESCAPE SHOULD BE IMPOSSIBLE...
YOU'RE INCREDIBLY SWEATY, VICE PRESIDENT. PERHAPS YOU REALLY SHOULD GO CHANGE CLOTHES.
AH... NO, I'M ALL RIGHT...
I SEE... THEN WHY DON'T WE CHECK THE OTHER ROOMS?
YOU CHECK THE TOILET... I'LL CHECK THE WARDEN'S ROOM.
GU (TUG)
GU
MMF...
GU
DAMN... IT...
GU
THE ZIPPER GOT STUCK SOMEWHERE...

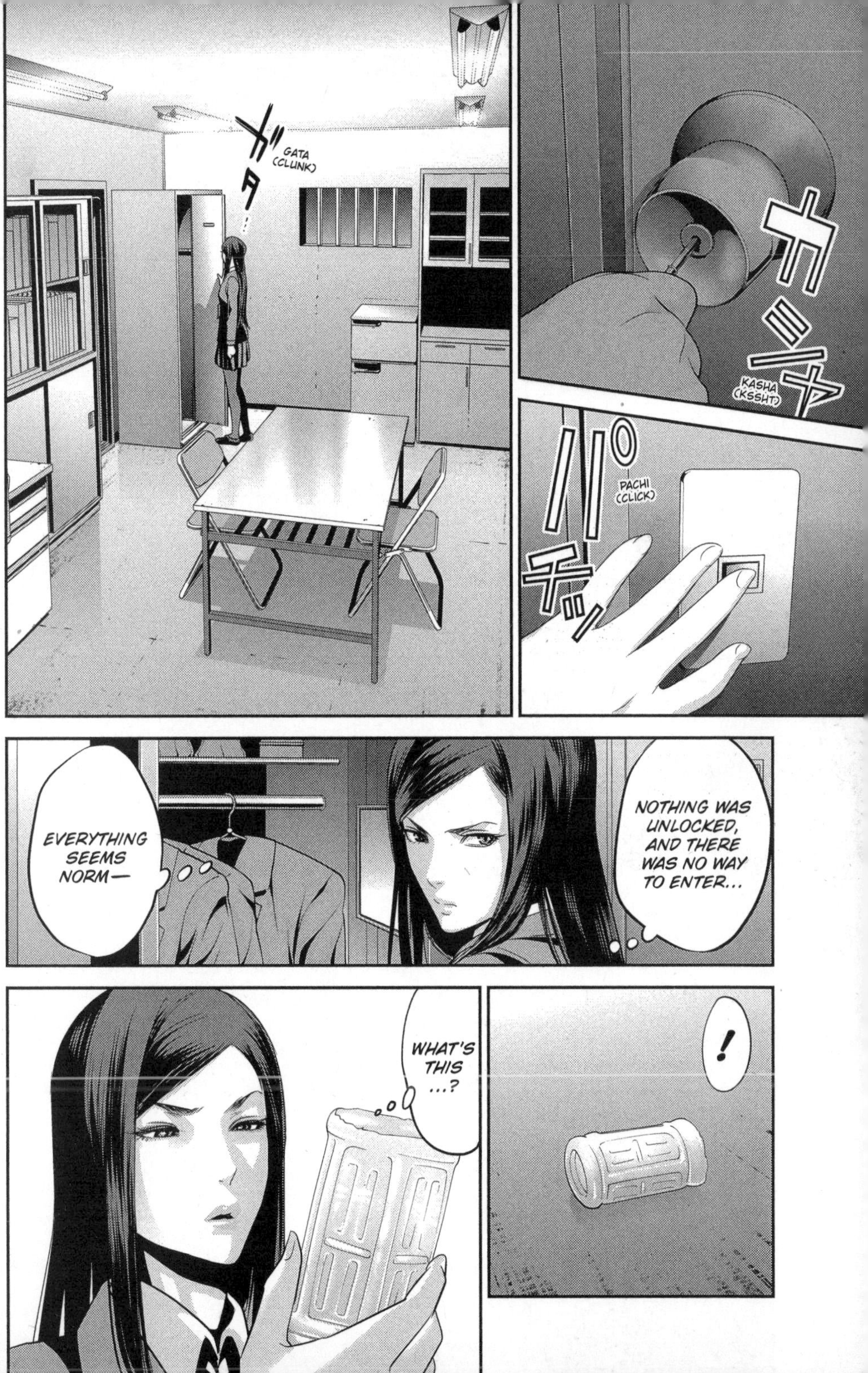
カシャ
KASHA (KSSHT)
パチッ
PACHI (CLICK)
ガタ
GATA (CLUNK)
NOTHING WAS UNLOCKED, AND THERE WAS NO WAY TO ENTER...
EVERYTHING SEEMS NORM—
!
WHAT'S THIS ...?

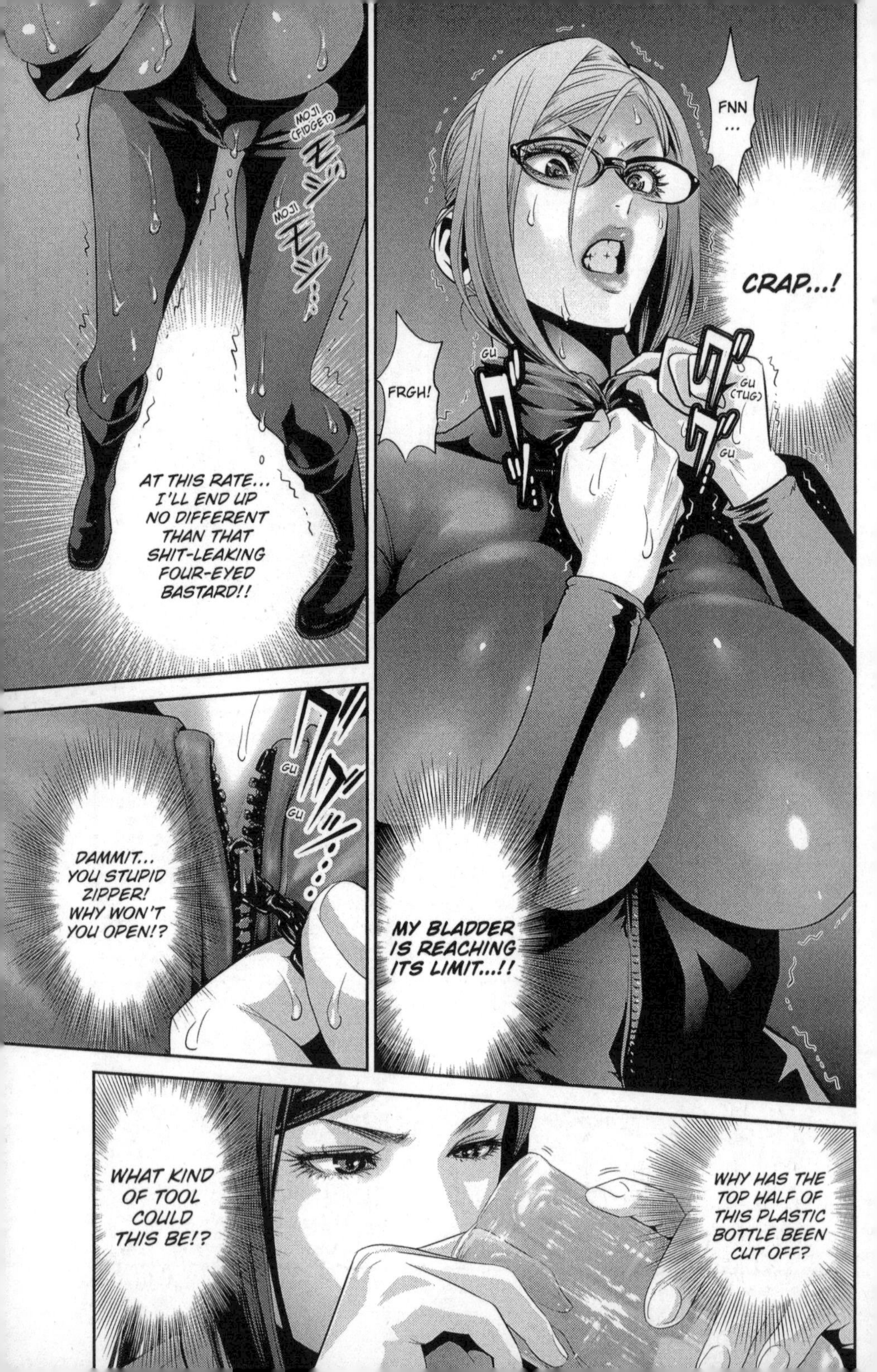
FNN ...
CRAP...!
GU (TUG)
GU
FRGH!
GU
MY BLADDER IS REACHING ITS LIMIT...!!
MOJI (FIDGET)
MOJI
AT THIS RATE... I'LL END UP NO DIFFERENT THAN THAT SHIT-LEAKING FOUR-EYED BASTARD!!
GU
GU
DAMMIT... YOU STUPID ZIPPER! WHY WON'T YOU OPEN!?
WHY HAS THE TOP HALF OF THIS PLASTIC BOTTLE BEEN CUT OFF?
WHAT KIND OF TOOL COULD THIS BE!?

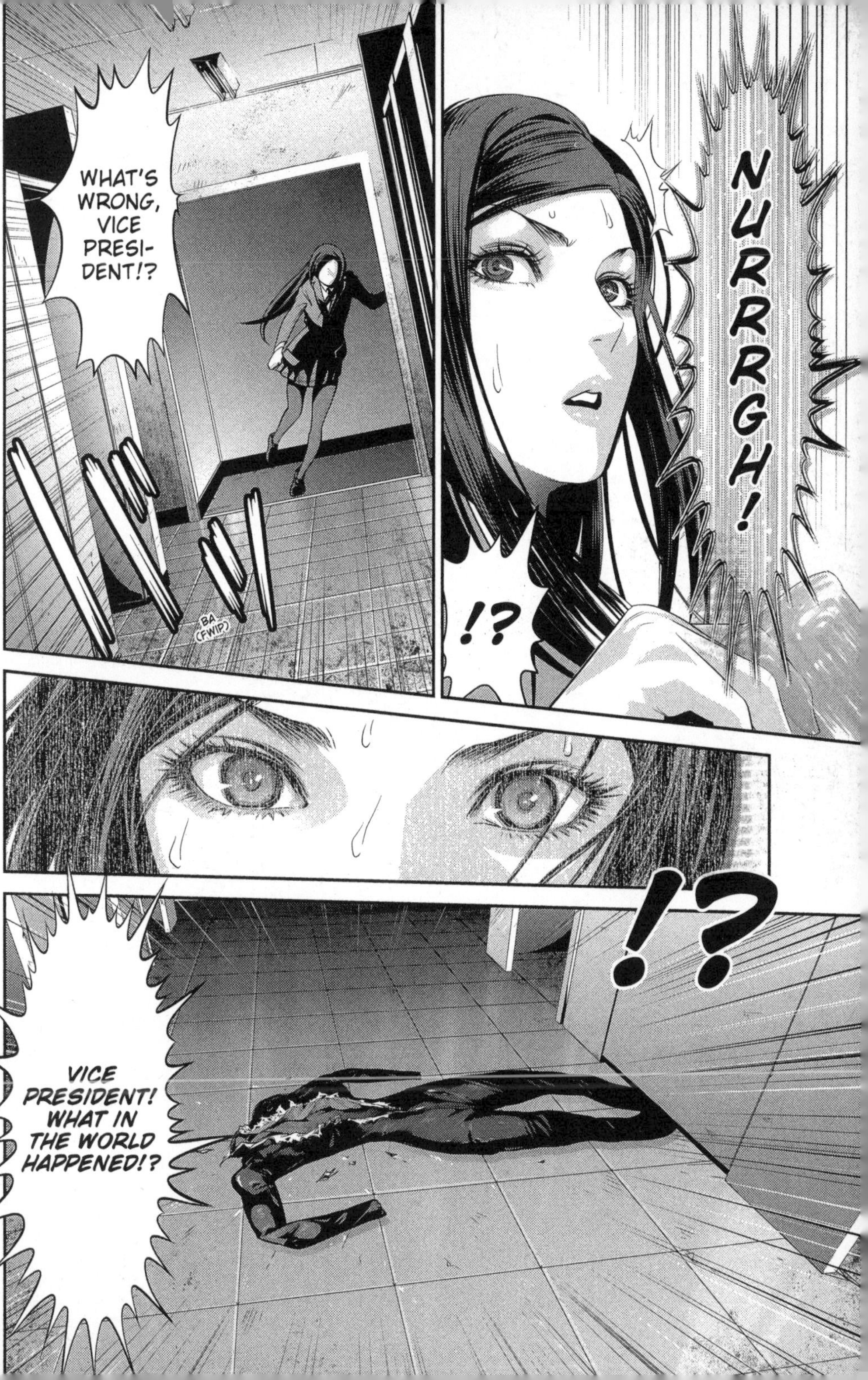
NURRRGH!
!?
WHAT'S WRONG, VICE PRESI-DENT!?
BA (FWIP)
!?
VICE PRESIDENT! WHAT IN THE WORLD HAPPENED!?

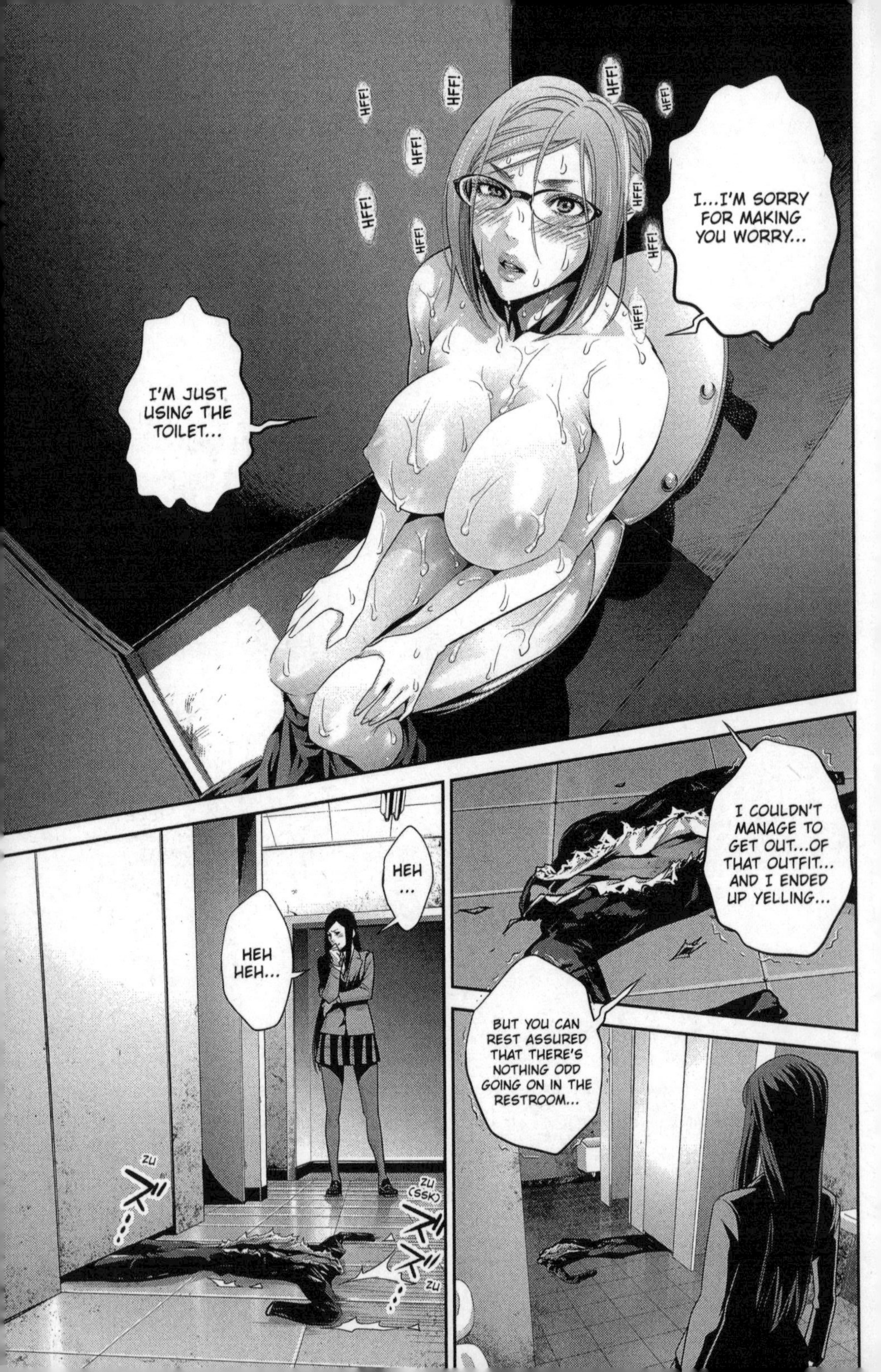
HFF! HFF! HFF! HFF! HFF!
I...I'M SORRY FOR MAKING YOU WORRY...
HFF! HFF! HFF! HFF!
I'M JUST USING THE TOILET...
I COULDN'T MANAGE TO GET OUT...OF THAT OUTFIT... AND I ENDED UP YELLING...
BUT YOU CAN REST ASSURED THAT THERE'S NOTHING ODD GOING ON IN THE RESTROOM...
HEH ...
HEH HEH...
ZU
ZU (SSK)
ZU

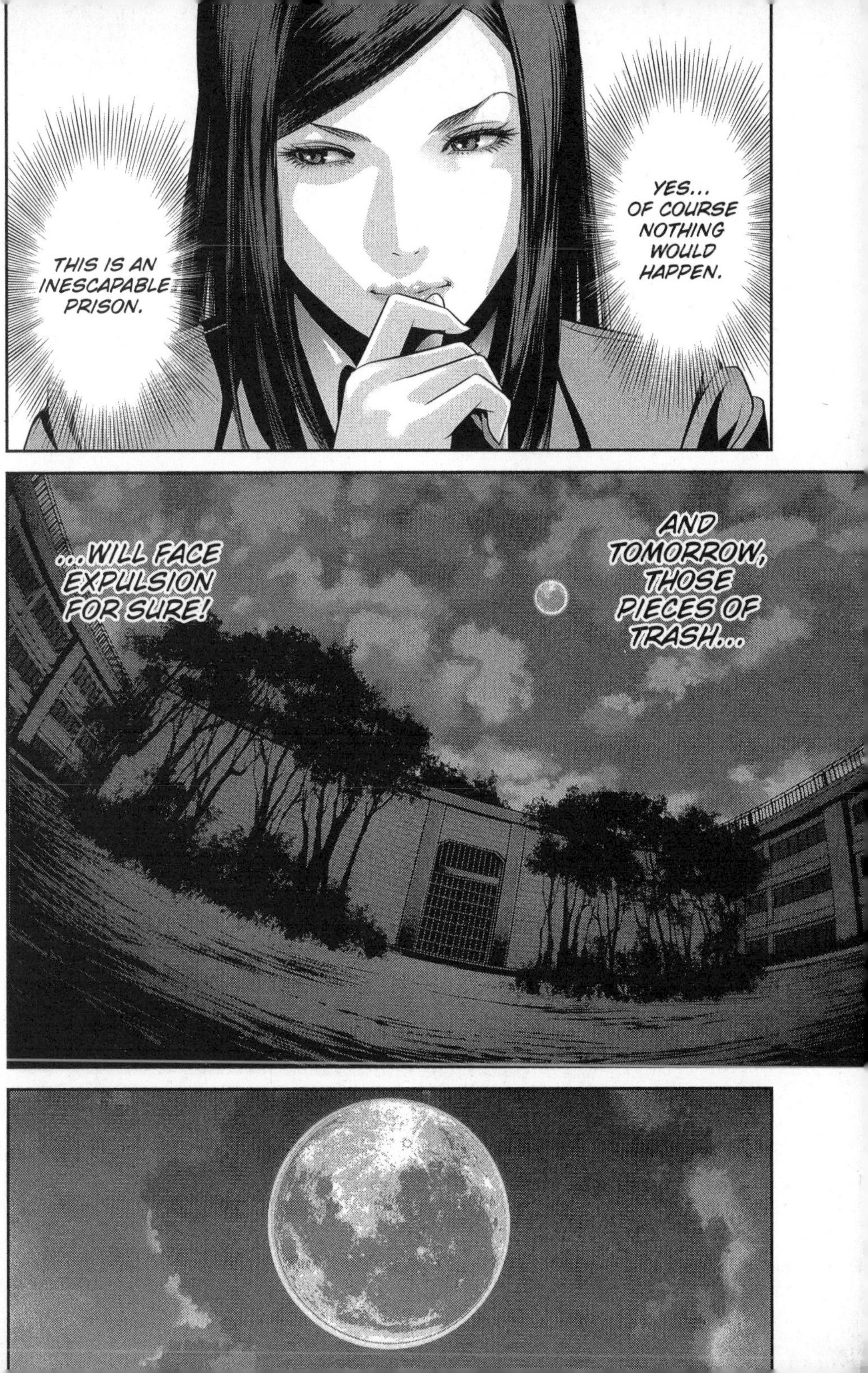
YES... OF COURSE NOTHING WOULD HAPPEN.
THIS IS AN INESCAPABLE PRISON.
AND TOMORROW, THOSE PIECES OF TRASH...
...WILL FACE EXPULSION FOR SURE!

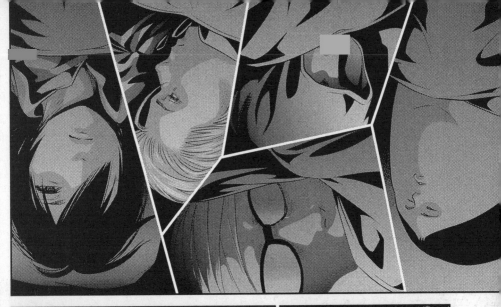

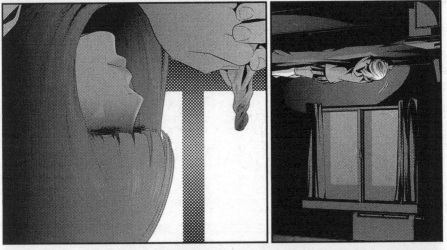

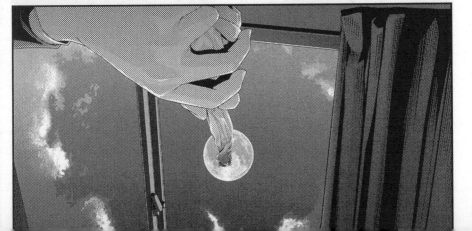

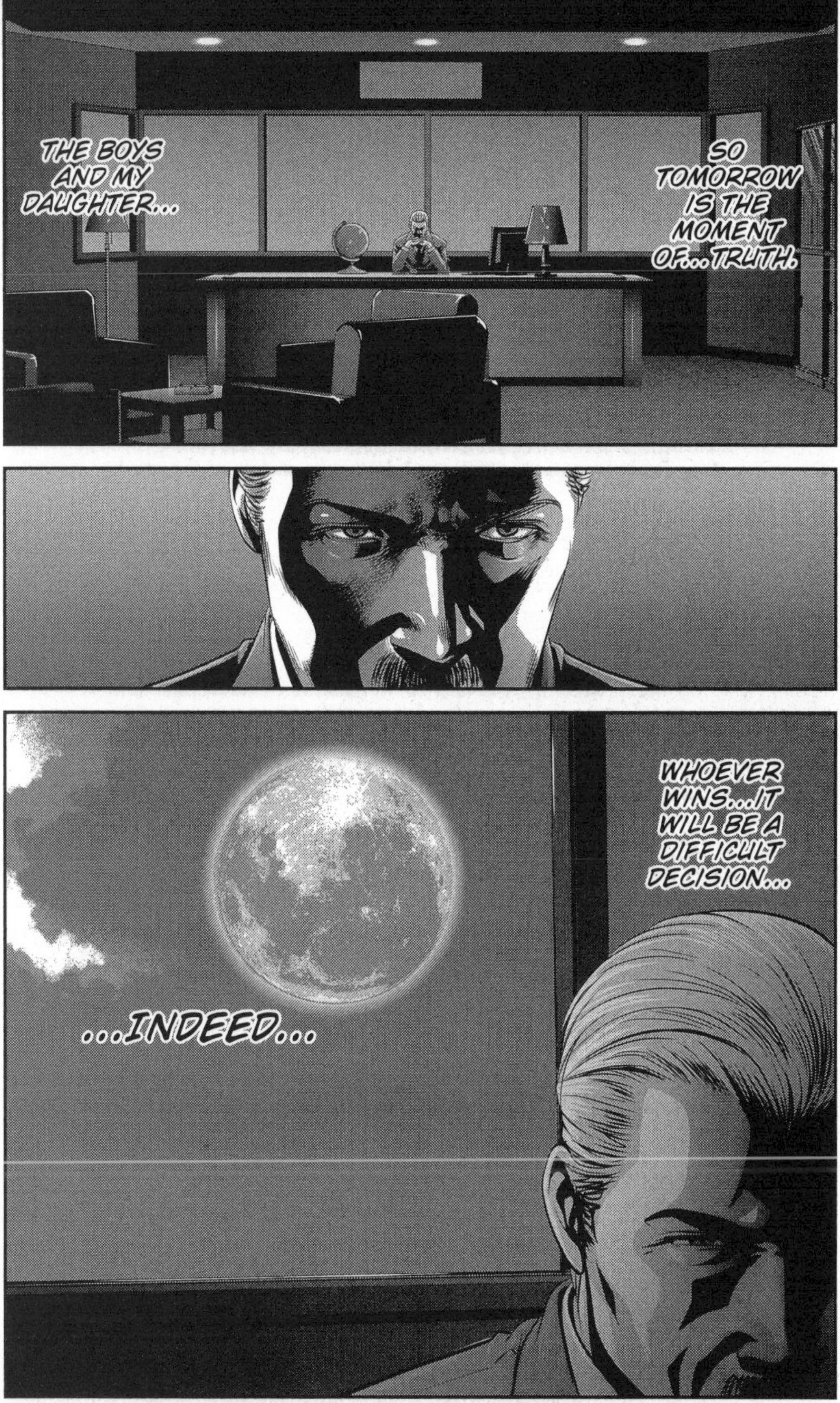
SO TOMORROW IS THE MOMENT OF...TRUTH.
THE BOYS AND MY DAUGHTER...
WHOEVER WINS...IT WILL BE A DIFFICULT DECISION...
...INDEED...

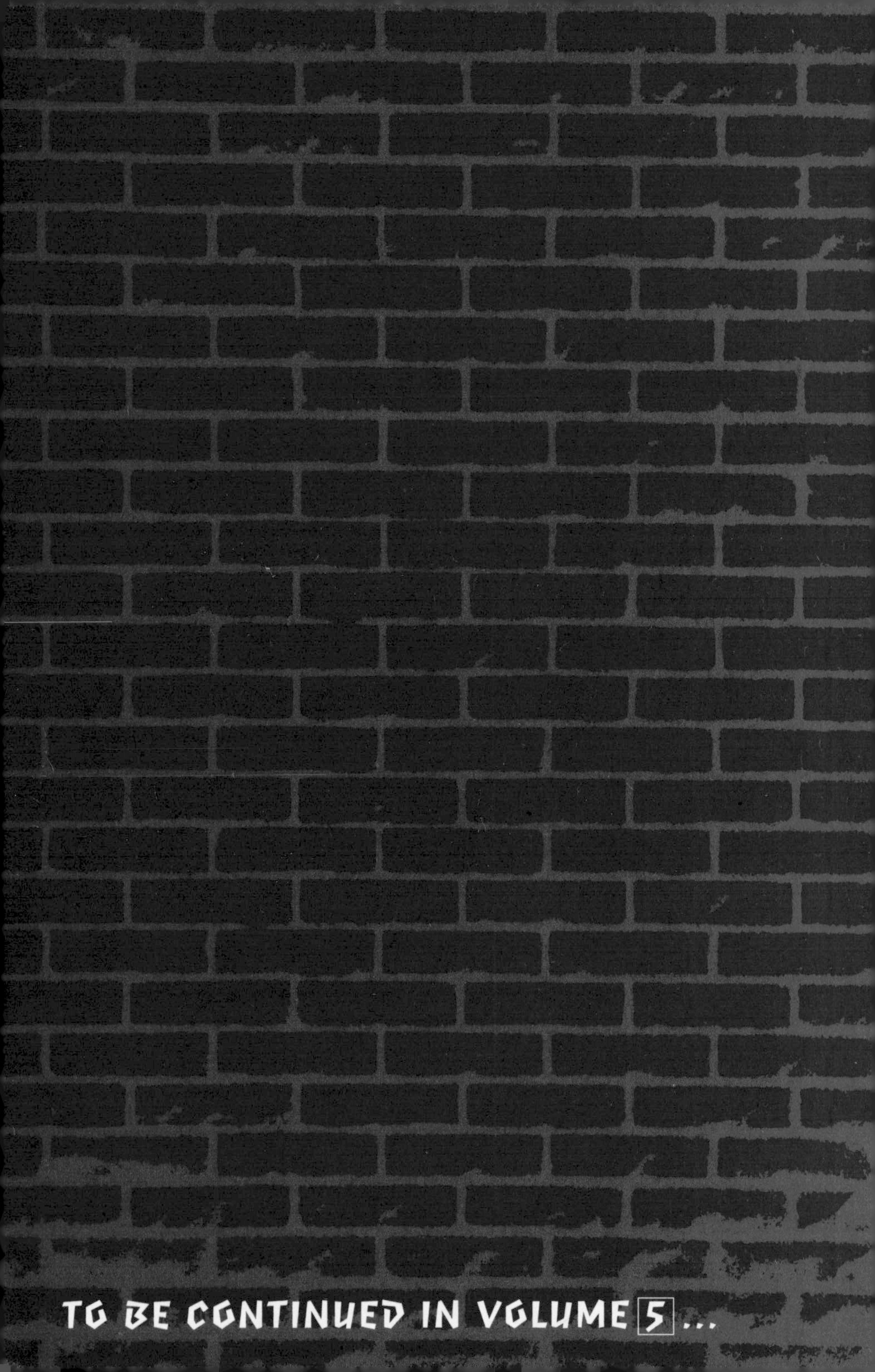
TO BE CONTINUED IN VOLUME 5 ...

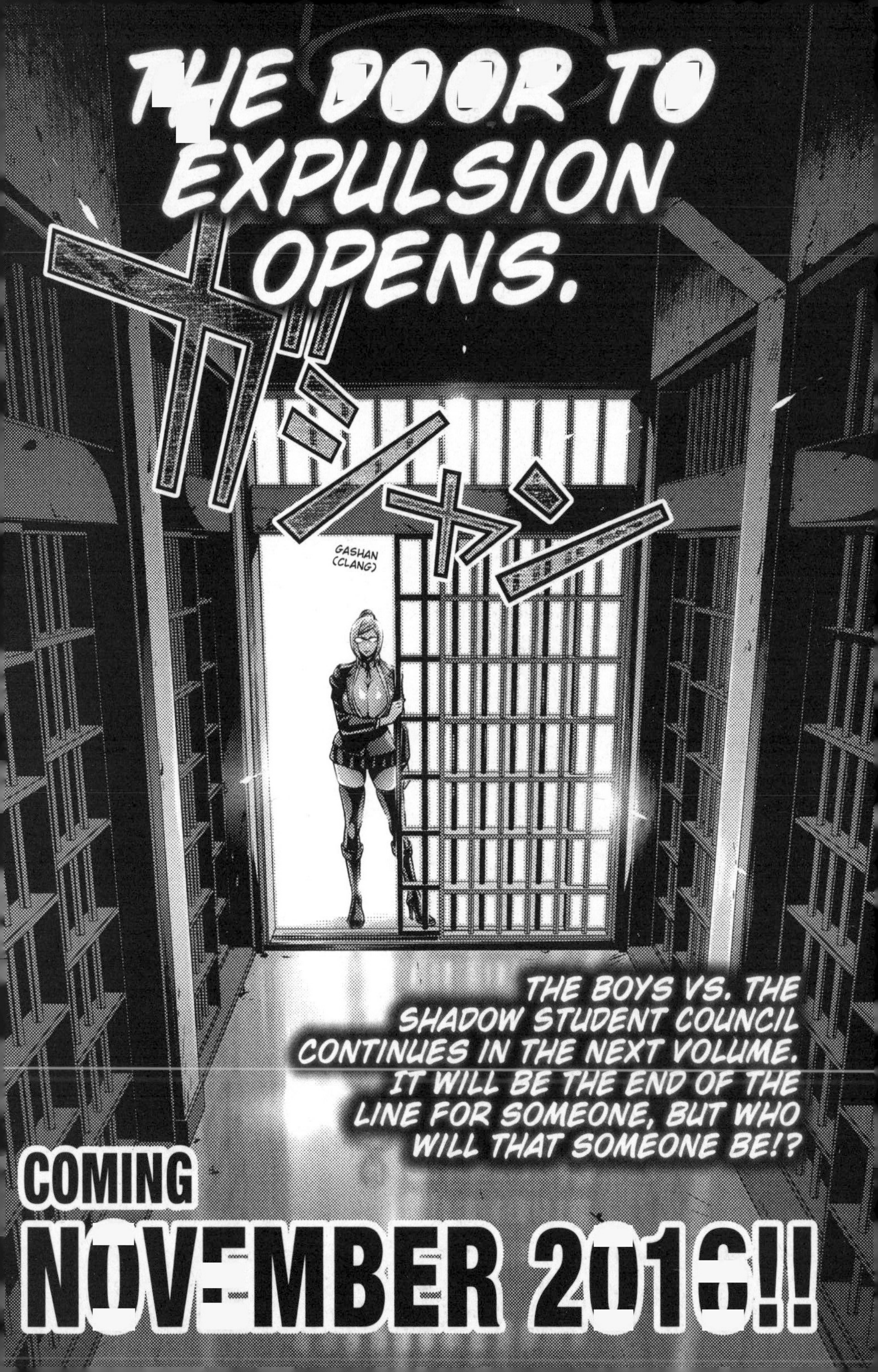
THE DOOR TO EXPULSION OPENS.
ガシャン
GASHAN (CLANG)
THE BOYS VS. THE SHADOW STUDENT COUNCIL CONTINUES IN THE NEXT VOLUME. IT WILL BE THE END OF THE LINE FOR SOMEONE, BUT WHO WILL THAT SOMEONE BE!?
COMING NOVEMBER 2016!!

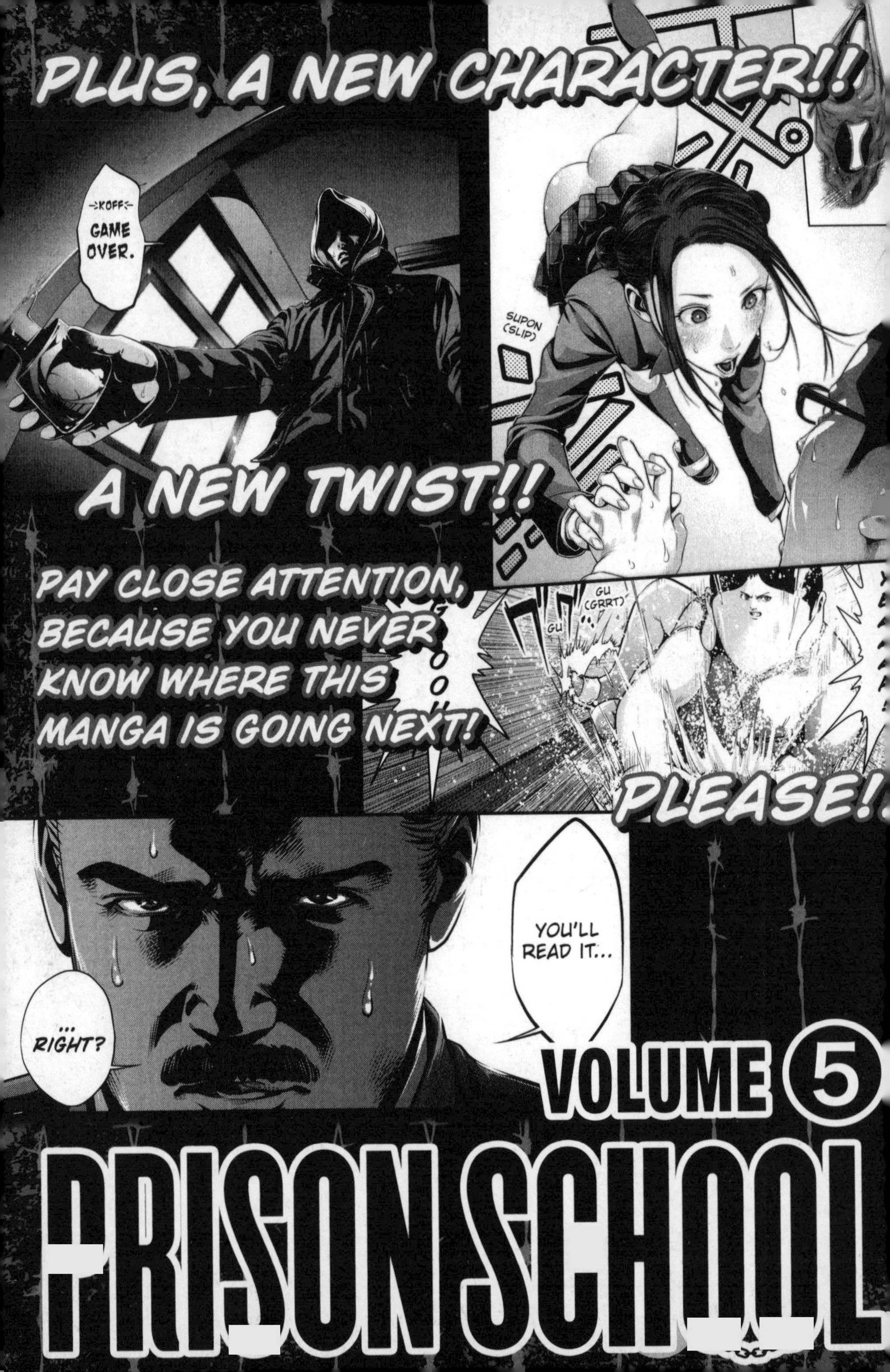
PLUS, A NEW CHARACTER!!
SUPON (SLIP)
—KOFF— GAME OVER.
A NEW TWIST!!
GU (GRRT)
GU
PAY CLOSE ATTENTION, BECAUSE YOU NEVER KNOW WHERE THIS MANGA IS GOING NEXT!
PLEASE!!
YOU'LL READ IT...
...RIGHT?
VOLUME 5
PRISON SCHOOL

TRANSLATION NOTES

Common Honorifics

no honorific: Indicates familiarity or closeness; if used without permission or reason, addressing someone in this manner would constitute an insult.

-san: The Japanese equivalent of Mr./Mrs./Miss. If a situation calls for politeness, this is the fail-safe honorific.

-dono: Conveys an indication of respect for the addressee.

-kun: Used most often when referring to boys, this indicates affection or familiarity. Occasionally used by older men among their peers, but it may also be used by anyone referring to a person of lower standing.

-chan: An affectionate honorific indicating familiarity used mostly in reference to girls; also used in reference to cute persons or animals of either gender.

-senpai: A suffix used to address upperclassmen or more experienced coworkers.

PRISON SCHOOL

PRISON SCHOOL ④

AKIRA HIRAMOTO

D1240409

Translation: Ko Ransom

Lettering: Alexis Eckerman

This book is a work of fiction. Names, characters, places, and incidents are the product of the author's imagination or are used fictitiously. Any resemblance to actual events, locales, or persons, living or dead, is coincidental.

PRISON SCHOOL Vol. 7, 8
© 2013 Akira Hiramoto. All rights reserved.
First published in Japan in 2013 by Kodansha, Ltd. Tokyo.
Publication rights for this English edition arranged through Kodansha, Ltd. Tokyo.

English translation ©2016 by SQUARE ENIX CO., LTD.

Yen Press
1290 Avenue of the Americas
New York, NY 10104

Visit us at yenpress.com
facebook.com/yenpress
twitter.com/yenpress
yenpress.tumblr.com

First Yen Press Edition: July 2016

Yen Press is an imprint of Yen Press, LLC.
The Yen Press name and logo are trademarks of Yen Press, LLC.

The publisher is not responsible for websites (or their content) that are not owned by the publisher.

Library of Congress Control Number: 2015373915

ISBN: 978-0-316-34615-3

10 9 8 7 6 5 4 3 2 1

BVG

Printed in the United States of America